AN IRISH READER IN MORAL THEOLOGY

AN IRISH READER IN MORAL THEOLOGY

The Legacy of the Last Fifty Years

VOLUME 1: FOUNDATIONS

Edited by Enda McDonagh and Vincent MacNamara

Research and Editorial Assistants:
Aoife McGrath and Siobhán Mooney

First published in 2009 by
the columba press
55A Spruce Avenue,
Stillorgan Industrial Park,
Blackrock, Co. Dublin
Email info@columba.ie
Website www.columba.ie

Cover by Bill Bolger
Printed by SPRINT-print

Second Printing

ISBN 978 1 85607 656 2

Dedicated to the next generation of
Moral Theologians in Ireland

Contents

Biographies

GARRETT BARDEN studied and taught abroad until joining the Milltown Institute, Dublin (1970–1972) and University College Cork (1972–1999). He is now a visitor at the University of Akureyri in Iceland.

HUGH CONNOLLY, a priest of the diocese of Dromore, is the President of St Patrick's College, Maynooth. He lectured in its Department of Moral Theology from 1997, and was appointed Professor in 2007. He is the author of *The Irish Penitentials and their Significance for the Sacraments of Penance Today* (1995) and *Sin* (2002).

W.J. CONWAY was Archbishop of Armagh and Primate of All Ireland. He was head of the Catholic Church in Ireland during the reforms of the Second Vatican Council, and was Professor of Moral Theology from 1943–1958 at St Patrick's College, Maynooth.

WILLIAM COSGRAVE received his doctorate in Moral Theology at St Patrick's College, Maynooth. He lectured in Moral Theology at St Peter's College, Wexford. He is parish priest of Monageer, Co. Wexford, and the author of *Christian Living Today* (2001).

KIERAN CRONIN is a Franciscan friar who has taught Moral Theology and Ethics at the Mater Dei Institute, Dublin, and the Irish School of Ecumenics, Trinity College, Dublin. He is currently Acting Head of the Centre of Philosophy, Milltown Institute, Dublin.

M.B. CROWE was born in Cahir, Co. Tipperary in 1923. He was ordained a priest for the Archdiocese of Dublin in 1949. He lectured in Philosophy at University College Dublin until his death in 1980, having previously done research at Boston College and lectured at the University of Louvain.

SEÁN FAGAN is a Marist priest. He is the author of *Has Sin Changed?* (1977), *Does Morality Change?* (1997), *What Happened to Sin?* (2008), and of numerous articles on theology, spirituality and religious life. He was Secretary General of the Society of Mary in Rome from 1983–1995.

AMELIA FLEMING is a graduate of St Patrick's College, Maynooth, and lectures in Theology at Carlow College. She has published in *The Furrow, Doctrine and Life* and the *Irish Theological Quarterly*. Her current research centres on the relationship between Christian faith and contemporary culture.

SEÁN FREYNE is Professor Emeritus of Theology at Trinity College, Dublin, and was formerly director of the Centre for Mediterranean and Near Eastern Studies there. Since his retirement he has been a Visiting Professor of Early Christian History and Literature at the Harvard Divinity School. His most recent book is *Jesus: a Jewish Galilean* (2005).

RAPHAEL GALLAGHER, an Irish Redemptorist priest, is currently Visiting Professor at the Alphonsian Academy, Rome. He is the co-author of *History and Conscience: Studies in Honour of Fr Sean O'Riordan* (1989), and author of *Understanding the Homosexual* (1985) and *Sean O'Riordan: A Theologian of Development* (1988).

PATRICK HANNON, a priest of the diocese of Cloyne, is Professor Emeritus of Moral Theology at St Patrick's College, Maynooth. He is the author of *Church, State, Morality and Law* (1992), *Moral Decision Making* (2005) and *Moral Theology: A Reader* (2006), and of the forthcoming *Right or Wrong? Essays in Moral Theology* (2009).

DONAL HARRINGTON was a lecturer in Moral Theology at the Mater Dei Institute and Holy Cross College, Clonliffe. He is the author of *What is Morality?* (1996).

WILFRID J. HARRINGTON OP is Professor Emeritus at the Milltown Institute of Theology and Philosophy. He is also Visiting Lecturer at the Church of Ireland Theological College.

LINDA HOGAN is Professor of Ecumenics at the Irish School of Ecumenics, Trinity College, Dublin. She is the author of *Confronting the Truth: Conscience in the Catholic Tradition* (2000) and *From Women's Experience to Feminist Theology* (1995, 1998).

MAUREEN JUNKER-KENNY is Associate Professor of Theology at the School of Religions and Theology, Trinity College, Dublin. She is co-editor of the *International Journal of Practical Theology, Ethics and Education,* of the series *Practical Theology in the Discourse of the Humanities* and of the *Encyclopedia of Applied Ethics.*

JAMES P. MACKEY is Thomas Chalmers Professor of Theology (Emeritus) at the University of Edinburgh, and Visiting Professor at Trinity College, Dublin. He is the author of *Jesus of Nazareth: The Life, the Faith and the Future of the Prophet* (2008).

VINCENT MACNAMARA has taught in theological institutes in Ireland and Rome. He is the author of *Faith and Ethics: Recent Roman Catholicism* (1985), *The Truth in Love: Reflections on Christian Morality* (1988) and *New Life for Old: On Desire and Becoming Human* (2004).

PATRICK MASTERSON is former Dean of the Faculty of Philosophy at University College Dublin and former President of UCD and of the European University Institute, Florence.

ANDREW D.H. MAYES is Erasmus Smith's Professor of Hebrew at Trinity College, Dublin. His chief research interests are in the Hebrew Bible and in early Israelite history and religion. He is the author of *The Old Testament in Sociological Perspective* (1989) and the co-editor of *Recognising the Margins: Developments in Biblical and Theological Studies* (2007).

ENDA MCDONAGH was Professor of Moral Theology from 1958–1995 at St Patrick's College, Maynooth. He is the author of numerous publications, including *Immersed in Mystery: En Route to Theology* (2007), and the editor of *Remembering to Forgive: A Tribute to Una O'Higgins O'Malley* (2008).

P.J. MCGRATH lectured in Philosophy at University College Cork, St Patrick's College, Maynooth, Carlow College and the University of Surrey. He is the author of *The Nature of Moral Judgment* (1969), *The Objectivity of Morals* (2003), *Believing in God* (1995) and *The Justification of Religious Belief* (1997).

JAMES G. MURPHY SJ lectures in Philosophy at the Milltown Institute, Dublin. He has worked in the Jesuit Centre for Faith and Justice and has published both on philosophy and on public and social justice issues.

Biographies   3

DENIS O'CALLAGHAN has had long and varied experience in academic and pastoral life over half a century. A former professor of Moral Theology at St Patrick's College, Maynooth, he was a frequent contributor to theological journals in Ireland and abroad. He is the author of *Putting Hand to the Plough* (2007) and *Gone Fishing: Anecdotes of an Angler* (2008).

NOEL DERMOT O'DONOGHUE was a priest of the Diocese of Kerry. He was Professor of Ethics in the Faculty of Philosophy at St Patrick's College, Maynooth. He subsequently joined the OCD (Carmelites) and was a lecturer in Theology and Spirituality at the University of Edinburgh until his death. One of his publications is the much-admired *Heaven in Ordinarie: Prayer in Transcendence* (1979).

PATRICK RIORDAN is a Jesuit of the Irish Province and former President of the Milltown Institute, Dublin. He is currently lecturer in Political Philosophy at Heythrop College, London. His research interests include the philosophy of justice, religion and politics, and the Common Good.

D. VINCENT TWOMEY, a priest of the Divine Word Missionaries, studied Philosophy at Donamon and Theology at St Patrick's College, Maynooth, before doing his doctorate in Regensburg. He taught Theology in Papua New Guinea, Austria, Switzerland, Germany and finally at St Patrick's College, Maynooth, where he was Professor of Moral Theology until 2006.

Research and Editorial Assistants

Aoife McGrath is a graduate of the Pontifical University, Maynooth, and lectures in the Department of Religious Studies in St Patrick's College in Thurles. Her teaching interests are in the areas of sexual ethics and bioethics. Her current research centres on ecclesial and experiential sources of the theology of marriage.

Siobhán Mooney is a graduate of the Pontifical University, Maynooth, and an occasional lecturer in its Department of Systematic Theology. She is currently a recipient of the Scholastic Trust Doctoral Scholarship in Theology. Her research concerns the topic of transcendence in the work of Jean-Luc Marion.

General Introduction

The Historical and Global Context

The immediate origins of this work lie in a conversation between the editors almost four years ago now. They were conscious of the large amount of material published in Ireland in the area of moral theology over their academic lifetimes but which lay scattered across a wide range of publications and so were no longer readily available to colleagues, students or interested lay readers. Given the innovative character of much of these writings in method and content, reflecting broader changes in Church and society, such a work could also provide some historical picture of the achievements, challenges and interests of the Ireland of its time. Although we considered ourselves familiar with much if not all of the relevant literature and its authors, we took the precaution of writing to those authors still active, explaining the project. We invited them to propose some appropriate articles or chapters and we also suggested some titles of theirs chosen by ourselves. The vast majority were extremely cooperative and we were flooded with titles and even texts.

Although the thrust of this work is to present Irish writers and writings in moral theology, these were inevitably influenced by the wider global context in which they were studying and writing. Several very significant events for the whole of Irish life took place early in this period: the Second Vatican Council, 1962–1965; the onset of the 'Troubles' in Northern Ireland in the late 1960s; the Republic of Ireland joining the European Common Market (now the EU) in 1973; and all this within the maelstrom of the social upheavals of the 1960s and 1970s from civil rights to feminism, particularly in Europe and North America. Liberation movements in Latin America, de-colonisation in Africa, and a range of developments in Asia, including at one end of the spectrum the Vietnam War and at the other fresh interest in Eastern religion and meditation, fuelled the spiritual as well as the political and cultural upheavals in the West and in the Christian churches world-wide. On top of all this came economic globalisation and Ireland's participation in the boom and now the bust, amid the growing fears of climate change.

Inevitably a theology of Christian living, or moral theology as it has been usually called in the Roman Catholic tradition, faced powerful new challenges and had to draw on new or at least renewed resources. Ireland was never entirely removed from these broader developments. Its missionary presence in Latin America, Africa and Asia ensured that their crises and challenges were felt back home. These global religious, cultural and political affairs did, as we hope will be obvious, play their part in Irish writings in moral theology and partly explains the desire to publish this extensive if necessarily incomplete anthology of them.

The thrust of the previous paragraphs has been to emphasise the impact of critical developments in society and Church on the living and believing conditions of Christians both as individual agents and members of an intimate community, the Church and Body of Christ. This work in its moral focus is primarily concerned with Christian belonging, behaviour and transformation, both personal and communal. As Christian it is intrinsically connected to Christian belief and worship. As belonging it reveals the centrality of membership of Christian and human community. As behaviour it is individual in its responsibility but conscious of its continuing practical and theoretical interchange with traditions of morality which have originated and developed outside its ambit.

It is assumed that 'Christian' in this discussion has a Jewish dimension as originating in the Jew, Jesus Christ and his early Jewish disciples. The Hebrew summary phrase 'the Law and the Prophets' is invoked to express the moral continuity between the two great traditions, the Old Law and the New, the Jewish and the Christian, although not without discontinuity as well. A rather different continuity–discontinuity between the religio-moral traditions of Jews and Christians and that of their non-religious or other-religious contemporaries informs both Old and New Testaments and their scriptures. The complex pre-history of the decalogue and still more the sources of some of the Wisdom literature in the Hebrew scriptures testify to that fertile if critical exchange. In the Christian scriptures this Hebrew heritage carries the interchange further. Fresh dialogue with and integration of Stoic and other moral ideas and ideals are obvious in the writings of St Paul for example. While the Hebrew and Christian scriptures remain standard reference points for future generations of Christians, practical and theoretical developments without as well as within Christianity have explicitly through eventual dialogue (e.g. human rights) or implicitly through changing political and cultural contexts (e.g. justification of war) resulted in crucial developments in Christian morality and moral theology. Clearly these developments are far from finished. Just as the moral life of the Christian individual has a narrative or historical form, so have the moral life of the Church and its systematic analysis and presentation in the Church. Indeed in all human societies, moral analysis and presentation, however abstract or absolute and self-sufficient they may seem, have their own narrative and historical character. Over the fifty years with which this work deals, the narrative dimension in its theological, secular and practical forms must be kept continuously in mind if rigidity and fundamentalism and consequent misjudgement are to be avoided.

Although it had its antecedents in the Irish and other Penitentials in the eighth and ninth centuries and more particularly in the *Summae Confessorum* of the Middle Ages, moral theology as a discipline with its specialist authors and writings emerged primarily in the Roman Catholic tradition in the aftermath of the Reformation and the Council of Trent. In this form it issued in manuals for the training of confessors, a form which predominated until the time of the Second Vatican Council.

In the decades immediately prior to that Council, attempts to break out of the manual tradition and develop moral theology as a theology of the Christian life with explicit roots in the scriptures were beginning to have an impact through the work of Tillman, Leclercq, Häring, Gilleman, Fuchs and others. Indeed some of this renewal had already begun to surface in Ireland. For the Reformed churches a formal discipline had not developed in the same way, mainly due no doubt to their exclusion of Penance as a sacrament. The Church of England was the exception here and maintained with difficulty a distinct tradition of moral theology. The other churches dealt with this area as practical theology or Christian ethics or theological ethics but often without the stress the Catholic Church laid on it. In these volumes we are dealing mainly with the Catholic tradition as it developed over the last fifty years in Ireland, from just before Vatican II until the present day. We do however try to integrate important material from Anglican and other Church scholars in Ireland in the same period.

While we retain the term 'moral theology' as still in general usage, a more accurately descriptive term would be a Theology of Christian Life or of Christian Living. This would both distinguish it from and relate it closely to that other dominant and traditional Catholic discipline of dogmatic or systematic theology, the theology of Christian belief or Christian believing. Their sharp separation from each other, and particularly in the case of moral theology, their separation from scripture in the centuries between Trent and Vatican II was an impoverishment which recent developments have been attempting to correct. This Irish anthology seeks to record some efforts at such correction. The fuller integration of these disciplines is still in process, while account must also be taken of their relation to liturgy and spirituality.

Of course all theological disciplines must take account of a range of cognate secular disciplines such as philosophy and philosophical ethics to ensure their own intellectual relevance and integrity. Scientific disciplines, both hard and soft, challenge Christian believing and living as never before and have been addressed by Irish theologians, especially moral theologians, as these volumes also demonstrate. The imaginative works of writers and artists frequently illuminate the mystery and the morality of the human condition and its Christian dimension. So the relation between ethics and aesthetics has received some attention from Irish theologians during this period.

This brief sketch of the background and concerns of the Reader is also an indication of the shape of the work as a whole. The first volume, entitled

'Foundations', deals with the origins and development of the current renewal of the basics of moral theology, including its scriptural and philosophical foundations. Critical to that renewal has been the move from the focus on actions to the focus on agents, personal agents, persons. The further two volumes elaborate on this personal moral agency. Volume II deals with personal issues of life and death, of medical and bioethics, of gender, sex and marriage. Volume III deals with social, economic and ecological issues, including those of human rights, discrimination, peace and war. In concluding with reflections on Christian morality's relation to liturgy, spirituality and personal prayer as well as to art and aesthetics, the third volume and the work as a whole will be seeking to give a more complete account and analysis of the Christian moral journey through the human life cycle in person and community.

THE EARLIER IRISH TRADITION

Like the sexual revolution or the reforms of Vatican II, moral theology and its renewal did not begin even in Ireland in the 1960s. The complete tradition in Ireland is coterminous with the coming of Christianity in the fifth century, although it was of course then derivative from the Latin tradition of presenting and applying the Christian way of life. Particular Irish innovations arose somewhat later through the dominant monastic structure, the repetition and then privatization of the sacrament of Penance, with the Penitential Books to which this gave rise. The introduction of these practices and books by Irish missionaries into Europe had a powerful impact. Some modern scholars, including Bernard Häring, have been inclined to blame the deficiencies of the later manuals of moral theology after Trent on this original Irish influence. This is however, given the complex developments from the Lateran Council of 1215 to the Council of Trent in the sixteenth century, much too simple an explanation.

In the post-Trent period up to the nineteenth century there was no opportunity to develop Catholic theology in any form in Ireland, and the Reformed churches, including the established Anglican Church of Ireland, had little distinctive tradition of such a theology. Later in the century Professor George Crolly at Maynooth (1844–1878) produced his own volume on justice presented in *Disputatio* form and including discussion of the relevant civil law. *Disputiones Theologicae de Justitia et Jure* was published in Dublin in 1870. Crolly had been one of those accused of Gallicanism.

William Walsh, Professor of Dogmatic and Moral Theology (as was then the practice), afterwards President of Maynooth (1867–1885), later Archbishop of Dublin and first Chancellor of the National University of Ireland, published such serious material as the volume *De Actibus Humanis* (1889), which was well received internationally and reflected in quite a sophisticated manner the current return to Thomas Aquinas. He also played a notable role in seeking to resolve the critically moral land question for Ireland in the 1880s. His intervention on the

Roman Rescript, which seemed to condemn a vital part of the Irish National League and its land programme known as the Plan of Campaign, was crucial to the further success of the League and its land restoration and wider political objectives.

A successor in Moral and (Dogmatic) Theology and later Prefect of the Dunboyne Institute of Postgraduate Studies at Maynooth, Walter McDonald (1881–1921) helped establish the *Irish Theological Quarterly* (1907). He was at one stage accused of modernism. He published several books of his own and in one of these, *Some Ethical Questions of Peace and War* (1919), he criticised the use of violence in the struggle for Irish independence, although some of the Irish bishops had come to accept it. About this time also a sharp theological debate emerged on the ethics of hunger strike, as employed by people like Terence McSweeney in protest at British rule in Ireland. This debate was initiated by Canon John Waters, a Dublin moral theologian, in the *Irish Ecclesiastic Record* in 1918, and continued there and in the *Tablet* for some time. Another participant was Maynooth moralist, Patrick Cleary, later a bishop in the Nancheng province in China with the Columba Missionary Society. In the following decades Fathers Edward Cahill SJ and Eddie Coyne SJ, moral theologians both, were prominent in a number of moral debates, including for Coyne that of the Mother and Child Bill proposed by then Minister for Health Dr Noel Browne in 1950. I mention these events to illustrate the kind of lively moral debate for good and for ill that did emerge in Ireland over the previous century, which had few parallels in the wider Church.

The *Irish Ecclesiastical Record* (IER), first published in the 1860s and lasting into the 1970s, carried regular features on moral theology, particularly in the question and answer form practised in many journals of this era. John MacCarthy of Maynooth was widely quoted for his IER answers to current questions in English-speaking journals during the 1940s and 1950s. Other journals such as the *Irish Theological Quarterly* and *Studies* sometimes carried more extended and systematic treatments of moral issues. This very scrappy account of the earlier Irish moral theology tradition may serve as a reminder of historical scholarship still to be undertaken, and of our own earlier roots. The only example of this work included here is an article by William Cardinal Conway, Professor of Moral Theology at Maynooth (1943–1958). Apart from just about fitting into the chosen timeframe, he had written about the new developments of moral theology in Europe. His most quoted piece however is a discussion of 'The Act of Two Effects', which he published in 1951 and which is included in this volume.

Even the full three volumes could not cope with the range of authors and materials published over the fifty years or be sure of selecting only the best of even individual authors. A decision has been taken to include as many worthwhile authors and topics as possible without giving undue coverage to any particular author or topic. Yet when the final selections were made, we realised that many valuable pieces had to be omitted, and that others, and this we particularly regret, could be included only in part. Such are the limitations of space and still more of editorial judgement. If this of its nature and genesis be not the very best collection possible of the material published by Irish moral theologians over the last half-century, we hope that it may be sufficiently interesting in itself and truly illuminating of a road well travelled, though the journey is far from complete. Mistaken omissions and inclusions, for which we apologise in advance, will be picked up by the alert professional reader with her or his own set of criteria.

Enda McDonagh
February 2009

Introduction

Volume 1: Foundations

Two issues dominated the area of Catholic moral theology, which we refer to as Foundations, over the last fifty years. They were both, not surprisingly, concerned with method. The first was about the sources of moral knowledge. Neo-Scholastic moral theology was framed by the notion of a creator God who was the human being's ultimate end and who instituted the moral order as a way towards that end. That moral order was to be found in scripture, in natural law philosophy and in canon law as articulated by the Church. The appeal to scripture, if it occurred at all, was as a corroborative proof to conclusions already arrived at by reference to Church teaching.

Outside the textbook tradition there was a richer, more directly scriptural approach in the German-speaking countries. Gradually, during the 1940s and 1950s of the last century, this began to exercise a greater influence. The manual tradition, which was dominant for centuries, and which is traced in one of our articles, was criticised as a mixture of philosophy and jurisprudence, that was minimalist in its view of the moral life. Specifically, it was seen as a failure to breathe the spirit of Christian life as found in the scriptures and in the early Church. The basic error, it was said, was that it sought its inspiration and method in the wrong source – in philosophy and natural law – the assumption being that revelation should make a difference to morality and give it a different content. There was a call for a morality 'out of the middle of the revelation', as one author put it. The climax of this was the direction of Vatican II that the teaching of moral theology was to be reformed. Its soul, the Council said, ought to be scripture. Such a move was facilitated by the very considerable development in scripture studies, recently freed from official suspicion.

So Catholic authors embraced a scriptural approach. There were brave efforts, notable studies in the moral theology of the Bible, particularly by biblical scholars. But because the theologians had little serious tradition to guide them, the project proved to be more difficult than was envisaged. It was one thing to elaborate the moral teaching of the scriptures, another to determine the significance of that for moral discernment today. Very soon, as the problem of method emerged, there were misgivings of various kinds. A number of the articles in this volume witness to that ongoing effort of renewal, to the reactions which it provoked, and to the extension of the question to the broader issue of the relationship between morality and religion.

Whatever position theologians took about the bearing of the biblical culture on Christian judgement, they found that they could not absolve themselves from a serious engagement with the traditions of ethical theory. This was the second major issue. The manual that was in use until the 1960s continued the dependence on natural law theory. The notion of natural law has a long and honourable history. But the version in vogue was heavily physicalist. Disenchantment with this led to major disagreements: disagreement about particular issues, such as birth control, was in part a disagreement about moral method. There are better understandings of natural law that that of the manuals and, indeed, the Vatican itself has more recently sought to distance itself from a physicalist/ biological approach, though not wholly satisfactorily. It is important therefore that Part Three of this volume offer reflection on moral theory. It begins with two major articles on the natural law in Aquinas, which will be a useful research source. Other articles reflect developing thinking on natural law through a half-century, and modern approaches to moral theory. Many of the authors in this section are themselves professional philosophers. But they all show an interest in the theological question and, in particular, in how natural law fares in the moral tradition of the Church.

There follow, finally, some more practical issues. If notions of morality change, so do notions of sin. If there is debate not just about moral particulars but about fundamental method, the question of conscience becomes more acute. The theological climate of fifty years ago did not suffer much diversity of opinion in the area of morality. More than most other areas of thought, it was always an area of special concern for Church authority. The imposition of a common, universal morality on Catholics was seen as crucial to the unity and coherence of the Church: the task of the moral theologian was very much regarded as the elaboration and defence of Church teaching. As theologians gradually found courage openly to question received positions, and a greater diversity of opinion emerged, the question of conscience became more critical. It remains a live issue for many Catholics. Parallel to that was a questioning of received teaching on sin. A significant part of the manual text-book was concerned with sin – the notion of sin, its distinctions, and its gravity. Changing notions of morality, and questions about the relationship of religion and morality, necessarily gave rise to changing notions of sin. Theologians were soon suggesting that some of the accepted teaching was less than credible. About such matters there has been much discussion over the last fifty years. The articles of this section offer interesting commentary.

Vincent MacNamara
February 2009

An Irish Reader in Moral Theology

Part One
Scriptural Approaches

1   The Law, the Prophets and the Gospel

Wilfrid J. Harrington

(Enda McDonagh (ed.), *Moral Theology Renewed: Papers of the Maynooth Union Summer School 1964,* Dublin: Gill & Son, 1965, pp. 31–54.)

It is still too readily taken for granted that the legalistic religion of pharisaism, so severely criticised by Our Lord, is a fair enough picture of Old Testament religion and morality – a way of life all hedged about by futile and soul-destroying laws. The truth of the matter is that, until the later stages of Judaism, the Torah was not at all regarded as an oppressive burden but was gladly accepted as God's gift to his people. Jesus did not reproach the scribes and pharisees for their attachment to the law but for their failure to grasp the spirit of it; immersed in their casuistry they had neglected the 'weightier matters of the law, justice and mercy and faith'.[1] Indeed, the pharisaic outlook is more in harmony with bare and bald casuistic teaching than it is representative of the biblical moral doctrine. The renewal of our moral theology can be forwarded by a study of the Old Testament as well as of the New.

The object of this paper is to indicate something of the depth and breadth of the Torah, the will of God for his people, and to trace its pervasive influence through life and literature of Israel. It will be shown that the moral teaching of the prophets developed in harmony with the law and that there is no conflict between prophet and priest. Finally it will be seen that Christ brought a new dimension into human life and that ever since the moral life of the Christian is, or ought to be, guided by the law of Christ – a commandment of love.

THE LAW

The Hebrew word *torah* has a wider signification, one less strictly juridical, than the *nomos* of the LXX or the English 'law'; it is a 'teaching' given by God to men in order to regulate their conduct. That is why the whole Pentateuch, and not only the legislation, is called the Torah. In fact, framed in a narrative setting, the Pentateuch contains the ensemble of prescriptions which ruled the moral, social and religious life of the people. All of these prescriptions, moral, juridical and cultic, have a religious character, and the whole corpus is presented as the charter of a covenant with Yahweh and is linked with the narrative of happenings in the desert where the covenant was made.

While it remains true that the basis of the legislation goes back to the time of Moses, the Pentateuch, in its present form, includes many laws of later ages. It is simply not conceivable that a legal code, drawn up for a small nomad people in the thirteenth century BC, would have remained unchanged for over a thousand years while that people became successively an agricultural community, a monarchy and a church. Laws are made to be applied and must necessarily be adapted to changing conditions. So, for instance, much of the priestly legislation found in Exodus 25-31, 35-40 bears the stamp of later times. The Covenant Code[2] is the law of a pastoral and agricultural society, and it met the conditions of Israel already settled in Palestine. The ritual laws of Ex 34:14-26 date from the same time but show some influence of Deuteronomy. Leviticus took its final shape after the Exile, in the Second Temple, but the basis of it goes back to the primitive ritual of the desert. The Law of Holiness[3] seems to have been codified towards the close of the monarchy. The deuteronomical code[4] is earlier than the fall of Samaria in 721, and though it shows a development that is influenced by an appreciation of the love of Yahweh for his people and of Israel's consequent obligation to act as he would act, it is basically a reinterpretation and a new presentation of earlier laws.

It seems possible to identify some of the earlier laws of the Pentateuch on the basis of form. Two general types are readily noted: casuistic (or hypothetical) law and apodeictic (or categorical) law. Both types are well represented in Ex 22; the hypothetical type in vv 1-17 ('If ...' with the provision in the third person) and the apodeictic form in vv 18, 21f. ('Thou shalt not ...', with the injunction in the second person). Hypothetical law was common throughout the ancient world, especially in Mesopotamia and among the Hittites, and is best represented in the Code of Hammurabi.[5] Apodeictic law is peculiar to Israel. This fact powerfully strengthens the argument that the decalogue (to take a striking example) goes back to Moses. The Ten Commandments, in Hebrew the 'Ten Words,' are given twice;[6] both versions are in apodeictic form – though several of the commandments have been expanded in later times – and both go back to a common primitive form set out in sharp, terse language. In general, it may be said that the apodeictic laws are early and may well represent a nucleus that originated with Moses. However, for our purpose, instead of analysing and comparing the various codes within the Pentateuch, it is more profitable to set that work in its covenant background and to examine the four great strands of which it is woven.

The Covenant

To express the nature of the link which exists between God and his people, the Old Testament uses the word *berith* (rendered in the Greek by *diath?k??* and in Latin by *testamentum*). In English it is generally translated 'covenant'. This term 'covenant', which in its technical theological sense concerns the relations of man with God, was borrowed from the social experience of men, from the fact of treaties and alliances between peoples and individuals. In practice, the religious use of the term regards a special type of covenant, that in which one partner takes the initiative and imposes the conditions. This is exactly the pattern of the Sinai covenant.

At Sinai the people, delivered from Egyptian bondage, entered into a covenant with Yahweh and the cult of Yahweh was established as the national religion. A study of Hittite treaties has shed light on the nature of this covenant.[7] Two types of treaty may be distinguished: the parity pact and the suzerainty pact. In a parity covenant both partners, standing on equal terms, bound themselves by bilateral obligations. The suzerainty covenant, on the other hand, was made between a king and his vassal and was unilateral. The suzerain 'gave' a covenant and the vassal was obliged to accept and obey the conditions of the suzerain. Yet such a covenant was not just an assertion of power and authority on the part of the suzerain; it was explicitly regarded and presented as an act of benevolence, and the vassal accepted the obligations in a sense of gratitude. In keeping with this conception the covenant was couched in an 'I-Thou' dialogue form.

At the vision of the burning bush Yahweh revealed to Moses both his name and his plan for Israel; he willed to deliver Israel from Egypt and to install his people in the land of Canaan.[8] This plan presupposed that Israel was the object of his choice and the recipient of a promise; the Exodus demonstrated that God was capable of imposing his will ('You have seen how I bore you on eagles' wings and brought you to myself' – Ex 19:4) and the people responded by faith.[9] Then God revealed the terms of the covenant: 'If you will obey my voice and keep my covenant, you shall be my own possession among all peoples; for all the earth is mine, and you shall be to me a kingdom of priests and a holy nation.'[10] Israel will henceforth be his kingdom, his people will render him due cult. In return, God will 'tabernacle' in the midst of his people: 'They shall know that I am the Lord their God, who brought them forth out of the land of Egypt that I might dwell among them.'[11] The Sinai covenant, however, was conditional. In granting this covenant to Israel and in making promises God imposed conditions which Israel must observe. But these laws and institutions were laid down and established in order that Israel should be a holy people; they are an expression of divine benevolence, even though failure to observe them will entail a curse.[12]

The covenant of Sinai revealed in a definitive manner an essential aspect of the plan of salvation. God had willed to join himself to men by establishing a cultic community dedicated to his service, ruled by his law, the recipient of his promises; the New Testament will fully realise this divine project. Although the covenant was God's free gift to Israel it became enmeshed in the historical destiny of Israel to such an extent that salvation tended to be regarded as the reward of human fidelity to the law. Its limitation to one nation tended to obscure the universal scope of God's plan, while the promises of temporal rewards could cause men to lose sight of the religious object of the covenant – the establishment of the kingship of God over Israel and through Israel over the whole world.[13] Nonetheless, the covenant of Sinai dominated Israel's history and the development of revelation. It is the inspiration of the Torah.

The Yahwist[14]

The work of the Yahwist is a synthesis, both in form and in substance, and yet this writer is one of the most creative literary artists of Israel. He gathered together the traditions of the tribes and of the sanctuaries and reworked them in order to make the old relevant to the new. Many of these old narratives are aetiologies, that is, their purpose was to explain, in a popular way, some facts in tribal history, or the names of places, or certain aspects of the cult. The Yahwist combined these different materials in a new literary structure, a great epic extending from the creation of the world to the conquest of Transjordan. Some of the individual stories taken by themselves, for example, the angel marriages[15] and the Tower of Babel,[16] betray a primitive theological outlook; but, as used by the Yahwist, they play their part in the presentation of his elevated theology.

The Yahwist is keenly aware of the forces of evil at work in the world; he has no illusions about humanity and he unpityingly exposes human weakness, but he is an optimist at heart. He has confidence in nature and her laws which will not be disrupted by another deluge. He shows the persistence and expansion of life, the good fortune of the sons of Jacob, Israel delivered from slavery, the twelve tribes on their way to a land flowing with milk and honey. This optimism is based on a knowledge of Yahweh, on confidence in his plan and in his power. Yahweh is transcendent but draws near to men, and this nearness is expressed in bold anthropomorphisms. God demands of men faith, courage and confidence in the traditions and in the life of the nation.[17]

The Yahwist's epic falls into three parts: primeval history, the patriarchal tradition, the Mosaic tradition. The primeval history, constructed from elements of very different kinds, proclaims that all evil comes from sin and testifies to a growth in evil. Yet the widening chasm between God and man remains spanned by a bridge of mercy and is matched by an increasing power of grace. In the call of Abraham[18] primeval history is linked with sacred history and finds its meaning in this link.[19] The Yahwist continues his theological synthesis by utilising the patriarchal traditions. In his eyes Abraham is the model patriarch, yet the promises of God are destined not for him but for his posterity. Right through the patriarchal epoch run the cult of the same God (the 'God of the fathers') and the participation of successive generations in the same divine promises. Similarly, the God who revealed himself to Moses at the burning bush is the 'God of the fathers'[20] and it is Moses who communicated to the people the will of God, his words, in the form of a ritual decalogue.[21]

The Elohist

The Elohist begins with the call of Abraham and so does not have a primeval history; in this he lacks the scope of the Yahwist. Similarly, the Elohist does not show the theological depth, much less the literary artistry, of the Yahwist. Yet what he loses in vividness and brilliance he gains somewhat in moral sensibility. His sense of sin is more refined than that of the Yahwist. So, for instance, he avoids the impression that Abraham had lied to Abimelech by stating explicitly that Sarah was the patriarch's half-sister.[22] For him the law is more moral than cultic. The basis of it, as it finds expression in the decalogue, concerns man's duties towards God and towards his neighbour. These duties are made more explicit in the Covenant Code[23] where the respect of one's neighbour and of his goods is regulated by customs and precepts that have been sanctioned by God. The Elohist tends to emphasise the distance of God from men, at least in comparison with the Yahwist's approach. Anthropomorphism is restricted. God does not walk among men[24] but speaks from heaven[25] and in dreams.[26] Indeed it is stated explicitly: 'Let not God speak to us, lest we die.'[27] In the story of Joseph the Elohist brings out the religious significance of the events: 'As for you, you meant evil against me; but God meant it for good, to bring it about that many people should be kept alive, as they are today.'[28]

The Deuteronomist

The kernel of Deuteronomy is the legal code,[29] of northern origin, and going back ultimately to the Mosaic age; the narrative part, the three discourses of Moses, are much later, from just before and after the Exile. The second discourse[30] is especially fitting in the mouth of the great leader because the essential purpose of Deuteronomy is a revival of Mosaic teaching as it was understood in the seventh century BC; it is a reform programme, not an innovation. Hence the appeal for covenant renewal, made with urgency, the repetition of 'this day'– the here and now of the divine election – and the involvement of the present generation of Israel in the covenant made at Horeb.[31] The law of the one sanctuary[32] is inspired by the same reforming spirit: to preserve the purified code of Yahweh from all contamination.

In the discourses characteristic turns of phrase keep cropping up. God is always 'Yahweh thy God' or 'Yahweh your God'. Canaan is described as 'a land flowing with milk and honey', and, in order that they might possess it, God had delivered his people from Egypt 'with a mighty hand and an outstretched arm'. That is why the people are admonished to 'hear the voice of Yahweh your God' and to 'keep his statutes and his commandments and ordinances' and to 'fear Yahweh your God'. Above all, they are exhorted: 'You shall love Yahweh your God with all your heart, and with all your soul and with all your might' – the manifest influence of Hosea. And throughout there is the frequent reminder that faithful observance of the commandments of Yahweh will ensure a blessing and the warning that neglect of the commandments will bring upon them the anger of a loving but just God.

That warning should have been unnecessary, for these 'statutes, commandments and ordinances' are not a heavy burden imposed from without, but are intimate, interior: 'For this commandment which I have commanded you this day is not too hard for you; it is in your mouth and in your heart, so that you can do it.'[33] Yahweh is a Father who gives his life-giving word to Israel, the word that brings happiness and long life.

A characteristic of Deuteronomy, and one which witnesses to the northern origin of the tradition, is the influence of Hosea. Indeed, together with the whole deuteronomical history,[34] it becomes a commentary on Chapter II of Hosea:

> When Israel was a child I loved him, and out of Egypt I called my son. But the more I called them the farther they departed from me … How can I give you up, O Ephraim![35]

Hosea is not the only prophet whose influence is evident. Jeremiah[36] had foreseen a deliverance, a return, a new covenant; it was in the light of his vision that Deuteronomy was completed. And in its final chapters too our book joins Second Isaiah who described the new journey across the desert and the victory over the nations now summoned to adore the God of Israel, the only true God. Other images are borrowed from Ezekiel who also described the return from the Exile and the new division of the holy land around the new sanctuary.[37] Thus inspired by the prophetic message Deuteronomy, in its final edition, is a witness to a crucial stage in religious history when a monarchy yielded place to a church.[38]

The Priestly Tradition

At much the same time that the deuteronomical code took shape in the north, the traditions of the Jerusalem priests were compiled in the Holiness Code.[39] Like the deuteronomical code it opens with the law of one sanctuary and then gives several series of prescriptions regarding morality, the priests, the sacrifices and the feasts; it closes like Deuteronomy with blessings and curses.[40] Israel is conceived as an *edah*, a worshipping community, ruled by the priests. The object of the priests was to raise men to God by fidelity to the traditional laws and prescriptions. Their guiding principle was the command: 'You shall be holy; for I Yahweh your God am holy.'[41]

During the Exile the deported priests, cut off from the elaborate ritual worship of Yahweh in his Temple, saw that their duty was to organise the religious life of the community in these different surroundings and circumstances. It seemed to them that the foundations on which the religious life might be built must be a common national origin, common traditions and an authentic priesthood. So the priestly history took shape. The religious institutions of Israel were authorised and given greater force by being set in a historical framework, and by projecting all these institutions back into the Mosaic age it was dramatically emphasised that they had their beginnings at Sinai. The whole presentation is pervaded by a theology of the divine presence and by the demands of a God of holiness.

If we look at the priestly history as a whole we see it as the fruit of a theological reflection on the ancient liturgical traditions and customs preserved by the Jerusalem priests. Fidelity to these traditions is the only guarantee of a life in union with God, the only means of bringing about the fulfilment of God's purpose for Israel. This follows from a consideration of that plan as it gradually unfolded.

There was a covenant of God with all humanity in the person of Noah – it assured earthly existence if men would respect the life of creatures. There was a covenant with Abraham – it guaranteed his descendants a future in the promised land if they would observe the Sabbath and circumcision. There was a more personal covenant with the Aaronitic priesthood which made of them the associates of God and the dispensers of the divine benefits; the cult is the sensible sign of divine grace. The monarchy had failed; in the mind of the priestly writer Aaron must henceforth take its place – Israel in exile is sustained by the priesthood in her fidelity to the national and religious traditions. For Israel is 'a kingdom (ruled by) priests and a holy nation' (Ex 19:6).[42]

The Pentateuch

The religion of the Old Testament, like that of the New, is a historical religion; it is based on the revelation made by God to certain men in given places and on the interventions of God at certain determined moments. The Pentateuch, which traces the history of these relations of God with the world, is the foundation of the Jewish religion, its sacred book *par excellence*, its law. In it the Israelite found the explanation of his destiny and a way of life.

The Pentateuch is drawn into a unity by the threads of promise and election, of covenant and law which run through it. To Adam and Eve, after the Fall, God gives the assurance of salvation in the distant future; after the Flood he reassures Noah that the earth will never again be so disastrously stricken. Abraham is the man of promises: for himself and for his posterity and through them for all mankind. In God's free choice of Abraham the election of Israel is foreseen and included. The Pentateuch is also the book of covenants: tacit with Adam, explicit with Noah, Abraham and Moses. Each covenant is a free exercise of divine initiative, an act of benevolence; God demands in return fidelity and obedience. The law which he gives will make explicit the divine demands and prepare the way for the fulfilment of the promises. The unifying themes of the Pentateuch continue into the rest of the Old Testament, for the Pentateuch is not complete in itself. It tells of the promise but not of its fulfilment, and it closes before the entry into the promised land. But even when the Conquest is achieved the fulfilment is not yet, for the promise looks ultimately to Christ, to the new covenant and to his commandment.

Though in its earliest forms prophetism in Israel was little different from the same phenomenon in Mesopotamia, and especially in Phoenicia and Canaan, it developed into something distinctive, into something unique in fact, and became one of the most significant factors in the history of the chosen people. Indeed the prophetic movement, by itself, goes far to explain the survival of the Jewish nation. But the prophets did more than assure the survival of a people. They carried on a religious tradition which they had inherited, fostered its development between the eighth and fourth centuries, and passed it on, immeasurably enriched, to Judaism. They were entirely faithful to the dogma fixed in the Mosaic age, ethical monotheism,[43] and exploited it to the full. They were guides, carefully chosen – specially raised – along a vital and precarious stage of the spiritual journey that led to Christ. Here we shall be content to sketch the moral doctrine of some of the greatest of them.

Amos, the earliest of the 'writing' prophets, is the champion of justice. He took his stand on the essential justice of God and vindicated the moral order established by God and enshrined in his Covenant. So he mercilessly castigated the disorders that prevailed in an era of hectic prosperity. To his eyes the symptoms of social decay were glaring: wealth, concentrated in the hands of a few – the leaders of the people – had corrupted its possessors; oppression of the poor was rife; the richly endowed national religion with its elaborate ceremonial provided a comfortable atmosphere of self-righteousness. 'The ordinary Israelite, we may be sure, felt that he had the privilege of belonging to an uncommonly religious nation, which was properly rewarded for its piety by this unwonted prosperity.'[44] It is this dangerous complacency that the prophets set out to shatter.

The series of oracles[45] shows how dramatically he could accomplish his task. The people listened, doubtless with approval, to the threatened punishment of God on six neighbouring nations. Then comes the climax, the seventh oracle (the oracle against Judah – Amos 2:4f. – is a later addition) and, out of the blue, the prophet's thunderbolt strikes Israel! Yahweh is clearly shown to be the master of all peoples,[46] but he has chosen one people: the whole family which he brought up out of Egypt.[47] With the privilege of that choice goes a corresponding obligation: 'You only have I known of all the families of the earth, therefore I will punish you for all your iniquities.'[48] Israel has received more and of her more will be required; divine justice demands it.

Hosea was profoundly aware of the Mosaic past and looked back with nostalgia to the beginning of Israel's tradition, to the desert, to the 'days of her youth'[49] and to the Covenant.[50] The baneful influence of a materialistic society had caused Israel to forget Yahweh;[51] so Yahweh will bring her back into the desert and speak to her heart.[52] Hosea was the first to represent the covenant relations of Yahweh with his people as a marriage. It is out of his own personal experience that the marriage image came to the prophet, and that he realised its aptness in describing the relations between Yahweh and his people. He understood that the psychology of human love can wonderfully illustrate the mystery of God's relations with men, the reality and depth of his love. The divine husband has been betrayed by his wife who has given herself to adultery and prostitution. Yet he seeks only to win her again to him, and if he chastises her it is with that sole end in view. As a last resort he determines to bring her back once more to the conditions of the Exodus, the honeymoon period of their love.[53] In fact, he ultimately goes beyond this and promises to bring her into the harmony of a new garden of Eden[54] where their love will be the crowning and fulfilment of the mutual love of the first couple.[55]

Hosea has to speak of judgement too and warns of the approaching Assyrian danger.[56] But his leading idea remains the divine goodness (*hesed*) which explains the origin of Israel[57] and which will have the last word.[58] This divine *hesed* is demanding; what God asks is 'steadfast love (*hesed*) and knowledge of God';[59] true religion is a practical, loving acceptance of God, an affair of the heart. 'The word *hesed* evokes a relation similar to that denoted by *pietas*; it implies a dedication to someone.'[60]

The God of Isaiah is the 'Holy One'; this holiness, thrice proclaimed by the seraphim, expresses the moral perfection of the deity, but above all, it indicates his inaccessibility and his majesty. Furthermore, for Isaiah, Yahweh is the 'Holy One of Israel'; this transcendent God is a God who acts in history on behalf of his chosen people. The title, by itself, expresses the mystery of an all-holy God who yet stoops down to frail and sinful man.

Isaiah insists on faith – the practical conviction that Yahweh alone matters; one must lean on God alone.[61] He vainly sought, in Ahaz, the faith which would turn the king from human alliances and enable him to stand, unperturbed, in the midst of threats and even in the presence of hostile armies. In place of humble acceptance of God he found wilful self-sufficiency, and he warned Ahaz: 'If you will not believe, surely you will not be established.'[62] This truth is stressed again by Micah who in his most famous saying[63] presents his message as a synthesis of the preaching of his predecessor and contemporaries: 'He has showed you, O man, what is good; and what does Yahweh require of you but to do justice (Amos), and to love kindness (*hesed* – Hosea) and to walk humbly (Isaiah) with your God?'[64]

It is possible to trace the spiritual progress of Jeremiah and to see in him the purifying and strengthening effect of suffering, for the real message of the prophet is his own life. He was a man of rare sensitivity with an exceptional capacity for affection; and his mission was 'to pluck up and to break down, to destroy and to overthrow'[65] and to cry out, without respite, 'violence and destruction' against the people he loved.[66] Jeremiah's efforts to bring his people to their senses failed; but it is the greatness of the man, and the grandeur of his faith, that precisely during the most tragic moment of his life he spoke his optimistic oracles, notably those of chapters 30–33. He saw that the old covenant will be replaced by a new one[67] when God will act directly on the heart of man, when he will write his law on that heart, and when all men will know Yahweh.

That is one of the epoch-making utterances in the history of religion. Jeremiah had in his youth been a witness of the reformation under Josiah, and had no doubt shared the enthusiasm with which it had been greeted by idealists of the time. It seemed that at last the aim for which good men had striven for a century and a half had been attained. The nation had returned to the Lord their God and sealed their repentance by the solemn acceptance of a high code of social morals such as the prophets had taught. But in the period of disillusionment that followed he came to the conclusion (trite enough by now) that 'you cannot make men good by Act of Parliament'. It was not enough to write good laws into the statute-book. They must be written 'on the hearts' of men. In other words, the only adequate basis for right relations of men with God is in an inward and personal understanding of his demands, an inward and personal response to them. It would not be true to say that Jeremiah first discovered the role of the individual in religion; for it is implicit in all prophetic teaching. But his clear emphasis upon it at the moment when the whole apparatus of public 'institutional' religion had been swept away, was of the first importance for all subsequent development.[68]

Ezekiel showed himself more uncompromisingly still the champion of individual responsibility,[69] and during the first part of his ministry his message was very like that of Jeremiah. After the fall of Jerusalem Ezekiel sought to encourage the exiles and went about it in his own way. His portrait of the faithful shepherd, the new David, who tends his sheep with justice and love,[70] is not only the inspiration of the passage in John 10, but expresses the ideal that will find its realisation in Christ. In the promise of a new heart and a new spirit[71] he again approaches Jeremiah.[72] Then, in the last nine chapters of his book[73] he not only describes the New Temple and its rites but goes on to describe the division of the country among the sanctuary, the prince and the twelve tribes. These chapters, from our viewpoint neither very interesting nor very intelligible, have really had more influence than the rest. They express a political and religious ideal that, in large measure, set the pattern for the restoration of Israel.

We shall be content to note two major contributions of Second Isaiah. By his clear-cut and sweeping definition of the concept of ethical monotheism he marked the culmination of the Mosaic movement.[74] And his doctrine of vicarious suffering, as presented in the figure of the servant of Yahweh, not only immeasurably deepened the concept of Messiah but also foreshadowed the Christian victory over suffering: 'In my flesh I complete what is lacking in Christ's afflictions for the sake of his body, that is, the Church.'[75] We have reached the

An Irish Reader in Moral Theology

high-point of the prophetic movement, for though the voice of prophecy will be heard until the fourth century, it no longer has the vigour and resonance of the past.

While we must, in the interests of space, leave aside any treatment we may note, at least, the pervasive influence of the law. Throughout the Old Testament the law is everywhere present and it directly or indirectly influences the thought of the sacred writers.[76] The priests are, *ex officio*, guardians of the Torah and specialists in its interpretation[77] and it is their duty to teach the people.[78] Under their authority the Torah developed and was compiled. The prophets recognised the authority of the Torah.[79] Their high moral doctrine was nothing more than a profound understanding of the demands of the Mosaic law. The historians of Israel clearly saw the birth of the nation in the covenant of Sinai. Among them the deuteronomists judged events in the light of the deuteronomical code while the Chronicler was guided in his work by a complete Pentateuch. The wisdom of the sages is enlightened by the Torah, and Sirach states explicitly that the true wisdom is nothing, other than the Law.[80] The palmists extol the law.[81] Finally, Ezra set the Torah as the authoritative rule for the faith and practice of the post-exilic community and as the centre of its life. Attachment to the law inspired the Maccabaean revolt and supported the martyrs and heroes of that rising.

However, we must face the fact that prophetic religion has often been represented as the complete antithesis of priestly religion. It has even been held that the prophets rejected the whole institution of sacrifice and all the ritual of the Temple.[82] Several prophetical texts have been urged in support of these views.[83] An important consideration is that all the prophetical books were finally edited in post-exilic times, when the priestly influence was dominant, and the later compilers and editors are not conscious of any fundamental variance in outlook between priestly and prophetical writings. The Book of Deuteronomy is of paramount interest here. We have noted that it is strongly marked by the influence of the prophets, especially Hosea and Jeremiah; yet that book is built around a legal code and regards the existence of a central shrine, with the attendant cult, as a prime article of faith.

When we look again at the passages that allegedly point to a conflict between prophet and priest we find that all of them reflect the unambiguous declaration of Samuel to Saul:

> Has the Lord as great delight in burnt offerings and sacrifices as in obeying the voice of the Lord? Behold, to obey is better than sacrifice, and to harken than the fat of rams.[84]

Here is no rejection of sacrifice but a manifest appreciation of the fact that sacrifice as an external act, unrelated to an attitude of heart, had no value and was an insult to God. It is a measure of the moral perception of Israel that this truth had been clearly grasped at such an early date. Of course, the prophets had to combat formalism in worship, as they had to preach against moral lapses of all kinds, but their stand is a witness to the uncompromising demands of the Law, demands that did not stop at external conformity but which reached to fundamental attitudes. And it was in the Torah that Jesus found the two commandments on which all the law and the prophets depend.[85] The 'great and first commandment' is given in Deuteronomy 6:4f.: 'You shall love the Lord your God with all your heart, and with all your soul, and with all your might'; and the second is read in Leviticus 19:18: 'You shall love your neighbour as yourself.'

All the same, we must admit that the law is much concerned with involuntary acts and ritual uncleanliness where no moral considerations were involved, and we must acknowledge that priestly religion did tend towards formalism. In fact, the post-exilic devotion to the law had its dangers, and the tragedy of Judaism is that it ended by succumbing to these dangers.

When we speak of post-exilic Judaism we may not ignore the key figure of Ezra for he, more surely than Ezekiel, is the father of Judaism. The 'book of the law of Moses'[86] which Ezra brought from Babylon is most likely the Pentateuch in its final form. This 'book of the law' was accepted by the people as the law of the community, and Ezra, by his cultic and moral reforms, brought the life of the community into conformity with that norm. From this time the life and religion of Jews was directed and moulded by the Torah and Judaism assumed its distinctive characteristic of strict adherence and fidelity to the law.

This does no mean that Ezra is responsible for the extreme legalistic outlook of pharisaism; though it is not altogether surprising that his reform should have led to legalism and isolationism – it is not easy to maintain a balance in such matters. If we are to judge Ezra's role aright we shall need to make certain observations.[87] He did not introduce the emphasis on obedience to the law; that went right back to Moses and the Sinai tradition. Then there is Israel's attitude to the law to be taken into account; the Torah was not regarded as a code to be obeyed, a long list of commands and prohibitions. Rather, it was seen as the will of a law-giver who is the redeemer of Israel; the goodness of God moved the Israelite to serve him freely and to obey him gladly. It follows that the law was not counted as a burden: it was a gracious gift of God and a source of delight.[88] Nor does attachment to the law conflict with the prophetic outlook and spirit. The long prayer of Ezra[89] shows that the post-exilic priestly view was quite in sympathy with the prophetic demands.

In the light of these observations we may appreciate Ezra's attitude to the law and the cult and realise the true place of the Torah in Judaism. If the elaborate Temple ritual did, for many, become an empty form and if devotion to the law lapsed into legalism, these deviations were due to the weakness of Judaism, to the weakness inherent in any community of men. The first manifestation of this weakness was the setting of all precepts, religious and moral, civil and cultic, on the same plane instead of ordering them, in correct hierarchy, around the one precept that would give meaning and life to all of them.[90] As a result the law became the preserve of casuists and became so overloaded with minutiae that it had turned into an insupportable burden.[91] The second danger, and a more insidious one, was to base man's justification on a meticulous observance of the law rather than to visualise it as the work of divine grace, freely bestowed; it meant that man could justify himself. It needed the forceful teaching of St Paul to make clear once for all that man is not justified by the works of the law, but by faith in Jesus Christ.[92]

THE GOSPEL

Paul fully understood and appreciated the truth that the coming of Christ had brought in an entirely new phase of God's dealing with men, a new epoch in *Heilsgeschichte*. The new divine economy is not a continuation of the old along the same plane. Though Christianity strikes its roots deep in Judaism it moves on another level of reality; Christ has made all things new. The regime of the law was transitory, a time of preparation and education, and the law itself was powerless to justify men. Paul not only points to the uselessness (in the Christian era) of the cultic observances of Judaism; he also argues that the moral precepts, within the framework of Judaism, have no real value, while the 'law of Christ'[93] unlike the old law, fulfils the promise of a covenant written on the hearts of men.[94]

Jesus formulated the special character, the new spirit of the Kingdom of God, in the Sermon on the Mount.[95] The new law of Christ does not stand in sharp antithesis[96] to that given on Sinai; it is a fulfilment of the Law of Moses.[97] Indeed Matthew did see the Jesus of the Sermon as a new Moses, but also as more than a Mosaic figure. The Sermon is not another version of the law, it is a definitive formulation. Suggestive of the law of a new Moses, it is also the authoritative word of the Lord, the Messiah; it is the Messianic Torah.[98] We have to be aware too that the Sermon is not primarily *kerygma*, a first missionary Preaching of the good news to Jews or pagans[99] but *didache*, a preaching to the Christian community, to those already within the fold. We find in the Sermon on the Mount a compilation of sayings of Jesus which forms an instruction addressed to Christians, one aimed at their Christian formation.

When the Sermon is compared with the rest of the New Testament, it becomes clear that these words of Jesus, his moral teaching, were preserved primarily because they were part of the essential structure of the gospel. Jesus did make demands, he did lay down the law of the Messiah. There is no conflict between gospel and law, the law of Christ.

The gospel is not only *kerygma* and *didache*; it is also a moral code, and this was so from the beginning. We might put it another way and say that the *kerygma* includes the acceptance of Christ and his demands and that the *didache* includes precepts and rules of conduct for Christian living. 'For some in the primitive Church, if not for all, the penetrating demands of Jesus, no less than the great kerygmatic affirmations about him, were part of "the bright light of the Gospel", that is, they were revelatory.'[100] Jesus revealed himself not only in his works and words but also by the exigency of his demands.

We may justly regard the Sermon as a classic example of *didache*. It is a collection of sayings of Jesus, compiled for the Purpose of Christian formation, and it most likely served for the instruction of catechumens or for the further direction of the newly baptised. It follows that something is presupposed: the proclamation of the Lord, crucified, risen and to come; the declaration that Jesus has reconciled us with God and that he is our life. What is presupposed is the conquering attraction of the 'Good News, a sincere conversion; what has already taken place is the witness which Jesus has given, in words and works, to what he is; what is presupposed is faith in the risen Lord'.[101]

That is why Jesus is so demanding, that is why he goes so far beyond the law.[102] His teaching is addressed to men who have been rescued by the good news from the power of Satan, men who already stand in the kingdom of God. He addresses men who have been pardoned, prodigal sons who have been received back into the house of their Father. Men who have received that gift and who have experienced the love and mercy of God, are urged, by inner compulsion, to do the will of that heavenly Father. The commandments of Christ are not further reminders of our sin,[103] but carry with them the divine help that enables us to obey, and the possibility of living as children of God.

The Sermon on the Mount shows us the spirit and the demands of the gospel of Jesus, demands far more exacting than those of the law and a spirit of freedom unknown to the most sincere observer of the law. Above all, he who listens to the demands of Christ, and earnestly seeks to carry them out, is given the means to achieve that task, the liberal gift of grace. Here we put our finger on the difference between law and gospel. The law makes demands but does not, itself, give the means of carrying them out; it leaves man to himself; the gospel sets man before the gift of God (salvation through Jesus Christ) and demands of him that he should make that ineffable gift the sole foundation of his life. Yet, in the new life there is still room for precepts, there is still need for law, the 'law of Christ'.[104]

Since, however, the quality that Jesus looks for in a faithful disciple is a boundless love, we may (in the language of John) claim that Christ has given not a law but a commandment.[105] In the Good Samaritan he has taught the lesson in a way that may not be mistaken and cannot be forgotten.[106] He implies that the lawyer's question, 'Who is my neighbour?' has no place in the Christian life. True charity does not pause to weigh up matters of colour or race or creed, but goes without reserve to one in need. The Christian's neighbour is Everyman; his love can have no limits.

But Christian love has deeper reaches still. The true disciple, like the woman who was a sinner, is conscious of being the recipient of great mercy[107] and the effect of this realisation is underlined, by contrast, in the Unmerciful Servant.[108] A man who has been freed of a crippling burden, who has experienced the wonder of divine forgiveness, must surely feel compelled to pardon the trifling offences of others. 'Love is not resentful ... love bears all things';[109] otherwise it is not love. The charity of Christ is the inspiration, and the stuff, of Christian life and of Christian living.

Notes

1   Mt 23:23.
2   Ex 20-23.
3   Lev 17-26.
4   Deut 12-26.
5   Cf. J.B. Pritchard, *Ancient Near-Eastern Texts*, New Jersey: Princeton, 1955, pp. 163–80.
6   Ex 20:2-17; Deut 5:6-18.
7   G.E. Mendenhall, 'Law and Covenant in Israel and the Ancient Near East', *The Biblical Archaeologist*, 17 (1954), pp. 26–76.
8   Ex 3:7-10.
9   Ibid., 14:31.
10   Ibid., 19:5f.
11   Ibid., 29:46.
12   Lev 26:14-39.
13   *Vocabulaire de Théologie Biblique* (ed. Leon-Dufour), Paris: Éditions du Cerf, 1962, p. 21.
14   The earliest of the four traditions which make up the Pentateuch is named the *Yahwistic*; it is of Judean origin and took its final form in the tenth century BC. The *Elohistic* tradition developed in Israel and was fixed in the ninth century. The *Deuteronomical* tradition is confined to the Book of Deuteronomy. The nucleus of it was formed in Israel before 721 BC; it was promulgated in Judah during the reform of Josiah (640–609) and an enlarged edition of it was prepared during the Exile (586–538). The *Priestly* tradition is particularly interested in the organisation of the sanctuary, in the sacrifices and in the sacred personnel. It developed during the Exile and took its final shape after the return. The priests, who were responsible for fixing this tradition, also gave its definitive form to the whole Pentateuch. We may say briefly that Genesis, Exodus and Numbers are a combination of the yahwistic, elohistic and priestly traditions; Leviticus has the priestly tradition only, and the deuteronomical tradition is found in Deuteronomy alone.
15   Gen 6:1-4.
16   Ibid., 11:1-9.
17   H. Cazelles, *Introduction a la Bible I* (ed. A. Robert A. Feuillet), Paris: Tournai, 1957, pp. 348–80.
18   Gen 12:1-3.
19   G. von Rad, *Genesis*, London: SCM Press, 1961, pp. 148–50.
20   Ex 3:16.
21   Ibid., 34:10-28.
22   Gen 20:12.
23   Ex 20:22-23:19.
24   Gen 3:8; 18:1ff.
25   Ibid., 21:17.

26   Ibid., 20:3, 6; 15:1; 18:12.

27   Ex 20:19.

28   Gen 50:20.

29   Deut 12:1; 26:15.

30   Ibid., 4:41; 28:64

31   B.W. Anderson, *The Living World of the Old Testament*, London: Longman, 1958, p. 313.

32   Deut 12:1-14.

33   Ibid., 30:11, 14.

34   The books of Joshua, Judges, Samuel, Kings (with Deuteronomy as an introduction) form the deuteronomical history. The first edition of this great work was made during the reign of Josiah (640–609); the final edition was made during the Exile.

35   Hos 11:1f.

36   Jer 31.

37   Ezek 37:40-48; cf. Deut 3:12-17.

38   H. Cazelles, *Le Deutoronome* (BJ), Paris, 1958, p. 17.

39   Lev 17-26.

40   Ibid., 26.

41   Ibid., 19:2.

42   H. Cazelles, *Introduction a la Bible I*, p. 376.

43   Ethical monotheism: belief in one God who imposes a moral order; the one God of Israel is a just God who demands of his people obedience to his righteous law.

44   C.H. Dodd, *The Bible Today*, Cambridge: Cambridge University Press, 1961, p. 39.

45   Amos 1:2-2:16.

46   Ibid., 9:7.

47   Ibid., 3:1.

48   Ibid., 3:2.

49   Hos 2:17(15).

50   Ibid., 13:5.

51   Ibid., 13:6.

52   Ibid., 2:16(14); 12:10.

53   Ibid., 2:16f.

54   Ibid., 2:18.

55   Ibid., 2:21f.

56   Ibid., 13:15.

57   Ibid., 11:1-9.

58   Ibid., 2:21(19).

59   Ibid., 6:6.

60   A. Gelin, *Introduction a la Bible I*, p. 498.

61   Is 8:13, 28:16, 30:15.

62   Ibid., 7:9.

63   Mic 8:6.

64   A. Gelin, op. cit., p. 500.

65   Jer 1:10.

66   Ibid., 20:8.

67   Ibid., 31:31-34.

68   C.H. Dodd, op. cit., p. 46f.

69   Cf. Ezek 18:20.

70   Ibid., 34.

71   Ibid., 36:23-28.

72   Jer 31:31-34.

73   Ezek 40-48.

74   W.F. Albright, *From the Stone Age to Christianity*, New York: John Hopkins University Press, 1957, p. 327.

75   Col 1:24.

76   *Vocabulaire de Théologie Biblique*, pp. 544–6.

77   Hos 5:1; Jer 18:18; Ezek 7:26.
78   Deut 33:10; Hos 4:6; Jer 5:4f.
79   Hos 9:12, 4:1f; Jer 11:1-12; Ezek 22:1-16, 26.
80   Sir 24:23, 8; cf. Bar 4:1.
81   Cf. Ps 19(18):7-14, 119(118).
82   The falsity of these views is clearly demonstrated by H.H. Rowley, *The Unity of the Bible*, London: Carey Kingsgate Press, 1953, pp. 30–61.
83   Cf. Amos 5:21f; Hos 6:6; Is 1:11ff; Jer 6:20, 7:22; Mic 6:6ff.
84   I Sam 15:22.
85   Mt 22:36-40.
86   Neh 8:1.
87   B.W. Anderson, op. cit., pp. 457–60.
88   Cf. Ps 1, 19(18):7-14, 119(118)
89   Neh 9.
90   Deut 6:4.
91   Mt 23:4; Acts 15:10.
92   Gal 2:16; Rom 3:28.
93   Gal 6:2; cf. I Cor 9:21.
94   2 Cor 3:3.
95   Mt 5-7; cf. Lk 6:20-49.
96   The designation 'antitheses' applied to Mt 5:21-48 should not be overstressed.
97   Mt 5:17.
98   W.D. Davies, *The Setting of the Sermon on the Mount*, Cambridge: Cambridge University Press, 1964, p. 93.
99   Cf. 1 Cor 15:3-5.
100   W.D. Davies, op. cit., p. 437.
101   J. Jeremias, *Paroles de Jésus*, Paris: Éditions du Cerf, 1963, pp. 15–48.
102   Cf. Mt 5:21-48.
103   Cf. Rom 7:7-13.
104   Gal 6:2.
105   Jn 13:34, 15:12; 1 Jn 2:7f.
106   Lk 10:30-37.
107   Ibid., 7:47.
108   Mt 18:23-35.
109   I Cor 15:5, 7.

2   The Decalogue of Moses: An Enduring Ethical Programme?

Andrew D.H. Mayes

(Seán Freyne (ed.), *Ethics and the Christian*, Dublin: Columba Press, 1991, pp. 25–40.)

I

The liturgy for the baptism of children in the Anglican tradition includes this charge to the godparents of the newly baptised child: 'You are to take care that this child be brought to the bishop to be confirmed by him so soon as he can say the creed, the Lord's prayer and the ten commandments, and be further instructed in the Church catechism set forth for that purpose.' The presupposed function of the ten commandments in this context is clearly that of the definition of the Christian life, a function which has a long history in Christian tradition. On the other hand, the ten commandments also appear in the Anglican tradition in the order for the Administration of the Lord's Supper or Holy Communion with a different function. Near the beginning of that service there is provision for the recitation of each commandment by the celebrant, following which the people respond 'Lord, have mercy upon us, and incline our hearts to keep this law'. Here there is perhaps reflected that especially strong tradition in the Church that the law performs the negative function of revealing sin.

Both of these functions of the law, and indeed perhaps of the decalogue in particular, are to be traced back into the New Testament. The response of Jesus to the rich man who asked him, 'What must I do to inherit eternal life?' was in the first instance 'You know the commandments: do not kill, do not commit adultery, do not steal, do not bear false witness, do not defraud, honour your father and mother' (Mk 10:19); the rich man's continuing dissatisfaction, reflected in his protest, 'Teacher, all these I have observed from my youth', may indicate that it was only in its negative function that the decalogue had meaning for him. Certainly for Paul the decalogue, with the other Old Testament law, performed that negative function of producing a sense of sin and guilt (Rom 1:29-31), although even for Paul within the context of faith in Christ the decalogue has a positive function: 'The commandments, you shall not commit adultery, you shall not kill, you shall not steal, you shall not covet, and any other commandment, are summed up in this sentence "You shall love your neighbour as yourself"' (Rom 13:9).

Whether negatively or positively understood, the decalogue has had a fundamental significance, a significance which, of course, is highlighted in different ways within the Hebrew Bible itself. It stands at the very foundation of Israel at Sinai; it is not directed to any special group, priests, judges, or whatever, but to the whole undifferentiated people of God; it is the direct and unmediated communication of God himself to Israel while the rest of the law is mediated through Moses; it is given its own special name, 'the ten words'; it is repeated in Ex 20 and Deut 5.

Despite this fundamental significance however, it is perhaps the case that the decalogue no longer has that centrality and foundational significance with which the tradition invests it. It maintains at least a formal place in the liturgy, but it is rarely, if ever, recited; insofar as people still have a knowledge of it, it is more a knowledge of the idea of it than of the decalogue itself; within the framework of a general discouragement of learning by rote, the decalogue, like much else in religious tradition, has perhaps been marginalised to the edge of consciousness; within the context of a general distrust and suspicion of all authority as more or less arbitrary restraint on individual freedom, the decalogue is seen, like the Bible as a whole, as just another authority, our relationship with which is highly problematic.

Our task, then, seems to be a dual one: on the one hand, to seek out the ground and nature of the central significance which the decalogue has traditionally enjoyed; on the other hand, to ask with what continuing significance we may regard it. I think that these questions are by no means unrelated, and even if as a biblical scholar of a historical sort I concentrate on the first aspect of our task, the understanding of the decalogue to which that may lead us has, I believe, something to say in response to the question that defines the second aspect of our task.

II

In our consideration of the decalogue I would like to start with a brief discussion of some general formal issues, then move on to some general questions of substance, before focusing in on more particular issues associated with the decalogue. Our formal considerations relate first to the decalogue as a series of ten commandments, and second to the way in which these commandments are brought to expression.

Everybody used to know the ten commandments; at least, those of us brought up by the traditional rote-learning methods knew the ten commandments. Or did we? The fact of the matter is that the ten commandments are not the same for everyone. This apparently single collection of ten commandments bearing the title 'the decalogue' comprises slightly but significantly different content for different religious traditions. The Hebrew Bible speaks of ten 'words', rather than commandments, and it finds one 'word' in the following: 'You shall have no other gods before me. You shall not make yourself a graven image, or any likeness of anything that is in heaven above, or that is in the earth beneath or that is in the water under the earth; you shall not bow down to them or serve them.' This is followed also by the Catholic and Lutheran religious traditions, but not by the Reformed tradition. According to the latter there are two commandments here: 'You shall have no other gods before me', and 'You shall not make yourself a graven image', and these are in fact reckoned as the first two commandments of the decalogue. The Hebrew Bible takes as its first 'word' 'I am the Lord your God who brought you out of the land of Egypt, out of the house of bondage'; the Catholic and Lutheran traditions, on the other hand, maintain the number ten for the total by finding two commandments in 'You shall not covet your neighbour's house; you shall not covet your neighbour's wife, or his manservant or his maidservant, or his ox, or his ass, or anything that is your neighbour's'; all of this, on the other hand, is taken as one 'word' in the Hebrew Bible and as one commandment in the Reformed tradition.

All of this seems a bit nit-picking, and perhaps we should not make too much of it; in any case, surely it is quite unrelated to what is certainly the really significant thing: the decalogue is a fundamental rule of life understood to have divine origin. In one way or another surely the same substance is there whatever esoteric differences there might be in the organisation of it. In fact, however, these formal points do suggest an important consideration of substance: the decalogue is not a fixed entity, a clearly defined text, but is rather something more fluid. We cannot simply take the decalogue for granted, as something known, and then go on to discuss the question of its meaning and application; rather, the questions of meaning, understanding and application belong right at the heart of the decalogue, right at the point of the very definition of the decalogue, and are not secondary questions that we bring to it as to a given accepted entity.

Maybe I exaggerate the problem, for surely there is a decalogue, a fixed single entity, a quite definite text, and the differences I have been speaking of are themselves secondary differences, differences in the way in which this once-fixed text has been interpreted and transmitted in the various religious traditions. It is, however, more complicated than that. The term 'ten commandments', or, to use the terminology of the Hebrew Bible, 'ten words', is not used in Ex 20 where the decalogue first appears; rather, this chapter refers simply to 'all these words'. The term 'ten words' first appears in Ex 34:28 (where it is used in relation to a quite different collection of commandments) and then next, with reference to our more familiar decalogue, in Deut 4:13; 10:4. In fact, the term 'ten commandments' or 'ten words' never appears in immediate connection with the decalogue, but belongs rather in secondary contexts which make reference to this collection of commandments. If we relate this to the difficulty there most evidently is in finding here ten words or commandments, then the conclusion to which we seem to be pointed is that the use of the term 'ten words' appears to be an attempt to impose order and uniformity on what was essentially a much more fluid and unstable collection which could be looked at in different ways. It seems almost to be an attempt to bring canonical order to what was by origin and nature much less fixed and determined. It represents an attempt to create a recognisable and memorable statement by imposing order on existing material which was essentially much less ordered and defined. There is, if you like, a process of finding meaning and order going on right at the heart of the decalogue. The decalogue is a statement of meaning, almost a statement of intention, rather than an immediately clearly defined set of regulations.

This seems almost to undermine or contradict what we understand by the term 'commandment'. Surely this, of all forms of speech, must embody clarity and precision, and yet just this quality seems to be questioned by the uncertainty over what is meant by the decalogue. This brings me to the second aspect of our formal considerations, the way in which these commandments are brought to expression, for it seems to me that the customary use of the term 'commandment' itself introduces implications which are not necessarily present.

Even a superficial perusal of those parts of Exodus and Deuteronomy which contain laws will reveal the variety of forms of expression which these laws use. Here are two of these. Ex 21:18-19 reads: 'When men quarrel and one strikes the other with a stone or with his fist and the man does not die but keeps his bed, then if the man rises again and walks abroad with his staff, he that struck him shall be clear; only he shall pay for the loss of his time and shall have him thoroughly healed'; Ex 23:9 reads: 'You shall not oppress a stranger; you know the heart of a stranger, for you were strangers in the land of Egypt.' On the one hand, there is a law which in an impersonal way describes a particular case in some detail and then prescribes an appropriate punishment. This is case law and we can understand how it could well have been used in the administration of justice in the concrete conditions of daily life in ancient Israel; collections of such laws would have constituted the precedents by which order and uniformity would have been brought to judicial administration. On the other hand, however, there is a prohibition which is direct and personal; it gives no detailed description of a case and it does not prescribe any punishment. Indeed, whereas in the first instance an offence is presupposed as having been committed and a punishment is then provided for it, in the second instance no offence is presupposed as having been committed. This is a prohibition directed to future behaviour rather than a law which attempts to deal with past behaviour.

The decalogue clearly belongs with the type of the prohibition rather than the type of case law. Even in the case of those two commandments which have a positive formulation rather than a negative ('Remember the Sabbath day to keep it holy', and 'Honour your father and your mother'), the address is still direct and future-oriented and no punishment is prescribed. There is in the decalogue no case law; there is no precedent here on which a judge in a court situation could rely. Not only is no punishment prescribed for any breach of the prohibition, but the prohibition is expressed in such general and all-inclusive terms as to be virtually useless in the concrete circumstances of any given situation. 'You shall not kill': does this include the slaughter of animals; does it apply in a situation of war; does it have any relevance to capital punishment? These prohibitions and commands are not laws; they give expression to the most general directions for life in the context of one person instructing another.

Our formal considerations thus lead to the conclusion that the decalogue is teaching rather than law, into which a certain order and uniformity has been brought by the attempt to mark out ten words or ten commandments in this teaching.

III

Let us try to lead this on a little further by gradually introducing issues relating more to the general substance of this teaching. We cannot immediately terminate our more formal considerations, however, for these are inextricably connected with the questions of substance. Formally, the decalogue commandments have been seen to be teaching rather than law, instruction appropriate to a setting different from the law court situation to which case law belongs. What is this setting for the teaching of the decalogue?

The Old Testament context within which the decalogue is set is that of God proclaiming the law of the covenant on Mount Sinai. The decalogue is the only part of this law that is given directly by God to Israel. Insofar as the decalogue contains direct, personal prohibitions and commands, it is presupposed that God is the speaker and Israel is the addressee, and this, indeed, has sometimes been considered to be the explanation of this particular expression of Israel's law. The direct form of address presupposes a speaking authority and an immediate addressee; so the setting of the decalogue, and indeed of all direct prohibitions and commands in the Old Testament, was always that of God addressing Israel and declaring the terms of his covenant with his people. 'You shall have no other gods before me' could never have been uttered in any other context than that of God addressing his people and declaring to them the terms of his covenant relationship with them. This form of law has, therefore, a religious context of origin: it originated in and belongs to a religious festival of covenant making and covenant renewal in the course of which the decalogue was proclaimed by a priest uttering the direct word of God to the assembled people.

This understanding of the decalogue is correct so far as it goes, but it seems to me that a lot more can be said which can lead to a better appreciation of the nature of the decalogue. In the first place, while the decalogue as such may always have been presented as the direct speech of God, this is not true of all the commands and prohibitions of the Old Testament which have the direct form of address. In other words, as a form of speech, the commands and prohibitions are not necessarily rooted in this religious context. A closely analogous form is to be found in the book of Proverbs, as in Prov 22:22ff: 'Do not rob the poor ... make no friendship with a man given to anger ... remove not the ancient landmark', and here the setting is explicitly that of the father instructing his son or the wise man his pupil. This more secular setting of instruction is presupposed also in Jer 35:6ff. Here, we read, the conservative clan of the Rechabites lived according to the teaching of their ancestor Jonadab, who prescribed: 'You shall not drink wine, neither you nor your sons for ever; you shall not build a house; you shall not sow seed; you shall not plant or have a vineyard.' This last context of use is particularly significant for it clearly suggests a setting for this form of instruction which is old and original, *viz.* that of the clan elder instructing his followers, or those being initiated into the way of life he represented. The speaking authority which the form presupposes is that of the clan elder with the whole weight of clan tradition behind him; those addressed are the members of the clan, those responsible for the maintenance and transmission of that way of life. The instruction comprises the basic principles, the fundamental truths, which have traditionally defined and constituted that way of life.

Now this suggests a much more comprehensive framework within which to examine the decalogue once more. The form in which the decalogue is expressed is the form used in order to express the fundamental principles which traditionally characterise a particular life context. Thus, it is the form used for the clan ethic of the Rechabites; it is also the form used in a series of prohibitions in Ex 23:1-3, 6, 8-9, 'You shall not utter a false report; you shall not follow a multitude to do evil; you shall not be partial to a poor man in his suit; you shall not pervert the justice due to the poor; you shall take no bribe; you shall not oppress a stranger'; all of which are related to the administration of justice and constitute a kind of *vade mecum* for judges. The basic purpose behind these prohibitions is to make explicit the constitutional rules of conduct, the limiting principles, within the framework of which the one who adheres to the life context addressed by these principles is to work out his way of living. The teaching enshrined in these principles does not cover every issue; it sets the external limits, the boundaries beyond which one may not pass and still remain a member of the particular community addressed by that teaching.

One cannot set the decalogue apart from considerations such as these and simply claim it as the word of God to Israel. At the very least, it uses human speech forms, and, moreover, human speech forms which carry over with them into the decalogue context quite particular implications. But the connection between the decalogue and those other uses of prohibitions and commands is even closer than that suggests, for it is clear that the decalogue cannot be understood independently simply as the original and founding word of God to Israel. It is not consistently formulated as the word of God; rather, it speaks of God in the third person in three commandments ('You shall not take the name of the Lord your God in vain'; 'the seventh day is a Sabbath to the Lord your God'; 'Honour your father and your mother, that your days may be long in the land which the

Lord your God gives you'), and so presupposes a setting other than one in which God himself is speaker. What this suggests is that the decalogue is a mixed composition in which existing speech forms, existing commands and prohibitions, have been secondarily brought together into a collection. Many of these commands and prohibitions already existed before they were brought into this decalogue context.

Like the commands and prohibitions in general, so also the decalogue seeks to formulate a set of basic principles, a constitution, within the framework of which those addressed by it must live. Unlike many of these other commands and prohibitions, however, the decalogue is not addressed to a specific group, Rechabites, judges or whatever; rather, it is addressed to a total community which may comprise all of these or none of these.

The community addressed by the decalogue is defined neither by socio-economic lifestyle, like the Rechabites, nor by professional occupation, like the judges; it is a community defined by its common adherence to 'the Lord your God who brought you out of the land of Egypt' and by its adherence to a principle of respect for integrity of the other which is understood to flow from that; it is a community which finds its unity not on the basis of particular common social, economic or professional interests, but on the basis of a unity of faith which both transcends and also holds in check the ultimately selfish divisions characteristic of social, economic and professional life.

IV

Our general considerations relating to the form and substance of the decalogue have led to the following conclusions: that the decalogue is teaching rather than law; that the notion of ten specific commandments may be a secondary attempt to bring clarity and order to a more fluid collection; that decalogue in the wider context of commands and prohibitions expresses the fundamental and traditional rules of life in community, defining its boundaries; and that the community addressed by the decalogue is one that is not restricted by social, economic and professional interests. Now, let us turn our attention finally to the decalogue much more specifically with some quite definitive historical, literary and religious questions in mind. There are two concluding issues which I wish to discuss: first, the general context of origin of the decalogue and what this means for our understanding of it; and, secondly, the ongoing significance of the decalogue.

The decalogue is presented to us in Ex 20 as the word of God to Israel at Sinai, at the time of the foundation of Israel. It is a founding document serving to call the people of God into existence. Is this historically verifiable? Attempts to provide a critical justification for deriving the decalogue from the beginning of Israel's history have not been lacking, but they have never coped successfully with the following points. First, from a literary point of view, the decalogue in Ex 20 is quite isolated: its context makes no reference to it and does not presuppose its presence. Second, the early history of Israel, insofar as it is known from the traditional material in Joshua, Judges, Samuel and Kings, makes no reference to the decalogue, and, indeed, in that a story such as Jg 17f presupposes the use of images in Israelite worship, it might be argued that this history excludes the decalogue. Third, although an early prophet, Hosea, castigates behaviour which is prohibited by the decalogue ('There is swearing, lying, killing, stealing and committing adultery; they break all bounds and murder follows murder', 4:2), it is much more likely that this prophet is anticipating the decalogue prohibitions rather than depending on them. Fourth, the particular corpus of Israelite literature with which the decalogue has its closest links is the deuteronomic corpus, and that corpus belongs at the end of Israel's pre-exilic history rather than at the beginning.

Such a late dating for the decalogue implies that it is a distillation of Israel's ongoing tradition and teaching rather than that it is the basic text which was foundational to that tradition and teaching; it represents a breakthrough to a recognition of what constituted the people of God, which was won only at the cost of painful experience, it is not a divine gift which came independent of history and experience. In fact, it is almost a summary expression of two prophetic traditions in Israel: on the one hand, the tradition represented by Hosea and Jeremiah which emphasised the absolute demand for the worship of God alone; and, on the other hand, the tradition represented by Amos and Isaiah which is so strongly characterised by its ethical demand. As the concise distillation of so much that stands in the earlier Israelite religious and literary tradition, the decalogue takes on the character of a classic expression of faith, which, like the creeds and like the biblical canon in general, has behind it theological dispute and confirming experience. It grew out of the thinking and reflection of different religious and cultural streams in Israel, and is then a point of arrival rather than departure. It represents a breakthrough to an expression of basic religious and ethical teaching, which is at a level of generality sufficient for it to transcend cultural distinctiveness and historical particularity.

Now, I am very much aware that by describing the decalogue in these terms I imply that it is something very different from the revealed word of God to Moses on Mount Sinai; it is, rather, an insight which was formulated in deuteronomic circles only at the cost of experience and dispute. This experience and this dispute includes prophetic preaching, and insofar as one thinks of the prophets as messengers of God, then the preaching which found its deposit in the decalogue may be considered the word of God. Such a description must, however, be defined more closely.

The preaching of the prophets cannot be understood as the imparting of divine revelation in the sense that the prophets were privileged recipients of private and esoteric knowledge. Their condemnations of Israel arise, not from private revelation of something new but rather from their insight into and recognition of what is known to be wrong behaviour. The first two chapters of Amos, for example, contain a series of oracles in which the activities of the nations around Israel are held up for condemnation. It is a condemnation uttered in the name of God and the crimes mentioned are understood as violations of the will of God. These crimes did not necessarily involve Israel in any way, so it is not because of this that Amos condemned them. Rather, the focus is on the crimes themselves, which are understood to violate the will of God. But on what grounds can Amos condemn Edom, Moab, Damascus, the Philistines and others? These are non-Israelite peoples; they had received no revelation of law from God. Surely, the very foundation of the condemnations of Amos must be what can be called 'natural law'. There is a way of behaviour built into the created order that is there to be perceived by all peoples, and by this all men must live; it is the foundation of all life and integral to all life; it is not something additional to creation but flows from creation. Amos appeals not to Moses but to fundamental ethical standards to which all men are bound.

Indeed, this must be the basis also of his comprehensive denunciation of Israel. Again, no Mosaic revelation, and no private prophetic revelation, forms the foundation of his preaching; rather, it is norms of behaviour which people know to be right. Psalm 19 declares that 'the law of the Lord is perfect, reviving the soul; the testimony of the Lord is sure, making wise the simple; the precepts of the Lord are right, rejoicing the heart; the commandment of the Lord is pure, enlightening the eyes; the fear of the Lord is clean, enduring for ever; the ordinances of the Lord are true, and righteous altogether ... Moreover, by them is thy servant warned; in keeping them there is great reward.' Again, however, it is most unlikely that it is a Mosaic revelation on which the psalmist is reflecting. There is no reference to Moses or Sinai, no reference to God's making a covenant with his people, to his coming down on the mountain to deliver his law. In fact, the most appropriate way to interpret it is by reference to the beginning of the same psalm: 'The heavens are telling the glory of God; and the firmament proclaims his handiwork. Day to day pours forth speech and night to night declares knowledge. There is no speech, nor are there words; their voice is not heard; yet their voice goes out through all the earth, and their words to the end of the world.' This law is the law of the natural order; it is the way of life to which human beings as part of that natural order are bound; it is the fundamental principles of behaviour which are to be discerned through experience and reflection.

Amos and the other prophets do not represent an isolated tradition within Israel in this respect. Their appeal to known fundamental principles of behaviour has a close relationship to Israel's wisdom tradition. The proverbs of wisdom are the literary expression of the basic assertion that there is a moral order in creation, and that violation of that moral order is destructive of order in creation. There is no appeal here to a revealed law backed up by the authority of a punishing God; rather, the consequences of violation of the moral order are immediate and direct, forming an integral part of that violation: 'These men lie in wait for their own blood, they set an ambush for their own lives. Such are the ways of all who get gain by violence; it takes away the life of its possessors' (Prov 1:18f); 'The integrity of the upright guides them, but the crookedness of the treacherous destroys them ... The righteousness of the blameless keeps his way straight, but the wicked falls by his own wickedness. The righteousness of the upright delivers them, but the treacherous are taken captive by their lust' (11:3, 5f); 'He who closes his ear to the cry of the poor will himself cry out and not be heard' (21:13); 'He who digs a pit will fall into it, and a stone will come back upon him who starts it rolling' (26:27). This proverbial wisdom, with its characteristic understanding of the synthetic nature of human action, in which act and consequence together form a single whole, is the background of prophetic preaching. Its particular expression reflects a particular historical and cultural context, and stands in considerable conflict with the later reflections of Job and Ecclesiastes. Yet, its presupposed assertion of a moral order in creation remains as the ultimate foundation of the decalogue: 'You shall not kill' is not a law requiring the judicial execution or life imprisonment of murderers, but a prohibition which warns against the destructive violation of what is recognised to be a basic element of that moral order.

This brings me to the second of my two concluding concerns: the ongoing significance of the decalogue. The decalogue is a point of arrival, a breakthrough to what is generally valid; it emerged as a statement of meaning and intent which was to a limited extent fluid and changeable in itself, but which certainly always had to be interpreted for changing religious and historical situations. That it was to some extent a fluid rather than a permanently fixed statement is indicated by a number of points which I have already hinted at, and which have considerable intrinsic interest. First, there is some indication that individual commandments have experienced modification within the framework of the decalogue. Near the beginning of the decalogue the prohibition 'You shall not make for yourself a graven image' was probably originally an independent prohibition referring specifically to images of Israel's God, Yahweh; as a reference to images of other gods it would be superfluous after the immediately preceding prohibition of the worship of these other gods. Yet it is clear that at a very early stage the image prohibited was understood to be that of another god. The elaboration of that prohibition in the words 'or any likeness of anything that is in heaven above or that is in the earth beneath, or that is in the water under the earth' expands the application of the prohibition beyond the bounds of the worship of Yahweh; the further elaboration 'You shall not bow down to them or worship them' firmly links the prohibition of images with the prohibition of having other gods, binding the two together as one single prohibition of the worship of other gods. This unity of concern is then presupposed by the motivation 'for I the Lord your God am a jealous God', for the jealousy of Yahweh is always related to his exclusive claim on Israel and his absolute intolerance of her turning to other gods.

At the end of the decalogue, the commandment 'You shall not covet ...' seems originally to have referred not simply to feelings of envy but rather to the concrete steps taken in order to appropriate what belongs to another. This sense of the verb 'covet' is presupposed in Ex 34:24 which commands that all Israelite men should go to the sanctuary three times a year, and declares 'no man shall covet your land when you go up to appear before the Lord your God three times in the year'. If this is the older sense of the verb 'covet', however, it implies a major overlap with the prohibition 'You shall not steal', both meaning effectively the same thing. Since such duplication is unlikely in a summarising and generalising statement like the decalogue, it may be that the prohibition 'You shall not steal' originally had a specifying object, 'a man', and that its concern was to prohibit not theft in general but kidnapping in particular. This is a concern of laws outside the decalogue, and is, in fact, an early Jewish interpretation of the commandment in its present form. If this does represent its original concern, then a coherent sequence of topics results for the second half of the decalogue: they protect, in turn, the life of the individual, his marriage, his freedom, his reputation and his property, so including all the basic spheres of the individual's experience. It was when the meaning of the verb 'covet' eventually developed, as it did develop, to have reference only to feelings of envy and desire, that the general subject of theft then ceased to be covered by the decalogue; it was this loss that was made good by dropping the specifying object from the original commandment 'You shall not steal a man'.

Now this is quite obviously a fairly speculative reconstruction of part of the internal history of the decalogue; but much less speculation is involved in the second indication that the decalogue was open to internal modification. There are some important objective differences between the decalogue as it occurs in Ex 20 and its form in Deut 5. These differences illustrate the nature of the decalogue as a statement of meaning which was itself open to interpretative organisation and expression. The major differences are these: the motivation for the observance of the Sabbath in the Deuteronomy version, unlike that in Exodus, refers to the exodus from Egypt, and in so doing provides a catchword link with the reference to Egypt in the beginning of the decalogue; that same motivation adds a reference to the ox and ass, which should likewise benefit from the Sabbath rest, and this makes a catchword link with the final commandment of the decalogue; in the Deuteronomic decalogue the commandments 'You shall not kill, you shall not commit adultery, you shall not steal, you shall not bear false witness, you shall not covet', do not appear as separate commandments as in the Exodus version, but are all joined into a single literary unit by the use of the conjunction, and this provides a balance for the long literary unit found at the beginning of the decalogue. The result is a regular alternation of long and short literary units in which the central, long unit has catchword links with the beginning and end of the decalogue. The overall effect of these modifications is to create a new literary structure, known as a chiasm or ring pattern, which has the intended effect of pushing forward and emphasising the centre as the focal point: in the case of the version of the decalogue in Deut 5 it is the Sabbath commandment which receives this emphasis.

It is because the decalogue represents what we might call a charismatic breakthrough to a general interpretation of what it means to be a member of the people of one God that it maintained a general stability and uniformity while at the same time was open to some internal adaptation: its basic requirement of what might be called a practical monotheism, embracing both religious and ethical behaviour, remained constant even if its expression received now one new formulation and now another, now one new emphasis and now another. It is this openness to new understanding, within a constant basic framework, belonging to the very nature of the decalogue, which is the foundation for the radical reinterpretation of the demands of the decalogue in the Sermon on the Mount; it is that same openness which is the justification for the continued reinterpretation and extension of the demands of the decalogue in the history of the religious communities which valued it. The decalogue is a classic statement of the life of a community of faith; like the classic in any context it is a total statement in which now one part, now the other, may be highlighted. Ultimately, however, it is valued for the basic single insight which it reflects: that the worship of one God implies respect for the integrity of others, that respect for the integrity of others implies the worship of one God.

FURTHER READING

Alt, A., 'The Origins of Israelite Law', *Essays on Old Testament History and Religion*, Oxford: Blackwell, 1966.

Childs, B.S., *Exodus (Old Testament Library)*, Canterbury: SCM Press, 1974. *Interpretation,* Vol. XLIII, No. 3, July 1989.

Johnstone, W., 'The "Ten Commandments": Some Recent Interpretations', *Expository Times,* 100, 1988–89, 453ff.

Mayes, A.D.H., *Deuteronomy (New Century Bible),* London: Marshall, Morgan & Scott, 1979.

3   The Ethic of Jesus: The Sermon on the Mount Then and Now

Seán Freyne

(Seán Freyne (ed.), *Ethics and the Christian*, Dublin: Columba Press, 1991, pp. 41–57.)

THE PRESENT SITUATION IN SOCIETY AND CHURCH

These are heady times for the idealists among us – those who like to think about the emerging world as one family, all living happily together in a single global village. For Europeans in particular, the collapse of what from the outside appeared to be an immovable and impenetrable socialist block has been a very strange, even weird experience. Nobody seems quite sure how to react, whether to rejoice or be scared. The demise of the old enemy, Communism, has left us somewhat breathless, unsure of the future and where we might all be headed. For those of us who operate under the liberal democratic philosophy of the West, all these developments could easily be seen as a vindication of our dominant world-view – the success of the free-market economy and its myth of progress, leading to a better world for all.

I recall these political facts of our times merely to point up some of the ironies of our contemporary situation which apply not just to the political sphere, but to the religious and the ethical as well. In different ways, we are all faced with the question of how to subscribe to universal dreams while retaining the identity that is part of our particular experience – be it political, cultural or religious. The collapse of the universal dreams of a socialist Europe imposed by force is due in no small measure to the reassertion of much older ethnic and cultural differences that could not be wiped out or glossed over. It would be ironic indeed if such events should give rise to a different form of liberal universalism that would seek to ignore differences in human life as these express themselves in so many aspects of our experience – everything from language to the ways we think about the universe and its ultimate destiny. In many cases of resistance, religion played a significant role in ensuring the non-acceptance of a totalitarian regime. The question now is: will it be a divisive or a creative factor in the shaping of the new Europe, either by attempting to control and dominate, or by continuing to challenge some of the new ideologies of progress that are on offer?

For two centuries now, two opposing tendencies may be discerned in the way that Christians everywhere in the West have dealt with the problem of living within an increasingly secular environment. Either Christian values were assumed to correspond with universal human ones, and so there was nothing distinctive, at least in the domain of public morality, about being Christian, or alternatively, Christians so cut themselves off from the world and from each other that they developed highly individualistic, anti-world value systems, which had little to say to the emerging secular ethos of the Enlightenment and modern humanism.

It was during the same centuries, and faced with that same secularisation process, that 'the eclipse of biblical narrative' occurred, to use the title of Hans Frei's influential work. By this he means that in the wake of the changing scientific understanding of the universe and the emergence of the sense of the self as being wholly free and autonomous, people's self-understanding was no longer grounded in the biblical account of human and world origins. The story of Jesus, likewise, had to be shorn of the outdated mythological trappings in which it had been handed down in the gospels. In the many lives of Jesus that emerged in the nineteenth century he was made to represent the dominant value system of the day, that of liberal humanism. Such lives were written for the best of motives, to salvage something from the wreckage that the Enlightenment was deemed to have caused to Christian faith through the apparent discrediting of its foundational documents. Thus, Jesus was seen as a wise teacher/philosopher whose life and teachings embodied the best liberal ideals in the pursuit of freedom and equality. Of course, both Catholic and Protestant orthodoxies in their different ways reacted to this liberal response. Within Roman Catholicism the anti-modernist crisis of the late nineteenth and early twentieth centuries represented a return to the medieval world-view as this had been defined in the Counter-Reformation period. Almost contemporaneously the work of Karl Barth attempted to reaffirm the reformation principle of justification by faith, understood as a surrender of the self to God's saving action in Christ, as witnessed in scripture.

Both positions can be seen as a reassertion of the quest for a timeless truth whereby Christian faith could ignore the vicissitudes of human history and culture. Though adopting very different starting points, both tend to ignore the changing historical and cultural circumstances within which human life is lived and human responses to God's call are fashioned. Neither takes seriously the subjective dimension of all truth claims, and the consequent need for careful attention to the linguistic, social, psychological and other conditioning that must be seen as substantive rather than purely accidental features of all human understanding in the world. In this paper, however, I propose to develop a different line of argument, because I am persuaded of the necessity for Christians, even in Ireland, to explore anew their own resources, spiritual and ethical, as a way of being challenged to enter into dialogue with other value systems.

Dr Jeanrond has suggested that a conversation model, in which competing truth-claims in ethics as in other spheres of life can be debated publicly, is a pressing need for our times. This demands that Christians can articulate their own distinctive vision, without on the one hand reducing it to a set of generalised truths, or on the other rejecting out of hand all other claims as false or unworthy. In the past, especially in Ireland, it has been a particular temptation for all the churches here to want to control the total ethos of the society in terms of its ethical values – for the best of reasons of course! In the changing culture that now obtains here, traditional norms are breaking down more rapidly than in societies that have for long been accustomed to questioning and change. We are threatened with a dangerous vacuum, in which the very question of values is likely to be dismissed, simply because the authority by which the traditional ones were imposed is now rejected. As Christians we must make more modest claims to universal truth, especially in ethics, while at the same time taking our own vision more seriously than heretofore.

EXPLORING THE ETHICAL VISION OF JESUS

But what have we got to offer? What particular insights from our tradition might be of special significance at the present juncture. That Jesus of Nazareth was one of the great 'classic' religious figures would be acknowledged by all thinking people, irrespective of their personal allegiance to him or to the religion that has emerged in his name. In the nineteenth century, as previously mentioned, it was as a teacher of ethical truths that Jesus was seen by many 'enlightened' investigators. Certainly, the ethical teachings of Jesus have almost from the very beginning been singled out for attention, especially as they had been distilled to the early Church through Matthew's gospel in the famous Sermon on the Mount (Mt 5-7), with some of the great early Christian fathers such as Origen and Augustine writing special commentaries on it. Luke, in his gospel, has another, much shorter version, which he locates on a plain (Lk 6:19-49), something that reminds us that the career and teaching of Jesus have come to us through the interpretative activity of the early Christian community in often quite different circumstances. This already alerts us to an important aspect of Jesus' teaching, namely, that he was not a teacher of timeless moral truths of an unchanging and unchangeable character, but rather a prophetic figure who applied his particular vision of the kingdom of God to very specific and concrete situations and problems within everyday life of the Galilean country folk amongst whom his public ministry was conducted. If Jesus' life and teaching are to be accorded the status of the classic then he fulfils admirably the first condition for that epithet, namely, particularity of origins.

In view of the modem interest in Jesus as a teacher of ethics it may come as some surprise to hear that the role of teacher was not by any means the most obvious description of him by some at least of his contemporaries. True he is addressed in the gospels frequently as Rabbi/*didaskale*/teacher, but only by outsiders. Thus, Matthew at least would seem to want to distance Jesus from the role of the scribe, the official teachers within Judaism, who were a professional and elitist class according to one of their early representatives, Jesus son of Sirach from

Jerusalem. By such standards Jesus did not rank. He had not studied, nor as a *tecton* or craftsman was he likely to have had the leisure to acquire the necessary knowledge to give him the status of a scribe (see Sir 38; Jn 7:15).

This observation points us in another direction in trying to identify the significance of Jesus for ethics. It is his life and ministry, his praxis, if you like, that distinguishes him, since, as has often been observed, many of his recorded sayings echo those of other great teachers, Jewish and Greek, emanating from that culture. His originality lay not so much in the sayings themselves but in the context within which they were uttered, a life that lived out the radical implications of these utterances, to the point that the saying became a commentary on the one who spoke them.

The story of Jesus then is the important factor; it is a story of the one who in the name of God's kingly rule gathered around himself the messianic community that, according to the Israelite prophetic tradition, would be purified and restored, so that the great ideals of her communal life could at last be realised. Insofar as that vision was based on the restoration of right relations – with God, with the earth and its creatures and with fellow human beings – it was indeed a utopian vision; not utopian in the sense of being unrealisable, but as reflecting the most primordial longings of the human spirit faced with the reality of greed and selfishness distorting the way that things ought to be and could be, we are convinced, in our world. In the gospel stories about Jesus, therefore, we should hear again echoes of the stories of Paradise, not in terms of the mythological expressions of a lost Golden Age, but as realised historically in and through the career of Jesus of Galilee. We will never grasp the full meaning, and therefore, the full challenge of the sermon if we do not constantly remind ourselves that it is only in the setting of that story and all its implications that this particular ethical synthesis is intended to make full sense.

Mention has already been made of the contrasting settings – mountain and plain – that Matthew and Luke choose for the sermon. Like all good storytellers they are seeking a suitable backdrop for the account, in order to stimulate, provoke and challenge their readers to be opened up to new possibilities, as they leave the everyday world (Matthew) or remain within it (Luke). Matthew's setting is particularly suggestive for our present purposes. Horizons of meaning as well as of vision change as we climb the mountain, and new and hitherto unexplored vistas are opened up before us. However, for the first readers of his work 'the mountain' and its association with 'city' and 'house' a few verses further on had other resonances emanating from the Hebrew scriptures. According to Isaiah, at the end of days the mountain of the house of the Lord, that is, the new Jerusalem with its new temple, would raise itself higher than all other mountains and attract the nations there to learn the wisdom of the Lord (Is 2:2-4). That this futuristic imagery was intended to pervade the whole sermon is confirmed by the closing image of the wise person building a house on the rock, in contrast to that of the foolish person building on sand. Jesus, as Wisdom incarnate, builds himself a house on a rock that is a community to which all are invited to enter and learn of wisdom.

As well as having imaginative evocations from the prophetic and wisdom traditions, houses and cities were also the places where the early Christians lived out their communal existence together. In such settings they undertook a radically alternative lifestyle that was subversive of the traditional value systems of Greco-Roman culture, as we shall see. It was only within such caring communities that such ideals as turning the other cheek, loving one's enemies, sharing beyond the call of duty make sense. It is only when these extremes are undertaken within the context of communities bonded together in faith and love in the name of Jesus Christ, and thus providing a supportive ethos, that they become possible and viable, not foolhardy undertakings of a highly individualistic nature.

It is sometimes suggested that Matthew wanted to present Jesus as the giver of a second law to fulfil the Mosaic dispensation. While some of the utterances do indeed suggest such a contrast, it is clear from the overall tone and style that to interpret the whole in a legal fashion would be seriously to misconstrue the intention of Jesus, even as Matthew understands it. Unfortunately, that is what has happened in Christian history with some of the sayings such as those on divorce, whereas others like turning the other cheek have been largely ignored, even as possible ideals for Christians who have had no difficulties in fighting so-called just wars! General instruction is interspersed with personal address; warnings, exhortations and declarations of blessedness arising from the pursuit of certain values are to be found side by side with practical wisdom, rules, admonitions, examples of correct conduct in prayer, fasting and almsgiving, within this new vision. Here is neither the precision of a sustained law code nor the detached and abstract reflections of a philosophical ethician. Rather, it is the passionate, direct appeal of a charismatic preacher, the urgency of whose language betrays the sense of finality about the message.

Despite this very distinctive tone and language that marks the sermon as unmistakably Jewish, one can also detect an opening out to the larger world of discourse on ethical and other issues that was such a feature of the Mediterranean world generally, and which certainly marked Jesus' Galilean ministry. The golden rule – as you would that others should do to you do to them in like manner – was a commonplace among both Jewish teachers and pagan philosophers. Besides, such terms as justice (*dikaiosyne*) and perfection (*teleios*) were also much debated issues. In Matthew's account however, the justice that Jesus talks about is that of the kingdom and the ideal of perfection that is proposed is that of the heavenly Father (6:53; 5:48). Even the golden rule is thoroughly Judaised, since after its citation, Matthew adds: 'For this is the law and the prophets' (7:10). Thus, the central ethical values of the culture were grounded theologically in Jesus' vision, but in such a way, however, that his lifestyle as an articulation of those values and their theological grounding proved to be a severe threat, not just to the received understanding of justice and perfection, but to that of the kingdom of God, the law and the prophets and even the concept of God itself. It was because he was seen to be engaged in an attack both on the received value system of the Roman world and the religious symbols of his own tradition that Rome and the Jewish religious establishment could join forces against this prophet from Galilee. Establishments, religious and political, can tolerate theoretical discussion as long as it remains isolated from so-called 'real life'. However, ethical stances always imply a particular belief system and world-view, and it is in the resultant behaviour that these can be most easily identified, as every social reformer has learned, often to their cost, from Socrates in fifth-century Athens to Nelson Mandela in contemporary South Africa

As an experiment in identifying more precisely the distinctive ethic of Jesus we can attempt a comparison with the Greek ideal in regard to these two central categories of the sermon, justice and perfection.

Justice was an ideal that was particularly dear to the Greeks within the context of the *polis*, or city-state. For them it was a matter of fulfilling one's duties as these were defined within the particular social realms of the household or the city: 'giving to each its own in accordance with the laws' as Aristotle expresses it. The symbol of the scales was highly appropriate for such a notion since it was largely a matter of balancing the rights and duties of each, but in accordance with the structured patterns of rank within the particular setting. These ranged from males who were full citizens and who took precedence over all others, to women, children, slaves and aliens. According to the prevailing view, it was those who were in a position to take on some *leitourgia* or service on behalf of the *polis* that were on the top rung of the ladder as far as justice was concerned. In the family hierarchy there was a similar structure with the paterfamilias as the first in terms of rights.

Jesus' vision was not based on abstract ideas of justice but on the prophetic ideal of *sedaqah*, which, as articulated by several prophets, entailed a radical social programme. In their view justice was first and foremost a righting of the social ills within Israel. This, rather than worship of Yahweh in prayers, fasting and other religious and cultic practices, was essential for a right relationship with Israel's God, who, unlike many other gods in her neighbourhood, had a strongly ethical character. 'I desire mercy (in the sense of deeds of loving kindness) not sacrifice' is Hosea's declaration, and this is twice quoted by the Matthean Jesus as the correct expression of his understanding of God's will also (Mt 9:13, 12:7). Later prophets such as Third Isaiah continue to spell out the same message after the restoration from the Babylonian exile. In a passage that touches on many topics developed in the Sermon on the Mount we read, 'If you take away from the midst of you the yoke, the pointing of the finger and speaking wickedness, if you pour yourself out for the afflicted, then shall your light rise in the darkness ... and the

Lord shall satisfy your desires with good things ... and your ancient ruins shall be rebuilt' (Is 58:1-12).

In this and other passages, the justice that is demanded is 'my justice'. God had entered into a partnership with Israel in slavery and thus justice was ongoing faithfulness to that relationship, no matter how badly Israel had failed. Justice as an ethical norm within Israel must always mirror God's justice, and that meant particular care for the poor, the needy and the socially outcast. Since God had not considered rank in the choice of a people, justice built on that memory had to be concerned with a radical reordering of all social relationships, including economic ones.

The realisation of such a justice had been long delayed. In the centuries between the Babylonian captivity and the first century AD the repressive experience of successive kingdoms, including for a time a Jewish national one, that of the Maccabeans, had only heightened the expectation among pious Jews of God's kingdom as opposed to all human kingdoms, when such a society could at last be realised. It was in the name of this kingdom that Jesus preached and lived his own ethical vision, not as some distant ideal, but as a reality now. Among his Jewish contemporaries others too proclaimed the dawning of the new era, but in terms very different from his. To take one example, not without its relevance for our world, the Zealots, or extreme nationalists, espoused a militant overthrowing of Roman rule and destruction of those who collaborated with the enemy. In Jesus' words, they sought to force open the kingdom of heaven by violence. There is ample evidence from Josephus of the manner in which that particular ideology expressed itself throughout the first century, leading up to the revolt against Rome in the year AD 66. In God's name they espoused the annihilation, whereas Jesus called for love of the enemy, so startlingly portrayed in the images of turning the other cheek, or going an extra mile beyond that which one was constrained to do – a frequent form of harassment of a native population by an invading army.

As with justice, so also with perfection, the other general ethical category that Matthew's gospel shares with its larger environment. In the Greek ideal perfection was a matter of achieving the correct balance between the good and the beautiful, and therefore it had an aesthetic as well as an ethical dimension. Alternatively, in certain circles it had become an elitist ideal that separated 'the perfect' from society at large. Either way, it was a highly individualistic ideal achieved through self-restraint and training rather than in and through a life shared with others. The gods had achieved this inner harmony which expressed itself in detachment, and the individual could be exhorted to imitate God by living in accordance with nature (Stoics) or achieving an inner freedom from all passions and desires (Epicureans).

By contrast the perfect God of Jesus as Matthew portrays it is deeply involved with the world. This is emphasised by the fact that the same ideal, perfection, can be achieved through following Jesus. 'If you would be perfect,' he tells the rich young man, 'sell what you have, give to the poor and come follow me' (Mt 19:21). In the sermon itself the God of Jesus, 'the heavenly Father', is portrayed as totally involved with and in control of creation. In an extraordinarily evocative passage, Jesus contrasts the freedom of the animal plant life with the care-ridden existence of humans, expressed in terms of concern for food, drink and clothing. This passage expresses no romantic idealism about nature, however, but is rather deliberately provocative in terms of prevailing discussions about true and false cares. The Christian disciple is being challenged to let go, not just of daily cares, but of the care for existence itself, expressed under the metaphors of food, drink and clothing – the very basic necessities of life (Mt 6:25-34). In Paradise nakedness was natural, not because of the absence of sexual desires, but because total trust in and openness to God prevailed. Food and drink were present in abundance also. Against such a mythological background the God of Jesus is totally involved with creation, human anxiety has been taken care of and the possibility of a human community based on the sharing of God with the creation is once again a practical possibility. This is the perfection of God that the disciple is to imitate as it is defined in the ethic of Jesus.

We shall have to terminate at this point our exploration of the ethic of Jesus based on comparisons with similar ideals, pagan and Jewish. In this light its distinctive character, its radical demand and theological grounding stand out in clearer perspective. While it shared considerably with the other great traditions within which it was fashioned, its values, vision and communitarian character clearly *differed* from these in a very essential way. As Matthew views it, Christian disciples are to essay a more radical lifestyle than either Jewish or pagan standards; there was a 'more' demanded that was defined by Jesus himself. And yet this did not mean a 'holier than thou' attitude, since according to Isaiah, on whose vision it is based, all would want to ascend God's holy mountain and learn there the wisdom of Zion. Thus, the ethical vision of Jesus is not a perfectionist ideal for the few, but a radical statement of human possibility for all that will generate its own dynamism, if only it is attempted. 'People will see your good works and glorify (not you) but your Father who is in heaven' (Mt 5:16).

FUSING THE HORIZONS: THE ETHICAL VISION OF JESUS IN OUR CULTURE

Karl Marx has declared that the object of all human reflection should be, not to interpret reality, but to change it. This of course presumes that those who do the reflection are unhappy with the status quo and feel called on to do something about it. The reflection will both help to identify the problem and determine what one ought to do. As Christians, we are pilgrim people, restless, struggling to ascend the mountain so that we get a clearer view of the farthest horizons and what lies between us and it. It is not however, as, though we are struggling to ascend in order to catch a first glimpse, we have in fact already crossed over. As German theologian Jürgen Moltmann declares, with reference to the liberation that Christians claim in Christ: 'When Freedom draws near, the chains begin to hurt; When Life has passed by, Death becomes deadly.' We Christians cannot, or at least should not be satisfied with our world, or its *laissez-faire* attitudes, once we have been confronted with the ethical vision of Jesus and the possibilities for human transformation that it both envisages and proclaims as a possibility now.

We are, I submit, faced with two questions that are intimately related. First, how are we as Christians to appropriate the ethical vision of Jesus today, and second, how might such an appropriation contribute to a more serious debate about ethics within contemporary life? This second question is all the more urgent if, as I (and others) have suggested, the Christian churches have for the most part opted for the neo-conservative response of reasserting past orthodoxies, without listening to other voices in our culture that are also struggling with genuine ethical dilemmas.

First, however, we must begin to put our own house in order, taking seriously the advice of the sermon itself: do not seek to remove the speck from others' eyes, without removing first the log from our own. Interpreting the sermon has almost always in Christian history been seen as a task of negotiating its radical demands within the context of everyday life, either watering those demands down, choosing between them or seeing them as unattainable ideals. Thus, interpreting the ethics of Jesus is itself an ethical exercise, and for this we are recommended, again by the sermon itself, to have our eye simple rather than evil, in order to hear its demands fully, and open ourselves up to the perspectives it unfolds before us (Mt 6:22f, 7:3-5).

Earlier, I stressed that as Christians we should not be tempted into the position of divorcing the ethic of Jesus from his story, which is the strange, paradoxical and profoundly disturbing story that in the life, death and resurrection of Jesus of Nazareth, God's ultimate purpose for this world has been disclosed. The fact that others ignore, dismiss or find this story unconvincing is ultimately not the point. It is our story and we are called on to affirm it by allowing our own personal and communal stories be judged by its radical demands and supported by its profound sense of hope in the midst of human failure and suffering. In practice this means that we feel called on to participate together in a radically new venture, called on, not as individuals, but in community, the messianic community that Jesus has gathered around him in order to live out his shared vision of human togetherness in the world.

We have already alluded more than once in passing to the image of climbing the mountain as an invitation to change our perspective. Useful as this image is, it is to the language of the sermon that we must look for its transformative effects, since language is not just descriptive of the way things are, but creative of the way things can and ought to be. As in all the utterances of Jesus, equally in his ethical statements, there is a strange, even paradoxical quality: the persecuted are declared blessed; disciples who are contrasted with hypocrites are themselves called hypocrites; birds and flowers can be used, not as romantic images of innocence, but as analogues for human activity – sowing, reaping, gathering into barns; logs of timber in the eye blocking one's vision are scarcely a normal occurrence! But then so much of the conduct that is enjoined is not 'normal' either – turning the other cheek, letting coat as well as cloak go, loving one's enemy. There is a strangeness about these demands, even hyperbole, but it is hyperbole that is not merely ornamental but which goes to the heart of the matter, literally as well as metaphorically. Here language is being used in a recklessly extravagant manner in order to shock us into seeing new and hitherto unperceived possibilities for human conduct. Their only logic is that of superabundance, as Paul Ricoeur puts it, a logic that gives rise to extravagance in doing and thinking. At crucial points we are directed to pay attention to the eye and the heart as focal points of vision and intention. We are invited to embark on a journey inwards as well as upwards. What would it be like if our eye were really simple, that is single minded, and we tried out this vision, but together, as a way of overcoming our self-centred and self-grounded super-egos, the product of both the Enlightenment's legacy of the totally free and autonomous self, and of the scientific revolution's myth of human self-sufficiency and control over our own destiny? The last enemy to be conquered is Death, declared one of the leaders of the French Revolution, and modern medicine seems hell-bent on taking him seriously!

Of course the sermon does not answer directly our specific ethical questions, since many of its examples are time-conditioned and are not (often at least) part of our culture. There is no substitute for the task of discerning, often painfully, what our detailed Christian response should be, but it does give us very clear directions if we really want to know. Justice, in terms of radical concern for human need wherever and in whatever form it is encountered, will be the keynote; concern with the other will increasingly define the self, and thus the values that will inform the lifestyle will often be in direct conflict with those that motivate the progressivist modern world, where 'greed is good' functions as the most fundamental principle of life. Our actions for and on behalf of others will always be anti-ideological, that is opposed to all forms of discrimination: sexism, racism, ageism, classism, monetarism. We will be deeply conscious that too often the Christian churches have been the propagators of these very ideologies, despite our most noble declarations that there is neither Jew nor Greek, slave nor free, male or female (Gal 3:24), and conscious also that ours is at best a highly ambiguous history in terms of the liberative praxis that we are called to as followers of Jesus, the prophet of liberation for all.

If Christians in Ireland, as elsewhere within western democracies, were to embark on such a messianic lifestyle, what difference would it make to our world? While each of our cultures has its own distinctive ethos, due to circumstances of geography and history – to name the most obvious determinants – ours is on the whole a monochromic world that is shaped by universal myths which are the product of the Enlightenment and its successor, the scientific revolution. The shallowness and ego-centrism of so much of modern life are the direct results of our failure to replace the medieval and renaissance world-views and their in-built ethical programmes, with new and responsible alternatives that could seriously address in our own time the age-old questions of what is the good life, what is the nature of happiness, how and where can we find meaning in time and history.

This should not be interpreted as though I regard the advances of the Enlightenment and scientific progress as evil or to be rejected. Much has been achieved through the freeing of the human subject from outmoded, authoritarian structures that sought to control human thinking and acting in the world. It would be difficult to imagine even the possibilities of various feminist liberation movements today for example, without the understanding of human freedom and dignity that have been hammered out over the past two centuries. And who could deny the advances for human life in the world that science in its many forms has achieved over the past 150 years in particular. What has been wrong is not that such intellectual and scientific advances have occurred, but that we have allowed them to go unchallenged in terms of their meaning for all of human life in this world. The gloriously free and autonomous self of Kant, having failed in some of its more ambitious projects, has become the feckless, disillusioned and in the end irresponsible self of some post-modernist writers. The unbridled exploration and use of our natural resources that has followed in the wake of much scientific advance has brought us to the very brink of ecological disaster on a global scale. Nuclearism may have receded temporarily from our list of ideologies that have to be resisted, but nevertheless we are for ever doomed to live in the last age of the world. We and our children must always live now in the realisation that we have at hand the capacity to destroy ourselves irrevocably.

In the midst of such competing ideologies, many of them literally life-threatening, the Christian churches are faced with new challenges, but also new possibilities. Ecumenical hair splitting, debates about women's ordination and other inner Church conflicts are almost obscene luxuries, by comparison with the tasks that confront us. Where the Christian messianic vision is being lived today, as in the third world countries, we can hear again, and more importantly, see again, the reality of Jesus of Galilee's prophetic critique and the transformative power for human living in the world of its radically alternative lifestyle. We have as yet hardly begun to discern what shape it might take in our own more affluent cultures or how we might begin to learn from the voices of the oppressed among us.

What if Christians in Ireland were to take seriously the messianic lifestyle of Jesus? What changes to Church and society could we expect? A number of subsequent papers [in the original collection] attempt answers to these pressing questions in the areas of justice for the poor, especially for poor women, the ecology and politics. As background to those more detailed discussions it may be appropriate here to recall that insofar as Ireland has experienced social revolutions in the past – Davitt's 'land war' of the last century and Larkin's campaign for the urban workers in this – these never coalesced to bring about a total revolution for all within our society. Sectional interests still vie with each other while appealing in a highly selective manner to a notion of justice that smacks more of the 'I'm-all-right-Jack' philosophy of the middle classes than of Jesus' vision of a justice that is biased in favour of the needy.

In attempting to envisage a new society inspired by such a vision we might do well to recall the values that were embedded in the old Irish notion of *muintearas*, a concept for which neighbourliness is a rather bland translation. Mutual help, support and sharing were the hallmarks of the peasant economy of the countryside. This suggestion is not prompted by any nostalgic looking back to the past, but by the awareness that any viable alternative to the current dominant trends of our macro-economic practitioners must draw on our own well-springs, while always for Christians also recalling the radical challenge of Jesus' vision. Europe and 1992 is no panacea for the deep-seated social ills that beset our society, despite the increased affluence for those in the privileged position to avail of the new opportunities.

In rural Ireland *muintearas* could be narrow-minded, inward-looking and self-interested, yet its heart was in the right place. With limited resources life's necessities had to be shared and mutual help was based on mutual trust. As such it was grounded in social realities similar to those that prompted Jesus' radical vision which we have been exploring in this paper. His first followers attempted some daring experiments in putting this ideal into practice in the new urban environments of the Mediterranean cities, thereby providing a home for the homeless, status for non-persons such as women and slaves, and a welcome for strangers. The conservative moral economy of the peasant took on a radical dimension when translated from the kinship society of peasants to the open and free associations of the city. Were Irish Christians to embark on a similar imaginative venture based on the memory of togetherness that our forebears practised (*'ní neart go cur le chéile'* – 'Our power comes from our cooperation'), yet continuing to be challenged by the older memory of Jesus, they would certainly be a transforming force in our churches and our society.

One has the distinct impression that at present the 'alternative vision' which the churches have to offer is stifled by their own failures at the institutional level to take that vision seriously. They can hardly expect society, either north or south, to be too impressed by words when, with some notable individual exceptions, deeds of justice and caring seem to be lacking. One is reminded of the prophetic words of Dietrich Bonhoeffer, as relevant today for the European churches as when they were uttered in a German prison fifty years ago: 'Our Church that has been fighting in these years only for its self-preservation, as though that were an end in itself, is incapable of taking the word of reconciliation to the world ... Our being Christian today will be limited to two things – prayer and righteous action in the world ... We are not yet out of the melting pot, and any attempt to help the Church prematurely to a new expansion of its organisation will merely delay its conversion and purification.'

FURTHER READING

Davies, W.D., *The Setting of the Sermon on the Mount*, Cambridge: Cambridge University Press, 1964.

Betz, H.D., *Essays on the Sermon on the Mount*, Philadelphia: Fortress Press, 1985.

Lambrecht, J., *The Sermon on the Mount: Proclamation and Exhortation*, Wilmington: Michael Glazier, 1985.

Moxes, H., *The Economy of the Kingdom: Social Conflict and Economic Relations in Luke's Gospel*, Philadelphia: Fortress Press, 1988.

Crosby, Michael H., *House of Disciples: Church, Economics and Justice in Matthew*, Maryknoll: Orbis Books, 1988.

Freyne, S., *Galilee, Jesus and the Gospels. Literary Approaches and Historical Investigations*, Dublin: Gill & Macmillan, 1988.

Meeks, W., *The Moral World of the First Christians*, London: APCK, 1986.

Mieth D. & Pohier, J., 'Changing Values and Virtues', *Concilium*, 191, Edinburgh: T. & T. Clark.

Horsley, R., *Jesus and the Spiral of Violence: Popular Jewish Resistance in Roman Palestine*, New York: Harper & Row, 1987.

Ricoeur, P., 'The Golden Rule: Exegetical and Theological Perplexities', *New Testament Studies*, 36 (1990), pp. 392–397.

Part Two
Theological Reflection

4   The Fate of the Moral Manual since Saint Alphonsus

Raphael Gallagher

(Raphael Gallagher and Brendan McConvery (eds), *History and Conscience: Studies in Honour of Father Sean O'Riordan CSsR*, Dublin: Gill and Macmillan, 1989, pp. 212–39.)

When analysing literature as voluminous and technical as the moral manuals since the death of St Alphonsus the initial temptation is to deal in generalities. One could simply accept the broadly agreed divisions: an attitude vacillating between suspicion of and opposition to Alphonsus' method that is tempered with his canonisation in 1839, a gradual rallying round the moral views of Alphonsus that reaches a symbolic climax when he is declared *Doctor Ecclesiae* in 1871, a period of controversy centring on the precise status and exact interpretation of Alphonsus' views that begins with the controversy surrounding the publication of the *Vindiciae Alphonsianae* (1873) and ends only with the turn of the century, and finally the acceptance of Alphonsus as the preferred ecclesiastical authority in casuistic moral theology comparable, in an analagous sense, with the authority of St Thomas in dogmatic theology.

There is truth in those broad divisions, with the reservations one normally has about too general notions. It would be possible, methodologically, to chart the systematisation of the Alphonsian moral method by applying those broadly accepted divisions to particular manuals of various schools, e.g. Redemptorist, Jesuit, Dominican, and thus discover what was transformed, abandoned or rejected in the Alphonsian method. This paper approaches these questions in a more limited way. Because of the great number and often intimidating length of these manuals, it seemed advisable to opt for some principles of control in the material to be examined.

The twenty or so manuals referred to in some depth in this article represent publications from most of the decades between 1800 and 1960: that is, the period when the manuals were very definitely 'in possession' after the bitter systems controversies of the 1700s and before the dramatic and virtually universal collapse of the manual in the 1960s. Within the kaleidoscope of interesting questions treated by the manuals, one is particularly considered here: *de habituatis et recidivis*. Why? The major methodological concern of the manuals was the preparation of future confessors for the juridically correct administration of the sacrament of penance; on the basis of that fact it is fair to make the further assumption that the manual treatment of *habituati et recidivi* (perhaps numerically the majority of penitents?) would give a reasonable indication of the overall method of the manual writer and thus show in what way the teaching of Alphonsus was transformed, abandoned or rejected. The perspective from which the questions of this article are asked is, therefore, limited. There is, also, an inevitable subjective bias and arbitrariness of selection in choosing both the manuals themselves and the main questions from them which are studied here. Within those limits, a chronological assessment of some major moral manuals from the optic of their treatment of the *habituati et recidivi* is, I believe, a plausible way of looking at the development of the moral manual since Alphonsus.

SAINT ALPHONSUS

The *Theologia Moralis* went through nine editions in the saint's lifetime, the first in 1748, the last in 1785. In the century after his death there were, at least, sixty-six editions, the majority being in France and Italy.[1] With the edition of Leonard Gaudé in 1905 a standard critical version was established and it is to this that reference is made here.[2] Alphonsus treats the question of the *consuetudinarii* and *recidivi* in Volume 3 of *Theologia Moralis*. The treatment bears the marks of pastoral realism and prudential balancing of opinions which were later seen to be a characteristically Alphonsian approach.

With regard to the *consuetudinarius* (one confessing a bad habit for the first time), the presumption is given to the penitent in that coming to the sacrament is, in itself, a good sign and absolution is to be given unless sorrow is absolutely lacking. In giving his opinion on the *recidivus* (one who relapses into the same sin after confession of the sin), Alphonsus, characteristically, searches for the middle ground that avoids dangerous extremes. Not for him the lax view that will allow absolution as often as one confesses, nor the strict view that demands total emendation before any absolution. The laxist view is rejected on the grounds that such a practice would not give the basis of a prudent assessment for the priest-confessor to have moral certainty in his judgement; the strict view is rejected because it implies that doubt or suspicion is equivalent to certainty in forming a judgement on the penitent's dispositions. The middle position espoused by Alphonsus states that absolution is to be refused to the *recidivus* unless there are extraordinary signs of sorrow.

These extraordinary signs are then listed: tears/weeping, a lessening in the number of sins, notable efforts at emendation such as fasting or almsgiving, evidence of a search for new means of moral improvement, spontaneous confession, special motivation such as the fear of some impending disaster, confession of sins previously and culpably omitted, prior restitution or the signs of a new awareness of guilt. It is evident that there is a flexibility of applying the apparently rigid principle 'no absolution for the *recidivus*' within these extraordinary signs of repentance. And Alphonsus urges the confessor to have great confidence in applying the principle within these circumstances.

　　　　　　　　　　　　　An Irish Reader in Moral Theology

Between the positions of giving and refusing absolution, Alphonsus next discusses the possibility of deferring absolution. Absolution is to be deferred when the confessor is morally certain of the wrong disposition of the penitent. What is required is moral, not absolute, certainty: that is, the certainty of a prudent and probable judgement. Moral certainty is sufficient to proceed with since absolution should be deferred only when there is clearly positive doubt about a total lack of sorrow. Delaying absolution is less a question of the juridical requirements of confession than of acting in the interests of the penitent's spiritual health. Absolution is not to be deferred if there is a danger of more harm than good being done.

Alphonsus rejects the stern rigidity of absolutist principles for the milder view of pastoral sensitivity to the circumstances of the case, particularly if there is question of a penitent reverting to the same sin more through the intrinsic causes of human weakness than through voluntary and extrinsic causes. The reason is, again, a pastoral one: in the sins of human weakness the grace of God is always more helpful than a harsh moralism. Alphonsus acknowledges that, at times, absolution should be deferred; he is, however, at pains to stress that this should never be done in a way that deprives the penitent of God's grace if there is a prudent possibility of the penitent responding to this. In *a cri de coeur* the pastorally minded Alphonsus acknowledges that deferral of absolution may often lead the penitent to despair and to a neglect of the sacraments. Legally speaking, the confessor may be within his rights in deferring absolution; ordinarily speaking, however, the properly disposed penitent who shows some extraordinary sign of sorrow should be absolved at once.

This cursory summary of Alphonsus' views on the *consuetudinarii et recidivi* highlights some important points from his total manual system:

1. The selection of the mediate position between the Scylla of laxism and the Charybdis of rigorism marks the characteristically Alphonsian search to avoid extremes of theological expression.
2. Alphonsus' abiding concern is the spiritual welfare of people. This spiritual welfare is to be based on sound common sense; the loose views of the laxists lack a firm foundation for moral growth while the stern views of the rigorists lead only to despair. The former view lacks a sense of Christian realism, the latter a sense of Christian hope.
3. Alphonsus had great trust in the power of God's grace, more so than he had in any moral self-righteousness. As long as there is a prudent possibility of good will on the penitent's part, the grace of the sacrament should be given.
4. Moral principles are to be clearly articulated, but they are to be applied prudentially in view of the prevailing circumstances. That is why Alphonsus upholds the legal requirements of the priest as judge on the one hand, while on the other, through his comments on the extraordinary signs of sorrow, he

goes to great lengths to find ways of understanding the human condition, especially in terms of the weakness of human nature.

5. The concern of Alphonsus is to uphold the sovereign goodness of God along with a patient understanding of how humans grow in a painful and often sporadic way. He will defer absolution – but only if it is unavoidable. The reason is that he does not wish to deprive any properly disposed penitent of grace, nor to make a bad situation worse by inducing despair.

6. He writes, as is customary for him, more to clarify a problem for ordinary people than to achieve stylistic elegance of expression. He presents the views of other theologians in a fair-minded way in order to reach his own reasoned opinion of prudent and pastoral judgements.

The treatment of the *consuetudinarii et recidivi* is a useful example of the overall spirit of Alphonsus' moral system. How later theologians treat the same question will show, in however limited a way, what ideas of his were later transformed, abandoned or rejected.

THE STRUGGLE FOR ACCEPTANCE 1800–1850

The authors chosen to represent the first half of the nineteenth century include some re-publications from the eighteenth century as well as representatives of the new writing in Europe and North America. The juxtaposition of the older and established authors, which were still widely used, with the modern moral writing of the early nineteenth century, will indicate how Alphonsus influenced the development of the manual through the treatment of the question of the *habituati et recidivi*.

Published in the previous century, the work of Paul Gabriel Antoine[3] was still very popular in the 1800s. Over sixty editions of his work appeared after 1726. It carried a recommendation from Pope Benedict XIV, and an '*approbatio multiplex*' from Italian and French sources, which prefaces the first volume, indicates that he was an established authority.

Characteristic of his general approach, Antoine first decides on those to whom absolution is to be refused because of defect of matter or of disposition. Ten categories are given, all in a rigorist tone: little room is left for a prudent interpretation of circumstances. The concern is with the legal requirements of the confessor rather than with understanding a problem from the penitent's viewpoint. Even if the penitent does not know what is binding in law he cannot be absolved; the penitent's own word is not to be trusted. Quoting Suarez, Antoine gives the primary consideration to the role of the priest as judge and the need for material integrity, with scarcely a mention of other roles and needs. The presumption is against giving absolution, thus making it difficult to positively conceive the circumstances when absolution can be given.

An Irish Reader in Moral Theology

When he comes to the possibility of deferring absolution, the same harshness prevails. The emphasis is on external appearances, not on internal grace; no flexibility is given to understand, for instance, the psychological pressures on young people. One senses that the main concern is with the confessor as controller of the confessional tribunal; the penitent's own testimony is untrustworthy and evidence of good works seems more important than the converting grace of the sacrament. The overall tone is of the great difficulty in granting absolution; even when it is a question of a *per accidens* occasion of sin, absolution is ordinarily to be deferred, and when the lesser threat of deferral fails the confessor is to force the penitent towards repentance with the greater threat of total refusal. There is a begrudging attitude even towards those who are contrite and rightly disposed; the overall tone reflected a restrictive access to the grace of the sacrament and such a concern with the judicial role of the priest that the other aspects of the confessor's sacramental position, e.g. healer, teacher, are virtually obscured. Antoine represents those harsh moralists whose narrow concern for the externals of orthodoxy contributed to despair among ordinary people and, in time, to the great pastoral problem of the neglect of the sacraments. In Antoine, the perspective on the *habituati et recidivi* is predominantly that of *a priori* judicial requirements rather than the actual and pressing needs of people. There is no evidence, in this revised edition of Antoine, that the thinking of Alphonsus has influenced the treatment of the question.

Born near Antwerp in 1690, Peter Dens died at Malines in 1775; he is, thus, broadly a contemporary of Alphonsus. He taught at the Benedictine Abbey of Afrighen and later in the seminary in Malines, of which he was President from 1735–1755. In his zeal for the moral and scientific training of the clergy, and in his simple piety and love of the poor, he is quite like Alphonsus. The work mentioned here[4] was first published after his death and remained popular well into the 1800s. We can take it that the work is substantially his, though an uneven style and presentation suggested posthumous editors. This, combined with a didactic question-and-answer style, do not make it easy to read now; on the other hand, the casuistic treatment of practical questions no doubt contributed to its popularity as a work of reference for the busy priest of those days. What the book lacks in consistency and coherence of presentation is compensated for by the wide base of its learning and the practical bent in the application of principles.[5]

Before treating the question *de consuetudinariis et recidivis*, Dens examines the qualities of the confessor. These include virtue, wisdom and prudence, which are to be exercised through the offices of the confessor as father, teacher, doctor and judge. Great care is to be taken in analysing the dispositions of the penitent, and Dens tries to avoid the extremes of rigid and lax abuses in his general principles regarding the refusal and deferral of absolution. Though clear in articulating the principles, he avoids rigidity of application. Though I could find no evidence of Dens being familiar with the works of Alphonsus, the treatment of these questions is fairly similar to that of Alphonsus in the *Theologia Moralis* and the *Praxis Confessarii*.

In the actual treatment *de consuetudinariis et recidivis* Dens is a benign anti-probabilist. He takes the main questions in turn – refusing absolution, giving absolution, deferring absolution – and treats them in a casuistic way. That means that he is strict in the formulation of the principles, but shows pastoral sensitivity in the application; this is particularly notable in his analysis of the possibility of granting absolution. His starting points are often restrictive, but in practice he is more flexible within the limitations of his casuistry. In this he is unlike Antoine who is restrictive in both the articulation and application of principles. Dens, at least, shows an awareness of the pastoral care of tortured individuals.

Because Dens' work is written in a catechetical question-and-answer style it is hard to evaluate as a manual of moral theology. Overall, the cryptic legal tone dominates, giving the impression that the questions are asked less from a theological than a canonico-legal point of view. He avoids the harshness of an Antoine: yet he fails to integrate the theological emphases of an Alphonsus.[6]

Constantine Roncaglia (1677–1734), an Italian moralist from Lucca, was a prolific writer on moral, dogmatic and scriptural questions: his moral theology was known and respected by Alphonsus and it was republished well into the 1800s.[7] The treatment of the question of the *habituati et recidivi* is prefaced by an extended exposition of the priest as minister of the sacrament of penance; the tone is very legalistic, with the main emphasis falling on the obligations of the confessor. He is strict with regard to the articulation of principles: this is evident when he discusses people in a proximate voluntary occasion of sin. Such people are judged to be in a continual state of actual sin; the consideration, for instance, that the occasion, though voluntary, may be necessitated by other unavoidable circumstances does not substantially lessen Roncaglia's harsh expression of the principle. The same strictness applies to the habit of sin due to internal human weakness; absolution is to be denied to these. First, as judge, the priest is forced to doubt the disposition of such people. Second, as doctor, the priest must at least defer absolution until there is positive evidence of emendation. The impression is given of the priest as a strict controller of people's lives, with little emphasis on the present, actual needs of penitents themselves. The penitent will always be judged on the basis of the past, with little attention being given to the possibility of all sin being taken away by the grace of God.

A milder approach is evident when he deals with actual confessional practice. Though he, like Antoine, quotes Bellarmine on the dangers of too easily giving absolution, he adverts to the harm that is done by those of an overly rigid view as well. He professes, in practice, to follow a middle view: it is this, perhaps, that enabled Alphonsus to recommend Roncaglia as a moralist.

There is no evidence that the later editors of Roncaglia incorporated any specific points from Alphonsus. Though there are certain similarities with

Alphonsus, as noted above, overall Roncaglia appears more harsh than Alphonsus, at least to the extent that there is a more rigorist articulation of the principles. The rules to be followed in practice, though milder, lack that sense of pastoral awareness of the actual human problems which permeates the writing of Alphonsus.

As the other authors to be considered all wrote at least fifty years after the death of Alphonsus, an interim comment is appropriate. The beginning of the nineteenth century shows a variety of views on the question of the *habituati et recidivi*. The views of Alphonsus are in contrast, to varying degrees, with the other popular moralists of the time. There is a clear choice facing the moral theologian after 1830: does one follow the views of Alphonsus, or the more rigorist views of the likes of Antoine, Dens and Roncaglia?

The Irishman, Francis Patrick Kenrick, is a good example of the new generation of nineteenth century authors who would have been familiar with the writings of both the rigorists and of Alphonsus. Born in Dublin in 1797, Kenrick studied at the Propaganda College in Rome before his ministry in America where he was, first, Professor of Theology at Bardstown, Kentucky and, in turn, Coadjutor Bishop of Philadephia, Bishop of Philadelphia and Archbishop of Baltimore (1850) until his death in 1863. His moral theology was widely used, not least because it was clearly the work of a pastor engaged with the problems of his own day.[8]

Kenrick's fundamental principle in discussing the *habituati et recidivi* is that the properly disposed penitent has a right to absolution even though the confessor, as physician of the soul, may at times defer it. His statement contrasts with the rigorists who so hedge this right as to make it virtually meaningless. The emphasis is on the state of the conscience of the penitent at the time of confession, a view very close to that of Alphonsus whom he quotes on the matter. The confessor's duty is to concentrate on the essential rather than the peripheral. Kenrick's overall analysis of the occasions of sin is also close to that of Alphonsus; he tries, understandably, to translate the views of the saint, culturally conditioned by the kingdom of Naples in the mid-eighteenth century, to the differing conditions of mid-nineteenth-century America. For instance, the fact that a particular maid may be an occasion of sin for a male employer does not necessarily mean that she has to be dismissed, since the problem may not be the maid but the man's lust. It is this which must be remedied, and dismissing one maid, though she be the present object of the lust, leaves the basic problem untouched. Kenrick's concern is with the spiritual growth of people above all else. A further example is his rejection of Alphonsus' views on betrothed couples going to each other's house, something which Alphonsus thought would almost inevitably lead to sin. Kenrick thinks that Alphonsus' harsher views were necessary because of the depraved morals of the Italians and suggests that a milder view might be possible for the Americans who are, presumably, to be more trusted in these matters! In general Kenrick's moral doctrine on sexual matters is milder than that of Alphonsus. Kenrick writes as a practical pastor with the care of souls, rather than as a scientific theologian. Though, clearly, he does not wish to see people sinning, he shows a tolerance of the human condition and he tries to avoid making life more complicated than is necessary.

Consuetudinarii should be absolved if they show some signs of sorrow, but absolution is not to be given indiscriminately. In the case of the *recidivi* the decision to absolve or to defer absolution is to be based on the penitent's conscience and the possibilities for future growth. Less indulgence is to be shown to the latter than to the former, but this implies that some indulgence be shown. Kenrick envisages deferral until such time as the confessor is morally certain of the penitent's good disposition, since the confessor is both judge and doctor; deferral is recommended only if it helps the penitent's spiritual growth. This is close to Alphonsus' teaching, a point further evidenced by the quotations from St Thomas and the Roman Ritual on the power of grace over that of good works and on the benefits of frequent communion. Kenrick is aware that although, legally speaking, one may consider deferring absolution, there may be spiritual dangers in so doing; a person left without sacramental grace may be worse off than before. Prudence is to be exercised. Sometimes the case is clear cut (total lack of sorrow, no sense of faith, no minimal purpose of amendment) but the confessor must avoid rash judgements. For instance, lack of external signs of sorrow is not necessarily lack of sorrow.

In the preface Kenrick had acknowledged Alphonsus as one of his chief sources, and this is borne out in the treatment of the *hatibuati et recidivi*. Kenrick was writing before it was commonplace, indeed fashionable, to acknowledge the importance of Alphonsus, and in this his pioneering insight is to be acknowledged. In large measure Kenrick simply repeats Alphonsus' doctrine, though in matters of a practical import he was not afraid to state his own view. In combining a loyalty to the central Alphonsian principles with a liberty to vary their application to a new culture, he shows a sense of judgement that was not always matched by later writers.

Review of the authors of the first half of the nineteenth century ends, appropriately, with Thomas Gousset. Born in 1792, he taught for thirteen years at the seminary of Besançon and was progressively Bishop of Perigueux, Archbishop of Rheims and Cardinal (1850) until his death in 1866. The symbolic appropriateness of Gousset is that, having been educated on the principles of rigorism, he made a chance discovery of the works of Alphonsus in 1829 and he took a vow the following year to consecrate himself to the defence and spreading of the views of Alphonsus. Gousset came to appreciate the errors of the rigorists and found, in Alphonsus, the theological expression of those principles of practical moral wisdom which he wished to follow. His moral theology had thirteen editions in his lifetime and was a major influence in establishing Alphonsus as an accepted author for the pastoral solution of moral problems.[9]

Gousset distinguishes between those with the habit of sin and the recidivists *'pour la direction'*: that is, for him it is not simply a legal distinction but more a matter of spiritual discernment. His teaching on those with the habit of sin, following Alphonsus and the Roman Ritual which he quotes, is that, generally speaking, absolution is not to be deferred or refused. His approach is thoroughly pastoral. A habit of sin is not, in itself, a presumption of bad will since it may be the result of human weakness rather than moral depravity. Even though the confessor may feel that the penitent will sin again, absolution should be given if there is a prudent probability of good dispositions. Gousset combines an understanding of human weakness with a great belief in the power of God's grace that allows him to act in favour of the present good conscience of the individual. Of course, Gousset acknowledges that prudence may at times dictate a deferral of absolution; but this is to be done rarely, and only in favour of the penitent's spiritual health. Interestingly, at this point Gousset refers to confession as *'la sacrement de la réconciliation'*, thus anticipating by over a century the currently preferred nomenclature.

With regard to recidivists, the same awareness of the sensitive application of basic principles is evident. Just one of the extraordinary signs suffices, each case is to be treated on its own merits, full reversal of a habit is not easily achieved. Though he does not use the precise term, what he is concerned with in the case of recidivists is the establishment of whether there is a basic option for sin. Otherwise, one can consider the possibility of absolution; for example, if there is a diminution in the number of sins. He repeatedly distances himself from the harsh views of the rigorists which he sees as not properly understanding the nature of human weakness or the strengthening power of God's grace. Rigidity is not necessarily a gospel virtue. Gousset is very understanding of the problems of young people and of the fact that conversion is often a gradual process. One must uphold moral principles, but equally one must avoid counsels of desperation: as far as is morally prudent and spiritually beneficial one must act in favour of the freedom of an individual's present good conscience.

The same Alphonsian spirit of prudent judgements comes through in his treatment of the occasions of sin. His analysis of the principles governing occasions of sin – proximate and remote, necessary and voluntary – is standard. What is noticeable in him is the way the principles are applied: distinctions are necessary; there are always exceptions to the rule; one must take local customs into account.[10] Gousset avoids the rigoristic restatement of principles by emphasising that judgements are relative to particular cases and must be in favour of the spiritual health of the individual.[11] Gousset is a classic exponent of the Alphonsian spirit: knowledge of the principles must be combined with a knowledge of the human heart and individual circumstances. Prudence is that virtue by which one combines and preserves both, in favour of the individual's good conscience empowered by God's grace in the sacrament.

The Fate of the Moral Manual since Saint Alphonsus

By the middle of the nineteenth century it can be said that the moral theology of Alphonsus was established as a solid pastoral guide for confessors. As yet, not much of Alphonsus' system was transformed, abandoned or rejected. The reason is that the arguments centred on the general acceptability of Alphonsus rather than on the particularised examination of his views. The theological disputes of the time were more limited (though not, for all that, less important) in their focus; was Alphonsus a solid guide for moral practice? At the beginning of the century the rigorist heirs of Arnauld, Pascal and the anti-Probabilists were in the ascendant, particularly so in France. The delay of absolution was the norm rather than the exception and this was justified on the basis of a rigid theory of the role of the confessor-as-judge. The undermining of the dominance of this view, which owed not a little to the Jansenistic theories of grace and predestination, came from the pastoral experience of those priests who saw that such a restrictive view of the sacrament led to despair, a decline in the practice of the faith and, ultimately, the decline of faith itself. Their arguments were, at first, more the reflective instinct of pastoral insight than the result of the sustained argument of scholarly theology. That is where the importance of the Alphonsian manual lies in the early nineteenth century. He was seen by people like Kenrick and Gousset as an authoritative expression of what their own pastoral instincts were telling them.

The acceptability of Alphonsus was, of course, helped by the interventions from Rome in 1803 and 1831.[12] These were seen as official approval of what was already beginning to happen pastorally and, later, theologically. But it is here, precisely, that the seeds of future problems were being sown. The focus of attention too easily shifted from the intrinsic merits of Alphonsus' theological method to the extrinsic acceptability of his position as an ecclesiastical authority. One can understand Kenrick and Gousset using Alphonsus in a somewhat extrinsic sense, though, as was shown, not even they took Alphonsus 'literally'. They were, after all, trying to refute the rigorists and they needed all the help they could get, even if it was based on authority. The difficulties will arise later when it is only the extrinsic authority of Alphonsus that seems to matter.

By 1850 there was a widespread acceptance of the moral manual of Alphonsus, at least in contrast to the position at the turn of the century.[13] That this later proved to be more the use of Alphonsus as an extrinsic authority than a promotion of the study of Alphonsus in the original text and spirit is not to be attributed directly to the pre-1850 moral theologians. They were trying to establish the acceptability of Alphonsus in opposition to the rigorists: the development of the manual in the early nineteenth century is the story of that gradual acceptability.[14]

TRANSFORMATION AND FOSSILISATION 1850–1900

To assess the influence of Alphonsus on the moral manuals in the second half of the nineteenth century the same, admittedly limited, method used for the first half of the century is followed here. Publications from each decade will be taken, again focusing on the question of the *habituati et recidivi*.

Peter Scavini (1791–1869) was professor of theology at the seminary of Novara, and he presents his moral theology as a faithful reproduction of Alphonsus.[15] This acknowledgement of Alphonsus, now becoming commonplace, is a reflection of the growing acceptability of Alphonsus, a position that was to be copperfastened with his being declared a Doctor of the Church in 1871.

The *consuetudinarius* is defined as 'the one who is in a proximate and intrinsic occasion of sin' and is, generally speaking, to be absolved: notable, however, is Scavini's belief that, with sexual sins, a harsher definition of what constitutes a habit is proposed. The recidivist is not to be absolved unless extraordinary signs of sorrow are shown. This rule is to be taken as generally true but there are exceptions in the line of the extraordinary signs of sorrow which he accepts when they are solid and well based. He acknowledges the power of God's grace conferred in the sacrament.

Scavini's moral theology is straightforward, even perfunctory. It is not original, and lacks personal insights. He repeats the traditional teaching of Alphonsus, but in a very cursory way that, perhaps, does damage to the spirit of Alphonsus. The theological content of Alphonsus is replaced by dry formulae; the nuances of Alphonsus' argument are lost, with the result that Scavini appears more rigid than the master he professes to follow. Those who would have known Alphonsus only through Scavini would have had a truncated vision of the saint's original insight.

John Peter Gury (1801–1866) taught moral theology at Vals in France from 1833 until his death, apart from a one-year professorship at the Collegio Romano which was abruptly terminated by the revolutionary disturbances of 1848. A follower of Busenbaum, Alphonsus and Gousset, he had, firstly, urged the Abbé Neyraguet to publish the Alphonsian *Compendium Theologiae Moralis*, before publishing his own in 1850. It was to be extraordinarily successful; on the basis of forty-three editions between 1850 and 1890, James Healy estimates that there were 200,000 copies printed in that time.[16] The success of the work is due to a combination of factors: the clear presentation, the evident scholarship and, not least, the fact that it was written by a theologian who was very active pastorally, evidenced by the fact that he died while conducting a parish mission.[17]

In explaining the differences between the *consuetudinarius* and the *recidivus* Gury, characteristically, gives an extended historical footnote to explain the possible different nuances. One with a habit of sin can be absolved even before improvement actually takes place: Gury rejects the rigorist view as unrealistic, on the basis that everyone is constantly affected by sin. The possibility of occasional refusal is granted. Extraordinary signs of sorrow may be grounds for the absolution of the recidivist, though not always. Even with the ordinary signs of sorrow absolution is possible if delay is dangerous and immediate absolution may be beneficial. He is at pains to show that his interpretation of Alphonsus is the correct one, thereby showing the beginning of future controversies on the exact meaning of Alphonsian texts. In doubt, one must defer absolution but there is always need for mercy and patience. Gury tries to establish a benign application of the accepted principles. The method of Gury's exposition – short enunciation of principles together with long historical footnotes – was to cause controversy later among those who questioned his historical interpretations. Overall, Gury is at pains to administer the sacrament in a benign way, showing God's mercy and proving that the good of the penitent is always greater than any particular rule. His common sense approach is transparent. Good examples are his treatment of those who refuse to go to frequent confession and his way of listing the extraordinary signs of sorrow.[18] The work of Gury represents a further stage in the evolutionary influence of Alphonsus on the moral manual. It is no longer a question of giving an apologia for the defence of Alphonsus; such is clearly no longer necessary. What is now in the forefront is the disputed interpretation of Alphonsian texts. Gury (and his adversaries, later) will claim that they have the correct interpretation of the matter. The hidden agenda of many of these controversies was the older question of the probabilist and equi-probabilist opinions. By raising these questions, however, indirectly, Gury and others were to take the focus away from the Alphonsian spirit to the more literal questions of correct interpretation.

The work of Ernest Müller,[19] though never as popular as Scavini or Gury, has its own merits. He treats, firstly, the occasions of sin according to three principles: those in remote occasions are not to be denied absolution; those in necessary proximate occasions are not to be denied absolution if they use the normal remedies; those in voluntary proximate occasions are to be denied absolution. Most of his examples are sexual ones, thus representing the growing identification of moral questions with one area of life. His language is more legal than theological, again indicative of the further identification of moral theology with canonical terminology.

His factual definitions of *haituati* and *recidivi* are the by now common ones. His basic principles are that those with a habit of sin are usually to be absolved though occasionally, if prudence demands, one may defer, and recidivists are not to be regularly absolved though occasionally, if prudence demands, one may absolve. Having enunciated the principles he counsels consideration of particular circumstances. In doubt, one may consider a conditional absolution, as the power of God's grace and mercy are never to be underestimated. He finishes with a *casus* on masturbation, which he solves in a sensitive way.

A casuist, Müller tries to apply the principles in favour of the individual. His method is: firstly give the factual definition of terms, secondly give the moral principles, and then deal with individual cases. It is a classic presentation of casuistry. Though he quotes Alphonsus, one can note in him a certain transformation and rejection of the Alphonsian method. Gone is the overall theological basis and the sense of Christian discernment. In their places are legal formulae and a deductive, though benign, application of the principles to the case. The question is not the acceptability of Alphonsus (which is presumed) nor the precise interpretation of disputed texts (in which Müller shows no apparent interest). The method of Alphonsus is here transformed into neat categories and definitions, denuded of a sense of theological depth and spiritual insight which one finds in the original Alphonsian texts. The transformation has occurred, largely, because the focus of the manual is now more clearly the didactic purpose of the moral classroom. This dictates a definite approach and many of the nuances of the original Alphonsian synthesis are lost.

The Dutch Redemptorist, Anthony Konings (1821–84), had a varied career as teacher, prefect of students and Provincial in Holland before his transfer to America in 1870 to teach in the Redemptorist seminary at Illchester, Maryland. It is interesting that, like Alphonsus, he was in his fifties when he wrote his moral theology[20] which he intended to be a less bulky work than the older manuals, and more adapted to the particular problems of North America. A didactic work intended for the ordinary student, his moral theology does, however, show the experience of one familiar with practical pastoral problems.

A factual and commonplace definition of the *consuetudinarius* and *recidivus* is followed by an elaboration of four principles governing confessional practice. Because a habit is not per se a sign of bad disposition, such people are to be absolved on a regular basis, though the possibility of deferral can at times be considered. A recidivist who is only materially such is to be granted absolution; but the disposition of the recidivist who is formally such is questionable, and absolution is to be usually refused, unless some extraordinary sign of sorrow is given. The fourth principle is concerned with the deferral of absolution which the confessor uses in his role as physician of the soul if such is the prudent judgement on the penitent's spiritual health. He finishes with some practical examples (people who are of a frivolous disposition or who are weak-hearted); kindness is to be shown to all.

In Konings a transformation of the Alphonsian manual can be noted similar to that already seen in Scavini. Technically, Konings follows Alphonsus but, somehow, it is more a material repetition than otherwise. Lacking is the Alphonsian feel for the prudential moral judgement and the emphasis on the power of grace. It is as if discipline is brought to Alphonsus' thought in order to make moral theology more easily memorised by the student. All is neatly worked into principles, explanations and examples. Though Konings is clearly reliant on Alphonsus, he lacks the flexibility of the Alphonsian position. He seems more anxious about the duties of the confessor (who should, of course, be prudent and kind) than about explaining the forgiving power of God's grace. The transformation that is occurring in a manual like Konings' is one dictated by the didactic focus of the manual as an accessible textbook. It is not that Konings is, as such, unfaithful to Alphonsus; indeed, he did much to explain the Alphonsian theory of equi-probabilism. In reducing Alphonsus to a compendium-style presentation however, the theological perspective and spiritual discernment of Alphonsus are lost in the principles and examples which, however neat, miss the inner spirit of Alphonsus' broader vision. The external forms of some of Alphonsus' teachings are still there, but the inner vitality is missing.

The final author chosen to represent the second half of the nineteenth century is the little-known Anthony Haine.[21] Precise definitions of the *consuetudinarius* and *recidivus* are given; the definitions are more legal than strictly theological. In treating the *consuetudinarius*, he, again, uses legal terminology full of intricate distinctions. His practical conclusions are benign, but his arguments are extrinsic, authority-based and legal. He is concerned with what is legally possible and though he may come to some of the same conclusions as Alphonsus, his way of reaching them is very different. The same general remarks are true of his treatment of the *recidivus* who is, again, defined in a legalistic way, though, in practice, Haine wishes to be benign.

We are at a further stage of the transformation of the Alphonsian manual here. Legal precisions have replaced nuanced theological arguments; extrinsic authority has taken the place of the intrinsic merits of an argument; the nominal duties of confessors take precedence over other considerations. Haine, no doubt, reflects the mood of the times. Neo-scholastic formulae are now commonplace in the theological textbooks and fear of the anti-modernist watchdogs had driven most theologians to the calm, but stagnant, waters of authoritarian harbours. There is not a conscious transformation of Alphonsus evident in an author like Haine. But, in fact, the tenor of Haine is so different from Alphonsus that one is hard put to see a continuity of spirit between the manuals both of them wrote.

Why did this transformation of the Alphonsian manual take place? To try to answer this question one must, firstly, be aware of the nature of the change and the general historical influences that were at work throughout the nineteenth century. The nature of the transformation is more easily stated. Looking at the later nineteenth century manuals, the outward presentation of an issue like the *habituati et recidivi* has not changed substantially. What has happened is that, materially, the presentation becomes more ordered (in terms of 'definitions', 'laws', 'principles' and 'cases') and the primary emphasis of Alphonsus on the prudent application of principles within the primacy of grace becomes less pronounced, with the result that the later manuals appear more rigid. Historical reasons contributed to this. At the turn of the century, the struggle was for the acceptance of Alphonsus as a legitimate moral theologian, as shown in Gousset and Kenrick. With the growing ecclesiastical approval of Alphonsus within a church that was becoming more centralised, an ironic change takes place in that Alphonsus, once under suspicion for over-liberal views, is an establishment theologian by the latter part of the century, as noted in people like Konings. The

An Irish Reader in Moral Theology

focus now becomes: what is the proper interpretation of Alphonsus, and in what sense is he to be seen as probabilist or equi-probabilist? That becomes clear in a manual like Gury's. The more distant they are from Aphonsus, the less theologians seem to rely on his primary text. The debates that dominate are what particular schools believe that Alponsus said. It is in this limited sense that the prudential moral spirit and dominance of God's grace and mercy, so evident in Alphonsus, becomes less pronounced, even though, in a material sense, the manuals increasingly seem to be 'Alphonsian'.

Three areas of misunderstanding, unrelated in themselves but interconnected in their cumulative influence, contributed to the process by which Alphonsus' teaching was, in part, transformed, abandoned or rejected: 1. misunderstandings, on the part of Catholic theologians, as to the precise authority of Alphonsus in moral theology; 2. misunderstandings, on the part of Protestant theologians, as to the theological method of Alphonsus; and 3. misunderstandings, between moral theologians, as to the sense of Alphonsus' equi-probabilism. I will comment briefly on each of these in turn.

The three major Roman statements on the authority of Alphonsus already referred to (those of the Sacred Congregation of Rites 1803, the Sacred Penitentiary 1831 and the official declaration as *Doctor Ecclesiae* in 1870) need to be carefully parsed. Positively, these statements show that Alphonsus' moral theology is in accordance with Catholic teaching, can be safely followed and is a practical guide for Christian living. Given the opposition to Alphonsus on the part of many rigorists and the lingering suspicion that, being tainted with probabilism, Aphonsus was a laxist, these statements, undoubtedly, represent official approval of Alphonsus. That said, one needs to be careful in analysing this approval. Alphonsus is free from error, that is, at the time he wrote and according to knowledge then available about matters of faith and morals in Church teaching; he can be safely followed, but he is not the only moral theologian who merits respect; he is a sure guide for pastoral practice, but that does not mean he has a pre-eminence in all areas of theology. It is my impression that not all Catholic theologians of the nineteenth century subscribed to these caveats in the interpretation of Alphonsus. On the one hand, the defenders of Alphonsus took an ahistorical view of his growing Church approval that led, in time, to the fossilisation of Alphonsian thought. On the other hand, the opponents of Alphonsus too easily dismissed his importance simply because he had not the speculative genius of an Aquinas or was not in tune with the new insights of the positive and psychological advances of the late nineteenth century. The approval of Alphonsus is a nuanced one, relating to the practical genius of his moral theology in the context of the eighteenth century confusion in that science, and it is limited in the scope of its intentions. To approve of Alphonsus is not to disapprove of Aquinas. To value the insights of the patristic era is not to undervalue Alphonsus who was writing at a different time and for a different purpose.[22] The passions aroused by the theological debates of the nineteenth century did not, unfortunately, allow for such eirenic assessments.

Accustomed, as we now are, to an ecumenical tone in our theological discussion we can forget the debates of a former age when Catholic and Protestant theologians attacked each other with a virulence akin to the tribalism of a 'holy war'. Alphonsus was a major victim of Protestant misunderstanding in mainland Europe, Britain and America during the nineteenth century.

The pamphlets of Grassman, Hermann, Harneck, Von Hoensbroech and the German Evangelical Alliance may now cause more amusement than annoyance, but their influence was substantial in the nineteenth century popular Protestant press. Alphonsus was, in particular, seen as dangerous: 'Whatever remained of St Augustine's thinking in the nineteenth century had been thrown aside by Ligouri. Casuistic morals, together with the doctrine of attrition, have forced all dogmatic teaching into the background. It has been torn to shreds by probabilism and papalism. It is at the present time a legal system either rigid or elastic as circumstances demand.'[23] This is one of the milder quotations that I could use, but one can infer from its tone that Alphonsus was, in Protestant eyes, a symbol of the unbiblical and deceptive morality of Rome. Alphonsus' cause was not, admittedly, helped by some of his defenders who were as vehemently anti-Protestant as the attackers were anti-Catholic. Not all Catholics defended Alphonsus in a literalist sense,[24] but for many Protestants on mainland Europe Alphonsus was seen as an exponent of all that was evil in the modern Roman Church.

An extraordinary book by R.P. Blakeney[25] is typical of a certain type of fundamentalist Protestant reaction to Alphonsus in Britain. Some quotations give the flavour of the book: 'No attempt has been made to rebut the charges of immorality which are brought against the saint's moral theology. The conclusion may fairly be drawn that the attempt is regarded as hopeless'; 'We the undersigned beg to state that the Latin not translated in this volume, especially that on the Confessional, is unfit for Protestant eyes or ears and must therefore be left in the original'; 'Thus the moral theology of Liguori has received in the most marked manner the imprimatur of Rome. That Church, by her authority, has proclaimed with one consent that his works are worthy of the highest praise and that they contain not one word worthy of censure ... the principles of Liguori are the principles of Rome'; 'Oh, how different is the morality of the Bible! The religion of Jesus will make no compromise with sin, nor will it, under any circumstances, or for the accomplishment of any good, recognise and adopt the principle of doing evil that good may come.'[26] Blakeney's work has the appearances of scholarship, comprising eighteen chapters that purport to analyse the text of Alphonsus. In fact, the point of Alphonsus' method is altogether missed: that is, the enunciation of principles and their application to particular circumstances with a view to the good pastoral administration of the sacrament of confession. What, for a standard Catholic moralist, is the interpretation and application of principles taking the human situation into account, appears to the fundamentalist Protestant, like Blakeney, as anti-gospel equivocation.

In America it was possible, in the nineteenth century, for Protestants and Catholics to live and die without ever meeting each other. In that atmosphere total misunderstanding was possible, and for the poorly educated Protestant Alphonsus represented the worst of the 'harlot Rome': 'To American Protestants, Liguori stood for the threat that Catholic immorality could overwhelm American virtue.'[27]

Distant from the theological perspective of today, also, are the quarrels over the interpretation of probabilism and equi-probabilism and the precise role of Aphonsus in these debates. But in the late nineteenth century this was still a very live issue, as is instanced by the publication of *Vindiciae Ballerinianae* and the *Vindiciae Alphonsianae* in 1873. These works generated immediate and widespread controversy.[28]

This is not the place to argue the merits of either of these voluminous tomes, as I only wish to comment on them in the context of the development of the manual. It is clear, from the *Vindiciae Alphonsianae*, that the status of Alphonsus was a very sensitive issue for the Redemptorists of the time and there is a hint of wounded pride that the founder of their congregation could be in any way maligned. Much of both *Vindiciae* now seems like an arid debate, far removed from the realities of the time. It seems strange to have leading moral theologians quibbling over the niceties of probabilism when the major issues of the day were political upheaval, the industrial revolution and growing religious indifference. The *Vindiciae* debate cemented the tendency towards the use of Alphonsus as an external authority in moral matters: what was at stake, particularly in the *Vindiciae Alphonsianae*, was the need to uphold the authority of Alphonsus against any other authority that did not have Alphonsus' ecclesiastical standing. The Redemptorist authors of the *Vindiciae Alphonsianae*, aware that probabilism was equated with laxism in many minds, wanted to preserve the authority of Alphonsus from being tainted with a laxist brush. This positive aim was, however, advanced more by arguments of extrinsic authority than intrinsic merit.

Some conclusions, based on the manual analysed, can now be made as to how the Alphosian moral system was transformed, rejected or abandoned by the end of the nineteenth century. Alphonsus was open-minded in the terms of his own day and his moral theology was part of a wider theological and spiritual vision. Because of the misunderstandings just mentioned, the text of Alphonsus was, increasingly, used in a defensive way as the century progressed. Anxious to prove Alphonsus' orthodoxy, his defenders used extrinsic arguments to avoid any expression of ambiguity in the Alphonsian interpretations. Conscious of Protestant objections, Alphonsus' defenders were all the more anxious to protect his position as a Roman Catholic theologian: and within the narrow confines of the moral schools, the defenders of Alphonsus tried to protect their master from the contamination of dubious, especially probabilist, authors. Taken together, these meant that, by the end of the nineteenth century, Alphonsus was interpreted in a more rigid sense than his own text implies. The theological context and inner spirit of Alphonsus' own moral theology were obscured, at least, by the effort to condense his thought into compendia of statements, laws and principles.

What were the concerns of these late nineteenth century manualists? They wished to be seen as supporting Alphonsus' views; they were anxious to incorporate relevant Roman legislation and citations of approval in Alphonsus' favour and they wished to provide textbooks that were concise and easily studied with a view to the sacramental administration of confession. In themselves, all these are obviously laudable concerns. In practice, however, they obscured the purpose of the Alphonsian manual. Support for the Alphonsian view is not as easy as stating that one writes '*secundum doctrinam S Alphonsi*' or even as easy as quoting him: interpretation of Alphonsus demands a knowledge of the original texts and an evaluation of their historical setting, qualities not immediately obvious in the later manuals. Incorporating new Roman decrees can, too easily, become a litany of references grafted on to a basic text in a way that the focus of the original text is obscured by the addition of many details. A compendium is attractive in that its brief formulae are easily learned. The summary of a complex theological problem (like the *habituati et recidivi),* without reference to the underlying psychological and theological problems, can, over time, become quite ambiguous.

By the late nineteenth century the moral manuals had become introverted. Their agenda was set *a priori* and they were little interested in the new scientific knowledge or the new social and economic problems. It is not that they are unaware of these, but the presumption is that, within themselves, they have the principles to solve any new problems. A further stage of isolation occurs with the tightening control of the moral schools by the respective religious orders; many opinions appear to be 'commonly accepted', possibly because only authors of a certain view were studied.

It is a major irony of the nineteenth-century development of the moral manual that Alphonsus, in his own time the seeker of the pastorally viable middle way according to intrinsically meritorious arguments, became, after his own time, an establishment theologian quoted as an extrinsic authority to head off any further arguments. The problem, looked at from this safe distance, was that there was little knowledge of the primary Alphonsian texts and little appreciation of their historical context.

DECLINE OF THE MANUAL TRADITION 1900–1960

As in the previous sections, editions of manuals for each decade of this period were taken to chart the systematisation of the Alphonsian manual. My comments will be brief, as there is little of note in these manuals in that they represent, for the greater part, a consolidation of the changes that have already taken place in the late nineteenth century, rather than any notable evolution in their own right.

Thomas Slater's manual[29] is broadly within the then accepted interpretation of Alphonsus: he seeks the middle view and tries to uphold the good faith of the penitent's conscience. By placing the question of the habitual and recidivist sinner within the discussion of the roles of the priest as physician and counsellor he is able to take a more realistically pastoral view than some of the more rigid manuals. The manual of Jerome Noldin[30] is representative of the probabilist tradition. The particular emphasis is on the obligation of the confessor more than the power of grace operative in the penitent.[31] His method is careful and legalistic though, within the tight formulation of principles, he tries to apply them in a benign way. Overall, the impression is of a manualist more concerned with exactitude of legal formulation than with the liberating power of God's grace. Reading Joseph Aertnys and Cornelius Damen[32] one is aware of their Redemptorist loyalty to Alphonsus: a learned work and up-to-date with Roman legislation, it is more in conformity with the material words of Alphonsus than with the inner spirit. The emphasis is, too often, on negative fear rather than on the positive power of love. Louis Wouters,[33] also a Redemptorist, is more of a casuist than Aertnys-Damen; the emphasis is on extrinsic authority and upholding the views of one particular school of moral theology.[34]

Representative of the main alternate moral school, the Jesuit Edward Genicot and his nephew Joseph Salsmans produced a manual still being published in the 1940s.[35] It is in the tradition of Gury and Ballerini, though written in a more popular vein. There is not much difference in the practical conclusions that Aertnys-Damen or Genicot-Salsmans come to, but their way of argument represents two differing strands in the tradition, an indication that the internal tensions of the nineteenth century moral debates still lingered on. Our final manual by Herbert Jone and Urban Adelman[36] shows the poverty of theological vision and moral prudence to which the manual had descended by the middle of the twentieth century. Questions are seen from the narrow perspective of the confessor's legal duties rather than from that of the conscience of the penitent.[37] The possibility of sin is everywhere seen, rather than the opportunities for love.[38] Good works seem more important than the power of grace. A cryptic legal tone takes the place of the theological and moral categories evident in Alphonsus. The transformation of Alphonsus is now so marked that, even if one cannot say that Jone-Adelman reject Alphonsus' views explicitly, in practice these views are abandoned.

The transformation of the Alphonsian manual to the point where Alphonsus' views were neglected, as in the question of the *habituati et recidivi*, left the manuals incapable of incorporating the new psychological and theological insights that were being articulated in the 1940s and 1950s: for instance, the psychological factors involved in defining sin; the distinctions between venial, grave and mortal sin; the degree of freedom and knowledge necessary for sin in the moral sense; and the replacing of a juridical model of confession by one that sees it as a sacrament of joyful reconciliation.[39] All of these insights could have helped the manuals in their treatment of the *habituati et recidivi*. Because of the transformation of the manual in the late nineteenth century, a transformation that became fossilised in the twentieth century, such new insights were seen as incompatible with the manual system, as it had become. Had the manuals remained more in the spirit of Alphonsus, these would have been seen as organic developments, and some of the practical advantages of the manuals could have been saved. Instead, they wrote their own death sentence by, in practice, abandoning some of the Alphonsian views.

NOTES

1   A list of the editions is found in M. De Meulemeester, *Bibliographie générale des écrivains Rédemptoristes,* première partie, Louvain, 1933, pp. 62–8.

2   Alphonsus de Liguori, *Theologia Moralis,* ed. L. Gaudé, Rome, 1905. Referred to henceforth as Gaudé.

3   P. Antoine, *Theologia Moralis Universa,* revised edition, 1818; the references here are to tom. 5, pp. 28–301.

4   P. Dens, *Theologia Moralis et Dogmatica,* Dublin, ex. typ. Richardi Coyne, 1829, pp. 150–213.

5   Brief notes on Dens are to be found in *New Catholic Encyclopedia,* Vol. 4, London, 1908, and *Dictionnaire de Théologie Catholique,* tom. 4, Paris, 1911.

6   A notable difference would be the emphasis of Alphonsus on grace and the sovereign goodness of God throughout the whole treatment of the question. It is not that Dens would deny these, but the categories of thought with which he works, being legally casuistic, do not easily highlight them.

7   C. Roncaglia, *Universa Moralis Theologia,* editio absolutissima a P. Optato Bellotti, Luca, 1834. There is a short note on Roncaglia's life in *Dictionnaire de Théologie Catholique,* tom. 13, Paris, 1937.

8   F.P. Kendrick, *Theologia Moralis,* Vol. 3, Philadelphia, 1843, pp. 208–21. Short biographical material in *Catholic Encyclopedia,* Vol. 8, and in J. Healy, *The Just Wage, 1750–1890,* The Hague, 1966.

9   T.M. Gousset, *Théologie morale à l'usage des cures et des confesseurs,* tom. 2, Brussels, 1849, pp. 251–68. Also, his earlier work, *Justification de la théologie maorale du Bienheureux Alphonse Marie de Ligorio,* 1832. Biographical details in J. Healy, op. cit., and in *Dictionnaire de Théologie Catholique,* tom. 6, Paris, 1920.

10   He distances himself, somewhat, from Alphonsus' views on the sexual conduct of fiancés: if young people are to prepare for marriage how are they to avoid seeing each other?

11   Ibid., p. 267.

12   These dates refer to (a) the Decree of the Sacred Congregation of Rites of 18 May 1803, 'super revisione et approbatione operum Ven Alphonsi in ordine ad eius beatificationem' and (b) Responsum S. Poenitentiariae super Doctrina Morali B. Alphonsi, 5 July 1831. These statements (particularly the much quoted 'nihil in his censura dignum repertum fuerit') were, in time, used in a fairly literalist way, ignoring the theological subtleties needed in the interpretation of such Roman documents.

13   The standard account is J. Guerber, *Le ralliment du clergé à la morale francaise Liguorienne,* Analecta Gregoriana 193, Rome, Gregorian University, 1973.

14   Besides the theological arguments of Lanteri, Gousset and Pallavincini, all mentioned by Guerber and which were most definitely crucial in this regard, one should not underestimate the impact of the popular missions preached by congregations like the Redemptorists at this time. The great appeal of these missions was, in part, due to the sensible pastoral practice of confession which they incorporated.

15   P. Scavini, *Theologia Moralis Universa,* Vol. 4, Paris, 1859, pp. 118–125.

16   Healy, op. cit., p. 313.

17   Further biographical details can be found in *Dictionnaire de Théologie Catholique,* Vol. 6, Paris, 1920.

18   In his list of the extraordinary signs he does not start, as most others did, with the sign of weeping/sighs. In fact, he places this sign last, as if to suggest slight French distrust of the exuberance of the Italian moralists.

19   E. Muller, *Theologia Moralis,* Vol. 3, Vienna, 1879, pp. 355–65.

20   A. Konings, *Theologia Moralis,* Vol. 2, London, 1880, pp. 179–84.

21   A.J. Haine, *Theologia Moralis Universa,* Vol. 3, Rome: Louvain, 1899, pp. 363–73.

22   Balanced assessments of Alphonsus' status can be found in 'Theologie Morale', *Dictionnaire de Théologie Catholique,* tom. 10, Paris, 1928, and in T. Bouquillon, *Theologia Moralis Fundamentalis,* Vol. 1, New York, 1890, p. 43–128.

23   A. Harnack, *Dogmengeschichte,* 4th ed., 3, p. 755; quoted in J. Mausbach, Catholic moral teaching and its antagonists, New York, 1914, pp. 57–8.

24   One can note J.H. Newman's opposition to Alphonsus' views on reservation (*Apologia,* 1902 ed., 279) and the careful assessment of Alphonsus in Mausbach, op. cit., pp. 57–65.

25   R.P. Blakeney, *St Alphonsus Liguori,* London: Reformation Society Office, 1852.

26   Blakeney, op. cit., iii, xiii, 31, 89.

27   P. Gardella, *Innocent Ecstasy,* Oxford University Press, 1985, p. 102.

28   A list of articles in the Vindicia Alphonsiana, xii–xiv and lxi–lxvii, is an indication of this.

29   T. Slater, *A Manual of Moral Theology,* Vol. 2, New York: Benziger Brothers, 1908, pp. 216–25.

30   H. Noldin, *Summa Theologiae Moralis,* Vol. 3, Rome, 1912, pp. 469–90.

31   Art. 5 (*De absolvendis consuetudinariis,* pp. 476–7) and Art. 6 (*De absolvendis recidivis,* pp. 477–81) follow as applications of Art. 4 (*De obligatione absolvendi poenitentes in genere,* pp. 468–76).

32   J. Aertnys and C. Damen, *Theologia Moralis secundum doctrinam S Alfonsi de Ligorio,* tom. 2, Turin, 1920, pp. 346–90.

33   L. Wouters, *Manuale Theologia Moralis,* Bruges, 1933.

34   Roman documents are often quoted, without their theological weight being assessed. His theological sources are, in the main, Redemptorist ones, especially Ter Haar on the question of the *recidivi et habituati.*

35   E. Genicot, *Institutiones Theologiae Moralis,* Vol. 2, quam recognovit I Salsmans, Brussels, 1940, pp. 321–35.

36   H. Jone and U. Adelman, *Moral Theology,* Cork: Mercier Press, 1955, pp. 422–33.

37   'Thus, if the invalidity of a marriage is commonly known the penitent must be told even though he has been till now in good faith, and even if it is foreseen that he will not pay any attention to the information.' Jone-Adelman, p. 424.

38   'One necessary proximate occasion of sin is company-keeping with the prospect of an early marriage', ibid., p. 428.

39   Bernard Häring, *The Law of Christ,* Vol. 1, Cork: Mercier Press, 1961. Chapters 8–12 discuss many of these questions. While he does not deal with the *habituati et recidivi* in the limited sense that the manuals of the time dealt with them, it is the same human and theological problems that he grapples with. His language of dealing with the problem is so new that many manualists simply did not understand what Häring was trying to say.

5   Moral Theology:
The Need for Renewal

Enda McDonagh

(Enda McDonagh (ed.), *Moral Theology Renewed: Papers of the Maynooth Union Summer School 1964*, Dublin: Gill and Son, 1965, pp. 13–30.)

Today we readily admit that the Church, and theology as the servant of the Church, are in constant need of renewal. In its role of faith in search of understanding, theology tries to interpret and present God's revelation of himself in Christ in a way that is intelligible and relevant to the contemporary world. The renewal issues from the tension generated between two forces in the mind of the Church or the theologian, the never-ending quest for a fuller understanding of the Christian message and the need to expound that message in the light of the prevailing ideas, needs and problems of the men of a particular time and place. The task of theology then is to provide the intellectual and scientific basis for a fruitful dialogue between the Word of God and his world.

This task has become more urgent in recent times because of the remarkable progress at the tension points, the Word and the world. The increasing understanding of God's Word which modern biblical scholarship provides, and the radical developments in politics, philosophy, psychology and the physical sciences which this century has witnessed, have placed a great responsibility on the Church and its theologians to keep these two points in fruitful contact. Otherwise the Church will be isolated with a theology that, however rich it is in the biblical scholarship of today or yesterday or the speculative thought of another time and place, will be irrelevant and unintelligible to the man to whom God wishes to speak through the Church today, that is, modern man with his own mental and emotional make-up, his own interests and needs. It will have a non-theology in fact.

Attempts to meet the more urgent demands of renewal in theology have been in existence at least since the beginning of the century, although they suffered a serious set-back at an early stage owing to the excesses of Modernism. Today Vatican II has given a new status and impetus to such attempts, and adopted as its own many of the theological developments which preceded it.

Some of these developments affect moral theology in an intimate way. The purpose of this paper is to outline the reasons why any such renewal should be necessary in moral theology, which seemed to be so clearly and completely presented in the various manuals or *Institutiones Theologiae Moralis*. Apart from particular new problems such as the atomic bomb and the contraceptive pill or some changes in the law about the eucharistic fast and the like, there might not seem to be any room for more radical rethinking and presentation. Yet it is in moral theology that some of the most far-reaching attempts at renewal have been made and some of the most intense controversies have arisen.[1]

THE NEGATIVE APPROACH

The case for renewal in moral theology might be presented in a completely negative way. This would consist in a direct criticism of the *Institutiones* or manuals as determining the approach and character of most writing and thinking in moral theology as well as the form and content of the seminary courses in recent centuries. And it would be possible to list in a damaging way the more obvious defects of the manuals. They have been criticised for their failure to emphasise the supernatural, Christian character of moral theology, for a tendency to reduce it to a combination of natural ethics and canon law, for their heavily legal (if not legalist) framework, and for their preoccupation with sin and their emphasis on casuistry.[2] And these criticisms have considerable justification, even if they are sometimes presented in an exaggerated way without sufficient understanding of the historical purpose and development of the manuals. Allowing for all this, the criticisms still add up to a convincing case for some renewal in moral theology.

THE UNITY-OF-THEOLOGY APPROACH

A different approach could start from the developments in other areas of theology, which because of the unity of theology must also affect moral theology. This would be a more positive and perhaps more profitable approach than the previous one.

There are many obvious connections between these other theological developments and moral theology. The biblical movement has given all theologians a new awareness of their obligation to base their thinking on the fullest understanding of the Bible available through modern scholarship. Such an increased understanding must also throw fresh light on the foundation and practice of Christian morals. The liturgical movement and the new insights in sacramental theology highlight the community worship of the Father through Christ as central to Christian living and morality. All other human acts acquire their basic Christian significance from this worshipping unity with the son. The related theology of the laity makes clear the vocation and responsibility of the individual Christian to live his life in the Church and in the world as a member and witness of Christ. The implications of the ecumenical movement for Catholic theology will only gradually be realised. But already, and even in moral theology, the efforts to explain oneself to Christians who are without any strong legal or Aristotelian tradition in morals and the meeting with a morality couched in more personal terms, have had enriching results. In general the renewed theology of the Church and of the Christian in the world has considerable importance for the behaviour of Christians and for the theology that deals with it, namely, Christian moral theology.

Moral Theology: The Need for Renewal

A more profound and satisfying method of approach would be to examine the nature and structure of Christian moral theology and see what properties should characterise it. In this way it will be possible to judge how far the conventional presentation of the manuals is in need of renewal. The criticisms of the first approach will appear in their true context without the same danger of exaggeration, while the influences of other theological developments will be given cohesion and unity.

Morality concerns men's behaviour. Christian morality concerns how men called to be Christians should behave and live. The theology of Christian morality then is a theology of Christian life. It investigates and presents in scientific, organised fashion, the way of life revealed by God in Christ. It studies Christ and the Christian revelation as a way of life.[3] From the basic structure of this way of life made known in Christ it is possible to derive the characteristic properties of Christian moral theology.

The distinction between dogmatic and moral theology is a relatively late development, which, for all its usefulness for study purposes, has tended to obscure the unity of theology as the one scientific study of God's revelation of himself to man. It is tempting to describe dogmatic theology as the study of this revelation as a system of truth, and moral theology as the study of it as a way of life.[4] But the truth is the life. And the distinction is artificial, whereby dogmatic theology stops short of presenting the truth as life, allowing moral theology to deal with the immediate life-giving consequences of this truth, how it affects man's life and behaviour. It is therefore sometimes difficult to decide whether to treat a particular section of theology (for example, grace) in dogma or moral. Where one actually draws the line of division is of less importance than the insistence on the unity of theology and on the fact that the truths of the Christian faith form the springs of Christian life. So the truths elaborated in dogmatic theology must be examined as sources of life in moral theology.

This can be expressed in a slightly different manner. Theology by definition is basically about God, for us the God of Revelation, God as he has revealed or communicated himself to man. This communication took the form of a series of interventions in human history. All earlier interventions were preparatory to and derive their meaning from God's supreme communication of himself to man, in the incarnation, death and resurrection of his Son. Christian theology studies Christ as the primary manifestation of the divine to man and all other manifestations in the light of Christ. But this communication or manifestation of himself to man by God was at the same time an invitation to man to respond by giving himself to God and so sharing divine life. Man's self-giving and sharing like God's self-manifesting and inviting are achieved in Christ. And this whole complex reality forms the subject-matter of Christian theology. Moral theology concentrates on man's response to God in Christ through his life and behaviour, but it must study it in terms of invitation-response because it is a response to a definite invitation.[5]

The life of the Christian is organised or structured in this way about these focal points – God communicating himself to man as an invitation in Christ and man responding in Christ to God. And moral theology, if it is to be true to the lines of the reality which it studies, must allow this inner structure to stand out clearly in its scientific presentation of the life and behaviour demanded of man in the Christian revelation. This will not be achieved by a brief introductory paragraph, or even chapter, on this structure in outlining the general principles of moral theology. The general principles must be seen as built into this structure and each special section of moral theology should be discussed in terms of God's invitation through Christ to man in this particular area and man's response again through Christ. And it is from this invitation-response relationship between God and man founded in Christ that the properties of a scientific presentation of Christian moral theology may be derived.

1. God-centred

God, not man, and certainly not any impersonal institution like the law, should be at the centre of moral theology. It is through his giving himself to God that man attains perfection. But the perfection of man should not appear as the primary and guiding principle in presenting moral theology. This perfection is important and a necessary consequence of the Christian life but it is not of first importance. It can be maintained that ontologically man's perfection implies the love and service of God and his glory. But it is the way of implication that is objectionable – with its appearance of a subordination of God to man's satisfaction. It is to those who first of all seek the kingship of God, who give themselves unconditionally to him in response to the invitation he issues in Christ, that all other things (man's complete perfection) will be added.[6] And the most enlightened self-seeking is no substitute for God-seeking.

The search for self-perfection as the principle of morality easily issues in exaggerated emphasis on the law and the works of the law as a tangible assurance of perfection – the very attitude Christ came to condemn.[7] The true meaning of the divine (and human) law is obscured. It tends to be regarded as self-explanatory instead of being understood as a necessary guide in reading the divine invitation in any given situation. It is only within the limits of divine law that man can truly respond to God. But the observance of particular laws is no substitute for and no guarantee of this loving response. Unless a man responds to God out of love, the fulfilment of law will profit him nothing.[8]

2. Based on Christ

The mediating link in the structure of Christian living and so of Christian moral theology is Christ. It is in and through Christ that God has issued his invitation to man, and it is only in and through Christ that man can accept and respond to this invitation.[9] A proper appreciation of God whom man seeks, in his unity and trinity, in his activity in the world, in his invitation to man to share his life, and his gift to man of the power to understand and accept the invitation, depends on an ever-deepening understanding of the divine self-disclosure in Christ. The role of the person Christ, God become man, God communicating himself to man at the supreme level and man in utter response to God, should dominate any scientific account of moral theology, any account that organises moral theology about its central truths. And it must shape the general outline as well as each individual section of moral theology.

Recent attempts at renewal in moral theology have illustrated the need and effectiveness of this approach. The pioneer work of exegete and moral theologian Fritz Tillmann[10] was centred on the evangelical idea of the imitation and following of Christ (*die Nachfolge Christi*) as the determining principle of moral theology. Emile Mersch SJ had a similar inspiration for his *Morale et Corps Mystique*.[11] And the most influential single work in the whole task of renewing moral theology, that of Bernard Häring CSsR was simply called *The Law of Christ*[12] (*das Gesetz Christi*) and placed great emphasis on the invitation-response structure in Christ as its cardinal idea.

The position of Christ as the corner-stone on which the Christian life and moral theology must be erected will be expounded more fully.[13] Here it is sufficient to derive from it two subsidiary properties which should characterise the moral theologian's thinking and writing. Christ as the basis of Christian life is present to man today in the Church. And here he is encountered in two primary and divinely given forms, word and sacrament. In the word of God as recorded under divine inspiration in the Bible and in the sacraments instituted by him as effective signs of grace in the Church, the Christian and the theologian find their most immediate contact with Christ and Christian life. To be true to its Christian character, moral theology must be biblical and sacramental.

(a) *Biblical*

All Christian theology must be biblical, based on the divine account of Christ, of the preparation for his coming and of his life and teaching. No other source of theology can compare with the Bible. It must of course be studied in the Church of Christ, faithful to his guidance of the Church, but it must be studied, constantly invoked and referred to in all attempts to develop theology. The Bible is obviously not a theology textbook. And reading the Bible is not a substitute for theology. What is called biblical theology, the systematic study of the truths of the Bible in the context and terms of the Bible, is not what we understand by a developed Christian theology. A developed theology takes account of all the available sources of knowledge about God and man, and of the world and the civilization in which Christ's message must be preached and lived. But the Bible as the word of God is necessary reading for all literate Christians. For the professional teachers of the Christian message a scientific understanding of the Bible is indispensable. Today, understanding of the Bible has increased considerably. In its growth and composition, in its gradual manifestation of God to man, in the dominant ideas which that manifestation reveals and the immediate contact with the person of Christ which it gives, the Bible must dominate the moral theologian's thinking, if he is to present Christ and his message as a way of life.

Referring the reader to a dogmatic tract for anything more than can be derived from natural ethics or expressed in a legal framework, invocation of isolated texts on a particular virtue or sin, do not suffice to make a moral theology textbook biblical. And it seems hardly unfair to criticise the manuals of recent vintage as lacking in this biblical character.

(b) *Sacramental*

As a theology of the Christian's living and behaviour, moral theology must be sacramental. The sacraments are at once signs and sources of man's sharing the life of Christ himself. Performed in the church, they are events of real significance in which the Christian encounters Christ. In their different ways they form the high points of God's communicating himself to the man responsive in Christ. By this sacramental communication man is assimilated to Christ and united with him in all his activity.

This activity becomes Christian activity, Christ-activity, expressing the Christ-life which man now enjoys and which demands expression in his every act.

The sacramental source of Christian life and activity emphasises its character as a divine gift.[14] We have nothing that we have not received.[15] Of ourselves we can do nothing. It is only as branches of the true vine that we can bear fruit.[16] The true, Christian and gratuitous character of every one of our good actions, thus revealed, will not tolerate any impression of self-justification through the observance of laws. Such moralism is not Christian morality.

As man's union with the Son in the worship of the Father is the apex of his vocation, so the Eucharistic liturgy, as the fullest realisation of that in the pilgrim days of the Church,[17] assumes its rightful place at the centre of Christian living, in which every human act is an act of worship, giving glory to the Father through the Son. The liturgical renewal will remain the preserve of the esthete or *élite* unless consciousness of the worshipping character of his every act is awakened in the Christian.

This human act of his has a further sacramental value. It bears witness before the whole world to the life that is in him. It is the sign of Christ's grace at work in the world, especially for those for whom the Church's sacramental rites are not yet signs of faith. Elaboration of this witness or sign-value of the Christian's human act gives a new dimension to life and morality. And it provides a remarkable antidote to the legalism and minimalism sometimes found in Catholic presentations of morality and frequently a source of scandal to Catholics themselves and other Christians. To manifest the full implications of the sacramental character of Christian life and activity in every sphere is one of the tasks of a renewed moral theology.

3. Personal to Man

As the study of man's activity in responding to God's invitation, moral theology should be presented in a way that takes account of man's dignity as a person. The third focal point in the structure of moral theology, man, may never be treated as an object or as an impersonal source of material actions, the morality of which are judged independently of the person performing them. The human response which these actions express is as personal as the divine invitation which prompts them. In the moral theology which studies and judges them, this personal character should emerge very clearly.

The personal quality of Christian morality is very evident in the biblical writings on which it is based. The appeal of Christ called for man's ???????? (conversion), complete personal turning to God.[18] The acceptance of God's final communication of himself in Christ involves total personal commitment. God in Christ does not ask for the lip-service of those who say Lord, Lord.[19] He cannot be satisfied with those who honour him with their lips while their hearts are far from him.[20] The external observance of laws, even the physical offering of sacrifices by those who have refused this personal self-giving, is of no account.[21] It is what comes forth from a man's heart that is of value for man and to God.[22] The whole law of morality, of the human response which God demands, is summed up in the total gift of self through love.[23] And this love must exceed all human ties and be prepared to follow in Christ's way of the Cross even unto death.[24]

Conversion through personal commitment to God in Christ is the beginning of Christian life for each man. But it is a response which has to be renewed and deepened every day. Conversion is a permanent demand in the life of the Christian. Daily he must take up his cross, accept the challenge of the moment and follow Christ.[25] In every situation in which he can accept or reject, each human act will express this acceptance (generously or weakly) or it will reject it. And face to face with this decision, the Christian is not alone. Through his union with Christ, he enjoys the guidance and strength of the Spirit of Christ[26] who has been poured forth in his heart.[27] In fulfilling the highest demands of his personality by responding positively to the divine call in each situation, he is allowing the Spirit who has been given to him to act through him. The life and grace of Christ which is his, finds its expression in his personal action.

The biblical stress on the personal quality which moral theology should have is confirmed by many of the philosophical and psychological developments of today. The deeper understanding of the individual human person and of his particular situation, activity and vocation, to which various modern philosophical movements have drawn attention, is extremely valuable to moral theology. The insistence of the personalist movement for instance on the supreme value and dignity of the person, who may never be treated as a mere functionary, still less as an object or thing, harmonises with and enriches a theology of invitation-response, while it is quite alien to a purely legalist system of morality. Similarly the existentialist movement, for all its deviations and distortions precisely in the field of morality, has given the (moral) theologian an increased awareness of the importance of the concrete, individual man existing in all his uniqueness as this particular man in this particular situation. And the growth of value-philosophy enabled theologians to present moral realities in a way that was truer to the full moral reality, for example, of justice or chastity, and less dependent on legal expression. It is significant that the successors to Tillmann, in his attempt at a purely biblical renewal of the theology, have tried to integrate the positive elements of these philosophical movements into their work. This is clear in the work of the influential professional moralists like Häring,[28] Gilleman,[29] and Fuch.[30] It is even truer of Karl Rahner[31] whose work has been the most searching dialogue yet composed between modern man and the Christian message, and who, while he may be professionally described as a dogmatic theologian, is one of the most fertile influences today in moral as in all Catholic theology.

These insights of the philosophers existed in some degree already in theology, even if they had been largely ignored or undeveloped. But the radical developments of modern psychology from Freud to the present day, revealing new and unsuspected regions in man's personality, present a new challenge particularly to the theology of man's personal activity. The ideas and discoveries are still incomplete, still the subject of great controversy; but at the practical and therapeutic level we have an immediate impression of the importance of personal maturity through the recognition and acceptance of oneself, one's gifts and limitations, and through growth in the capacity to love as the highest personal act.

Psychological health and maturity free man from certain irrational forces or rather enable him to harness his sub-rational forces and to give himself in love to God and his fellowman in a fuller way. Any developments in knowledge and technique which help man to grow in this way are welcome additions to the moral theologian's picture of the human person responding to God. While he must take account of the emotional and other forces which inhibit man's freedom and so reduce his responsibility, he is primarily interested in the advances of psychology or psychiatry, not as providing excusing causes or impediments to voluntariety, but as providing help to each man in attaining the fullest measure of maturity and freedom possible to him, so making that complete personal response in Christ to which God is calling him. The integration of the established conclusions of modern psychology into moral theology is a task that demands a very personal presentation of the Christian agent. A predominantly legal presentation will be unequal to it. It is only in a moral theology that is true to the personal and living character of Christian morals as derived from Christ and the New Testament, that the psychological and philosophical concepts of today can find their real home. The place of the legal precept or prohibition may never be ignored, but it cannot address the full reality or be given first place in the moral theology of a Christian person.

(a) *Positive*

As a theology of personal response to an invitation, moral theology should be presented in positive terms. God does not invite man to no-thing, to not-do things, to avoid things. He invites man to a personal love of himself. This love man manifests by responding to the manifestations of the divine which, summed up in Christ, are now mediated to man through word and sacrament and Christian moral values. In seeking the moral values of, for example, truth or justice or chastity inherent in any situation with which he is faced, man is responding in love to the God whom they reflect and mediate. It is from the supreme value, the *summum bonum* which is God, that these intermediate perfections or values, really the objects of the Christian virtues, derive their goodness for man. In seeing them as reflections of the divine, man expresses his loving response to God and perfects himself by increasing in himself the image of God and likeness to Christ.

The true Christian significance of these values has been frequently diminished in the legalist framework of moral theology and distorted by the manual preoccupation with sin or non-value.

The extent of this preoccupation may be deduced from a recent (1961) edition of a standard and in general comparatively balanced manual of moral theology.

The half-volume entitled *De Sexto et Nono Praeceptis* contains more than sixty-five pages and deals with four questions. After an introductory paragraph, quoting the sixth and ninth commandments from the Book of Exodus, *Quaestio I* dealing very properly with the virtue and headed *De castitate et pudicitia*, begins on p. 8 and runs to p. 10; *Quaestio II* headed *De luxuria in genere*, runs from p. 11 to p. 20; *Quaestio III De peccatis luxuriae consummatis*, pp. 21–43 (including an appendix *De sexualitate abnormi*), and *Quaestio IV De peccatis luxuriae non consummatis*, pp. 43–58, complete the theological treatment of chastity. Three questions on the vice, comprising forty-eight pages, are balanced by one question on the virtue comprising three pages, of which almost one page is taken up with the question *Quomodo virginitas amittatur*. No matter how excellent the opening two pages on the virtue might be, they could scarcely counterbalance the other almost fifty pages dealing with the vice or sins against the virtue. And this predominantly negative treatment has not been confined to the virtue of chastity, although it was here that it may have been most harmful.

In defence of such treatment it is sometimes alleged that the purpose of the manuals is the training of confessors. This defence is not altogether convincing. The manual itself claims to be a textbook of moral theology and should be criticised as such. In particular there is no comparable positive treatment of chastity at a theological level to which the seminarian may turn in his course. And even as a guide for confessors the predominantly negative treatment is inadequate. Sin is a negation, and the negative has meaning only in relation to the positive. Sin in general must be described as man's personal rejection of God as he communicates himself to man. This communication may be perceived only in a general, unreflecting, implicit way. But there must be some such implicit understanding of God and his summons to a particular act, before you can have the rejection of God which sin always involves.

God himself has revealed how this communication of himself is implied in each good act to which man is obliged. It is the business of the moral theologian to make as explicit as possible in each area of human activity the implicit divine invitation, by clarifying the positive value involved as it reflects the divine goodness and becomes a suitable term of man's act of loving God. In sex as in every other area of human activity moral theology seeks to understand how God manifests himself and how man may recognise and respond to that manifestation. It is the rejection of the divine invitation enshrined in chastity or of the reflection of God in sex that is the sin of unchastity. But the meaning and malice of unchastity can be understood only in so far as chastity is understood. The negative as always derives its meaning from the positive it denies. This has always been assumed in our teaching of morality. The principles of morality were first of all statements of the obligatory values proposed to us by God and the Church in each sphere of our activity. But this became obscured in the elaboration of the legal and negative expression of the limits within which these values could be realised. To train priests in the discernment of sins of unchastity or any other sins the primary requirement is a full study of the virtue itself. As a preacher as well as a confessor this positive understanding of the riches of the divine invitation in each area of Christian living will be indispensable to the priest.

(b) Dynamic

In attempting to present a programme of living, moral theology must reveal the dynamism of life. Life is a process of growth and development. It has an inner dynamism. The Christian life as a personal response to God has a dynamism also. It is a going somewhere, not just staying somewhere. It is dynamic, not static. A Christian is either going forward, however gradually, towards God or backwards away from him into sin. A static theology distorts the reality by ignoring this movement and presenting the Christian as staying somewhere, out of sin, within the law or vice versa. It tends to become preoccupied with the limits dividing sin and non-sin, while its attention is distracted from the central reality, God in Christ, who gives the limits their meaning and whom man should be seeking. In this way it can create insoluble problems for people who may become obsessed with the limits beyond which lie the sins they know they should but feel they cannot avoid, while they never turn their eyes to the merciful God who is calling them and to whom they will come a step at a time.

(c) *In community*

Finally the personal character of moral theology implies that it should have a community or social aspect also. A person is not an isolated individual. By birth and baptism he belongs to society or community. He is bound to other persons by multiple ties of blood and dependence and common destiny. All these ties find a deeper significance in Christianity. As Christ was raised up to draw all men to him,[32] all men are bound more closely together under their new head, with whom they should form one body.[33] In man's response to God's invitation in Christ, the community context must colour his every action. This was long ago proclaimed by Christ himself in summarising the response under love of God and the neighbour,[34] and its implications spelled out by St John, as he denied the possibility of loving God without loving one's brother.[35]

At the human level the corporate destiny of mankind was never more intensely felt than it is today. This destiny is ultimately a Christian one. And it makes it all the more necessary that commitment to the community should be evident in every section of Christian moral theology, so that no suspicion of a spiritual or material self-centred individualistic attitude may colour our moral teaching.

CONCLUSION

The central mystery of Christianity is the expression of the one God in three divine persons. It is through their roles in his salvation that they are revealed to man. The Father out of mercy for man in his sinful helplessness initiates the plan of human salvation which is accomplished in the sending of the Son. The radical salvation or reconciliation of man with the Father is extended to the individual man by the giving of the Holy Spirit to Christ's Church. In the salvation of the race then, as well as in the salvation of the individual human person, the Father communicates himself to man and realises his plan for man in the Son. Man responds to the Father in the Son through the power and guidance of the Spirit. It is with the understanding of and cooperation with this activity of the three divine persons in the world and in each person that Christian moral theology is concerned.[36] It is to enable man both to understand and cooperate more fully that the present efforts at renewal are directed. By respecting the structure of moral theology and its characteristics as indicated here, renewal may be profitably attempted.

NOTES

1   There is already a vast literature on this subject. Here I can only indicate a few most recent articles. The more important fuller works are referred to later in the article and may be consulted for fuller bibliography.

Cf. Bernard Häring, CSsR., 'Heutige Bestrebungen zur Vertiefung und Erneuerung der Moraltheologie' in *Studia Moralia* I, Roma, 1963.

P. Anciaux, 'Religion et Morale' in *Collectanea Mechlinensia* 49 (1964–5), 409ff.

P. Delhaye, 'Morale et Moralisme' in *Suppl. La Vie Spirituelle* 70 (1964), 243ff.

F. Böckle, 'Bestrebungen in der Moraltheologie' in *Fragen der Theologie Heute*, Einsiedeln, 1960.

The most useful single work treating of the different needs and aspects of renewal is still, perhaps, *Moral Chrétienne et Requetes Contemporaines*, Paris: Tournai, 1954. A similar type of work is V. Redlich (ed.), *Moralprobleme in Umbruch der Zeit*, Munich, 1957.

2   The best known and most extreme presentation of this critical approach is J. Leclercq, *L'Enseignement de la Morale Chrétienne*, Louvain: Louvain University Press, 1950.

3   'I am the way, the truth and the life.' Jn 14:6.

4   For a comprehensive account of the different approaches to this problem cf. R. Hofmann, *Moraltheologische Erkenntnis- und Methodenlehre*, Munich, 1963.

5   Cf. Neuhäusler, *Anspruch und Antwort Gettes*, Dusseldorf, 1962.

6   Mt 6:33; Lk 12:31.

7   Lk 18:10ff; Mt 21:31. Cf. Gal 2:16, 21; 3:10.

8   1 Cor 13.

9   Cf. Jn 14:6ff etc.

10 F. Tillmann, *Handbuch der Katholischen Sittenlehre; Bd. III Die Idee der Nachfolge Christi; Bd. IV Die Verwirklichung der Nachfolge Christi*. Dusseldorf, 1933 (4th ed. 1952). A summary of his ideas may be found in his single volume work, *The Master Calls*, London, 1962. Cf. Schulz, *Nachfolgen und Nachahmen*, Munich, 1962.

11 3rd ed., Brussels, 1949.

12 In English translation Vols. I, II. Cork, 1961, 1963.

13 *The Law of Christ*, p. 70.

14 Jn 1:16; Rom I:5, etc.

15 2 Cor 3:5; Gal I:12.

16 Jn 15:4-5.

17 *Const. De Sacra Liturgia*, § 2.

18 Mk 1:15, par.

19 Mt 7:31.

20 Is 29:13; Mt 15:7-9.

21 Mk 12:33; Mt 9:13; 1 Sam 15:27; Hos 6:6.

22 Mt 12:34f; Lk 6:45.

23 Mk 12:28-34, par.

24 Mt 10:34-9, par.

25 Lk 9:23, par.

26 Cf. Rom 8.

27 Gal 4:6; Rom 8:15; 2 Cor 1:22.

28 *Vide supra* note 12.

29 G. Gillemann, *The Primacy of Charity in Moral Theology*, London: Burns and Oates, 1959.

30 J. Fuchs, *Theologia Moralis Generalis*, Rome, 1963.

31 Rahner's relevant works are scattered through his articles and the various collections of them. Some of those most directly concerned with moral theology may be found in translation in *Nature and Grace*, London, 1963; *Mission and Grace* I, II, London, 1963, 1964; and *The Dynamic Element in the Church*, London, 1964.

32 Jn 3:16.

33 I Cor II: 3; 12:12, etc.

34 Mk 12:28-34, par. Jn 13:34ff.

35 I Jn 4:7ff.

36 Cf. Ceslas Spicq, *St Paul and Christian Living*, Dublin: Gill and Macmillan, 1964.

6   Morality and the Christian Faith

Patrick Hannon

(Patrick Hannon, *Church, State, Morality and Law,* Dublin: Gill & Macmillan, 1992, pp. 30–49.)

In looking at morality as the art of right relationship with each other and the world around us we saw that it is a natural accompaniment of human living. It may be accounted for without reference to religious belief and indeed there are many people who subscribe to and achieve a high moral standard without being committed to a religious faith in any usual sense. But Christian faith sheds light on the moral life, and in this chapter we look more closely at how this is so.

Perhaps the best point of entry is by way of relevant biblical material, for the Bible is the source and reference point *par excellence* for Christian theologising. According to Roman Catholic tradition, 'the divinely revealed realities which are contained and presented in the text of Sacred Scripture have been written down under the inspiration of the Holy Spirit'.[1] But even for those who do not see the Bible in this light, its books are the formative and normative expression of the Judaeo-Christian religious heritage. Its perspectives and emphases no less than its explicit teaching remain instructive in the shaping of theology in our time.

TWO QUESTIONS

Two questions will be of particular interest to us. The first is the general question of what was made of morality during the formative phase of the Church, the second the more particular question of the relationship between the Church and the civil power. But from the outset it is important to place these questions in context. It is a basic theme of this book that the primary work of the Church is to bear witness to a gospel of human salvation; and all its other concerns, including its concern with morality, are in aid of that witness. This is evident from even the most rudimentary summary of the biblical data.

THE CONTEXT

The Christian religion is founded upon the belief that God is disclosed uniquely in Jesus Christ. According to a modern theological emphasis that disclosure took place in the personal *history* of Jesus; as the Constitution on Revelation of the Second Vatican Council has it, Jesus revealed God 'by the total fact of his presence and self-manifestation – by words and works, signs and miracles, but above all by his death and glorious resurrection from the dead, and finally by sending the Spirit of truth'.[2] What this means is that God is disclosed, and his design for his creation, in the detail of the personal history of Jesus.

That history itself took place within the history of a people who had already experienced themselves as especially chosen. God, they believed, was already revealing himself in the unfolding story of their 'deliverance' in accordance with a promise which he made to Abraham and ratified in a covenant with Moses. Although their expectations were in time no longer crassly political, most of them were unprepared for the claim that their deliverance was less from temporal enemies and evils than from the bondage of sin, and that their saviour was a travelling rabbi from Nazareth who said he was the Son of God.

So they crucified him, but 'God raised him up',[3] and later he was seen by some of the disciples.[4] Later again they came to recognise that he had left them definitively and had gone back to the Father.[5] And then what came to be called the Church was born in the coming together of Jesus' disciples, following his injunction to remember in the breaking of bread'[6] what he had done, or what God had done in him. The core of the disciples' belief was that Jesus was Lord, who had died and was risen and would some time come again. They were at first fearful and inhibited but, transformed by the Pentecost event, at length went forth to tell others of their faith and hope.

Their message was called 'good news – the Greek *evangelion* and the English 'gospel' have comparable roots. In classical Greek the term was often used in reference to the announcement of a victory, and in a religious context it could signify a divine utterance. But the sense in which the expression came most readily to the disciples was a strictly biblical one: it echoed exactly a word used in Second Isaiah to signify that the time of salvation was at hand.

Salvation was a familiar theme in the religious patrimony of Israel. The complex history of the theme is beyond our purpose; essentially the concept signified the action of God in the life of the chosen people in virtue of which they were to achieve the destiny promised the descendants of Abraham. The shape of that destiny disclosed itself only gradually, and only gradually did it come to be associated with the expectation of a messiah. But by the time of the prophets it had begun to appear that salvation was primarily in the spiritual order, and the saviour was seen in the role of a suffering Servant.[8]

This was the backdrop to the events which are the subject of the narratives which we now call gospels. These books, each from its own viewpoint, document the impact of Jesus of Nazareth upon his first hearers. They tell the story of Jesus, a story which was perceived by himself and by those who became his disciples as continuing and completing the story of God's dealings with the people of his choice.

And so Luke portrays Jesus early in his public ministry announcing in the synagogue at Nazareth that the words of the prophet Isaiah were that day fulfilled:

'The Spirit of the Lord is upon me, because he has anointed me to preach good news to the poor. He has sent me to proclaim release to the captives and recovering of sight to the blind, to set at liberty those who are oppressed, to proclaim the acceptable year of the Lord.'[9] That *this* is the salvation which Israel was waiting for was a main theme in the spreading of the good news.

It seems that a brief telling of the story of Jesus was a central feature in the early proclamation of the gospel. Several of Paul's letters and some passages in the Acts of the Apostles incorporate such a narrative, and Peter's speech to Cornelius as reported in Acts will serve to exemplify this here.

> You know the word which [God] sent to Israel, preaching the good news of peace by Jesus Christ (he is Lord of all), the word which was proclaimed throughout all Judaea, beginning from Galilee after the baptism which John preached: how God anointed Jesus of Nazareth with the Holy Spirit and with power; how he went about doing good and healing all that were oppressed by the devil, for God was with him. And we are witnesses to all that he did both in the country of the Jews and in Jerusalem. They put him to death by hanging him on a tree; but God raised him on the third day and made him manifest; not to all the people but to us who were chosen by God as witnesses, who ate and drank with him after he rose from the dead. And he commanded us to preach to the people, and to testify that he is the one ordained by God to be judge of the living and the dead. To him all the prophets bear witness that everyone who believes in him receives forgiveness of sins through his name.[10]

So we have a community – or, more exactly, communities – gathering in remembrance of the story of Jesus' life, and especially in what would come to be known as the paschal events; and then going out to spread the word that in him is salvation accomplished. It took a little time before the new 'churches' realised their distinctiveness in the common Jewish tradition, a little longer before it was clear that subscription to that tradition was not a prerequisite of entry into the Christian 'way'. And it took yet longer before their community of faith and worship generated a community of organisation: before, that is, the churches became the Church, which in time would be one in government as well as in worship and faith.

But from the outset the churches saw themselves as charged with proclaiming the good news. The disciples were conscious of being 'sent', as Peter's speech just quoted shows. Matthew records a sending,[11] and later he presents the risen Lord on a mountain in Galilee bidding the eleven 'go and make disciples of all nations, baptising them in the name of the Father and of the Son and of the Holy Spirit, teaching them to observe all that I have commanded you'.[12]

It is a commonplace of modern ecclesiology that the Church 'is mission' – so much a commonplace that one is tempted to try to find another way of saying what is meant. Yet there is hardly a more exact way of saying that in its very

An Irish Reader in Moral Theology

coming together to celebrate Jesus as Lord it is meant to go forth to affirm what it celebrates. 'As the Father has sent me I also send you.'[13] In a later theological perspective the Church would be seen as a visible expression in history of the saving work of Christ.

AN ETHICAL RELIGION

It is time now to turn to the first of the questions in which we must be especially interested: what was made of morality itself in the formative phase of the Church. The Christian religion, wrote C.H. Dodd, 'is an ethical religion in the specific sense that it recognises no ultimate separation between the service of God and social behaviour'.[14] What this means is that you cannot claim to love the God of Jesus Christ unless you love the neighbour. Of course the link between religion and morality had already been affirmed in Judaism, and there was much in the tradition inherited by the first Christians to remind them of it. V. Warnach has summarised the data: 'In the Old Testament the love which God bestows upon men, above all on the chosen people, is for the most part understood as faithfulness to the covenant. In view of this it is not surprising that the reciprocal love of men should likewise be conceived of as consisting essentially in the acceptance of covenant obligations.'[15]

These obligations included worship; but no less did they stress the need for a right relationship with the neighbour. And indeed it was to be a constant theme, especially in the preaching of the prophets, that the God of Israel was not placated by mere ritual in the absence of a conversion of heart expressed in right conduct toward others.[16]

And so it was not as it were out of the blue that Jesus preached repentance. 'Repentance' translates a Greek word *metanoia* which is much richer in its signification than the English. Its chief Old Testament antecedent is a Hebrew word *shuv*, whose literal meaning is to return to the place from which one has set out – that is to God. When Jesus called for repentance he was calling on people to turn about, to re-orientate their lives, to make a fresh beginning, to go back to God.

Yet the call to repentance was not the primary motif of the message; that motif was, rather, the coming of the kingdom of God. Again we must be careful of the English word: 'kingship' or 'reign' or 'rule' are better guides to the biblical sense. For in the tradition God had often been thought of as king, and in time the hope of Israel was expressed in terms of the setting up of his kingly rule in Israel and among the nations. But the rule would not be a merely political dominion. Isaiah's vision of it is summarised by Rudolf Schnackenburg: 'The peace of paradise will be brought back (Is 11:6-9), and, in general, this kingdom of God fulfilled in the last age takes on universal characteristics even though Israel has always the place of honour. It also has cosmic dimensions and a clearly religious and moral character – salvation and peace and the law established as the basis of the world order.'[19] It will simplify matters if we indicate its meaning by calling it the universal reign of God's love.

In Jesus' preaching the advent of that reign is the context of the call to repentance. Mark's portrayal of the opening of the public ministry shows this: 'The time is fulfilled and the kingdom of God is at hand; repent, and believe in the gospel.'[20] The time of the promise is here, the rule of God's love is inaugurated, and the people are called to turn again to him. The turning implies a change of heart, the change is expressed in walking along the right path. But the turning is in another sense only like a first move, a step within a larger process. For Jesus asks them also to believe in the gospel – to entrust themselves to the word that God has saved his people. They are invited to recognise their salvation *and then* walk in salvation's way.

The call to repentance therefore is at root a call to acknowledge the presence of God's love and its power. To see it merely as a summons to moral rectitude is to impoverish it. What is announced first is that God loves us, and in the very announcement we are asked to return that love. If we want to return it we are thereby committed to love of the neighbour. In the gospel accounts, as a glance will show, Jesus repeatedly reiterates the love-commandment and places it at the heart of the religious and moral response which he asks of his disciples.[21] It is, however, important to remember that Jesus was not primarily a moral teacher. True, as we have seen, what he taught had a bearing on morality. And he did sometimes teach morality directly: the primacy of the love-commandment, the scope and quality of the love which it enjoins, something of what it precludes as well as what it asks to be done. But as with the call to repentance his moral teaching is consequent upon his gospel. It opens up the path of love for one in whom God's love has resonated.

GOSPEL AND LAW

The first hearers grasped this well, and it is reflected in the way they shaped their own teaching. First they announced the good news, as had Jesus in announcing the coming of the kingdom; then they explained what this meant in terms of the expectations and preoccupations of Jew or Gentile as the context called for; and then they bade the new disciples to 'let your manner of life be worthy of the gospel of Christ'.[22] Sometimes too they gave specific indications of the kind of behaviour which this required.[23] But always the moral instruction was subordinate to the announcement of the gospel.

Biblical scholarship furnishes a terminology for analysing the foregoing approach. The statement of the essence of the good news is called *kerygma*, a word which means the message of a herald and so is suitable in reference to the *euangelion*. Jesus' own *kerygma*, as we have seen, was characteristically expressed in terms of the coming of God's reign, explicitly or implicitly identified with his own presence. That formula or some version of it featured too in the spreading of the good news by the disciples, and as we saw in Peter's speech to Cornelius its link with Jesus was made by a recital of the main events of his life, with special emphasis on the death and resurrection. What the first preachers were intent above all to convey was that Jesus is the Christ the Son of God, so that their hearers, believing, might have life in his name.[24]

But the preaching of the *kerygma* inevitably gave rise to a need for explanation, called by the scholars catechesis; and this assumed a typical shape at an early stage. Our interest is in its ethical component, usually called *didache*, a word which meant teaching – in this context moral instruction. Another biblical term for it is *paraenesi*, meaning, literally, moral exhortation.

I have stressed that in Jesus' teaching moral instruction must be seen in the context of his proclamation of God's reign. The same point is made in the way in which in the gospels, moral teaching is set within a narrative which presents Jesus as inaugurating that reign. But the subordination of moral instruction to religious message is perhaps most clearly seen in the structure of the Pauline and other New Testament letters. The letter to the Romans will serve as an example.

The letter to the Romans is 'the record of the maturing thoughts of Paul, written on the occasion of his impending visit to Rome, in which he formulated the more universal implications of the gospel that he had been preaching'.[26] Paul first considers the way in which God through Christ 'justifies' the person of faith. He goes on to show how God's love assures salvation to all thus justified, paying special attention to the threefold liberation which life 'in Christ' brings: freedom from sin and death, freedom from self through union with Christ, and freedom from the Law. The role of the Spirit in this new life is explored, and the Christian's destiny in 'glory'. The reflections conclude with a paean: 'O the depth of the riches and wisdom and knowledge of God! How unsearchable his judgements and how inscrutable his ways! ... For from him and through him and to him are all things. To him be glory for ever. Amen.'[27] Only then does Paul turn to moral exhortation.

I chose the letter to the Romans to illustrate the structure of which we have been speaking, the pattern which makes moral *didache* subordinate to the affirmations of the *kerygma*, for in that letter the pattern is seen at its plainest. But the structure may be detected in the other letters too, as theological reflection, often in a mood of thanksgiving or of celebration, leads on to exhortation about good living. We must now look at the exhortation's content.

According to C.H. Dodd the soundest method of determining the contents of the early Christian pattern of teaching is to examine the ethical portions of a number of epistles, and see whether the material common to them all shows any sign of originating at a stage antedating the particular piece. Dodd's own analysis leads to the conclusion that the ethical portions of the epistles are based upon an accepted pattern of teaching which in fact goes back to a very early period, and he considers that the form and content of this teaching can be determined with considerable probability. We can do no better here than reproduce this great scholar's account.

The convert is first enjoined to lay aside certain discreditable kinds of conduct, especially some which were common and easily condoned in pagan society. Sometimes lists of such vices are inserted, lists which can be shown to have been drawn from popular ethical teaching of the period, quite outside Christianity. The convert is enjoined to abandon these vices and to be prepared for a total reorientation of moral standards in a Christian sense. This is sometimes expressed in the terms, 'to put off the old man and to put on the new'.

Next, some of the typical virtues of the new way of life are set forth, with special emphasis upon such virtues as purity and sobriety, gentleness and humility, generosity and a hospitable temper, patience under injuries, and readiness to forgive.

Then various social relationships are reviewed, in particular those which constitute the family as the primary form of community; the relations of husband and wife, parents and children, master and servants – for, in the social structure of the time, a servant, even if he were a slave, was a member of the *familia*. The proper Christian attitude in all such relations is briefly indicated: husbands are to love their wives, children to obey their parents, masters to treat their servants with consideration, and so forth.

Then the wider 'family' of the Christian community itself comes into view. The new member is enjoined to respect the leaders or elders of the society and is taught that each member has his own special function in the body, for which he is responsible.

Looking farther afield, he is given some counsel about behaviour to his pagan neighbours in the delicate situation in which the members of an unpopular sect were likely to find themselves. He must be prudent, nonprovocative, seeking peace, never flouting the social or moral standards of those among whom he lives, while using any opportunity of doing a kindness to them even if they had not been friendly to him.

Like other subjects of the Empire, he is told, he owes obedience to the constituted authorities and should make it a matter of conscience to keep the law and pay his taxes. But there are limits beyond which a higher allegiance claims him: he must be loyal at all cost to his faith, and prepared to endure persecution with inflexible determination and fortitude.

Finally he is reminded of the extremely critical time in which he lives, which calls for constant watchfulness and lays upon him the most solemn responsibilities.[28]

What we need to notice at this point is the *character* of the ethic associated with the preaching of the gospel. It is at once plain that the 'change of heart' was meant to affect day-to-day living and to permeate it through and through. The ambit of that living was manifold: the family and other domestic relations, the larger community of Christians, pagan neighbours, the civil authority. No part of life is untouched by the new experience of faith in Jesus Christ, and all of living is somehow judged by it.

The writings show that the new experience suffused the view of life of the first hearers, and the developing Christian imagination sought ways in which to express the sense of newness engendered by the gospel. And so the early writers spoke of dying and rising with Christ, a second birth, adoption into the family of God's children, putting on the new man. 'The radicality of the metaphors bespeaks a real experience of sharp displacement which many of the converts must have felt.'[29] The first Christians are no longer at ease here, like Eliot's magi after the birth.[30]

And yet there is an ordinariness about the imperatives of the earliest instruction, a kind of modesty which keeps it earthbound. The vices condemned are those which any sound ethic might condemn, the virtues by and large are of a kind aspired to by anyone wishing to live humanely. Christians are not to be conformed to this world, Paul wrote; yet, as one commentator has put it, 'his typical admonitions, which follow those words, are sprinkled with topics and turns of phrase that would be instantly recognisable in the moral rhetoric of his time and place'.[31] Scholars have long acknowledged, as Dodd does in the passage above, that the early writers made use of existing ethical writing in setting out the demands of the Christian way of life.

For of course the early Christian writers were able to draw on a wealth of ethical wisdom from more than one tradition. There was in the first place the Jewish tradition, which formed Jesus himself, and was the background to the first post-pentecost spreading of the gospel in the Jewish homeland and the diaspora. Then there was the moral content of the Graeco-Roman heritage, a natural resource for those who like Paul took the message to the chief cities of the empire. Not that the Christian way was simply identical with that of Israel: and before long that point was tested in the controversy over circumcising gentile converts. Nor that, for example, the detachment from the world prized by the Christians was in the same spirit as that espoused by some stoic philosophers. Yet it was from the moral perceptions of Israel and of Athens and Rome that the early Christians fashioned their 'way'.

Wayne Meeks has expressed the foregoing in these words: 'The meaningful world in which those earliest Christians lived – the world which lived in their heads as well as that which was all around them – was a Jewish world. But the Jewish world was part of the Graeco-Roman world. If therefore we are looking for some "pure" Christian values and beliefs unmixed with the surrounding culture, we are on a fool's errand. What was Christian about the ethos and ethics of those early Christian communities we will discover not by abstraction but by confronting their involvement in the culture of their time and place and seeking to trace the new patterns they made of old forms, to hear the new songs they composed from old melodies.'[32]

Meeks' words serve to warn against the danger of imposing an alien schema upon a process so complex as is here described. Yet it happens that a modern theological debate offers one way of coping with a key issue, as for our purposes, however summarily, we must. The debate concerns the precise character or as it is sometimes called the identity of Christian morality. In view of the account of morality with which this book opened, the way in which the question arises might be put as follows: if morality is a matter of general human experience and if its prescriptions are accessible to reason, what role does Christian faith play? The question is often put in the form, is there a specifically Christian morality?

WHAT WAS NEW?

Here we can only try to simplify a complex and continuing debate; and this account is based in the main upon the Roman Catholic experience of the question. In that experience the debate began when moral theologians, critical of accounts of Christian ethics which scarcely referred to Christ or Christian sources, called for a return to the Bible as the sourcebook of all Christian theologising. There ensued a recovery of focus on the person and teaching of Jesus Christ; and his emphasis upon the love-commandment was taken to be the essential mark of any account of morality which wished to be Christian.

But what *was* this love? It was soon seen that to give concrete content to the love-commandment one needed to have recourse to specific prescriptions such as those of the decalogue and of the ethical teaching of the gospels and other New Testament books. And so love of the neighbour was seen to be expressed in concrete norms: negative, as in prohibitions on killing, say, or stealing or lying; positive in injunctions to be just or peaceful or truthful, or whatever the particular virtue or action.

But then a new kind of question suggested itself. Are not these precepts of peace and justice and respect for life and truthfulness, whether positively or negatively expressed, what anyone who thought about the prerequisites of a good life would see as necessary? The emergence of this type of question was influenced by two quite diverse (though of course sometimes overlapping) developments.

One was the work of scripture scholars who were finding parallels between the moral teaching of the scriptures and that from other religious and even secular sources. It was noted for example that the main provisions of the decalogue were the same, if differently formulated, as those of the Babylonian Code of Hammurabi. And I have already alluded to Paul's use of the stoic lists of virtues and vices, and mentioned the secular origins of other parts of the early Christian ethic. Such scholarly findings gave point to the question, is there anything in the moral teaching of the Bible, even of Jesus himself, that is not available to reason reflecting on human experience in the world?

A second stimulus came from quite another direction. It is again somewhat of a simplification but I hope not unfair to say that in the 1960s and 1970s

Anglo-American moral philosophy began to make an impact upon Catholic moral theology for the first time. And one of the ways in which it impinged was in creating an awareness of the ways in which a particular type of moral prescription is inevitably time-bound and culture-bound. Thus was raised a question about the present status of some of the biblical teaching: obvious examples are Paul's injunctions concerning slavery and concerning women. Inevitably it came to be asked, is there anything in the biblical moral teaching which is not in the end to be judged at the bar of reason? Which is another way of asking whether there is anything in the moral teaching of the Bible, even of Jesus himself, that is not available to reason reflecting on human experience in the world.

TWO APPROACHES

The two lines of response which this question has evoked have been called respectively the 'Autonomy' and *Glaubensethik* schools. The former are so called from the apparent autonomy which they attribute to morality vis-à-vis religion – though, as we shall see, the autonomy is relative and not absolute. The latter school gets its name from the German word for faith, and the name implies a view of morality which connects it closely with religious belief. One of the ways in which the issue between them is often formulated is whether or to what extent 'revelation' is necessary to morality.

In answering this question writers of the Autonomy school are in general reluctant to grant that the revelation made in Jesus Christ has contributed anything to our knowledge of morality's *content*. Another way of putting this is to say that one does not need Christian faith to know what morality requires. These writers concede that revelation and faith give a *context* to moral striving, as the Covenant gave a context to the Israelites' keeping the Torah. Many of them grant that a Christian vision gives additional *motivation* for right behaviour: we love the neighbour for him/herself, but also as brother or sister in the Lord. And of course the Christian has, in the person of Jesus, a model and an inspiration for moral endeavour. But what to do or refrain from doing, in the cause of justice or peace or any other moral value, is in its substance the same.

Writers in the *Glaubensethik* school agree with the autonomists concerning context and motivation and the exemplary significance of Jesus. Where they disagree is upon the question of content, for they maintain that in the Christian moral way there are requirements whose existence and character and binding force are known only because of revelation. Of course the substance of morality's claims are accessible to reason, they say, and so shared by all people of good will. But in the *Glaubensethik* view it is nevertheless the case that there are things asked of Christians which are recognised only in faith.

One might think that this must be an issue of fact which could be settled by recourse to the sources of the revelation. One might expect, that is, that the

Glaubensethik authors could provide a list of moral demands which are known only from scripture and/or from the tradition of the Church, and which cannot be perceived as obligatory by the use of reason alone. If they can do this, one might think, their position is vindicated; if not, the autonomists have it.

The matter, however, is not so simple. The authors of the *Glaubensethik* do indeed provide a list (or lists, for they differ a little as between themselves).[33] But the autonomists respond by contending that some of the items on the list are instances of religious rather than moral obligation, while others are taught in the Catholic tradition as grounded in reason as much as they are in faith.

In order to decide between the two positions we should have to agree in the first place upon the respective scopes of religion and morality and to consider the import of the tradition's grounding of positions in faith as well as in reason. We should also, as Vincent MacNamara has done, analyse each side's use of such terms as 'content' and 'motivation'.[34] But this task is too vast in the present context so for the sake of later argument I shall sketch summarily a working position.

THE MAKINGS OF A RESPONSE

We might begin by recalling the incontrovertible. It is incontrovertible that the Judaeo-Christian theological inheritance provides a context in which the moral pilgrimage of humanity may be seen in a way which enhances it. There is the doctrine of creation, with its view of humans as made in the image of God and so called to take part in the very making of the world. There is the theme of human stewardship of creation, suggestive of an accountability for what is in our power and charge. Then there is the doctrine of sin, the 'sin of the world' and personal sin, a dark shadow on the *imago dei* which threatens death to the human spirit. And of course there is salvation: the news of a gracious God who has not left us in the prison of our sin but in Christ has freed us to 'return'.

It is incontrovertible too that in the moral teaching of Jesus the love-commandment is primary: all the Law and the Prophets are summarised in it. And in the teaching of Jesus we find abundant illustration of the quality of the love which is called for. It is in the first place a matter of the 'heart' (a Hebrew metaphor for the core of the personality) but it is expressed in action which is provident and caring. It is universal in its scope: the disciple is asked to love even the enemy. It is compassionate and forgiving and persists even in the face of rejection. It is radical and boundlessly generous. It is like God's love; indeed it *is* God's love, for we are capable if it only because God first loved us.

It can perhaps be said that the love thus characterised exceeds the 'merely rational', if rational in this context bespeaks something which may be concluded as a result of reason's reflection on human nature. And it makes demands which appear to transcend what might 'reasonably' be expected: one of its distinctive features, for example, is an unlimited readiness to forgive even those who have done us great wrong. *Agape*, to use the New Testament's word for this kind of loving, is more than urbanity.

It may be said also, on the evidence of the biblical material, that the translation of this love into action displays some characteristic emphases. There is the readiness to forgive just mentioned; there is also a concern with 'justice', and a special concern for the widow and the orphan – Hebrew metaphors for the specially needy. There is the message of the parable that unless the grain of wheat dies it does not bring forth fruit.

But it will no doubt be noticed that all of these features – unlimited readiness to forgive, a preoccupation with justice, a bias towards the specially vulnerable, an openness to the 'cross' – are in the first place matters of quality and emphasis and orientation. They indicate the *character* of the love to which a disciple is called: the readiness to forgive is 'unlimited', concern with justice is a 'preoccupation', service of the poor is by way of 'bias', crucifixion for most is metaphorical. These pointers to the way of the Christian disciple do not on their face say anything about the *content* of concrete actions.

Not that the Bible lacks concrete precepts: that is, precepts which name acts or attitudes or states of affairs or omissions enjoined on us or prohibited by *agape*. 'Thou shalt not kill', for example, is a plain statement of the kind of action excluded under the new as under the old covenant.

'Love is patient and kind,' says Paul; 'love is not jealous or boastful; it is not arrogant or rude.'[35] 'It has been reported to me by Chloe's people that there is quarrelling among you,' he writes reprovingly to the Corinthians.[36] 'I was hungry and you gave me no food,' the King will say to those on his left hand; 'I was thirsty and you gave me no drink, I was a stranger and you did not welcome me, naked and you did not clothe me, sick and in prison and you did not visit me.'[37]

But the precepts of the 'second table' of the decalogue – those which concern our innerworldy relationships – and the concrete norms of the earliest Christian teaching are found also outside of the biblical books, for they belong too to the currency of other ethical traditions. We might say that they are the kind of imperative which any well-meaning, right-thinking person might recognise. Reverting to an earlier perspective, we might say that we do not need revelation or faith to know of them or to see how they could oblige us. And of course the concrete norms of biblical times must be interpreted with care, for they were forged in the life of a distant time and place. Paul's injunctions to slaves have outgrown their usefulness, as has certain of his teaching about the relationship of husband and wife. The Bible says nothing concrete about nuclear weapons or computer ethics or test-tube babies or public education programmes on AIDS.

So even if it be agreed (and agreement, as already said, would presuppose a considerable clarification of terms) that there is some revealed content at the core of the Christian moral scheme, we are not relieved from thinking through the practical demands of morality as these disclose themselves in each age. Our path will be illuminated by the great Christian affirmations about the world and about humanity, our thinking shaped by what has been handed on to us out of generations of experience of life in the Spirit of Christ. But in this as in other dimensions of the human task grace builds on nature, and there is no shortcut to moral wisdom or achievement.

We turn next to an aspect of early Christian experience which has a more particular bearing on our theme: the Christian community's relationship with outsiders and especially with the civil authority. Earlier we glimpsed an unease felt by converts in the religious and secular environments in which they found themselves. Their sense of urgency in regard to spreading the gospel was considerable and it was reinforced, it seems, by a belief that the form of this world was in any case passing away. But we have seen also that the typical *didache* included some instruction upon their relationship with neighbours who were not of the faith, and that its tone was moderate and forbearing. We shall see now that there emerged also a gradual recognition of the need to make terms with the requirements of life in the *polis*.

CHURCHES AND SYNAGOGUES

The first neighbours were Jewish, and the converts' relationships with them were bound to be sensitive: think of how we can feel when a family member or friend changes religious allegiance. At first the members of the new community continued to live outwardly in the ordinary Jewish way. As Rudolf Schnackenburg has remarked: 'How else would it have been possible for their people not to look upon them as a disloyal separate community, but to look on them with benevolence (cf. Acts 2:47) and for many, including even priests (6:7) and Pharisees (15:5) to join them?'[38] But in time it was necessary to insist upon a radical theological difference between the ancient tradition and the new way, as the Christians were forced to an explicit rejection of the belief that salvation came through observance of the Law.

The way in which this came into prominence is told in the Acts of the Apostles. 'Now the apostles and the brethren who were in Judaea heard that the Gentiles also had received the word of God. So when Peter went up to Jerusalem, the circumcision party criticised him, saying "Why did you go to uncircumcised men and eat with them?"'[39] The circumcision party were those who contended that converts had to observe everything which the old law prescribed. This particular complaint can be looked at both as objecting to the violation of a traditional dietary law and as requiring circumcision for entry into what would soon be called the Christian community. Peter's reply is to recount the vision which had brought him to see that salvation was for the gentiles too. The vision included a repudiation of another dietary regulation – that which pronounced certain foods unclean – and led Peter's hearers to acknowledge that 'to the Gentiles also God has granted repentance unto life'.[40]

But the dispute did not end there, and chapter fifteen opens with the information that some men came down from Judaea and were teaching the brethren, 'Unless you were circumcised according to the custom of Moses, you cannot be saved'.[41] The result was what became known as the Council of Jerusalem, at which after 'much debate' Peter reiterated the freedom of the gentiles from merely ceremonial or cultic traditional observance. The question of eating with gentiles itself was to surface again, as it came to be asked whether Jewish Christians living according to the Mosaic law should share a common table with gentile Christians. And Paul tells the Galatians how he stood up to Peter who for fear of the circumcision party had begun to vacillate. Paul's own position was uncompromising: 'I said to Cephas before them all, "If you, though a Jew, live like a Gentile and not like a Jew, how can you compel the Gentiles to, live like Jews?"'[43]

Yet the stance vis-à-vis the Jewish environment was respected, and neither Paul nor the others denied the right of Jewish Christians to live after the Jewish manner.[44] Paul shows a like sensitivity in a well-known passage in the letter to the Romans. Of this Schnackenburg has written: 'Probably we should identify the "weak" in Rome (Rom 14:1-15:3) mainly with former Jews who could still not accustom themselves no longer to observe certain days (14:5) and the distinction between clean and unclean foods (14:14, 20). Paul was even ready to show them consideration.'[45]

The early letters gave instruction too on the behaviour of the Christians toward their pagan neighbours. On matters of principle there was to be no compromise: they were not, for example, to take part in pagan sacrifice, for 'what pagans sacrifice they offer to demons and not to God'.[46] But a sectarian fanaticism is inappropriate. So the Corinthians should 'eat whatever is sold in the meat market without raising any question on the ground of conscience'.[47] Moreover, 'if one of the unbelievers invites you to dinner and you are disposed to go, eat whatever is set before you without raising any question on the ground of conscience'.[48] Both these injunctions refer to the possibility of the Christian's being offered, at the market or as dinner guests, food which has been sacrificed to idols. The Christian is not to make unnecessary fuss. Yet if acceptance is accorded a potentially scandalous significance ('If someone says to you "This has been offered in sacrifice"'), then 'out of consideration for the man who informed you, and for conscience' sake – I mean his conscience, not yours – do not eat it'.[49]

CAESAR'S COIN

More precisely to the point of our concern is the attitude of the new community toward the civil authority and its institutions. Mark records this as having come in question explicitly during the mission of Jesus himself.[50] Jesus' activities had aroused the anger of the chief priests and scribes and elders, and they sent some Pharisees and Herodians 'to entrap him in his talk'. The subject of their intervention was a census tax which the Romans had levied upon the inhabitants of Judea, Samaria and Idumea. The tax was controversial among the Jews for in addition to being a permanent reminder of their subjection to Rome it provoked religious scruples. This was because it had to be paid in coins bearing the Emperor's image, whereas the Jews acknowledged only God or his representative as sovereign. The question 'is it lawful to pay taxes to Caesar, or not?' was intended to discredit Jesus among both nationalistic Jews and those who favoured the link with Rome.[51]

A full account of the meaning of Jesus' reply – 'Render to Caesar the things that are Caesar's, and to God the things are God's'[52] – is beyond our present purpose. It will be enough to observe that Mark took Jesus' pronouncement as an endorsement of the principle that loyalty to the civil authority need not contradict obedience to God.[53] The point is made by Schnackenburg thus: 'Emperor and God, State and divine rule are for Jesus two realities, belonging to two different orders, though not juxtaposed unrelatedly, and there is no question which of the two for him is the higher, incomparably higher. He leaves the secular and at that time the pagan State its rights in its own sphere, but only to the extent that the all-embracing rights of God over man are not thereby violated.'[54]

Schnackenburg elsewhere remarks that though Jesus' reply showed the early Church the line it should take in its attitude to the public authorities, 'that terse saying did not relieve it of the task of determining its actual relationship with those in authority'.[55] Something of what the emergent community made of that relationship may be gleaned from a reading of other New Testament writings.

Of course we need not expect to find a full-blown doctrine of Church-State relations. For one thing it took time for the little communities of Christians to develop sufficiently defined mutual bonds to generate a sense of 'Church', as distinct from 'churches'. And issues of relationship with civil society arose only piecemeal and incidentally. Alec Vidler has described the general situation: 'After Pentecost, the Church of Christ soon became a distinct society, but in the New Testament period it was never more than a small minority within the Roman Empire. All it looked for, so far as civil government was concerned, was freedom and security for its missionary work. There was no question yet of formal relations between civil government and ecclesiastical organisation.'[56]

CHRISTIANS IN THE POLIS

We have already touched on what Meeks called the sense of displacement which the gospel engendered in the converts. And any sense of estrangement was bound to have made itself felt especially in the domain of their relationship with temporal power and its institutions. Jewish Christians had already had to contend with the fact that the land of a proud people must now count as no more than a province of Rome. And we have seen that the religious claims of the emperor were in direct conflict with the religious role of Jewish civil leadership, as well as with the most basic conviction of the followers of Jesus. Add to this a sense of the imminence

An Irish Reader in Moral Theology

of the last times, and an impatience with and detachment from secular institutions must have been inevitable.

Indeed we get a glimpse of this in the early Paul, as when he conveys to the Thessalonians a sense of their apartness: 'But we exhort you, brethren ... to aspire to live quietly, to mind your own affairs, and to work with your hands, as we charged you; so that you may command the respect of outsiders, and be dependent on nobody.'[57] Later, more pointedly, he reproves the Corinthians for taking their quarrels before the pagan courts. Yet, as we have seen, the Corinthians are not to comport themselves eccentrically in the secular environment. And by the time of writing the letter to the Romans Paul is speaking of the authority of the civil government as being from God.

It is interesting to read this passage in full.

> Let every person be subject to the governing authorities. For there is no authority except from God, and those that exist have been instituted by God. Therefore he who resists the authorities resists what God has appointed, and those who resist will incur judgement. For rulers are not a terror to good conduct, but to bad. Would you have no fear of him who is in authority? Then do what is good, and you will receive his approval, for he is God's servant for your good. But if you do wrong, be afraid, for he does not bear the sword in vain; he is the servant of God, to execute his wrath on the wrongdoer. Therefore one must be subject, not only to avoid God's wrath but also for the sake of conscience. For the same reason you must pay taxes, for the authorities are ministers of God, attending to this very thing. Pay all of them their dues, taxes to whom taxes are due, revenue to whom revenue is due, respect to whom respect is due, honour to whom honour is due.[59]

This has puzzled commentators, partly because it seems a little out of place in the context in which it occurs, in the letter to the Romans, partly because of its apparently unreserved and unexpected regard for the secular authority. Some have thought it an interpolation, but this seems unlikely.[60] For a proper grasp of its import it is necessary to keep some points in mind.

First, it is natural that Paul should have addressed matters of civic duty; these were, after all, an aspect of life in community with others, meant to be regulated by justice and by love. And the Christians of Rome were bound to have been especially conscious of the imperial authorities and institutions. Second, the passage is not at all at odds with the general tenor of Paul's teaching: 'Despite St Paul's not always satisfactory experiences, there is not a word in his writings against the empire.'[61] Third, it assumes throughout that the authorities are 'conducting themselves uprightly and are seeking the interests of the community'.[62] As Fitzmyer writes: 'The possibility is not envisaged either of a tyrannical government or of one failing to cope with a situation where the just rights of individual citizens or of a minority group are neglected.'[63] Fourth, Paul is here concerned solely with the duties of subjects of legitimate authority, and not with duties of its bearers.

The same teaching is found in the first letter of Peter: 'Be subject for the Lord's sake to every human institution, whether it be to the emperor as supreme, or to the governors as sent by him to punish those who do wrong and to praise those who do right. For it is God's will that by doing right you should put to silence the ignorance of foolish men. Live as free men, yet without using your freedom as a pretext for evil; but live as servants of God. Honour all men. Love the brotherhood. Fear God. Honour the emperor.'[64] Similar exhortations are found in the letter to Titus,[65] and in the first letter to Timothy,[66] where prayer for the authorities is called for.

What we see expressed in the data here reviewed therefore is a sense both of apartness and of continuity. The sense of apartness is stronger in the earlier writing, as might be expected, given the belief that the end of the 'present age' was imminent. As the believers came to discover that the parousia was not yet, they settled down to make Christian sense of the secular life around them. This process included a recognition of the role of government and its institutions, and of the fact that membership of a Christian community did not exempt people from the usual civic duties.

Upon one point however the converts were unrepentantly at odds with the ethos in which Christianity was making its way, and that was the the religious pretensions of civil rulers. The key text here is the Apocalypse – composed, according to the majority of scholars, during the persecution of Christians which occurred towards the end of the reign of the emperor Domitian (d. AD 96).[67] The gradual apotheosis of the emperor was a product of the religious spirit of the time[68] and was soon seen by the State to be an important instrument in consolidating the unity of the empire. A religion which was both exclusivist and supra-national was bound to draw the wrath of the authorities, and from the time of Nero (54–68) Christians began to be persecuted.

A refusal to worship the emperor was probably what immediately occasioned the persecution of Christians under Domitian,[69] and the Apocalypse may be seen as expressing the Christian reaction to this. Schnackenburg comments that it is significant that the Apocalypse ascribes the power of the State which is blasphemously abused, not to God but to Satan. 'The State that deifies itself, the ruler who exceeds his competence and treads the honour of God under his feet, is an instrument of Satan.'[70]

The import of the main material from the New Testament concerning the developing relationships between the new faith and the civic setting in which it was forged has been expressed by Rudolf Schnackenburg in these words: 'The early Christian conception of the state ... remains unharmonised to a certain extent; but Jesus' exhortation to give to Caesar the things that are Caesar's, and to God the things that are God's lies at the point of intersection of the two lines, one leading to God and the other leading to Satan. Romans 13 and Apocalypse 13 are not two mutually exclusive pictures, but rather the two different sides of one coin ...'[71]

Our review of the biblical data was meant to achieve two things. First it was intended to give a sense of what the emergent Christian community made of morality. Their gospel was that a new reign of God's love was begun in the work of Jesus Christ; and this had implications for daily living. For love begets love, and the news that God loves is an invitation to love in return. The central Christian commandment was that we are to love both God and the neighbour. Indications of what this meant in practice are in the teaching and example of Jesus; and what it further meant in the concrete was worked out in the unfolding experience of the earliest Christians. The new Church was concerned with right moral living therefore; but its concern was secondary to its witness to the saving love of God.

Among the specific concerns of the early Christians was that of relating to the civil authority; and a sense of what they made of this was the second objective of our review. The Christians' task was complicated by the Roman dimension of political existence in the territories in which the first churches made their way. It was further complicated by a widespread if temporary belief that the world as they knew it was coming to an end. But what we find on the whole is a readiness to render to Caesar and to God respectively what was seen as belonging to each.

NOTES

1   *Dei verbum*, par. 11. The translation used is as in A. Flannery OP (ed.), *Vatican Council II, The Conciliar and Post-conciliar Documents,* Vol. 1 (hereinafter Fl). Par. 11 of *Dei verbum* is at p. 756.
2   par. 4, Fl 752.
3   Acts 2:24. The translation used is that of the Revised Standard Version.
4   Mk 16, and parallels.
5   Mk 16:19.
6   Lk 22:19. Cf. 1 Cor 11:23-26.
7   Acts 2.
8.   Isa 42.
9   Lk 4:18, 19.
10   Acts 11:36-43.
11   Mt 10:5ff.
12   Mt 28:19, 20.
13   Jn 20:21.
14   *Gospel and Law*, New York, 1951, p. 13.
15   In Bauer (ed.), *Encyclopedia of Biblical Theology*, London, 1976, art. 'Love' (pp. 522–3).
16   See, for example, Isaiah 1.
17   Cf. Bauer, op. cit., art. 'Conversion'.
18   In Bauer, op. cit., 'Kingdom of God', at p. 458.
19   In Bauer, ibid.

20   Mk 1:15.
21   Mt 22:23-40; Mk 12:28-34; Lk 10:25ff.
22   Phil 1:27.
23   e.g. Rom 12, 13; 1 Cor 5-8.
24   Jn 20:31.
25   See for example, A. Robert and A. Tricot, *Guide to the Bible*, Vol. 1 (Paris etc., 1963).
26   J.A. Fitzmyer SJ, 'The Letter to the Romans', *The New Jerome Biblical Commentary*, ed. Brown, Fitzmyer and Murphy, New Jersey: Englewood Cliffs, 1990, p. 830.
27   Rom 11:33, 36.
28   Dodd, op. cit., p. 17.
29   Wayne Meeks, *The Moral World of the First Christians*, London, 1987, p. 13.
30   T.S. Eliot, 'Journey of the Magi'.
31   Meeks, op. cit., p. 13.
32   op. cit., p. 97.
33   Vincent MacNamara, *Faith and Ethics*, Dublin: Gill and Macmillan, 1985, p. 55ff.
34   op. cit.
35   1 Cor 13.
36   1 Cor 1:11.
37   Mt 25:42, 43.
38   *The Moral Teaching of the New Testament*, tr. J. Holland-Smith, London, 1965, p. 198.
39   Acts 11:1-3.
40   Acts 11:18.
41   v. 1.
42   15:6-11.
43   Gal 2:14.
44   Schnackenburg, op. cit., p. 200.
45   ibid.
46   1 Cor 10:20.
47   1 Cor 10:25.
48   v. 27.
49   vv. 28, 29.
50   Mk 12:13-17.
51   D.J. Harrington, 'The Gospel according to Mark', *New Jerome Biblical Commentary*, p. 621.
52   v. 17.
53   Harringtom loc. cit.
54   op. cit., p. 118.
55   op. cit., p. 235.
56   Art. 'Church and State', *A New Dictionary of Christian Ethics*, London, 1987, p. 91.
57   1 Thess 4:10-12.
58   1 Cor 6.
59   Rom 13:1-7.
60   cf. Schnackenburg, op. cit., p. 241.
61   Ibid.
62   Fitzmyer, *New Jerome Biblical Commentary*, p. 864.
63   Ibid., cf. Schnackenburg, op. cit., p. 241.
64   1 Pet 2:13-17.
65   Tit 3:1-3.
66   1 Tim 2:1-3.
67   A.Y. Collins, 'The Apocalypse (Revelation)', *New Jerome Biblical Commentary*, p. 998.
68   Philip Hughes, *A History of the Church*, Vol. 1, London, 1956, p. 157.
69   Schnackenburg, op. cit., p. 243.
70   Ibid., p. 244.
71   Ibid.

An Irish Reader in Moral Theology

7 Who are the Authors of Christian Morality?

James P. Mackey

(*Irish Theological Quarterly*, No. 62, 1997, pp. 297–313, originally a paper delivered at the Annual General Meeting of the Irish Theological Association in May 1996.)

I. THE STATE OF THE QUESTION: THE STATE OF THE CHURCH

Some twenty-seven years ago I edited a volume, published by Michael Gill in Dublin, and entitled *Morals, Law and Authority*. It topped the bestsellers' list (non-fiction) for a couple of weeks. A month or so ago I reviewed for *The Furrow* a volume edited by Sean Mac Réamoinn, entitled *Authority in the Church*. Both volumes were, in part at least, responses to crises caused by official Church teaching on matters of morals, and by swells of negative public reaction to it. The later volume complemented the earlier in significant ways – mainly in its critical analysis of the structures and modes in which Church authority is actually exercised on this island; and in its addition of lay to clerical voices, and of voices from the other churches to those of the Roman Catholic Church – and for this alone, it deserved to top the best-sellers' list even more than its predecessor did. And yet, for all of that, the impression remains that the fundamental debate about morality, Christian morality, and authority has not advanced very much in the quarter of a century between.

Yes, of course, in these years the primacy of charity in moral theology had been secured, and the scriptures had been designated a more basic source of Christian moral insight than the collections and commentaries of the Canon Law, and more basic also than the more abstruse reasonings of that more mysterious source of moral insight known as the Natural Law. And yes, indeed, Vatican II and its aftermath saw bold declarations and even some promising practical moves, all of which seemed to augur well for more widespread and participative involvement in the development and implementation of Christian morality. Collegiality was the watchword in the theory and practice of Church government; and, although government remained as strictly hierarchical, clerical and male in its composition as it had been before Vatican II, the Decree of that Council on 'The Apostolate of the Laity' went very far indeed to correct any implied imbalance in the allocation of responsibility for the progress of Christian morality in the modern world.

For that decree declared quite roundly:
- that lay people should develop the qualities and talents bestowed on them according to their condition in life, that is to say, their status in marriage and

the family, in professional, economic and political life; for in all of this they would be making use of the gifts of the Spirit so liberally poured out especially on them in their places and states for this very purpose;

- that they should bring to the Church community at large their own and the world's problems, and that these should be 'examined and resolved by common deliberation';
- that 'the effort to infuse a Christian spirit into the mentality, customs, laws, and structures of the community is so much the duty and responsibility of the laity that it can never be properly performed by others', and that the laity themselves should set up and run the groups and associations that would promote such an essential and comprehensive lay apostolate.

When one adds the declaration that the renewal of the temporal order is the laity's 'own special obligation', one seems to have a veritable charter for lay initiative and leadership in the whole of the Christian moral enterprise – for that phrase 'the renewal of the temporal order' is broad enough to include all that could pass for morality, Christian or otherwise, at least for this life. Whether there is a segment of Christian morality which is directed to a life other than or after the one we now live, a life so different from this that it requires of those who would one day be born into it and thereafter live it, a quite separate set of moral actions, ideals and prescriptions, is something I incline to doubt, but it would take a much longer paper to consider such a suggestion. It is sufficient to note now that the declarations of just one Vatican II decree promised a very wide-reaching and fulsome answer to our titular question: who are the authors of Christian morality?

And yet ... and yet ... in spite of all that, when push came to shove, and the Christian community in the world faced crucial moral decisions, and moral decisions, moreover, which concerned matters so central to the temporal order as sex, marriage and the family, the implicitly promised and prominent involvement of all those Spirit-filled experts and would-be co-authors of such moral decisions either failed to materialise, or found itself stage-managed or marginalised by a legislating hierarchy.

It would not be a good use of our time to try to tease out in detail the causes of this retrograde process; and it would be entirely invidious to try to apportion the blame for it amongst all the parties involved, since we must each shoulder our own share of the blame.

Undoubtedly the much vaunted primacy of charity in moral theology allowed people to hide behind the sentimental rhetoric of love when hard, concrete moral decisions had to be made on quite specific issues. For there are great practical differences between one kind of loving and another; and the purer and higher my love the more, not the less, anguished must be my choice of criterion and method, and of the ensuing, concrete moral response in any given situation.

If I aspire to high Christian love for the women who share this Roman Catholic Church with me; if I say that this love makes me open, indeed vulnerable to the discrimination these women suffer in life, in Church as well as in state, but I stop well short of facing the issue of the right or, more likely, wrong of excluding them from priesthood and hierarchy, I can well stand accused of sentimental rhetoric, in which the invocation of charity holds less the position of primacy in moral theology, and more the function of a rhetorical smoke-screen designed, at worst, to save my miserable skin from the reaction of those whose often pathetic theological reasoning is calculated to keep these women in their traditional place in the Church. Love, as the poet put it, must be made real in act; it is no substitute for hard moral thinking; in fact it exercises its primacy by driving me towards hard moral thinking and the implementation in act of the best inkling of the good that such hard thinking may yield.

Undoubtedly also, the preferment of Scripture as source over canon or 'natural' law, while unable in itself to deter those fundamentalists who elevate particular moral propositions in Scripture to the status of divine edicts for all times and places, did direct people towards that most promising form of hard, concrete moralising which takes the form of creative imagination operating through story and drama; the parables of Jesus and the drama of his life, death and destiny. *Homo Ludens*, play as our first, and last, means of testing the world and registering its realities, of learning how to do good and to be well, with and within it, and with all others who are within it. The story-teller and the dramatist, above all the dramatist, as the one, then, who best pursues the moralising task in word and text. Yes, indeed; but perhaps some of the people who embraced this better means of Christian moralising too easily forgot that only those gifted in these ways can do it; in the hands of the less gifted, the re-heated stories and the re-enacted dramas lost all the heuristic power of the critical encounter of precise emotions and of hard-held positions, and congealed once more into sentimental evocations of Love.

And there were, no doubt, reasons other than these relative failures to implement good moral theological moves, to help explain our retrograde experience over against the promises we all thought we had been made some thirty-odd years ago. At the very highest levels of Church government a reaction set in, which ran counter to the theory and incipient practice of more collegial and communitarian processes, those we associate, already with a tinge of nostalgia, with Vatican II. The clearest expression of this reactionary tendency is found in Pope John Paul II's encyclical, *Veritatis Splendor*, in which, as it happens, his topic is Christian moral teaching; the first time, he states, that the Magisterium of the Church has set forth its fundamental elements (n.115; although he also states that the recently issued *Cathechism of the Catholic Church* 'contains a complete and systematic exposition of Christian moral teaching', n.5).

The twin leitmotifs of the encyclical are surely these: the essential bond between freedom and truth, and the manner in which Christian morality lives in

Who are the Authors of Christian Morality?   113 the light of Transcendence. Now these are two motifs that strike a chord in the heart of every human being. The bond that binds freedom to truth is sensed by every human being engaged in the moral quest, who feels that the good that is sought is beyond individual whim, and a matter of truth rather than arbitrary human decision. And the often dim perception that the human moral quest is anchored in some truly transcendent prospect and promise for this world, a prospect and promise that are spiritual in nature, is one which is shared, not just by non-Christians, but by many a so-called secular humanist who is otherwise agnostic with respect to all established faiths. And so, even if we prescinded from Pope John Paul II's unique positioning, ability and determination to bring to the whole world a witness to the deepest moral and spiritual truths it most desperately needs and is always prepared to acknowledge, we should expect the encyclical to be addressed to all people of good will, as even *Humanae vitae* was, and to contain such an account of the basic elements of Christian morality as would elicit some serious level of cooperative agreement from Catholics, other Christians and non-Christians alike.

Sad to say, what we get instead is such a self-centred account of the basic elements of Christian morality, that the human moralist in all of us, Christian or not, is quite unable to see what we should surely expect to see, namely, an account of the common basic elements of all morality, enhanced by the Christian experience of faith and life, on the model of grace perfecting nature. Instead, what we see is what can only be called a retarded version of these basic elements of morality, where the retarding factors consist in certain allegedly Christian revelations concerning God's moralising activities carried out through his chosen authorities on earth. The resulting account of the basic elements of morality in the increasingly dominant terms of law and obedience is such as to make the human moralist in all of us demand, in the name of that intrinsic authority to moralise which, as I hope to show, is the birthright and the highest dignity of every human being, that we should all as soon as possible outgrow it. It is well worth focusing, then, on some of the central features of *Veritatis Splendor*, in order to assess the rather unsatisfactory point we have reached, and to try to plot a way forward.

First, the truth, the splendour of which the very title of the encyclical promises to reveal, is insistently and repeatedly glossed as being in the form of norms, prescriptions, in short, formulated laws, universal and immutable. The stage is set for this preferred form of truth by the question-and-answer format of the opening paragraphs. The fundamental question, we are told, is 'what must I do?' and although the decisive answer is given by Jesus, indeed *is* Jesus (n.2), who shines on the Church (here is the splendour), and sends the Church (more of this shortly), that answer is then subdivided, and each subdivision glossed in the manner just indicated. God gives us answers through natural law, and although that is rightly first identified with *recta ratio*, the light of understanding by which all human beings discern the good and the bad (n.12), that too is later unpacked in terms of positive and negative precept the latter are said to be as universal and immutable as the former, and then include, of course, some of the Pope's own favourites, those concerning divorce and 'artificial' contraception (n.51–2). Divine answers to our question in the Old Testament are epitomised in the so-called Ten Commandments. And the crowning work of Christ in answering our question is described as a new law inscribed by the Spirit in our hearts; Jesus reaffirmed the decalogue, and issued negative precepts (the Pope, without analysing Scripture evidence to the contrary, insists that Jesus legislated definitively against divorce), though all of this was given more positive content in his Sermon on the Mount (n.12). Even the Pope's description of conscience itself presents it as that which enables us to detect a law, an objective norm, which holds us to obedience (n.54, 60). The truth, therefore, is primarily and persistently thought of in terms of formulated precepts, promulgated law.

Second, the bond between freedom and truth – the first important leitmotif of the encyclical – despite all the talk of love and personal relationship to God, Jesus and others, yields a view of freedom which is as restrictive and restricting as the view of moral truth to which it corresponds. The freedom described is basically the freedom to obey the laws divinely promulgated. At the very opening of the encyclical there is already the impression that freedom is to be negatively construed; it is such freedom from our inherited darkness of intellect and weakness of will as would enable us to obey the moral laws laid down in the light of reason, in the Old Covenant, and in the coming of Christ. And that of course entails the freedom to disobey, to sin, though not, presumably, to take or not to take the consequences which God has also decreed. The bond between freedom and truth, then, is forged by obedience. And a similarly retarded view of human morality is sustained; for as everyone knows, obedience is the dominant virtue only of those who have not arrived at adult moral stature. For freedom of conscience in this encyclical does not entail freedom to dissent in theory or practice from promulgated moral law: that cannot happen without incurring guilt and the state of sin, unless there is invincible ignorance – we should have to say such a person's conscience was sunk in ignorance rather than free – and since Catholics in particular are constantly made aware of their duty to inform their consciences by reference to the teaching of their hierarchy, it would not at all be easy judge any of them without guilt if they appealed to conscience in disregard of promulgated moral law.

This leads naturally to a third feature of the encyclical's contents which is of interest to us here: the role of the Church in relation to moral freedom and truth. The moral truth in the preferred form of promulgated law which we are free only to obey or disobey, the answer to our fundamental moral question, 'what must I do?' which comes in its definitive, i.e. Christian form in Jesus, comes to the Church on which he shines and which he sends. And although at the outset that assertion is taken to imply that the whole Church as the people of God can offer to everyone some answers which come from Christ's truth in a manner appropriate to each time (n.2), so that vistas of truly cooperative moral enterprise seem to open again before us, repeated glosses upon that assertion once more restrict and constrain the ensuing vision of morality, until it recedes even further towards that retarded stage of moral development already so distressingly obvious from the two previous features of the encyclical's analysis and argument.

The first set of glosses on the theme of the Church as the benificiary of revealed answers to our fundamental moral question are triumphalist indeed, not only in their high praise of the Church's moral teaching and influence, particularly over the last two centuries, but also in the predominantly and harshly negative assessment of moral theory and influence from a world outside the Church from which a more generous and cooperative spirit might acknowledge and expect so much. The Church we are told has contributed continually to a better understanding of human sexuality, of the family, of social, economic, and political life (n.4). By contrast, there is constant carping about trends in 'the world', all loosely indicated in mixum-gatherums of vague references to subjectivism, individualism, atheism, procedures of scientific objectification, technological progress, certain forms of liberalism, and so on, and all somehow connected with some otherwise unidentified tendencies to break the bond between freedom and truth. In fact at one point the Pope accuses some of these currents of modern thought of attributing to conscience 'the status of supreme tribunal of moral judgement which hands down categorical and infallible decisions about good and evil' (n.32). I have long been a student of secular humanism, and I have never seen a serious suggestion about conscience in such terms. Which leads to a second set of glosses on the Church as recipient of all the moral answers. But first one really must pause to remark on the sheer insensitivity of the failure to acknowledge the moral damage done by the Church in both moral theory and practice in every century of its existence, and the often superior moral witness, again in both vision and practice and in every age, that comes from those outside the Church.

In the second set of glosses, the Church is persistently replaced by the Pope and bishops as the ones who propose moral teaching in all the important areas of life; for the task of interpreting divinely revealed moral prescriptions was entrusted to the Apostles and their successors (n.25) as part of their general task of authentically interpreting the word of God (n.27). And is it not significant in this context that this encyclical is addressed, not to all people of good will, nor even to all Christians or all Catholics, but to the bishops of the Church, and that it ends with a section on sanctions to be applied by the bishops to those persons or institutions which show any signs of non-conformity? Even those allegedly errant Catholic moral theologians who depend upon human reason in their moralising, but without due dependence in turn, the Pope alleges, upon divine revelation of specific and determined moral content, are ipso facto, and for that very reason, involved in denial of specific doctrinal competence on the part of the magisterium (n.37). The Church, then, for all practical purposes of moral teaching, is the Magisterium.

Put these three features of the encyclical's argument together, then – the preference for moral truth in the form of universal and immutable laws; the persistent evocation of obedience at the opening and close of the encyclical and in all its major parts, as the primary moral element which for all of us relates our freedom to the truth; and the constant gloss on the Church, the repository of revealed moral answers, as consisting primarily of the hierarchy – and there can be little doubt left about the fact that this encyclical is a statement and a stout defence of all that is reactionary in the Church since the promises of Vatican II concerning openness to the world and involvement of the whole People of God were made, and began to be realised so very tentatively.

The resulting tragedy for the world at large is likely to be less than that for the Church; although any tragedy for the Church's own moral witness is bound to affect the world at large eventually also. This Pope [John Paul II] on his pilgrim way has constantly offered the world a sense of the reality and objectivity of moral truth, particularly that truth which most closely concerns the justice and dignity which is the birthright of every human being; on his journeys he has constantly borne witness to the transcendent goal and ground of human moral striving; and for these two things so many perceptive people, in the Two-Thirds World in particular, are profoundly grateful to him. And they will remain grateful, despite the fact that they recognise, sometimes with a rueful smile, that he treats his own flock as moral children whose main access to the truth is still through simple obedience; that he gets some of his particular moral prescriptions, concerning contraception for instance, quite wrong; that in his internal dealings in the Church he pictures the relationship of God to humans on the model of legislator-judge-sanctioner, and that this is a very poor model for the Transcendent in which every moral human being would dearly want to believe.

We need a quite radical critique, then, if we are to counter those moves and influences which have tended to retard the progress of the moral task in the Church; and if we are to redeem the earlier promise. We need to go deeper than the analyses mentioned at the outset – the analyses of morals, law and authority in the contemporary Church – we need to go to the roots of morality itself. We need to see morality itself as a process that belongs to the very essence of being human; and since it is certainly not confined to Christians, we need to examine its very nature and structure in order to find out who are its authors, and how they are so; and then go on to discover its distinctively Christian form – if, as we assume, there is such a distinctive form – and then, and only then, try to say who are the authors of Christian morality, and how they are so, and how, if many, they are to relate to each other in the Church, and to the authors of morality in the world at large. That is, of course, a tall order, and one which would need a small book to fill it, rather than a lecture or two. All that can be offered here, in the time-honoured fashion of theses nailed to real or imaginary doors, is a series of key propositions concerning the nature of morality, its Christian form, and its authors. I did develop these themes in a book called *Power and Christian Ethics*, but that is too tedious a book to recommend to friends or even to mere acquaintances, and the themes would in any case be better developed cooperatively in a series such as that to which Seán Mac Réamoinn's *Authority in the Church* belongs.

II. SOME THESES CONCERNING THE NATURE OF (CHRISTIAN) MORALITY AND THE IDENTITY OF ITS AUTHORS

1.   As our Scholastic mentors used to tell us in their dry, analytic fashion, morality itself is the product of the practical intellect, although theories about the nature of morality, such as the one on which we are now engaged, are products of the speculative intellect. And the practical intellect refers simply to the human mind as it is actually engaged in acting, in doing. Doing what? Everything and anything, all that belongs to the praxis of being with others, of living with others in our common world. We are, in essence, as Heidegger would say, a thrown project; and the world into which, already in the womb, we find ourselves thrown, is itself a great, all-encompassing project. Our first and most elementary description of the very nature of morality, then, is this: it consists in mind-impregnated cooperative praxis.

A fuller analysis of this first thesis would require two large elucidations and one general implication, each of which can but be noted here.

1.1   The first elucidation is this: it seems that a certain level or kind of consciousness is required for that mind-impregnated praxis which would count as morality. This is a kind or level of consciousness intrinsically characterised by transcendence. That is to say, negatively, no particular content or number of particular contents can exhaust it; more positively, it can look beyond (that is what transcendence means) any content it enjoys, and envisage something further, different, other. Some link this innate transcendence with a feature of consciousness known as reflexivity, self-consciousness. Because I can make my very consciousness *and* its contents the 'object' of my consciousness, in that reflexive (bending-back-over-) act known as self-consciousness, I transcend both self-as-project and its interrelated wider reality-project, both as currently known, and can therefore envisage for both further possibilities, which are in principle limitless, infinite. Hence I, together with all conscious beings at my level of consciousness or higher, am aware of my self-project, the local projects, in which that is implicated, and the widest project of the world which forms, as Marx put it, its inorganic body, as entities or a comprehensive entity to be suffered, maintained, aided, rejected, resisted, altered, in so far as any or all of this is possible.

1.2 The second elucidation is this: within that general consciousness of a self-project which is always implicated with other reality-projects and indeed with the encompassing world-project in which I inevitably participate with all other entities, a particular kind of self-project is always as central as my own self-project and just as indelibly focused. It is the self-project of another self, or selves, of the same or a similar level of consciousness as my self. Whether it is the sensed presence of such an other self that enables me to be conscious of my own self in that peculiar experience which I call self-consciousness; or whether the opposite is the case, namely, it is my intrinsic constitution as reflexive or self consciousness that enables me to detect or recognise the presence to me of other selves at the same level of mind or consciousness; I do not know. What I do know is that I cannot reach so deep in my present experience, or so far back in my memory, as to find myself without the presence of a comparable other, without my awareness of being an integral part of the conscious project of a community of at least two. As inevitably as I participate in the general reality-project I call world, I participate in this cooperatively in a community. Morality, then, is a communally structured mind-impregnated praxis, by its nature.

1.3 The general implication is this: that if one follows the path already laid down by these two elucidations, if one continues to analyse that admittedly complex but yet most intimately known centre of the whole reality-project which we inevitably occupy, all the features of moral living, of morality in its primary form, will reveal themselves. The project I call myself, of which I am conscious, is already a driven thing, striving according to its nature and structure, for being and for well-being. So are the other projects of which I am concomitantly conscious (for I am never conscious of myself except in the process of my self being conscious of other projects). And all of these, first myself and those other persons with whom I am always in communion, then the local reality projects of my situation, and finally the whole interconnected and encompassing reality-project which I call world or universe; all of these reveal themselves to me as I cooperate in and with them; in fact, in revealing not only their present achievement but their possibilities, their limitless promise, they shine for me. This is the shining, the splendour, of the Pope's title; it is the hallmark of beauty, and to the drivenness already experienced in my innermost self it adds a drawnness which Plato hypostatised as Eros. This Eros, which drives and draws all things, takes the form of instinct in levels of consciousness lower than the highest human level; but at the highest human level it takes the form of the sense of obligation, that is a driven-drawnness, not to biologically pre-determined results, but to projects envisioned always with their aura of further possibility and limitless promise; and hence operated and cooperated, not merely physically or chemically or instinctively, but creatively.

Consequently, all of these interconnected projects which constitute reality as we know it – individual, communal, local, universal – are values. *Ens et bonum convertuntur*, as the perennial philosophy put it. In more homely terms, since reality in its local and universal reaches, as we know it and in the only way we can know it, is person-centred project, every entity and event that constitutes it is a value, for each can contribute or take from the well-being of all. My reading of this paper in this hall, and your hearing it, is not just an empirical fact which can be verified; it is a value in which we ought to be engaged as we are. Moral value is just as much a feature of reality as is, say, atomic structure. There is no real dichotomy between 'ought' and 'is'; only a simple-minded empiricist like Hume would think otherwise. What I actually do is as much what I ought to do (what I do in relatively free creativity under the influence of Eros), as is anything I think I should do tomorrow.

2. Since morality, then, in its primary and universal form consists in all of those projects of which reality is made up, precisely in so far as each and all are person-centred, that is to say, accepted, sustained, rejected, attacked, or altered for better or worse by self-conscious beings, the question as to who are the authors of morality quite easily finds its first and most basic answer. The primary authors of morality are all persons who are engaged of their nature in all of those manifold and interconnected projects that make up reality in its most localised as well as its most universal form, in so far as they are so engaged. Hence, to take one localised form of a reality project as an example, the primary authors of the morality of married life are married people: it is for them, and for them alone that marriage is a communally structured, mind-impregnated praxis, a project towards their well-being which engages their sense of obligation in relatively free creativity. No others can hold the primacy in the authorship of the morality of marriage which these hold; although, as we shall see shortly, there are other, secondary ways in which non-married people can contribute to the morality of marriage. And if there is a special dimension to marriage as a result of the partners to the marriage being Christians, then the primary authors of the Christian morality of marriage are married Christians. This is the deep, philosophical ground for the necessary truth of that more general

statement of Vatican II's Decree on the Apostolate of the Laity: 'the effort to infuse a Christian spirit into the mentality, customs, laws, and structures of the community, is so much the duty and responsibility of the laity *that it can never be properly performed by others.*'

3.   How is morality in this primary form communicated or taught? How, in other words, do its primary authors or makers become authorities in the lives of others? Is there any room at all for such authority in morals? Of course, there is; but it must be exercised primarily on a model that accords with the primary form of morality itself; a model for which the term 'example' is perhaps too slight, and which could best be conceived as the master-apprentice relationship, in which the master has shown significant mastery of the area of morality in question. Obedience enters here as an element corresponding to the authority of the master practitioner; but it is a kind of obedience that accords with the moral stature of the apprentice and with the primary form of morality of which each and every agent is an author. It is the obedience of the apprentice willingly submitting herself to an imitation of the master; not a slavish imitation, but one which is expected from the outset to show increasing signs of its own creativity. At this point I usually express my appreciation of the work of an international group of developmental psychologists, led by my Edinburgh colleague, Colwyn Trevarthen, who have shown that the human neonate, on its entry into the world is already operating consciously in interpersonal terms with significant adults, and that it actually takes the initiative in 'wheedling culture out of them', as Trevarthen puts it; the human neonate, even at the pre-verbal stage, is already a communally structured, mind-impregnated little project initiating itself into a certain subjection to the influence and direction of those who already enjoy some mastery of life. But this is a very different kind of obedience to that which the Pope has in mind, the assent in theory and practice to an imposed regulation with its sanctions attached. The latter is a very secondary form of obedience, which has a minor part to play in the moral project, but which should never be mistaken for one of the basic elements of morality at any stage.

4.   There are other, secondary and derivative forms of morality; other forms in which the moral project is carried forward; and, correspondingly, there are other, secondary forms of moral authorship and authority. These are three or more, depending on the categorisation adopted; and they are all in general due to the fact that the human mind or spirit is self-conscious. In short, that same reflexive ability which enables the mind to survey its own contents in the very course of praxis, thus to see an aura of possibility and promise beyond the status quo, and consequently to exercise that creativity which is of the essence of the whole moral project of reality; that same ability can be exercised more reflectively still: outside the immediate

context called praxis, I call to mind representations of some of the interlinked reality-projects that I experience, and in this more reflective and detached mode I try to envision their creative possibilities and promises.

4.1   The first of those secondary and derivative forms in which the moral project is carried forward, the one closest to the primary form of morality itself, is the work of imagination. I do not mean imagination in the sense in which some faculty-psychologies distinguish it from intelligence, as something more childish and errant. I mean imagination as Wordsworth understood it, as 'Reason in its most exalted mood'; in the sense of *intelligere/intus legere*, the ability to *see into* (read into) the project of self, of other, and of further related events in the world, to *envision* their inner dynamism and larger promise. The immediate result may be an artistic creation of some kind; in which case I become a moral authority for others, not because art is a moralising process in itself – *ars gratia artis* – but because I thus enable others to envision this transformation of some part of the project that is reality, and thus give impetus and direction to their own moral enterprise, if they wish to take it. The most comprehensive instance of this secondary and indirect form of moral authorship and authority is that of the drama. It is no accident that it shares the term 'play' with the earliest means by which the neonate apprentice learns to negotiate that moral project which is the world. ('Play with me, daddy.') As we know from all the great practitioners of drama, literature and the other arts, it is not necessary to be directly engaged in life in the project envisaged in order to make this contribution: celibate authors have had some of the best insights into marriage. But it is necessary to have those unusual gifts of the imagination which recognised artists have, in order to exercise at all this secondary authorship and this authority, at one remove now from that foundational and primary authorship which is the source of all morality.

4.2   A related, and perhaps even more secondary way, in which one can contribute to the overall moral project, while still in the reflective mode detached from the primary form of moral authorship in praxis, is by engaging in what is called the morality of virtue. Much favoured by Christian moralists these days, this concentrates on those habitual patterns of behaviour called virtues, and on such patterns of these in turn as would constitute a concrete picture of a good moral character operating in the world. 'The just man justices,' as the poet put it; or, as Aristotle said, the criterion of justice is the just man. The composition of such character-pictures requires rather less ability than the genuine artist possesses; and they tend to be correspondingly stereotyped and lacking in formative influence. Some would add here a third secondary form of moralising. This is related to a morality of virtue because some of the names of the virtues recur in this form also – I mean the evocation and description of moral ideals, such as justice and love itself. But it is necessary to pass quickly to a final form of secondary moralising, very secondary indeed and the most detached of all with respect to that communally structured mind-impregnated praxis in which our primary moral authorship and authority consists. I mean moralising in the form of law.

4.3   Laws are propositions of a prescriptive kind, which of their nature aim at a certain universality in application. They are produced, not by the imagination as *intelligere*, but by the analytic/abstractive powers of the mind, which surveys the rich diversity of human action in the world, and reduces much of it to definitions, defined categories of action, to be imposed or, more usually, proscribed. Now this very secondary and detached form of carrying forward the moral project has two very substantial drawbacks, which should be enough to dissuade anyone who would like to think of it as the primary form of morality, or a primary form for the exercise of moral authorship or authority; but it does have one very practical and necessary use which gives it an inescapable if severely restricted role in the overall moral project.

First, law achieves its universality of application – it never achieves immutability; all legal systems need constant reform – at the cost of such an abstract definition of a class of human actions that its application to the always concrete and complex human activity in which we all engage needs a further exercise of judgement before we know what to do or not to do (what makes contraception artificial, and not 'natural'; which instances of killing constitute murder?). In societal terms this involves a judicial system designed to determine guilt or innocence in individual cases in which the law is alleged to have been broken.

Second, its very prescriptive form tends to elicit that kind of obedience which reduces its subjects to the lowest tolerable level of moral stature; and that before the sanctions with which it is often accompanied are taken into account.

Yet these very drawbacks fit law for the role just mentioned, at the same time as they severely restrict the playing of this role and the exercise of this function to a minor and conditioned contribution in the overall pursuit of the human moral project. For that moral project requires for its pursuit freedom from those threats to life and the supports of life which are posed in any society by the unruly. Hence, in order that the general human moral project proceed, it is necessary to prescribe, and perhaps more often to proscribe, certain kinds of conduct, so that essentially communal human cooperation may be unhindered and secure. Negative prescriptions such as the law against murder provide examples here, but also positive legal prescriptions, such as divorce legislation which is designed to prevent further damage to the lives of partners and children in relevant circumstances. In short, the exercise of legislative power, particularly if enforced by sanctions, is designed to protect the perimeters of that larger communal life which comprises the main moral project of our kind, but it never constitutes the substance of that project and can never become its paradigm.

It is the business of the state through its legislature to provide such legislation, its supports and sanctions. It is doubtful if a Church should ever allocate such business to itself; a Christian Church in any case. It would certainly be a grave mistake for anyone to model morality as such on law of this nature; as it would to conceive of an alleged divine revelation of the answer to our moral quest as consisting of promulgated laws. Such inherently reformable legal systems have always been and always are the product of organised human societies, to serve the restricted purposes for which they are designed.

5. What, then, of Christian morality? What needs to be added to this general account of morality in its primary and derivative forms in order to cover its specifically Christian character?

5.1 The relationship between morality and religion in general is too vast a subject for this paper, but this may be said. The relationship emerges, I would say naturally and inevitably, from within morality; it does not come upon morality from any vantage point outside morality, and certainly not by way of divine dictation of regulations. At the heart of morality itself, and a matter of its very essence, is a sense of that communion with other selves as the centre of a cooperative, creative process which makes up reality as we know it. The sense of transcendence which is intrinsic to each self moves it quite naturally to wonder how deep and high, how original and final, is this person-centeredness of the universe. We do not move in this vast universe at all without an experience of the interpersonal dimension, which is instanced, but never exhausted, by those named and numbered persons who are closest to us; and no region of real-ity in which we move is without traces of creativity inviting us to cooperate, making us feel addressed and responsible. If morality, as

An Irish Reader in Moral Theology

our opening description of it suggests, is coextensive with reality itself as person-centred project, then it has a spiritual dimension; and in so far as we are enabled in our growing moral experience to believe, or even to hope, that that spiritual dimension belongs to its first origin and final goal, we are already in the realm of religion; we are already on the brink of religious language, already anticipating a sense of the limitlessness of moral aim and ambition which can have the most immediate, practical effects on our dealings in this life with 'all poor foolish things that pass away' (as Yeats might say, for in these he too was able to detect, 'eternal beauty wandering on her way').

5.2 Correspondingly, the Christian version of religious faith is incarnational in essence. Its fundamental claim is that the character of the personal centre at the source of the universe is more closely known, indeed historically speaking definitively revealed, from the life, death and destiny of one Joshua or Jehoshua of Nazareth.

From this foundational Christian centre the more concretely delineated character of creator and creation, and consequently of that creativity in which the essence of reality as project consists, can be variously desribed: as unconditional grace, for example; or, if we see the cross rather than the conception of Jesus as the high point of incarnation (as Paul does in his reference to 'the Word of the cross' in I Cor 1:18), as self-emptying love. And the most concrete and practical implications can then emerge for the way we are to behave in all areas of life, in family, society, and the world at large. We shall not judge others and treat them according to their narrow moral deserts; but rather as God's sun warms alike the good and the bad, and his rain refreshes the virtuous and the wicked – unconditional grace; and we shall in general seek the fulfilment of our lives in pouring them out to others, rather than absorbing everything into our inflated selves.

But the important point here is this: this specific version of the deepest moral truth to which we are thereby given access is in the form of a life or a way; its transmission is through a living of that life, a walking in that way, by would-be followers of Jesus; its first derivative expression or, better, evocation, is ritual drama (primarily the Eucharist), and story. Other derivative expressions, secondary formulations of that life, occur also from the beginning: think of Paul forming lists of virtues into character portraits for Christians; and of the odd attempt at legislative formula, as when Matthew legislates for divorce (Matthew 19:9), presumably out of discontent with the laxity of some current law in existing society. The specific character of Christian morality, therefore, entails no specific differences in the account already given of the primary form of morality itself, and of the primary and secondary, derivative forms of moral authorship and authority.

As far as the primary authorship of Christian morality is concerned, then, and the primary authority in developing and passing it on, all who live the Christian life under the influence of the Spirit of Jesus, breathed on all, according to John's gospel, from his cross, all of us from Pope to peasant, all are on all fours together. Secondary forms of authorship and authority may be exercised by those who have the relevant gifts – parable tellers, gospel writers, creators and developers of ritual dramas, and the more abstract analysts of patterns of virtue and moral ideal. But authorship and authority in these forms must always be exercised in such a manner as to let their derivative and secondary nature be realised and be seen to be realised. For all such forms of contribution to the moral task are derived by means of a more detached reflection on the primary form of morality which, in the case of a Christian morality, consists in the lives of Christians. Furthermore, these secondary forms of imaginative and intellectual construction must allow themselves to be proven true (or false) in the course of these same Christian lives, in the experience of life and life more abundant in which they result (or life more stunted and threatened).

And all of this is all the more true of that final and most derivative form in which Christian moral authorship and authority may be exercised, the formulation and imposition of positive law, as it is called. If it is necessary for a Christian Church to engage in this at all – and it will surely be necessary only if the secular authority in societies, to whose remit it primarily belongs, fails significantly in the task – it will be all the more necessary that the secondary and derivative nature of this be realised and be seen to be realised in the terms stated above (and above all the terms of verification, as, for example, in the case of recent regulations concerning contra-ception); and it is additionally necessary in this case that such legislation be restricted to such basic areas of moral conduct as are necessary to secure the peace and security of life in society as such. Undoubtedly, in the age of Caesaro-Papism, during the long centuries of Christendom, Church officers assumed hugely exaggerated degrees of this kind of power of jurisdiction. That is an accident of western history, and has little to do either with the founding of the Church or with the nature of morality, Christian or otherwise. Hence any attempt to exercise this power of jurisdiction

An Irish Reader in Moral Theology

which does not reveal its derivation from the Christian lives of the primary authors of Christian morality, and which fails to submit itself in turn to the verification of Christian living, will result simply in the diminution of the authority of the office of the one who so acts. We are seeing some of the clearest examples of such loss of hierarchical authority in moral matters in the Roman Catholic Church at the present time, a loss which no amount of lecturing on obedience is in the least likely to reverse. Which leads me to remark on the obvious: 'it is obvious that the account of moral authorship and authority offered above is quite at variance with that which is both stated and implied in *Veritatis Splendor*. The differences between this paper and *Veritatis Splendor* in the accounts of moral authorship no doubt derive ultimately from deeper differences in the way in which relationships between freedom, splendour and truth are construed. So let me conclude with a reminder of the manner in which these relationships are construed here.

For freedom substitute the more comprehensive term 'creativity'. My self-conscious self transcends every present content and so envisages it to be repeatable and changeable, and it is driven to secure such continuity and change for the better in ways to which it can set no prior limit. In my first and always most basic apprehension of it, reality is this person-centred project towards well-being; good, better, best. *Ens et bonum convertuntur*. But then also in my most basic apprehension, I sense another like myself, not reducible to my imagining; on the contrary, active in constituting my sense of self by that very irreducibility, its own autonomous being and structure and project intact in the most intimate reaches of that interpersonal relationship which is foundational for both of us; and further, if only through this now communally structured project which we are, I sense with the other, structures of a wider reality given simultaneously to the both or many of us, and so irreducible to our individual imaginings, requiring from us acknowledgment of its own autonomous being and structures, demanding of us in its very being-for-us, the kind of relationship that is called truth. *Ens et verum convertuntur*. And finally, in my most basic apprehension, I see these structures of self, other and wider reality, not as static things in this most intimate relationship, but as dynamic things, each and all surrounded by that aura of past, present and possible transformation, like a light that shines from some high ideal, like a beauty that draws me along a way wider and steeper and longer than that along which my lonely drivenness could ever move me. *Ens et pulchrum convertuntur*. And so the circle is closed upon that comprehensive account of reality, of Being, which the scholastics so well understood through the trinity of transcendent characters: goodness, truth and beauty.

NOTE

This paper was given as the opening lecture of the annual conference of the Irish Theological Association in May 1996. One particular criticism of its content, voiced by one respondent, would be noted: this was to the effect that my reading of *Veritatis Splendor* concentrated so excusively on impressions of obedience as that which related our moral freedom to a transcendent truth in the form of law, that all reference to contexts in which the Pope invoked the counsels of Christian perfection were buried from sight, and the whole encyclical was then convicted of a more restricted view of Christian morality than that which the Pope in fact managed to present. I happily acknowledge that the reading of any complex document involves the choice of a perspective within the document from which the rest of the document is interpreted, and that different readers will see, and interpret from, different perspectives. But I would say this in defence of what I believe to be the dominant perspective in this document from which the whole of it is to be interpreted:

Look closely again at the sections of the encyclical in which the perfection to which Jesus calls us, and hence the 'counsels of perfection', are treated (nn.16–24, e.g.). The discussion is framed by the story of Jesus' discourse on marriage which ends in the reference to celibacy, both in Matthew 19 (only obedience is missing from the triad of monastic perfection; and that is hardly missing from the encyclical as a whole). The point of invoking perfection in this section seems to be, first, to demonstrate 'the openness of the *commandments* and their orientation towards the horizon of the perfection proper to the Beatitudes' (n.16), and 'to bear witness to the fundamental relationship between freedom and divine law' (n.17).

8   Moral Renewal Through Renewed Moral Reasoning

D. Vincent Twomey

(*Josephinum Journal of Theology*, Vol. 10, No. 2, Summer 2003, pp. 210–29.)

Moral theology seems to be a peripheral activity within an increasingly secular society. Existentially, moral theology seems to have become irrelevant. This has not a little to do with the prevailing ethos of society in the western world, characterised as it is by moral relativism, which, due to its (mostly practical) denial of objectivity,[1] especially regarding truth in the ethical realm, renders a search for moral principles redundant. But the increasing irrelevance is also probably due, within the Church at least, to two not unrelated factors: the fall off in confessional practice and the prevalence of a kind of moral theology that seems increasingly more like secular ethics than theology. One could also mention the singularly 'dull' nature of much writing in moral theology, due not least to the internal, unfortunately necessary, but potentially sterile, debates on moral theology since the Council.[2] Once the preserve of clerics, for whom moral theology was a requisite for their professional activities, in particular for hearing confessions, moral theology today rightly strives to become another discipline in the academy, studied and taught more by lay experts than by clerics. It is increasingly seen to be of merely 'academic' interest, using the term in the pejorative sense of the word. Since moral philosophers increasingly dominate the (rather limited) public discussion of contentious moral issues,[3] moral theologians, eager to join in that debate, tend to adopt the presuppositions of the secular ethicists, and so render moral theology quite simply peripheral. Some reflection on the task of moral theology seems to be required. But the articulation of that task will depend on one's understanding of (a) what morality is and (b) what is meant by moral theology.

THE RECOVERY OF VIRTUE

Recent developments in philosophy and (to a lesser extent) theology[4] have led to the reappraisal of morality primarily in terms of virtue (including its preconditions). The recovery of the original, Aristotelian/Thomistic notion of virtue as the context for moral reflection, it seems to me, has yet to make any significant impact on the mainstream of the academic discipline of moral theology. The latter is still dominated by the rival schools of a teleological approach (proportionalism) or the deontological approach (principles).[5] This is despite the fact that the methodology of its moral section of the *Catechism of the Catholic Church* (Section III, Part I) is determined by an understanding of morality arising from its nature as virtue, a fact that few commentators seem to have appreciated when it was first published. And even today, there is little reflection among theologians on such central themes of 'virtue ethics'.[6] These include the role of the passions in morality[7] (a subject not even mentioned in recent handbooks of moral theology) and the essential political or communal context of human behaviour (incorporating the main tenet of Catholic Social Teaching into fundamental moral theology).[8] These are areas of study that, it seems to me, moral theology might address with profit. Be that as it may, the *Catechism* also helps implicitly to answer the question regarding the specific nature of Christian morality by its recovery of the New Law, the life of grace, including its relationship with natural law (which grace presupposes and perfects).[9] Grace, it might be said, is a subject in need of immediate attention by moral theologians, if moral theology is to recover its authentic theological dimension.[10] But the most important aspect of the recovery of virtue for moral theology is the recovery of the original teleology of Aquinas, namely beatitude as the goal of all human behaviour. Like the manualist theologians, their successors, be they deontologists or proportionalists, could in a sense be said to be preoccupied by sin – the former in defining it, the latter in trying, if not to erase, at least to mollify sin. Virtue ethics makes happiness the central concern of morality.

Moral theology may be defined as the systematic reflection in the light of revelation, carried out within the existential context of the Church, on the nature of human behaviour and the specific moral demands arising from our human nature now transformed in Christ. But what is its standing? I will argue that moral theology is by nature peripheral, though indispensable – once we understand the precise nature of that peripheral position in Church and society. In order to locate the essential, as distinct from the existential, 'peripheral' standing of moral theology within the Church and society, we must take a closer look at the nature of virtue. Following Aristotle, we will sketch how virtues are typically acquired and then take a closer look at the nature of moral knowledge, practical reason.

MORAL DEVELOPMENT AND ITS PRECONDITIONS

To learn how to play football or play a musical instrument, or to acquire any other practical skill, a knowledge of the rules or theory quite evidently will not suffice. One must simply tog out and try to play the game, or pick up the violin and start scratching the strings. The same applies to any other activity, such as music. The very shape of the violin the aspiring young violinist places under her chin for the first time is likewise the product of a tradition, not to mention the musical scores, composers, and master performers who invite imitation, no matter how absurd the comparison between child and virtuoso performer may seem. And that is what

An Irish Reader in Moral Theology

training effectively amounts to: initiation (by way of imitation of the skills of others) into a tradition, and so into a community and vice versa, whose top exponents (models) usually extend the range and depth of that traditon. In other words, inherent capacity for a particular skill means little without the structures needed to develop them, as talent only flourishes within a living tradition with its rules, regulations, standards – and indeed authorities, both in the material sense of the best exponents of that particular skill and in the formal sense of some decision-making body to make and interpret the rules within that living tradition.

The first point to note, then, is that in order to develop any inherent human capacity or talent, we need institutions, namely those structured communities which, determined by needs of the nature of that particular activity or practice, make it possible for individual talents to flourish. The structures characteristic of those institutions emerge from and embody the particular activity for which the institution exists. With regard to specific talents, institutions are, in the first place, communities of interest with a history and tradition, which provide standards and models for contemporary practice and find a quasi-legal expression in rules and regulations that are subject to constant review. That process of review arises from the needs of the practice, the experience gained (tradition), the achievements of its greatest exponents, and the demands arising from new possibilities opened up not only by external conditions but by the very skill of the best achievers. These needs and demands are subject to widespread discussion (and reflection), leading to a resolution by a duly constituted, authoritative body according to previously agreed procedures. Let us take a closer look at this process.

Inherent human capacities or talents can only be developed by *practising* them within those structures, or more correctly, institutions, which are the *sine qua non* for every human *praxis*. Thus, the first step is always a submission to the authority of the tradition, embodied as an ideal in the shape of a particular game or artistic activity. Empirically, tradition is embodied in the trainer or teacher who teaches the rules of the game not by theoretical discourse or even reciting the rules, but showing us how to play, by providing a model. He also corrects one's faults and gives approval of one's performance, usually by external punishment and awards (various penalties, examination results, prizes, etc.). Implicit in all this is submission to whatever authoritative body makes the final decisions (regarding the written and unwritten rules of the game and their interpretation). In time, and only after constant repetition, does the neophyte eventually internalise the practice (the rules or inherent principles of the game or artistic activity) so that the practice becomes an end in itself, something we enjoy for its own sake and exercise with a certain spontaneity. As a result, we can say that I *am* what I practice: an athlete or a musician. The practice has become second nature to me, an acquired disposition. Depending on the quality of one's talent and the opportunities at one's disposal to pursue a given activity, but also on the quality of the more immediate structures available, athletes or musicians or scholars continue to develop their talents, improve their 'spontaneous' performances. Each actual performance, in turn, is always at the same time unique and unrepeatable, not just an automatic repetition – until one has reached the height of one's powers. Furthermore, one can at any moment 'miss the mark', fail. The object of the whole exercise, from the first submission to the authority of the tradition to the creative interpretation of the concert violinist or the spectacular yet always unexpected performance of the top athletes at their best – true *virtuosos* – is the achievement of excellence in that particular field. The Greek word for it is *aretê*, which the Romans called *virtus*, that (inner) strength and excellence which engenders *autarkeia*.[11] Discussions regarding changing the rules of a sport or theories of music are in a real sense quite peripheral to the acquisition of excellence; yet they are essential to the development of a sport (or art form or any other genuine human *praxis*) demanded by changing circumstances and the result of the greatest exponents, who explore and extend its inherent possibilities.

The same applies *mutatis mutandis* to virtue in the strict sense of the term. Moral theology or philosophy are thus by nature remote from moral behaviour. And yet, they are indispensable. Before we try to refine our understanding of how this is so, enough has been said for us to draw some initial conclusions about the nature of moral theology as such, namely the systematic analysis of human behaviour in the light of faith.

At the root of all morality is a vision of what it is to be human, an anthropology that articulates the truth or purpose of human existence in all its fullness. This is where faith first enters in, faith here understood as the truth about human existence as revealed by God: God our origin, God our goal, and God as the means to achieve that goal; Christ the way, the truth and the life. That goal or *telos* is what in the final analysis determines what is good, good for us. Good actions are those that lead us to our goal by transforming us from within so that we achieve the transcendent fullness of our humanity, thus satisfying our deepest desire for happiness or beatitude. Faith is handed on in that structured community or institution we call Church through the entire sacramental matrix of its life, within which theology has its own limited but indispensible role arising from the nature of faith as ever seeking understanding.[12] Theology, reflecting on human experience in the light of faith, ensures that the vision of our ultimate end remains fresh in our memory, igniting our deepest desire, and that the light thrown on human existence by revelation finds its contemporary expression in terms of the cultural conditions peculiar to each place and generation.

The analogy between virtue in the strict sense of the term and any partial human excellence such as sport and music, which I have chosen for the basis for my exposition, does not only limp rather badly. Like every analogy, in the final analysis it collapses altogether, since the source and ultimate goal of human excellence is not human but divine. And it is, perhaps, in trying to articulate in the light of revelation the deepest yearnings of the human heart amid the tragedy of

An Irish Reader in Moral Theology

our (sinful) human condition that moral theology might in time rediscover its authentic social relevance and be less existentially peripheral.[13] Thus, one possible starting point for moral theology might be sympathetic attention to the world of contemporary (in particular post-Holocaust) literature. Such attention to contemporary literature may well be an essential prerequisite for doing moral theology, but as a starting point it would seem to be more suited to philosophical ethics, well illustrated by the way Martha Nussbaum incorporates literature and social studies into her philosophical enquiries. Others might argue that a more appropriate starting point for theological ethics should be an examination of our *telos* as human beings, eternal beatitude, following the lead of Aristotle and Aquinas (but now, once again, the *Catechism of the Catholic Church*). This, I think, would be true of any systematic treatise on the subject, which is beyond the scope of this essay. Our limited concern, I think, might best be served by concentrating on another forgotten aspect of *arete*, namely the hallmark of the accomplished athlete and virtuous person alike. And this is spontaneity. According to Aquinas,[14] the distinguishing mark of virtue is doing good 'with promptitude and with pleasure' (*delectabiliter et prompte*).

Virtus enim est spontaneus in bonum bonae voluntatis assensus[15]

Our spontaneous reactions reveal our true character, who we are. In the words of one Pre-Socratic quoted by St Thomas, 'mastery reveals the man'.[16] Virtue ethics is essentially about human character, about our integrity as human beings. The virtues are our acquired predispositions to do what is upright and just as well as respond to good and evil with whatever level of passion is appropriate. Virtuous action and feeling thus become 'second nature' to us, second nature, because our 'first' nature as such is incomplete.[17] To be human is to act and feel in harmony with reason, but this is not automatic. Animals are born with their behavioural instincts intact. Humans do not (with one important exception I will mention later). They have to acquire them. The fully human 'instincts', we might say, are the various virtues: habitual dispositions to feel and behave rightly, i.e. in harmony with our goal as humans, and make us good people. The failure to acquire virtue results in dispositions of a negative nature: vice, weakness, or malice.

The raw material, if you wish, out of which these dispositions (good and bad) are fashioned is that unique mixture peculiar to the 'rational animal': sense and sensibility, intellect and freedom on the one hand, and, on the other, the more primal instincts of self-preservation embedded in those 'passions' which make us creatures of flesh and blood. But the actual fashioning of such dispositions involves a long process of education and formation by which the child learns from its interaction with its human environment, its parents and family, or their substitutes. Parents are the initial embodiment of a historically formed political and cultural community whose traditions they *nolens volens* mediate to their children. What is natural to the animal – its instinctual pattern of behaviour so that it achieves its end – must be acquired over time by rational animals, so that we can be said to be truly human.[18]

Only in a limited, though important, way can morals be 'taught', namely primarily, though not exclusively, by clarifying or correcting what has or has not been already 'caught' in interaction with the child's moral authorities (parents, teachers, role models – and peers). Imitation is the source of moral growth. But moral theory, i.e. systematic reflection on the nature of morality, on the demands of the various virtues, is a condition *sine qua non* for its flourishing and perfection, and this for two interrelated reasons. In the first place, systematic moral reflection sharpens our intellectual (or, better, prudential) potentiality to make the right moral judgement in particular situations, just as study of the theory of music opens up new possibilities to the accomplished musician, or literary criticism acts as a self-corrective faculty to the writer or poet. In the second place, reflection – both systematic and informal – is also needed at the public level (both in Church and society) to inform that public discourse and debate which modulates public attitudes and values, and influences both the formulation and the interpretation of legislation. All of this forms the larger environment for the acquisition and practice of (or, where such public attitudes and laws are deficient, the undermining of) the virtues. Within the Church, this public debate will necessarily concentrate on crises of conscience arising out of new social developments (such as in the area of bioethics or justice) that call for an adequate response. But its traditional role in the professional training of candidates for priesthood remains. The need for guidance in helping to resolve difficult cases of conscience to be dealt with in the internal forum requires, among other things, dialogue between pastors and theologians. Beyond the task of clarifying specific moral questions, moral theology also has an, as yet, unexplored area of research open to it. This is the exploration of the great exemplars of heroic virtue, the saints, who are in a sense the living 'authorities' of tradition, the great exponents of virtue within certain historical situations and cultural conditions. These men, women, and children are canonised (they become a 'rule' in the Aristotelian sense of the virtuous man), among other things, to inspire us and to prompt us to imitate them. Their model (and our's) is Jesus Christ, *the* exemplar. They embody the Christian life as 'imitation' (cf. 1 Cor 4:16; 11:1; Eph 5:1; 1 Thess 1:6; Heb 6:12), and can play an as yet largely unexplored role in moral theology.[19] The lives of the saints, liberated from the exaggerations of earlier hagiography (such as Peter Ackroyd's *The Life of Thomas More*) and used critically,[20] should enable us to plumb depths of the workings of grace within human condition and show what human beings are truly capable of. These are the perfect exponents of virtue. They demonstrate what heroism 'ordinary' people can and do achieve as politicians, housewives, priests, or nuns. The memory of their character and integrity under duress can be the decisive factor in our decisions taken in extreme situations.[21] To understand the nature of 'daily heroism', attention must also be given to the study of the various vices, and the real malice in people and society, without which study, moral theology can seem if not irrelevant then certainly unreal.[22]

Within contemporary society, the role of moral theologians may seem even more peripheral, though in fact it is more urgent. But to identify that role more closely, we must look at what might be one of the most pressing tasks for contemporary moral theology, identifying the nature of moral knowledge.

THE NATURE OF MORAL KNOWLEDGE: PRACTICAL WISDOM

Leaving aside for the moment any specifically theological issues, what does the above account of moral development, provided it is generally accurate, tell us about the nature of morality? In the above account, we have been constrained to use terms which are part of the vocabulary of morality: good and bad behaviour, virtue and vice, freedom and the lack of same, etc. Each term needs to be teased out, and indeed has been subject to debate since the dawn of time. But since morality, like language, belongs to the very essence of our human nature, and we tend to subject these terms to critical examination, this means that we must have some in-built critical capacity to do so, one that we all share and makes dialogue possible. We possess, in other words, some common pre-understanding of what morality might involve, however we may differ in our actual behaviour, in our (basically inherited) moral codes, or in our theoretical analysis of the latter. The source of this common pre-understanding would seem to be conscience understood as *synderesis* as distinct from conscience as prudential judgement. Joseph Pieper called it *das Urgewissen* or primal conscience, a notion taken up by Ratzinger, who, echoing Plato and Augustine, calls it *anamnêsis*, our primordial memory of the true and the good arising from our being created in the image and likeness of God.[23] This primal conscience may be (necessarily inadequately) expressed in, but it cannot be reduced to, abstract principles, as it tends to be in both traditional and modern moral theology. It is, rather, an ontological capacity that urges one to seek the truth. It is the most elemental human instinct. Though in essence a primal drive or instinct to know the truth, it is distinctly passive in that it cannot produce truths but only re-cognise[24] the truth it encounters and submit to it in such a way that one's person is transformed in the depths of one's being.[25] Unless prevented (we can choose not to see), this 'primordial conscience' needs the external stimulus of articulated truth, as found in the sapiential traditions of humanity, but above all in the Church's authoritative tradition (into which these traditions flow like tributaries of a river) in order to be activated. The truth it recognises is always experienced as being both particular (culturally expressed) and universal (transcendent in nature) at the same time. In this, it is similar to language, always particular, and yet allowing great thinkers express the truth of the human condition in their own languages. Since they articulate universal truths in local guise, they can be translated into other languages.

One cannot reflect on, or discuss the nature of, language, its style and syntax, without having acquired a particular 'tongue' of one's own, with all its cultural and historical baggage, and yet one can also criticise it and in so doing 'transcend' it to a certain extent. So too, one cannot discuss ethics or morality without being in some sense moral, i.e. knowing something about right and wrong and acting accordingly – and without possessing a given moral code which is in great part due to one's upbringing and particular environment and culture, though never simply the product of that cultural environment.

In the case of the moral philosopher, the situation is rather more complex, since he or she approaches the subject within a particular tradition of moral reflection acquired by studying and reflecting on one or more of the many competing schools of thought, all of which are in fierce disagreement. These schools are part of the larger western tradition with its history of conflict and contradiction which, according to MacIntyre, has produced the dominant view of morality today, namely emotivism with its implicit denial of a universally valid, objective moral order as is such. Moral theologians, too, are necessarily influenced by this situation. (Indeed, this situation, it could be argued, gives such theories as proportionalism their apparent evidence; it is sometimes claimed that their propositions 'resonate' with modern man.) But the situation of Catholic moral theologians is complicated by other factors. These arise from the upheaval brought about by the various attempts by different schools of moral theology to respond to the demand made by the Second Vatican Council for the renewal of moral theology, already mentioned.[26]

In other words, when the moral theologian approaches his subject, the attempt to say anything has already been pre-empted by various interpretations, and one's own approach is just one of them. It cannot be otherwise: there is no position 'out there', above the fray, from which we can view the matter with quasi-scientific 'objectivity'.[27] This does not mean that we are condemned to relativism, or pure subjectivity in moral matters, a question which would take us beyond the scope of this paper. What is does mean, briefly, is that objectivity in the moral sphere is of a different nature to that found in the natural science. In science, objectivity is the product of 'disengaged reason' (Charles Taylor) characterised by its essentially measurable nature, while in morality objectivity is the product of practical reason (prudence), the acting subject's perception of what he or she objectively ought to do in a particular situation with a view to realising one's ultimate goal in life, 'engaged reason', as it were. It is life's ultimate goal that in the final analysis determines the objectivity of morality.

Moral reason is not an abstraction. This brings us to the classical distinction concerning the nature of morality, that between speculative and practical reason. This is a distinction, it seems to me, that is largely neglected in contemporary moral discourse, especially discourse of a theological nature. It is rarely recognised that moral theology, such as this particular essay in the subject, is an exercise in speculative reason. But my decision to write about morality and (renewed each time I sit down to write and continuing as long as I am engaged in writing and its attendant exercises, research and reflection) is an exercise of practical reason. The factors feeding into the myriad of 'decisions' I have to make continually are my professional responsibilities, the time available to me, the demands of competing duties such as arise from teaching, friendship, religion, citizenship, etc. Engaged in the process of writing are other, morally even more significant, factors that continually impinge on that underlying decision. Such factors are those relating to the truth or falsity of what I write, my attempts to be objective, my self-control over my emotional response to what I or others write (envy, discouragement, rage, etc.), my courage to name the unnamable, my readiness to acknowledge my sources where possible, etc. All of these factors feed into the on-going 'judgements' of practical reason. Finally, practical reason involves keeping a check on my motives for engaging in this enterprise in the first place, or persevering in it – a much more difficult process than is often assumed, since motivation tends to be singularly opaque. The end result (if it is ever satisfactorily concluded) of this moral effort will be in great part determined not only by the literary, philosophical, theological and other skills that I may or may not have acquired. It will also be even more decisively formed by the quality of my own moral dispositions to be honest, fair, self-critical, temperate etc. These dispositions are not themselves the product of introspection or reflective thinking. This point needs to be stressed, since one often gets the impression that, for theologians, morality is assumed to be a process of conscious reflection or time-consuming deliberation.[28]

Now, there are occasions when one literally has to stop and think about what one ought to do. This would apply to unusual moral dilemmas caused either by complex human situations, such as those caused by a vocational crisis, an unexpected event of major proportions (personal tragedy or war), or a decision to be made by someone in authority with major implications for others. Thus, for example, a patient with an illness that responds to no standard treatment might be offered a 'treatment', which is the product of unprecedented developments in medicine or biotechnology, where the relevant moral response may be either unknown or unclear. It should be mentioned, in parenthesis, that most moral dilemmas are not between good and bad, right and wrong, but, as Greek tragedy illustrates, between two goods making conflicting demands at the same time.[29] The problem is complicated by the so-called hard cases. Hard cases not only make bad law, they leap-frog the issue of moral character, character being the often forgotten but in fact the decisive context for any such deliberation, one which cannot be reproduced even in the best forms of casuistry.

Contemporary moral theological reflection, when not otherwise concerned with fundamental principles, tends to be primarily concerned with how to make moral judgements in the face of moral dilemmas, which modern technology, especially biotechnology, has thrown up in abundance. As Jonathan Sacks once pointed out, the danger is that taking moral dilemmas as one's starting point, one invariably ends up a relativist, denying that there are any objective demands of a universal nature. A theoretical or rationalistic discussion of moral dilemmas – a modern, sophisticated form of casuistry,[30] but casuistry nonetheless – suffers from being precisely that: abstract and hypothetical. Such a discussion is not really based on the demands of practical reason but rather speculative reason of a particularly narrow range, more rationalist than reasonable. The object of the discussion is to arrive at general principles of human action from mostly imaginary situations of an exceptional nature. Even if these situations involve the reconstruction of actual cases in the lives of historical personages, they remain hypothetical reconstructions dependent on the necessarily limited information available and on the greater or lesser imagination of the one who reconstructs the case. They do not and cannot reflect the moral predisposition of the person faced with the dilemma or the capacity of that person for self-transcendence in the face of such a dilemma. It is not surprising that the end product of such reflections tend to be vague generalisations, often rationalisations, with only one 'moral absolute', namely the denial of moral demands of a universal applicable in every conceivable circumstance. If you start with exceptional situations, you tend to end with exceptions to all moral principles. For these reasons, applied ethics seems to a non-starter, indeed a dubious activity, unless it is frankly seen as refined casuistry, which, as already admitted, has its uses. But the tendency towards moral relativism of this kind is aided and abetted by another weakness in this hypothetical, basically casuistic, not to say rationalistic approach, namely a failure to take account of the innate moral weakness of the moral theologian himself, or at least his consciousness of this weakness.[31]

There are situations when what people ought to do invariably places huge demands on frail human beings, demands we personally might often feel unable to live up to, demands we would not wish to impose on others, even theoretically.[32] This highlights an often forgotten aspect of morality: its inherent difficulty, which has wider implications beyond the immediate discussion of moral dilemmas. Hesiod once wrote: 'Before virtue the gods placed sweat.'[33] This may mean quite simply that virtues are not easily acquired. But it probably also refers to the fact that, for everyone, doing what is right is enormously difficult and challenging. (When Aristotle defined virtue as the mean between two extremes, he referred to the enormous tug exercised by one or other of the opposing extreme passions of repulsion and attraction.) Is this the aspect of morality that causes us most unease today? Is there an existential reluctance to face up to the often harsh demands of trying to live an upright life, trying to act with integrity, making the right choice in extreme situations despite the 'foreseen' negative consequences?[34] Even the words 'character' and 'integrity' have vanished from common coinage, like so much that was discarded as hypocrisy, morality masquerading as respectability, words such as heroism and humility. Instead, the businessman or banker, for example, who tries to act honestly and fairly is becoming more and more rare, since everyone bows to the demands of the 'real' world, where deception, unbridled market forces and corruption are accepted as the norm. The final abandonment of moral responsibility by parents and teachers is their despairing acceptance that the children in their charge cannot be expected to resist peer and other social pressure to engage in sexual activity. And so parents reluctantly agree that their teenagers should be provided with some 'protection' from either unwanted pregnancy or sexually transmitted diseases.

Be that as it may, the student of morality is invited to participate in an abstract deliberation to resolve a particular difficult dilemma; we are invited to judge in theory how *others* (in such circumstances) should behave. Since few would demand of others a heroism they know they might not show if they themselves were placed in a similar situation, a form of situation ethics advocating the easy way out of the moral dilemma becomes very attractive. The outcome is generally some form of 'theology of compromise' (Charles Curran) such as a 'principle of the practical ideal' (Raphael Gallagher),[35] an approach that, in addition, appeals very strongly to the modern notion of compassion.[36] This, it seems to me, is a peculiar perversion of the Golden Rule, now understood as 'do not expect of others what one would not expect of oneself'![37] This is also where Kant's theoretical attempt to reduce morality to what is potentially universalizable (as perceived by the acting person), is shipwrecked on the rock of human experience.

Nonetheless, it is important to stress that, generally speaking, moral judgement does not involve such painstaking, heart-rending and time-consuming deliberation, even in unexpected and unusual situations, though a certain amount of 'mulling over' might be needed. To return to our analogy with sport, accomplished players have to make instant judgements on the field, judgements which they can later recall in detail though it will take them much longer to relate than the split-second decision that produced the triumphant (or fatal) movement. The greater the 'vision' of a given football player (their ability to note exactly where everyone is on the pitch at that particular moment and their likely movements), the better the judgement and the decision. But 'timing' is of the essence of the act. It, too, arises from experience (*praxis*) or skill, the acquired disposition of the players which forms both their vision and their judgement, and that will determine the risk to be taken, *and* when and how they should take it. There is only one right judgement, one correct action, which in retrospect will be seen to be such, i.e. after it has found its intended target. While to sin is to miss the mark (as Aristotle recognised, presumably using archery as an analogy), and thus the possibilities of doing wrong are legion, yet there is only one right action – as there is only one right emotional response. Only the person of good character can make the right judgement as to what, when and how he should do it. Only such a person experiences the right or appropriate emotional response. 'For the man of good character judges every situation rightly; i.e. in every situation what appears to him is the truth,'[38] namely what he ought to do here and now: 'to feel and act towards the right person to the right extent at the right time for the right reason in the right way.'[39] This kind of knowledge is, technically speaking, practical or moral knowledge. It involves both insight in the imperative of the moment and the required emotional response to what gives rise to the imperative.

In contrast, rationalism is a manner of thinking characteristic of a mechanistic understanding of reality as presupposed by (classical) scientific and technological knowledge in its efforts to explain everything in accordance with certain laws of causality. When, in the area of human behaviour, contemporaries ask the reason why certain people acted in a particular way (e.g. criminal behaviour), the answer is often given in some deterministic fashion. Environment, psychological or social development, historical circumstances, genetic factors, etc. are said to be the cause of a person so acting. In other words, a quasi-mechanical causality is attributed to what are simply conditions. But, as the ancients knew so well, a cause is not a reason.[40] The influence of moral character and the role of freewill are ignored or denied.[41] Where the element of freedom of choice is nonetheless stressed, rationalism reduces moral decision-making to a conscious or reflective calculation.

This is a weighing-up of the circumstances, of the good and bad foreseeable consequences of a certain action, in order to opt for the greater good to be expected as the outcome of a decision in a particular situation that always involves a percentage of 'evil'. What is of note, first of all, is that such an understanding of moral decision-making ignores the possibility of 'spontaneity', which, as we saw, is the defining characteristic (admittedly in different ways) of both virtue and vice. More significant is the fact that what are being calculated are the external effects of an action, not the effect of the action on the acting person him or herself, namely whether or not one is a better person by so acting. In other words, moral quality is no longer defined by whether or not one is thereby brought closer to one's ultimate goal in life, the purpose of being human. But 'judging the circumstances and weighing up the consequences' implies that these are quantifiable and so measurable entities.[42] Rationalism is essentially quantifiable, mathematical. It is abstract or hypothetical reason.

Speculative or contemplative reason for the Greeks, who were the first to make the distinction, was the capacity to reach the immutable truth or reality behind appearances or phenomena. Its object was *theoria*, a certain insight into reality, to see things as they really are beyond or behind the continually changing visible or empirical reality. As already mentioned, this is what we exercise when we engage in philosophy or theology. Ethics and moral theology are essentially exercises in speculative reason on matters relating to practical knowledge. But practical knowledge itself, though ultimately rooted in speculative knowledge,[43] is that unique kind of knowledge we have in a particular situation as to what we ought to do there and then. It is '... *the* "state of capacity to act"...',[44] as distinct from the underlying general capacity for truth. It has an imperative character, though we may choose to ignore it and do anything but what we ought to do. That imperative character is itself molded by the depth of a person's vision of reality or speculative knowledge, which throws light on the demands of the particular situations, *logos* having a certain primacy over *ethos*, as Guardini in another context pointed out long ago.[45] And it is at this level that the truth of faith and its theological articulation provides a kind of enlightenment or illumination that characterises Christian morality.

Practical knowledge itself, however, is a virtue, an acquired disposition marked by spontaneity in its fully developed form. Its technical name is *phronesis*, inadequately rendered into English by the term 'prudence'.[46] It is to be distinguished, following Aristotle, by that other type of practical knowledge or technical skill which is characteristic of making things. In other words, there are two kinds of deliberative or calculate reason, the knowledge we require in order to make some *thing* and the knowledge we require to act in a human or moral fashion. Modern moral theory of a utilitarian or consequentialist nature, it seems to me, has effectively identified practical knowledge of a prudential nature with the kind of practical knowledge used in the making of things, since it tries to calculate the good and bad foreseen consequences of particular acts. But only practical knowledge understood as prudence deserves to be called moral reason.

Practical reason is the first of the cardinal virtues: prudence. It is generally found in its perfection only in the old and the wise, though child prodigies are as frequent here as in all areas of human endeavour: Thérèse of Lisieux being an obvious example. Again it is marked by that spontaneity which is characteristic of all habitual dispositions. It is generally not a process of reflection, as rationalist philosophy or theology would have us believe. Even when faced with extraordinary moral dilemmas, practical reason first spontaneously reacts by prompting us to stop and think again. Extraordinary moral dilemmas, or major decisions affecting the course of our lives, do demand conscious reflection, when we have to discover or tease out the implications of some decision to be made (generally by being able to recognise all the relevant factors), and seek help from people renowned for their own prudence, perhaps even moral theologians. Whereas some decision are instantaneous, others (usually involving major decisions) require a quiet but sustained quest for the right thing to do. Such a quest takes time and involves a certain 'incubation period' before it becomes clear what one should do, often by what Newman might have described as the force of converging evidences coalescing into a decision.[47] Practical reason is our acquired capacity to be objective in this reflection, to seek out and face up to what we *ought* to do rather than what we *want* to do. The latter produces its own 'reasons', attempts to justify a decision, in other words, rationalisations. Practical reason, in a sense, transcends one's feelings, or rather judges the adequacy or inadequacy of one's emotional response to that particular situation. Thus, it presupposes a measure of self-control over one's feelings and passions (the virtues of temperance and fortitude), so that our inordinate fears or desire for pleasure do not cloud one's reason. But above all, practical reason is sensitive to the *when* and *how* we ought to act. The (spontaneous) tact or finesse needed to ensure the necessary 'timing'– sensitive to the concrete circumstances and persons involved or affected – can only be determined by someone who has acquired virtue. *Bonum ex integra causa, malum ex quocumque defectu.*[48] For an act to be good, every aspect of it must be good: the act itself, the motivation, and the circumstances. Only the virtuous person can so act – and does so spontaneously, promptly and with pleasure.

Nonetheless, practical reason is marked by an element of risk-taking (as in sport), since the kind of knowledge one has about what one should do (moral certainty) will always include an element of uncertainty. Only thus can practical reason, or prudence, reveal the demands of reality, of what one ought to do, though one may not want to so act. Practical reason helps us discover the moral response demanded of us after taking into consideration the reality of the situation in which we find ourselves, a situation that is always particular and unique. And yet what is demanded in that situation is of a universal nature, such as telling the truth, giving to others what is their due, not taking innocent human life as a means to an otherwise good end. But it is precisely here, at the level of moral demands of a universal nature – which leads us back to primal conscience (*anamnêsis*) and the *theoria* of the magisterium – that we find the existential heart of the contemporary crisis in ethics. Society is profoundly ambivalent about the existence of moral demands of a universal nature – in effect, the denial of speculative truth – and this in turn undermines practical reason.

Practical reason, we saw, is neither acquired nor exercised in a social vacuum. Its formation (in the family and local community, especially the school) and its exercise (in adulthood) are both greatly determined by the quality of the political community, which formulates its standards of what is and what is not generally accepted moral behaviour. Practical reason can be more easily cultivated and exercised in a community and within a tradition where the ground rules are more or less generally unquestioned,[49] where certain actions are known to be ruled out in all circumstances (adultery or stealing or lying). Such a community is not made up of the perfect, but weak imperfect sinners who (publicly) recognise the great exponents of virtue in the past (such as the saints or heroes) and cultivate their memory as models for themselves and future generations. But where there is an all-pervasive ambivalence about what is right and wrong in society, and where the models for emulation are primarily the rich and successful, including the wielders of power and influence in the present, then the acquisition and exercise of practical wisdom becomes more difficult (though, of course, not impossible). Where the existence of any universally binding rules and regulations – a moral code that includes a framework of moral absolutes – is denied in theory or accepted in practice, then practical knowledge becomes extremely difficult either to acquire or to exercise.[50] And it is here, in the realm of public debate (i.e. primarily at the university), that moral theology has it indispensable function. What is specific to it, what it has to offer society, is the divinely assured certitude of the authoritative Christian tradition rooted in God's self-revelation of himself in Christ, who, as the Council taught, 'revealed man to himself'. The last statement will be, for many, quite scandalous. Do they have a point?

THE PUBLIC RESPONSIBILITY OF MORAL THEOLOGIANS

Virtue is acquired within the human commuity. But it is a more difficult task to define more precisely what we mean by 'the human community'. In the first place, as was pointed out above, it is or should be the family. But the family does not live in isolation. It exists within a particular culure and society defined in large part by the political community, the State with its complex of institutions and laws. Though in a very important sense the family precedes and transcends the State, the State as the political community is the 'perfect society', which does not mean that it is 'perfect' (or self-sufficient) but rather it encompasses all aspects of life including the family – at least it should. In the modern world, the growth of various supranational 'unions' and 'organisations' of states, and the growing interdependence of all states on each other highlight in different ways the growing imperfection of the 'state', its inability to function autonomously or with real sovereignty.[51] Mass communications and the increasing internationalisation of commerce, law, culture, and the arts likewise exercise enormous influence on the life within individual states. And yet, it is still the state that defines 'the rules and regulations', namely the laws, which to a large extent define our humanity and are the framework within which we acquire and exercise virtue. It is only recently that an awareness has grown that the modern, liberal democratic state is imperfect in another, even more important sense. It depends on moral resources that it cannot produce of itself, but without which it cannot survive.[52] For all western countries, that resource is primarily Christianity, be it Protestant or Catholic, with its roots in Hebrew faith and Greek reason. It is the living local churches that provide such moral resources – and one aspect of moral theology's indispensible role is to articulate and clarify them, often removing the incrustations of time that deface the Church's moral teaching, so that the *traditio*, the handing-on of the moral patrimony of the faith in the home and in the schools is facilitated.

And yet, the state enjoys a certain existential primacy in the moral order. The political community exists (or should exist) for the flourishing of those who make up the community. This in turn presupposes a general consensus about the nature of human flourishing. For the ancients, it was the promotion of virtue. For Aristotle, the purpose of the *polis* is to enable its citizens not simply to live (i.e. to exist in material security) but to live *well*, that is virtuously. The good life is the common good or weal, the common goal of all who made up the commuity. Goodness, truth and beauty are its goal. In a word: God. This anthropological order of society[53] was taken up and enlarged by Christianity. Like the leaven in the dough, it transformed over the centuries western European culture from within. And so the bulk of the laws which still define most modern liberal democratic states were framed within a culture that recognised God as the ultimate end of all human endeavour and Christianity as the authoritative witness to that end. This is so because Christianity, as Newman recognised, is based on the primacy of conscience understood not as the subjective judgement of opinion or the final arbiter of the truth of values, but as '… the window that for human beings opens onto a view of the common truth, which truth establishes and sustains us all and so makes community of decision and responsibility possible thanks to the common ground of perception'.[54] Christianity appeals to that conscience, it speaks to the 'heart'. Even though moral consensus no longer exists, consensus is recoverable because of the 'structure of reality' (namely primal conscience, the capacity for truth that defines us as human being), provided the moral theologian literally has the courage of his convictions (and finds the right language) to challenge contemporay cultural assumptions.

Though perhaps largely peripheral to the actual exercise of the virtues, moral theology, it seems to me, has its indispensible role percisely in the public realm both inside and outside the Church.[55] Within the Church, moral theology has the task of renewing the vision of what it means to be fully human and of clarifying specific moral demands that arise from, or are obscured by, contemporary culture, including those actions that are intrinsically at enmity with our basic humanity and our final end and which cannot be even entertained by a virtuous person.[56] As already mentioned above, such actions, though powerfully seductive, the virtuous may not seriously contemplate. Refusing to even consider them makes heroes of us all, martyrs to the truth and so sharers in the Paschal Mystery. Ruling them out *a priori* is an act of faith in the inherent dignity of every one that enables the most 'ordinary' when 'put to the test' to rise to greatness, as any chaplain in a hospital can confirm. A theory of compromise undermines human dignity and promotes lives of quiet desperation. But moral theology has an even more important contribution to make.

Paradoxically, what philososphers see as the 'weakness' of any faith-based position, namely its unique certainty, might well be the real strength of moral theology in the public realm. In a culture where the centre no longer holds (relativism), moral theology's herculean task is to help society recover its centre, to convince society (indirectly, though its students) of the indispensible moral parameters for its flourishing and for the well-being, ultimately the happiness of all. This, of course, moral theology will fail miserably to achieve if that same certainty engenders complacency, reducing Catholic moral theology to an unthinking repetition of 'what the magisterium teaches', a kind of Catholic ideology masked under the claim to orthodoxy. More is needed – originality and creativity in dialogue with contemporary philosophy and literature and the drama of the human condition – and that 'more' is part of what constitutes moral theology. That 'more' arises in the final anlaysis from the inspiration the moral theologian personally takes from scripture, liturgy, and tradition (including the great saints and thinkers of the past and present), once he or she has been alerted to the nuances and ambiguities of the human condition by the great thinkers of past and present. That 'more' could, perhaps, be characterised by its capacity to touch the human sensorium for transcendence in others since one has oneself been touched by Transcendence: *cor ad cor loquitur.* In the public realm, what counts in the last analysis is not a clever intellectual system – such, indeed, is sufficient to undermine commonly accepted truths, if propagated by sufficient numbers of opinion makers – but rather the voice of a man or woman who has been stirred in the depths of his or her soul and in some sense seared by truth. Only such a one has the courage to stand up and be counted when called to give a reason for the hope that sustains them.

Thus, within the political community, moral theology has the task of entering public debate and of witnessing – through the quality of its writings, the depth of its arguments, and (yes) the personal integrity or character of the theologian – to the truth that alone makes people free. The present 'crisis of values' (Ratzinger) will be overcome when people recover a sense of the ultimate goal in life, namely God, a recovery that, of coure, is in the final analysis in his hands. But moral theology has its own limited but real contribution to make by helping society to rediscover how the happiness all people desire can indeed be attained in the midst of apparently mundane lives, namely by virtue, which is its own reward in this life – the seed of the life to come.

Conclusion

More implicit than explicit in the above discussion is a topic rarely mentioned in contemporary moral theology: holiness as the ultimate object of morality.[57] Moral theology, it seems to me, will cease to be *existentially* peripheral to the inner life of the Church once moral theologians realise that what is truly 'specific' to moral theology is its humble (but daunting) role in helping to define (and continually to refine the definitions of) what constitute the moral conditions for the acquistion of holiness. All morality is finally measured by that goal. Indeed, the moral life itself is spiritual worship,[58] which ultimately grounds the specific role of the Church's magisterium. But this raises many other questions, which we have not even touched on. What, for example, is the role of Providence in the moral life, corresponding, according to Aquinas, to what the Greeks understood as 'chance' whose role in determining human happiness was so great that they made a goddess of it. How is conversion to be understood in the context of virtue as an acqured disposition or character trait? What are the implications of the claim that the human virtues are rooted in the theological virtues?[59] What is meant by the axiom that charity (divine love) is the form of all the virtues? And how can one integrate into moral theology the need to become docile to the promptings not simply of conscience but of the Holy Spirit?[60] Perhaps it is a false humility that prevents us as moral theologians from examining the radical implications of being Christian and the unique dignity (and danger) this implies. Is it too much to suggest that we might ponder again the significance of the fact that the *Catechism* begins its moral section with the words of St Leo the Great: 'Christian, recognise your dignity ...'[61]?

NOTES

1   See Allan Bloom, *The Closing of the American Mind*, New York: Simon & Schuster, 1987. Few, if any, theoretical ethicists are thoroughgoing relativists. Regarding the long-term political consequences of the all-pervasive moral relativism, cf. Francis Fukuyama, *The End of History and the Last Man*, New York: Penguin Books, 1992, pp. 328–39, especially 332.

2   The causes of such sterility are many. On the part of the so-called liberal or dissident Catholic moral theologians, one imporant factor, it seems to me, must be their preoccupation (not to say obsession) with justifying their own denial of absolute moral norms, which denial itself produces a kind of minimalist ethics and lends itself to a selective reading of tradition. Such miminalist ethics finds its expression in that refined type of casuistry known as 'applied ethics' and so it is restrained to remain within the narrow confines of the legalist tradition, while at the same time trying to break out of it, but failing to do so. On the part of their more traditional or conservative opponents, who tend to be more original and creative since they acknowledge a complexity of moral principles and are more open to the broader tradition of Catholic morality, the increasing sterility would seem to be due to their assumption of being 'faithful to the Magisterium'. In recent times, the Magisterium has indeed been extraordinarily creative in this area, even at a philosophical and theological level, the very impressiveness of which tends to make those who claim to be faithful to it (the 'orthodox') somewhat lazy, if not ideologues. Both schools have in varying degrees developed their own 'establishments', each of which claims to be the authentic expression of modern Catholic moral theology and so ignore the criticism of the other school, thereby cutting themselves off from any radical questioning of their assumption or, indeed, any self-criticism.

3   These public debates tend to be limited to ethical dilemmas posed by the more dramatic developments in biotechnology, which developments still stir the embers of western society's moral sensitivity when first made public – only to be dampened in time by the all-prevailing crisis of values, usually resolved by an appeal to compassion (such as the potential 'therapeutic' value of such things as experimentation on human embryos), and/or an appeal to the 'experts' and various 'bioethical commissions'.

4   What follows has been greatly influenced by the notion of virtue as articulated by Josef Pieper in the 1930s and as recovered in recent decades by philosophers, above all by Elizabeth Anscome and Alasdair MacIntyre, and by theologians such as Servais Pinckaers.

5   See note 2.

6   I use this term for want of a better one, though it can be misconstrued as just another 'school'.

7   Cf. *CCC* 1767–70.

8   Catholic Social Teaching was once confined to a discipline of questionable integrity, namely 'Catholic sociology', that in time regained its integrity by becoming, quite simply, sociology, and has been searching for a home. 'In *Sollicitudo Rei Socialis* 41 John Paul II brings social teaching or social doctrine, which at times has been somewhat isolated, back to "moral theology"' (Jean-Yves Calvez SJ, article on the encyclical in Judith A. Dwyer (ed.), *The New Dictionary of Catholic Social Thought*, Collegeville, MN: The Liturgical Press, 1994, p. 917). Its essential principles have been incorporated in Part III, the moral theology section of the *Catechism* (cf. *CCC* 1877–1948; 2234–2246; 2419–2457).

9   It is of note that the *Catechism* deals with the role of the Magisterium only at the *end* of the fundamental moral theology section (cf. *CCC* 2032–2040), after its treatment of law and

grace.

10   The implications of the inclusion of the teaching on grace in Section Three (cf. *CCC* 1987–2029), the moral theology section of the *Catechism* rather than in Section One (corresponding to dogmatic theology), have yet to be examined by mainstream moral theology.

11   A modern equivalent might be 'autonomy', understood however not as the opposite of heteronomy, namely subject to an essentially alienating authority, but rather as a 'self-realising' agent acting with inner liberty within a tradition characterised by recognised authorities both informal (recognised models) and formal.

12   Cf. Joseph Cardinal Ratzinger, *The Nature and Mission of Theology: Approaches to Understanding Its Role in the Light of Present Controversy*, translated by Adrian Walker, San Francisco: Ignatius Press, 1995, esp. pp. 13–29.

13   Fergus Kerr OP reminds us that the late Herbert McCabe OP (*Law, Love and Language*, London and Sydney: Sheed and Ward, 1968, Chapter 3) once argued 'that ethics is a "kind of literary criticism of human behaviour, seeking not so much to classify it as right and wrong as to explore its significance, trying to discover what 'love' means"' (*New Blackfriars*, Vol. 83, No. 977/978 [2002], 316).

14   *S.Th.* I-II, 107, 4.

15   Wilhelm von Saint-Thierry, *Meditationen und Gebete. Lateinisch-deutsch*. Trans. by Klaus Beger and Christine Nord, Darmstadt: Wissenschaftliche Buchgesellschaft, 2001, p. 40.

16   As quoted in Josef Pieper, *Justice*, London: Faber and Faber, 1957, p. 51.

17   Human beings are by nature 'incomplete', as distinct from the disabling effects of original sin.

18   'Man's "inborn instincts" are drives, fragments to be assembled, given meaning, and organised during a prolonged childhood by methods of child training and schooling which vary from culture to culture and are determined by tradition. ...[M]an survives only where traditional child training provides him with a conscience which will guide him without crushing him and which is firm and flexible enough to fit the vissitudes of his historical era ...' Erik Erikson, *Childhood and Society*, New York: Norton, 1963, pp. 95–6. I am grateful to my confrere, Fr Franz Gassner SVD, who drew my attention to this author.

19   In *Veritatis Splendor* 90, Pope John Paul II uses the story of Susanna from the Old Testament and that of John the Baptist in the New to make an often forgotten point regarding the link between moral integrity and martyrdom.

20   See also its modern equivalent, such as Robert Bolt's *A Man for All Seasons*, which glorifies a peculiarly modern understanding of conscience that, in my opinion, is radically at variance with More's own understanding, and tells us more about Bolt's radically subjectivist idea of conscience prominent in the 1960s. Yet Bolt is used in modern moral theology textbooks quite uncritically, not to say selectively (to bolster a similar view of conscience), as though the play incorporated only the *ipsissima verba* of the one-time Chancellor of England and newly proclaimed Patron of Politicians.

21   This was illustrated recently by Peter Shaw, a Welsh businessman aged fifty-seven and a non-practicising Christian, who was held hostage by armed bandits in Georgia for five months, during which time he was continually beaten by his captors (his skull was fractured on one occasion). He spent four months (manacled to the wall by his neck) in a pitch black hole somewhere in the mountains of Georgia. Food was scarce. Light was provided for forty-five minutes each day by a candle. For days, he became obsessed with the idea of suicide, but did not succumb. 'In the end,' he recalled after his dramatic escape, 'I got the impression that God wanted me to survive, so I started living day by day. I knew I would probably freeze to death and it made everything more bearable. I thought of Captain Scott [and his doomed expedition to the South Pole] – he didn't commit suicide, so nor would I. He knew he was not coming back [from the Antarctic] so he and his men snuggled down in their tents and waited for the cold to kill them. He became an inspiration.' (*The Sunday Times*, 11 November 2002; text in first square brackets inserted by this writer). It is instructive to compare this case with the general approach of modern Catholic moral theologians to the famous *casus* of the married woman in the Nazi concentration camp, who was offered a chance of freedom, if she would commit adultery.

22   The study of moral evil in history opens up the depths of human depravity, consciousness of which seems to be singularly lacking in much modern moral theology, which reduces it to something that can somehow or other be 'accommodated', acounted for, or even tolerated, so that compromise is always an option (cf. the comments by Josef Pieper, *Fortitude and Temperance*, London: Faber & Faber, 1955, pp. 11–15). See, however, the attempt by Gordon Graham, *Evil and Christian Ethics*, Cambridge University Press, 2001; see also the instructive philosophical study by Jonathan Glover, *Humanity. The Moral History of the Twentieth Century*, New Haven and London: Yale University Press, 1999.

23   Joseph Cardinal Ratzinger, *Conscience and Truth*, Braintree, MA: Pope John Center, 1991. This is the deepest level of conscience as rediscovered by John Herny Newman, cf. Nicholas Madden OCD, 'Newman: Conscience, the Matrix of Spirituality' in *Irish Theological Quarterly* 67 (2002), pp. 145–51.

24   Cf. Boethius, *Consolat. Phil.* V, Poem III.

25   Cf. Hans Urs von Balthasar, *Science, Religion, and Christianity*, translated from the German by Hilda Graef (London: Burns and Oates, 1958), pp. 31–9, especially 33.

26   See footnote 2.

27   See von Balthasar, op. cit. 33 and 37.

28   This view is well analysed, and corrected, by Rosaline Hursthouse, *On Virtue Ethics*, Oxford: University Press, 1999, Ch. 6 and 7, pp. 121–60.

29   Cf. Hursthouse, op. cit.

30   Despite justified criticism, casuistry (from the Latin *casus* = case), the discussion of either typical or unusual legal or moral cases in order to test or develop legal or moral principles remains a most useful tool for (training in) ethics and jurisprudence. However, it is not, strictly speaking, an exercise in prudence. (It may be what Aristotle meant by *sunesis* or even *gnômê*, both of which are closely related to *phronesis*, but even that is doubtful.) Casuistry is rather a form of speculative reason, speculating on what the relevant factors an upright person in that situation should consider in the formation of a prudential judgement and how he or she should act.

31   There is also a reaction to the rigorism of the pre-Vatican II manualist tradition and an alertness to the Lord's injunction not to place burdens on people's backs, while doing nothing to help them carry them.

32   Take the question of whether or not suicide would be a morally justifiable option in the case of Mr Peter Shaw (note 21 above).

33   Plato, *Protagoras*, 340d.

34   The fact is, we cannot foresee the effects of our actions. Someone recently talked about the 'law of unintended consequences' as a main characteristic of human behaviour.

35   Cf. Raphael Gallagher CSsR, *Understanding the Homosexual*, Dublin: Veritas, 1985, p. 24.

36   Re. this notion of compassion, cf. Oliver O'Donovan, *Begotten or Made?*, Oxford: Clarendon Press, 1984, pp. 1–13.

37   This only applies to an abstract consideration of future possibilities, since in practice many people surprise themselves when they do in fact rise to challenges they wouldn't or couldn't contemplate beforehand in the abstract.

38   Aristotle, *Nic. Ethics*, III iv (Thompson, 121).

39   Aristotle, *Nic. Ethics*, II ix (Thompson, 109).

40   Cf. W.T. Stace, *A Critical Histoy of Greek Philosophy*, London: Macmillan, 1969 (originally 1920), p. 64; also John Henry Cardinal Newman, *An Essay in Aid of a Grammer of Assent*, London: Longmans, Green and Co., 1909, pp. 66–72. I thank Professor Emeritus Thomas Canon Finan for drawing my attention to Stace and Newman.

41   Re. the most recent contributions to the debate on the existence or non-existence of free will ('liberarianism' versus determinism), cf. Hugo Meynell, 'Some Recent Books on Free Will' in *The Heythrop Journal*, Vol. 43, No. 4 (2002), pp. 496–501.

42   This, of course, is not to deny that there are moral situations when the consequences must be taken into consideration – for which such principles as that of double effect were developed as guides – and when the proportionality of the foreseen consequences have a vital part to place in the moral decision – as in the case of trying to establish the conditions for a just war.

But even here, the character of the acting person, his or her experience as a statesman, the degree of acquired wit and keeness of vision (prudence) will be the decisive elements in the decision, not the quantifiable measurement of what are often incommensurable goods.

43 For what seems to be the classical account of the complex relationship between speculative reason and practical reason, cf. Josef Pieper, *Die Wirklichkeit und das Gute*, Munich: Kosel Verlag, 1949 (7th printing, 1963).

44 Werner Jaeger, *Aristotle. Fundamentals of the History of his Development*, translated by Richard Robinson, London/Oxford/New York: Oxford University Press, 1962 (2nd edition), p. 239.

45 Cf. Romano Guardini, *Vom Geist der Liturgie. Zur aktuellen Situation*, Frieburg imBresgau: Herder, 1983, pp. 127–43 (originally published in 1918).

46 See in particular the classic work of Josef Pieper, *Prudence*, translated by Richard and Clara Winston, London: Faber and Faber, 1959 (and reprinted in *The Four Cardinal Virtues*, Notre Dame: University of Notre Dame Press, 1964).

47 As already mentioned, excluded *a priori* are certain acts which by their very nature are *intrinsece inhonestum* (*Humanae vitae*, no.14). They cannot be entertained as legitimate options, however strongly one may be attracted to them 'as a way of' getting out of a dilemma or achieving a legitimate goal; the end does not justify the means (cf. Rom 3:8). Incidentally, *intrinsece inhonestum*, it seems to me, is a term that might best be rendered into English as 'intrinsically shameful' or 'essentially ignoble', i.e. contrary to our inherent dignity and inherent *telos*, and so incapable of furthering our human flourishing. It is unfortunate that the controversy surrounding this basic notion (better: this 'bottom line') tends to translate the term 'intrisic evil', which seems to be a rather blunt instrument for moral discourse in the English language. It is passing strange that, in his revised version of *Denzinger* (Freiburg im Bresgau, 1991, 37th edition, corrected, expanded and translated into German) Peter Hünermann leaves out the paragraph containing this and other basic principles of fundamental moral theology in his selective account of *Humanae vitae*, 14 (cf. *DH* 4476).

48 Pseudo-Dionysius (*Div. Nom.* iv), as quoted in Thomas Aquinas, *S.Th.* I-II, q,18, a.4 ad 3.

49 Even the most perfect community is no guarantee that its members will be virtuous. Human freedom may refuse to cultivate it or, more likely, opt to be led by feelings devoid of reason.

50 This, of course, is the very good reason for the intense moral theological debate on this subject over the past thirty years, the negative effects of which I mentioned above.

51 This applies more to the intermediate state of individual nations merging into some kind of confederation or union. When the process is complete, then that bigger unit – the union or federation – effectively becomes the state in the tranditonal sense, which seems to be the path Europe is taking at the moment.

52 Cf. Supreme Justice E.-W. Böckenförder, *Staat – Gesellschaft – Kirche*, Frieburg, 1982, as quoted by Jospeh Ratzinger, *Church, Ecumenism and Politics. New Essays in Ecclesiology*, Slough: St Paul, 1988, p. 206; the same sentiments are expressed by Chief Rabbi Jonathan Sacks, *The Persistence of Faith. Religion, Morality & Society in a Secular Age* (The Reith Lectures 1990), London: Weidenfeld and Nicolson, 1991: 'Our political structures need a moral base which they cannot themselves create but without which they cannot survive' (91).

53 Here I allude to Eric Voegelin, *The New Science of Politics, An Introduction*, Chicago & London: The University of Chicago Press, 1952, who distinguishes between the cosmological and the anthropological orders of societies. The former is characterised above all by a political society's claim to represent the truth of human existence and the resulting collecivity, the assumption of the primacy of society over the members who make up that society, as in the Marxist political order of the former Soviet Union or Maoist China. The anthropological order affirms the primacy of human beings due to philosophical reflection on the experience of the soul as the sensorium of transcendence, i.e. endowed with the capacity to know ultimate truth and so in a sense transcend society. The sensorium of transcendence, it seems to me, is what is meant by 'primal conscience' or *Urgewissen* mentioned above. The anthropological principle, according to Voegelin, found its completion and fullest existential realisation in the soteriological princple, Christianity, the western version of which provided the required matrix for the emergence of democracy in the course of western society's historical articulation.

54   Joseph Cardinal Ratzinger, *Wahrheit, Werte, Macht, Prüfsteine der pluralistischen Gesellschaft,* Freiburg: Herder, 1993, p. 32 (my translation).

55   By public realm, I mean primarily the academic world, secondarily education in general, and finally (if at all) the public media.

56   Aristotle recognised that there were certain actions *and feelings* which, he asserts, are essentially wicked (*tôi auta phaula einai*) and, futhermore, 'nor does acting rightly or wrongly in such cases depend upon circumstances', cf. Nic. Ethics II vi (1107a; Thompson translation). Recent attempts by some proportionalists to use Aristotle to bolster their cause seriously misinterpret the Stagirite, due, it seems to me, to their rationalist, not to say basically pragmatist understanding of practical reason.

57   There are promising signs that this situation is about to change. The *Catechism of the Catholic Church* leads the way, cf. in particular *CCC*, pp. 2012–6. But, apart from the writings of Pinckaers, who has devoted his life's work to articulating a moral theology orientated to holiness, see James Keating and David McCarthy, 'Habits of Holiness: The Ordering of Moral-Mystical Living' in *Communio. International Catholic Review*, Vol. 28, No. 4 (2001), pp. 820–42. Despite their own distinctly different approach to the issues, the authors in fact put flesh on much of what is proposed above. They situate contemporary moral reflection within (post-Kantian) political thought, before they go on to situate the moral life within the complexity of so-called ordinary life and the universal call to holiness. Virtue, they point out, is not an abstraction but the acquisition of a *habitus* within a particular habitat. Virtus follows practice – or rather practices – not the other way around. And practices are determined by the complexity of the particular roles we play (as parents, teachers, politicians, musicians, sportspersons, etc.). Virtue gives unity to those otherwise disparate practices. That unity is rooted in the underlying theological virtues, namely virtues that relate us to God and are acquired within the matrix of the Church's sacramental, communal life in all its (seeming) ordinariness and imperfection. This communal life relates us and all we do to our Source and End, transforming us within, making us in the course of an often emotionally turbulent life, simultaneously whole and holy. Perhaps I overlooked it, but I found little indication that, within 'ordinary life', there is also considerable drama and tragedy (the passion and cross), and thus, so much real heroism (resurrection), the sign of true holiness and the only antidote to boredom and alienation. Further, the notion of conscience found here needs further clarification to take into consideration what Pieper calls the primal conscience. But these reservations do not take away from the article's singular achievment and importance.

58   Cf. *CCC* 2031.

59   Cf. *CCC* 1812.

60   Cf. *CCC* 1830–1.

61   *CCC* 1691.

9   Christianity and Creation: Code

James P. Mackey

(James P. Mackey, *Christianity and Creation: The Essence of the Christian Faith and its Future Among Religions*, London: Continuum, 2006, pp. 243–65 [extract].)

THE NEW COVENANT RATIFIED IN THE BLOOD OF THE CHRIST: THE (RE)NEW(ED) CODE GIVEN DOWN FROM THE MOUNTAIN

However all analysis of previous covenants may fare, persuasively or not, one thing at least is beyond doubt in the Bible. The prophet Jesus of Nazareth considered that by his time the covenant of God with his people had been radically distorted, particularly by the religious leaders of Israel. It had become distorted particularly with respect to the cult, with respect to the code, and most tellingly of all perhaps, with respect to that intermingling of cult with code that so often in religious *Weltanschauungen* make these two seem to constitute a seamless garment. Rather than a set of separates, one of which could be worn, and might indeed be better worn, without the other.

So there was by Jesus's time this inter-weaving of Temple and Torah. As the story goes, the Temple when first built by Solomon was designated to house the ark of the covenant, the ark that contained the written terms of the covenant, the terms which in turn guaranteed the presence of God with his people, forever giving them life and making them whole. An ark and a covenant and a Presence that they had before that carried with them wherever they went, but that was now stabilised in the Temple in the capital city of the land that God had promised them, forever. An ark and a covenant that therefore made the Temple the principal, if not the only house of the one, true God in the world. A covenant that defined in the details of both ritual and moral law the terms and conditions that were Israel's as the partner people in the covenant. It was this whole complex, constituting the religion of his people as it was formulated, taught and practiced in his time that Jesus criticised in virtually every encounter he had with the leaders of that religion. According to John in particular, he accused that version of his religion of being little less than idolatry. Satan, he said, was the father of these leaders, not the Father whose kingdom he, Jesus, had been sent to restore. Of course, they answered him in kind: accusing him of being a false messiah, a blasphemer whose ruling spirit was Satan, an idolator.

Now as then people can only judge between these Jewish opponents on the issue of the true God and the true version of the Jewish religion, by considering the case that Jesus made and died for. The case ranges over all connected issues of temple, ritual observance and moral response, and much of it has appeared already on previous pages. It needs but a brief recall here, together with some additional attention to the more specifically ethical principles involved in any overview that focuses primarily on the centrality of the covenant myth to that whole complex of co-involved issues that runs from temples to moralities.

So we have already seen that Jesus was understood, and rightly so, to have rejected the idea that the Presence could be confined to, or even considered predominantly available for worship in, the Jerusalem temple. Or anyone else's temple, for that matter. (A Roman Catholic may think at this point about the pretence that the Real Presence can be encountered in their churches where the eucharistic bread is reserved, but not in other Christian churches.) In reality of course the house in which the Presence can be felt and followed was, and ever is, the house of creation. And although temples could help focus that cosmic encounter – like the sacred building built and then burned down at Emain Macha – if they provided for worship of the one, true God of all creation, no one of them could ever be said to be essential to that blessed, demanding and most promising of all experiences in that same creation. It is also already obvious how that intersection of ritual and moral obligation known as the Sabbath observance became a focal point of the deadly disputes between Jesus and contemporary leaders of his faith. For the Sabbath ritual of abstinence from all was so interpreted as to suspend a moral obligation which, as it turns out, is the most fundamental moral obligation of the most fundamental covenant. It is the obligation imposed in the very act of God's creating creators and rulers plenipotentiary, to co-create in the course of God's own continuous creation and, as a crucial part of that very obligation, to make whole that which had suffered diminution of life. And, in this respect, as we have also seen, Jesus gave an even more general and radical instruction on the nature of the relationship between cultic/ritual precepts and moral precepts as these occur in the context of presenting religions as covenants.

The true nature of the relationship between ritual and moral precept was formulated by Jesus in his insistence that the Sabbath was made for man, not man for the Sabbath, and that principle is both general and radical in the following manner: Not only does it prevent the setting aside of a moral precept in any individual case, such as this one of Sabbath observance. It sets up a general, moral principle to the effect that ritual precepts must always give way to the needs and applications of moral principles. In more concrete and practical terms, ritual precepts must be constantly interpreted and critically assessed in the light of humanity's developing moral precepts. This would mean, for example, that the Hindu rite of suttee, according to which the dead man's wife joined him, as in life, now on his funeral pyre, would have to be revoked as soon as the evolving moral sensibility of humankind arrived at the stage of extending the moral precept, thou shalt not kill, to this scenario also. Indeed the extension of this precept, thou shalt not kill, to more and more scenarios in human life is probably the best barometer of the rising or falling of human moral sensibility in general.

There is a further and more general and radical example of the effect of allowing humanity's obviously evolving moral sensibility and subsequent legislation to act as critic and judge of ritual precept, according to the principle laid down by Jesus. As one can see from covenant texts in particular, ritual and moral precepts are set out as if they constituted one seamless whole, covering the whole response of humanity to God's gracious will and testament. And as such, if ritual precepts are not placed above moral precepts since they seem to have to do directly with what we owe to God rather than how we are obligated toward our neighbour, these two codes are placed on all fours together. Both are in consequence treated as expressions of the irrevocable will of the covenanting God, and the moral precepts then appear also as straightforward divine impositions. Rather than what these moral precepts are in reality, namely, inevitably developing codification of the rules of relationships to God through other creatures that equally inevitably change, as human beings engage in their most fundamental covenant response of co-creating God's world – 'that (the human spirit) may become creator and evaluator and lover and benefactor of all things'. This form of failure to observe the critical primacy of humanity's evolving moral sensibility and its correspondingly changing legal codification, by placing ritual and moral precept on all fours together, is unfortunately reflected in many, if not most of the so-called world religions, and mostly, to take one salient example, in the discrimination against women, if not their actual and daily oppression. All of which leads us to examine the purely moral precepts in the covenants now under discussion at this stage of the biblical story. For what we do find there, in Jesus's sermon from the mountain, is the most radical revision of the moral precepts recorded in the covenant according to Moses, and never more radical than in the interpretation of the precept, thou shalt not kill.

In the revised code of the covenant according to Moses, in the revision by Jesus that is designed to perfect, or to fulfil that code that has by now become in part at least obsolete and counterproductive in interpretation and praxis, the moral precepts are entirely predominant (Mt 5-7). There is no repetition by Jesus of his explicit views on what has by now gone wrong with the understanding of the cult and the distorting domination of ritual. Except obliquely perhaps, when Jesus decrees that people should prefer prayer in private to public performances of ever more elaborate liturgical prayer in synagogues, and offers instead the brief 'Our Father' prayer as an example of all we need to say. Or when he insists that being reconciled with a fellow human being that one has injured in some way takes priority over any and all sacrifices formally offered in temples (or churches that have altars). The moral precepts, it can do no harm to repeat, that define the human response to God's covenant are entirely dominant in the Torah now handed down by Jesus from the mountain. It does no harm to repeat this if only because few accounts of what Jesus did and taught give to this sermon on the mount the pivotal place it should enjoy in Christianity, the religion and the moral system. Furthermore, whenever this sermon is commented upon in the relevant literature, certain of its most demanding precepts are treated rather as counsels of perfection, as they are then called. Anything but the straight moral precepts that they are, and requiring, as moral precepts do, the compliance of any who would keep the covenant that Jesus restored and sealed in his own blood.

'You have heard that it was said to the men of old, "you shall not kill," ... but I say to you': the contrast with the Sinai covenant could not be more stark than it is in this new interpretation of the Fifth Commandment. (Matthew does not include a statement of the Ten Commandments here in this sermon, though he does state it in summary elsewhere, and clearly presupposes it here.) And the contrast is all the starker because of the number of circumstances in which the older formulation of covenant law allowed one to kill legally. 'Whoever strikes, or curses his father or mother ... whoever steals a man (into slavery?) shall be put to death.' And then the *lex talionis* is invoked: 'you shall give life for life, eye for eye, tooth for tooth, hand for hand, foot for foot, burn for burn, wound for wound, stripe for stripe' (Ex 21:15-24). And then Jesus: 'But I say to you,' that we are not even to be angry with each other. We are not to deliberately diminish each other in any way. If we do, we are to make up to each other as a priority to our cultic obligations. In sum, we are obliged to do nothing less than to love all enemies who intend and do evil to us, and to pray for those who persecute us. So that we may be sons and daughters of God, true offspring of our Father who is in heaven, who makes the sun to offer its life-giving light and heat to the evil and the good alike, and who sends the rain to furnish the necessities of life equally to the just and the unjust. And it is particularly important that we do not return evil for evil in those cases where we are maligned, made subject to false accusation and positively persecuted precisely for living out this law of the covenant in God's kingdom, the world. Because in these cases we reach the stature of God's prophets, and in sharing their fate we give the most complete testimony to that trust in the Creator in which the limitless hope of all humankind consists.

And that is the first and foundational precept of the reformulated response to the divine covenant according to Jesus: trust in the Creator, eternal giver of life and existence to all. Trust in God forever for life and all the supports and enhancements of life. This trust is not a passive trust. Rather does it involve our assuming our full role as best-equipped creators among all creatures. Becoming people who can themselves be trusted, and who are prepared to trust others to share life and all the affordances of life with each other. For what is at issue here is a trusting response to the eternal life-giving source that results in our ruling the creation in the wisdom and the justice toward all that is transmitted to us in the very rationale (*logos*) of the creation itself. 'Seek first his kingdom and his righteousness, and all these things (needed for life) shall be yours as well.'

The corresponding, negative precept reads, in two versions: 'do not lay up *for yourselves* treasures on earth,' and 'you cannot serve God and Mammon.' Here in those twin precepts the horrendous prospect comes into view of people acting as if they were sole creative providers and guarantors of life for themselves, the prospect of idolatry in one or other of its many mythic forms, worshipful trust in oneself, in a creature-god, in a satanic power. And the prospect of all the destruction and death-dealing that then inevitably flows from this upon human life and upon the good earth that now supports it. For us plenipotentiaries of the Creator God on this earth these precepts mean then that we take our true trustful part in God's own project and rule, in pouring out life and existence unstintingly to all things. And in particular to give of ourselves and of God's good things even to those who would try to take them from us by force, to those who would steal them, as well as 'to him who begs from you, and do not refuse him who would borrow from you'. For all God's creatures are so inter-related and inter-dependent in this one universe that each comes into being, flourishes and even dies at the expense of others. But only if that expense – at once bodily-material and emotional-spiritual – is freely paid by each, can all continue to flourish and life continue to evolve and to abound. With no limit other than those an eternal God might wish to impose, but shows no signs whatever of wishing to do so. In what is possibly the oldest surviving fragment of western philosophy, Anaximander, who said that the source of all things was *to apeiron*, The Infinite, was quoted also as saying: 'Into that from which things take their rise they pass away once more, and they make reparation and satisfaction to one another for the "injustices" [i.e., what they have to take away from each other], according to Time's decree.' Or old Heraclitus, who put it even more succinctly in his aphoristic manner when he imagined in the case of both mortals and immortals, 'the one living by the other's death, and dying by the other's life'.

There is one other precept of the decalogue that Jesus specifically subjects to a revised interpretation in the course of handing down the new law from the holy mountain. The new terms of the new covenant that looks more and more like the oldest, original covenant of all. It is the so-called Sixth Commandment: thou shalt not commit adultery. Jesus's revision of this precept consists in decreeing that divorce, which Moses allowed as a concession to people's hard and unrepentant hearts, is not to be sought. It is forbidden under the terms of the new (old) covenant from the mountain, and so, if any one marries a divorcee, the result for both is the sin of adultery. In other passages from Matthew and Mark Jesus claims as his authority for therefore forbidding divorce the ordinance of God's creation: 'He who made them from the beginning [or, as Mark puts it: 'from the beginning of creation'] ... said ... "the two shall become one"' (Mt 19:3-9; Mk 10:2-9). This reference to an ordinance of creation in support of a straight ban on divorce finds its rationale in the following analysis: God in creating the world does so out of an eternal, steadfast love for all, the self-same steadfast love we are asked to exhibit in always returning good for evil, so that God expects nothing less from us. All the more then does God expect such steadfast love from the two who join together in the most special activity of procreating the very species that represents (to the best of our present knowledge) the highest form of co-creation in the universe. Under the renewed reign of God, in the terms of the renewed covenant of creation, married couples will exhibit such steadfast love for each other, for their children, and for all of God's creatures, for as long as they live.

In the text of Jesus's sermon from the mount as we now have it, an exception to Jesus's total ban on divorce is included in the form of the phrase 'except on grounds of unchastity', whatever that may be taken to mean. Scholars of the text suspect that the legal loophole was inserted in the very early Church for its own reason and benefit. And this could very well be true. Because Paul says clearly that Jesus simply banned divorce, without qualification ('not I, but the Lord'). Yet a few sentences later Paul himself is permitting divorce for converts to the faith of Jesus, under certain circumstances. But in doing so he specifically adds that he has no record of a saying of Jesus to support such an innovation ('I say, not the Lord': 1 Cor 7:10-15). So it is best to deal later with these and other changes to Jesus' remembered formulations of the ethical terms of the covenant that he mediated, when the handling by the followers of Jesus of these terms of the renewed testament comes up for investigation.

Finally, some further precepts from Jesus to guide our relationships to God and to the world that God created. First, we are not to swear, not to call on God as guarantor of the truth of what we speak or do. We are simply to speak and do the truth. By the fruits of our speech and action people will know whether it is true or right or not, and no ceremony of calling on God will change that fact. Anymore than our calling God our Lord, our Lord, will do anything whatever to make us in the least bit whole and hopeful of eternal life, if we do not keep to the moral responsibilities laid on us in and by the covenant of creation itself. For if we are not living truly and rightly, and not expressing that truth and right, then calling on God in order to profess our allegiance or to promote some advocacy for our cause is to try to make God complicit in our own evil. 'Let what you say be simply Yes and No; anything more than this comes from evil.' One's word must be one's bond. The fundamental precept of the old Irish religion under the aegis of God in the persona of Fionn comes to mind here: *ceart 'nar gcroidhe, neart 'nar ngeag, agus beart do reir ar mbriathair:* truth, right in our hearts; strength in our arms; and our deeds in accordance with our words. Words that are the expression of the truth and right that is in our hearts and that governs all our deeds, bringing the precept full circle. And that is all that is necessary; anything added to it may more likely take from it. Particularly, perhaps, distorted motivation. For the good that I do, whether in pursuit of moral or of ritual participation in the covenant, may be done purely for purposes of my own self-aggrandisement once again. I may pray ostentatiously from the front pews in church, or make a public display of my charity to the poor, or even parade my fasting with gaunt looks before an admiring populace (though this might not work these days, when the ideal woman is meant to look like a stick insect), and the oldest temptation is in control once more, the fertile source of the oldest sin. God may not be used, nor right and justice bent in the direction of satanic service. Truth must be upheld and right secured, for their own sakes, in the mutual steadfast love that binds the Creator and the creation. And anything below or beyond that is of evil.

In the actual sermon, in the actual formulation of the terms of the divine covenant, the whole text of it is prefaced by Matthew with a picture of the perfect human respondent drawn along the lines, not now of moral precept, but of moral ideal and virtue. This preface has become known as 'the beatitudes', simply because those who comply with the terms of the covenant, now couched in these alternative moral categories, are assured in every verse of this hymn-like composition, of companionship with all whose happiness in the presence of the eternal God is thereby guaranteed, now and in the future. For they are already citizens and agents of the kingdom of the eternal God: blessed are you.

'Blessed are the poor in spirit, for theirs is the kingdom of heaven.' The poor in spirit, because the poor in fact only are just as likely as the de facto rich to be self-centred, greedy and willing at first chance to take by deceit or violence what others have, including at times their lives.

'Blessed are those who mourn, for they shall be comforted.' God will keep on creating life for those deprived of it in any measure.

'Blessed are the meek, for they shall inherit the earth.' The virtue of temperance best translates into the categories of ideal or of virtue what is at stake here, namely, the opposite of going to excess and lording it over others in the quest for control of the sources of life and consequent power.

'Blessed are those who hunger and thirst after righteousness, for they shall be satisfied.' The virtue and ideal of right, truth, justice will prevail.

'Blessed are the merciful, for they shall obtain mercy.' The forgiveness, the first and most difficult exercise that is undertaken for the sake of the ideal and virtue of love will, like love, prevail also, blessing 'both him that gives and him that takes'.

'Blessed are the pure of heart, for they shall see God.' Clear sightedness, and single-mindedness are meant here, closest perhaps to the cardinal virtue of prudence in that this concerns knowing what to do, and nothing in particular to do with Christian churches' obsession with sex, as if sex were the most important thing in the world to get right. The heart, the emotions are the foundational heuristic devices where moral insight is concerned. Their cleansing of all excessive or distorted accretion is something that can be encouraged by education and acquired like any other virtue.

'Blessed are the peacemakers, for they shall be called the sons of God.' Not war-makers of any ilk or hue, or for any reason whatever.

Like Jesus, people who make peace – *shalom* – are sons of God, because, as the phrase connotes, they share in the Creator's prime characteristic of giving life, even through the very gates of death.

'Blessed are those who are persecuted for righteousness' sake, for theirs is the kingdom of heaven; blessed are you when men revile you and persecute you and utter all kinds of evil against you falsely on my account. Rejoice and be glad, for your reward is great in heaven, for so men persecuted the prophets who were before you.' The ideal and virtue of fortitude is now unquestionably in view, though not of course on its own. For virtues and ideals, like precepts, must travel in convoy if they are to have any hope of picturing at once in detail and in the whole that most precious and promising thing that can then be called a good moral life. So, if in the face of persecution one can muster the fortitude to go through it, loving and forgiving the persecutors, with faith in the eternal Source of life and the consequent hope in one's heart, one can find no better way of living out the terms of this covenant established by God in the activity and results of creation itself. And if the persecution is to result in nothing less than death, and one can go through the gates of death with that same fortitude, that same faith, love and hope, then like Jesus in this also, one can seal the covenant in the shedding of one's blood. For there is no more definitive form of testimony than to die for that in which one believes, to die keeping faith more fully than one ever did during life. That then is the definitive seal on the human side; on God's side the definitive seal consists in bringing out of human death life eternal, as Christians believed happened in the case of the man, Jesus, because it happens for all – as Paul put it: 'if the dead are not raised, then Christ has not been raised.' (1 Cor 15:16)

THE COVENANT MEDIATED BY JESUS AND ITS MORAL PRINCIPLES

There can be no doubt about the fact that Jesus quite deliberately reformed (fulfilled) the covenant according to Moses as it had been interpreted by his time. There can be no doubt either about the fact that he did so in all instances by using as his criterion the covenant in creation. This is clear from his references to sun and rain, to the birds of the air, the grass and the lilies of the field, and the single sparrow that falls to the ground. It is especially clear from his references to the beginning of creation – beginning in the sense of source – from which we can learn all the most important lessons about God's ways with the world, and ours with the world and with its God. It is also clear from the work that Jesus was sent to do and did, namely, the continuation of God's work in creating, most commonly in the form of making whole what had been subjected to self-inflicted or suffered destruction.

Further, there can be no doubt about the fact that the moral prescriptions, virtues and ideals, set out by Matthew as part of the mythic picture of the making of this re-new-ed covenant, do represent the strict terms of the moral obligations incurred by all who would be party to the only covenant God ever offered, does or will offer. And who would hope for the ultimate blessedness that this testament of God promises: eternal life from life's eternal Source.

There should be no room for vacillation here. What has been summarised and commented upon here, what would be far better read and meditated upon in Matthew's original report and, most likely, Jesus's own powerful and memorable imagery, this does present us with the strict terms of the covenant. None of these terms can be sidelined as counsels of perfection meant only for those who as a consequence can be described as more perfect Christians than are those who live their lives 'in the world'. Instead, what can and must be done with them continually is to specify and modulate them, if only because ideals and virtues and even sets of precepts are often very general and difficult to relate to the very concrete situations that in sequence make up most of our ever-changing lives. Jesus in the course of that collection presented by Matthew as a single sermon, does just that for some of the general precepts, concerning killing and adultery for example. But that does not complete the task for all time, even in the case of these two precepts. For, apart altogether from the fact that people must forever be prepared to correct sets of rules that they are always liable to corrupt for their own self-centered purposes, life evolves, creativity continues, and therefore codes must constantly change in order both to facilitate and to reflect the advances of life in length and quality.

The most general and fundamental moral principle in the covenant of creation is this: act only so as to preserve and advance life for all, and accept or cause only such diminution of life as is necessary to pursue the constant transformation of life for all. That most general and fundamental principle, implicit in the Creator's will and testament to continuously create and advance life for all, cannot be deemed to be addressed solely to human kind. All other species play their due part in the general creativity of the universe, and as a consequence, as individuals, die gradually that others might live and, as species, are transformed and sometimes die out in the process, that other (versions of) species might emerge. The covenant then is with all, and certainly with all living things, as the creation covenant with Noah makes explicitly clear. The human race, endowed with reflective consciousness, is explicitly aware of these terms of the covenant of creation, and so these terms take on with humans the form of moral precepts to which they can willingly conform, or not. And that places the further obligation of the charge upon them to rule themselves and the rest as vice-regents of the One who rules with the love that moves the sun and the other stars. To rule the other species in justice, to enable them to live as all subordinate co-creators must live and die.

The covenant implicit in creation is then not simply between individual species and God their Giver of life, but also between the species themselves, and primarily in this respect between the human species and those less endowed with reason and a corresponding moral sensitivity. From this point of view, it might have been preferable if some of our biblical authors who quoted Jeremiah as the prophet of the covenant that came (again) through Jesus, had chosen Hosea instead. Hosea, picturing the day when Jahweh woos Israel back from her idolatry, back to the relationship that obtained 'when she came out of the land of Egypt,' has Jahweh declare: 'I will make for you a covenant on that day with the beasts of the field, the birds of the air, and creeping things on the ground; and I will abolish the bow, the sword, and war from the land; and I will make you lie down in safety ... I will betroth you to me in righteousness and justice, in steadfast love and mercy I will betroth you to me in faithfulness; and you shall know the Lord' (Hos 2:14-20).

It is here, incidentally, where it is a matter of extending to others, to all other co-creative creatures, to all other dynamic forms of reality, the steadfast love that is the defining characteristic of all creators of life both original and derivative; it is here that the third intrinsic character of the whole of reality comes into its own: the character of beauty. Truth and goodness have already gone together, in every reference to truth and right or righteousness, justice: *omne ens est bonum; omne ens est verum.* The truth and goodness of all reality coincide in that the truth of a thing consists in its being and remaining itself through its formation, deformation, reformation, transformation, on its journey to its perfection and in the course of its mutual adaptation to other forms of reality during the evolutionary process. Truth and falsehood in accounts of things consist in success or failure to account accurately for such existential truth and falsehood. Good and bad consist in the same process by which things are formed, deformed, reformed and at all events transformed, again in the general process of mutual adaptation. Good and evil then are the names for that reality-as-process and all parts of it, and its outcome in transformation seen from the point of view of any of the agent-things involved in it. And because all the truth we may ever know of all these things with which we share the world comes from our interaction as thrown-projects with them, that truth is also formulated in an account of the matter in which, in fact, such fulfilment is or is not achieved, and can or cannot be achieved by each and all. And moral discourse – for that is the form of the account of the world-project that is now at issue – is then true or false as such, and adequate or inadequate, to the extent that it accurately or misleadingly accounts for the processes by which transformation does and can, or does not and cannot, come about.

Yet, in spite of how fine that sounds, the fact of the matter remains that the character of goodness in the whole of process-reality is always inclined to be seen predominantly in terms of the transformation of the human viewer. Just as the ancient, indeed original temptation with respect to that steadfast love that drives all transformation through the inevitable deformations on the way, and that is therefore the first, foundational moral ideal and virtue, is the temptation to cage that love within the confines of the self. To confine the most steadfast love to self-love, if not of the individual self, then of one's national or ethnic neighbours, or at the very most of one's fellow human beings, and excluding enemies of course in all cases. And that is where beauty, together with its contrary ugliness, comes in as the third universal category, the third metaphysical character of all reality, that as such then coincides with the other two: *omne ens est pulchrum*. And that is also where art comes in, creative art and the artists who produce it, the seers who see the beauty and ugliness of creation-in-process and are then the indispensable agents of the revelation to those who, caged in their very self-centeredness, stain the otherwise translucent world with their selfish yearning. As Brendan Kennelly, thinking of his own art, put it:

> Words are innocent,
> And are never free from man's power to corrupt them.
> Out of his cage he sends his cries,
> Impressing his slavery on free things.
> Fields, cities, seas
> Are stained with his yearning,
> His blood stains the summer sky
> And he wonders why
> He tries to glorify
> Himself
> By turning the rattle of his chains
> Into the music of a word called freedom.
> Yet when I consider the stain
> I know that only the same grimed heart
> Stumbling on its happy words
> Will wipe it clean.

For beauty it is that elicits love, even in the grimed heart, love which cannot be commanded, and is the source of all commands that have the least claim to be obeyed. For beauty truly is a matter of form, and not simply of the integrity of the dynamic form of the individual agent or species that drives it to pro-create and evolve according to its kind, but of the harmony, the fittingness of forms of agencies that interact and are so interdependent, that must mutually adapt for the transformation of what constitutes after all one world, a universe. To picture such beauty, together with its oft-attendant ugliness, in words or in any of the media of the visual arts, or in the elegant formulae of deep mathematics, or to compose its harmonies and disharmonies and their reconciliation in music, is to enable the greediest of grime-clogged hearts to expand toward love of 'all poor foolish things that live a day' (in Yeats's phrase), and to cherish them in their own right and their rightful place in the transformation of the world.

This in itself is the participation by the appointed vice-regents and co-creators of the world, whether they recognise themselves as such or not, in the steadfast love that characterises the ultimate Creator of all. For even the deformations that comprise the transient badness and ugliness that all transformation requires can be beautiful and are rightly portrayed as such. The deformation of the woman's body in pregnancy, even the slight heaviness or grossness of the facial features, have the beauty of the advent symbolism of promise of a new creation, a new world. The true artist, the true seer, can detect and present the beauty of such deformations in contra-distinction to the ugliness of deformations and stains inflicted upon the beauty of the world by evil-doing. All part and parcel of art's general ability to enable us to love the one and to be repelled by the other, even as we are moved to compassion for those who are afflicted by it. The truest education of our emotions and our moral sensibilities occurs here, without the least intrusion of overt moralising, and indeed all the better for being without that, merely by enabling us to see the light of goodness and truth that shines in all true creation, and the darkness that occludes it upon the entrance of evil.

That is not to say that without a goodly exposure to good art, we cannot come upon that vision of the beauty that shines through all things, and its vulnerability in particular to the incursions of ugly, evil forces. For one thing, art that is technically quite good can glorify evil by beautifying both its processes and its results: think only of the age-old artistic glorification of soldiering and killing in war. For another, any experience of true love in response to natural beauty, and most especially to the beauty we love in a partner or child, can literally change the world for us, instantly and utterly, opening our eyes at once and simultaneously to the fragile beauty of all the earth, to the joy of its goodness, and also to the sorrow of its constant and universal exposure to forces that could then look either indifferent or downright malicious, and might well be either or both.

Very few poems in the whole history of poetry express the beauty-born love of another human being and reveal the manner in which it infuses all of the natural world with the joy of its grace and sorrow for its threatening transience than Yeats' paired poems, 'The Pity of Love' and 'The Sorrow of Love'.

THE CODIFICATION OF JESUS' RENEWED COVENANT OF CREATION AND WHAT THE CHURCHES MADE OF IT

The fundamental principle of morality is not now sufficiently captured in the old formulation: do good and avoid evil. That principle stands of course underneath all, but it needs immediate supplement for purposes of any and every practical application, and practical application after all is what all moral principle and precept is about. The suggestion has already been made that the immediate supplement should read something like this: create always, as a derivative and dependent creator engaged in the task; and create in such a manner and degree that the benefits are there for all fellow creatures, and that any diminution of life and existence incurred is only such as can be seen to be an inevitable part of that progressive transformation of life and existence, that evolution of life and existence that is so obviously the result and goal of the continuous Creator of all. There is not much difficulty in formulating that fundamental principle, and it could be formulated more elegantly and more clearly than that by someone more gifted in such matters.

It is in the further formulation of that fundamental principle, it is at the point at which it can be made to guide our actions in any and every one of the concrete projects we face, it is there that the difficulties crowd in. We can begin by reminding ourselves that everyone who engages with the world in which we exist as thrown projects will benefit from faith in this evolving world and in all the powers co-active in it. Everyone can benefit from the hope to which such active faith gives rise, and above all perhaps, from a steadfast love of all involved, born of the beauty of transformation ever already evident in the world. And we can remember that it takes prudence to judge what must be done in these conditions of existence. It takes courage to do all of this in face of countervailing sufferings either natural to the process or maliciously increased by those whose god is self. It takes temperance to ensure that one's aim in action is moderate, that one's own god is not self. It takes justice to see to it that one's creative input is to the benefit of all involved and in due proportion in each case. And that is all very true, and very practical and concrete. But it all still raises rather than settles the question for each particular project in which we engage: what in particular ought one to do here and now? My justice makes it obligatory on me to answer that question in particular detail. My love makes me want to answer without any talk of obligation. Yet, although love can make it a joy to do what I ought to do, and can guide me to some extent as to what I ought to do, if only by holding my imagination to that beauty and harmony between all things that first and always arouses love, the precision of particular precept remains a permanent task. That is why human societies should have, not just legal systems, but permanent legislatures, and judicial systems that are independent of the legislatures.

This is not the time or place to talk any more about moral codes made up of precepts, of their well advertised and inherent limitations, despite their prevailing necessity, and certainly not the time nor the place to offer even in broad outline such a code for this age. It is the place only to look once more to Jesus' reformulation of the code that was then attached to the Mosaic covenant, and to see what the followers of Jesus then did with his code of precepts. It is clear from the rNT – yes, the re-NEW-ed Testament, because of all that has been said about the covenant mediated through Jesus as the renewal of the ... no, not the Old Testament, but the Original Testament, still OT, the terms of which had become corrupted by the time of Jesus – it is clear from the rNT itself that Jesus's followers already revised in important respects and often, it would appear, in a backward direction, his code, his formulation of the terms of the covenant of creation. Paul revised Jesus' anti-divorce precept, as did Matthew. And Matthew also modified quite radically Jesus' precept to the effect that we should never return evil for evil, but that, in preparation for doing nothing but good to those who do us harm, we should always forgive all who do us wrong.

Matthew's revision reads as follows: if your brother offends against you, try first for reconciliation between the two of you. If he does not cooperate, try again before witnesses. If he still will not cooperate, bring him before the Church, and if the Church does not succeed with him, let him be treated as 'the heathen and the publican'. Now this revision occurs within a few lines of Matthew's text that contains Matthew's clear account of Jesus' precept that there should be no limit to the amount of times we should forgive our enemies, seventy times seventy, as a symbol for infinity. And in a context in which Matthew had apparently already decided either to forget or to ignore Jesus' precept and practice of accepting as one of ourselves, by breaking bread with them, publicans and other sinners. In short, Matthew replaces an ethos of limitless forgiveness with a strictly judicial system in which failed appeals to offenders to come to heel would be followed by judicial trial and specific sanction (Mt 18:15-21). These cases of backward revision are due no doubt to the unwillingness, or at best the inability of the first followers of Jesus to accept fully his version of the reign of God, and the consequent inability to accept Jesus' moral portrait of a true son of the true God. More of this unwillingness and inability may be seen when the theme of judgement and second (third ... ?) comings come up for perusal. But it is in the case of the precept against killing, as Jesus radically revised it, that we have already seen the most radical retro-revision by the community that claimed to follow Jesus in the early centuries after his death. Particularly as that killing is instanced in wars, and especially in the wars of conquest in which Christian nations, like other religious peoples, engaged. For war is the most obscene example of killing, involving as it does managerial killing on a massive scale.

Take the case of a British army arriving in the land of the Zulu in order to bring that land under the aegis of good Queen Victoria. The commander of that army announces that just invading Zululand and 'killing a few thousand Zulus' should be sufficient to accomplish the annexation. What further formulation of our most general moral principle, thou shalt not kill, should govern the behaviour of the Zulu in this case? According to Jesus, that further formulation should read: we must not resist the evil of this newly arrived killing machine; we must not kill them that would kill us; we must instead give them what they would take from us, and more. Give them some land, or give them a livelihood, or enough to live on. And if they insist on ruling over us, let them have their share in government, but insist peacefully that such rule must be a rule of justice for all. Something like that? Gandhi's pacifist policy of rebellion against injustice? One has to be very resourceful and, yes, imaginatively creative, in order to prescribe for the kind of conduct that can adapt the precept, thou shalt not kill, to such extreme circumstances.

It does seem to be the case that over the first two centuries of its existence the Christian Church did understand Jesus to have forbidden warfare. Christians therefore would not take up the profession of arms. But then, it also appears, at a time that suspiciously coincided with the movement to make Christianity the established religion of the Roman Empire, Christian theologians began to adopt from Platonised Stoicism the morality of the just war. The fact itself of borrowing moral method and moral precept from Platonised Stoicism should not surprise us. For Christians had already borrowed the Stoic-Platonic theology of God. On the grounds that, in both systems, one discovered the ethical rules that should govern the world, from one's daily and cooperative experience of the way in which God's Word/Wisdom continued to create and re-create that same world. Except that Jesus interpreted such creative activity of the Word that his followers said was incarnate in him, in a way which showed that God never returns evil for evil, but only does good equally to all, and so all sons and daughters of God should do likewise. Whereas Christian theologians now began to adopt instead the contemporary Stoic-Platonic reading of God's Word revealed in nature, and thereby claimed a share in the prevailing 'just war' theory. Conveniently so, for secular rulers seldom fail to require some quid-pro-quo for their patronage of religion. Political theology prevails over natural theology, as the Greeks would have put it. Or else some other Jesus or Socrates must die.

So Christians borrowed such arguments as would make the wholesale, managerial killing called war 'just', in just such general circumstances as the British in Zululand and later, the Germans of the Third Reich created. This was and remains throughout history and to this day the most massive betrayal of Jesus's vision and mission to restore the true covenant of the reign of God. There seemed to be some fleeting hope of ending the maleficent reign of just war theory when nuclear arms were invented and used. For people began to argue that such weapons were so massively widespread and indiscriminate in their destructiveness, they simply could not be reconciled with the 'just war' embargo on targeting innocent civilians. It soon became clear, however, that people like the so-called Allies in the Second World War were prepared, as Hitler and countless other war-mongers before him, to commit such crimes against humanity as the deliberate targeting and bombing both by conventional and nuclear weapons, of hundreds of thousands of civilians in Dresden, Hiroshima, Nagasaki ... The same Allies who have since been prepared to terrorise hundreds of thousands of innocent Iraqi civilians, killing thousands of them in a 'war against terror', while displaying the nauseating hypocrisy of presenting the killing of some three thousand in New York on 9/11 as 'the day the world changed'. In truth 9/11 was just another normal day in a persistently war-mongering world, and just another instance of what Americans themselves describe often in tones of moral righteousness, as 'what goes around, comes around'. In other words, the words of Jesus: those who live by the sword, will die by the sword. And there is no end in sight of that disastrous delusion of 'just war' with which churches and states replaced the morality preached by Jesus.

But there are more common and everyday circumstances in which the same Fifth Commandment needs more concrete formulations and applications. These circumstances refer once again to the general moral principle of the divine covenant in creation, and in particular to that part of it which enjoins on all to keep to the minimum the expense to others of their living well and living ever better. Look now to the most basic, physical necessity of life, food and drink. Is it permissible to kill other living things for food? Does the Fifth Commandment apply only to humans, and only quite conditionally to these other living things? Or does it apply to all sentient animals, birds, fish, but not to other living things like plants, if they are not sentient? And as humanity comes into more extensive control of the whole earth, what further responsibilities must then devolve upon the shoulders of this species, with respect even to other animal species that currently live, as does humanity also, 'red in tooth and claw'? The covenant envisaged by Hosea will not come about by direct divine action. God the Creator creates through creatures, and specifically through human creatures, in the course of that creative response. And that means that we have to be as continuously creative in formulating precepts for what we have to do, as we are in doing for what we are responsible for doing as derivative creators. There are no sets of absolute immutable moral principles. And if a precept such as 'thou shalt not kill' looks like one, that is only because in such brief and simple formulation it is still lacking in the necessary interpretation and in the concrete details necessary for its application in a constantly evolving and highly complex universe. The same is true, even more so, of that general principle already announced as the fundamental moral principle of the covenant of creation.

A current illustration of the first and more positive part of that fundamental moral principle – thou shalt create life ever more abundant for all, acting as a derivative and dependent creator – is found in the present and increasing knowledge and mastery of the genetic infrastructure of the evolution of life. And more especially in the awesome and, more often than not, largely unknown prospects of incipient genetic engineering. There are many who would say, and do say, that we human creatures should not engage in such activity at all. That to do so is in itself a form of idolatry, a prime form in fact of the original sin of humanity: playing God. To such people human beings have no properly creative role at all in God's creation. They are at best maintenance workers reading off from the natures that come from a static divinity's assembly line the unchanging rules for dealing with each and all. And any attempt on the part of human beings to initiate a creative contribution or to alter in any way the pro-creative process in which certain creatures, including themselves, engage would be tantamount to posing as rivals to God who is sole and exclusive Creator of the world.

This kind of false Christian moralising is traceable to the fact that when Christians first borrowed the Stoic-Platonic theology of God the Creator, they took in wholesale also the damage that an inferior dualist Platonism had already done to the original Stoic theology. As the chapter on creation above explained, the wholly immanent and ever-dynamic, spirit-like, fire-like *Logos* was gradually removed beyond the world, having created it originally through the immutable Ideas or Forms in the divine mind. So now Logos/Word squatted outside the world, distinct both from the world (and the World Soul) and from the ultimate One – the application in Christian theology of the term *person* helped here. Leaving human beings, now no longer real co-creators, to read off immutable moral principles from the largely static natures of things that make up creation.

The classic example of that false theology of creation, and its consequently straightforward 'reading off' from a certain current feature of human nature, namely, the human reproductive cycle, a misleading, in fact a false moral ruling, occurs in the case of the papal prohibition of the use of any form of 'artificial' contraception, rather than the 'natural safe period'. The hidden reasoning behind this latest example of misleading the faithful in matters of morality must be something like this: one must leave it to the divine Creator alone, to create new human beings as and only when the Creator alone wishes. The best way to do this is to keep on copulating regardless; the next best way is to abstain from sexual intercourse, perhaps by confining sexual intercourse to the notoriously unreliable 'safe period', which nature, and therefore God has ordained for this purpose.

But it is the attempt to ban in the name of Christian morality all potentially salvific-creative genetic manipulation, it is this that represents the more serious outcome of a false theology of creation, and consequently false fundamental principle of human morality. If only because the vast majority of the people to whom it was addressed have long ceased to pay any attention to the papal decree on contraception in any case. For one thing, such comprehensive condemnation of creative-salvific genetic manipulation distracts from a most urgent moral task of the moment. This is the task of detecting and weeding out the real immoralities that are only too prevalent at this time in the practice of genetic modulation. These are, first, the cynicism of pretending that the solution to the problem of world hunger lies with genetically engineered crops, rather than the reform of persistent economic pillaging and oppression by the developed countries for the sake of their own enrichment and self-aggrandizement. Second, the consequent use of the so-called developing countries as guinea pigs for growing GM crops well before sufficient research has been carried out in order to calculate the risk of the whole enterprise. And, third, for the same greedy, self-centered Mammon-motives, the patenting by business enterprises of the kind of knowledge and know-how from which, of its very nature, all human kind, and indeed other living species, should benefit equally and simultaneously. And so it is that the most advanced instance of humanity's exponentially growing powers of co-creation becomes at one and the same time a show-case for the persistent destructiveness of the oldest form of fundamental sinfulness, and the fullest and most persuasive example of the nature of human moralising as a continuous creative elucidation of the fundamental moral principle of divine covenant in ever-changing sets of concrete precepts. 'No more to will and no more to evaluate and no more to create! Ah, that this lassitude may ever stay far from me.' Yes indeed, and Ah also, that this newest prospect of human creativity at the genetic level be rescued from the sinners, and pursued properly by the just.

Is what has been outlined just now as the ever-evolving ethic that goes with the covenant that Jesus renewed, a Christian ethic then? Well, yes and no. Yes, in the sense that in so far as it is a morality that maintains and develops as necessary the moral principles that Jesus himself bequeathed to his followers. But no, in so far as one can see that the priests and teachers of the new religion, called Christianity, which Jesus neither intended nor even foresaw, have reversed in many instances the moral directions explicitly laid down by Jesus, and have furthermore over the centuries so changed for the worse the true biblical and theological context for right ethical thinking, that their moral teaching can result in wrong rather than right valuation and conduct to this day.

And no, also, in a more general sense. In the sense that the moral positions that Jesus adopted and outlined, and by which he lived and died, are quite recognisably derivable from the covenant in creation, as part and parcel of our human response and responsibility. Being, as we are, beneficiaries and subordinate partners in that covenant. In other words, the Word that was enfleshed in Jesus is the self-same Word that creates the world and thereby enlightens everyone who is born into this world – as John put it in the prologue to his gospel. Therefore, the moral vision and formulation that occurs in and with the imaginative, reflective creativity to which all humans are called in this covenant is both a possibility and a vocation for all of humankind at all times and places. As the epistemologist says, we know the world and all that is in it – including God – when we imagine and know simultaneously what it is and what it can and indeed ought yet to be, in so far as our limited human spirits can at any time know all of this. Human beings as such are natural moralists, equipped for this vocation by their very nature and position in creation. And they are designated moralists in and through the very course of being whatever else they are: scientists, politicians, farmers, entrepreneurs, tinkers ... And whether they are members of some religion or of none. And they are none the less fully qualified moralists for being none of the above, being numbered perhaps among the unemployed, those described by the poet as the ones 'who only stand and wait'. Those who follow Jesus take him to be a special revelation of the true morality of creation, especially to those of them still partially (never totally) blinded by the original evil that forever seems to afflict our race.

10 Virtues and the God Who Makes Everything New

Maureen Junker-Kenny

(W.G. Jeanrond and A.D.H. Mayes (eds), *Recognising the Margins*, Dublin: Columba, 2006, pp. 293–320.)

At a time where disciplinary boundaries are shifting, new affinities are being discovered, and immediate interaction takes place between, e.g. New Testament Studies and Christian Ethics, it is worthwhile to probe some of the assumptions behind the new flourishing of such co-operations.[1] The reality of such joint ventures may be a sign that historical enquiries can meet with contemporary concerns; history is not just antiquarian and ethics not merely ruled by the urgent demands of today's world. The 'ugly ditches' between history, truths of reason and theological appropriations may have actually been filled in and made passable through the hermeneutical awareness that all sciences, be they secular or biblical and theological, start from presuppositions they have to lay open and justify. Thus, the assessment of historical processes depends on one's horizon of expectation and cannot be passed off as 'objective' without giving account of how a scholar construes the relationship between the present, the past and the future.[2]

But the directness of the new links sought between historical and practical disciplines across a previously gaping precipice may also betray a problematic loss of the willingness to engage in systematic perspectives;[3] 'systematic' in the sense of seeking a coherent thought form in which the ongoing significance of the biblical heritage is outlined with regard to contemporary self-understandings. Yet it is true that such coherence has not even been achieved in Systematic Theology. The following observation of the simultaneous use of alternative paradigms shows that it still remains very much a project:

> The *ad hoc* use of arbitrary means of thought is not an adequate method; e.g. to conceive of the celebration of the mysteries of faith with Platonic, of the Eucharistic presence of Jesus Christ with Aristotelian categories, to go on to grasp the unity of divinity and humanity in his being in Neo-Chalcedonian or in Hegelian-speculative terms, and at the same time apply some thought forms from a theory of freedom to the proceedings of revelation, tradition and grace. Since in changing from one thought form to another also the content of what is thought changes, this manner of

proceeding either overlooks the objective interference of the content of the themes treated, or the incompatibility of the thought forms used.[4]

In view of this analysis of irreconcilable methods, can Christian Ethics be blamed for not wanting to get bogged down in the quagmire of never-ending systematic quarrels? What is wrong about reaching for uplifting biblical concepts and images such as 'covenant' or 'city on the mountain' to inspire the types of practice and disposition Christian Ethics is held to reflect on? The accompanying move away from a mainly prohibitive style of Moral Theology towards a Christian Ethics of capability, from 'ought' to 'can do', may have sound theological reasons behind it. Yet on the other hand, counter-movements to what is perceived as the ruling modern orthodoxies may not be free from ideology themselves. There could be just as much cultural drivenness behind the position that sees modernity solely in terms of decline as in the opposite desire to be fresh, innovative and daring in aiming to create a discipline as fetching in its own way as contemporary appeals to market attraction and fun. Can a balance be struck between the aims of rehabilitating understandings of ethics that have been sidelined unjustly and to the detriment of contemporary moral experience, and the urge of Christian Ethics to be cutting-edge or at least not behind the times?

Praxis-oriented disciplines such as Ethics cannot wait for all conceptual disputes to be resolved before they venture what may turn out to be premature and wrong conclusions. Yet, by eclipsing systematic theological reflection one runs the risk of short-circuiting Christian ethical argumentation by jumping from the ancient world straight into the postmodern: from pre-secular to post-secular, Patristic to post-liberal, from early Christian to late modern ecclesial communities, or from antique philosophical to (early and modern) Christian virtue ethics. I am going to investigate the claim that Christian Ethics should take the form of virtue ethics by comparing the classical philosophical tradition of virtues and its theoretical underpinnings to exegetical accounts of the Jesus who proclaimed a Creator who makes everything new. Here, Theological Ethics can learn from systematic theological enquiries into the gradual change of Greek philosophical concepts of God effected by the biblical testimony to a God of liberation, faithfulness and of the unique power to begin. By illustrating the need to go back to such issues of systematic reflection, I am hoping to upset the easy alliance between the decidedly non-speculative self-understandings that historical and practical disciplines display of themselves.[5]

My enquiry into current attempts to recast Christian Ethics as a whole in the antique 'virtue' mode will take the following steps: in order to clarify in what the distinctiveness of Christian Ethics consists (1), and starting from the discontents expressed with modern, i.e. 'liberal' approaches to deliver on this (2), I will discuss the charges of individualism versus community (a), and of rule-definition versus character-orientation (b). The position resulting from these options will be examined in the light of the status that ethics receives in a hermeneutical-contextual framework over against a critical deontological one (c).

1. DEFINING THE DISTINCTIVENESS OF CHRISTIAN ETHICS

It is remarkable how differently the distinctiveness of Christian Ethics can be configured with regard to its historical origins. The feature familiar to all hermeneutically conscious reconstructions that the terms used are inevitably predetermined and loaded will be exemplified by comparing two definitions. Such basic descriptions influence the way in which the conceptual and hermeneutical difficulties are portrayed that arise when guidance is sought from the New Testament for contemporary ethical problems.

What was distinctive about the approach of the people of the Bible to morality? How did faith determine and enlighten its conduct; how much better off is it than its neighbours in discovering how one should lead the good life and in what that good life consists? Such a use of the Bible in theology seems best to take account of its historical and time-conditioned nature, on the one hand, and yet accept its normative value as God's word for the Church of every age, on the other … One could answer what is distinctive about biblical morality by briefly saying that it regards man's behaviour as the direct and immediate response to God's revealed will.[6]

From the background of subsequent decades of debate in Christian Ethics, two features are distinctive in this short formula offered at the end of the 1960s by Seán Freyne: what is specific for biblical, including Christian, particularity, is sought in the *approach* to morality, not first of all in a totally different *content* from the surrounding cultures. It is a specific way of dealing with the moral element in the human constitution, not necessarily a different set of instructions.

This approach typical for Jewish and Christian monotheism is marked, secondly, as a human response to the prior self-expression of God, and more precisely, of God's will. The voluntaristic turn thus introduced into antique thought structures will merit further attention.

Leaving aside the article's subsequent development of differences in content and motivation from the specific eras and sources of biblical morality, I want to turn to a more recent basic description which shows the traces of the last quarter-century's debate between Liberalism and Communitarianism. The Belgian moral theologian Jef Van Gerwen concludes his overview of the origins of Christian Ethics as follows, anchoring the understanding of morality following from the person and practice of Jesus firmly in the tradition of virtue ethics:

> Early Christians all agreed that morality was a matter of training in the basic virtues, rather than just the application of a universal set of rules or rational principles. These approaches stress the particular features of moral education in a concrete sociohistorical community. Morality depends on

the training of character, and seeing and imitating concrete examples, such as Jesus Christ, the saints, or the ordinary faithful.[7]

The beginning of the article makes it quite clear that there is more continuity with antique understandings of ethics than with modern ones. The fact that these later interpretations were developed in the history of reception of Christianity does not invite closer attention to their content.

> (E)thics for early Christians was a matter of attitudes or habits, rather than just rules and commandments. Although the Jewish Law (especially the Ten Commandments) played a central role in it, Christian morality was primarily based on the practice of a number of virtues, such as love, hope, justice, forgiveness and patience … Consequently, it was committed to fight vices such as hate, envy, lust, sloth and anger. Early Christian Ethics resembles more closely other antique schools of ethics, such as Aristotelianism or Stoicism, than our modern Kantian and utilitarian paradigms. (204)

Jesus' practice and proclamation is seen as continuing the 'virtues' chosen by the prophets:

> The ethical teaching of Jesus of Nazareth fits perfectly into the tradition of prophetic and early rabbinical representatives of Jewish ethics. In the line of the prophets, Jesus stresses the importance of the virtues of justice and mercy over the ritualistic ethics of purity and cult offerings that had been developed in the Jewish Law (the books of Leviticus and Deuteronomy). In his interpretation of the Mosaic Law (Mt 5-7) he focuses on the purity of intention of the agent, rather than on the mere act of trespassing a rule of law. (205)

What stands out in this position are the alternatives against which the Christian moral view is constructed as belonging to the virtue tradition. As in similar attempts, the deficiencies to be overcome always include individualism (a), the understanding of ethics as legislation centred on acts (b), and 'abstract' or 'universal' criteria, i.e. standards of evaluation that are independent of the context and 'situatedness' of agents and communities (c).

2. VIRTUES AS AN ALTERNATIVE TO AUTONOMY

In contrast to other rehabilitation projects that seek to integrate Aristotelian elements such as striving for the good life, or the rationality of virtuous practices into a comprehensive understanding of ethics,[8] it is clear that it is not a matter of complementing but of challenging the modern foundation of ethics on the autonomy of the subject. The programmatic embrace of pre-modern ethics as a way out of current impasses raises the question whether such a return is philosophically desirable and possible, and whether it is theologically appropriate for Christian Ethics. While not all sympathy for the virtue mode of ethics (e.g. Dietmar Mieth's) and not all communitarian leanings (e.g. Charles Taylor's) are dismissive of modernity's principle of freedom, the folio against which the renaissance of virtue is called for most often is modern liberalism.

a) Community orientation versus liberal individualism

In societies marked by structural differentiation and individualisation, it will be part of the service of self-enlightenment that philosophy can offer to reassess models of linking individual and political life. When each person is forced to become the stage manager of their own life under market conditions, where community ties are subordinated to demands of mobility and the local is devalued as peripheral to the centre, a counter-move is necessary to do justice to requirements of human existence that can only be fulfilled in an intersubjective, communicative way.[9] Education, cultural self-expression, political participation and religious practice need a community that is valued not just as a conduit to a next 'higher' stage.

If the current revival of virtue ethics was just a matter of balance and of critiquing the degeneration of the moral subject to a bearer of rights but not of equal original obligation to others, this dissatisfaction would find resonance in Kantian objections to the liberal emptying of the moral concept of autonomy to mere choice. Virtue ethicists and deontologists could agree on the need to foster 'virtues' in the sense of intersubjectively shared proposals of attractive human models of being and would thus have convincing alternatives to offer to a public culture in danger of reducing itself to a cult of celebrities. However, even then it will be necessary to clarify in *philosophical* terms the two constitutive poles of the individual and the community, or of human reflexivity and sociability, and explain the model pursued in relating them (1). When it comes to the *theological* appropriation of the philosophical turn to 'community', it is even more urgent to come clear on one's implicit claims. If the Aristotelian bent towards the existing ethos that Hegel named '*Sittlichkeit*' is already problematic as a foundation for ethics, it does not help if ecclesial communitarians claim this ground for the Christian Church as the seat of salvation. The three dangers Theological Ethics should avoid are to reduce the kingdom of God to the visible Church, thus denying its universal claim and the legitimacy of relating to civil society; to downplay the role of individual conscience over against dispositions acquired within a supportive ethos; and to dismiss the ongoing role of an autonomous morality of respect for human dignity in critiquing in-group ideologies, be they ecclesial or issuing from other politics of identity that claim exceptions for themselves from the rule of mutual recognition (2).

(1) Two poles: reflexivity and sociability

The current emphasis on community in social ethics has evident advantages: life stages other than full autonomy are recognised, attention is paid to the genesis and renewal of values, and the political element in human nature is emphasised as part of its fulfilment. Yet, there are two significant draw-backs in communitarian analysis:

- Without an equal consideration of the pole of human reflexivity, it remains one-sided and in danger of promoting social conformity with no regard for individual conscience.
- By conceiving all social relations in terms of community, it ignores the 'most important *non*-Aristotelian element in our modern ethos: the concept of legality'.[10]

There is no need to cry 'atomism' when a transcendental analysis of human freedom distinguishes its formal unconditionality from its concrete, embodied, intersubjectively nurtured existence. Without this distinction of levels, there could not even be any specific appropriation of a surrounding ethos, but only an unquestioning connectedness, a seamless belonging or primary embeddedness that could never be regained as, in Paul Ricoeur's words, a second *naiveté*. As little as it is necessary to devalue the ethos in which one was socialised as a preliminary stage to be left behind for a 'post-conventional' identity,[11] as unconvincing is the identification of the goal of self-determination with that of self-invention or even self-production. The ability to distance oneself from the community's ethos is a condition also for its conscious and critical appropriation.

The second shortfall in communitarianism is the lack of regard for mere 'legality'. Arising from the Kantian turn to subjectivity, respect for personally espoused convictions, developed in the interaction of individual reflexivity with culturally transmitted values, has the consequence that 'legality' denoting not substantive communal, but formal legal relations, becomes a valued condition of personal freedom.[12] The reverse side of 'legality' within a neutral *state* is religious freedom within *society*.[13] The familiarity and social bondedness that are lost in this transition can be transferred to a different register; one can work at being willing to live together with anonymous others even without an already given social vision of the good. The end of the *polis* does not have to spell barbarism, as for Alasdair MacIntyre in the last pages of *After Virtue*; it is also possible that a diverse civil society without pre-established alliances is born. Then, it is the matter of the resources of each conviction whether mutual respect can be created. In a pluralist culture one feature of Christian religious convictions may even come out stronger: that their claim is not simply directed to members of an in-group ethos but to 'all people of good will'. This key expression, familiar to all hearers of the nativity stories and oratorios, contains a second significant difference that an anti-modern project of virtue ethics cannot appreciate: the change from a cognitive, intellect-oriented model of ethics to a will-based one.

(2) Consequences of the communitarian vision for the concept of Church
The Aristotelian and Hegelian starting-point of the existing ethos over against a deontology of imperatives that can never be fulfilled completely, results in a focus on the Church as the framework of the ethical life of the faithful. This setting has several advantages: it avoids the interpretive practice of 'norm hunting' in the New Testament[14] by focusing on the shared self-understanding of the community 'prior to legislation'. It abandons 'quandary ethics' and has an interest in formation, socialisation, spiritual and ethical growth.[15] Its subject is not simply a deliberating individual, but a participant and contributor to a shared enterprise of faithful hope. The main dangers to be avoided, however, are an apotheosis of the Church, a denial of its internal differences, and a corresponding loss of interest in contributing to the spheres outside the *communio*. A further consequence, to be treated in section c), is the reduction of the status of ethics to a hermeneutics, in this case of Church life.

Setting up the Church as the counter-model to a liberal society seen as consumerist, permissive and aggressive in defending its wasteful lifestyle, risks sacralising it and isolating it from the 'world'. The price of this contrasting of ideal types is that, the more the Church becomes a fortress against moral degeneration, the more its instrumental character for the kingdom of God disappears. The unity of faith gets stressed to an extent that faithful practical and theoretical conscientious dissent from what has been defined as orthodoxy and orthopraxy is hardly conceivable. And the possibilities of mutual learning and critique, instead of constant correction of secular society, as well as the chance for the world to repent are no longer held open.

Seán Freyne's account of the dispute about the proper content of 'Zion' gives helpful biblical pointers on how to conceive the service of the Church beyond its own confines. In his discussion of 'Jesus' Disciples as the Servant Community' he shows how Jesus aligned himself with the 'servants of Yahweh' understanding of Zion that Isaiah raised as a challenge to the triumphalist view held by the circle that dominated the cult. For Isaiah, a 'genuinely inclusive universalism' of both Israel and the nations was the proper goal.

> The catalyst for this understanding of what Mother Zion could mean was a changed understanding of Yahweh and the nature of his demands. The 'servants of Yahweh' group certainly did not espouse a notion of tolerant syncretism in which Yahweh would merely be one of the many different names for God. Ironically, that was the position of the dominant group, while at the same time exploiting the Zion symbol to regard the nations as their servants. For the 'servants of Yahweh', on the other hand, Yahweh

alone was God, but this one God was concerned for all because he had created all ... Isaiah's Yahweh and Jesus' God is no tribal warrior, but one whose 'eternal covenant' was with all the children of Noah, as well as with the earth.[16]

The line of demarcation does not run between those in the community and those outside, but between those who answer the needs of the vulnerable and those who do not:

> The beatitudes are cut from the same cloth as Yahweh's oracle to the temple authorities, declaring that it was the poor and those who are broken in spirit and not they, who will eat, drink, and rejoice. (118)

No-one's openness is discounted:

> The Queen of the South (Sheba) coming to hear Solomon's wisdom, and the Ninevites repenting at Jonah's preaching are adduced as evidence of 'outsiders' seeking wisdom and taking the prophetic warning seriously (Mt 12:40-42; Lk 11:30-32) ... Wisdom is available to all and repentance is a possibility for non-Jews. (118-20)

Isaiah's and the Synoptics' critiques of those who 'do not understand the universal scope of their own tradition' are a telling precedent in an on-going interpretive struggle. Emphasis on the resources of one's particular religious *communio* should not blind one to its shortcomings. The implicit repristination of the *extra ecclesiam nulla salus* model cannot be supported, however justified current prophetic critiques of market-bred lifestyles and the cognitive marginalisation of religion in liberal states may be. But if the claim of the community on a member's allegiance is not tempered by the distinction of legality from legitimacy achieved by Kant, then communitarianism can degenerate into totalitarianism. The dignity of a believer's own personal assent can only be safeguarded if exterior conformity to the rules of the law that is obligatory for all is distinguished from interior appropriation which will always be particular, selective, contextual and developing. The possibility of legitimate interior dissent is the pass to an un-suffocating sense of ecclesial belonging. This reminder of the singularly individual character of religious response runs counter to the virtue ethicists' interest in minimising the difference between the person's and the community's ethical life. A holistic bent is also visible in their wish to relate 'acts' back to 'character' and to avoid the external authority of 'rules' in favour of habits that arise organically from virtuous dispositions.

b) From rules to 'character'

The move away from an ethics totally centred on acts to the being behind the agency lifts several impasses at once. An overemphasis on agency risks ignoring receptivity and facticity as constitutive features of human existence, dissects the moral life into a series of isolated acts regardless of any over-arching intention and vision, and neglects the issue of conditions for developing stable identities that put values into practice in a reliable instead of a once-off way. If the counter-model of a 'character' ethics is to fill these *lacunae* of act-centered moral theories, it is a helpful correction. But is the concept of 'character' or 'being' from which agency follows[17] sufficient to serve these different tasks? Or does the opposition of 'character versus decision' and 'being versus legislation' need to be related dialectically and embedded in a more comprehensive approach? Within the perceived alternatives, 'character' stands for steadiness over against disjoint decisions, and for the Hegelian shift from an ethics of obligation to one of confidence in people's own powers, competence, and ability to be good. The *philosophical* question here is whether 'character' is only one pole and has to be complemented by another element in a full theory of subjectivity. In P. Ricoeur's account of the ethical self, the '*idem*' element of recognisable sameness through time has to be related to the '*ipse*', the responsible and spontaneous centre of creativity. 'Character' as the '*idem*' pole is not a complete description of ethical selfhood; the *idem* does not exhaust the *ipse*, it is a basis that has to be made one's own. The task of shaping the open future out of the past is to be captured as the '*ipse*' aspect of the self.

The need for the subtle distinctions Ricoeur offers can also be shown from a *theological* perspective. Their relevance for a theological anthropology comes out most clearly when virtue ethics' antipathy to the 'legislation' mode of Kant's approach is analysed. If it only amounted to broadening ethics to include the narrative dimension of tracing a person's particular moral insights to his biographical identity, it could easily be compatible with a Christian appreciation of life as a journey in faith towards God. The perspective to which virtue ethics is committed, to include into the moral task also the level of affects and to sympathetically shape one's emotions within an over-arching vision of an authentic life, rather than denounce them as mere inclinations, can be seen as opening up a spiritual dimension. But the emphasis on 'growth' that they find missing in act-centred ethics is in danger of being contaminated by the residual legacy of a natural entelechy. We don't need 'rules' because we are already striving for the good life. This Aristotelian assertion is less harmless when it comes as Hegel's critique of Kant, as a triumphalism of reason against the evidence of human brokenness and disposition towards violence. Theologically, the issue in need of assertion is not that 'being' is more than 'acting', but that the person is more than the sum of her acts and that God distinguishes between our deeds and our selves in need of redemption.[18] Jesus' emphasis on God's forgiveness that creates a new beginning for us cannot be captured in the terms of a natural entelechy, of organic development, and growth without conversion. Here, John Barton's doubt about whether a scheme of virtues and vices can be a suitable model for a biblically inspired ethics that turns on 'conversion' points in the right direction.[19] 'Conversion' denotes a re-orientation of the will which cannot be grasped in categories of striving. That exterior actions arise from an interior source does not tie us to the conceptual framework of virtuous dispositions. The Aristotelian cast of virtue ethics can hide the decisive difference between this antique philosophical and Christian ethics: the shift from ends towards which we strive naturally to an emphasis on the will. It results in repositioning the good from the cognitive sphere of insight to the quality of the will. Its volatility poses other limits than a mere lack of understanding did.

c) The status of ethics

My final point starts with reclaiming the modern, Kantian measure of the 'good will' as the origin, in contrast to the Utilitarian outcome, of acts, as founded on a new anthropology arising from the Jewish and Christian religious heritages. Concluding with a comparison of the status of ethics in a hermeneutical to a deontological framework, I want to show that context-independent criteria are needed at a time when a previously existing moral consensus on the inviolability of human life, itself the fruit of historical struggles, is represented as an outmoded and indefensible taboo.

What MacIntyre sees as the deplorable emphasis of modernity, the voluntarist bent of ethics, can also be deciphered as a paradigm shift in Greek thinking resulting from the encounter with the religious experience of a saving God and free creator. While not offering any views on the roots of this change, Otfried Höffe analyses the new ground that is broken by the idea that striving can acquire a distance from itself (*Idee einer Distanz des Strebens in sich selbst*) introduced by the concept of the will. Without it, change in patterns of action that are deemed ethical could only be explained as arising from outside, e.g. from modifications in needs, or of the means of satisfying them. Value change and critique for moral reasons, radical reform, or the proclamation of a 'new law' such as that of the New Testament would be unthinkable.

> [The] concept of striving lives off an unproblematised presupposition: the (individual-spontaneous) finality of human agency. Interpreted as striving, human praxis is always already assigned a goal … In phenomena such as moral criticism out of morality or ethical-political protests, in the giving of a 'New Law' (cf. New Testament), in constitutional reforms, political revolutions or in an explicit renewal of personal and political value priorities aims are no longer pursued in the framework of a lived ethos. Rather, the ethical-political basic framework itself is up for decision. An inherited

system of institutions and patterns of behaviour and the activities of striving that correspond to them is put up for disposition with regard to the principles themselves. Such a process can no longer be conceptualised as agency due to internalised basic orientations, as a spontaneous affirmation and pursual of ends, i.e. as an act of striving. It is rather a case of a distance of striving within itself, i.e. an act of the will … due to which ends are not only pursued but first of all posited.[20]

The human dignity of agency in the sense of 'positing' goals can only be captured in the modern idea of self-determination, as a 'strictly non-necessary movement'. Virtue as an acquired disposition of character may presuppose some appreciation of freedom besides reason,[21] but it is caught in the framework of Aristotle's metaphysics of movement which does not allow for a clear distinction between the quality of action authored by human beings and that of every other part of the universe. The constraints of a model of continuity between the natural world and the sphere of human reason become clear when compared to the image of the human person arising in biblical monotheism. As a 'summoned self' (P. Ricoeur) she stands in a counterpart relationship with a personal God to whom she is responsible. In this anthropology, failure is not first of all weakness of insight but a denial of response, an act of the will, not a lack of reason. In his comparison of a 'Greek ethics of insight' with a 'biblical ethics of command' the New Testament scholar Gerd Theissen characterises the main difference as that between founding ethical judgements on the nature of things as opposed to vocation by God. 'It is said: "You shall love your neighbour like yourself; I am Lord." Israel shaped human behaviour not through rational insight into the world, but through disciplining the will through God's will.' What is decisive for the subsequent development of ethics is where human frailty and goodness is located: in the power of the will.

> Important for the biblical ethics of command is a difference in the view of the human person: One can oppose a command – also against good insight. The human person has an independent will that can be good or bad. Wrong behaviour does not originate from an incorrect judgement, but from an evil will. This ethics is voluntarist.[22]

One interesting conclusion from this contrast is that what sounds more authoritarian than liberating to modern ears, the emphasis on God's command and discipline, allowed a break-through in the understanding of the interior dynamics of being human. Just as the idea of creation out of nothing (that the Christian apologists defended against the Greek conviction that matter was as eternal as God) underlined God's absolute power to begin, and thus the origin of the world in God's free motivation of love, so is the human person seen as endowed with the power to posit, not just to follow the given goals of nature. There is more tension, but also more freedom in seeing the human person as the addressee of God's call than governed by the anonymous laws of the cosmos that human reason seeks to explore and live by.

Höffe's reference to 'principles' by which existing social arrangements and personal orientations can be judged and discontinued, rather than only ever evolved and adjusted, gives an important clue to the new understanding of the status of ethics. Are context-independent principles possible, or is all that reflective reason can achieve the self-exploration of the internal logic of one's ethos? Is moral judgement always a situated, *a posteriori* elucidation of the self-understanding of a community and its agents, or is an evaluation led by independent criteria possible? That is the point of debate between universalist and hermeneutical approaches. Schnädelbach's critique of what he calls the '*phronesis* ideology' of contemporary Neo-Aristotelianism shows the danger of emphasising the contingent, singular nature of human action so much that no general evaluation according to recognised criteria is possible. Contingency, skepticism and an ethics favouring the status quo are intellectual neighbours.

> If it is no longer possible to attach strong normative claims to an idea, a radical critique can also no longer be founded. Theoretical skepticism always favours the power of what is established; thus, it is not by chance that Descartes is the inventor of a provisional morality. The historically enlightened Neo-Aristotelian can in fact only be a skeptic ... leaving praxis – in equal distance both to a Kantian ethics of obligation and to platonising ethics of value – to practical cleverness and unburdening himself and us from normative challenges as far as possible.[23]

For Schnädelbach, the advantage in Aristotle's admission that the realm of praxis does not allow for standards of exactness similar to theoretical *episteme* is that common sense is allowed a chance against the expert knowledge of elites and of 'the philosopher kings and their dictatorship of theory'(212). But the price of disallowing any relevance of "theory" (which also includes principles) for praxis is an embedded *phronesis* that can never go beyond the confines of the community ethos. An entirely hermeneutical model of ethics thus resigns itself to the polis's internal limits to moral growth and is hermetic to radical outside questioning. But is it really a choice between dictatorial *a priori* normativists and insular ethos interpreters?

The context-sensitivity of *phronesis* could be safeguarded without the cost of minimalising ethics to a normatively and prescriptively powerless explication of the existing self-understandings of agents in a community if one follows a model that seeks to combine the strong points of each approach. Ricoeur's use of the term 'practical wisdom' does not denote a return behind Kant, but intensifies the unconditionality of his concept of respect for each person as an end in himself by focusing on singularity. The deontological unconditional norm is independent of the context and 'situatedness' of agents and communities, but it is possible to make exceptions from the 'rule' precisely to honour the concrete person as an end in herself. The 'ought' is maintained, but its potential rigorism softened, while the tacit background assumption of a virtue ethics, the primacy of the given ethos with the weak and context-dependent justifications it implies, is avoided.[24]

Wayne Meeks' advice to understand ethics as an 'interpretive exercise'[25] can be theologically defended insofar as it points to the givenness of salvation which was not created by human reason. It is attractive and especially apt to portray the Church as testifying to this givenness, and constituting its social tradition. However, 'interpretive' can also mean an exclusive focus on its own resources. But can these be separated so clearly from its history of reception and secular conversion? A touchstone for any group ethics is the question as to whether any relationship is to be conceived between its own legal system, in this case Church law, and Human Rights. While it is true both that the proliferation of 'rights' talk constitutes a problem and undermines the core application of the term, and that there is, e.g., no 'right' to be ordained, even if there should be a right to have one's vocation tested, a Church distancing itself completely from the standards it establishes would be suspicious. The fate of the concept of conscience in Hegel's ethics should be a warning.[26] His view of 'conscience' as mere subjectivity and as an almost terrorist singularity against the established mores of a community is not the example a Christian ecclesial ethics should follow. Yet, if Christian Ethics is to be seen not only as an interpretive, in-house exercise, its internal relation to the discovery and ongoing determination of who counts as a subject, and what constitutes a violation, of Human Rights will be part of its brief.

To come clean on this part of the secular heritage of Christianity is all the more urgent in view of the ethical debates arising under the pressures of global market conditions. Are virtues enough to stem the tide from Shanghai to Cambridge that is swallowing every moral standard achieved in long processes of historical struggle inspired by the Jewish and Christian values of justice and compassion for the vulnerable? Is 'Europe just a suburb of Shanghai?'[27]

If 'Shanghai' stands for the willingness to compromise principles for the goal of the successful competition of one's own *polis,* it is just on our doorstep. Aubrey de Grey, a biomedical gerontologist at the University of Cambridge, admits:

> I don't have much time for the Hippocratic Oath myself. I think it's something that made a lot of sense when the understanding of medicine was primitive and people could spontaneously recover from illnesses for reasons that the doctor could not identify. That's where the 'do no harm' idea comes from. That becomes less reasonable as we become more knowledgeable about how to intervene in the body's metabolism. One also

has to remember that around the world there are very different versions of medical ethics. There's good reason to believe that many of these therapies will be first developed in countries where they are more forward-looking about cost-benefit ratio.[28]

CONCLUSION

I have tried to show that Christian ethical interpretations of the message of Jesus in terms of virtue are in danger of downplaying the shift to an emerging new paradigm of thinking that broke with many plausibilities especially of Greek high culture. To encompass such revolutions of attitude in the framework of a virtue ethic that in its inherited form only knew one context, the existing *polis*, risks short-changing the message of Jesus on two counts:

(1)   The emphasis on the will that the call to conversion implies is smoothed into a new set of personal habitual practices, which are held to express the person's 'character'. The challenge to forge one's personal identity out of the dialectic of *idem* and *ipse*, i.e. to unite the recognisable, familiar traits of character and life story with the internal working out of selfhood is reduced to just one pole. The idea of personal 'growth', however, so dear to the new advocates of virtue ethics in theology, asks for categories that go beyond natural striving. The shift towards an interiority engaged by God is better expressed in terms of reflexivity and personal calling than in those of an ethos-ethic.

(2)   The new social framework of the Church in which Christian (ascetic) virtues are to be exercised is deemed the only existing one; the result is that any emphasis on the autonomy of the world and the recognition of civil society as a proper setting beside the Church for living the Christian calling seems to be misplaced. Ecclesial virtue ethicists such as Stanley Hauerwas transpose previously secular virtues completely into religious ones, thus breaking with the classical tradition of practical reason. The route taken by Thomas Aquinas, however, does not sanction this denial of reason. Modern virtue ethicists who accept both world and Church as equally important vineyards to plough have already tacitly extracted virtues from the grip of their ancient civic setting to be able to relate them to the dimension of faith in a saving God that transcends local alliances.

The task that remains, to determine the relationship between ethical and theological virtues, can be accomplished with greater promise if the shift in thought forms engendered by Christianity to categories of freedom is taken as the matrix of reconstruction. Once the entelechy of nature in human and other creatures is changed into a human-specific teleology of the quest for meaning, the orientation of nature towards grace can be assumed without resulting in a contradiction for the creator, that to withhold grace would leave the creature incomplete.[29] If God's offer is addressed to human freedom, the superabundant shape that it takes may disappoint a strict regard for the virtue of egalitarian justice but engage the imagination to come up with different measures for justice than a meritocratic one. It opens up the possibility of new self-interpretations and projects that are 'out of character'.

The turn to the reliable and more or less verifiable guide of virtues at a time when all other measures of goodness seem to be controversial is to be welcomed. It trusts in the evidence of personal authenticity, opts for prevention rather than repair,[30] reinvests in the building of long-term basic attitudes over against individual decision-testing, and in steady personal responsibility over against the anonymous forces of unrelated systems. But it takes moves for granted that virtue ethics on its own could never have achieved: the prophetic, in many ways anti-communitarian break with practiced modes of living, the discovery of individual irreplaceability in one's own singular response to God's personal calling, the foundation of ethics on the good will of the autonomous morality of each human being, not on the striving for a happiness congruent with the typical features of human nature.

Do these distinctions underestimate the power for innovation and change inherent in the traditions of Homer, Antigone, Socrates, and the idea of a good life governed by justice? We cannot know how antique traditions would have evolved without Jesus' faith in a God who makes everything new. It is likely that the virtù which Nietzsche admired in the Renaissance would not have had to suffer the interception of the 'slave morality' of the Beatitudes. Would the ability to understand oneself in a new framework once the old one had collapsed in irresolvable conflicts of compatibility, as in Antigone, have arisen? Or would the last word have been Zarathustra's 'deep midnight' of the human mode of being coming to an end, as not worth saving? The promise of a 'new heaven and a new earth', instead, is for a humanity redeemed, invited to a new mode of self-understanding, and not abandoned.

NOTES

1   See for example, M. Welker/F. Schweitzer (eds), *Reconsidering the Boundaries between Theological Disciplines. Zur Neubestimmung der Grenzen zwischen den theologischen Disziplinen*, Münster: LIT-Verlag, 2004.

2   Cf. P. Ricoeur, *Hermeneutics and the Human Sciences. Essays on Language, Action, and Interpretation* (ed. and trans. by J. Thompson), Cambridge: Cambridge University Press, 1981, pp. 63–100. In *Memory, History, Forgetting* (trans. K. Blamey/D. Pellauer) (Chicago: University of Chicago Press, 2004, pp. 333–42), he distinguishes between the historian's task of 'representation' over against 'interpretation' as a 'second order reflection on the entire course of this operation' (333). A parallel to this critical philosophical insight into historical reconstruction can be found in the distinctions offered by Halvor Moxnes, *Putting Jesus in his Place. A Radical Vision of Household and Kingdom*, Louisville and London: J. Knox Press, 2003, which Seán Freyne quotes in *Jesus, a Jewish Galilean*, London: T. & T. Clark, 2004, p. 18: Instead of taking location positivistically as a geographical given, the concept of 'place'

needs to be reconstructed in three dimensions: 'the *experience* of place, namely, how it is managed and controlled; the *legitimation* of place, i.e. the ideological underpinning of the dominant controlling view; and the *imagination* of place or the way in which an alternative vision of place can be developed'. The ethical relevance of such critical hermeneutical reconstruction of the present in the light of past legitimations and alternative futures is evident. The theological question about the 'the imaginative resources available to Jesus' for 'his version of Galilee' (18-19) leads to the creation and prophetic traditions in the Hebrew Bible. How their interplay is traced by S. Freyne will give clues further below as to how the concept of Christian community can and cannot be defined.

3   For a parallel concern from the discipline of philosophy when its genuine task and method of reflecting on the genesis and validity claims of products of the human spirit gets levelled down in the comparatistic perspective of 'cultural studies', see esp. Birgit Recki's contributions to the discussion on 'Die kulturwissenschaftliche Wende' with Thomas Goeller, Ralf Konersmann and Oswald Schwemmer in *Information Philosophie,* 33 (2005), pp. 20–32.

4   Th. Pröpper, 'Zur vielfältigen Rede von der Gegenwart Gottes und Jesu Christi', in *Evangelium und freie Vernunft,* Freiburg: Herder, 2001, pp. 245–65, 245–46. All translations from German titles are my own.

5   'Systematicians beware!' is how Seán Freyne ended a public lecture on 'The Bible and Christian Theology: Inspiration, Projection, Critique?' In his 'Introduction: Understanding the Issues of Unity and Diversity of Scripture Today' to the Concilium issue *The Many Voices of the Bible* (eds S. Freyne/E. Van Wolde, London: S.C.M. Press, 2002, pp. 7–8), its diversity and conflicting voices are explored 'as a challenge to a monistic understanding that is often imposed on the Bible in the name of canonical orthodoxy'. His warning in the lecture was issued against the tendency to downplay 'differences and disputes', such as those between Paul and the Judaisers of Galatia and within the Johannine community, and to 'seek to establish agreement between them in the name of a pure Biblical theology'. Seán Freyne's invitation, instead, is to see ambiguity 'as a blessing rather than a curse. Questions need to be asked as to the theological significance of such diversity in terms of an understanding of God and of Jesus Christ, and what these different understandings might mean for Christian praxis in the community and in the world.' I agree to the definition he gives of the task at hand: an 'adequate Christian Theology rooted in the Bible ... would involve exploring the larger world of the text, not simply as a way of providing a background, but rather *as a theological necessity* ... Such a contextual approach helps to avoid modernising and individualistic readings, and clarifies the distinctive point of view and critical stance that the biblical writers adopted in terms of their own worlds and the value-systems that they encountered and challenged.' The only qualification I would want to add is that the advantage of a consistent systematic theological approach is to be able to pinpoint where tacit projectionist readings from one's own contemporary concerns creep in even under the guise of reconstructing the Ancient Near Eastern and Mediterranean context of beliefs and practices. The programmatic attempt to regain the 'unsystematic' perspective of a virtue ethics as the only adequate framework for contemporary Christian Ethics is one such case.

6   S. Freyne, 'The Bible and Christian Morality' (1969), repr. in R.P. Hamel/K.R. Himes (eds), *Introduction to Christian Ethics. A Reader,* Mahwah, NJ: Paulist Press, 1989, pp. 9–32, 9–10.

7   J. Van Gerwen, 'Origins of Christian Ethics', W. Schweiker (ed.), *The Blackwell Companion to Religious Ethics,* Oxford: Blackwell, 2005, pp. 204–213, 213. Further page numbers are included in the text.

8   P. Ricoeur combines a theory of self with an ethics that proceeds from the first level of spontaneous striving 'to live with and for others in just institutions' to the moral awareness of the human reality of violence. Thus, it is the limit that the other poses to each person's self-expansion that calls for the second, deontological level of ethics. The third, 'practical wisdom', applies both in a judgement that balances moral rule and each person's singularity. Cf. *Oneself as Another,* Chicago: University of Chicago Press, 1992, Ch. 7–9, pp. 169–296.

      O. Höffe marks his reintegration of eudaimonistic insights into a full understanding of the ethical life clearly as complementary and not as an alternative to modern autonomous ethics. His critique of Kant for his near-exclusive focus on morality and disregard of the rational guidance available in eudaimonistic reflections on the limits of human fulfilment is matched by an equal dismissal of the arbitrariness of Political Liberalism in making goals of life a totally private and unaccountable affair, and of the over-dramatised contrast some Neo-Aristotelians draw between the antique tradition and the Enlightenment. Otfried Höffe, 'Zur Rehabilitierung einer eudämonistischen Ethik' in *Moral als Preis der Moderne*, Frankfurt: Suhrkamp, 1993, pp. 137–50.

9   Ulrich Beck's sociological analyses in *Risk Society. Towards a New Modernity* (London: Sage, 1992, esp. Ch. 5), depict the double face of modernisation that Jürgen Habermas criticises as the colonisation of the life-world by system imperatives. The triumph of purposive rationality can only be counter-acted by developing the resources of communicative action in civil society.

10   H. Schnädelbach, 'Was ist Neoaristotelismus?' in *Zur Rehabilitierung des animal rationale*, Frankfurt: Suhrkamp, 1992, pp. 205–30, p. 228.

11   See Hille Haker's critique of Habermas's previous stance that goes far beyond Kant's test of universalisability, in her *Moralische Identität*, Tübingen: Francke, 1999, p. 67.

12   Herbert Schnädelbach points out how legality is the condition under which modern citizens can be reconciled with the ethos of their societies. 'Legality concerns the conditions of freedom in the *exterior* relationships of people to each other. Exactly this element of exteriority bemoaned by the traditionalist we experience subjectively as the *basic condition of our individual freedom in the modern life-world* (228) ... A life-world in which universal principles that guarantee individual freedom are institutionalised, embodies not only a *historical-contingent* but a *rational-universalist* ethos ... with which an individual who insists on his rational autonomy can be "reconciled"'(227).

On the basis of this clear appreciation of the universalism inherent in a modern-day ethos, I find the hostility overdrawn that he presumes between Kant's understanding of freedom as self-determination and any existing ethos as denoting heteronomy. The enemy against which autonomy is defined as self-obligation is not an ethos, or conventions, as in Discourse Ethics up to the 1980s, but inclination. 'The controversy between morality and *Sittlichkeit* can only be resolved if one comes to an agreement on the concept of freedom. When freedom is grasped as subjective self-determination as in Kant, ethos and *Sittlichkeit* can only appear as heteronomy; when freedom is understood with Hegel as being with oneself in being with the other (*Beisichsein im Anderssein*), subjective autonomy is a misleading goal.' This sounds as if Kant had no idea of interaction between free subjects, despite his conceptions of a '*Commercium der Freiheit*' and the 'kingdom of ends.' Ricoeur's critique of the unbridgeable contrast between morality and convention in Discourse Ethics also applies to Schnädelbach's alternative between self-determination and ethos.

13   W. Huber, 'Die jüdisch-christliche Tradition,' in H. Joas/K. Wiegand (eds), *Die kulturellen Werte Europas*, Frankfurt: Fischer, 2005, pp. 69–92, 91: 'The secular state thus saves society from having to be secular. Rather, society is the space in which a guaranteed freedom can flourish equally as a freedom for religion as it can as a freedom from religion.'

14   T. Deidun, 'The Bible and Christian Ethics,' in B. Hoose (ed.), *Christian Ethics. An Introduction*, London: Cassell, 1998, pp. 3–46, 22.

15   C. Deane-Drummond admits that 'virtue theory requires some modification in order to be compatible with Christian thought. For example, concepts such as reconciliation, forgiveness and the need for God's grace are essential components of a Christian ethic.' *The Ethics of Nature*, Oxford: Blackwell, 2004, p. 22.

16   S. Freyne, *Jesus, a Jewish Galilean*, London: T. & T. Clark, 2004, pp. 116–21, 117. Further page numbers in the text.

17   J. Keenan explains the appeal of A. MacIntyre's critique of the 'depersonalisation' present in contemporary action ethics to Christian circles by applying the scholastic axiom of *agere sequitur esse* to Jesus' call to become disciples. 'If action follows being (*agere sequitur esse*), where was being?... Who more than Jesus beckons us to consider the question about the people we can become? In Scripture, Jesus invites us to become his disciples, children of God, and heirs of the kingdom.' (24) Virtue Ethics is thus seen to provide a 'method for building bridges between Scripture and Moral Theology', which the book *Jesus and Virtue Ethics*,

Lanham, MD/Chicago: Sheed & Ward, 2002, co-authored with the New Testament scholar Daniel Harrington, constructs from both sides.

18 In his discussion of H. Arendt's claim that forgiveness is a natural condition of action, Paul Ricoeur insists on its origin 'from elsewhere' and the need for it to be given, not just presupposed. See the 'Epilogue: Difficult Forgiveness' in *Memory, History, Forgetting* (pp. 457–506) and his lecture 'The Difficulty to Forgive' in P. Kenny/M. Junker-Kenny (eds), *Memory, Narrativity, Self, and the Challenge to Think God. The Reception within Theology of the Recent Work of Paul Ricoeur*, Münster: LIT-Verlag, 2004, pp. 6–16.

19 J. Barton, 'Virtue in the Bible,' *Studies in Christian Ethics* 12 (1999), pp. 12–22.

20 O. Höffe, *Ethik und Politik*, Frankfurt: Suhrkamp, 1979, pp. 329–32.

21 J. Rohls, *Geschichte der Ethik*, Tübingen: Mohr, 1991, p. 68.

22 G. Theissen, 'Urchristliches Ethos. Eine Synthese aus biblischer und griechischer Tradition.' The only version published up to now is in Swedish, under the title 'Urkristet etos – en syntes av biblisk och grekisk tradition' *Svensk Teologisk Kvartalsskrift* 79 (2003), pp. 1–12.

23 Schnädelbach, *Rehabilitierung*, p. 214.

24 In *Oneself as Another*, Ricoeur thinks through the famous humanistic formula of the Categorical Imperative and discovers a conflict between a 'universalist' and a 'pluralist' reading of the norm to treat 'humanity in one's own person and in the person of others' as an end in itself. Under the headings, '2. Respect and Conflict' (pp. 262–73) and '3. Autonomy and Conflict' (pp. 273–96), he analyses 'the *caesura* so carefully concealed by Kant between respect for the rule and respect for persons. This *caesura*, which will become a gaping tear in the case of the conflicts we shall mention, was probably not able to appear along the path where we subsumed actions under maxims and maxims under rules. The tear cannot help but attract attention, however, once we take the return path from the maxim, sanctioned by rules, to concrete situations,' (268) such as what telling the truth to a fatally ill patient can mean. Once the possible split between 'respect for the law and respect for persons' has been admitted, the task for 'practical wisdom may consist in giving priority to the respect for persons, in the name of the solicitude that is addressed to persons in their irreplaceable singularity (262) ... Practical wisdom consists in inventing conduct that will best satisfy the exception required by solicitude, yet betraying the rule to the smallest extent possible ... Practical wisdom consists here in inventing just behaviour suited to the singular nature of the case. But it is not, for all that, simply arbitrary ... Never can practical wisdom consent to transforming into a rule the exception to the rule.' (269)

25 W. A. Meeks, 'The Christian Beginnings and Christian Ethics: The Hermeneutical Challenge,' in *Bulletin European Theology*, 9 (1998), pp. 171–81.

26 Here, Schnädelbach's quotations (222–3) from paragraphs 139–41 of Hegel's *Philosophy of Law* are apposite.

27 This is the question with which the ex-European commissioner Mario Monti is quoted by Josef Joffe in his lead article in *Die Zeit* No. 26, 23/6/05, p. 1.

28 EMBO, 'Interview: Curing Aging and the consequences', EMBO Reports 6 (3) (2005), on line, p. 4 of 7, quoted in C. Deane-Drummond, 'Future Perfect? God, the Trans Human Future and the Quest for Immortality,' in C. Deane-Drummond (ed.), *Fabulous Humans*, London: T. & T. Clark, 2006.

Her critical conclusion is that 'in order to foster a technology that will ultimately benefit western societies the most ...' Grey makes the remarkable suggestion that those who are less squeamish about ethical objections in other parts of the world will subject inhabitants of less regulated countries to medical experimentation for First World 'rejuvenation treatment'.

29 Th. Pröpper, *Erlösungsglaube und Freiheitsgeschichte*, München: Kösel, 3rd. ed., 1991, p. 279.

30 D. Mieth, *Moral und Erfahrung II*, Fribourg/Freiburg: Universitätsverlag/Herder, 1998, p. 127.

11   Christian Moral Life

Vincent MacNamara

(J. Dwyer (ed.), *New Dictionary of Catholic Social Thought,* Collegeville, MN: Liturgical Press, 1994, pp. 635–50.)

This article is intended as a general reflection on the place of morality within modern Catholic life and theology. In stating the matter in that way I am deliberately opting for a broad canvas. There has been much debate in Catholic theology in recent times about the Christian ethic. It has concentrated on specificity, that is, on whether Christianity proposes a different content to moral life from that proposed by human morality – in effect, by those who do not explicitly subscribe to Christianity. My concern here certainly includes that, but it is wider.

There is a general assumption among Christians that there is something that can be called a Christian ethic. A recent work begins with the assertion: 'The foundations of Christian ethics must be evangelical foundations; or, to put it more simply, Christian ethics must arise from the gospel of Jesus Christ. Otherwise it could not be *Christian* ethics'.[1] So convinced are many believers of this that they regard the promotion of its ethical vision as the chief point of Christianity, and they are bewildered if one even raises the question of specificity. It comes as a shock to them to find that some Catholic moralists regard efforts to insist on specificity as a mistake.

It helps to pause and look at the very conjunction of the words 'Christian moral life', and 'Christian ethics'. Whether they be valid expressions or not, they ought not be taken for granted. If there be a Christian ethic it is one instance of a wider phenomenon – religious ethic. There are other religious ethical systems – Jewish, Muslim, Buddhist, animist, and so forth. Should we expect morality to occur with religion, and why?

Religion and morality are formally distinct. They have different concerns, different objects. They deal with different clusters of questions. There are many who acknowledge the ethical claim, who seek to listen to it and lead their lives in accordance with it, who develop ethical theories, but who firmly deny the religious dimension and refuse to have any truck with organised religious morality. They often claim that their morality is superior. In particular they claim that their moral motivation is purer, their state of moral development more advanced. An article in a relatively recent book on Christian ethics and contemporary philosophy begins with the remark that 'the thesis of this paper is that religious morality is infantile'[2] – infantile above all in its general conception and as diminishing the responsibility and autonomy of the subject. Our approach to Christian moral life, then, might set it in the broader context of religious morality and puzzle over such questions as how do these two relatively independent areas, religion and morality, encounter each other; what happens to morality when it is incorporated into a religious system; what is the borrowing from one to the other?

PART 1: CONTEXT

The fact is that most religions have an ethical strand. But the ethical is only one part of the composite picture. Sociologists of religion list various elements that tend to recur – myth, cult, organisation, ritual, behavioural rules of an ethical and non-ethical kind. Religions incorporate the ethical in quite different ways. Their basic myth and their general cosmogony bear on it differently. Major themes that relate to morality – the creation of the world, of human beings and human institutions, of good and evil – are envisioned differently. In some religions evil is an aspect of God, in others there is a qualified semidualism, in others a full dualism in which there are two opposed cosmic systems. In some the deity is otiose or indifferent, in others it is generally benevolent and concerned; in some, creation is devoid of moral purpose, in others the deity is lord of history. Not all religions believe the soul to be immoral or dependent on the deity, and not all have notions of reward or punishment in an afterlife. So they enshrine different views of the origin of morality and of its possibility. They weigh it differently with respect to other elements of the system. They have different notions of salvation – perhaps the basic quest of religions – and in particular of the significance of moral life for that.

All this is the subject matter of the discipline of comparative religious ethics. We might ask how Christian ethics looks against this background. That sets our own concern in clearer focus. It sharpens our wits. It questions assumptions that may have lain unexamined in the expression 'Christian ethics'. It provokes us to pursue issues that affect the contours of our moral lives: why is Christianity an ethical religion; how, in what way, and to what extent; where does it get its morality from; how do we conceive of the relationship between God and morality; what is the significance of moral life for salvation – and what salvation; can we be moral and with what means; how does our Christian anthropology, in particular our view of good and evil in our human constitution, affect our view of the whole moral enterprise? It is because Christianity answers such questions in its own way that there is in the first instance something that can be called 'Christian ethics'. Not all these questions can be treated here, but I hope to advert to the major ones.

An Ethical Religion: A Religious Ethic

Not all religions are equally ethical: in some ethics plays a prominent role in the story – in the daily life, in the discipline, and in the way to salvation. It is a commonplace that biblical religion is ethical and biblical ethics religious. However

Israel arrived at its Decalogue, that code is represented as standing at the very foundation of its history and as the direct and immediate communication of God. The context was the covenant. So, OT ethics is strongly historical: the sages may have had prudential reasons for some stipulations but they are subsumed under religious reasons; the law gives its orders in the name of the covenant God. God's demands for pity for the poor, the warnings against luxury and the abuse of wealth are so insistent and overpowering that cult becomes worthless unless it goes hand in hand with ethical life. Behind those sayings lie God's authority and love for the people.

> 'What to me is the multitude of your sacrifice?'
> says the Lord.
> 'I have had enough of burnt offerings of rams
> and the fat of fed beasts; ...
> cease to do evil, learn to do good;
> seek justice, correct oppression;
> defend the fatherless, plead for the widow' (Isa 1:11ff).

> Shall I come before him with burnt offerings
> with calves a year old? ...
> What does the Lord require of you
> but to do justice, and to love kindness,
> and to walk humbly with your God? (Mic 6:6-8).

If your deity is capricious your religion might not give a high priority to morality, and ritual might well predominate. But the God of Israel was good, faithful and merciful towards the poor. The covenant people were to be like God.

The religion-ethics dynamic is further accentuated in the NT. God is good, benevolent, has a care for the world, communicates with us, has a plan for a kingdom of justice and peace, wishes us to turn from selfishness and division and live with others in love. We are to show total and undivided obedience to God, but it is to a Father who has graciously approached us, who has first loved us in his saving action in Christ and called us to grace. The content of the ethics of Jesus may be found already in the OT or in extrabiblical sources, but it is the preaching of the kingdom that forms the fundamental presupposition and basis of it. The acceptance of the kingdom makes ethical demands on us. It is true that Jesus promises reward – not the reward of human favour (Mt 6) but of God's – and that just requital has its place in his preaching. But the overarching symbol is a merciful Father: God's mercy has been shown to us; we are called to show mercy in turn. By the Spirit who has been given to us we are enabled to live such a life: it is the fruit of God's Spirit. In the end this is what will matter – not bringing one's gift to the altar, not being able to call oneself a child of Abraham, not saying

'Lord, Lord' but having fed the hungry, cared for the sick, visited those in prison (Mt 25).

There is no moral life in the Bible without reference to the faith that motivates one to respond to God. So it is today: the moral life of Christians is shot through with religion. Take some remarks that are the everyday currency of Catholic moral life: 'I confess to Almighty God that I have sinned'; 'I absolve you from your sins in the name of the Father'; 'This murder is a crime against the sacred law of God'; 'I want to make my peace with God'; 'God can bring good out of evil'; 'We love others in God'; 'We see Christ in the neighbour'; 'What would Jesus have done in the circumstances'; 'Lord I am not worthy to receive you'; 'I have discerned this in the Spirit'; 'A Christian ought to ...' In all there is an intriguing intermingling of religious and ethical considerations. Indeed it is not always possible to distinguish them: there are experiences and terms – sin, holiness, wholeness, sacrifice, worship, salvation – that are not clearly one or the other.

Such matters are not usually the focus when the issue of Christain moral life is discussed. The focus is rather the content of morality, the question of moral norms, and of whether Chrisitanity does and must of its nature propose something different from other ethical systems. But it should be obvious that this more general context, the overall manner in which we conceptualise and situate morality, is of considerable importance. It is important both for morality and for faith: either or both can be distorted or diminished. Faith can be – and often is – reduced to morals or its understanding of the deity distorted. Morals can lose all autonomy. Rupert, in Iris Murdoch's novel *A Fairly Honourable Defeat*, 'disapproved of belief in God which he felt to be the weakener of the moral sinews'. But one can point to a whole battery of philosophers who felt that religion was antithetical to morality: Hume ('the steady attention alone to so important an interest as that of eternal salvation is apt to extinguish the benevolent affections and beget a narrow, contrasted selfishness'), Kant (morality based on the will of God 'would inevitably form the basis of a moral system which would be in direct opposition to morality'), Feuerbach ('whenever morality is based on theology ... the most immoral, unjust, infamous things can be justified and established').

The task of religious ethics is not an easy one. It brings together two of the most profound, most significant, and to some extent most elusive human experiences; two great symbol systems; two languages, the language of ethics (right, wrong, duty, obligation) and the language of religious myth (salvation, grace, justification, sin). They are deep concerns of the human spirit, and it is hardly surprising that we find it difficult to hold them together in a manner that does justice to both: the deepest concerns do not easily yeild themselves to neat definitions. How we hold the elements together has implications that go deep into our psyche. You see it in the notion of sin, for example, the shadow side of morality. It is a flash point because it brings together so many critical elements –

God, moral law, failure, repentance, sanction, satisfaction, salvation, Church discipline. The catechism definitions that we trade, the language and imagery we use, the prayers we teach our children, the role and signficance we attach to the sacrament of reconciliation, affect not only our understanding of morality but of God. Which is why we constantly need a hermeneutic of our symbols and why also it is enlightening as well as humbling to do our morality – as our religion – in dialogue with other religious traditions.

So let me try to follow in a little more detail the general contours of Catholic morality. It might be helpful to stand back from it and ask such questions as what kind of deity emerges from the Catholic moral tradition – benevolent, accepting, understanding of human weakness, or the opposite? (What are one's memories of a Catholic childhood? Remember the famous sermon in James Joyce's *Portrait of the Artist as a Young Man*.) Does God first love us or do we have to merit God's love by moral righteousness? And if we do not, what then? One thinks of the remark of the bishop of Woolwich in his *Honest to God* that we cannot rethink our notion of God without rethinking our notion of morality, so much is one a function of the other. As an example take this paraphrase from the moral philosoher Cathrein, who greatly influenced the moral textbook and catechism of late nineteenth and early twentieth-century Catholicism. Law, he says, requires a sanction: if God wished the moral law to be kept the only way to do so would be to impose a reward and punishment for it; only the eternal punishment of hell or reward of heaven would be sufficient stimulus; to impose a lesser punishment would be contrary to the wisdom of God. It would be hard to overestimate the influence that kind of thinking has had – and it was the common coin of all the philosophers and theologians of the period – on our idea of God. It is at the root of our most basic fears. It *is* many people's concept of God.

Morality as Law of God

We are here on what has been called the theological frontier of ethics and are engaged in a particlarly thorny piece of God-talk. The language that suggested itself most easily to the Christian tradition was that of law: morality is a law made by the ruler-God; sin is a crime, deserves punishment, and can only be discharged by pardon or penalty. Noldin gives a fair summary. 'God constituted himself the human being's ultimate end; but by the very fact that he did so, he imposed on them an obligation of tending to the ultimate end ... The moral order instituted by God is the way by which one is to tend to the ultimate end and the means, by observance of which, one achieves it'.[3] Neo-Scholastic moral theology went to some trouble to demonstrate that the external and natural laws exhibit the features of a *vera lex*: they are determined by someone in authority, they derive their binding force from the will of the legislator, they require a sanction, they can be dispensed from by the legislator. That particular metaphor has had grave consequences of Catholic moral life.

Such a religious morality is held together by a number of key concepts – morality as law of God, human righteousness as merit, beatitude as reward. The overall language model is a particular raid on the inaccessible mystery. Like all such, it is limited and bears the marks of its time and culture. It is an attempt to catch in symbolic form deep things of the spirit – belief in a transcendent, longing for salvation, recognition of the sacredness of the moral claim. The trouble is that we might read the symbol too sharply: to take it literally is to run the risk of distortion of our religious and moral sensibilities. One can only speculate what a different culture – Eastern for example – might have made of the biblical datum or how a female theological tradition – because the concepts and images have been severely male – might have shaped an understanding of the intermingling of the religious and the ethical. In the Roman Catholic tradition the language of 'sacred law of God' remains the favoured way of talking about morality.

Karl Rahner gave much thought to the Christian language of law-sin-guilt-punishment. He was unhappy about it because of the forensic model it espouses: it is predominantly and heavily the language of the law courts.[4] How appropriate is that to catch God's relationship with us or to do justice to the notion of morality? A Christian, of course, needs to contextualise his/her moral life, like everything else, within his/her overall world-view, and the Catholic tradition sees God as origin, exemplar, final grounding, and ultimate end of all human choice. It needs somehow to say that. But we need to remember that one cannot without great logical caution transfer the everyday language of 'law' or 'will' to God and morality. We do not do justice either to God or to morality unless we somehow preclude the notion that God is a man with a 'will' who issues commands like a monarch and arranges for punishment for those who do not obey. It is not surprising that it was along this particular fault line of the relationship of God-morality-salvation that the greatest upheaval in the history of Christianity occurred in the Reformation.

There are, of course, logical problems about morality as law. Already in Plato's *Euthyphro* they had been posed: 'whether the pious or holy is beloved by the gods because it is holy, or holy because it is beloved by the gods.' There are further objections that a divine-command theory of morality destroys responsibility and the very possibility of authentic response to the moral claim because it reduces morality to obedience to the will of a superior. There are varieties and nuances of divine-command theories, and much depends on what one's understanding is. But it has to be conceded that religious morality does open the way to crudities. One sees them in some of the more naïve approaches to the 'wiping away' of sin in confession. Moral fault cannot be wiped away or undone by God or by anyone else: what is done is done and one must take on the burden of one's failures. One can contextualise one's moral failures religiously, and the sacrament facilitates this. But to suggest that one can feel and behave as if one had not done wrong is to encourage the magical mentality and to do a disservice to morality and to the human spirit.

There were – and are – more nuanced understandings of law. For the great Scholastics it signified essentially guidance toward an end. 'Law' is, after all, an analogical term, and we use it to describe the law of the seasons as well as the law of nature or physical laws. It can refer to morality as the law of my being, as a thrust in me, a tendency to move or grow in a particular direction – a thrust, for example, to act in a way that brings about human good or flourishing or development. And I can of course say that in this sense morality is the law or will of God my Creator. But there is all the difference in the world between thinking of human beings listening to a thrust in them to behave in a particular way and finding it appropriate to refer to this also as the will or law of God, and thinking of morality as the law of God because it is a set of ordinances issued by God. It is in the former sense that the great Scholastics could refer to morality as law, and in this attenuated sense as the law of God. We can still do so today provided we know what we are doing.

Morality as law, sin as crime, redemption as satisfaction to offended majesty, form a triad. It is one model. There are others. For example, there is in the tradition a kindlier view of our human and religious history that sees sin as sickness rather than as crime, as weakness rather than as willfulness, and that sees God as healer rather than as judge. Such a view does not regard us as born into guilt for something for which we were not responsible, as classic theology of an original Fall did. It does not regard us as answerable for the weakness and ambivalence with which we were born. It calmly accepts our evolution from prerational and unconscious animality with its indispensible drives, passions and defense mechanisms. If this is the plan of our Creator it must be that God freely accepts the limitations, the imbalance, the lack of integration, to which we are all heir. It is the human condition. It can oppress ourselves and others. It can do harm. We need to be healed in order that the kingdom may come within us and around us. But there is a difference of perspective here that has far-reaching effects in human consciousness – in our sense of God, of ourselves, and of our relations to God.

It can be seen, then, how our particular creation and salvation-redemption myths – and even within the Christian tradition there are several of them – affect how we see the whole moral landscape. Salvation is a primary interest for religions: how it is envisioned and thought to be attained affects how moral life is situated. Not all religions place it in an afterlife, and not all relate it to morality. Traditional Catholicism did. For it, Christian life had one point, the heavenly salvation of the individual soul, and that was to be achieved by moral rectitude. So the moral theology manual began with the tract *De fine ultimo hominis*, which is the vision of God in heaven. What was the way thereto? Prümmer put that succinctly: 'By virtue of his supreme authority God prescribed for us the way by which we can reach him and our own beatitude. That way is made known to us by the laws made by Him … whence it follows that we cannot reach our beatitude except by obeying just laws'.[5] Two issues especially arise here and suggest themselves for consideration – the stance of the Christian toward the world and the problem of merit and justification.

Salvation and the World

There are varieties of moral life. There are individual vocations and ideals. But let us speak generally. For most of its history Catholicism has regarded the world as a vale of tears, and exile after which 'these poor banished children of Eve' would be shown the blessed fruit of the womb of the Virgin Mary – to quote a well-known and oft-used prayer. The world was a sad stage on which the drama of each one's individual salvation was played out. What happened to the world did not matter very much. What mattered was that each individual would strive to be preserved from its contagion and would ideally store up merit by the practice of virtue. The Christian was to ensure that nothing of his/her life in the world was lost to salvation by the practice of offering everything to God. If there was a thrust outward it was to save souls, to entice people away from moral depravity so that they too might reach salvation to the glory of God.

It is no longer so. There has been a shift in the community's perception and in theological reflection. One could interestingly trace the various theologies and the retrieval of biblical themes, particularly in relation to promise, salvation, history and kingdom, that have brought about the shift. The net result has been that it has come to be seen that the Church's concern is not just religious – the forms and structures of its own life – that it is not just an institution that offers salvation to the individuals, not an ideology that legitimates the status quo, but that the Church is for the kingdom and that the kingdom is for it a horizon and a judgement. It has to engage politicallly. Moral life has to become creative. In particular, justice can no longer be regarded as the preservation of the status quo. Hope cannot be for private salvation alone but for the cosmic peace. And because things will never reach the harmony that is God's dream for the human community but will always be under the eschatological proviso, Christians, far from trading opium, cannot settle for any human utopia but must be ever restless for the bringing about of the elusive kingdom.

Much of that received a blessing at Vatican II, notably in *Gaudium et spes* (39): 'The expectation of a new earth must not weaken but rather stimulate our concern for cultivating this one.' Even if in recent years there have been moments of hesitation – and interestingly, these at heart seem to focus on unease about the notion of salvation – post-Vatcan II Roman statements have in the main retained this thrust. The emphasis on social analysis and on praxis as a hermeneutical key to the meaning of some of our central religious concepts – salvation, liberation, sin – has accentuated the new orientation. It has all modified our religious myth. It has given us a reshaped religious cosmogony. It tells a different story about the world, about body and soul, about human growth, about our environment, about the future. It offers us a different God. It gives a different orientation to Christian moral life.

Moral Life and Beatitude

The second issue that suggests itself for consideration concerns the model that the community has of the relationship between moral life and beatitude. It is an old problem. It will be remembered that it was a problem for Aristotle to link the perfection of moral life with the supreme perfection of contemplation: if perfect bliss is not simply a matter of moral flourishing, how are they related? For the Christian, perfect bliss is union with God (*De fine ultimo hominis*). The Catholic tradition that saw morality as the law of the supreme legislator sat comfortably with the notion of bliss as reward for goodness and of loss of God as punishment for disobedience to the law – the 'forensic metaphor'. Part of his objection is that there is no intrinsic connection between moral life and beatitude: this is extrinsically granted by One who has power to legislate and reward. One has to win the favour of God: one could lose it. There is no need to labour the anxiety with which this has infected relations with God. However much a more benign pastoral practice has tried to soften the rigid logic of all this by appealing to more comforting areas of relevation, many Catholics down the ages have lived and died in fear of this God. Their hope was the confessional: the One whose authority gave binding force to the moral order could pardon, or wipe away, moral waywardness and had delegated this power to the Church. That, too, crucially affected the perspective on Christian moral life.

Again, we are dealing with a model – but a dangerous model. At the theoretical level one finds something more satisfactory in Aquinas. He views moral life as a preparation for vision: only those who are morally good are in an apt condition to receive beatific vision. But vision is still a matter of reward. Rahner, Fuchs, and others take a different line suggesting – and here they are recovering an insight of Catholic philosophy – that those who respond morally to the individual (categorial) situations that life presents are in truth really, though unthematically, responding to the divine offer of God's own self. It is not, in Rahner's view, that one loves God and then – in accordance with the will of God – is disposed to do good to the neighbour. It is not that we have been commanded to love the neighbour and do so out of love of God. It is not that the love of God is the motive for love of neighbour. There is even a more radical unity between the two. The explicit love of neighbour is the primary act of the love of God: one can love God, whom one does not see, only by loving one's visible neighbour.[6]

There is obviously much in the NT to support such a picture. It accords with and gives powerful philosophical sinew to the twenty-fifth chapter of Matthew: 'Just as you did it to one of the least of these who are members of my family, you did it to me.' It has the considerable virtue, too, of taking entirely seriously the spontaneous emergence of morality in interpersonal life rather than seeing it as issuing from divine edict. It gives that morality a profound metaphysical and religious interpretation, so much so that the whole incalculable mystery of our lives is seen to be contained within the drama of our love for one another.

I said that it was along this particular fault line that Christianity's greatest upheaval occurred. Luther had stood matters precisely on their head by his doctrine of grace and justification. For him moral life was more the result of justification than the means to it. The emphasis was on a God who first loved us and who reconciled us without any merit on our part: the Christian is at peace with God through graced faith in the redeeming Christ. Such forgiveness, however, is to beget forgiveness: the justified are to produce the works of justification in a eucharistic spirit. One thinks of the comment of Joachim Jeremias on the Sermon on the Mount as a splendid example. We do not appreciate the ethic of the Sermon, he says, because we have torn it out of its proper context. The context is the story of the kingdom, and that is one of forgiveness. Thus we are to preface every demand of the Sermon with the comforting assertion, 'you have been forgiven', which is also a challenge to adopt the kingdom's way of forgiveness.

There seems to be a small revolution taking place in Catholic life on these matters. There is a more optimistic view of God's relationship to us. It does not please everyone. One hears complaints about the loss of a sense of sin or about the fact that people do not go to confession anymore or that whole congregations approach the Eucharist confidently without prior confession. Certainly one can record a shift in theological thinking. One finds theologians trying to introduce into this theology of deterrence by threat of eternal damnation some glimmer of hope, saying that faith does not imply a religious performance by which one attempts to please God but an abandonment of any performance on our part and an admission that we can do nothing ourselves (Böckle). Or that the purpose for which we must discern good and evil is not to secure God's welcome, which is assured us in any case (Burtchaell). One thinks also of Küng's reexamination of the Catholic position on justification and Rahner's large agreement with him. We have lived through interesting times – interesting in respect of our fundamental concern about the relationship of religious faith and moral experience.

Part 2: Content

I have raised some questions about the general context of Christian moral life. That seems to me to be as important as the question of content, which has dominated recent theological discussion. It deeply colours our sense of God and of our meaning, purpose and possibilities. It runs far into our emotional life and evokes hope or fear, peace or anxiety. If crudely fashioned it can easily become a point of unbelief. It is especially useful for Catholics to stand back and view the contours of their lives, since in their tradition morality has occupied the high ground. Not only does one find a rigid position on the relation of works to salvation but also a very considerable emphasis on moral orthodoxy, on moral discipline, and on the competence of Church authority in moral matters. The arena where these came starkly together was the confessional. It was there that the weight of Church authority was felt. It was there that moral orthodoxy was checked and insisted upon and that discipline was imposed. To sin was to lose God's favour and to be exposed to damnation unless absolution was obtained. One who did not repent of mortal sin – as that was interpreted by Church authorities and the manuals of moral theology – could not receive absolution. There was no other route to grace and normal Church life; it was the second plank after shipwreck. It was a system that was terrifying in its simplicity and in its implications. The stakes could not have been higher.

The fear of the confessor himself was equally great. His training had been such that he was obliged to ensure that sins were confessed according to their number and lowers moral species, that is, in precise detail. His role, it was insisted, was not just declaratory – to be the visibility of the mercy of God. The confessional was a tribunal, the priest a judge. He was to judge the authenticity and adequacy of the confession, to impose a grave penance for a grave sin, to refuse absolution to those who were not disposed. So it was a large part of his professional competence to know what actions might jeopardise the salvation of his people. The teaching of the Church and the moral theology manuals were his guide. If he found the system depressingly severe he raked through the textbooks to find authors of more kindly disposition whose 'probable opinion' might afford him some latitude in dealing with the weaknesses of his penitents.

New-Scholasticism

It was this system that shaped the content of Christian moral life in the Catholic tradition in modern times, and it is reaction to it that is the starting point of contemporary reflection. The growth of the practice of private confession after Trent heightened the grace-sin drama, it highlighted the training of confessors, it exalted the role of the moralist. And the moralist concentrated on confessional dilemmas – on the fundamentals required for salvation. More disastrously, moral theology had over the centuries come adrift from its moorings in the great medieval syntheses. It had assumed a life of its own. It had become ever more assimilated to jurisprudence and had taken a positivistic turn.

So what was the Christian to do? What was to be the content of his/her moral life? The manuals set their sights low. They were concerned mainly to determine the boundary between mortal and venial sin. Their sources were Church teaching, philosophical ethics (a version of natural law), and canon law. Canon law was prominent. The growing centralisation of Church power and authority in the late nineteenth and early twentieth centuries had produced a detailed system of canon law that affected the daily life of the individual. Law bound under pain of sin, and it was the job of the moralist to weigh the significance of various laws. (One result was the recent bewilderment among Catholics about the abrogation of laws that they were once told bound gravely. To this day Catholics find it difficult to distinguish between morality and Church law.) The concern was with what was necessary for salvation, and that generated a sharp distinction between law and counsel. Laws, Noldin says, are necessary to obtain eternal life, they bind all and bind by the will of God. Counsels only bind those who freely bind themselves and merely help one to reach eternal life more securely. It can be seen how sharply focused all morality was on personal salvation.

So the souces of the teaching were narrow. One would be hard put to find a reference to Christ in the general principles of morality. There was appeal to the Bible, not as an inspiring source of moral discernment but as providing authoritative corroborative texts for positions already assumed. That, however, was important. It meant that there was an ultimate source and grounding for morality in the will or law of God as found in revelation. That silenced argument and gave the system a confidence about its moral positions. The Catholic position then as now was one of qualified confidence in the power of reason. The main lines of morality, it says, can be discovered without recourse to an explicit revelation, but such a revelation is necessary in order that even the truths of natural law be discovered securely and with certainty. So there remains the need of a revelation. And since that has its obscurities, the faithful need the authentic interpretation of Church authority. The effect is that the final appeal is not to the authority of human reason but to revelation – to the fact that God has made known authoritatively how we are to live. It also means that the reasons for a moral position proposed by the Church may remain opaque, that in the end Church teaching about morality does not have to defend itself at the bar of reason. It can adopt a superior attitude.

It has to be admitted that what the manuals presented was an arid and cheerless account of moral life. One could find in the Christian community more exalted teaching; it came under the rubic of spirituality and was treated in ascetical, mystical and devotional works. But it was an optional extra, and it went with a cast of mind that suggested that the basic commandments were the rule of life for the faithful while the further reaches of Christian life were the preserve of priest and religious.

Renewal and Reaction

In the 1940s and 1950s there emerged a strong current of dissatisfaction with the morality of the manual and an urgent call for a renewal of moral theology (Thils, Tillmann, Mausbach, Gilleman, Häring etc.). The central criticism was that what had been proposed as moral theology was merely a mixture of philosophy, psychology and jurisprudence and failed to present the distinctive character of the Christian vocation. It was negative and minimalist, so the criticism went, concerned with what some called the science of sin rather than with the riches of Christianity. It lacked the dynamism and inspiration that one would expect from Chrisitianity. Its basic error, it was said, was that it sought its inspiration and method in the wrong sources – in philosophy and natural-law ethics. The assumption was that religion should make a difference to morality, that it should give it a different content from philosophical ethics.

It was a primary tenet of the renewal movement that morality, if it was to be Christian, must be dependent on or derived from revelation. Above all, it was claimed that it must become biblical through and through. It must concentrate on the key themes of the Bible and not be satisfied with random quotations to bolster positions arrived at philosophically. It was a point of view that was canonised in the recommendations of Vatican II about the study of theology in general and of moral theology in particular: 'Sacred theology rests on the written word of God, together with sacred tradition as its primary and perpetual foundations ... The study of the sacred page is, as it were, the soul of sacred theology' (*Dei verbum* 24). 'Dogmatic theology should be so arranged that biblical themes are presented first. ... Special attention needs to be given to the development of moral theology. Its scientific exposition should be more thoroughly nourished by scriptual teaching. It should show the nobility of the Christan vocation of the faithful and their obligation to bring forth fruit in charity for the life of the world' (*Optatam totius* 16).

Much of the discussion of the 1940s and 1950s was about the possibility of finding one basic Christian principle on which a whole structure of Christian morality could be built. Several candidates were advanced. Christian moral life, it was proposed, should be based on the new life of grace. This view depended on the accepted interpretation of grace as an entitative elevation of the soul and its faculties, which was seen as giving the human being a new *esse*; we should bring about in our lives the moral demands of the new being. Ethics and moral theology, it was said, differ in essence. Or, Christian morality should be primarily a morality of charity: the supernatural virtue of charity should be the root, form and foundation of all moral life. Or, Christian life should be the following of Christ and moral theology the scientific presentation of that in individual and social life – Christ as the norm of morality. Or, Christian morality should be a morality of the mystical body or the elaboration of our sacramental vocation or, as Aquinas had said, an expression of the new internal law, which is primarily grace in us seeking to find its true realisation. This renewal movement marks an important point of development in modern Catholic thinking about morality: the current debate centres on its wisdom and validity.

These approaches all insist that there is a specific content to Christian life that is different from and higher than the natural-law morality that has been favoured by the manual – a position encouraged by the teaching of Vatican II that the fundamental vocation is that of baptism and that all Christians are called to the fullness of life in Christ. They all take the Bible as their starting point and are heavily dependent on reference to it. In spite of their claims, however, they did not adduce any significantly different content. They often confused content with motivation or with the general context and spirit of morality. Their use of the Bible was uncritical: it sometimes consisted merely in gathering together the scriptural texts and themes relevant to their subject, so that the bearing of Scripture on the moral argument was not clear.

There appeared in the late 1960s and early 1970s a reaction to this attempt to 'Christianise' morality (Fuchs, Auer, Schüller). This was in part due to a dissatisfaction with what was seen as a lack of rigour in the writings of the previous two decades, especially in the use of the biblical material. The criticism noted that it is one thing to elaborate the moral teaching of OT and NT – that had been done successfully and inspiringly by several biblical scholars – but another to delineate what bearing this was to have on moral argument. On this methodological issue the renewal movement had been less than successful, so that the whole project of elaborating a morality 'from the middle of revelation' (Böckle) was put in doubt. An equally important factor in the reaction was the feeling that the attempt to 'Christianise' morality gave the impression that Christians are a ghetto and Christian morality something esoteric. How could Christians then engage with all people of good will as Vatican II had proposed? There was also a desire to counter the biting criticism that Christian morality is a childish and unthinking acceptance of the Bible: revelation morality was stigmatised as a morality from beyond, naïve biblicism, revelation positivism, theological positivism, obedience morality; this, it was alleged, was destructive of human autonomy and genuine moral response.

The concern was in part about the content of Christian moral life, in part about method, and in part about the Christian's understanding of the structure of moral experience. The immediate questions here push us back to deeper issues – to the stance of our religious story about God and human possibilities. Does our religion contain laws given and made binding by God? If not, if morality arises spontaneously in human nature, if human beings can distinguish right and wrong, does the binding force of such morality arise in human reason or does it arise from the binding will of God? Can we discern the content of such morality, or do we need a special revelation so that the Bible becomes an authoritative source of moral information? Is the content of moral life then what is available to human reason (in the present order of salvation), or is it different from or more than that – so that there is a morality that arises out of Christian faith and may in some manner be found in the Bible? Or does the nature of morality demand that the norms of Christian life be fundamentally intelligible without reference to such faiths?

These authors take their stand on the autonomy of morality, albeit a relative autonomy. That position has two basic strands: (1) the norms of moral life are the same for Christians as for human morality and must therefore be accessible to reason; (2) morality makes its own demand and does not immediately require belief in God or appeal to the binding force of divine law. So morality arises out of the very human condition of being with others. And just as Christianity (as Vatican II also states) involves the recognition of earthly realities with their internal coherence and autonomy, so too it involves a recognition of the autonomy of morality. It is in essence the recognition that being with others makes a claim on us and that the acknowledgement of that is a primordial thrust of human reason and therefore a critical element in human wholeness.

The rejection of a Bible-based morality did not mean a return to the moral theory of the manualists. Theirs had been an impoverished form of natural-law morality. In particular, their dependence on the normativity of nature (physicalism) had come to be questioned. The emphasis now was on person; what is normative is what makes for the flourishing of the person in society. This easily expresses itself as a morality of agape: one of the insights of the renewal movement that perdured was Gilleman's suggestion (after Aquinas) that moral virtues are all a mediation of charity. To say that the person is the norm is, however, to leave many problems unresolved. There is a continuing debate between those who find the moral way in respect for individual human goods, none of which can be sacrificed or subordinated to another (Finnis, Grisez), and those who adopt a proportionalist calculus (Fuchs, Schüller). Both sides, however, reject the physicalist norm of the neo-Scholastics.

The autonomy position recognises that Christians will situate morality – as everything else – metaphysically. Moral life is religious: the Christian must take 'the natural ethical norms of life' into theologal life (Schillebeeckx). It is in and through response to the other that one lives in love with God, the ground, ultimate justification, exemplar, and final intentionality of moral life. But morality has its own internal coherence. Christians are to contextualise it in a manner that does not impair or devalue that.

This position was viewed with alarm by other theologians (Ratzinger, von Balthasar, Stoeckle, Delhaye) who allege that it is a diminution of revelation, a denial of the Church's teaching of authority, and even an undermining of Christianity itself. Their stance stresses that the Bible is an indispensable moral authority for Christians, that there are in the Bible (as official Church teaching declares) material moral norms that are universal and valid for all time – or at least Christian values and ideals and a Christian moral core. There is involved here, as well as the general issue of the bearing of the Bible on Christian discernment, the crucial issue of the source of Church teaching, of its moral methodology. It is no coincidence that it was dissatisfaction with the methodology of *Humanae vitae* that occasioned some of the early articles of the autonomous position.

There is obviously much ethical material in the Bible. What is in question is how it is used or whether it can be regarded as authoritative. The autonomy position saw its significance as parenetic or as contextual. But the position of

Ratzinger and the other critics reiterates the neo-Scholastic conviction that God is telling us through the Bible what to do, although different strands of it regard the biblical material as authoritative in different ways. To say the Bible gives us values, dispositions, or ideals is a weaker claim and gives more scope for a varied application to daily life than to say it gives universal rules (as does *Persona humana*). Values can be variously realised from one age to another; ideals do not bind with the same implacable rigour.

The difficulties of appeal to the Bible particularly for universal rules have been well documented. One faces problems about the dependency of the biblical writers on the philosophy of the time, about the cultural limitations of their horizons, about the distinction between normative and parenetic material, about exegetical and hermeneutical questions. In particular it is argued that in discriminating between still-valid percepts, for example, regarding adultery, and directives that the community has jettisoned, for example, regarding slaves or the position of women, one has to step outside the Bible and subject it to the criterion of common sense or of common moral experience.

Reflection

In reflecting on the current debate it is helpful to keep in mind three general over-lapping questions: (1) How are Christians to understand morality? (2) What is the source of their moral code (is it 'from above', decreed by God)? (3) How are they to go about moral discernment (by reference to the Bible or not)? The autonomy position insists on the recognition of morality as a human institution making its own claim. It seems to me to be important to drive that down as a deep pylon in Christian moral understanding. Christian faith enhances and transmutes that, but it is necesasry to recognise that it can and does exist without faith. Faith situates it in an ultimate scheme of things. It tells stories – of the rationality, goodness and fidelity of God, of hope in a final kingdom that will transform our earthly efforts, of providence that can bring good out of evil, of ultimate forgiveness – which are kind to and which sustain and support the whole institution of morality. Faith offers powerful motivation: Christians are confronted in their holy books with the elemental stories of the patience and fidelity of God ('He makes his sun rise on the evil and on the good, and sends rain on the righteous and on the unrighteous,' and 'Since God has loved us so much, we too should love one another'); of the self-forgetfulness of Christ (who 'emptied himself to assume the condition of a slave', who 'laid down his life for us when we were still sinners'); of the presence of the Spirit in us ('keep away from fornication … your body, you know, is the temple of the Holy Spirit').

But all this material must be garnered and communicated to and by the community in a way that respects the internal coherence and autonomy of morality. The authority of morality is the authority of the truth. Its claim is the claim of the truth, and genuine moral response is some recognition of that claim.

An Irish Reader in Moral Theology

It is not simply obedience to the will of another, even to the will of God. Not all doing right is authentic moral response. To do the right, to avoid evil is something. But if we are concerned not only about what happens but about those who make it happen, then why people act, out of what kind of consideration, with what reason or motive, is important. There are levels of moral response as of moral development. There is a danger that in Christian ethics precisely moral considerations will be clouded. Reward, sanction, fear, can move and deter. They may be necessary to prevent evil. They may be the only thing that works in a situation. That is something, but it is not yet developed moral response. It is significant that both Christian and philosophical morality have recently shown a marked interest in the recovery of the category of virtue. Virtue concerns itself not only with what is done but with why and how.

What this means, therefore, is that for religious people there are different kinds of reasons for being moral. There are moral reasons. These are central to morality, all morality, including Christian morality. They are what morality is about. There are also religious reasons. One does good because it is the will of God or as an act of love of God or to imitate God or to bring about God's purposes or kingdom or to gain a heavenly reward. Both kinds of reason are good. But to be moral solely for (religious) reasons extrinsic to morality appears to lack true awareness of what morality means. Aquinas has the striking statement: 'He therefore who avoids evil not because it is evil but because of the commands of God is not free, but he who avoids evil because it is evil is free' (see 2 Cor 3).

The emphasis of the autonomy position have set such matters in sharp relief. They have also rightly pointed up the problems of direct appeal to the Bible. But to admit to difficulty with the Bible as a source of authoritative moral rules is not to reject its authority in morals entirely but only to reject a certain kind of authority. It might be more profitable for Christian moral life to see the Bible primarily as nourishing faith rather than as imposing moral imperatives. We depend on the Bible for the great formative stories that tell us who God is, who we are, and what the world and the human community are about – for our cosmogony. They have a bearing on ethical judgement because they shape the self-understanding and the outlook on reality of the subject of moral discernment, of the 'I' who judges. Judgements are not made in a vacuum. They are made by people who see the world in a particular kind of way: moral disagreement is due in part to the fact that we see the reality in question differently or weigh differently aspects of that reality. One's evaluative description of the field of action and the responsibility experienced in a situation depend on the sort of person one is. That in turn depends on the stories and symbols that shape one's consciousness and imagination. It is only if you can understand a people's story that you understand what they see as the logic of their choices.

Religious faith nouished by the Bible might be seen as forming or having the potential to form a particular kind of character and therefore to suggest values and to evoke certain kinds of awareness and sensibilities that affect moral judgement, so that the Christian subject's experience of life in Christ becomes the hermeneutical centre of his/her ethics. One might see the Christian community, then, as having its own character shaped by stories of what God has done for it in Christ and therefore as having its own ideals and demands. And that is why there must be for us as there was for the Jews a close link between the liturgical recital of the good news of God's deeds and moral expectations.

So Christians are to discern as faith-people: they are to allow their faith to bear on their judgement. But we are not the first to seek the implications of faith for moral choice. We live in a tradition, and the Bible is the classic of that tradition. To make a sharp distinction between its religious and moral message is to do less than justice to the coherence and consistency of the life of the apostolic community. What we have in the Bible are impressions of that community's experience of the in-break of the kingdom in Jesus, of its resultant self-understanding, and of its attempts to see that through into practice or behaviour. So we need to notice how the faith-story issued in the ethical perspectives of the Bible. It has much to say, however elusively, about action; about living, loving and dying; about world, flesh and devil; about wholeness and flourishing; about welfare and happiness; about success and failure; about weakness and sin – concepts that are the common coin of the moralist.

Christian moral life calls, then, for dialogue between faith today and the complex faith of the apostolic community. It requires that we enter into the interplay of ethos and the ethic that we find there to discover its dynamic of believing and doing. It is not only what the texts say to us that is important. It is why the writers say what they say. It is their understanding of themselves in the cosmos, their symbolic and social world, and the delicate way in which they see the implications of that for living. We need to allow the biblical text to open up for us the new and wider world of meaning tht arises out of the experience of the divine irruption into history in Jesus Christ. We can only do so if we keep in mind that the ethical material of the Bible is rich, diverse and chaotic. It comes at several levels. Its language is not that of a scientific treatise but of literature – imaginative, colourful. Its mode is indicative, imperative, parabolic, mystical. It is more story than history, more wisdom than law. It says what it has to say in a bewildering profusion of forms and genres. It has to be taken on its own terms.

One who enters the world-view of the Bible will receive not just encouragement and motivation for moral life but light on judgement. The faith of the apostolic community issued in sayings that remain instructive for us about the one thing necessary, about losing and finding one's life, taking up the cross, taking no thought for tomorrow, regarding others as better than onself, seeking not one's own rights but those of others, laying down one's life, rejoicing in mourning and persecution. One who shares the story and does morality in fidelity to it finds a justification for choices about friendship with God, about prayer, poverty, detachment, celibacy, forgiveness, humility, as well as for a wider range of dispositions of joy, gratitude, hope, trust, patience.

There will be considerable areas of agreement between Christian and non-Christian, between all who have a concern for rights, justice, fairness and benevolence. This will be especially so at the level of negative moral norms – 'the minimum content of natural law' (Hart). But moral life cannot be adequately caught in negative norms. It is not only about what one must do but what one can do, about individual potentialities and responsibilities. It is for several reasons more satisfactorily seen in terms of character – as a settled disposition of seeing and making judgements according to one's story, as an attention not only to what is done but to why, as an unrest until the perfect shape of moral wholeness is realised. The Christian tradition says that while the details of our lives will not coincide with Christ's, his fidelity to his story as expressed in the kingdom ethic of the Sermon on the Mount remains the only entirely valid norm of morality, against which all else is to be measured.

The Christian discerns the moral way within the community of faith. There is no need to apologise for that: all who do morality do it out of a particular world-view or stance that in some way affects judgement. Indeed, there is much talk nowadays in philosophical ethics that it is only within a community of shared vision that values and judgements can be satisfactorily vindicated. This is not to advocate some esoteric discernment. If there is, as Rahner says, a faith-instinct in moral matters, it is the fruit of the stories and symbols that create the Christian imagination. The Christian 'facts of life' are public facts. The logic of Christian judgement can be understood, even if not subscribed to, by those who do not share the vision. Nor is Christian morality a ghetto morality. The Christian seeks to affect society, to bring about the kingdom. That very mission calls for its own virtues: tolerance of others, a readiness to work with all people of good will, and patience when one's point of view is not accepted in the public forum. But with due respect for different perspectives, Christians have to do their morality in fidelity to their own religious myth. That enshrines their ultimate concern and provide their basic cosmogony. It would be strange if it did not have something to say about how life is to be lived.

NOTES

1   O. O'Donovan, *Resurrection and Moral Order*, Leicester/Michigan: Inter-Varsity Press/Erdmans, 1986, p. 11.
2   Nowell-Smith in I. Ramsey, *Christian Ethics and Contemporary Philosophy*, London: SCM, 1966, p. 75.
3   H. Noldin and A. Schmitt, *Summa theologiae moralis,* Vol. 1, Barcelona: Heder, 1951, pp. 38, 40.
4   K. Rahner, *Theological Investigations*, trans. Kruger, Vol. 6, Baltimore/London: Helicon/Darton, Longman & Todd, 1969, p. 214.
5   D. Prümmer, *Manuale Theologiae Moralis,* Vol. 1, Barcelona: Heder, 1946, p. 98.
6   Rahner, op. cit., p. 247.

BIBLIOGRAPHY

MacNamara, Vincent, *Faith and Ethics,* Dublin/Washington DC: Gill and Macmillan/Georgetown University Press, 1985.

Noldin-Schmitt, *Summa Theologiae Moralis,* Vol. 1, Barcelona: Herder, 1951.

O'Donovan, O., *Resurrection and Moral Order,* Leicester/Michigan: Erdmans, Grand Rapics, 1986.

Prümmer, D., *Manuale Theologiae Moralis,* Vol. 1, Barcelona: Herder, 1946.

Rahner, Karl, *Theological Investigations,* trans. Kruger, Vol. 6, Baltimore/London: Helicon/Darton, Longman and Todd, 1969.

Ramsey, I., *Christian Ethics and Contemporary Philosophy*, London: SCM, 1966.

Part Three
Moral Theory

12 The Thomist Concept of Natural Law

Noel Dermot O'Donoghue

(*Irish Theological Quarterly*, 1955, No. 2, pp. 89–109.)

Within the last few years the subject of Natural Law has come to receive a great deal of attention. Those philosophers and historians whose aim has been to establish contact with that Christian intelligence which had been obscured by the Renaissance and the Enlightenment have found that Natural Law was one of the great disputed questions all through the Middle Ages, and that we are the heirs to a large treasury of ideas, carefully elaborated and contrasted. Philosophers of law have come to see that Positivistic theories do not provide a basis for Civil Law and have been forced to return to the Natural Law of Pufendorf and Kant, and in some cases have gone further back to the theocentric medieval concept. The growth of Social Philosophy has centred attention on Natural Law from another point of view; it has come to be realised that if the Social Philosopher is to make moral judgements he must have recourse in the final analysis to Natural Law. As a result of this general renewal of interest, scholastic textbooks of Ethics and Moral Theology have come to give a fuller treatment of Natural Law and are careful to set down what appear to be the more important statements of St Thomas on the subject.

St Thomas's doctrine of Natural Law has received more attention than that of any other medieval author. The study of his teaching has been facilitated by the fact that he dealt with the subject of law *ex professo* and at length in the *Summa Theologiae*.[1] We are spared the labour of piecing texts together in order to arrive at the answer to a question he did not pose. He asks the questions which we would ask; he deals with them satisfactorily and meets the relevant objections. His terminology is sometimes puzzling but historical research has shown us how he came to use the terms he used, and with what meaning.

Nevertheless, the reader of St Thomas' treatise on law may find himself faced with difficulties and paradoxes and it may happen that the darkness is rather deepened than lightened if he has recourse to contemporary expositions of the Thomist doctrine. In particular, he may find himself asking with increasing irritation: What exactly *is* Natural Law? What is the central notion from which all else derives, in relation to which everything else is properly understood? This general difficulty will probably present itself in an individual way to the individual reader for whom it arises. The following reflections are concerned with expressing a certain line of difficulty and with proposing from the point of view of this line of difficulty an answer to the question: *What is St Thomas' concept of Natural Law?*

I

The first difficulty arises from the definition of Law with which the treatise on Law opens: *quaedam rationis ordinatio ad bonum commune, et ab eo qui curam communitatis habet, promulgata.*[2] How are we to arrive at a notion of Natural Law which satisfies this definition? If Natural Law is something by which the individual governs his own life – *quo quis agit*[3] – how can it be said to be ordered to the common good by the head of the community? And in what sense can such a Law be said to be promulgated?

This difficulty has been explored very thoroughly by Dom O. Lottin:

> La loi selon saint Thomas est une dictée de la raison discursive; la loi naturelle, de son coté est une dictée de la raison naturelle. La loi, selon la définition thomiste, poursuit comme but le bien commun, non le bien des individus; la loi naturelle, au contraire, poursuit le bien de la nature humaine, lequel est, il est vrai, commun à tous les hommes, mais en même, temps est strictement personnel à chaque homme. La loi, selon saint Thomas, a comme auteur le législateur, que est chef de la communauté: notion essentielle à tel point qu'on ne peut comprendre la moralité des actes prescrits et leur caractère obligatoire qu'en recourant à la notion de législateur. Quant à la loi naturelle, on peut comprendre la moralité des actes prescrits par elle et même leur caractère obligatoire sans recourir directement à la notion du législateur divin ... La loi enfin, d'aprés saint Thomas doit etre promulguée ... La loi naturelle, au contraire n'a nul besoin d'etre promulguée; elle est connue par ellememe, du seul fait que l'homme est raisonnable.[4]

Dom Lottin is so impressed by these differences that he wishes to detach Natural Law altogether from the general definition of law. Natural Law consists simply in the dictates of natural reason, directing human action towards its end. It must be considered apart from Divine Law, as well as from the definition of law in general. The treatise on law in the *Summa Theologiae* is coloured by scholastic tradition; in order to discover the personal thought of St Thomas – *la pensée vraiment personnelle de saint Thomas* – it is necessary to go to the fourth book of the Sentences, which was inspired by the teleology of Aristotle.[5] *Il n'y a donc aucun inconvénient a abandonner les cadres de la Somme de théologie, si l'on veut saisir la notion de la loi naturelle.*[6]

We are not concerned here with Dom Lottin's thesis insofar as it might be put forward as a *correction* of St Thomas. As an *interpretation* of St Thomas, as a presentation of his 'truly personal thought', it is not convincing. We are asked to believe that St Thomas does not really understand Natural Law as fulfilling the definition of law which he elaborated so carefully and that his close relating of Natural Law to Eternal Law was somehow *praeter intentionem*. And yet, in one of the articles in which the definition of law is elaborated we have an objection which contains the statement: *lex naturalis maxime habet rationem legis*, and St Thomas does not deny or in any way qualify the statement.[7] And, in the second next article he states categorically that natural law is law in the strict sense – *proprie lex vocatur*.[8] As regards the relation of Natural Law to Eternal Law we find that the former is in fact defined in terms of the latter – *lex naturalis nihil aliud est quam perticipatio legis aeternae in rationali creatura*.[9] Indeed, so close is the relation between the two that at one point they are almost identified.[10] It is clear therefore that in order to accept Dom Lottin's thesis it is necessary to change, not only the general framework and terminology of the treatise on law in the *Summa*, but the whole substance of the treatise as well.[11]

If we do not accept Dom Lottin's interpretation, we are left with the difficulties which he has so forcefully expressed. How can Natural Law be seen to fit the definition of law in general?

Let us pose the question a little differently. How can the definition of Natural Law be seen to fit the definition of law in general? It is true that St Thomas does not provide a direct definition of Natural Law, but he defines it indirectly, as a participation in External Law, which is in turn defined as *summa ratio in Deo existens*.[12] *Lex naturalis nihil aliud est quam participatio legis aeternae in rationali creatura*.[13] The way to the understanding of Natural Law would seem to be clearly indicated: we must first arrive at an adequate notion of Eternal Law and then see what is meant by saying that Natural Law is a participation of the Eternal Law.

II

The Eternal Law is outside time, in the mind of God, directing all creatures towards their end, which is the Divine Essence.[14] It differs from providence in this that while Eternal Law is the plan of creation, *ratio operis*,[15] providence is the detailed carrying out of this plan, *ordo in finem artificiati*.[16] The Eternal Law gives its direction to the created universe and the activity of all created things participates in this direction. And so we have the definition: *lex aeterna nihil aliud est quam ratio divinae sapientiae, secundum quod est directiva omnium actuum et motionum*.[17]

It is clear that this law which has for its end the universal common good and which is promulgated by the fact of creation comes under the definition of law in general.[18] It follows that Natural Law will participate in the nature of law as defined by St Thomas in the way and to the extent that it participates in Eternal

Law. Accordingly we must examine carefully what is meant by this participation in Eternal Law.

There is a sense in which all things participate in Eternal Law *inquantum scilicet ex impressione ejus habent inclinationes in proprios actus et fines*.[19] The precepts of the Divine reason are found receptively in the things which they direct. But the creature which itself possesses reason participates in Eternal Law in a more excellent way *inquantum et ipsa fit providentiae particeps, sibi ipsi et aliis providens ... in ipsa participatur ratio aerterna ... Participat eam intellectualiter et rationaliter*. This participation of Eternal Law in a rational creature is law in the proper sense; that participation which is in irrational nature can be called law only *per similitudinem*.[20]

Natural Law, therefore, is a *rational participation* in Eternal Law. But – and this is our second difficulty – there are two ways of understanding rational participation. We might see it as *receptive* participation: created reason is receptive of Eternal Law just as irrational nature is receptive of Eternal Law, though in a higher way, *excellentiori modo*. The mode of reception is higher, since the rational is higher than the irrational, but there is none the less question of receptivity, of *being* regulated. Rational nature has its rational inclinations just as irrational nature has non-rational inclinations: in both cases there is the *impression* or direction of Eternal Law. *Or* we might see rational participation as *legislative*, as participation in the very activity of legislating. That which participates in reason participates in that which lays down Eternal Law and therefore lays down this law for itself. The role of reason is preceptive, regulative, the measure of the rightness of human acts – *ratio mensurans* rather than *ratio mensurata*.

That we must understand rational participation in the second sense, seeing human reason as regulative rather than regulated, is clear from the fact that St Thomas identifies the Natural Law with the 'propositions' or 'precepts' of natural reason.[21] The matter is put beyond doubt by the discussion in Q.93, a.6 where a sharp distinction is drawn between participation in Eternal Law by way of *inclinatio naturalis ad id quod est consonum legi aeternae* and *ipsa naturalis cognitio boni*. The Eternal Law is impressed on all creatures, irrational and well as rational, by way of natural inclination, and this participation is both active and passive.[22] This inclination in man is rational and has therefore a special character, but this special character does not affect the mode of participation: it is still receptive participation – *per modum obedientiae*.[23] That which differentiates Natural Law from natural inclination and makes it law in the proper sense is the fact that it is the work of reason, expression rather than impression. It comes from God, as all human things; it is a light given to the mind, *impressio divini luminis*; but the mind receives it; not as itself an object which is revealed by it, but as becoming a source of light, discerning and declaring the truth for human activity – *lumen rationis naturalis, quo discernimus quid sit bonum et quid malum*.[24]

This notion of rational participation *per modum cognitionis* is misunderstood or simply not arrived at in most current expositions of Thomist Natural Law.[25] Some authors distinguish between Natural Law considered *objectively* and Natural Law considered *subjectively*. Objectivity considered Natural Law is Eternal Law received *per modum obedientiae* as explained in the preceding paragraph; subjectivity considered Natural Law is awareness of this objective law as obligatory.[26] Others see Natural Law as the promulgation of Eternal Law by human reason.[27] In neither case can reason be said to be legislative; it simply recognises and accepts a law which is already there. It may be said that, nevertheless, reason lays down this law with a certain force and assurance. But in this its role is that of an interpreter and not that of a legislator, as if a lawyer spoke with certainty on the precepts of human law.

Natural Law is not simply a set of judgements or observations; it is a set of imperatives or precepts.[28] An imperative does not merely recognise what is to be done; it lays down what is to be done. It contains within itself that moral force which is obligation – *movet cum quadam intimatione denuntiativa*.[29] It is essentially an intellectual act, since it imposes order in view of an end, but it has within it the force of the will which desires the end. Since Natural Law is law in the proper sense and since it is the work of human reason, it follows that it is constituted by imperatives of this character enunciated by the reason as ruler of human activities.

III

We have arrived at a partial understanding of what St Thomas had in mind when he defined Natural Law as a participation in Eternal Law. There is question of participation in the legislative activity itself. As man is made to the image of God, so man's reason enunciates precepts after the manner in which the Divine Reason enunciates precepts.

But our understanding is only partial. We are faced with new difficulties. How does man's reason come to enunciate these principles? Is there question of a special illumination, or do we remain within the ordinary ways of knowledge? Further, the precepts of Natural Law seem to bind or oblige us. What is the source of this obligation? Has it the quality of Divine authority, or is it something human and personal? Clearly, we must arrive at an answer to these questions in order to understand what Natural Law is, and what is the manner of its participation in Eternal Law.

In describing how reason comes to enunciate the precepts of Natural Law, Thomas uses language that is oddly coloured by metaphor. Reason is illuminated, comes under the influence of a Divine irradiation, has these precepts inscribed, implanted in it. If this language is taken too literally, it will seem that there is question of Divine illumination, or a direct vision of the Divine Eternal Law, or at least of some special and extraordinary type of knowledge. Thus Professor d'Entrèves thinks that St Thomas' notion of the light of reason 'probably goes back to Platonic and Augustinian sources,' and favours the suggestion that 'St Thomas rationalised the illumination doctrine which St Augustine had derived from Plato'.[30] The notion is quite common that, in the very act of enunciating Natural Law, we see God as its author, we see it *as* coming from God.[31] The authors who put forward this notion do not seem to find it necessary to discuss what it implies, viz. that the person who does not accept God's existence is incapable of enunciating any principle of Natural Law, not even 'good is to be done and evil avoided'.

In a recent book, M. Maritain has put forward an original interpretation of St Thomas on the point under discussion, one which is apt to commend itself to an age impatient of abstraction:

> I think that Thomas Aquinas' teaching, here, needs to be understood in a much deeper and more precise fashion than is common. When he says that human reason discovers the regulations of natural law through the guidance of the *inclinations* of human nature, he means that the very mode and manner in which human reason knows natural law is not rational knowledge, but knowledge *through inclination*. That kind of knowledge is not clear knowledge through concepts and conceptual judgements; it is obscure, unsystematic, vital knowledge by connaturality or affinity, in which the intellect, in order to form its judgements, consults and listens to the inner melody that the vibrating strings of abiding tendencies awaken in us.[32]

These interpretations of the knowledge of Natural Law as non-rational or as transcending abstraction from sense data, or as, in some way special and extraordinary are given a certain plausibility by the *language* which St Thomas uses. Nevertheless, they are contradicted by the *teaching* of St Thomas as presented in the following texts:

> … Praeexistunt in nobis quaedam scientiarum semina scilicet primae conceptiones intellectus, quae statim lumine intellectus agentis cognoscuntur per species a sensibilibus abstractas, sive sint complexa, ut dignitates, sive incomplexa, sicut ratio entis, et unius, et hujusmodi, quae statim intellectus apprehendit. Ex istis autem principiis universalibus omnia principia sequuntur sicut ex quibusdam rationibus seminalibus.[33]
> … Anima humana, quantum ad id quod in ipsa supremum est, aliquid attingit de eo quod proprium est naturae angelicae; ut scilicet aliquorum cognitionem subito et sine inquisitione habeat, quamvis quantum ad hoc inveniatur angelo inferior, quod in his veritatem cognoscere non potest nisi a sensu accipiendo … Unde et in natura humana, inquantum attingit

angelicam, oportet esse cognitionem veritatis sine inquisitione et in speculativis et in practicis; et hanc quidem cognitionem oportet esse principium totius cognitionis sequentis sive speculativae sive practicae, cum principia oporteat esse stabiliora et certiora; unde et hanc cognitionem oportet homini naturaliter inesse, cum hoc quidem cognoscat quasi quoddam seminarium totius cognitionis sequentis.[34]

The first principles of practical reason are the primary precepts of Natural Law. These principles arise in the mind through the operation of that power which governs all our thinking, the active intellect. The active intellect does not discover these principles within itself, nor within the passive intellect, nor does it find them written in human nature. Neither does it arrive at them by way of a vision of an intelligible world or through contact with the *veritas incommutabilis* of St Augustine.[35] It arrives at them by addressing itself to the data provided by the senses. Through the abstractive power of the active intellect, the intelligible element in these data is disengaged. This intelligible element – *species intelligibilis* – is impressed on the passive intellect, which finally operates, expresses itself, by forming concepts and judgements. These concepts and judgements have for their direct object the external world which was presented in the first place by way of the sense data. The intellect which forms these concepts and judgements is passive and receptive all the way up to the final act of knowledge. The principal agent in the whole process is the active intellect; the sense data – more exactly, the *phantasmata* – are the instrumental or secondary agent.[36] Both agents are essential to the process; the sense data are unintelligible until they come under the light of the active intellect, just as sense objects are invisible apart from physical light; the active intellect is of itself merely illuminative of objects and cannot provide or create objects … *Conceptiones intellectus … lumine intellectus agentis cognoscuntur per species a sensibilibus abstractas.*

The process which we have outlined is that which is at the basis of all intellectual knowledge, as St Thomas sees it. This doctrine respects both the interiority and exteriority of knowledge; it accords to the mind that rich and varied immanent activity which results from the conjunction of matter and spirit, of activity and receptivity; it asserts that the act of knowledge, of conception or of judgement, has for its object the intelligible structure of the world presented through the senses. There are some corollaries of this general theory which are specially relevant to our present discussion. The active intellect is part of the mind, *aliquid animae*; it is not therefore a light which has its proper source inside the mind. Nevertheless, it is a *participation* in the light of the Divine intellect – *quaedam participata similitudo luminis increati.*[37] Moreover, it depends in its operation on the Divine light to such a degree that the Divine light is the primary agent, and the active intellect only a secondary and instrumental agent. And so, St Thomas can say that the first principles are caused by God and that the light under which they come to be enunciated has its source in God.[38] But it must be remembered that every human activity, even that of free will, has God as its source; he is the primary cause of the effect. Moreover, the active intellect has a role in all intellectual knowledge, so that all knowledge may be said to be a participation in the Divine light. Finally, the *species intelligibiles* which the active intellect abstracts from the sense data, are intelligible by participation in the absolute intelligibility of God.[39] We can see, therefore, that St Thomas is not necessarily thinking of a special and extraordinary knowledge when he speaks of the precepts of Natural Law as *rationes quas Deus naturae inseruit* or *impressio divini luminis in nobis.*

Nevertheless, our knowledge of the first principles of Natural Law has a special character. It has something of the quality of angelic knowledge in that it is attained immediately and without labour. In its normal operations the human intellect arrives at definite concepts and sure judgements as the result of a process, more or less laborious, of investigation and comparison. The sense data provide the intellect with a report on the externals of things merely – accidents, properties, effects; by way of these the intellect advances towards some knowledge of the essence, and towards judgements approximating to certainty. Our first conception of 'man', for example, will be vague and inaccurate, based on externals, and our judgements bearing on 'man' will be correspondingly uncertain and inaccurate. Similarly, our conception of 'law' will, prior to reflection, be based on this and that particular law or on certain effects or external trappings of law. We do not have a clear vision of a world of ideas; we are in the position of the prisoners in the cave of Plato's allegory. The sense world veils from us the intelligible structure of reality and the light of intelligence which we possess enables us to see the truth only with difficulty and in part. Yet the truth is there, the ideas are there, ultimately and properly in the Divine mind, derivatively and by way of participation in the material world. Now St Thomas' doctrine is that there are *some* conceptions which the mind comes to possess immediately and without difficulty. There is in the mind a special quality relating it to these conceptions, so that once it is presented with the appearances or species which open the way to these conceptions, it forms the conceptions immediately and with absolute certainty. It does not have to *search* for these conceptions within the sense appearances; it sees them immediately as if it were in the position of the search having been made for it. *Anima humana quantum ad id quod in ipsa supremum est, aliquid attingit de eo quod proprium est naturae angelicae; ut scilicet aliquorum cognitionem subito et sine inquisitione habeat.*[40]

The special quality or habit of mind whereby the mind possesses immediate knowledge of the first principles of Natural Law is called by St Thomas *synderesis*. It is the counterpart in the order of actions to the 'habit of first principles' in the order of speculation. These qualities are the source of all knowledge; their light radiates through all subsequent knowledge to such an extent that its certainty is in proportion to its proximity to the principles attained through these qualities – *principium totius cognitionis sequentis*.[41] The principles of Natural Law are not innate, but the habit of *synderesis* is innate and it is in this sense precisely that we have a *naturalis conceptio* of Natural Law, that this law is *indita, cordi impressa, naturaliter cognita*.[42]

These then are the elements involved in the enunciation of Natural Law by the intellect as practical: the habit of synderesis in the passive intellect, the data presented by the senses and the light of the active intellect which renders the sense data intelligible and uses them as the instrument for bringing the powers of the passive intellect into operation. In other words, the mind has a special *aptitude* for enunciating the law, but it must wait on sense experience, which it nevertheless interprets for itself. It is only by sense experience that the mind is in contact with reality and its first speculative operation is that of recognising this, of seeing what is presented to it *as* reality.[43] Similarly, in the practical order, it is through sense experience that the mind comes in contact with a world which is the field of action, where it has its own part to play purposing and planning, deciding and directing. Faced with this world of action, the mind forms immediately and without difficulty the concepts of good and bad, distinguishing 'that which is to be done' and 'that which is not to be done'. There is no question at this stage of seeing any particular thing or line of action as good or bad, but of forming general concepts through which, or in the light of which, everything in the world of action can be judged. In face of the world of action, the mind does not remain disengaged, interested only in the truth about action, though this is the proper object of the practical intellect as intellect.[44] The mind is tendency as well as understanding, and it knows itself as tendency, as appetite; in Thomist terms, the intellect reflects on the will and on the will's inclinations.[45] Immediately, and with absolute certainty, the mind judges that good is the object of appetite, that there is complete identity between that which is good and that which the will desires. This is the first principle enunciated by the practical intellect. *Primum principium in ratione practica est quod fundatur supra rationem boni; quae est: Bonum est quod omnia appetunt*.[46] This first principle is not tautologous, for in its most simple concept the good is seen as the end or goal of action, while the judgement asserts further that it is the end of desire.

The first principle of the practical reason is not a law; it is merely a judgement. Law is preceptive, imperative; that is to say, it is a judgement which has within it the force of the will in motion towards the end presented by the intellect. Moreover, a precept is regulative; it imposes a rule on subordinates. Once the good *as* good is revealed it attracts the will necessarily and irresistibly. But the good is not *possessed* by this adhesion towards it as known, for goodness, unlike truth, is in the object, not in the intellect. Good can only be attained by action; indeed it first appears as the goal of action. All man's various powers of action must be mobilised towards its attainment. Since the good is the *only* object of desire, no action of any power can be directed towards what is not good. And so, the intellect lays on every member of the domain of action which it governs this rule, which suffers no exception: *Good is to be done and sought after, evil is to be avoided*. There is question of the good generally, *as* good, not of any particular good, but it is nevertheless a human good in that it is the object of the individual human will. All other precepts arise within this; it contains them all in germ – *quasi quoddam seminarium*.[47] The other precepts arise by way of the recognition of certain things as human goods, or as necessary means to human goods. Since the first principle stated that the good is the object of desire, the intellect discovers human goods by considering human desires or inclinations, according as each has its place within the complete tendency of the will.[48]

IV

An understanding of St Thomas' teaching on the way in which Natural Law is enunciated leads us to see more clearly in what sense Natural Law is a participation in Eternal Law.

Natural Law is enunciated through the light of the active intellect working on the passive intellect by way of species or forms derived from the senses. Once the first precept of Natural Law is enunciated, it becomes the instrument whereby the active intellect illuminates the world of conduct and enunciates further principles.[49] At its origin, then, Natural Law is a source of illumination lighting up the domain of action. This light is something created and human; nevertheless it is a similitude and participation of the Divine light which contains the precepts of Eternal Law, *quaedam participata similitudo luminis increati, in quo continentur rationes aeternae*.[50] The human mind is an 'image' or 'mirror' of the Divine mind.[51] This does not mean that the light which is in man's mind is a reflection of the Divine light; the created light is a distinct though dependent source of light; it is not itself mirrored, but rather mirrors the truth which is in the Divine mind.[52] This mirroring of the Divine truth is not immediate, as if the created mind saw the truth in God, or was receptive of Divine illumination. The human mind mirrors Divine truth, not as the moon mirrors the sun, nor as the sea mirrors the sky, but after the manner in which that which is generated mirrors it parent. There is a light in the human mind which is so closely fashioned in the likeness of the light in the Divine intellect that it forms principles which are in fact an exact copy of the principles in the Divine intellect. There is that in man's mind which forms the concept of the good, the practical first principle, the first imperative within which further imperatives naturally arise; in this the precepts which are being enunciated are in fact the precepts of the Eternal Law that governs creation, yet the law is being enunciated by human reason as an imperative governing human action, and concerned only with the world of human action.[53]

We can see from this how it is that Natural Law is law in the proper sense and yet is not 'diverse' from Eternal Law – *(non est) aliquid diversum a lege aeterna*.[54]

Natural Law is in man's mind, and is, therefore, distinct from Eternal Law in the mind of God. Nevertheless, in stating the precepts of Natural Law, we are in fact stating precepts of Eternal Law.

It must be emphasised that Natural Law participates in Eternal Law *as law*. This means that Natural Law possesses all the elements which go to constitute the definition of law. It is easy to see that Natural Law is an *ordination of reason;* its precepts are enunciated by the practical intellect. It is also clear that Natural Law is *promulgated,* since the mind not only enunciates it but knows or recognises that it is being enunciated; the promulgation consists in the fact that the precepts are presented to the mind in such a way that it recognises them.[55] It is more difficult to see Natural Law as containing the other elements which go to form the definition of law: direction to the common good and enunciation by the head of a community. Natural Law is in the individual man who seeks his own last end and who has no authority over the community. It would seem that, even if Natural Law participates in that which contains these elements, it does not participate in it *as* containing these elements.

It must be remembered, however, that, although the good towards which Natural Law is directed is the object of the individual human will, nevertheless, since the will is a spiritual faculty, its object is not any limited or particular good, but the good in general, *bonum in communi, bonum universale*.[56] Since man is spirit, open to universal reality, it is only in *the* good that he can find *his* good. The first concept of the good which man forms naturally, and which is an image of the idea of the good in the Divine mind, is a concept of the good *as such*, not of something that merely participates in the good; it is the good towards which the whole work of creation moves *bonum commune divinum*.[57] It follows that the precepts of Natural Law which arise from the conception of the good are directed towards the common good in the most complete sense, so that this element of the definition of law is found properly and formally in Natural Law.[58]

Similarly, Natural Law is *ab eo qui curam communitatis habet*, not because it participates in Eternal Law which has *in fact* this quality, but because it participates in this very quality in Eternal Law so as to possess it properly and formally. He who legislates in view of the common good not only has the idea of the common good and the desire to accomplish it – a private person can have that – but has a function in its accomplishment. The idea which he has of the common good is directive, architectonic, and he is a legislator because he has been placed in a situation in which his activity is governed by this idea. Now the activity of man in enunciating Natural Law is governed by the idea of the good as *bonum commune universale*; he participates in the architectonic idea in the Divine mind. It is therefore quite exact to say that man in enunciating Natural Law has the care of the community. He has a legislative function in relation to the common good, since his activity is naturally controlled by the idea which engenders this function.[59] He does not merely direct his actions to the common good in accordance with law; he lays down the law by which the common good is safeguarded.

It is clear, therefore, that all the elements which constitute the definition of law are found formally and properly in Natural Law and that, if we would have an exact notion of what Natural Law is as law, it is these elements that we must consider. We can see, further, how St Thomas came to define Natural Law, in so far as it is a special kind of law, as *participatio legis aeternae in rationali creatura*. This participation has to be understood formally as participation in law *as* law, that is to say, participation in all the elements that constitute law.

V

There remains the question of obligation. What is the source of the obligation which attaches to Natural Law? That there is within us a force which may be called Obligation or Duty or Conscience is generally admitted. 'As we have naturally a sense of the beautiful and graceful in nature and art, though tastes proverbially differ, so we have a sense of duty and obligation whether we associate it with the same certain actions in particular or not.'[60] That we have this sense at least in relation to the primary precepts of Natural Law may be taken as a fact and starting point of discussion; it is in the interpretation of this fact that differences arise.

Leaving aside those interpretations which would reduce obligation to non-ethical impulses and feelings, we find that there are two main attitudes to the question of obligation. These attitudes provide the terms of the antitheses: right and good, rule and end, deontology and teleology which have been at the centre of ethical discussion in England for the last fifty years. Is an action good ultimately because it obeys a rule or because it brings about an end? Does obligation arise from a law to be obeyed or from an end to be followed? Does moral law oblige of itself (deontology) or because it serves some end good in itself (teleology)?

Is St Thomas' ethical system a deontology primarily or a teleology? It has been interpreted both ways. It is pointed out that, for St Thomas as for Aristotle, an action is good or bad only in relation to the last end; there is no question therefore of seeing its goodness in terms of law. On the other hand, it is clear that St Thomas attached great importance to the first precept: do good and avoid evil, and it would seem that actions are good or bad insofar as they obey this precept.

We cannot attempt a full discussion of this question here, but it will appear that some of the points that have come up in our previous discussion help towards a solution. It is clear that for St Thomas all law carries with it a force of obligation – (*praecepta*) *legis habent vim obligandi ex ipso dictamine rationis*.[61] This obligation is within the law so that the law imposes itself on conscience, on will and intellect as considering a particular action. An action is good or evil according as it agrees or does not agree with right reason, that is, with reason informed by law.[62] Thus law imposes itself as a rule of action.

But what is the source of this obligation which is a quality of Natural Law? We shall discover St Thomas' answer to this question if we reflect on the fact that for him law is an ordination of reason *in view of the end*. It is because the end imposes itself that the law imposes itself. The end moves the will and it is this motion of the will that is the force of obligation within the law. *Praeceptum legis, cum sit obligatorium, est de aliquo quod fieri debet. Quod autem aliquid debet fieri, hoc provenit ex necessitate alicujus finis.*[63] Natural Law has its source in the conception of the good, which imposes itself on the will as its adequate object. And so, the primary precept which arises immediately from the apprehension of the good as such is an absolute or categorical imperative and subsequent precepts derive all their force from this first precept.[64] When a particular line of action is commanded it is commanded only because and insofar as it is good. The first precept imposes itself absolutely as suffering no condition or exception. Moreover, it arises through a sort of physical necessity, since the will when confronted with the good cannot but choose it. We must not forget, however, the role of the intellect in the primary and natural operations of the practical mind: the good which attracts the will is the *true* good, that is to say, the good of the will as a rational faculty. This true good is presented *formally;* with the precept which it engenders it is a light which can be brought to bear on particular goods to judge them; there is no immediate vision of that in which the true good is found in the concrete. Further, the primary precepts are not always in operation; they may be merely present in the mind *habitually.*[65] In a particular instance, the will may be presented with apparent good, a good appealing to sense inclination, and is free to bring reason and precept to bear on the situation or not; the precept is present with its imperative force, but only habitually, and the will in its actual choice can disregard it.[66] The first precept has absolute force if it is allowed to operate fully, but the will is free in the particular case not to allow it to operate fully.

It would be interesting to consider more closely how the binding force of law bears on the particular choice, but we are here concerned directly with the source of obligation as a quality of Natural Law. This source, we have seen, is the good as the primary concept in the practical order. The good in its purity, unparticipated, is God; no other object can satisfy the man who follows the light of natural reason consistently to its source. For such a man, or for anybody who has been taught from childhood to identify the true good, the precepts of Natural Law appear as Divine precepts carrying Divine authority, and demanding obedience as the expression of the Divine will. Thus the voice of Conscience is heard as the voice of God and it is possible to argue with Newman that this voice assures us most convincingly of the existence of God. This is so for the man who has been trained to see where the natural light leads, or who is willing to follow it with full sincerity. Yet it is possible to recognise Natural Law and to feel its obligation without admitting the authority of God or believing that God exists. Here Natural Law, stripped to its elements, has its obligation from the good as the adequate object of the will.[67]

VI

We have been concerned with the answer to the question: What is Natural Law for St Thomas? The question arises from the fact that St Thomas' teaching has been variously interpreted and that there are writers of great authority who say that the concept of Natural Law does not fit the general definition of law. Our investigation has led to the conclusion that Natural Law fits the general definition exactly. Natural Law is not merely a receptive participation in Eternal Law. It is a participation in Eternal Law *as law*, that is to say, it participates in all the elements whereby Eternal Law is law. It is not, immediately, a law received by human reason; rather it is enunciated by human reason. It does not come to be enunciated through a Divine illumination, yet that in man whereby it is enunciated is created participation in the Divine light. Within this light the precepts of Natural Law may be called a reflection of the precepts of Eternal Law. The first precept: 'do good and avoid evil' is a natural discovery of the mind as the image of the Divine mind, as participating in the Divine ideas. This first precept contains all other precepts within it *quasi quoddam seminarium*. This precept has absolute obligation since it arises through the apprehension of the good as the adequate object of the will.

Since we have been concerned with the *conception* of Natural Law, we have taken as example the precept in which this conception is most perfectly verified, the first precept from which the others arise. To consider other precepts would involve raising the question of the derivation of these precepts from the first precept, and the sense of the distinction between primary and secondary precepts. This is a large question and it demands separate treatment, though it can be examined only in the light of a clear conception of what Natural Law is. In particular it must be remembered that, for St Thomas, the first precept is not one among several primary precepts, but is the source or ground of all precept and all obligation. Other precepts bind only insofar as they embody the first precept; it follows that the obligation of what is called a secondary precept is no less strong than that of a primary precept, once the former is clearly seen to embody the first precept. It is generally recognised that St Thomas's doctrine allows largely for variety in moral notions and in the application of general principles. What is known by all, as part of essential human nature, is the first principle and the *conceptiones communes* which it involves.[68] All men know that there is a good and that it must be sought, that action must be ruled by principle rather than the impulse of the moment. Contemporary anthropologists have come to see that in fact all men are one in affirming this. As a recent writer puts it: 'Morality is universal in the sense that everywhere we find a recognition, implicit or explicit, that conduct has to be controlled or guided in reference to "principle".'[69]

Natural Law is a Divine light guiding conduct in that it is a participation by man in the light whereby the Divine intelligence orders all creation towards its end. The concept of the good which governs the whole moral life is not a laborious invention pieced together after the fashion of ordinary human concepts, neither is it formed according to the measure of particular and partial goods; it arises immediately and it remains to judge all particular goods. It commands action and binds it to itself, and this command and obligation it attaches to every pursuit that leads to the good. The will can only rest finally in the true good which is God, but if the principle of the good is not followed to its source, the will must narrow or deform itself to the measure of a partial good. Man seeks the true good insofar as he reflects the Divine idea and the Divine command, as God's image, and the image finds it proper truth in that which it mirrors.

NOTES

1 1-2, 90–108. The treatment in the *Summa Contra Gentiles* (3, 112–118 and 128–130) is brief and incidental. There is besides the *lectio* which deals with Aristotle's doctrine of natural and legal right in the Commentary on the Ethics (5, 12), and two incidental discussions in the Commentary on the Sentences (3, 37, 1–4, 33, 1 and 2).

2 1-2, 90, 4.

3 1-2, 94, 1.

4 'La Valeur des Formules de saint Thomas d'Aquin concernant la loi naturelle: Mélanges Joseph Maréchal', Paris, 1950, Tome II, p. 367.

5 Art. cit., pp. 368, 369 and pp. 375, 376.

6 Art. cit., p. 369.

7 1-2, 90, 4 obj. 1 and ad 1.

8 1-2, 91, 2 ad 3.

9 1-2, 91, 2.

10 1-2, 91, 2 ad 1.

11 Dom Lottin's contention that the truly personal thought of St Thomas is be found in the Commentary on the Sentences, Book 4, Dist. 33, is not easy to accept. We are asked to prefer an incidental discussion in an early work to a formal and lengthy exposition in the second part of the *Summa Theologiae*. There is in fact nothing in the Sentences that is contradicted by the exposition in the *Summa*, but the earlier doctrine is developed and clarified particularly by the use of the notion of *participation* which defines the relation between Natural and Eternal Law. This notion is elaborated by means of a verse from Psalm 4: *signatum est super nos lumen vultus tui, Domine*; we find the same text used to relate Natural Law to its source in *De Veritate*, 17, 3. In other words, the basic notion of Natural Law as a participation of the Eternal Law is implicit in some of St Thomas's earliest writing on the subject.

12 1-2, 93, 1

13 1-2, 91, 2.

14 1-2, 93, 1.

15 S.c.G., 3, 114.

16 *De Veritate*, 5, 1 ad 9. Cf. ibid. ad 6 … 'Providentia in Deo proprie non nominat legem aeternam, sed aliquid ad legem aeternam consequens.' Providence applies the Eternal Law to particular things just as Prudence in man applies the general principles of conduct to particular situations.

17 1-2, 93, 1. For a fuller treatment of Eternal Law see *The Natural Moral Law*, by Walter Farrell OP, Ditchling: St Dominic's Press, 1930. Fr Farrell points to the phrase 'servatis aliis quae supra esse diximus de legis ratione' as showing that, in speaking about Eternal Law, St Thomas was fully conscious of his definition of law in general.

18 1-2, 91, 2

19 Ibid. c. and ad 3.

20   Ibid. ad 3. This is what is now called Natural Law in the sense of Physical Law.

21   1-2, 94 *passim*. 'The conclusion is forced on us, then, that the natural law – can only be conceived as consisting essentially in the proposition of reason.' J. Cunnane, *The Catholic Notion of the Natural Law*, Maynooth, 1941, p. 30. 'The precept of practical reason, i.e. the proposition of reason resulting from this precept, would seem to be the Natural Moral Law in its very essence if we judge it by the principles laid down by St Thomas as applying to all law.' Farrell, op. cit., p. 98. The two monographs just cited are outstanding in that they are based on a careful and perceptive analysis of the relevant texts.

22   '... per modum actionis et passionis, inquantum participator per modum interioris principii motivi.' 1-2, 93, 6. It is clear from this that receptive participation may be either active or passive; what is received as law is not action but the direction of action.

23   1-2, 93, 5 and 2.

24   1-2, 91, 2.

25   The authors who understand rational participation as we think it must be understood are the exception. Dr Cunnane and Dr Farrell have been already cited (note 21 supra). It may be noted that Dr Farrell retreats somewhat from the position to which he has been led by an examination of 'the principles laid down by St Thomas,' and would make natural inclination part of the essence of Natural Law (op. cit., pp. 99–101); Dr Cunnane rightly rejects this amalgamation (op. cit., p. 50). Dom Lottin states unamiguously that Natural Law consists in the precepts of natural reason (art. cit., p. 361, *Principes de Morale*, Louvain, 1946, I, p. 125). As representative of those authors who see Thomist Natural Law in terms of natural inclination or, more generally, in receptive terms the following may be cited: Merkelbach: Lex naturalis non est lex quatenus est in legislatore ut regulante, ac proinde non est ipsa lex aeterna, sed est lex ut est in subditis ut regulatis, ac proinde est participatio, manifestatio, promulgatio passiva legis aeternae in nobis.' (*Summa Theologiae Moralis*, ed. alt., Paris, 1935, I, p. 226). Gilson: 'En nous, comme en toute chose, l'inclination qui nous entrain vers certaines fins est la marque non méconnaissable de ce que la loi éternelle nous impose. Puisque c'est elle que nous fait etre ce que nous sommes, il soffit que nous cedions aux penchants légitimes de notre nature pour lui obéir. La loi éternelle ainsi participee par chacun de nous, et que nous découvrons inscrite dans notre propre nature, recoit le nom de loi naturelle.' (*Le Thomisine*, Paris, 1942, p. 366) Davitt: 'Granted the act of creation, all things must somehow participate in this primordial ordering. They will participate in it passively inasmuch as their forms; irrational or rational, bespeak this divine ordering and constitute what is called the natural law, both physical and moral. Such a law is law, therefore, only by an analogy of attribution' (*The Nature of Law*, St Louis, 1951, p. 134).

26   Cf. Prümmer, *Manuale Theologiae Moralis*, Friburgi Brisgoviae, 1931 (ed. 7ima), I, p. 105, Noldin-Schmitt, *Summa Theologiae Moralis*, Barcelona, 1951 (ed. xxviii), I, pp. 119–20.

27   Cf. Cronin, *The Science of Ethics*, Dublin, 1909, I, p. 609. Cox, *Liberty – Its Use and Abuse*, New York, 1939 (2nd ed.), p. 64. Moral, *Philosophia Moralis*, Santander, 1952, (ed. 3tia), p. 213.

28   Cf. the penetrating analysis of the Thomist concept of law as *praeceptum* or *imperium* by Fr Collins OP, in *Aquinas and Law*, *Irish Theological Quarterly*, XVIII, 3, pp. 220 sq.

29   1-2, 17, 1 ad 1.

30   *Natural Law*, London, 1951, p. 40.

31   'Lex naturalis est lumen intellectus naturaliter insitum nobis, quo cognoscimus nos a Deo ad bonum faciendum et malum vitandum. adstringi.' Cathrein, *Philosophia Moralis*, (ed. 4ta), Fribourg, 1902, p. 134. 'We may define the Natural Moral Law as a rule of action, mandatory in form, which reason itself discovers as having been established by the Author of man's nature and promulgated by being imbedded in the nature of man.' Cox, op. cit., p. 64.

32   *Man and the State*, London, 1954, p. 83.

33   *De Veritate*, 11, 1. Cf. Q.D. de Anima, 5c ad finem: '... ipsa principia indemonstrabilia cognoscimus abstrahendo a singularibus.' In the text quoted St Thomas does not mention explicitly the concept of the good from which the precepts of Natural Law derive (1-2, 94, 2), but this depends on the concept of being which is prior to it (*De Veritate*, 1, 1) ; consequently the concept of good and the principles which it generates are acquired by way of abstraction from sense data.

34	*De Veritate*, 16, 1, cf. *De Div. Nom.* 711, 713 (ed. Pera).
35	It is only necessary to compare the texts which we have quoted with Book 2, chapters 9–12 of the *De Libero Arbitrio* to see that St Thomas's doctrine is sharply opposed to that of St Augustine.
36	I Cf. *De Veritate*, 10, 6 ad 7.
37	1, 84, 5c. Cf. Joseph Legrand SJ, *L'Univers et L'Honnize darts la Philosophie de Saint Thomas*, Paris, 1946, II, pp. 39 sq. Fr Legrand's illuminating exposition of the Thomist teaching on intellectual cognition is read more profitably if one takes account of a tendency to attenuate the role of secondary causes.
38	Cf. *De Veritate*, 11, 3.
39	1, 84, 4 ad 1. Cf. Legrand, op. cit., II, p. 49.
40	Cf. 97, note 2.
41	*De Veritate*, 16, 1.
42	3 Sent., 33, 1, 1; *Ethicor.* 1018 (ed. Spiazzi). Cf. 1-2, 93, 6; ibid. 100, 3. St Thomas distinguishes between the *habit* of first principles and the *habitual possession* of first principles. The habit does not operate except through contact with sense experience under the light of the active intellect; but once this operation takes place the mind possesses the principles of Natural Law, either actually when these principles are being used, or habitually as when a person is asleep. Thus it can be said that while Natural Law is *not* the habit of synderesis, nevertheless it can exist in us habitually as well as actually (cf. 1-2, 94, 1).
43	'Illud quod primo intellectus concipit quasi notissimum, et in quo omnes conceptiones resolvit, est ens.' *De Veritate*, 1, 1. Cf. 1-2, 94, 2.
44	'Objectum intellectus practici non est bonun, sed verum relatum ad opus,' *De Veritate*, 22, 10 ad 4 cf. 1-2, 94, 2: 'Bonum est primum quad cadit in apprehensione practicae rationis, quae ordinatur ad opus.' The practical intellect knows the good *sub ratione veri*. Cf. 1, 79, 11 ad 2; *De Veritate*, 3, 3 ad 9.
45	The intellect reflects on the will *rationally, conceptually*. Its operation does not in the slightest way partake of the irrationality and 'obscurity' of the will; its action is in no way conditioned by the action which is proper to the will. 'Cum aliqua potentia super aliam fertur, comparator ad eam secundum suam proprietatem; sicut intellectus cum intelligit voluntatem velle, accipit in seipso rationem volendi.' *De Veritate*, 22, 12. M. Maritain's conception of non-rational *knowledge through inclination* has no place in St Thomas's system.
46	1-2, 94, 2
47	*De Veritate* 16, 1
48	The foregoing is a commentary on the text beginning: *Hoc est ergo primum praeceptum legis*, 1-2, 94, 2. R.P. Sertillanges shows himself uncharacteristically impercipient in his interpretation of the first precept as equivalent to: *Ce qui est a faire est a faire* (*La Philosophie Morale de Saint Thomas D'Aquin*), Paris, 1946 p. 102.
49	'Ipsa principia comparantur ad intellectum agentem ut instrumenta quaedam ejus, quia per ea facit alia intelligibilia actu.' *Q. D. de Anima*, 5c ad finem. 'Id ergo quo cognoscimus sicut instrumento, oportet esse nobis primo notum; et sic cognoscimus conclusiones per principia naturaliter nota, ad quae comparatur intellectus agens sicut ad instrumenta.' *Quodl.* 10, 7.
50	1, 84, 5. Cf. *Quodl.* 8, 4.
51	Cf. 1, 16, 6 ad 1; 1, 93, 4c; 1-2, 19, 4 ad 3; *De Veritate*, 5, 5c; *Quodl.* 10, 7 1
52	'Anima judicat de rebus ... secundum veritatem primam, inquantum resultat in ea sicut in speculo, secundum prima intelligibilia.' 1, 16, 6 ad 1.
53	For a careful statement of this doctrine of exemplary illumination cf. 1-2, 19, 4. That in which the mind participates is, in the first place, the intellectual light, at once active and passive (*intellectus agens* and *synderesis*: cf. Quodl. 10, 7 and *De Veritate*, 16, 1 ad 5) and, in the second place, the primary principles, which become, as instruments of the active intellect, a source of illumination: the light in the first sense is *innate*; the light in the second sense is *natural*, but only partly innate.
54	1-2, 91, 2 ad 1.
55	'Promulgatio legis naturae est ex hoc ipso quod Deus eam mentibus hominum inseruit naturaliter cognoscendam.' 1-2, 90, 4 ad 1. *Inseruit* must be understood in the light of the

general doctrine on the way in which Natural Law comes to be enunciated; *cognoscendam*, does not seem to refer to the enunciation of the precepts of Natural Law but to our recognition of these precepts. In any case we must not confuse the act of *enunciating* Natural Law with the act of *recognising* the law as enunciated. The same person may be legislator and subject *quantum ad vim directivam legis*. Cf. 1-2, 96, 5 ad 3. There is no basis for the statement that 'la loi naturelle ... n'est pas promulguée par l'homme, mais a l'homme.' (Jacques Leclercq, *La Philosophie Morale de saint Thomas devant la Pensée Contemporaine*, Louvain, 1955, p. 387). Canon Leclercq's other tilts at St Thomas' doctrine of Natural Law are even more obviously misdirected.

56   'Appetites humanus, qui est voluntas, est boni universalis.' 1-2, 2, 7.

57   Cf. 1-2, 19, 10: 'oportet quod bonum commune divinum sit volitum formaliter.'

58   Law is related to community in that it is directed towards the common good but not in that it orders every member of the community to the common good. The *subject* of Natural Law is the individual who enunciates the law; the law which he enunciates does not directly and as such govern others. In this Natural Law differs from Eternal Law, since the latter governs every creature. But this difference is not concerned with what is essential to law. Cf. 1-2, 90, 3 ad 1 and 96, 1 ad I.

59   Cf. 1-2, 97, 4 ad 3 where Divine Law is differentiated from Natural Law on the grounds that man is related to the former *sicut persona privata ad legem publicam*.

60   Newman, *A Grammar of Assent*, London, 1895, p. 107.

61   1-2, 104, 1.

62   Cf. *De Malo*, 2, 4.

63   1-2, 99, 1. Cf. 1-2, 102, 1 and 2.

64   Cf. 1-2, 94, 2

65   See p. 100, note 2.

66   Cf. *De Veritate*, 24, 10

67   *The New Scholasticism* of January, 1955 carries a short summary of a paper entitled 'The Relations of Law and Obligation' by Dom Gregory Stevens, to be read at the 29th Annual Meeting of the American Catholic Philosophical Association (p. 96). Dom Stevens' conclusion is that 'the first moral principle which is the first precept of the natural law is a necessary judgement of the practical order, imposing a morally necessary direction on the will, and this is rooted in finality.' We should prefer to distinguish between the first principle and the first precept and see obligation as belonging to the latter, but would agree that obligation is rooted in finality.

68   Cf. 1-2, 94, 4.

69   Morris Ginsberg, *On the Diversity of Morals* (Huxley Memorial Lecture, 1953), London: Royal Anthropological Institute, p. 13.

13 Human Nature – Immutable or Mutable?

M.B. Crowe

(*Irish Theological Quarterly*, 1963, No. 3, pp. 204–31.)

The natural law is central in scholastic moral theory. The explicit references to it in the magisterium of the Church have been multiplied in modern times; and when moral theologians characterise certain types of conduct, artificial birth prevention for example, as 'against nature' or 'unnatural' they intend to condemn such conduct in the clearest terms. The assumption is that there is a determinate 'human nature' against which human behaviour may be measured and possibly found wanting. It is precisely this conception of human nature as an invariable, universal standard that so many of our contemporaries find impossible to accept. In a celebrated passage Jean-Paul Sartre argues that classical metaphysics has been vitiated by *une vision technique du monde*, by the assumption that there is a God, artificer of the universe, whose ideas define the parts of the universe as the idea in the mind of the manufacturer of paper-knives defines the object he makes; there is, in fact, no God and, so, no divine idea to define 'human nature'; man first exists and, then, is defined as what he makes himself.[1] Insofar as man has an essence he is freedom as opposed to 'nature'; this same paradox, that the nature of man is not to have a nature, can be found also in Maurice Merleau-Ponty and in Gabriel Marcel.[2] Nor has human nature fared much better with the logical positivists. A.J. Ayer began his *Language, Truth and Logic* with a chapter on 'The Elimination of Metaphysics' and followed it with a later one entitled 'Critique of Ethics and Theology'; between them they were thought to have disposed of human nature as a metaphysical conception and to have shown that statements about human nature, being neither tautologies nor empirically verifiable, were strictly meaningless.[3] The only function left to ethical terms and propositions is that of expressing emotion; and the emotive theory of ethics can claim a respectable background in empiricism going back to Hume. Even if the more extreme views of *Language, Truth and Logic* have been abandoned, even by Ayer himself, the prejudice against metaphysics has not.[4] And even if human nature be allowed, any effort to base moral statements upon it comes under the ban of the 'naturalistic fallacy', purporting, as it does, to derive moral imperatives from factual propositions, or 'ought' from 'is'. Add to this the rejection of any unchanging human nature by the Marxist dialectic, the difficulties raised by developments in the study of evolution, in psychology and in cultural anthropology, and the indictment of 'human nature' becomes formidable indeed. How far, one is led to ask, is the scholastic natural law based upon a totally unjustifiable 'platonic' essence of man?

I

It is by now a commonplace to note that the word 'nature' is one of the most ambiguous of philosophical terms. Lalande's standard *Vocabulaire technique et critique de la philosophie* lists some eleven meanings for 'nature' and thirteen for 'naturel'.[5] Raimundo Paniker, in 1931, recorded no less than twenty meanings for 'nature', meanings discussed and tabulated more recently by Philippe Delhaye.[6] In the context of natural law alone Erich Wolf listed nine meanings for 'nature'.[7] But almost any book on the natural law can provide a similar exposure of the ambiguities in the term. More often than not it is taken for granted that this effectively disposes of any idea of an unchanging natural law. Norberto Bobbio, for one, has pointed out that 'nature' is such an equivocal term that diametrically opposed laws have been thought natural and that a new *Praise of Folly* might be written by simply listing the institutions – slavery or liberty, private property or communism, polygamy or monogamy and so on – said to be 'in conformity with nature'.[8] It would, however, be a great mistake to think that the scholastics were unaware of the possible equivocations of the word 'nature'. St Thomas's handling of the word in the context of morals will be considered later in this paper; for the present it will suffice to notice an interesting reference to the matter in John Duns Scotus:

> ... naturale est aequivocum et non uno modo dictum. Hoc apparet ex pluralitate illorum, quibus opponitur. Nam *naturale* uno modo opponitur *libero* ... secundo modo *naturale* opponitur *supernaturali* ... tertio modo *naturale* opponitur *violento*.[9]

Still, while conceding that the word 'nature' holds more than a few pitfalls, it would seem essential to maintain that there is a 'human nature' which is the standard of natural morality; otherwise the entire system of natural law ethics, fundamental to scholasticism, crumbles. And therein lies the difficulty.

If there is a common nature, independent of the conditions of space and time, upon which natural morals are founded, then morals ought to be the same for all times and places. But in the experience of moralists no fact is more evident than the extreme diversity of moral ideas, codes and practice accepted in various parts of the world and during different periods in history. This fact, like the ambiguity of 'nature' just referred to, has often been taken to be a proof of the relativity of morals. Some of the examples of moral diversity frequently quoted in this connection may be found in John Locke's *Essay concerning Human*

Understanding as part of his argument against innate moral ideas.[10] Modern writers tend to be cautious in assessing the different kinds of moral variation and even point out that some, if not all, moral variations are perfectly compatible with the acceptance of absolute standards. The conclusion of Morris Ginsberg's 1953 Huxley Memorial Lecture 'On the Diversity of Morals' is that 'there is no necessary connection between the diversity of morals and the relativity of ethics'.[11] The diversity still requires explanation. There seem to be broadly three kinds of explanation:

> When St Thomas 'finds himself in the presence of different moralities, of contradictory laws, of diversely organised institutions', he neither regards every variation as an anomaly nor attributes all divergences to the same cause. The explanations scattered through his works may be grouped under three heads: 1. the influence of the passions; 2. the unequal development of reason, of insight and of civilization; 3. the diversity of conditions, of situations, and of circumstances.[12]

The possibility of moral variations arising out of 'passion' does not require much elaboration. Human nature, whatever it is, is not exclusively rational; there is an affective and emotional side, not to speak of the bodily aspect that must be taken into consideration when human behaviour is studied. For this reason Aristotle[13] rejected the Socratic identification of virtue and knowledge and discussed at length the paradox of the incontinent man, the man who knows what is right and yet does the opposite.[14] St Paul put it more concretely, and in a theological setting: 'the good which I will, I do not; but the evil which I will not, that I do ... but I see another law in my members, fighting against the law of my mind, and captivating me in the law of sin' (Rom 7:19-23). St Thomas accepted the position; for him it was a patent fact that men acted sometimes out of passion and in spite of knowledge: *experimento patet quad multi agunt contra ea, quorum scientiam habent.*[15] He repeats the point more than once when speaking of the natural law:

> aliqui habent depravatam rationem ex passione, seu ex mala consuetudine, seu ex mala habitudine naturae; sicut apud Germanos olim latrocinium non reputabatur iniquum, cum tamen sit expresse contra legem naturae, ut refert Iulius Caesar in libro de Bello Gallico.[16]

And even more striking is his insistence upon the necessity of moral precepts in the Old Law, brushing aside the objection that human reason ought to be able to discover these for itself:

> ratio ... propter consuetudinem peccandi obscurabatur in particularibus agendis; circa alia vero praecepta moralia quae sunt quasi conclusiones

deductae ex communibus principiis legis naturae multorum ratio oberrabat; ita ut quaedam, quae sunt secundum se mala, ratio multorum licita iudicaret.[17]

Here the reference seems to be to something more than the ordinary influence of passion upon conduct; it is not the one gust of passion that extinguishes reason but the habitual bias that corrupts the objectivity of reason. And St Thomas allows it full scope.

The second factor explaining moral variations is the caducity of human reason. The individual reason is fallible; we all make mistakes, in our practical decisions as well as in our theoretical conclusions. St Thomas seems to have accepted Aristotle's doctrine of the practical syllogism, moral decision being the conclusion drawn from moral premises. He therefore mentions, side by side with the evil customs that corrupt good manners, the erroneous convictions that produce wrong conclusions: *potest lex naturalis deleri de cordibus hominum vel propter malas persuasiones (eo modo quo etiam in speculativis errores contingunt circa conclusiones necessarias)*.[18] The deficiency of human reason, however, extends to more than simple error in the deductive process. There is the larger question of unequal development, not merely the difference between one individual and another, but, particularly, the differences between entire peoples at different stages of civilization. Jacques Maritain finds here the 'law of the progress of moral conscience', which he considers to be a most important law in the philosophy of history. He speaks, of course, of progress in the knowledge of the moral law, which does not mean that men necessarily behave better. He gives as examples of this progress the present-day awareness that slavery is contrary to the dignity of the human person, that prisoners of war have rights, that child labour is intolerable, that labour itself has its dignity, that authority does not need to be ruthless:

The sense of duty and obligation was always present, but the explicit knowledge of the various norms of natural law grows with time. And certain of these norms, like the law of monogamy, were known rather late in the history of mankind, so far as it is accessible to our investigation. Also, we may think that the knowledge of the precepts of the natural law in all of their precise aspects and requirements will continue to grow until the end of human history.[19]

This conception of progress and development in moral ideas is one that must be carefully distinguished from the view that moral ideas are simply products of evolution. This will be seen in its place. Meantime, the idea of growth points the way to the third of the factors that, in St Thomas's view, make for variation in morals – diversity of conditions, situations and circumstances.

An Irish Reader in Moral Theology

This factor proves to be the most radical of all in explaining why men have so differed, and still differ, in their moral convictions as well as in their moral behaviour. For it goes deeper than the blinding of reason by passion or prejudice, deeper than the inadequacy of human reason faced with the complexity of some moral situations, right down to the nature of moral reasoning and to the essentials of the moral order. Moral decision, in fact, differs essentially from the conclusion drawn from speculative premisses – this is where the practical syllogism breaks down – and the principles of morality do not share the kind of universality and permanence characteristic of speculative assertions. St Thomas accepted Aristotle's wise observation, at the beginning of the *Nicomachean Ethics*, that we should seek in each discussion only such precision as the subject-matter admits – 'it is evidently equally foolish to accept probable reasoning from a mathematician and to demand from a rhetorician scientific proofs'. With regard to 'fine and just actions':

> We must be content ... in speaking of such subjects and with such premisses to indicate the truth roughly and in outline, and in speaking about things which are only for the most part true and with premisses of the same kind to reach conclusions that are no better.[20]

St Thomas, in the *Summa Theologiae*, puts this view to work with interesting results. He is discussing the question whether the natural law is the same for all men and he has, of course, to find an explanation for the evident discrepancies between men's views of that law. His argument turns upon the difference between speculative reasoning, which proceeds from firm principles to necessary conclusions, and practical reasoning which, while it may be sure of its principles – *si in communibus sit aliqua necessitas* – has to do with contingent human action. In speculative matters truth is the same for all, although perhaps not equally available to all since it may require effort or ability to see it; it is true, for all who are capable of understanding, that the angles of a triangle are together equal to two right angles. But in practical affairs one cannot always say that there is truth, if only one could discover it; the very truth may be different for one man and for another. St Thomas's phrase is strong:

> In operativis autem non est eadem veritas, vel rectitudo practica apud omnes quantum ad propria sed solum quantum ad communia; et apud illos, apud quos est eadem rectitudo in propriis, non est aequaliter omnibus nota.[21]

It is right and true for all, without exception, that one should act in accordance with reason. From this it follows that goods held in trust should be returned when the owner claims them; and so it happens in the majority of cases. But the exceptional case may arise in which it would be harmful and, consequently, irrational to return the goods – if the goods were required by their owner *ad impugnandam patriam*.[22] In a word, the complexity of circumstances surrounding every human act is ineluctable and no law, not even the natural law, can cater for every contingency. The matter is plain in human law; no legislator can foresee all the possibilities his law may meet.[23] If he tries to do so his law becomes a thicket of qualifying clauses and – worse still – the more conditions it includes the greater is the chance of one or other being unfulfilled and so rendering the law itself nugatory.

St Thomas, then, had a more flexible conception of the natural law than he is sometimes credited with. Passion and human fallibility as sources of moral diversity are compatible with a rigid view of human nature and of its law; but if differences in circumstances and situations can provoke differences in moral solutions it becomes less easy to be firm about nature and law. St Thomas is, indeed, driven to say more than once in this connection: *Natura humana mutabilis est*.[24] The phrase will repay closer scrutiny.

II

The assertion that human nature is mutable is one that might be expected to find an echo in quarters influenced by evolution and by situation-ethics (and both evolutionary theory and the approaches of situation-ethics have stimulated valuable developments in moral theory). Three recent scholastic writers, who exploit St Thomas's phrase about human nature being mutable, provide a convenient introduction to the topic.

The most recent of these authors is Ludger Oeing-Hanhoff. In an article entitled 'Thomas von Aquin and die Situation des Thomismus heute'[25] his main concern is with the necessity of bringing Thomistic metaphysics into line with present-day developments, notably by abandoning elements that belong to the outdated Aristotelian physics. Towards the end of the article he refers to moral questions, to the problem of the historical changes in the natural law and in the moral obligations of peoples. The discussion of this problem, he suggests, may be linked with a phrase of St Thomas: *Natura humana non est immobilis sicut divina. Et ideo diversificantur quae sunt de iure naturali secundum diversos status et conditiones hominum*.[26] This is, doubtless – Oeing-Hanhoff goes on – *un mot à l'aventure* in Thomistic philosophy; but it is very striking. It allows us to glimpse, side by side with the timeless and invariable metaphysical principle in man, something of the cultural and social environment in which man must develop, something of the changing status and conditions of human existence, the 'historicity', that justifies our speaking of a changeable human nature.[27]

Another author to make this point is Josef Fuchs who devotes part of a chapter in his book *Lex Naturae – zur Theologie des Naturrechts* to the 'Philosophical Concept of Nature'.[28] The difficulty for a theologian in making any statements about 'human nature' is that, while our experience is of a human nature elevated to a supernatural order, fallen and redeemed, the concept of 'mere nature' or 'pure nature' must seem impoverished indeed, an abstraction, the invention of philosophers and incapable of verification. Still, the fact that 'pure nature' is not directly accessible to us does not mean that there can be no definition of the *physis* of man or no conception of the moral order corresponding to this metaphysical definition. It is important to know which of the properties of human nature are rooted in the metaphysical definition and which are related to the supernatural condition in which man actually finds himself i.e. are put in human nature by God expressly as a substratum for the supernatural. Fuchs contends that, at least in some cases, we can establish propositions concerning the essence, meaning and obligations of human personality on the basis of *natura pura*. In other words, we can make assertions about human nature despite the fact that the nature we experience is not mere human nature. Our judgements about, say, property, sex, marriage, natural religion, relations with God can be soundly based upon the nature of man. Admittedly the exact 'contour' of these judgements may be unknown to us in the sense that we may not know with certainty, or may not yet know, whether the elements in human nature giving rise to them belong to the permanent state of nature willed by God or to that *de facto* subject to historical change.[29] Further, philosophy, uninstructed by revelation risks erroneous interpretation of such propositions. But the possibility of arriving at valid conclusions about man's nature, conclusions that will not later be revised by the recognition of his exclusively supernatural destiny or by the possibility of supernatural experience, must be insisted upon. Fuchs is critical of those theologians – he mentions Hans Urs von Balthasar and Henri de Lubac – who unduly decry the natural in man in favour of the supernatural.[30] The point of present interest in this whole discussion is the suggestion that the nature of man, even the metaphysical nature, must be taken in its historical setting.

In another work Fuchs further expands his views on these matters.[31] Once again he defends the conception of metaphysical nature and of the natural law against those who would minimize both, whether Protestants who deny their value or Catholics *ducti tendentia unilateraliter supernaturali* who do not sufficiently see their value. There is a human nature, accessible to reason, and a natural law corresponding to it. But this human nature may be considered either as the abstract metaphysical definition of man, *animal rationale,* or as the historical realisation of that definition by God's creative act. The supernatural setting of human existence is something that, logically, comes later.[32] The precepts of the natural law are reason's conceptualizations and formulations of the moral order founded upon the *Esse* of man as man.

Some pages later Fuchs returns to the point and discusses the 'historicity' of the natural law.[33] He remarks that, as the natural law is rooted in the personal essence of man, one might take it to be something quite static and 'non-historical'. This, indeed, is the assumption of many opponents of the doctrine of natural law.

It is not, however, an assumption that can be justified; for human nature, historically, is in some sense changeable and, in consequence, so is the natural law. And this is said explicitly by St Thomas.[34] In support of the attribution of this view to St Thomas, Fuchs cites three passages. The first of these is the one given also by Oeing-Hanhoff – *natura humana non est immobilis sicut divina; et ideo diversificantur ea, quae sunt de iure naturali, secundum diversos status et conditiones hominum.*[35] The second, given as a cross-reference by Oeing-Hanhoff, is more explicit – *illud quod est naturale habenti naturam immutabilem, oportet quod sit semper et ubique tale. Natura autem hominis est mutabilis.*[36] The third is a passage in the *De malo* in which St Thomas is discussing the need for human positive law. He says that there are two ways in which things may be said to be right and good:

> uno modo formaliter; et sic semper et ubique sunt eadem, quia principia iuris, quae sunt in naturali ratione, non mutantur. Alio modo materialiter; et sic non sunt eadem iusta et bona ubique et apud omnes, sed oportet ea lege determinari. Et hoc contingit propter mutabilitatem naturae humanae, et diversas conditiones hominum et rerum, secundum diversitatem locorum et temporum.[37]

This last passage, because of the context in which it occurs, is the least useful to prove the point; it can be paralleled by a number of passages on the *Summa* where St Thomas discusses the mutability of human law. He says, for example, that *lex recte mutari potest propter mutationem conditionum hominum, quibus secundum diversas eorum conditiones diversa expediunt* (and he quotes St Augustine in support). But St Thomas does not say here that human nature is mutable – the nearest he comes to it is when he says, in the reply to an objection, that the eternal law is unchanging, for it shares in the divine reason's immobility and perfection; *sed ratio humana mutabilis est, et imperfecta; et ideo eius lex mutabilis est.* In fact, all through the discussion the contrast is made between the invariability of the natural law and the variability of human law.[38]

Still, St Thomas's statements that human nature may vary must be given their due weight; and this Fuchs proceeds to do. First of all, the natural law is more 'historical' than positive law, that is, it is more adapted to historical conditions. This is another way of saying that the moral order, against which every human action in no matter what historical conjunction must be judged, is founded upon the *Esse hominis*, which *Esse* is either that of man as such or that of this man together with the circumstances, internal or external, in which he finds himself.[39] When the natural law is formulated in moral propositions its historicity becomes even more apparent – for it is seen that some elements in human nature are always present, others not. One can distinguish between the absolute and the relative or contingent elements and consequently between those prescriptions of the natural

An Irish Reader in Moral Theology

law that are absolute and apply at all times, and those others that apply only in those periods in which the elements in human nature to which they correspond are verified.

The position is illustrated by examples. Society – the state, say, or the family – requires authority (*jus absolutum*). In the condition of fallen nature the right of coercion is needed (*jus elativum*); it would not be needed if the original, supernatural harmony had lasted. Again, the family living wage is owed in the social and economic conditions that obtain today (*jus relativum*) but not, however, under other possible conditions. What is required in all conditions (*jus absolutum*) is that a just wage be paid; what is a just wage depends upon circumstances. Fuchs concludes this argument with two observations: (a) man's nature absolutely requires this possibility of laws relative to the circumstances i.e. it is equally necessary that authority be not coercive in the state of original harmony and that it should exercise force in the state of fallen nature; (b) the relativity here described may be attributed to the inadequacy in the formulation of these laws; properly and fully expressed, the law is absolute, e.g. that society requires the right of coercion *when necessary for harmony*. Finally he remarks that original sin must be counted the greatest factor introducing the kind of change in the status of man to which natural law must be related. Some of the Fathers called the natural law relative to the condition of original justice primary natural law, and that relative to man's fallen state secondary natural law – but others use a different terminology, or use the same terms in a different sense. The fact to appreciate is that many of the prescriptions of the natural law are relative to our fallen nature; they presuppose a sin that has entered the world and are, in fact, the sign of it. Examples are the right of coercion already mentioned, slavery (in certain conditions), private property,[40] the liceity of material cooperation in evil in given circumstances, broad mental restriction as permissible sometimes.[41]

It is now possible for Fuchs to face the problem of the mutability or immutability of the natural law in the light of his extremely *nuancé* doctrine of human nature. It is clear, he says, that the natural law is neither intrinsically changeable, nor, properly speaking, extrinsically dispensable. This is true absolutely for the absolute precepts; and for the relative precepts it is true as long as the conditions of nature, to which they relate, persist. It is not unfair to say, then, that the natural law is in a sense mutable and in another sense immutable; mutable in the sense that its incidence is conditioned by the circumstances of human nature, immutable in that the intrinsic *ratio moralis* does not change. The formulations of the law frequently neglect the conditions that ought to be expressed, if the law is to be absolute. Hence the apparent difficulties or dispensations in the wide sense. 'Thou shalt not kill', for example, is not adequately formulated as a precept of the natural law, for it says nothing about killing directly or by private authority and, so, does not meet the cases of lawful self-defence, capital punishment, just war or divine authorisation as in the case of Abraham with Isaac.[42]

Human Nature – Immutable or Mutable?   235

A third contemporary scholastic, writing on the mutability of human nature mainly from the point of view of cultural anthropology, provides a most interesting commentary on the kind of discussion just summarised – C. Fay who, in an article entitled 'Human Evolution: a Challenge to Thomistic Ethics', chides the reluctance of Thomistic ethicians to come to terms with evolution and anthropology.[43] The article makes certain assumptions: (a) that evolution provides a partial explanation not alone of the development of the human body, but of much of human culture; (b) that human evolution is 'bio-cultural', i.e. both organic and super-organic; and (c) that it is meaningful to speak of progress in human as well as in organic evolution. Fay's finding is that, in general, the evolutionary approach confirms and complements the traditional conception of basic, unchanging principles in nature expressed, however, with different modalities.

He begins by describing the mutual relations of bodily and cultural factors in human evolution and justly remarks that this interplay of the organic and the 'more than organic' is precisely what a Thomist, given his theory of the soul, ought to expect. The fact that man has evolved in this fashion shows that he has a nature, and, so, an end, different from that of brutes. In the course of evolution life is lived at ever higher levels; but no essentially new mode of activity has arisen since Zinjanthropos. The changes introduced as man evolved are 'accidental' to his nature as a rational animal – a more upright posture, a less simian face, a central nervous system better organised for symbolic life. In contemporary humans there is abundant evidence for a common nature, despite racial and cultural diversities; language, technology, family, art, religion, are the universal traits of cultural life. These traits vary greatly – and some of the variations are more significant than others – but there is a limit to variation. Up to the present the changes introduced by culture in the direction and pace of human evolution worked, for the most part, unconsciously – the genetic mechanisms involved were not understood. Work at present being done on genetics may yield the knowledge necessary to regulate the further course of evolution – which is a possibility that may present new problems in moral philosophy. This is an aspect to which Fay returns later in his paper.[44] Before coming to it, he examines the effects of 'bio-cultural evolution', which modifies human nature as it concretely exists, so that 'its signification for ethics involves some sort of evolution in the sphere of morals'.[45]

The natural law is based upon man's nature; moral goodness is conformity to human nature as *it actually exists*, i.e. as affected by the conditions of time and place. In the course of bio-cultural evolution such conditions have modified – even radically modified – human nature. Primary urges, like those towards food and sexual activity, are differently experienced, even by contemporary men, as a result of differences in cultural conditioning. If the family, for example, represents a universal human situation, its determinate character is due to the particular circumstances obtaining when and where it is founded.[46] In general, human morality has its universal and invariable aspect and its aspect relative to this or that particular culture. The conflict is more apparent than real for it is simply a consequence of viewing human nature either abstractly and universally (and, so, univocally common to the entire human species) or concretely and realistically existing in individual men (and, so, subject to bio-cultural evolution as well as to the individuation by matter). In the first case the natural law will be invariable; in the second variable as is the nature on which it depends.

At this point Fay cites St Thomas's phrase: *Natura autem hominis mutabilis est*[47] and suggests that here at least St Thomas is taking the second of the above views of human nature; further, this view would be more prominent if St Thomas were writing today. For some of the changes introduced by bio-cultural evolution so alter the meaning of human knowledge and power (for example, agricultural and industrial revolutions), so transform relations between men and men (the urban revolution) and between man and nature (atomic energy, polymer chemistry) that certain acts which were formerly good become bad and vice versa. I do not deny that the species of morally significant acts are determined in the light of universal human needs which are stable: lying, stealing and murder are bad of their very nature, precisely because they frustrate universal human appetites. But I do deny that the species of moral acts is determined exclusively in the light of such needs; the species of good and bad acts are also determined by a constellation of biological and cultural conditions and emergent needs which are both variable and relative.[48]

The changes introduced by bio-cultural evolution may be accidental in the ontological sense; but morally they may be extremely important – as the ontological accident of relationship makes the same act with one person adultery and with another fornication. One example of a change introduced in evolution is provided by social organisation, at one time based exclusively upon kinship. In a modern society it would be wrong to favour relatives in the distribution of offices, whereas formerly it was not alone right but necessary. The difference is in the different ways in which men existed then and now, the changed historical situation. There are, nevertheless, some things that can be judged irrespective of the cultural situation, so that an individual in one culture can correctly judge an action performed in an alien culture as morally evil, despite his unfamiliarity with the cultural surroundings of the act. This is because as well as the changing factors stressed by bio-cultural evolution there are also universal and unchanging factors:

> Every society forbids lying, murder and stealing because of needs experienced by all men. But some acts are regarded as unjust homicide or theft in one culture but not in another: nevertheless, a stranger to a certain culture can ordinarily recognise that an act of theft, say, is stealing and is unjust; and he disapproves in the light of appetites shared with the members of the alien culture.

Human Nature – Immutable or Mutable?

There are cross-cultural parallels in human appetition, and these parallels impose limits on variability and evolution in morals …[49]

These views of Fay on the mutability of human nature are worth considering at some length because they represent an interpretation of evolution sympathetic to the demands of a natural law ethics; most evolutionary approaches to ethics are totally destructive of any system like the Thomistic one. Fay's conclusion should be taken to heart, that human needs and acts are proportionally similar rather than univocally the same, that, while there are profound similarities in human life and its moral requirements, 'to come to grips with similarities in moral philosophy will require a more extensive use of the data and theories of the sciences of man than ethicians have been accustomed to'.[50]

III

It is clear that there are certain advantages in being able to say that human nature is 'mutable'; and, for a Thomist, decided advantages in being able to quote St Thomas in support. But it may well be pertinent to ask whether a very few texts of St Thomas are not being pushed too hard in this matter. Only three texts have been adduced by the authors mentioned in the previous section. These texts – and one may add another *natura nostra variabilis est* unnoticed by those authors – have in common that they figure in replies to objections.[51] Oeing-Hanhoff, as has been seen, concedes that St Thomas's statement that human nature is mutable is hardly more than an *obiter dictum*. It is a just observation when account is taken of the enormous number of references to 'nature' in St Thomas and the great number of such references in the special context of human nature and natural law.[52] The significance of passing references to mutability must be measured against the overwhelming weight of emphasis upon the immutability of human nature and the consequent invariability of the natural law. At the outset of his career, in the *De ente et essentia* [53] St Thomas defined 'nature' in terms of immutability as 'the essence of anything according to which it has an ordination to its proper activity, for nothing lacks its proper operation'. In his major discussions of the natural law – even when he has to take account of moral variations including those biblical difficulties like the polygamy of the Patriarchs, the spoliation of the Egyptians in the exodus or the marriage of Osee to 'a wife of fornications' which so exercised the medieval theological mind – St Thomas tries to save the immutability of human nature. Thus in his first full-dress discussion of the natural law he defines it in terms of the intrinsic teleology of human nature:

> Lex ergo naturalis nihil est aliud quam conceptio homini naturaliter indita, qua dirigitur ad convenienter agendum in actionibus propriis, sive competant ei ex natura generis, ut generare, comedere et hujusmodi, sive ex natura speciei, ut ratiocinari et similia.

His solution of the difficulty of the Patriarchal polygamy turns, then, upon a distinction between the primary and the secondary ends of nature in marriage; polyandry, as contradicting the primary ends, is intolerable; but polygamy (perhaps one should say, more properly, polygyny) is only against the natural law in an attenuated sense for it is reconcilable with the primary, although not with the secondary, ends of nature and might, consequently, in given circumstances, be tolerated by God. A similar solution is offered to the problem of natural law and the Old Testament bill of divorce; inseparability is imposed, not by the primary but by the secondary ends of nature in marriage; exceptional cases, in which the spouses are separated, are therefore conceivable.[54] The finer points of the distinction between the primary and the secondary ends of nature – a distinction that St Thomas seems to have been the first to present in this form which has commended itself to scholastic moralists ever since – are not the issue at the moment; suffice it to say that the solution it affords to the problem of certain vagaries in Old Testament morality does not amount to a statement that human nature is variable. That phrase is incidental, in the reply to an objection.[55] Nor, in the *Contra Gentiles*,[55a] when he treats of actions that are good or evil 'by nature', does St Thomas say – he seems rather positively to exclude the suggestion – that human nature is mutable. And in his last major work, the *Summa Theologiae,* St Thomas's preoccupation is likewise with the immutability, not the mutability, of human nature.

The references to a mutable nature then are quite exceptional. Each must, therefore, be seen in its proper context. The first of them, chronologically, is that found in the Supplement to the third part of the *Summa*; for, as is well known, this work was left unfinished by St Thomas but was completed after his death by the expedient of taking the appropriate passages from the *Commentary on the Sentences* and shaping them, by a scissors-and-paste method, to the plan he had already outlined.[56] One must not forget that this Supplement to the *Summa* of St Thomas's maturity really represents the thought of his first years as a professor, twenty years before. The phrase: *Natura humana non est immobilis sicut divina* is here taken, like most of the Supplement, from the Commentary on the fourth book of the *Sentences* of Peter Lombard.[57] St Thomas quotes, as his source, the seventh book of Aristotle's *Nicomachean Ethics circa finem.*[58] The passage is one of those in which Aristotle discusses the status of pleasure. He is making the point that, if our nature were 'unchanging' like the Divine Nature, the same thing would always please us; but, since we are changeable beings, what gives us pleasure now may not do so at some future date. The point is not without its relevance for the present discussion; but St Thomas hardly develops it. Nor does he develop it when, much later in his career, he comments explicitly on this passage; his commentary is confined, as is so frequently the case, to eliciting the literal meaning of Aristotle's statement and does little to stress the mutability of human nature.[59]

There is, however, another passage in the *Nicomachean Ethics* that might seem more promising. It occurs in the fifth book, where Aristotle draws the distinction between natural and legal justice, natural justice having everywhere the same force ('as fire burns both here and in Persia') while legal justice varies from place to place. It must seem slightly paradoxical that this passage should inspire St Thomas to say – it is his next reference in the *Commentary on the Sentences* to a changeable human nature – *natura nostra variabilis est*.[60] But in its context the phrase is less radical than might appear. It comes in the discussion of polygamy, where St Thomas meets the objection that a genuinely invariable natural law if it at any time forbids polygamy (as it now does) must always have forbidden it. The reply – designed to cater for the Old Testament practices – is that while the natural law is always and everywhere the same it may *per accidens* fail in its application. So, as Aristotle said, the right hand is by nature stronger than the left *semper et ubique*, yet not so as to exclude the possibility of one's becoming ambidextrous. Indeed, in his later *ex professo* commentary on this passage St Thomas points out that, since we are not separated substances with unchanging natures, there is something changeable in our nature: *apud nos homines, qui sumus inter res corruptibiles est aliquid quidem secundum naturam, et tamen quicquid est in nobis est mutabile, vel per se vel per accidens*. What is natural is what happens for the most part – *ut in pluribus, sed ut in paucioribus deficiunt* – as the restoration of entrusted goods is almost always a natural duty, but occasionally not.[61]

To return, however, to the *Commentary on the Sentences*, it should be noted that St Thomas relates his phrase about human nature being variable to the well-known Aristotelian schema of the degrees of natural necessity.[62] There are those natural events that happen *semper* and cannot be impeded; there are those that take place *frequenter* and meet with occasional obstacles; and, finally, there are those that take place *raro*. In this *triplex cursus rerum* events of the first class are *causa et origo* of those of the other two classes. So, for example, the invariable motion of the heavenly bodies is responsible for weather conditions (e.g. rain) which, in turn, provide the occasion for digging one's garden and possibly unearthing a treasure! The illustration depends too much upon Aristotelian physics to hold much appeal for the modern mind. Still something can be learned from it; St Thomas's insistence that the natural law can be assimilated not alone to the invariable but also to the frequent course of nature (which admits of obstacles or exceptions) is not really an admission that natural law varies. Rather it is that the circumstances in which human nature finds itself that vary.[63] This may be gathered from another passage in the *Commentary on the Sentences*, where St Thomas discusses the possibility of dispensation in the commandments of the decalogue. The spoliation of the Egyptians and the marriage of Osee are inevitably mentioned. St Thomas meets such difficulties by saying that what happened was that God changed the subject matter of the precepts about property and marriage so that they no longer applied: *Potest tamen Deus in aliquibus factis conditiones contrarias decalogo auferri, qui et naturam mutare potest.*[64]

The passage from the *Quaestio Disputata de Malo* cited by Fuchs occurs in the article on indifferent acts.[65] The thirteenth objection purports to show that all acts are, in themselves, indifferent and that there can be neither natural justice nor injustice (for such ought to be the same always and everywhere whereas it is evident that what is just or unjust depends upon time and place). St Thomas's reply, as has been seen, involves distinguishing between the ways in which a thing may be said to be just and good, namely formally or materially. What is formally just is invariable; for the principles of justice, found in natural reason, do not alter. Materially, however, what is just may vary on account of the mutability of human nature and the different conditions of men and things, of time and place. In such circumstances it is left to the law to settle what is just. St Thomas's example is taken from Aristotle's discussion of the *dikaion phusikon* in the *Nicomachean Ethics*.[66] The tenor of the whole reply to the objection in showing the need for positive law has already been noticed; for this it was not, strictly, necessary to say that human nature is mutable – it would have sufficed to say, as St Thomas does elsewhere, that human nature finds itself in changeable conditions.

This last remark applies also to St Thomas's final reference to a mutable human nature in the *Secunda Secundae*. Here it is once again a question of justifying the existence of a law based upon nature and, at the same time, of explaining why it does not cover all possible contingencies. The article is headed: *Utrum jus convenienter dividatur in jus naturale et jus positivum.*[67] The first objection is that in human affairs nothing immutable is found and, consequently, there cannot be a natural law. In his reply St Thomas states that human nature is mutable; from which it follows that what is 'natural' to man *potest aliquando deficere*. He gives in support the example we have seen before, that of the obligation of rendering up goods held in trust. This would always be a duty *si ita esset quod natura humana semper esset recta*. But it does happen from time to time that, because of the depraved will of man, a case will arise in which such goods should not be given back, lest the perverse will of man abuse them *ut puta si furiosus vel hostis reipublicae arena deposita reposcat.*[68] Here, it will be noticed, the mutability of St Thomas seems to have in mind is that which makes possible a change in the will of the depositor, usually well-intentioned about the use to which he will put his property but possibly ill-intentioned. This is not quite the same as the objective mutability of the situation; still less is it a mutability in human nature as such. Cajetan's commentary on the passage is instructive. Three things, he says, should be noted: (1) the sense of the maxim: *Naturale est immutabile*; (2) the reason why a deposit should sometimes not be returned; and (3) the fact that the change from justice to injustice in the rendering of a deposit and in similar matters *assignatur ex parte alterius, ad quem dicitur iustum; ex mutatione namque ipsius mutatio fit in actu reddendi.* From which Cajetan derives the advice – *Et hoc ideo, vir speculative, specialiter notare debes* – that it is important to distinguish between the case when what is just varies (as a result of a change in the *ordo ad alterum*) and the case when the exhibition of justice is prevented (by reason of something in the agent concerned).[69]

IV

So far it has been suggested in this paper that St Thomas, perfectly well aware of the need for meeting the difficulty of moral variations, left room for a certain flexibility in moral judgements appealing to nature; that the phrase *natura humana mutabilis est* appears in this connection, although rarely and in a passing way; and that closer examination of those references counsels prudence in placing reliance upon the phrase as it stands. It may help at this stage to indicate how some contemporary scholastics, apart from those already mentioned as invoking the phrase about human nature being mutable, see the basis for flexibility in moral judgements. It is, to some extent, a matter of terminology. But the terms chosen by different writers to draw out what is held to be implied in St Thomas's principles may be instructive.

The problem is still the same one: in what sense is 'nature' invariable and in what sense variable? One obvious way of answering the question is by a distinction between 'abstract nature', which is quite invariable and 'real' or 'concrete nature' which is not. This is, in effect, what authors like Oeing-Hanhoff, Fuchs and Fay say when they use terms like 'historicity' in connection with the natural law, or when they refer to the 'concrete and realistic' consideration of human nature. But other authors who use the same terminology – 'abstract' as against 'concrete' or 'real' nature – seem to think of the distinction more in terms of changed conditions in which nature finds itself than in terms of a changed or changing nature. For some the distinction between abstract and concrete may not involve much more than the acceptance of the common doctrine about universals, namely that abstract human nature does not exist except as individualised – and that individuals are irreducible. This takes one back to the metaphysical distinction between essence and existence. Essences are invariable *per se*; but as concretely existing they may change *per accidens ad corruptionem individui.*[69a] This same universal-individual distinction has been used in a rather different way in connection with the natural law by Heinrich Rommen; individual institutions, marriage for example, may be regarded as more or less imperfect embodiments of the ideal essence; and progress consists in the approach towards the perfect realisation of the essence.[70] The metaphysical basis for this kind of thinking is found in the distinction between potency and act.[71]

It should be noticed, however, that authors such as those just referred to are not usually content to have indicated the basic reason for a certain mutability in the natural law; the reason for actual variations needs to be stated. It is not enough to say simply: *Natura humana mutabilis est*. That phrase may be a convenient compendium of doctrine, as no doubt it was for St Thomas too, but the variations in the natural law are explained on lines like those of St Thomas, namely as the influence of 'passion', the fallibility of human reason or, most important, the complexity of the material with which moral reasoning has to deal. One is struck by the frequency with which St Thomas's example – which St Thomas himself borrowed – of the obligation of returning entrusted property is used to illustrate the latter point. Here is an instance, according to Manser (to take one author), in which the matter of the precept changes.[72] This is, of course, the basis for the *dispensatio improprie dicta* often invoked to explain the moral difficulties in the Old Testament like the spoliation of the Egyptians or the sacrifice of Abraham; God's supreme dominion over life and property can 'change the material of the precept'. But such divine interventions apart, the matter to which natural law precepts applies is contingent and variable inasmuch as situations are contingent and variable; and some at least of the precepts of the natural law, frequently called secondary precepts, vary according to such circumstances. This is not a novel explanation, even in St Thomas. It can be discovered in St Augustine and the idea was developed by more than one writer in the interval between him and St Thomas.[73] The corollary is that precepts of the natural law may be more or less adequately formulated. So, it is pointed out, the rules of the natural law when adequately formulated are invariable. Josef Fuchs makes this point in the course of his discussion of variation in the natural law;[74] and it is instructive to compare his handling of it with the more conservative approach of Ludovicus Bender. Having proved the existence of a natural law, Bender meets a number of objections, including the objection that, since all *jus* is subject to evolution there can be no such thing as a *naturale jus* (this being *ex hypothesi* invariable). His reply is entirely unambiguous – *nos simpliciter negamus maiorem* – those who try to show that all *jus* evolves, appealing to history, are mistaken. Historians should confine their attention to positive law, which does evolve.[75] In the following section, treating of errors, Bender reaffirms this position categorically. Nature is immutable; hence natural law is immutable. The rules of natural law are founded upon the unchanging nature of things and in no way upon the changing circumstances in which individual natures may find themselves placed.[76] Nevertheless *haec immutabilitas bens est intelligenda*! The precept: Thou shalt not kill, is not, as it stands, adequately expressed and is not invariable. In order to exclude the cases of lawful self-defence and capital punishment, where killing is justified, one should say: Thou shalt not kill an innocent person.[77] Bender then proceeds to give the common doctrine about secondary precepts of the natural law, which may admit of exception, and primary precepts, which remain unchanged. The explanation lies in the difference between the way in which speculative and practical reason work from principles to conclusions. In the practical reason the conclusions, or the secondary principles, are valid and good, but allow exceptions. The principle that a man's property should be returned to him is a good principle and almost always applicable; but it is not applicable when a madman looks for the restoration of his sword. This is not, Bender says rather disingenuously, *mutatio* in the strict and proper sense; the natural law absolutely and immutably prescribes that deposits be given back except in such exceptional cases![78] It is clear that the realisation that there is a difficulty about adequately formulating natural law precepts does not necessarily involve a flexible notion of human nature.

It can, indeed, be argued that on this thorny matter of the rule of natural law and the exceptional case to which it does not apply St Thomas was more influenced by the Platonic conception of the idea and the singular than by the Aristotelian. For Aristotle the perfection of the rule was in its application to individual cases; for Plato the individual case is thought of as falling short of the ideal.[79] If this is so then there is even less reason than one suspected for thinking that St Thomas would stress that human nature is mutable; if human nature is thought of as a Platonic form, imperfectly imitated by individuals, the exceptions to moral rules are laid at the door of the circumstances that prevent individual human nature from measuring up to the ideal.

Enough has been said to show that widely differing approaches are possible, within the scholastic tradition, to the problem of moral variations. A fuller study would require to take much greater account of the theological fact of original sin – important for its effect upon human nature and for its commanding the attitudes of many of the Fathers about human nature. This study, however, has had the more modest aim of examining some representative tendencies in contemporary scholastic writers faced with this capital problem. It does seem as if certain errors of our time, situation-ethics or exaggerated views about the scope of evolution for example, have had the beneficial effect of focusing attention upon weak points in the traditional doctrine. This is hardly surprising; error always contains a germ of truth. An awareness of the contribution of new studies, such as that of cultural anthropology, must help towards a better-balanced and more valid and in con-sequence more effectively defensible, conception of human nature and natural law. Such a conception may, indeed, be implicit in St Thomas's handling of the theme of variations in morality; but it needs to be drawn out and exhibited in a dress that will appeal to modern speculation. Hence the great value of a careful study of the 'historicity' of the natural law, such as Josef Fuchs provides. Hence, too, the danger (although it is not suggested that any of the authors referred to has fallen into it) of making uncritical use of St Thomas's phrase that human nature is mutable as if it solved everything. The phrase is of great interest; but to exaggerate its import would be imprudent as well as facile.

An Irish Reader in Moral Theology

NOTES

1   J.P. Sartre, *Existentialisme est un humanisme*, Paris: Nagel, 1959, pp. 17–22.

2   '... cette nature de la conscience qui consiste A. n'avoir pas de nature'—Maurice Merleau-Ponty, *Phenomenologie de la perception*, p. 499: 'Ce n'est pas l'essence en tant que nature que j'atteins dans le toi. En effet, en traitant l'autre comme *lui* je reduis l'autre á n'être que nature; un objet animé qui fonctionne de telle facon et non de telle autre. Au contraire, en traitant l'autre comme toi, je le traite, je le saisis comme liberté, car il *est* aussi liberté et non pas seulement nature' – *Etre et avoir*, p. 154. Both passages cited in P. Foulquié-R. Saint-Jean, *Dictionnaire de la langue philosophique*, Paris: Presses Universitaires de France, 1962, s.v. 'Nature'.

3   A.J. Ayer, *Language, Truth and Logic*, London, Gollancz, 1936, ch. 1 and 6. Cf. M. Warnock, *Ethics Since 1900*, Oxford University Press, 1960, pp. 79–118.

4   '... a glance at the history of natural law will be more helpful than epistemological argumentation to see the arbitrariness and emptiness of metaphysical speculation. Strictly speaking, metaphysical assertions do not admit of being disproved, precisely because they disport themselves in a sphere beyond the reach of verification'. A. Ross, *On Law and Justice*, London: Stevens, 1958, p. 258.

5   8me édition, revue et augmentée, Paris: Presses Universitaires de France, 1960, pp. 667–673; cf. J.C. Piguet, *Le vocabulaire intellectual*, Paris: Centre de documentation universitaire, 1957, p. 67. Having given nine senses of 'nature' Piguet concludes 'L'emploi des termes "nature" et "naturel" exige les plus grandes précautions'. Cf. also P. Foulquié-R. Saint-Jean, *Dictionnaire de la langue philosophique*, Lc.

6   R. Paniker, *El concepto de naturaleza – analisis historico y metafisico de un concepto*, Madrid: Consejo superior de investigaciones cientificas, 1931; Philippe Delhaye, *Permanence du droit naturel*, Louvain: Nauwelaerts, 1960, Introduction, pp. 9–21.

7   *Das Problem der Naturrechtslehre*, Karlsruhe: Mueller, 1955.

8   'Le désaccord sur le point de depart se répercute dans le réponse que les jusnaturalistes ont donnée a la question: "quels sont les droits ou les institutions qui doivent être considérés comme naturels, et quels sont ceux qui ne doivent pas l'être?" Une liste complète des opinions en cette matière pourrait constituer, comme on l'a observe plus d'une fois, le sujet fascinant d'un nouvel éloge de la folie.' N. Bobbio, 'Quelques arguments contre le droit naturel' in *Le droit naturel, Annales de philosophie politique*, III, Paris: Presses Universitaires de France, 1959, p. 181.

9   *Reportata Parisiensia*, IV, d. 43, q. 4, scol. 1, nn. 2-5. Cf. David Hume, *Treatise of Human Nature*, Book III, Part I, section 2 (ed. L. A. Selby-Bigge, Oxford, 1888, pp. 473–6) where the exploration of the ambiguity of 'nature' takes the same form – Nature 'as oppos'd to miracles', 'as oppos'd to rare and unusual' and 'as oppos'd to artifice'.

10   Book I, ch. 3, n. 9; cf. ibid., n.10 – 'He that will carefully peruse the history of mankind, and look abroad into the several tribes of men, and with indifference survey their actions, will be able to satisfy himself that there is scarce that principle of morality to be named or rule of virtue to be thought upon ... which is not, somewhere or other, slighted and condemned by the general fashion of whole societies of men, governed by practical opinions and rules of living quite opposite to others.' Pascal had put the matter even more vividly, a generation before Locke – 'Le larcin, l'inceste, le meurtre des enfants et des péres, tout a eu sa place entre les actions vertueuses' (*Pensees*, n. 294, cf. L. Brunschvicq, *Blaise Pascal – Pensies et Opuscules*, Paris: Hachette, 1956, for parallel passages in Montaigne, Voltaire and Charron). Moderns, e.g. K.E. Kirk, *Threshold of Ethics* (London: Skeffington, 1933, p. 72), like to cite Westermarck's *Origin and Development of Moral Ideas* in support of this position.

11   M. Ginsberg, *On the Diversity of Morals*, London: Mercury, 1962, p. 97.

12   S. Deploige, *Le conflit de la moral et de la sociologie*, cited in H. Rommen, *Natural Law*, St Louis & London: Herder, 1947, p. 227, note 19.

13   *Nicomachean Ethics*, I, 13, 1102a26-1103a10.

14   *Nicomachean Ethics*, VII, 2-10, 1145b21-1152a35,

15   1-2ae, q. 77, a. 2.

16   1-2ae, q. 94, a. 4; cf. a. 6 reason may fail to apply the principles of natural law 'propter concupiscentiam, vel aliquam aliam passionem', secondary precepts may fail 'propter malas

persuasiones ... vel etiam propter pravas consuetudines, et habitus corruptos'. Caesar, though critical of the morals of the Germans, was not quite as hard on them as St Thomas appears to assume. The full reference is as follows: 'latrocinia nullam habet infamiam quae extra fines cuiusque civitatis fiunt, atque ea iuventutis exercendae ac desidiae minuendae causa fieri praedicant ...' (ed. Teubner, Leipzig, 1961, p. 191, VI, 23). On the praise of brigandage or piracy in the Greek ethnographical tradition cf. J.J. Tierney, *The Celtic Ethnography of Posidonius*, in Proceedings of the Royal Irish Academy, Vol. 60, C, 5, 1960, p. 218 where the present passage is briefly compared with Herodotus and Thucydides.

17   1-2ae, q. 99, a. 2 ad 2. Cf. J.H. Newman, 'Liberal Knowledge Its Own End' in *Scope and Nature of University Education*, Discourse IV, London: Everyman edition, 1915, p. 112: 'Quarry the granite rock with razors, or moor the vessel with a thread of silk; then may you hope with such keen and delicate instruments as human knowledge and human reason to contend against those giants, the passion and the pride of man.'

18   1-2ae, q. 94, a. 6.

19   J. Maritain, *On the Philosophy of History*, London: Bles, 1959, pp. 82–83. Cf. M. Ginsberg, op. cit., for a discussion of 'variations due to differences of moral insight and general level of development, moral and intellectual'.

20   1, 3, 1094b11-27. Both Aristotle and St Thomas return to this idea more than once. Cf. II, 2, 1104a2-7; 7, 1107a26-35; *In I Eth.*, lect. 3, (ed. R.M. Spiazzi, nn.32–36); *In II Eth.*, lect. 2 (Spiazzi, n.259); l.c., lect. 8 (Spiazzi, nn.333–4).

21   1-2ae, q. 94, a. 4. Cf. J. M. Cameron, *The Night Battle*, London: Burns and Oates, 1962, p. 93ff on 'the difficulty about where to place moral discourse on the logician's chart'.

22   Plato, *Republic*, I, 331C: 'If we had been given weapons by a friend when he was of sound mind, and he went mad and reclaimed them, it would surely be universally admitted that it would not be right to give them back. Anyone who did so, and who was prepared to tell the whole truth to a man in that state, would not be just.' A similar moral case is discussed in Xenophon, *Memorabilia*, IV, c. 2. But a more likely source for the scholastics is Cicero, *De officiis*, III, c. 25 – 'Si gladium quis apud te sans mente deposuerit, repetat insaniens, reddere peccatum sit, officium non reddere. Quid? Si is, qui apud te pecuniam deposuerit, bellum inferat patriae reddasne depositum ? Non credo: facias enim contra rempublicam, quae debet esse carissima. Sic multa, quae honesta nature videntur esse, temporibus fiunt non honesta; facere promissa, stare conventis, reddere deposits commutate utilitate fiunt non honesta.'

23   1-2ae, q. 96, a. 6 ad 3: 'nullius hominis sapientia tante, est, ut posit omnes singulares casus excogitare ... et si posset legislator omnes casus considerate, non opporteret ut omnes exprimeret propter confusionem vitandam ...'

24   2-2ae, q. 57, a. 2 ad 2; cf. Suppl. 3ae partis, q. 41, a. I ad 3; *De malo*, q. 2, a. 4 ad 13.

25   *Philosophisches Jahrbuch*, 1962 (70), pp. 17–33.

26   The reference given is 'St. theol. III Suppl. 41, 1, 3; vgl. 2–2, 57, 2, 1'. The passage in the Supplementum is, of course, originally found in *In IV Sent.*, d. 26, q. 1, a. I ad 3.

27   Op. cit., pp. 32–33: 'Zweifellos ist dieser Satz im Rahmen der thomistischen Philosophic, "un mot a l'aventure". Zu seiner Interpretation könnte man darauf hinweisen, dass zwar die substantiale Wesensform, die suzammen mit der materia prima das Wesen der Menschen konstituiert, ein von sich aus allgemeines übergeschichtliches, überzeitliches und unwandelbares metaphysisches Prinzip ist, dass aber auch ein geschichtliches Wandel der überindividuellen, kulturellen und gesellschaftlichen Bedingungen in etwa ein Wandel der menschlichen Natur ist; denn ist ein Wandel der Bedingungen, die zurn aktuellen Vollzug des Menschseins im actus secundus notwendig und naturhaft vorausgesetzt sind, da der Mensch von Natur aus animal sociale und notwendig auf Sprache und Gesellschaft angewiesen ist. Ein solcher geschichtlicher Wandel von 'status et conditiones hominum' bring nach dem zitierten Text auch einen Wandel dessen mit sich, was das Naturrecht vorschreibt. Ob damit ein Ansatz gewonnen ist, von dem her das Problem der Geschichtlichkeit des Naturrecht entfaltet und einer Lösung zugefiihrt werden könnte, mag dahingestellt bleiben ...'

28   Patmos, Dusseldorf, 1955, pp. 51–56.

29   Cf. the revised French translation J. Fuchs, *Le droit naturel – essai theologique*, Tournai: Desclee, 1960, p. 54.

30   Ibid., p. 53, note 2. In denying the possibility of *natura pura* one compromises the gratuitousness of grace. In *Humani Generis* Pius XII reproved those who held that 'God could not create intelligent beings without destining them to a supernatural order and calling them to the Beatific, Vision'. H. de Lubac, *Surnaturel*, Paris, 1946, appears to have held that *de potentia absoluta* God could have treated man in *statu naturae purae*, but *de potentia ordinate*. He could not do so. On this cf. S. Offelli, '*Natura pura*' in *Enciclopedia Filosofica*, Venezia-Roma, 1957, t. III, col. 821.

31   *Theologie Moralis Generalis*, Pars Prima, Roma: Universift Gregorian, 1960, pp. 66–88, 'De loge naturali in loge Christi'.

32   Op. cit., p. 68: 'Natura intelligitur essentia hominis, tum secundum suum *Esse metaphysicum* ("animal rationale", cum omnibus consequentiis inde necessario fluentibus), tum secundum suum *Esse physicum*, quo Esse metaphysicum ex voluntate creatoris de facto reale est, simul cum quibuscumque relationibus accedentibus. Haec natura, ideoque et lex naturalis, intelliguntur fundata in voluntate creatrice Dei, remotius in eius intellectup et essentia. Natura autem, et correlativa lex moralis, rationi humanae per se impervia non sunt. *Natura et correlativa lex moralis distinguuntur ab elementis supernaturalibus, cum correlativa lege morali,* quae, saltem ut talia, rationi prorsus imperviae sunt et revelationa necessario indigent.'

33   Op. cit., pp. 77–81.

34   Op. cit., p. 77: 'Lex naturalis, cum in ipsa essentia hominis personalis radicetur, videri posit esse aliquid plene staticum et non-historicum inde praecise sunt tot obiectiones contra doctrinam legis naturalis. Revers, natura humana historice, quodam sensu, mutabilis est, ut habet S. Thomas; consequenter, et eodem sensu, etiam lex naturalis; *quod autem recte intelligendum est.*'

35   *Summa*, Suppl., q. 41.a.1 ad 3; supra note 26.

36   2-2ae, q. 57, a. 2 ad 1.

37   *De malo*, q. 2 a. 4 ad 13.

38   1-2ae, q. 97, a. 1; ad 1, ad 3. Cf. S. Gagnér, *Studien zur Ideengeschichte der Gesetzgebung*, Stockholm: Almqvist & Wiksell, 1960, pp. 275–219.

39   J. Fuchs, op. cit., p. 77: 'Illud "Esse hominem" – quidquid accurate sit – *obiective fundat iudicium rations rectae*, quinam actus homini convenient: sive ratione solius "esse hominem", rive ratione huius "esse hominem" in relationa ad naturam realitatum accidentalium, quae – vel extra vel intra hominem – accedere possunt.'

40   Cf. Pius XI, *Quadragesimo Anno*, n. 49 (Catholic Truth Society translation) 'History proves that ownership, like other elements in social life, is not absolutely rigid ...' J. Messner, *Social Ethics*, St Louis-London, Herder, 1949, p. 170, note 28 comments – 'To find such evolutionary features of the natural law doctrine ... given explicit and decided expression in an authoritative ecclesiastical document like the papal encyclical *Quadragesimo Anno* (1931, Pius XI) was a surprise even for many who thought themselves acquainted with the traditional natural law school, not to speak of its opponents, all the more since the Pope deals with a topic always considered fundamental to the doctrine of natural law, namely private property.'

41   J. Fuchs, op. cit., pp. 79–81.

42   Op. cit., pp. 81–82: 'Exempli causa, propositio "depositum reddendum est" nondum respicit limitationem possibilem iuris; principium "non licet alios occidere" non addit conditiones "directe" et "propria auctoritate privata", negligens sic quaestiones poenae capitis, defensionis sui, auctorizationis divinae in materia iuris (cfr. casum Abraham-Isaac); norma "non licet auferre invito domino rem alienam" non indicat possibilitatem transferendi ius in aliud subiectum iuris, sive ex parte Dei sive per legitimam auctoritatem.'

43   *International Philosophical Quarterly*, 1960 (2), pp. 50–80.

44   Op. cit., p. 77: 'From now on evolutionary progress will not occur in humans without their awareness, but is initiated and controlled by them. Man is now on the verge of exercising human dominion over the bio-cultural modifications of human existence. It belongs to man that he complete, in the light of the finalities or evolutionary tendencies of his nature, his imperfect psychological structures, his largely potential principles of action.' He cites Teilhard de Chardin's saying that we are the players as well as the cards and the stakes in this great game and goes on (p. 78): 'While this moral perspective ethos is as yet inchoate in the minds of most

people, it does exist in the evolutionary humanists such as Julian Huxley, Herman J. Miller, as well as in Teilhard de Chardin's Christocentric approach.' Cf. J. C. Flugel, *Man, Morals and Society*, Harmondsworth, Peregrine Books, 1962, pp. 316–317.

45   C. Fay, op. cit., p. 61.

46   Ibid., p. 63: 'In spite of their unique and changing character, value orientations have universal foci; that is, all humans strive to keep alive as best they know how, to enjoy association with their fellows, to relate themselves cognitively and affectively to the universe of being.'

47   2-tae, q. 57, a. 2 ad 1.

48   C. Fay, op. cit., pp. 65–66. Compare P. Lumbreras, *De lege*, Rome: Angelicum; Madrid: Studium de Cultura, 1953, p. 49: '... etsi evolutionis qui dicuntur philosophi naturalem legem ... mutabilem praedicent, nobis indubium est naturam humanam non subdi mutationi, neque propterea legem huius naturae comitem.'

49   Ibid., pp. 64–65. Cf. C. Wellman, 'The Ethical Implications of Cultural Relativity' in *Journal of Philosophy*, 1963 (60), pp. 169–184, where it is argued that a human nature relative to culture does not entail ethical relativity. 'One may wonder whether the only alternatives are an entirely fixed and an entirely plastic human nature. It might be that enculturation could mould a human being, but only within certain limits. These limits might exist because certain parts of human nature are not at all plastic or because all parts are only moderately plastic. For example it might turn out that the need for food and the tendency to grow in a certain way cannot be modified at all by enculturation, or it might turn out that every element in human nature can be modified in some ways but not in others. In either case what a man becomes would depend partly upon enculturation and partly upon the nature of the organism being encultured ...' (pp. 173–4).

50   Ibid., p. 67. Cf. A. Verdross, *Abendländische Rechtsphilosophie*, Springer, Wien, 1958, p. 231: 'Jeder Mensch besitzt aber nicht nur die allgemeine Menschennatur, er is immer auch ein konkretes Einzelwesen, das Glied eines bestimmten Volkes in einer bestimmten Zeit und einer bestimmten Kultur ist. Im Laufe der Geschichte Ändern sich aber nicht nur die Verhältnisse, sondern auch die Menschen selb est (a footnote refers to *Summa Theologiae* 2-2, q. 57, a. 2 ad 1) da uns die Geschichte lehrt, dass primitive Völker allmäblich zu Kulturvölkern haranreifen können. Daher muss das naturlichë Rechtsgesetz, wenn es eine dem Menschen entsprechende Normenordnung ist, auch den Verschiendenheiten Rechnung tragen, die im, Laufe der Geschichte eingetreten sind.'

51   *De malo*, q. 2, a. 4 ad 13; 2-2, q. 57, a. 2 ad 1; *Suppl.*, q. 41, a. 1 ad 3 (=*In IV Sent.*, d. 26, q. 1, a. 1 ad 3). The additional text is *In IV Sent.*, d. 33, q. 1, 2 ad 1: 'Semper enim et ubique dextera est melior quam sinistra secundum naturam; sed per aliquod accidens conveniet aliquem esse ambidexterum, quia natura nostra variabilis est; et similiter etiam est de naturali justo, ut ibidem Philosophus dicit.' The reference is, of course, to *Nicomachean Ethics*, V, 7, 1134b30-35. For St Thomas's commentary on this passage cf. infra.

52   Cf. R.J. Deferrari and M.I. Barry, *Complete Index of the Summa Theologiae*, Washington, Catholic University Press, 1956, pp. 219–220. There are over 4,000 references to 'natura' and almost the same number to 'naturalis'; not all, it is evident, germane to a discussion of human nature or natural law. L. Schutz, *Thomas-lexikon*, Paderborn, 1895, reprint, Stuttgart, 1958, pp. 509–519, gives a systematised account of 'natura' and 'naturalis' in the works of St Thomas. He classifies the senses of these words rather as Lalande does (cf. supra, note 5).

53   C.1, n. 2: 'Nomen naturae ... videtur significare essentiam rei secundum quod habet ordinem vel ordinationem ad propriam operationem rei, quum nulla res propria destituatur operatione.'

54   *In IV Sent.*, d. 33, qq. 1-2.

55   Cf. supra note (5); O. Lottin, *Le droit naturel chez saint Thomas d'Aquin et ses prédécesseurs*, Bruges, Beyaert, 2nd ed., 1931, p. 76.

55a   See III, C. 129.

56   The author of the *Supplementum* was probably Reginald of Piperno. Cf. M. Grabmann, *Die Werke des hl. Thomas von Aquin*, Munster, Aschendorff, 1949, 3rd ed., pp. 296–301.

57   *Suppl. 3ae Partin*, q. 41, a. 1, ad 3 = *In IV Sent.*, d. 26, q. 1, a.1 ad 3.

58   *Nicomachean Ethics*, VII, 14, 1154b20; in the *Commentary on the Sentences*, l.c., the reference is given to the *sixth* book of the *Ethics*; in the *Supplementum* this is silently corrected to the *seventh* book.

59 In *VII Eth.*, lect. 14 (ed. Spiazzi, nn.1534–1537). There is still controversy about the date of the Commentary on the *Ethics*; it is much later than the Commentary on the *Sentences*, possibly as late as 1271–2. Cf. I.T. Eschmann, Catalogue of St Thomas's Works in E. Gilson, *Christian Philosophy of St Thomas Aquinas*, London, Gollancz, 1957, p. 405.

60 *Nicomachean Ethics*, V, 7, 1134bl 8-1135al3; *In IV Sent.*, d. 33, q. 1, a2 ad 1; *In V Eth.*, lect. 12 (ed. Spiazzi, nn.1016–1034).

61 Ibid., nn.1026–1028. Both in the *Commentary on the Sentences* and that on the *Ethics* St Thomas allows Aristotle's illustration less than its full force. Aristotle had said that, although the right hand is by nature the stronger 'yet it is possible that *all* men should become ambidextrous'; St Thomas speaks of *some* becoming ambidextrous.

62 *In IV Sent.*, d. 33, q. 1, a. 2 ad 1: 'Jus naturale semper et ubique, quantum est de se, habet eamdem potentiam; sed per accidens propter aliquod impedimentum, quandoque et alicubi potent variari, sicut ibidem Philosophus exemplum ponit de rebus naturalibus. Semper enim et ubique dextera est melior quam sinistra secundum naturam; sed per aliquod accidens convenit aliquem esse ambidexterum, quia natura nostra variabilis est; et similiter etiam est de naturali justo ...'

63 Cf. *Nicomachean Ethics*, III, 2, III 2a27. On the *triplex cursus rerum* in its application to the natural law cf. especially *In III Sent.*, d. 37, q. 1, a. 3.

64 *In III Sent.*, d. 37, q. 1, a. 4 ad 3. The passage may be regarded as a first sketch for the *Summa*, 1-2ae, q. 100, a. 8 ad 3 in which St Thomas takes a similar view but without saying that God can change nature.

65 *De malo*, q.2, a. 4: 'Utrum omnis actus sit indifferens.' The chronology of the *Quaestiones Disputatae* is still very much an open question. It seams, however, fairly certain that the *De malo* comes between the Prima Pars and the Prima-Secundae of the *Summa*. Cf. I.T. Eschmann, Catalogue of St Thomas's Works, appended to E. Gilson, *Christian Philosophy of St Thomas Aquinas*, London, Gollancz, 1957, p. 391; F. Van Steenberghen, review of O. Lottin, *Psychologie et morale aux XII it XIII siécles*, t. VI, *Revue philosophique de Louvain*, 1962 (60), p. 681.

66 *De malo*, q. 2, a. 4 ad 13 – '... alio modo materialiter; et sic non sunt eadem justa et bona ubique et apud omnes; sed oportet ea lege determinari. Et hoc contingit propter mutabilitatem naturae humanae, et diversas conditiones hominum et rerum, secundum diversitatem locorum et temporum; sicut hoc semper est justum quod in emptione et venditione fiat commutatio secundum aequivalens; sed pro mensura frumenti justum est ut in tali loco vel tempore tantum detur, et in alio loco vel tempore non tantum sed plus vel minus.' Cf. *Nicomachean Ethics*, V, 7, 1134b34: 'The things which are just by virtue of convention and expediency are like measures; for wine and corn measures are not everywhere equal, but larger in wholesale and smaller in retail markets.'

67 2-2ae, q. 57, a. 2.

68 Ibid. The example of the deposited goods was used by Plato – cf. supra note (22). St Thomas makes use of it, apart from the present context, in *In III Sent.*, d. 37, a. 1, a. 3; *In IV Sent.*, d. 33, q. , a. 2 ad 1; *In V Ethicorum*, lect. 12 (ed. Spiazzi, n. 1025); 1-2ae, q. 94, a. 4; 2-2ae, q. 51, a. 4; 2-2ae, q. 62, a. 5 obj. 1; 2-2ae, q. 120, a. 1. Cf. P. Antoine, 'Conscience et loi naturelle' in *Etudes*, 1963 (317), p. 165: 'Ce premier cas de conscience, que l'on pout lire daps la *Republique* de Platon, et qui remonte peut-etre a Socrate, ninon plus haut, sera indefiniment repris et commence par les moralistes. Il manifeste que l'on ne pout pas identifier simplement la justice A une formulation juridique.'

69 Thomas de Vio Caietanus, *Comm.* in 2-2ae, q. 57, a. 2.

69a G.M. Manser, *Das Naturrecht in thomistischer Beleuchtung*, Freiburg in der Schweiz, 1944, p. 60: 'Per se sind die Wesenheiten der kreatürlichen Dinge unveränderlich ... Aber ratione existentiae, kraft der kontingenten Existenz, kann auch die Wesenheit geschöpflicher Dinge, per accidens also, veränderlich genannt werden. So sagt in diesem Sinne präzis Thomas von Aquin: Das Naturrecht ist immer und uberall, "quantum ad se" unveränderlich dasselbe. Und dennoch kann es "per accidens" ad corruptioneñ individui' d.h. infolge seiner existentiellen Unvollkommenheit ausnahmsweise in diesem odor jenem. vordorbenen Individuum infolge der Leidenschaften und der gestörten normalen Erkenntnis Wandlungen unterworfen sein.'

For the phrase about accidental corruption 'ad corruptionem individui' Manser refers to *De verit.*, q. 1, a. 5 ad 14; *De spir. creat.*, a. 10 ad 8; 1a, p. 86, a. 3.

70   H. Rommen, *Natural Law*, Herder, St Louis-London, 1947, pp. 166–72. Cf. p. 168: 'The divine reason by thinking creates the essence of things. The divine will brings them into existence either immediately as first cause or indirectly through secondary causes. This is basic for the possibility of the natural law, because it means that the essential forms are not dependent in their quiddity on the absolute will of the almighty Spirit, but only in their existence. The essential forms of things are unalterable because they are ideas of the immutable God ...'

71   J. Funk, *Primat des Naturrechtes*, St Gabriel Verlag, Mödling bei Wien, 1952, p. 92: 'Ganz charakteristisch fur die Natur ist ihre Veränderlichkeit. Grundlage dafür ist vor allem ihre Zusammensetzung aus Akt und Potent, aus Wirklichkeit und Möglichkeit.'

72   G.M. Manser, *Das Naturrecht in thomistischer Beleuchfung*, p. 59.

73   S. Augustine, *De vera religione*, c. 31, n.58: 'Conditor legum temporalium ... illam ipsam consulit aeternam, ut secundum eius incommutabiles regulas, quid sit *pro tempore* iubendum vetandumque discernat,' cited by A. Verdross, *Abendlandische Rechtsphilosophie*, p. 61; cf. pp. 65–6.

74   Cf. supra note (42).

75   L. Bender, *Philosophia iuris*, ed. 2., Officium Libri Catholics, Rome, 1955, p. 176.

76   Op. cit., pp. 185–6: 'Regulae iuris naturalis fundantur in sola natura rerum et nullo modo fundantur in circumstantis accidentalibus, in quibus natura individualis versari potest, sed quae etiam abesse possunt.'

77   Ibid. and note 5: 'Dicentes "non licet occidere *innocentem*" exludimus casus, in quibus aliquis occidit violatorem iuris sui titulo exercitii iuris coactivitatis, praesertim in defensione cruenta, sive privata, sive in bello iusto, aut in applicatione poenae mortis. Sic enim haec verba ab omnibus intelliguntur. Non declaratur, solummodo prohibitum esse occidere innocentes. Saepe enim occidere hominem peccatorem erit iniuria et peccatum.'

78   Op. cit., p. 188: 'Ius naturale absolute immutabile praecipit: depositum est reddendum praeterquam in huiusmodi casibus exceptionalibus.'

79   Cf. M. Wittmann, *Die Ethik des hl. Thomas von Aquin*, Hueber, Munchen, 1933, pp. 346–52.

14   Natural Law Today

Patrick Masterson

(*Doctrine and Life*, Vol. 16, 1966, pp. 59–66.)

HUMAN NATURE

St Thomas describes natural law as the participation by a rational creature in the eternal law of God. In other words, he sees natural law as a special case in the overall divine plan.

All creatures below man are moved to the fulfilment of their purpose in a strictly determined and necessitated fashion. They are not free to perform actions contrary to their nature. An apple tree, for example, has no option in the matter of growing, blossoming and bearing fruit in due season. At the human level, however, we encounter a level of creation which is intelligent and free and which, consequently, is called to tend towards its perfection in a rational and free manner. In other words, it is called to discern for itself the sort of actions which are conducive to its welfare. The code of behaviour thus proposed is what is meant by natural law. Thus man, because he is rational and free, can come to some knowledge of the eternal law of God in his regard. However, since he is called by God to a supernatural life, which his reason by itself could never discover, he needs the help of Revelation and teaching of the Church in order to achieve a more complete understanding of his role in the plan of God.

When speaking to Catholics one can expect a sympathetic hearing for this introduction of the natural law theory of morality in terms of its ultimate theological setting. However, one may wonder how the theory can be defended at the present day when so many people question this ultimate theological setting. For example, could a Catholic doctor in discussion with an agnostic colleague convincingly explain his objections to abortion in terms of natural law? In principle the answer is yes. As Jacques Maritain remarks: 'Belief in human nature and in the freedom of the human being is in itself sufficient to convince us that there is an unwritten law, and to assure us that natural law is something as real in the moral realm as the laws of growth and decay in the physical' (*The Rights of Man*, p. 35). Certain misunderstandings, however, must be carefully avoided.

Let us return to our earlier remark that man, as a rational being, can discern the kinds of action which are conducive to his welfare. He can attain this knowledge without embarking upon a profound theological inquiry. An intelligent reflection upon the overall dynamic structure of human nature is sufficient to inform us in a general way of the natural moral precepts which must be observed if we are to live a truly human life.

However, it is important to realise that natural law is not something readymade in nature, to be discovered as one might discover an oil well in the back garden. Nor is it a written law to be found by somehow peeping into God's mind, or rummaging around in our own minds for a list of rules given to us at birth as part of our mental furniture. Unfortunately, babies, unlike motor cars, are not delivered with a list of rules or directions! And this is why St Thomas insists that coming to know the natural law is not simply like letting your hair grow but rather a task to be consciously accomplished, a task which man must accomplish if he is to live a fully human life It is accomplished by working out a rule of life based upon an intelligent scrutiny of the fundamental needs and tendencies of human nature.

Acting according to natural law is not simply a matter of following our natural tendencies and inclinations. It is rather a matter of living according to the truths which reason discovers to be relevant to human behaviour. In other words, following the natural law isn't a matter of giving indiscriminate consent to natural inclinations or conditions. Such an inadequate conception of natural law would preclude us from wearing clothes or devising institutions such as private property, since in his 'natural' condition, his 'state of nature', man has neither clothes nor possessions. In refuting this silly conception St Thomas points out that man is 'naturally' naked but that no natural law argument for or against clothing can be based on that empirical fact (*Summa*, 1-2, 94, 5 ad 5).

Likewise, he points out that our inclinations and tendencies, considered simply in themselves, are not always a sure guide to moral behaviour. He remarks that very often people, because of passion or dissipation or some constitutional disturbance, have strong inclinations and tendencies towards behaviour which is unbecoming to a human being. Christian thinkers who base their account of natural law simply on an analysis of inclination seem to have forgotten another part of theology, namely original sin. The 'naturalness' of my anger or the 'naturalness' of my concupiscence provide no moral justification for the actions that anger or that concupisience may suggest. St Thomas was realist enough and Christian enough to see that the narrow path of virtuous and moral action is not the one we tend to pursue with natural spontaneity and assuredness. Again we do not abandon moral beliefs simply because in our own enlightened times we find nations so intoxicated with passion and propaganda that they perpetrate the most fearful atrocities as though they were perfectly natural. Similarly, St Thomas was not inclined to abandon the doctrine of natural law simply because he read in Caesar's *Gallic Wars* that the German tribes treated robbing and plunder as something perfectly natural. For what he meant by natural moral law was something much more worthy of man than blind and irrational submission to

An Irish Reader in Moral Theology

natural impulse. Much misguided criticism of the Thomistic doctrine of natural law is strictly irrelevant because it is directed against caricature of the doctrine that St Thomas himself was careful to avoid.

When St Thomas speaks of natural law he is referring primarily not to man's needs and tendencies, but rather to the truths of life which reason discovers through reflection upon these needs and tendencies. Reason is man's specifying perfection and therefore the influence of reason should illuminate all his actions if they are to be truly human. First of all and spontaneously our reason tells us that in our actions we should do good and avoid evil. This is the first and most general truth of natural law, that one which constitutes the whole area of morality. For it is in virtue of this precept that man is forced beyond the realm of purely technical inquiry concerning what he *can* do – and impelled to consider what he *must* do in order to be a good man.

However, if we are to avoid a naïve presentation of natural law we must admit that the concrete determination of those actions which are good and those which are evil is a rational project of great difficulty and complexity. We must integrate all the pointers of our needs and tendencies into a unified rational vision of the overall meaning and purpose of human activity. Only when controlled in terms of this comprehensive framework can the various spheres of human activity, whether physical, biological, social or spiritual, be imbued with the quality of reasonableness and understanding which should be manifest in all human action.

There is no great difficulty in discovering the most general principles of such a rational framework. For example, from an understanding that the perfection of any individual presupposes continued existence and identity, follows the general principle that man should take appropriate measures to preserve and promote his survival and physical well-being. Likewise his understanding of the relationship between his procreative powers and the continuance of the human species enables him to formulate a general moral principle concerning the responsibility of the species to propagate and rear offspring. Again, realising the dependence of each individual on his fellow men for a truly human existence, a person can formulate a general moral principle concerning the moral obligation of instituting social relationships. Similarly, 'reason reflecting on man's nature as that of a rational being, promulgates the precept that he should seek truth and avoid ignorance, especially about those things knowledge of which is necessary for the right ordering of his life' (F.C. Copleston, *Aquinas*, p. 215). No special effort of the mind is required in order to recognise these fundamental moral truths. They are the *sine qua non* of a moral order.

However, the task of outlining clear and sure precepts becomes more difficult as we progress by intermediary stages from these general principles to their more specialised and concrete consequences. We can argue fairly easily to their not too particularised consequences such as the obligation to respect the person and liberty of others, to foster family life, to respect just authority, to promote education. However, the matter becomes much more difficult when, from these somewhat particularised principles, we turn to elucidate their even more particularised consequences and applications. The difficulty is encountered, not only because of the intrinsic richness and complexity of human nature considered absolutely in itself, but also because of the inescapably historical character of the human condition. Living the life of a man involves transforming the face of the earth. Man can humanise himself only by humanising the world around him. This, I take it, is part of the meaning of the command in the first chapter of Genesis, to 'increase and multiply and fill the earth and subdue it'. Inevitably, the moral principles which flow from man's existence must be constantly re-applied to the ever-changing cultural circumstances which he devises and inaugurates. In other words, the historical circumstances of a particular line of action are relevant to an assessment of its morality. For example, what might be just a social order at one time or in one place, might not be a just social order at a different time or place because of different economic or cultural circumstances. This does not mean that moral principles are constituted by historical circumstances, but rather that the application of the same universal moral principles in different historical circumstances may impose different lines of conduct.

CAN NATURAL LAW CHANGE?

This brings us to a very important question: can the natural law change? Clear thinking is essential on this point if the whole doctrine of natural law is not to seem suspect.

As we have already noted, moral knowledge – this is true of all knowledge – is not something readymade and known at birth. Although its more general truths are readily knowable, nevertheless it is knowledge which must be acquired. Hence, as in all other forms of knowledge, we must allow for growth and development. It must be emphasised, however, that what is involved here is growth and development in our comprehension of moral truths and not, as it sometimes suggested, a profound change or reversal of moral truths. When a physicist discovers a new physical law, nobody supposes that the structure of the world has changed. The change is in the refinement and development of the physicist's knowledge of the physical world. Likewise, there can be refinement and development in one's knowledge of the moral order.

It is of course true that the particularised formulation of a moral principle is influenced not simply by our more refined understanding of it, but also by the concrete requirements of cultural circumstances. All cultural development carries with it a moral development. Indeed, the development of culture is itself a moral precept. It is, or should be, a rational fulfilment of human potentialities and as such a fulfilment of the natural law. All authentic cultural development necessarily

An Irish Reader in Moral Theology

fosters the fuller realisation of the truths of life embodied in the natural law. Consequently, what the unchanging truths of natural law dictate will develop from one cultural context to another. For example, the absolute moral precept that we should be concerned about the well-being of our fellow men may, in primitive conditions, mean ensuring that everybody has a cave to live in, whereas in more developed circumstances it may mean ensuring that nobody has to live in a cave. The important point to bear in mind is that development of natural law means a development and concrete application of absolute moral principles, and not a denial or replacement of these principles. Whatever may be the changing applications of natural law to changing circumstances, every application must be analysable into the same absolute moral principles, which should always be respected by men precisely because they are men. Any cultural development which implied a disregard for the dignity of the individual, a total rejection of family life, a complete state of anarchy, or a systematic repression of the search for truth and authentic interpersonal relationships would always be morally wrong. It would be wrong because incompatible with the fundamental truths of life which follow from a consideration of the meaning and purpose of human existence.

THE TWO LEVELS OF NATURAL LAW

I have repeatedly mentioned that a defining feature of the natural law is that it is the work of reason prescribing the actions which are appropriate to the perfection of man's unchanging nature as it unfolds in ever-changing cultural circumstances. However, although this is true, nevertheless, Christians should avoid an exclusively rationalistic interpretation of natural law. It is sometimes suggested by believers that even for Christians natural law means exclusively the moral code which can be known by pure reason without adverting in any way to the life and teaching of the Church.

I believe that we should speak rather of two levels of natural law ethics. The first would be the moral code which is accessible to human nature. The second would be the moral code proposed by the rational reflection of a mind which is already refined by Christian awareness and Christian living. It would be the work of a mind fully stretched to show how far and how fully reason can go towards discerning that way of life which, as a Christian, he knows to be the true salvation of man. A man who has lived experience and conviction of the saving truth of Christianity will find more readily, and to a greater extent, that the morality inherent in Christianity is reasonable and natural, than will the man whose strictly rational reflection has no roots in Christian belief. They can agree on general principles but in more particular conclusions their account of natural law may differ. In other words, the particular conclusions of a strictly rationalistic theory of natural law on the one hand and a Christian conception of natural law on the other may differ, not indeed as incompatible, but rather as a less perfect to a more perfect understanding of the meaning and value of the human person. For example, in both a rationalist's and Christian's account of natural law there may be agreement on the importance of control in sexual behaviour. However, because of pre-reflective convictions, there may be disagreement concerning the nature and extent of that control. Moral argument, unlike mathematical demonstration, is influenced by a person's beliefs and way of life. A valid argument against adultery will more readily convince a happily married man than one who is unhappily married and perhaps committing adultery.

It would be unrealistic to expect that the rational ethical reflections of a convinced Christian should be totally immune to the influence of his Christian sensitivity. Consequently, when speaking of natural law ethics, it is important to distinguish the various levels of understanding which may be expected from a purely rationalistic foundation on the one hand and a profoundly Christian foundation on the other.

CONCLUSION

To summarise and conclude: when we talk about natural law as the criterion of morality we mean that, notwithstanding how often man in fact behaves viciously, it nevertheless remains true that every human act *should* be a worthy manifestation and fulfilment of human nature and human dignity. We mean that precisely because man is the sort of being he is and, as long as he remains this sort of being, his behaviour will be either true or false to the objective requirements of his life. We mean that the objective requirements of his life are one and all determined by a nature which is specifically and exclusively his. We know that the nature which characterises the human condition is that of an incarnate rationality or, in simpler terms, that of a rational animal. In particular, it is his intellect of reason which marks man off from the rest of the physical world and hence, all his actions, if they are to be truly human, should bear the stamp of reasonableness. We know that with a certain facility man can ascertain the general principles of action which must be respected if he is to live a truly *human* life. We know also that in particular situations it is not always easy to form a moral judgement with complete assurance that this is the action worthy of man and required of him in these circumstances. Much less is this likely to happen if the man making the judgement is involved in the problem. Objectivity here is rare indeed. Hence Aristotle's advice: 'Go, watch a good man.' However, we do know that every action is either true or false to the objective requirements of human nature. Moreover, however difficult the particular problem, we must hold fast to the goal of acting rationally in conformity with our humanity.

To abandon belief in the truth and efficacy of this goal is to deny that man is capable of living up to the dignity of his humanity. It is to open the doors of acting irresponsibly and in the dark. It is significant, perhaps, that after the last war, when the conquering powers sat in judgement on the Nazi atrocities, they were unable to condemn these atrocities logically in terms of their own prevailing ethical theories. Neither the pragmatism of the Americans, the emotivism or positivism of the British, the existentialism of the French, nor the communism of the Russians could provide an objective basis for the moral evaluation of gas chambers and concentration camps. Faced with the stark reality of dreadful evil, they had to have recourse to the theme of crimes against humanity to explain the nature of this evil. The positive counterpart of the notion of crimes against humanity is surprisingly close to what is meant by natural law.

Accepting natural law as the criterion of morality does not mean having a ready answer to every moral problem that presents itself. But it does mean knowing the ultimate criterion in terms of which the solution to a moral problem is possible. To reject the natural law doctrine does not mean always acting immorally, but it does mean lacking in ultimate rational criterion whereby one can measure and vindicate the morality of actions. To say that our understanding of the natural law is not always profound enough to enable us to encompass the whole range of our moral responsibilities, or to determine without doubt the morality of a particular action, is a just reflection on the finitude of our human condition, but it is not a refutation of the doctrine of natural law with its limited, but certain, claims. It is rather a reason for pursuing our investigation of this law with greater diligence and fidelity.

15 Natural Law and Moral Argument

P.J. McGrath

(J.P. Mackey (ed.), *Morals, Law and Authority*, Dublin: Gill and Macmillan, 1969, pp. 58–78.)

There are two ways of looking at an ethical theory. It can be looked at (a) as an account of the central concepts of ethics, that is, as an explanation of what it means to judge an action to be morally good or bad or morally right or wrong; and (b) as providing a pattern for valid argument in ethics. This second aspect will appear more clearly if we point to the parallel between a theory of ethics and a system of logic. The treatment of the syllogism in Aristotelian logic tells us which patterns of syllogistic argument are to be accepted and which to be rejected. Now an ethical theory does the same thing for ethical argument; it tells us which ethical arguments are to be accepted as valid and which to be regarded as invalid. If you accept Utilitarianism in ethics, for example, then you will regard as valid arguments of the form, 'This action or type of action is conducive to the greater happiness of the greater number: therefore it is morally good'; and you will reject as invalid the type of argument which is put forward by, say, natural law moralists or by those who accept hedonism in ethics.

This second way of looking at an ethical theory is one which normally doesn't attract much attention. The reason is that most ethical theories leave little or no room for doubt as to which type of ethical argument they permit and which type they reject. We may not be absolutely clear about the concept of happiness, for example, but at the same time we are sufficiently clear about it to know with certainty that certain types of action are conducive to the general happiness and certain types of action are not. And the same would be true of the concept of pleasure. This brings me to two points which I wish to make about natural law ethics. The first is that the natural law theory is an exception to the general rule we have just been discussing, that is to say, the natural law theory as it has been traditionally understood does not make clear which types of ethical argument the theory commits you to accept or to reject. The second point is that natural law moralists have not been aware of this, or at least have been insufficiently aware of it, with the result that the standard of argumentation within the natural law tradition has been and, I think, is, very unsatisfactory. It will be more convenient if I deal with the second of these points first.

I

If you examine the sort of reasoning employed by moralists in the natural law tradition, one thing that will strike you is the wide variety of argument that natural law moralists are prepared to accept. You might say, of course, that this is one of the virtues of natural law morality, for, after all, human nature is a complex reality and therefore ethical reasoning must of necessity be complex as well. This sounds reasonable, but there is another side to the coin – the greater the variety of reasoning one is prepared to accept in ethics the greater the necessity for being clear as to the sort of reasoning one is not prepared to accept and the greater the necessity for being clear on the relative merits of different types of ethical argument. Otherwise we will be unable to decide which ethical arguments have genuine force and which have not; and furthermore, when the situation arises where you have different arguments pro and contra the same moral principle, there will be no means of deciding the relative merits of these arguments. But there is little evidence that natural law moralists have been clear on these points and a good deal of evidence pointing in the opposite direction.

The first item of evidence is this: there is considerable disagreement amongst natural law moralists as to why certain courses of action are morally wrong. For example, there seem to be at least four different opinions concerning the fundamental reason why lying is immoral. It is claimed to be immoral (a) because it frustrates the function of the faculty of speech which is to communicate truth;[1] (b) because the words are naturally signs of thoughts and whoever lies violates the natural bond between a sign and the thing signified;[2] (c) because a lie violates the right of the person spoken to;[3] and (d) because lying frustrates a universal appetite.[4] You find the same situation with regard to suicide. Some say it is wrong because it violates the rights of the creator;[5] others because it is contrary to the natural human inclination of self-preservation;[6] and finally some say it is wrong because of its bad effects on society.[7]

One could attempt to explain away these discrepancies by saying that these arguments complement rather than exclude each other. But I do not think that this explanation is adequate. For while they do complement each other when considered simply as reasons why lying or suicide is immoral, when considered as basic or fundamental reasons they *are* incompatible. Moreover, when you speak of these arguments as complementing each other, you are envisaging a situation where an action is wrong for a number of different reasons. But this is possible only of individual actions, whereas what we are concerned with here, since we are dealing with universal moral principles, are types or species of actions. An individual act can be morally wrong for a number of reasons, since it may belong to several moral species at once. The same individual act can involve both a lie and the breaking of a promise, for example. But a morally wrong species as such cannot be morally wrong for a number of reasons for this would mean that it was simultaneously both one species and several species. Of course, there is nothing to prevent you speaking of a class or species of actions which belong simultaneously to two or more moral species. But the point is that, if we were considering the morality of such a 'mixed' species, we would first of all have to consider the morality of each 'unmixed' species separately. And here the consideration which I have been arguing for would apply, namely, that each species, if morally wrong, would be morally wrong for one fundamental reason. Or, to put this in natural law terms, if a species of actions is contrary to nature, then it is contrary to it in a certain specific way. The fact that there is little agreement within the natural law tradition, therefore, as to why lying or suicide is contrary to nature indicates a basic uncertainty as to how the natural law theory works; or, in other words, as to which ethical arguments are good and which bad.

A second item of evidence is the unsatisfactory character of much of the reasoning found in the natural law tradition. Some moral principles are supported by arguments which are scarcely arguments at all but merely reformulations of the principle. This is particularly true of actions such as incest or sodomy which are universally regarded, by Christians at least, as immoral. These actions are often said to be immoral simply because they are contrary to the order of nature or the rule of right reason; and this is only a concealed way of saying that they are immoral because they are immoral. It may be that the universal agreement concerning these actions means that moralists are rather careless in formulating arguments about them; at the same time, if it is obvious that these actions are contrary to nature, it ought to be obvious why they are contrary to nature, and this doesn't seem to be the case. Moreover, you occasionally find arguments from reason in the manuals which seem to have no connection with natural law – for example, the argument that lying is immoral on the grounds that it is repugnant to a divine attribute.[8] Apart from the merits of this argument, it is very difficult to see how you could connect it with natural law. Finally, many of the central natural law arguments are open to serious criticism. This is a point I must assume for the moment, since I want to postpone discussion of it until later on. But it all adds up to the suspicion that natural law moralists tend to regard actions as contrary to nature because they already regard them as immoral; and hence that their arguments are really rationalisations rather than genuine arguments.

It would be foolish to think that there is just one single explanation for the unsatisfactory state of the argumentation within the natural law tradition. One factor is that many of these moralists were theologians rather than philosophers and when they had what they believed to be a convincing argument from revelation in favour of a moral principle, they took little care in formulating the argument from reason. A second factor is the uniformity of opinion within the natural law tradition concerning the content of morality. When certain conclusions are universally accepted in a particular field of inquiry, there is little stimulus to examine critically the arguments on which these conclusions are based. It is like

An Irish Reader in Moral Theology

the emperor's clothes – if everyone accepts an opinion, nobody bothers to take a critical look at the evidence on which the opinion is based. This factor has obviously influenced the history of the Church's teaching on contraception. So long as the Church's stand was universally accepted by Catholics, there was no pressure on moralists to examine critically the arguments on which that stand was based. It was only after they began to doubt the truth of the Church's teaching that Catholics began to find flaws in the arguments. And, if we hadn't begun to entertain these doubts, we would probably still be happy with the arguments because we would never have bothered to think seriously about them. Now the greater part of the Church's teaching on morality is still immune from the sort of doubt which has arisen concerning her teaching on contraception. The result is that the Catholic moralist doesn't have to worry unduly about the standards of his argumentation in those areas. Since he knows that his readers won't question the truth of his conclusions, he can safely presume that they won't question the validity of his arguments.

But the principal reason for the unsatisfactory standard of natural law argumentation is, I think, something other than this. It is rather the fact that the natural law theory, unlike other ethical theories, does not make clear which types of ethical argument are valid and which are not. And hence acceptance of the theory does not make clear to moralists which forms of ethical argument they are committed to employ and which to reject. If we look at the natural law theory for a moment we will see why this is so. The natural law, as it has been traditionally understood, is an aspect of the eternal law of God; it is, in other words, that part of God's entire plan for creation which applies to man. The natural law theory, therefore, is based on an analogy between 'law' as it is understood by the physicist or chemist or biologist and 'law' as it is understood by the moralist. The irrational part of creation in obeying the laws of physical nature and man in obeying the laws of his rational nature are both carrying out the divine plan.

Exponents of natural law make it quite clear, of course, that this analogy is only an analogy and not a strict parallel. As St Thomas puts it, rational creatures participate in the eternal law in a manner which is quite different from that of irrational creatures, since they obey it consciously and freely, whereas irrational creatures obey it unconsciously and of necessity. At one crucial point, however, this analogy breaks down completely, that is, when the question arises of our knowledge of the eternal law. We can discover the eternal law for irrational creation by purely empirical methods. When we know how irrational creatures actually behave, we know how they ought to behave or how God wants them to behave, since the two things are identical. But how are we to discover how man ought to behave? Not by seeing how he actually behaves, since unless we already knew how he ought to behave, we would have no means of knowing whether his actual behaviour was morally good or bad. Well, then, how are we to find out how man ought to behave? Natural law moralists answered this question by saying that we find out how man ought to behave by seeing how his nature is constituted. The trouble with this, however, is that there is a logical gap between the facts about man's nature and the moral principles which tell us what he ought to do. Natural law moralists found various ways of bridging this gap, but none of these ways were actually implied by the natural law theory. Consequently, one could accept the theory and accept or reject as one pleased these ways of bridging the gap between human nature and the moral law, or even produce new ways if one wished. And this, I believe, is the fundamental reason why there is so much unsatisfactory reasoning in the natural law tradition and so many oddly divergent ways of justifying even such an elementary principle as 'Lying is morally wrong'.

I have said that the analogy between the eternal law as found in man and as found in irrational creatures breaks down when we come to explain how we acquire a knowledge of these laws. But I must qualify this by adding that natural law moralists would not admit that the analogy breaks down at this point and St Thomas goes to some pains to show how the analogy can be understood to continue. For St Thomas, every instance of the external law, whether in man or in irrational creation, is an expression of a natural tendency.[9] If water invariably boils at 100° or material bodies are attracted towards each other by the force which we call gravity, this is because they have a natural tendency to behave this way. Similarly, if man ought to speak the truth or ought not to commit suicide, this is because he has a natural tendency towards truth or towards the preservation of his life. For St Thomas, man has three basic natural tendencies.[10] As a substance he has a natural tendency towards self-preservation and it is from this that the moral principles concerning the preservation of life are derived. As animal he has a natural tendency towards reproduction and this provides the basis for moral principles concerning sex and family life. Finally, as a rational being he has a natural tendency towards truth and towards life in society and from this derive the moral principles which govern his social life.

The question which we must raise at this point is: does this concept of 'natural tendency' enable St Thomas to successfully bridge the gap between human nature as it is and human behaviour as it ought to be; in other words, does the natural law theory as understood in the light of this concept of 'natural tendency' commit you to accepting certain forms of ethical argument as valid and rejecting others as invalid? The answer to this question must, I think, be 'No'. For how are we to know what are man's natural tendencies? The only possible answer is that we discover what they are by looking at man's behaviour, just as we learn the natural tendencies of irrational creatures by looking at the manner in which they behave. But observation of human behaviour might lead us to conclude that man has a natural tendency to lie, or to drink too much, or to oppress his fellow man. We are faced then with the old difficulty that, before reaching conclusions about the content of natural law, we will be unable to distinguish in human behaviour between what is moral and what is immoral and therefore unable to base a morality on the tendencies which we find there.

St Thomas's classification of human natural tendencies seems to owe as much to the tree of Porphyry as to empirical investigation. But no one these days expects nature to subscribe to the canons of definition *per genus et differentiam*. Modern psychologists provide rather different classifications of the basic human drives or tendencies. According to Freud in his later period, for example, the two fundamental human tendencies are the life instinct and the death instinct, eros and thanatos. According to Adler, the basic human tendency is the will to power or to self-assertion. If you accepted one of these theories and also accepted St Thomas's conception of the ethical significance of the basis human tendencies then you would arrive, I feel, at some very odd ethical conclusions.

St Thomas himself does not seem to have taken this part of ethical theory very seriously since, if he had, he should have appealed to it in all his ethical arguments; an action for him should be morally good only if it accords with a natural tendency and morally bad only if it frustrates a natural tendency. But, in fact, he uses several other forms of ethical argument in his writings and I have been able to find only three instances where he uses this type of ethical argument explicitly – to show that love of one's neighbour is morally good, to show that sexual intercourse is morally good and to show that suicide is morally wrong. So I think we can conclude that St Thomas was aware of the difficulties of his own position.

II

I now wish to examine the various ways in which natural law moralists tried to span the gap between human nature as it is actually constituted and human behaviour as it ought to be, or, what amounts to the same thing, the principal forms of ethical argument found in the natural law tradition. There seems to be four main types at least – (1) the argument based on natural tendencies; (2) the argument from consequences; (3) the argument based on the natural function or purpose of a faculty; and (4) the argument from rights. This classification is not, of course, exhaustive; there are other forms of argument used, but these are either eccentric or exceptional and need not, therefore, be considered here. It is worth mentioning here that the second and third of these forms of argument were employed in the encyclical *Humane vitae*. I will now examine each of these four main types of argument in turn.

(1) The first type is the argument from natural tendencies. We have already pointed out the difficulty of deciding which are man's natural tendencies. But even if we overlook this point and presume that we have an accurate list of man's natural tendencies, further difficulties arise. If something is good or bad because it is in accordance with or contrary to a natural tendency, and if the natural tendency is in human nature because God has implanted it there, does it not

follow that the action is good or bad because God has willed or forbidden it? For example, if, as St Thomas argues,[11] love of neighbour is good because men have a natural tendency to love one another, wouldn't it follow that love of neighbour would be morally indifferent or even morally bad if God had implanted a different or contrary instinct in human nature? And this conclusion is obviously unacceptable. One could perhaps argue that the basic human tendencies follow of necessity from human nature and that therefore God had no choice in creating man but to implant these tendencies in him. But this would mean that the objects of these tendencies are not necessarily morally good. Every finite being endowed with free will might have, of necessity, a natural tendency to do wrong – if one were inclined to argue in this way, there would be no lack of empirical evidence to support one's position. So it seems that the natural tendency argument avoids ethical voluntarism only at the expense of depriving natural tendencies of their ethical significant.

In any event, natural tendencies seem incapable of bearing all the weight which moralists place upon them. For example, it seems impossible to understand how the natural tendency to reproduction could provide an adequate basis for a coherent sexual morality; if our sexual morality was really based on that tendency, wouldn't fornication be far more moral than celibacy?

Or take the argument that lying is immoral because it frustrates the natural appetite for truth. But if I lie, I don't frustrate *my* appetite for truth, but somebody else's. So, to complete the argument, one must introduce into human nature a natural tendency not to frustrate the natural tendencies of others. And at this stage the argument is in danger of becoming ridiculous; one could legitimately appeal to a variant of Ockham's razor – natural tendencies are not to be multiplied beyond necessity.

(2) The second type of argument is the argument from consequences. This is used in all sorts of different contexts by natural law moralists and it is also employed by the encyclical *Humanae vitae* (see paragraph 17), though it is not easy to judge how much weight the Pope attaches to it. The form of the argument is as following: lying or suicide or contraception are immoral because if they are not and people are free to indulge in these practices as they please, the effect on society will be disastrous. One thing that should make us suspicious about this type of argument is that, if it is valid, then many practices which are normally regarded as innocent should, in fact, be regarded as immoral – smoking, for instance, or driving a car or taking a drink. When one remembers that approximately sixty thousand people are killed each year in road accidents in western Europe and that most of these deaths would be avoided if cars were kept off the roads, then it is easy to see that there is a consequences argument against driving which is at least as strong as the parallel argument against suicide or contraception. But this example also shows the weakness of this type of

argumentation. For even though car driving has such horrifying consequences for humanity, this does not mean that every time one drives, one is behaving immorally. The fact that a certain type of action will sometimes be performed irresponsibly does not mean that every action of that type is morally wrong. The medievals summed this up in a neat phrase: *Abusus non tollit usum*. Even though a thing be abused by some, this does not prevent it from being properly used by others.

Has this type of argument then any part to play in ethics? The answer, I think, must be 'No', though it would be difficult to provide a complete justification for this view without drawing distinctions between different types of actions and different types of moral situations. Without going into this detail, however, one can, I think, say this: if the consequences argument is ever valid, it is because the doing of an action will induce others to do the same and the effect of this on society as a whole will be bad. But I do not think that this sort of argument could ever be validly used in ethics. For the effect on society will be bad only if some of these actions have bad consequences in themselves and therefore are immoral in themselves independently of whether they induce others to perform the same sort of action or not. But if the original action was of this type, then the consequences argument does not apply, since the original action is already immoral even if it does not induce others to do the same. But if it is not of this type, then we have no reason for thinking that it will induce others to perform the same action in such a way as to produce bad consequences. For how could the responsible performance of an action induce others to perform the same action irresponsibly? How could driving a car carefully, for instance, induce others to drive dangerously? One can, I suppose, conceive of this sort of thing happening, but it would certainly be an extraordinary occurrence and one which could not be used as the basis for a conclusion about the effects of driving in general.

The proponents of the consequences argument were obviously thinking, though not perhaps explicitly, along these lines: if I drive, I induce others to drive and since some of these are bound to drive dangerously, it follows that I cannot drive at all without inducing others to drive dangerously. But this argument is quite clearly invalid. One might as well argue that if I speak the truth, I induce others to tell lies, since if I speak at all, I thereby induce others to speak also and some of them are bound to speak falsely. It is clear, therefore, that if an action is performed responsibly, the consequences argument cannot be used against it to show that it is immoral, whereas if it is not performed responsibly, it is immoral in any case and appeal to the consequences argument is superfluous.

The use of this type of argument in the encyclical *Humanae vitae* exposes its weaknesses. For if, as the encyclical claims, artificial contraception is wrong in itself, that is, independently of its consequences for society, the consequences argument is irrelevant, since *ex hypothesi* it is not its consequences which make contraception morally wrong. If on the other hand, contraception is not wrong in itself, then we have no reason for assuming that the responsible use of contraceptive methods will lead others to use them irresponsibly and therefore no reason for thinking that contraception is immoral because of its consequences for society. So the consequences argument is either irrelevant or invalid. The encyclical's position on consequences is particularly weak since it is based on the unspoken assumption that those who would disobey the Pope were he to allow the use of the pill in certain well-defined circumstances within marriage, will obey him now that he has outlawed it completely; one has only to state this assumption to see how improbable it is. One might claim, of course, that the Pope is not really using the consequences argument, but merely asking his readers to contemplate the consequences of contraception for society so that they may be more easily convinced of its immorality. But even this presupposes the validity of the consequences argument, for otherwise how could contemplation of the consequences lead one to think that contraception is morally wrong?

The consequences argument could be validly used in a non-ethical context when it is a question of someone imposing a rule or a positive law. And its use in ethics is, I think, due to a confusion between the role of the legislator and the role of the moralist. A legislator could legitimately argue that a whole class of actions should be outlawed, not because each individual instance is harmful, but because this is the only way of preventing harmful actions of this type from being performed; this is what happens when a speed limit is imposed, for example. But the moralists cannot argue that he should declare a certain type of action to be immoral, for otherwise great harm will ensue. As a moralist he is not entitled to forbid or sanction anything, as is the legislator. His job is to make a judgement, not a decision; and the effects of his judgement are no more relevant to its truth than the effects of a declaration in favour of the Copernican theory would be to the truth of the proposition that the earth goes around the sun.

(3) The third type of argument is based on the purpose or function of human faculties. This type of argument is normally used by natural law moralists in dealing with sexual morality and the morality of lying. It is also the main argument appealed to by the encyclical *Humanae vitae*, though it is formulated there in an unusual way (par. 12).[12] The word 'meaning' (*significatio*) is used instead of 'function' or 'purpose', but this, I think, is an effort to forestall criticism that it is viewing sex in a purely biological manner. This type of argument faces some of the difficulties of the argument from natural tendencies. For how do we know what is the natural function of a faculty? The argument on lying claims that the function of the faculty of speech is to communicate truth. This seems to be based on the assumption that when we speak we invariably utter propositions – expressions which are either true or false. But many, perhaps most, of the things we say are not intended to be propositions; they are requests, questions, wishes, jokes, prayers, exhortations, commands, exclamations, insults and so on. None of these

An Irish Reader in Moral Theology

set out to be either true or false, so it is difficult to see how one could seriously defend the view that *the* function of the faculty is to communicate truth. Couldn't one make a more plausible case for saying that the function of speech was originally to enable man to survive? If you accept this, the argument against lying collapses. Or take the sex-faculty. Couldn't one make a plausible case for the view that one of its functions is to give pleasure? And, if so, couldn't one develop a natural law argument in favour of various types of behaviour which Christians invariably regard as morally wrong?

In his *Philosophical Investigations* Wittgenstein explained why philosophers so readily accepted a certain error in philosophy by saying, 'A picture held us captive' (par. 115). Natural law moralists, in putting forward this form were, I think, held captive by a picture, a picture of man's faculties as delicate instruments fashioned by a particular purpose by the creator. This led them to think of lying or the misuse of the sex-faculty as equivalent to using, say, a surgical instrument to pare a pencil. Now this picture of man's faculties is, I believe, inadequate for two reasons. In the first place it is inadequate for the purpose for which natural law moralists employ it. Using a surgical instrument to pare a pencil makes it unfit for use as a surgical instrument, but using the faculty of speech to tell a lie won't prevent you from telling the truth in future. In other words, the picture demands that misuse of the faculty renders it either defective or useless as far as its proper use is concerned, whereas the misuse moralists are thinking of is merely the using it for a purpose other than that for which it is intended. And so, even granted the picture, their arguments are defective. Secondly, the picture is, in any event, the wrong picture. Human nature and the human faculties were not directly created by God as the medievals believed; they have evolved. The human species has, in a certain sense, grown from very lowly origins. Hence, if you want to compare man and his faculties with human artefacts, you must compare them, not with things such as watches or pens or surgical instruments, but rather with a city or an institution which has grown to be what it is through a lengthy process of change and adaptation and development. And once you change the picture, the faculty argument disintegrates. For if you depart from the original plan of a city or institution, you are not necessarily going against the will of the founding fathers; what you are doing now may be precisely what they themselves would have done in similar circumstances. In the same way, if man alters the functioning of his faculties, he is not necessarily going against the will of his creator, since alteration and adaptation have been going on in nature from the very beginning.

(4) The fourth argument is the argument from rights. Again this is used in a variety of contexts by natural law moralists – in connection with property, with suicide, with the worship due to God and so on. The form of the argument is that an action is wrong because it violates the rights of another, whether the other is God, another person or society in general. There is another sort of argument

connected with this, which you occasionally find in the natural law manuals. This is that an action is wrong because it involves treating a person, not as a person, but as a thing. Fundamentally, I think, the two arguments are the same, since when you respect a person's rights, you treat him as a person and when you ignore his rights, you reduce him to the level of a thing. Rights are an expression of personality from the moral point of view. But what is so remarkable about this argument is that it is so very different from the others which we have been considering. For in the other arguments you were arguing from an 'is' to an 'ought', from the purpose of a faculty or the existence of a natural tendency or the effects on society of some course of action to the judgement that something ought or ought not to be done. The premises of these arguments were certain facts which were in themselves ethically neutral; the difficulty was to give these facts an ethical significance and it was on this difficulty that these arguments foundered. But this problem does not arise in connection with this fourth argument. For the facts on which this argument is based are of themselves ethically significant; they have an 'ought' built into them so that there is no logical gap to be bridged in drawing an ethical conclusion from them. To say that someone has a right is *eo ipso* to say that others ought to respect that right; if it does not say that, then to say that someone has a right is to say nothing at all.

There is a second way in which this fourth argument differs from the other three. The others place man on the same level as the rest of creation. They see man as a being with natural tendencies, with certain faculties each of which has a particular purpose and whose actions may have an effect on the entire group. Now there is nothing specifically human about all this; these features are also found in irrational creation. And, of course, this is part of the natural law way of looking at man; it sees him as governed by a code of laws which applies to creation as a whole. But when you begin to argue from rights and from personality, you are immediately on a different level. For rights and personality are what mark man off from the rest of creation; he is the only being in creation who is a person, who possesses rights. And once you realise this, you have to ask yourself whether this argument is really compatible with the natural law theory as it has been traditionally understood. And I think you would have to say 'No, it isn't'. If you accept this type of argument, then to be consistent you must reconstruct the natural law theory and place at its centre not the concept of nature, but the concept of person.

III

What form then should ethical arguments take? To answer this question satisfactorily one would need to write a full-scale treatise on ethics. But without going this far one can, I believe, lay down certain rules to which ethical argumentation must conform if it is to have any claim to be valid. The first is that moral judgements, whether they are general or particular, always need supporting arguments or reasons. Moral judgements are not like judgements of sense perception. We cannot perceive moral attributes like rightness or wrongness as we perceive qualities such as redness or whiteness, and it cannot happen, therefore, that one could know that something was right or wrong without having any reason for one's view. (This is not to be confused with having a reason without being able to articulate it, or with the situation where there are reasons for and against the rightness of an action and one knows intuitively that one reason outweighs the other.) To know that something is right or wrong one needs criteria for the application of these terms and these criteria constitute the supporting reasons for the moral judgement. If, for example, you say that an action is wrong because it involves stealing, you are using as a criterion for the application of the term 'wrong' the fact that the action involved the taking of property against its owner's wishes. And you are arguing implicitly in this way: whatever involves stealing is wrong (other things being equal). This involves stealing; therefore this is wrong.

There is one important corollary from this: appeal to authority is never sufficient justification for a moral judgement. This does not mean that someone might not be justified in acting on a moral principle which he accepts from authority rather than sees the truth of himself. What it does mean is that the authority must itself have a reason for its moral judgement and its opinions on moral matters are no better than the reasons which underlie them. This seems to undermine one line of approach to the teaching on contraception in *Humanae vitae*, that of those who say that while they cannot accept the Pope's reasons, they accept his teaching, since it was delivered under divine guidance. But since grace works through nature, would not divine guidance on moral matters necessarily take the form of enabling one to perceive the reasons why some course of action is right or wrong? It does not make sense to say that the divine guidance extended only as far as the judgement and left untouched the reasons on which the judgement was based, since the making of the judgement and the reasoning which underlies it are all part of the same process. Since one cannot accept, therefore, that the Holy Spirit aided the Pope to make the right judgement for the wrong reasons, if one accepts his judgement, one must also accept his reasons or provide better reasons in their place.

The second rule to which moral reasoning must conform is that the reasoning which underlies a moral judgement must be deductive in character. This follows from what we have said about criteria, since to apply a moral predicate in accordance with a criterion is implicitly to appeal to a more general moral principle; to say that something is wrong because it is x is to make implicit appeal to the principle, 'Everything which is x is wrong'. Nevertheless, the deductive character of moral reasoning is something which has come to be questioned by Catholic moralists, but this is partly due, I think, to the undue stress on deductive reasoning in traditional Catholic moral theology, where it was sometimes assumed that the conclusions of the moralist were as clear-cut as those of the geometrician. There can be no doubt that deduction by itself is not sufficient for arriving at ethical conclusions, since particular moral problems often involve a conflict of principles and can be resolved, not by deduction, but by what Aristotle called 'perception', something akin to good taste in artistic matters. But deduction is, I believe, the only possible way in which we could arrive at general moral principles, though the deduction here will not possess the lucidity of deductive reasoning in logic or in mathematics. If you do not accept this view, then the only alternative is to hold that moral principles are arrived at by induction, a view which has recently been put forward by John Coventry.[13] This would mean adopting an intuitional theory of moral judgement since, if we do not use criteria for the application of terms such as 'right' or 'wrong', then the only way for us to recognise rightness or wrongness is through some form of intuition; if our recognition of moral attributes is not indirect, it must be either direct or non-existent. The weakness of intuitionist ethics has, however, been very fully exposed in recent English moral philosophy and anyone adopting an intuitionist theory of moral judgement has a great many objections to answer before his position can be taken seriously, a task which has so far not been taken on by any supporter of ethical inductivism.

Besides, even if we overlook the weakness of intuitionism, it does not seem possible to form moral principles by means of induction. Any action may be described in various ways, and if it is immoral it won't necessarily be immoral under every description. Oswald's action in killing Kennedy, for example, was wrong, not because he pressed the trigger or released the spring or fired the gun, though these are all accurate descriptions of what he did from different points of view, but because he deliberately killed a man. If you condemn an action morally and are unable to state under which description it is morally blameworthy, you will be unable to use that judgement as the basis for a general principle; it is no use saying, 'All actions belonging to the same class as this action are morally wrong' if you do not know to which class this action belongs. But if you say that this action is wrong because it comes under this description, this is equivalent to saying that it is wrong because it is x. And this is the same thing as saying that you have arrived at this particular judgement because you accept the general principle that all actions which are x are wrong. So it appears there is no room for induction in moral reasoning.

The third rule to which moral reasoning must conform is that it must be concerned in some way with human welfare. An action cannot be morally wrong unless it is humanly bad, that is, detrimental to human welfare and it cannot be morally right unless it is humanly good. There is a passage in the *Summa Contra Gentes* which bears on this point. St Thomas is considering the objection that if two people commit fornication in such circumstances that they do no harm thereby either to themselves or to society, then they cannot be said to have done anything morally wrong. The objection goes on to say: 'Nor does it seem a sufficient answer to say that they wrong God, for God is not offended by us except by what we do against our own good; but it does not appear that this conduct is against man's good; hence no wrong seems to be done to God thereby.'[14] The significant thing is that St Thomas answers this objection on its own terms; he tries to show, in other words, that certain types of sexual behaviour are wrong because they are contrary to man's own good and not for any other reason. But this type of objection has not been taken sufficiently seriously by Catholic moralists since then. They have been shielded from it by the assumption that if an action is contrary to the order of nature, then it is morally wrong whether the order of nature has anything to do with human good or not. This too is the most serious defect in the reasoning which underlies the encyclical's condemnation of contraception. Even when it is discussing the consequences of contraception, it mentions only its bad consequences as if its good consequences were of no account. But this type of objection is one which Catholic morality will have to take more seriously in future.

Notes

1   Cf. Noldin-Schmitt, *Summa Theologiae Moralis*, II, 578. The references which I give here and in the following pages are, of course, merely sample ones.
2   Cf. St Thomas, *S.theol.*, IIa,IIae, q.110, art.3.
3   H. Grotius, *De Iure Belli et Pacis*, I.iii, c.i., nn.II
4   Cf. C. Fay, 'Human Evolution: A Challenge to Thomistic Ethics', in *International Philosophical Quarterly* (2) 1960, p. 66. Natural law moralists usually argue that lying is also wrong because of its evil effects on society, but I have found no one putting this forward as the basic reason for the immorality of lying.
5   Cf. Noldin-Schmitt, op.cit., II, p. 309
6   Cf. Joseph Rickaby, *Moral Philosophy*, London 1918, pp. 215–16.
7   Cf. W. Palely, *Ethics*, c.X, n.3, p. 178.
8   Cf. Noldin-Sch mitt, op. cit., II, p. 579.
9   Cf. *S.theol.*, IIa IIae, q.1, art.6
10   Cf. *S.theol.*, Ia IIae, q.94, art.2.
11   See *Summa Contra Gentes*, Book III, ch. CXVII.
12   In an article entitled 'The Arguments of *Humanae vitae*' (*The Month*, March 1969, p. 151) Timothy Potts says that the central argument of the encyclical is 'completely new and has not appeared in the literature before'. But this sounds most implausible. One can hardly accept that in paragraph 12 Pope Paul is claiming that the traditional teaching of the Church is based on an argument which has never previously been put forward. Moreover, in paragraph 13 the encyclical speaks of the meaning and purpose (*significatio et finis*) of sexual intercourse as if the terms were synonymous.
13   See John Coventry 'Christian Conscience', *The Heythrop Journal* (VII) 1966, pp. 145–60.
14   *Summa Contra Gentes*, Book III, ch. CXXII.

16   Is there a Natural Law?

Donal Harrington

(Donal Harrington, *What is Morality?*, Dublin: Columba Press, 1996, pp. 102–12 [extract].)

THE LAW OF OUR BEING

The fact remains that, even if we base our morality in reflecting on the nature of human reality, people still differ about what it is to be a human person. One school of thought will say that when we reflect on what we are, what we find is simply the inclination to seek pleasure and avoid pain. In contrast to this, traditional natural law theory speaks of the inclinations to preserve life, to procreate and educate offspring, to seek the truth and to cooperate in society. Another philosophy will hold that we find nothing pre-given, but that our human nature is nothing more than what we create through the exercise of our freedom.

But is there anything more fundamental that underlies such various interpretations? One promising approach would be to say that common to all such interpretations is the human spirit in search of moral truth. Natural law is about reflecing on human nature; but if reflection and deliberation are what is distinctively human, then natural law means most fundamentally our reflecting on our own reflecting. Whether our conclusions converge or diverge, we all seek and question according to the same pattern. If so, this pattern is itself the most basic natural moral law. Let us elaborate on this.[1]

At the heart of our moral consciousness there is questioning. First of all, our human experience of good and bad, right and wrong, raises questions for our understanding. As we seek to understand our experience, we come up with different ideas and insights, so that there arise questions for our judgement, which search to see if our understanding is true. This in turn raises questions for deliberation. These questions bring us beyond knowing and feeling to the moment of decision and commitment

This is the pattern of how we operate as morally conscious subjects, a pattern of experiencing, then understanding, then judging, then deciding. We can say that the pattern is invariant in that, if another were to disagree with the outcomes of our reflections and deliberations, that person would do so by coming to different understandings, judgements, decisions, commitments. Whatever the outcome, the pattern would be the same. Thus we can say that it is our natural orientation to inquire into our experience, to seek insight, to strive to arrive at what is true and what is good, and to commit ourselves to the good that we find.

One can readily see the 'law' that is contained in this pattern and how the pattern can be experienced as a source of obligation. It is the law of being open and attentive to our experience, of being intelligent and insightful in our inquiries, of being reasonable and comprehensive in our judgements, of being detached and responsible in our deliberations, of being committed to the good that we discover. If we observe these 'precepts' well, we will arrive at the true and the good. And this is what the natural law fundamentally is.

In the formulation of Thomas Aquinas seven centuries ago, the basic precept of the natural law is that we should do good and avoid evil. It may sound obvious, but what he was stating is that we are moral beings, that we are by nature oriented or inclined towards the good. The above formulation simply develops this, by elaborating on the pattern of our moral consciousness. It is this pattern of consciousness that differentiates us from the animals. They do not have to decide about themselves and about what is good. But we do, and this is how we go about it. For this reason, the human person might be described as 'the moral animal'.

From this we can say that the first thing that reason learns from reflecting on human nature concerns the 'how' rather than the 'what' of morality. Our basic learning concerns how to go about being moral beings, namely, by being attentive to our experience, insightful in our thinking, reasonable in our judgements, responsible in our deliberations, committed in our living. This is our nature, our natural inclination as moral beings. What this will tell us about right and wrong is a further question, but this is the path whereby we activate our nature as moral animals.

This much does, however, offer an explanation for at least some of the disagreement that exists about human nature and moral principles. That is to say, people attend, think, reflect, deliberate differently. People attend to different data; they understand differently and come to different conclusions. Some of this is due simply to the enriching fact of diversity. And some of it is the result of ignorance, inadvertence, oversight, blindspots, bias.

Some of the latter in turn has to do with the context, for it does happen that the blindspot or bias may affect a whole community or culture. It may be simply that the individual person has a distorted understanding of, say, property or of sexuality; or it may be that the person is a victim of the distorted understanding of the times he or she lives in. We do not reflect in a vacuum, apart from the culture we live in; on the contrary, that culture significantly modifies our moral sensibility.

This formulation also allows us to affirm a natural law while at the same time taking account of the centrality of change. The world we are in is constantly changing and so too, our perception of ourselves is on the move. But there is a bedrock, namely, our nature as experiencing, inquiring, understanding, knowing, deliberating, loving human beings. This bedrock makes for continuity amidst all the changes in our situation, in our perception of ourselves and in our moral awareness.

A FUTURE ACHIEVEMENT

The focus of our reflections has been on process rather than on content. We have been exploring the fruitfulness of thinking of natural law as the law of how we think about morality rather than as the results of that thinking. An advantage of this approach is that it avoids the impression of natural law as an immovable set of moral directives and emphasises instead the central role of the reasoning heart in the discovery of moral truth.

However, this approach is bound to feel frustrating to those who simply want a statement of what is right and wrong. The basic answer to that sense of frustration is that there is no way of setting forth what is right and wrong that bypasses human minds and hearts. There is no 'objective' formulation of the natural moral law, set in stone for all times and places and requiring nothing more than simple acquiescence on our part.

This is because of the nature of objectivity. In any area of inquiry there is no objectivity without subjectivity. We do not reach the objective truth without successfully negotiating the subjective processes of inquiry, understanding, judgement, decision. But in morality these processes are further complicated by the fact that what we are investigating is ourselves. The phenomena that scientists seek to understand are outside the scientists themselves. But in moral reflection we ourselves are the phenomenon that we are trying to understand.

There is no formulation of right and wrong that can be advanced so as to end all debate. Reflection on and debate about human experience is the only solution. If we start with people reflecting on what it is to be people; if we enter into conversation about our various viewpoints; if in a spirit of dialogue we grow to appreciate what has been called 'the light of disagreement', then we will be progressing towards truth.

For this reason the natural law, in the sense of the outcomes of our reflecting and conversing, could be said to lie ahead of us. It is something we strive towards rather than something we possess. In a sense it does not yet exist, because humanity has not yet attained a converging viewpoint as a result of its experiences, insights, judgements and decisions. Put more positively, the natural law exists insofar as people have come to a common perception of and commitment to the truth about themselves. The natural law is future because we as a race are still in the process of discovering who we are and learning to agree on what it means to be a human being.

One modest illustration of this comes from a gathering of people from the variety of world religions in 1993. The gathering styled itself the 'Parliament of the World's Religions' (though those present were not necessarily officially

An Irish Reader in Moral Theology

representing their religions), and it produced a declaration on what it called a 'global ethic'. The ethic consists of a 'fundamental demand' and four 'irrevocable directives'. The fundamental demand is that every human being must be treated humanely. The four directives are: commitment to a culture of non-violence and respect for life; commitment to a culture of solidarity and a just economic order; commitment to a culture of tolerance and a life of truthfulness; commitment to a culture of equal rights and partnership between men and women.[2]

To the enlightened this will seem unremarkable, yet something new is happening. People from vastly different cultures are beginning to come together and to agree on fundamental moral values. The values they articulate are very much what the natural law is about, or will be about in the future. These values are what emerge when people join together to attend and inquire, to reason and deliberate, in loving commitment. The results are not so much human constructions as what people discover when they activate their moral consciousness.

One thinks also of the United Nations Human Rights Declaration as a similar process in a secular context. But what it all amounts to is convergence. In one sense the natural law is there already, in the way we are and what we are for. But in another way it lies ahead of us, its unveiling hastened by the convergence of minds and hearts coming together from very varied backgrounds.

This is something that has never happened before in the history of the world. Whenever the natural law was formulated or articulated before, it was from within a single culture, that of Europe. Perhaps that is why the phenomenon of conflicting practices in far-off cultures was so hard to embrace. But now the world is becoming a single unit, a global community. The focus is on dialogue between different perceptions of the moral truth, on different accounts of our moral being coming into conversation. Here, truth is born from the enrichment of diversity.

The outcome of this emerging dialogue is not the kind of standardisation that capitalism is imposing on the world community, nor the kind of moral uniformity that might have characterised single cultures in the past. Rather, the possibility presents itself of diversity being recognised and cherished within a common perception of what it is to be human.

Nevertheless, to think of natural law in this way as a future achievement attendant upon the unity of humankind is far from implying that such an achievement is in any way imminent. Even though there is now a global context for ethical debate, it remains that some of the most intractable difficulties in moral discourse today stem from humanity's inability to agree on fundamental aspects of what it is to be a human being. It is one thing to speak as we have of natural law as being in the future; how short-term or long-term a future is another matter.

All of this echoes points that have always been acknowledged in the Catholic tradition about natural law. That tradition has acknowledged that we do not come to a knowledge of the natural law without difficulty, and that we should not expect that most people would agree on how to understand the natural law. The prospect of hordes of people easily recognising the rights and wrongs of whole ranges of issues, or even agreeing on the underlying principles, is not what natural law means. Confusion and disagreement are much more what is envisaged. The idea of natural law is that there is a moral truth to be found and that we will find it by activating our moral consciousness in communion with one another.

If this is the case then the clear need is that 'reason' be given the same attention at least as 'nature'. The idea of natural law holds that there is a law of our being that we are called to discover and to cherish. But it does not envisage an easy discovery. The key, then, is that we learn how to reason well with our reasoning hearts, and how to reason well together in a world that, for all its pluralism, is converging into a single community.

NOTES

1 Here we are drawing on the thought of Bernard Lonergan: see his *Method in Theology*, London: Darton, Longman and Todd, 1972, chapter one. Also: 'The Transition from a Classicist World-View to Historical Mindedness' in *A Second Collection*, London: Darton, Longman and Todd, 1974, pp. 1–9; and 'Natural Right and Historical Mindedness' in *A Third Collection*, New York: Paulist Press, 1985, pp. 169–83.
2 Hans Küng and Karl-Josef Kuschel, *A Global Ethic: The Declaration of the Parliament of the World's Religions*, London: SCM Press, 1993.

17 Ethics Making Sense

Patrick Riordan

(*Studies,* 91 (2002), pp. 7–14.)

Public life today involves the concerned citizen in a whole range of issues in which questions of morality overlap with practical stances in politics, diplomacy, business, medicine and the law. Whether it be the question of the justifiable use of military force in war, whether it be the issue of legislation permitting abortion in certain circumstances, whether it be the revelations of the extent of corruption in the echelons of business, public service, politics, and even the churches, the citizen is inevitably involved in ethical reflection. What resources are available for this reflection? In the midst of the seeming over-abundance of theories is there any way to cut through the layers of sophisticated intellectual analysis in order to get to the essentials? Given that the discussion involves many professionals with their own specialised competencies, are they able to rely on some shared language and shared presuppositions for talking to one another? Is it possible to clarify this shared language and these shared assumptions in order to proceed constructively with dialogue?

The following clarifications are offered in the service of intellectual housekeeping which philosophy traditionally performs. The housekeeping service to which I refer is the work of tidying up questions and issues. Distinctions are introduced, terms are clarified, to ensure that people are talking about the same matter, and applying the same criteria. For instance, it is one thing to discuss the morality of what is permitted by a proposed abortion law, it is another to discuss its political viability. Keeping these questions apart may be a help to ensuring a useful discussion. While the following tries to clarify and make as simple as possible, this should not be read as a disparagement of the value of sophistication in reflection and theory building in ethics. There is no simple blueprint or code available to us to direct actions and decisions in all the complex areas of modern life, from genetic manipulation to environmental protection. Any issue, once it is opened up, can lead ever deeper into discussions about the basic terms of our social life, about the criteria for our judgements and about the ultimate questions of the dignity and purpose of human existence. The following clarifications offer only a basic street map, to indicate the alternative paths the discussion might take, and the kinds of questions which are either opened up, or are blocked off, as one path rather than another is taken.

Distinguishing the moral from the ethical?

In ethics the potential for misunderstanding is increased by the fact that the terms used can be employed in an ordinary, everyday sense, as well as in a technical sense. For instance, the adjectives 'moral' and 'ethical' are sometimes used interchangeably, but many philosophers introduce these terms in such a way as to distinguish them. The misunderstanding might then be minimised by careful attention to the technical definitions, but this is made even more difficult by the fact that all philosophers do not distinguish these terms in the same way. Many distinctions and definitions are particular to the perspectives propounded by the thinkers, and so are incompatible with one another. For instance, some distinguish morality and ethics, by using the former term 'morality' to refer to the codes of rules and the set of practices etc. to which people conform (or better, attempt to conform) in their activity. The latter term 'ethics' is then used to refer to the reflection on the moral codes and practices which are operative in society. But even if ethics is used to identify reflection on the moral, this can also be done in various ways. The reflection involved can be the personal self-examination and commitment of the moral agent, the taking possession of one's own convictions and values, and resolution to abide by those principles. Alternatively, the reflection on morality might be the disciplined, structured discourse of the professional philosopher.

Which has priority, morality or ethics?

Not all who distinguish between the moral and the ethical do so in the same way. Some analysts will want to privilege the moment of reflection, seeing it as the more important. The 'ethical' person is then featured as one who has freed herself from mere conformity to convention, the demands of her society. Having reflected on the received norms of morality, she has chosen for herself the principles to guide her action, and so makes her decisions independently of the rules to which the masses conform. The reverse side of the high estimation of the autonomy of the individual is a disparagement of the conventional. What 'they' think, what society expects of one is treated with suspicion, as oppressive and restrictive. This tendency to privilege the ethical over the moral, so understood, is very strongly linked to the individualism of liberal political theory. It is also strongly influenced by the emphasis on freedom found in existentialism and personalism. The free person who acts well is one who is also thought to be free from the kinds of social pressure associated with threats of public disapproval or even punishment.

On the other hand, some thinkers are suspicious of the emphasis on reflection. They point out that we have obligations and that these require us to treat others in a certain way. We learn about our basic obligations, not to harm others, not to deceive, not to steal etc., before ever we have an opportunity to reflect on them. People have a fair idea of what they ought to do, and what is

An Irish Reader in Moral Theology

right and wrong, but getting them to reflect on this can lead to a distancing from it. Reflection can lead to a dilution of the sense of obligation, and a critical analysis of what is meant, for instance by 'justice', can lead not only to a greater precision in talking, but also to a reluctance to act. Where 'morality' is regarded as the forum in which right and wrong make their demands upon us, a philosophically reflective 'ethics' is seen as a dangerous distraction from the urgency to act.

No one correct distinction

Given that the distinction between moral and ethical can be drawn in several different ways, it is important when reading any philosopher on this topic to understand the way in which she uses the terms. But there is no correct definition and no uniquely right way of distinguishing these concepts. It is a mistake to expect a single and useful definition which encompasses this whole reality of human action and interaction. Different distinctions and definitions serve different purposes. We can test the usefulness of a distinction in terms of what it allows us to clarify and what questions it allows us to pursue.

In my teaching and writing I do not always distinguish between morality and ethics. It is not always necessary or indeed helpful to do so. The reference to the ethical can make a discussion of the moral unhelpfully self-conscious. In asking whether exaggerated promotional sales talk is a violation of the rule which forbids lying, I am in fact doing ethics, in the sense of reflecting on morality, but it does not necessarily help my investigation to advert to the fact. Better to confine the conversation to the moral matter in hand, unless of course some difficulty arises which makes it necessary to become explicit about what we are doing. If someone argues that the warning to the buyer, *caveat emptor*, let the buyer beware, releases the seller from the obligation to be truthful, then we will probably have to investigate the assumption implied here that one can be released from moral obligations in certain situations. To conduct this discussion further, we will have to be more explicit about our doing of ethics, and pay more attention to the principles, criteria and rules of argument and inference on which we rely.

Doing ethics as a disciplined reflection on moral talk is distinguishable from direct engagement in moral talk. But I would not wish to separate them, as sometimes happens when the reflection is seen as a purely academic exercise. Nor would I wish to give priority to the reflection over the direct engagement in morality. Reflection, whether in the personal search for authenticity or in the philosophical laboratory, serves the purpose of clarifying what is right and wrong, what is good and bad, what is to be done and what is better left undone.

Ethics as talk about morality

I suggest that it is helpful to see ethics as talk about morality. A large part of morality is talk about doing. This is the evaluative and normative talk about human action whereby we tell one another what is right and wrong, what is good and bad, what is helpful and harmful, what is convenient and inconvenient. This kind of talk is not only to be heard from pulpits, or to be encountered in the classroom. It is explicit in the instructions given by managers to new recruits, it is explicit in the speeches of politicians and political campaigners, and if not always explicit, it is implicit in the commentaries of journalists and the editorials of newspapers. But does this mean that all human action, insofar as it is subject to evaluation, is moral? I would say yes, given that we apply evaluative terms to every aspect of our activity. And while it is true that we sometimes find it useful to distinguish between the moral and the legal, the moral and the aesthetic, or between the moral and the prudential, these distinctions should not be taken to imply that the relevant categories of activity designated by these terms, aesthetic, prudential, legal, are outside of the scope of morality. These distinctions can be useful and contribute to clarifying certain questions, but if they are used to delimit the horizon of the moral, then the danger is that morality is confined to a very limited range of human doing. Our attention has often been drawn to the fact that the word 'immorality' had come to mean sexual misbehaviour. Other forms of abuse, exploitation and injustice disappeared from the moral horizon, because of this restriction in the language. Our speaking of what is good or bad, right or wrong, can apply to the full range of human activity, and so morality is equally broad in scope. My choice of jacket to wear to this evening's concert may not be as important as my choice of partner, either for the concert or for life, but who will deny that it is an element of living well?

Direction 1: the good life

What constitutes living well has been a key area of investigation since the beginning of philosophical reflection in ethics. What is it to live well, to enjoy a good life? Plato's *Republic* is an extended discussion of the question whether it is necessary to be just in order to live well in the sense of having a happy, fulfilled life. Aristotle's *Ethics* explores the nature of happiness, the flourishing human life. This very broad horizon remains the context for ethical reflection, even when the discussion is of a very specific issue or technical detail. The most fundamental question is 'how can I live well?', 'what must happen for my life as a whole to be considered a successful life?'. Aristotle is not slow to point out that many factors other than our own choices and actions contribute to making our lives happy. As well as the material and physical conditions for existence, a large measure of good fortune is also required for a happy life. It is not all under our own control.

But to the extent to which their own actions matter, people want to know whether the lifestyle they have adopted, or adapted to, is going to contribute to their fulfilment. And we notice how this question changes for them as they grow older. When young and energetic the exploration of possibilities and the realisation of their potential and their hopes loom large in the description of fulfilment. When older, and some commitments have been made, happiness and contentment evoke other images, which often involve the quality of life of others in the web of relationships which now characterise life. This question of the good life, the human good, is emerging in new ways. The practice of medicine is being challenged to rethink the notion of health in a more holistic manner, so that the patient as a whole is treated, and not only the disease. Business is having to consider a broad range of stakeholders whose interests are affected by its activity. So for business ethics now, the traditional definition of the purpose of business as maximising shareholder value is no longer satisfactory. Consideration must be given to the broader range of goods at stake, including the well-being of customers, suppliers, employees, and local community. Similarly, our consciousness of sharing a planet with limited resources is making us aware of the human impact on the environment. What in the past was ignored because taken for granted, must now be addressed explicitly. And so the question of the good is arising in many ways, in the question about the proper use of the natural environment, in the question about the ultimate purposes of our frenetic economic activity, and in the question of health as the well-being of the whole person in her relationships, among others.

Direction 2: which rules are binding

In recent centuries the focus in ethical reflection shifted away from the exploration of the good life and concentrated more on the rules to guide behaviour. One reason for this shift is to be found in the widespread disagreement about what constitutes the good for humans. The lack of a shared vision of the good life obliged people to attempt to find agreement on the rules to which they would be required to conform, even if they disagreed radically on religious, political or philosophical issues. This context affected political as well as ethical reflection. Accordingly, the law came to play an increasingly important part in moral thought. For instance, in the imagined discussion about truthfulness in advertising, someone making exaggerated claims for a product might argue in her defence that she is not breaking the law, or that she is prepared to be guided by the same legal constraints to which her competitors must also conform, or that she is willing to pay any penalty as required by law, if her advertisements are found to violate the required standards. The ethical reflection on such a moral discussion might then be an exploration of what the relevant laws should be, or more abstractly, what the bases and criteria for deciding on the law ought to be. Indeed, some philosophers maintain that the main task of ethics is the justification of norms or laws. Accordingly, elaborate theories are generated to provide for the required justification, and the literature invariably presents competing theories. The most familiar juxtaposition is that between theories of a consequentialist nature, on the one hand, such as the Utilitarianism of Bentham or Mill, which focus on the consequences of action, and deontological theories on the other hand, such as the thought of Kant, or analyses of human rights, which account for the sense of obligation to do what is known to be right, regardless of consequences, whether punishments or rewards. This polarisation between the two types of theories, and there are several versions of both kinds, is reproduced in manuals of applied ethics, such as business ethics. One reason why this debate seems so endless is that it is deprived of the resources of a more comprehensive ethics which would also include a consideration of the good.

Direction 3: the good guy: virtue and character

The history of ethics shows that while the justification of norms might be dominant in the literature today, other concerns have dominated in other periods. The fact that certain questions are not popular now does not mean that they are not real questions. Accordingly, a complete ethics will include questions about the human good, both in the sense of the purposes and goals of human action, and in the sense of the goodness of the human agent, as well as questions about the rules to be followed. The goodness of human agents is examined in virtue ethics, virtues being the acquired qualities of human characters, which equip them for the good life. And if living well means living in accordance with a valid and justified set of norms, then virtues are the qualities of character whereby people's behaviour exhibits conformity to rules. The just person is one who possesses the qualities of character whereby she spontaneously treats others justly, and so her behaviour is intelligible and predictable. It appears as consistent with the rules which specify what is just.

A comprehensive ethical reflection will include three elements, a theory of the virtues, a theory of the good (values) and a theory of rules or norms. The same arrangement of topics might be expected to recur in a comprehensive business ethic. The relevant theory of the good would explore the full range of goods to be realised in business activity. Neglect of this set of questions allows the accountant's view of business in terms of a balance sheet to dominate in discussions of business ethics. The range of goods and services which are produced and traded is enormous and growing, and it can be so self-evidently intrinsic to business that it is taken for granted. However, attention to this area is essential for appreciation of the human context in which business activity is located. Ethics as reflection I have characterised as talk about talk about the good. In this realm of ethics we reflect on what is spoken about spontaneously by people who in their business activities make assessments and evaluations of what is worthwhile and worth pursuing.

The same comment applies to the element of virtue ethics in business ethics. Who are the characters that in our society are considered to be good business people? What are the qualities of character which earn them this respect and recognition? Is it ingenuity, creativity, courage in risk taking, qualities of leadership, forcefulness in argument, ability to deal with a wide range of personalities? Or is it deceitfulness, dishonesty and the cleverness which enables this to be concealed, foolhardiness, aggressive behaviour towards competitors and employees? How might these features be analysed in terms of a broader understanding of the human person? Plato in *The Republic* has already shown how these evaluations of character depend on the shared assumptions in a society. Aristotle too argues along these lines when he correlates the good citizen with the corresponding constitution. And while a man may achieve greatness in his own city, the constitution in terms of which his greatness is measured may be fundamentally flawed, for instance, by its disregard for some essential human quality such as learning. The best citizen will be the best person in the city with the best constitution. Similarly, the best business person will be the one who stands out, not simply in the opinion of her peers in her own milieu, but in terms of the highest standards. Ethical reflection in this domain explores those standards. And so it might entail, not simply an evaluation of the performance of the salesperson according to established standards, but also an evaluation of the adequacy and appropriateness of the operative standards.

TO ACT WELL, OR NOT TO DO WRONG?

Concern about the best and the desire to be as good as the best are notably different from the minimalist mentality associated with the law. Typically, the law determines a minimum standard of behaviour below which participants in social activity should not fall. The law establishes a minimum standard for truth-telling in advertising, for protection of employees' rights, for consumer protection, and so on. Far from being able to ensure the protection of the natural environment, for instance, the law can only threaten with sanctions those who fail to conform to certain specific restrictions. And yet, because there are costs associated with the protection of consumers' and employees' rights, and with the provision of humane working environments and environmental protection, participants in business are concerned that they are not unfairly disadvantaged by assuming such costs when their competitors do not. And so there is considerable interest in determining what the minimum standards should be to which all participants conform. This can be a big part of the agenda of ethics.

NO-ENTRY SIGNS

I described this brief reflection as outlining a street map to indicate the directions in which ethical discussions might take us. There are three main directions opening up, which lead us into a reflection on the good and on value, a reflection on the norms and rules to guide our action, and a reflection on the qualities of good people. It is evident that these directions are complementary, and that a discussion which explores in one direction may find itself having to move into another. And while philosophy might be of assistance in offering helpful distinctions and clarifications, it can also be of use in challenging invalid no-entry signs. By that I mean that dialogue is often suppressed because someone says 'there's no point in bringing that up because we'll never agree on it'. Or possibly interesting areas of exploration are decreed out of bounds because some people would be uncomfortable with them. By calling into question the operative assumptions which block exploration we can liberate the dialogue and create greater possibilities for discovery and agreement. Unfortunately, such no-entry signs are to be found within the literature on ethics. One such is often posted in front of the concept of human nature. In exploring the question of the human good, what is good for people and what might constitute human happiness and fulfilment, we inevitably encounter the question whether there is some good appropriate for all human beings, insofar as they are human, having the same nature. This ancient question can be formulated as the question whether everything is conventional. The no-entry sign blocks discussion when someone asserts that everything is relative. It is said that the good and the right and the virtuous are understood differently in different cultures and at different times, so that the Australian Aborigine will think differently from the Irish Presbyterian. The popular current form of this remark goes under the heading of postmodernism. The complexity of the question and the difficulty in handling it properly should not allow a too hasty generalisation which effectively prohibits further discussion. It is legitimate to explore what I have in common with those men and women who are only known to me from media reports on their suffering or from TV programmes about their threatened culture.

Another dangerous block to dialogue is the related assumption that agreement is impossible. This no-entry sign diverts energy from reflection and discussion, and from the careful search for mutual understanding. The energy is diverted into dangerous channels. If discussion is pointless, since agreement is thought to be impossible, then people will seek other ways of protecting their interests, and so will seek for leverage in the power plays of the market or of politics. Then discussion and argument are abandoned; they are replaced at best by bargaining, and at worst by the blatant use of power to impose the will of the strong on the weak.

This last concern remains a perennial motivation to engage in ethics as reflection on morality. Engaged by the sense that I am obliged to give others what is due to them, I must think about the good and the bad that result from the activities in which I participate, I must examine the rules to which I expect others to conform, and I must be critical in evaluating the people of my world as good and bad. I owe it to them that I know what I'm talking about. And I owe it to them to do my best to ensure that we continue to talk, because the alternatives are too horrendous.

18 Of Natural Law or Reasonable Action[1]

Garrett Barden

(*Milltown Studies,* 56 (2005), pp. 71–86.)

In 'The Development of Moral Theology since the Second Vatican Council'[2] Joseph Selling, referring to the encyclical *Humanae vitae* and to the possibility of drawing 'moral conclusions based upon natural law arguments',[3] writes that 'moral *philosophers* who apparently felt the need to spring to the defense of the papal teaching, gave a resurgence to natural law thinking and the idea that morality was primarily about following norms and precepts'.[4] To allow him to develop his own position on the nature of morality he opposes this position even if, near the close of his article, he writes that 'we *have to* have two different perspectives in order to cover the entire field, because ethical discourse is fundamentally polar – that is, we are always trying to say two, different things at the same time'.[5]

Here I suggest that natural law theory as expounded by St Thomas in the *Contra Gentiles,* upon which I concentrate, and in the *Summa Theologiae* is not what Professor Selling thinks of as natural law.[6] It is true that there is a single theory neither of natural law nor of the naturally just.[7] Whether or not the natural law theory espoused by the writers referred to in his article is accurately presented is not here in question.

It is important to keep in mind that St Thomas's account of natural law is a theorem within his entire account of human action and his discussion of it should not be read, and will not be understood, in isolation from that account.

Professor Selling suggests that the writers he refers to 'gave resurgence to natural law thinking and the idea that morality was primarily about following norms and precepts'.[8] The expression is ambiguous. Is the claim that the writers did two things, namely (1) give a resurgence to natural law thinking, and (2) give a resurgence to the idea that morality was primarily about following norms and precepts? Or did they do only one thing, namely, give a resurgence to natural law thinking, that is, to the idea that morality was about following norms and precepts? The article as a whole seems to support the second reading.

I shall suggest that the idea that morality is primarily about following norms and precepts is very precisely and explicitly what St Thomas's theory of morality and of natural law is not. Chapter 129 of the third book of the *Contra Gentiles* is written in opposition to that moral theory. The title of this chapter is: 'That in the domain of human action some things are naturally right, that is, right in themselves and not simply owing to a positive law'.[9]

The question to which classical natural law theory is an answer is this: is it ever possible to discover whether or not a proposed course of action is good or reasonable without referring either to an established (positive) law or to an agreement?[10] Classical natural law theorists including Plato, Aristotle, Cicero and St Thomas assert that it is possible. So, indeed, do modern natural rights theories, however different are their arguments. The opposing theories, for there are several, commonly referred to as conventionalism or as positivism, assert that it is not.

St Thomas's context differs from his pre-Christian predecessors, including Aristotle to whom he is very close, in that he is a Christian theologian. From this difference flow two important consequences. First, his effort is to understand reasonable action in relation to God; and this because theology is for him the study of God and of other things in as much as they are ordered to God as to principle and end.[11] Second, because belief in a divine law revealed to Moses was part of the contemporary Christian tradition, his enquiry includes a discussion of this law, and primarily of the Ten Commandments or, as they are sometimes called, the Ten Words.[12]

In the two books of the Torah in which the story of the giving of the Ten Words to Moses appears, God is presented as lawgiver and so, in the Christian and Jewish traditions, these very basic, and for the most part very obvious, words of Yahweh are presented as precepts, commands, posited (positive) laws. This fact led easily to the question as to whether the acts commanded or prohibited in the laws given to Moses were good or bad because God had commanded or prohibited them (and thus indifferent in themselves) or were commanded or prohibited by God because they were good or bad in themselves. St Thomas's position was nuanced. He thought that, for example, the prohibition against graven images or the requirement to keep holy the Sabbath were bad or good because God had commanded them and, in both cases, could properly be, as they in fact had been, abandoned by Christians.[13] He did not, on the other hand, think that they had been prohibited or commanded irrationally and capriciously. The Golden Calf was a reminder that a graven image can become an idol to be worshipped. In the texts, whether originally or by later editors, a reason why the Sabbath should be kept holy is given. In Christianity, the day on which Christ rose from the dead is substituted for the Sabbath day upon which the work of creation was completed; common to both is the underlying precept the God should be worshipped which, for St Thomas, has its source in the actual, that is, natural, relation between Creator and reasonable creature; which natural relation includes the fact that human happiness is found only in God.[14] It must be perfectly obvious that we do not automatically know this; what is naturally so, is not

An Irish Reader in Moral Theology

necessarily automatically known; what is naturally good is not automatically known. What is good must be discovered. It is not easy to discover for we are fallible, biased and selfish.

In another approach to the way of thinking about God and, consequently, another way of thinking about human action, or morality, is to consider that for God everything, except contradiction, is possible and so to suppose that God simply decides what is good or evil, right or wrong, and could have decided otherwise. This is the Occamian position, the early modern, as distinct from the ancient, source of positivism: the idea that law is command and that the legitimate ruler's will determines the moral character of what is commanded. The good is what the ruler commands. Morality and positive law become identical. Morality becomes the following of norms and precepts; the basic moral precept, the axiom from which morality flows – and notice that it is an axiom, as Hans Kelsen acknowledges in his *Pure Theory of Law* – becomes: obey the law.[15]

William of Occam found support for his position in several stories in the Torah, perhaps most notably in the story of Abraham and Isaac told in the twenty-second chapter of *Bereshit* (Genesis) when Abraham is commanded to sacrifice his son.[16] Both he and St Thomas agreed that God could not command what was evil. Therefore, according to Occam, for Abraham to kill Isaac was good, because God had commanded him to do so. It would seem, therefore, that natural law is fundamentally changeable depending only on God's will. St Thomas's attempt to deal with the issue is found in the answer to the second objection in *Summa Theologiae*, Ia IIae, Q.94, article 5. It is clear that he does not think that God's command makes murder right; he thinks rather that God's command makes killing Isaac not murder and so, *mutatis mutandis*, for the other cases.

It is beyond doubt that St Thomas thought that most of the provisions of the divine law were commands or prohibitions enjoining actions that were in themselves good or right, and forbidding actions that were in themselves bad or wrong. This is assumed, and illuminates, his discussion, in chapter 128 of book III of *Contra Gentiles*,[17] as to how humans are ordered to one another according to the law of God, the law revealed to Moses.

In the first paragraph he writes:

From what has been said earlier it is clear that according to the divine law a person is led to follow a reasonable ordering of those things for which he can be responsible. Among those things for which one can be responsible are especially other people. Man is naturally a social animal who needs from others what alone he cannot provide. It is, accordingly, suitable that humans should be required by the divine law to be reasonably ordered towards one another.[18]

This is a rich paragraph and, despite the fact that St Thomas is writing of divine law, that is, of a set of commands revealed to Moses, it is perfectly clear that his conception of human action is far from a concept of morality as obedience to given norms and precepts. The basic feature of natural law in humans is that we, who are naturally social animals, are responsible for how we live and what we do. Natural law as it exists in animals or plants is different to the extent that they are not responsible for themselves.[19] It is natural to humans to be responsible for themselves, to discover intelligently, to judge reasonably, and to decide responsibly how they are to be. But reasonableness and responsibility are constant demands rather than constant achievements.[20] This is, in one sense of the term, a natural law although in no sense whatsoever a command. We must live in society; it is natural for us to do so. There is no vestige in St Thomas, as there was not in Aristotle, of society as the result of a contract between formerly isolated individuals. The question in chapter 128 therefore is this: how does the revealed divine law show the proper ordering of humans, who are naturally reasonable, naturally responsible and naturally social, among themselves?

Before discussing the commandments that order humans among themselves as distinct from those that order humans to God, St Thomas suggests that the good social order requires peace between those who live together. That humans are social animals is natural and unavoidable, that humans live together peacefully or, quoting St Augustine, in ordered concord, is by no means unavoidable but is the fruit of human decisions. A peaceful order is one within which each can pursue his goals without impeding others in the pursuit of theirs – which, when one reflects upon it, indicates the goals that one may properly have. A peaceful social order is the common good.[21] In passing, it is worth recalling that Thomas Hobbes, however different his political thought is from St Thomas's, considered 'the first, and Fundamentall Law of Nature [to be] *to seek Peace, and follow it*'.[22] Hobbes' natural condition is an imaginary world in which humans live in 'a time of Warre, where every man is Enemy to every man'.[23] Each seeks his own desire without reference to, or care for the desires of others, and everyone constantly impedes everyone. Hobbes' 'naturall condition' may be imaginary; although he thought that societies tended to it in civil war. St Thomas does not imagine such an original condition but, in actual human societies, there is the inevitable and constant danger of collapse into something like it. And the inevitable and constant source of that danger is the temptation to take one's own immediate interest as paramount, overriding the interests of others.

St Thomas understands these precepts of the Decalogue as indicating, and, since they are the law of God, also commanding, the kind of actions that maintain peace. Underlying them is the principle: take others' interests into account; that is, love one's neighbour as oneself. Why one should consider others' interests; why one should not take one's own as paramount is a question to which St Thomas returns in the final paragraph of the chapter.

First, however, he turns to those commandments in the Decalogue that look to our relations with one another.[24] For there to be concord between us 'each is to have what is his own; this is justice and so it is said (Isaiah, ch. 32, 17): *The work of justice is peace.*' Hence the precept against stealing. Adults commonly owe more to their parents than to anyone else. Hence the precept to honour one's parents, which St Thomas quite explicitly takes to be a special case of justice. There follow precepts showing how not to injure others. Hence the precepts against killing, adultery, stealing and bearing false witness. Finally, 'because God is judge even of our hearts' and lest 'we offend others in our hearts', there is the precept against coveting others' wives or goods. This last precept refers to an habitual and distorted attitude, that is, to a vice or source of distorted actions.[25] What is here forbidden is an attitude that disregards others' interests. In passing it may be said that when the synoptic gospels answer the question as to what one is to do to inherit eternal life, they give these precepts; but these are by no means 'a random list of Jewish prescriptions'.[26] St Matthew includes the command from *Wayiqra?* (Leviticus) (19:18): 'love your neighbour as yourself' which St Thomas makes the centre of his discussion as to why one would consider others' interests.[27]

St Thomas' discussion of these commandments is plainly from the point of view of justice and what is just.[28] Justice is for him the core virtue that sustains human society in peace and concord. Almost precisely five centuries later Adam Smith echoed the same thought when in *The Theory of Moral Sentiments* he wrote that 'Society may subsist, though not in the most comfortable state, without beneficence; but the prevalence of injustice must utterly destroy it'.[29]

There are, as everyone knows, many other precepts in the Torah. In the index of any good concordance under the word 'neighbour' one will find many others that have to do with justice,[30] for instance, in *Devarim* (Deuteronomy) (19:14) we find: 'You must not displace your neighbour's boundary mark, set by your forbears, in the inheritance you receive in the land Yahweh is giving into your possession.' Why not? To anyone who knows anything about a settled agricultural community, it is so obvious that the question seems distinctly odd. Is it not perfectly clear that wholesale displacement of boundary marks would lead to constant social unrest and, as happens, bitter litigation. Why did St Thomas consider the precepts of the Decalogue rather than this one? No doubt because the Decalogue, having been central in the Torah, had become central within Christianity. However the revelation of the Decalogue is understood, its precepts did not become central capriciously. They are both fundamental and ordinary. It is difficult to imagine any society without some version of them.[31] They are fairly commonplace and basic principles from which other more specific principles may be 'derived' or 'deduced' – I put inverted commas around these terms to indicate that when St Thomas uses them in this connection as he does in the discussion of law in the *Summa Theologiae* he does not use them as terms of a formal logic. To displace one's neighbour's boundary mark, for example, is a special case of theft, and a rule against it a special case of the rule against theft.

In the concluding paragraph of chapter 128 St Thomas takes up the question as to why one would want to be just. The question is why one '*would want to be*', not why one '*should be or ought to be*'. One may be just for one of two reasons – and perhaps in practice for a mixture of both. First, internally. Second, externally.

A person is just for internal reasons when he willingly does what is just; willingly does not steal, does not commit adultery and so on. 'The virtue of justice is the constant and enduring willingness to give to each what is due.'[32] But why would one try to attain this virtue? Why would one want to be just? St Thomas's answer is unequivocal: a person willingly observes the rules of justice, does what is just, is just, because he loves God and his neighbour and 'whosoever loves someone, spontaneously and with delight, gives what is due and even liberally more than what is due; hence the fulfilment of the entire law depends on love, as the Apostle has it: *love is the fulfilling of the law* (Rom 13:10); and the Lord says that o*n these two commandments*, namely on the love of God and one's neighbour, *hangs the whole law* (Mt 22:40)'.[33]

A person observes the rules of justice for external reasons – he *does* what is just, yet *is* not just[34] – when he is not internally disposed to be just, when he does not act justly spontaneously, but rather 'when he observes the rule and does the just thing out of fear of punishment. He fulfills the law not freely but in a servile manner; hence it is said (Isa 26:9): *for when thy judgements are made in the earth* – that is, when the wicked are punished – the inhabitants of the world will learn justice'.[35]

Those who observe the law from the internal reason: 'are the law for themselves, having love, which, in place of law, moves them and leads them to act freely. For such it was not necessary to impose an external law; hence it is said: *Law is not made for the just but for the unjust.* (1 Tim 1:9). This is not to be understood, as some have wrongly understood it, as if the just were not held to fulfill the law; but that these were moved by themselves to do what is just, even without the law.'[36] Here it is clear that love of one's neighbour not only inclines one freely to do what is just once what justice demands has been discovered but also so illuminates the situation that one is more likely to make the discovery in the first place.

In summary, St Thomas, in chapter 128, holds (1) that humans are social animals, (2) that internal peace is essential if a society is to survive, (3) that internal peace is the fruit of reasonable judgement and responsible decision, (4) the internal peace cannot be had unless most people freely act justly, (5) that the divine law commands those very fundamental actions that yield justice and prohibits those very fundamental actions that undermine it, (6) that the reason why people would freely follow the commandments is that they care for their neighbours' interests and thus love their neighbours as themselves, (7) that those who do not care for their neighbours' interests but make their own interests paramount do what is just merely out of fear and so act in a servile manner, and (8) that the coercive law exists to attempt to compel such to do what is just and to punish them when they fail to do so. Of these eight features, seven are explicit. The fourth is, I think, implicitly taken for granted. Certainly, a society in which most people most of the time acted justly only under compulsion would soon collapse.[37]

In chapter 129, he asks if some actions, including these provisions of the Decalogue, are naturally right or right only because commanded. He gives seven arguments to support the position that some actions are naturally right and to oppose the position that all actions are right and just only because commanded. He gives examples of actions that he considers to be naturally good; but he does not give either here or in the *Summa Theologiae,* a list of provisions of a supposed natural law conceived as a modern code or set of statutes enacted by the appropriate legislature. I shall refer to only one of his arguments but each is worth reading since they are not merely variations of one another.

In his third argument St Thomas holds that something is natural to a thing if the thing could not be without it. Humans are naturally social; this is shown by the fact that 'one man alone cannot provide all that is needed for human life'.[38] Notice that the fact that we are social animals is not understood to be an axiom or postulate; it is a justified empirical proposition, an hypothesis for which there is sufficient evidence. Because humans cannot live entirely by their own resources, those things 'without which human society cannot be sustained are naturally appropriate to us'. These things include: 'that each have what is his and that we abstain from being unjust to another.[39] Therefore, there are actions that are naturally right.'

The actions that are naturally right and just[40] are not right and just in some abstract universe but in human society which they tend to sustain.[41] And they are right and just precisely because they tend to sustain society which is the environment within which we live and outside which we cannot live. Human society can, of course, survive some injustice – precisely how much cannot be told in advance – but no human society can survive unlimited injustice. There will be unjust people, some of whom may be successfully compelled to do what is just, some of whom will be punished when they have been discovered to have acted unjustly, but no society can survive an indefinitely large number of such people. Most people, most of the time must freely act justly – that is, most people, on most occasions must care for their neighbours' interests. The common good is what is brought about when people act justly. But why on a particular occasion should I act justly when it is to my immediate benefit to act unjustly? Why if I see someone drop a €500 note without noticing: will I give it to him even though I feel it is to my immediate benefit to keep it? The answer is that which St Thomas gives in chapter 128: either because for some reason I am afraid not to do so, in which case I do what is just but in a servile way, or because I consider (1) that it belongs to him, and (2) that what belongs to him he should have[42] and (3) that I care for his interest and do not consider that my own must always prevail, that is, I love my neighbour as myself.[43] To act well freely, all three of these must be present. Without the first, I would not know to whom the money belonged; without the second, no question of giving the money to whom it belonged would arise; without the third, I would not give the money to its owner.

Thus, in St Thomas's account of knowing and doing what is naturally right, reasonable judgement evokes but does not determine responsible decision. St Thomas's theory of natural law is that it is sometimes possible to know what is right and just by examining the situation in which we find ourselves and that what is right and just is not determined only by positive law. The motive of right action is love. We cannot act rightly and justly – except by happy accident and then we simply do the just thing[44] – unless we know what is right and just in the situation in which we find ourselves, and we will not do so freely unless we love our neighbour as ourselves. There is no theoretical opposition between these.[45]

Finally, we cannot avoid deliberate action, we cannot avoid choosing what seems good to us, what seems valuable. We cannot, therefore, avoid trying to discover what is good. But it is we who enquire as to what is to be done, we who discover what seems good to us, we who decide. And what will seem good to us depends on what we have become, on how we see things, on how we feel about ourselves and others. Accordingly, one whose effective and affective[46] orientation is always to ignore others' interests in favour of his own advantage will find valuable what one whose effective and affective orientation is to take account of others' interests will find valueless. The choice is between taking account of others' interests and allowing one's own absolute primacy; between supporting society and subverting it. Thus, the choice between these orientations is the fundamental moral choice.[47] There remains the further question as to the mysterious presence and nature of God's action in human choice; hence St Thomas's account of law in the *Summa Theologiae* is immediately followed by his account of grace.[48]

NOTES

1   I am indebted to Professors David O'Mahony and Raymond Moloney SJ for their kind assistance. Inadequacies are mine.

2   *Milltown Studies*, 54 (2004), pp. 104–121.

3   Ibid, p. 110.

4   Ibid loc.cit.

5   Ibid, p. 120.

6   *Contra Gentiles*, III, CXXIX; *Summa Theologiae*, Ia IIae QQ. 90–100; especially Q. 94 and, on natural just, IIa IIae, QQ. 57–61; Q. 120; especially Q. 57. See also *In Decem Libros Ethicorum Aristotelis ad Nicomachum expositio*, Book V, especially Lectio XII.

7   In the *Summa Theologiae* St Thomas's account of natural law is within the set of questions on law at IaIae, QQ.90–108 and of what is naturally just within the set of question on the just

at IIaIIæ, QQ. 57–62. Michel Villey, who is at pains to distinguish natural law (*lex naturalis, loi naturelle*) from natural justice (*jus naturale; droit naturel*) and who concentrates on the latter, writes of classical and modern natural justice. His discussion illuminates a similar distinction between classical and modern accounts of natural law. See, for example, *Leçons d'Histoire de le Philosophie de Droit*, Dalloz, Paris, 1962 and *Seize Essais de Philosophie de Droit*, Dalloz, Paris, 1969. See also his article 'Le Positivisme Juridique Moderne et le Christianisme' in Luigi Lombardi Vallauri and Gerhard Dilcher (eds), *Christianismo Secollarizzasione e Diritto Moderno*, Nomos Verlagsgeselschaft, Baden-Baden and Giuffrè Editore, Milan, n.d., pp. 119–215; *Questions de Saint Thomas sur le droit et la politique*, PUF, Paris, 1987. The distinction between classical and modern theories of natural law and natural justices is that classical theory emphasises the jural relation between people within society while modern theory emphasises subjective rights. That some early writers were to an extent subjectivist is suggested by Brian Tierney in his, *The Idea of Natural Rights*, Edermans, 2001. See the review by David Gordon (*The Mises Review*, The Ludwig von Mises Institute, Alabama, Vol. 11. No. 2, 2005) of Roberto Modugno's selection and translation of essays by Murray Rothbard in her *Diritto,natura e ragione: scritti inediti versus Hayek, Mises, Strauss e Polanyi*, Rubettino, 2005. See also Richard Tuck, *Natural Rights Theories*, Cambridge UP, 1979. See Garrett Barden, 'Two Versions of Natural Justice' in Quinn, Ingram and Livingstone (eds), *Justice and Legal Theory in Ireland*, Oak Tree Press, Dublin, 1995, chapter 3.

8   Ibid, p. 110

9   My translation is not literal. The Latin reads: Quod in actibus humanis sunt aliqua recta secundum naturam, et non solum quasi lege posita. A more literal translation is: That in human acts some things are right according to nature and not only as it were by a posited law. See also, *Summa Theologiae*, IIaIIae, Q.57, art.4

10   It is, of course, not always possible. In some quite common situations the good action, although not arbitrary, is determined by agreement, e.g. the date upon which a loan is to be repaid.

11   *Summa Theologiae*, I.Q.1.article 7: 'Omnia autem pertractantur in sacra doctrina sub ratione Dei: vel quia sunt ipse Deus; vel quia habent ordinem ad Deum, ut ad principium et finem.'

12   See, for example, *Shemot* (Exodus), 34:28.

13   But not by all Christians; not by the Iconoclasts and, later, not by the Puritans.

14   Ibid. IaIIae, Q.2. art.8.

15   Kelsen is, of course, writing of metropolitan or civil law (roughly, what St Thomas calls 'human law' (*Summa Theologiae*, IaIIae,Q.91, art.3 and Q.95, *passim*), allowing for considerable differences in the importance of statute and legislation. See Hans Kelsen, *Reine Rechtslehre*, Deutike, Vienna, 1934 and 1960. *Pure Theory of Law*, University of California Press, 1967 is a translation of the 1960 edition. Particularly in Latin America, 'he was hailed as the defender of a nonidiological treatment of law against natural law theory'. Entry under Kelsen in Gray (ed.), *The Philosophy of Law: an Encyclopedia*, New York and London: Garland, 1999, Vol. II, pp. 477–80.

16   St Thomas (*Sum.Theol.* IaIIae, Q.94, 2nd objection) refers to two others: the Israelites' plundering of the Egyptians told in (Exodus) 12, 35ff and God's command to Hosea to marry a whore told in Hosea 1:2ff.

17   *Contra Gent.* Book III, Chapter CXXVIII. 'Quomodo secundum legem Dei homo ad proximum ordinatur.'

18   Once again my translation is not literal and the reader is recommended to consult the original.

19   See the second and third objections and their answers in *Sum. Theol.* IaIIae, Q.91, art.2.

20   See Bernard Lonergan SJ, *Method in Theology*, London: Darton, Longman & Todd Ltd., 1972 chs. 1 and 2.

21   The good social order, the common good, is not the result of legislative command or set of commands. It is not an organisation. The order emerges between people who act well together. See David O'Mahony, 'The Market: a social order', *Milltown Studies*, Nos. 59–60 (Summer/Winter, 2007), pp. 45–64 and F.A. von Hayek, *The Constitution of Liberty*, London: Routledge & Kegan Paul Ltd., 1990, *passim* but especially chapter 10. The common good is sometimes imagined as an aim or goal common to everyone; St Thomas's example

of victory being the goal common to all the soldiers in an army can mislead and must be read in the context of this and the second paragraph of chapter 128 where being ordered to God is said to be the goal common to all humans. But see his treatment in the *Summa Theologiae*, IaIIae, q.90, art.2, where he writes that law looks to the order of communal happiness: 'necesse est quod lex proprie respiciat ordinem ad felicitatem communem.' See also his discussion of the precepts of the old law in q.99. Think of the development of the idea of nuisance in the common law. Consult Patrick Riordan SJ, *A Politics of the Common Good*, IPA, Dublin, 1996; particularly his distinction between two assumptions: first, the interest common to players on the same team in a competitive game which is to win and, second, the common good of all the competitors that the game be fairly played (pp. 18–19). Notice that the desire to win may easily, and often does, undermine a player's commitment to the common good. See also the discussion of MacIntyre's distinction between the common good and public interest, i.e. 'reasons of state' in chapter 4.

22   Hobbes, Thomas: *Leviathan*, Part I, ch. 14

23   Hobbes, op. cit., Part I, ch. 13

24   In this paragraph all quotations, unless otherwise stated, are from the *Summa Contra Gentiles*, Bk. III, ch. CXXVIII.

25   A vice is an habitual attitude or disposition that is the source of evil actions, in contrast with a virtue which is an habitual attitude or disposition that is the source of good actions. Hence, the definition of the virtue of justice in Roman Law as 'the constant and enduring [that is, habitual] will to render to each his due'. *Institutes*, Lib.I, Title I, preamble. St Thomas's discussion of this definition is in the *Summa Theologiae*, IIaIIae, Q.58, art.1.

26   Selling, op. cit., p. 116

27   St Thomas's idea of the place of love in decision is investigated in Michael Sherwin OP, *By Knowledge and by Love*, Catholic University of America Press, 2005 and by Edward Collins Vacek in 'Passions and Principles', *Milltown Studies*, 52, Winter 2003, pp. 67–94.

28   This perspective is similar to Aristotle's in book five of his *Nicomachean Ethics*, at 1129b.26 where one sense of 'justice' is said to be 'virtue in relation to our neighbour'. See St Thomas commentary, V.II.906. St Thomas refers to the commandments that order our relations with one another as *praecepta iudicialia* (precepts having to do with what is just) in the *Summa Theologiae*, IaIIae, Q.99, art.4.

29   Adam Smith, *The Theory of Moral Sentiments* (orig. 1759), Oxford: Clarendon Press, 1991 edition, II.ii.I.9, p. 82.

30   In the *Concordance de la Bible de Jérusalem*, Cerf Brepols, Paris and Turnhout, 1982, p. 903, there are one hundred and seven entries under 'prochain' (neighbour), ninety-two from the Torah, most of which determine what in certain kinds of cases is just.

31   See Garrett Barden, 'Of the Naturally and Conventionally Just' in Tim Murphy (ed.), *Western Jurisprudence*, Dublin: Thomson Round Hall, 2004, pp.17–73, especially the section on the Decalogue, pp. 35–41. The question as to why there was a need for a law revealed to Moses is raised in the *Summa Theologiae*, IaIIae, Q.91, art.4.

32   *Institutes of Justinian*, I.I. preamble and *Digest*, i.1.10

33   *Contra Gentes*, III, CXXVIII. The demand others place upon us is the central theme of both Buber and Levinas.

34   Here he follows Aristotle who makes the same distinction between doing what is just in a servile manner, so to speak, unwillingly, out of fear or shame and the like and being just, that is, acting from within oneself as one with the virtue of justice. See Aristotle, *Nicomachean Ethics*, V.1135b5. Hence, in Roman Law, the emphasis on willingness in the definition quoted in footnote 28. Hence, too, St Thomas, who learned from, and often agreed with, both Aristotle and Roman Law.

35   Ibid. loc.cit.

36   Ibid. loc.cit. It is not easy to find a good English translation of 'sibi ipsi sunt lex'. I have given 'are the law for themselves' which is literal but not immediately clear. The idea, however, is clear. Those who love their neighbours, and act reasonably and responsibly will discover fallibly, and willingly accomplish what is just. Mistakes are inevitable but we can do no better than act as we think best.

37 See Garrett Barden, *Essays on a Philosophical Interpretation of Justice the Virtue of Justice*, Lampeter: Mellen, chapter 6: 'Justice in a Spontaneous Order'.

38 The references to the *Contra Gentes* in this paragraph are to Book III, Chapter CXXIX.

39 This may be translated as 'refrain from injuring another'. The Latin is 'injuria' which comes from 'jus' and a person's 'jus' is what is due to him. Compare Justinian's *Institutes*, Book I.Title I.3: 'The precepts of justice are these: live honestly, do not harm another, render to each what is his.'

40 In the final paragraph of this chapter, St Thomas associates the two.

41 The St Thomas thought that the good is to be discovered in the situation in which one finds oneself is clear from his discussion of *Epieikeia* in *Summa Theologiae*, IIaIae, Q.120, and in his commentary on Aristotle's *Nicomachean Ethics*, V.lectio 16. There are two senses in which the general rule that what someone owns is to be restored to him when he wants it, is not absolute; first, it is emergent within human society and, secondly, there are social situations when it is not to be applied literally; in one of St Thomas's examples, it is not good to restore his sword to someone maddened by rage. See Garrett Barden, 'Aristotle's Notion of *Epieikeia*' in Matthew Lamb (ed.), *Creativity and Method*, Milwaukee: Marquette UP, 1981, pp. 353–69.

42 That a person should have what belongs to him is what 'to belong to' means. There is no question here of deriving 'ought' from 'is'.

43 See Garrett Barden, op. cit., chapter 5.

44 See footnote 28 above. For example, Peter, thinking a painting to be a forgery, might sell it to Paul as genuine. If the painting turned out to be genuine, Peter would have done the just thing but would not have acted justly.

45 Cf. Bernard Lonergan, SJ, op. cit. loc.cit. And St Thomas *Summa Theologiae*, IaIIae, Q.13, art.1

46 On affectivity and choice see Edward Collins Vacek, 'Passions and Principles' in *Milltown Studies*, Dublin, No. 52, Winter 2003, pp. 67–94.

47 For a fuller analysis of this choice see my *Essays on a Philosophical Interpretation of Justice: The Virtue of Justice*, Lampeter: Mellen, 1999, ch. 9, 'Why be just?' and Garrett Barden, *After Principles*, Notre Dame: Notre Dame UP, 1990, Chs. 7–9. See also especially the chapter on the human good in Bernard Lonergan's *Method in Theology*, London: DLT, 1972 and note the place of love in the whole work.

48 Consider in particular the difficult question (addressed in the *Summa Theologiae*, Q.109, art.2) as to whether humans can, will, and do, what is good without grace.

19 Virtue Ethics and Christian Moral Reflection

James G. Murphy

(*Milltown Studies*, 55, Summer 2005, pp. 82–112.)

This essay makes two claims: (1) virtue ethics (henceforth abbreviated to VE) has substantial advantages over other systems of normative ethics, and (2) Christian ethicists would do well to use it. Since the first claim has been advanced by many in the last two decades, particularly in North America, I shall do little more than summarise what others have developed. On the other hand its impact in Britain and Ireland has been slight, so I hope this article will help to draw attention to it.

This essay does not offer a comprehensive ethical theory. Such a theory would have to include a theory of the Good (values) and a theory of the Right (norms and rules for action), as well as a theory of the virtues.[1] Nor do I provide a comprehensive theory of the virtues. My goal is to introduce VE, (a) drawing attention to some of its strengths, (b) suggesting that the good cannot be specified without giving due weight to the virtues as a constitutive part of human flourishing, (c) arguing that VE provides insights into how to develop norms for the assessment of action, and (d) proposing it as relevant to the Christian moralist's task of helping the Church grow in moral life and reflection.

VE derives from classical Greek philosophy, and has been enjoying a revival since 1980. Of the earlier works, Alasdair MacIntyre's *After Virtue* (1981) is probably best known, although the first shot was fired by Elizabeth Anscombe in her 'Modern Moral Philosophy' (1958). Peter Geach's *The Virtues* (1977) and Philippa Foot's *Virtues and Vices* (1978) were also significant. While many versions are Aristotelian in inspiration, there are modern versions based upon Hume, Martineau, Nietzsche, and others.[2]

VE is a normative ethic, giving a distinctive type of answer to questions about the Good (what is of value, what constitutes human well-being) and the Right (how to behave). The other normative systems are deontologism and utilitarianism, offering competing answers to those issues.[3] All ethical systems evaluate (1) acts, (2) outcomes (states of affairs), and (3) character and character traits, as reflected in motives, emotions, attitudes, beliefs and actions. What distinguishes one ethical system from another is which of (1)–(3) it takes to be the key category for ethical evaluation. For deontologism it is acts, for utilitarianism it is outcomes, while VE takes character.

While VE is treated today in undergraduate courses on ethical systems, it is not clear that most students understand it by the end of the course. As Henry Sidgwick, the most perceptive nineteenth century utilitarian, noted, the common-sense morality of ordinary people is explicitly duty-oriented (deontologist) and implicitly utilitarian, so that they tend to see morality as about actions and outcomes: about doing the right thing and making the world a better place.[4] In addition, the universal currency of deontologism's rights-and-duties language makes non-duty systems seem alien. Today, it takes quite a mental shift to reflect consciously, let alone react instinctively, in virtue-ethical ways.

THE HISTORICAL CONTEXT

How did western society get to the point where talk about character traits had become marginal and talk about virtues positively alien? The causes are multiple, some going back centuries, some of recent vintage.

One of the more remote causes has been the dominance of the Judeo-Christian ethic. Unlike Buddhism, it has a strong deontological stream, going back to the Ten Commandments: the concepts and language of the obligatory and the prohibited, duties and permissions, and a transcendent law-giver. The virtues were used in Christian thought, and Christian ethics as presented by Thomas Aquinas, adapting Aristotle, is to a significant extent a form of VE, where the key ethical concept is beatitude or happiness, playing a role not unlike that of Aristotle's *eudaimonia*, and human flourishing is found by pursuing the virtues, with the theological ones added on by Aquinas. But even in his time the Augustinian-Franciscan tradition, as represented by Duns Scotus, preferred an ethic whose central plank was that of God as a moral legislator.

Second, late medieval and early modern nominalism led away from the idea that human flourishing could be a moral goal: it sounded self-centred, and it seemed to limit God's absolute sovereignty.[5]

Third, the abandonment of Aristotelian metaphysics in the seventeenth century as a result of the scientific revolution led to the rejection of the notion of essences or natures (and hence too of the metaphysical underpinning for the moral ideal of fulfilment of human nature). The Reformation also led to a less optimistic view of human nature, where the idea of grace building upon nature to bring about moral transformation was less acceptable.

All this strengthened the deontological strain in Christian ethics. The virtues were still treated in moral theology, but within a deontological framework. While there was an awareness of Aristotle's idea that the virtues benefited their possessor, the context of that awareness was the idea that virtues were dispositions to obey God's laws.

In the nineteenth century, the secular ethics of Kant and the utilitarians, also duty-based, made inroads into wider culture. Now virtues were subordinated to universalizable norms, and seeking to make the world a better place.[6]

Virtue Ethics and Christian Moral Reflection

Normative ethics went through a lean time in the first two-thirds of the twentieth century, due in part to the dominance of logical positivism. Since positivists were anti-metaphysics (which meant they were anti-realist about value) secular philosophical ethics was reduced to discussing what meaning ethical terminology could still have. The dominant views were anti-realist (there are no moral facts) and non-cognitivist (moral judgements are only expressions of emotion, not genuine cognitions).

But by the 1960s, logical positivism was in terminal decline, and the revival of realism was under way. John Rawls' landmark book, *A Theory of Justice* (1971), put substantive issues on the philosophers' agenda again. In Britain, normative ethics was (and generally still is) heavily utilitarian, with Elizabeth Anscombe's and Bernard Williams' attacks on utilitarianism being voices crying in the wilderness. In the USA, Rawls' influence led in contractarian and deontological directions, i.e. in anti-utilitarian directions.[7] Since Rawls' work was concerned with the just society rather than the just individual, the type of ethical issues presented for ethical analysis in the 1970s tended to be those with a public policy angle, e.g. the morality of abortion, euthanasia, world hunger, etc. Most attention was paid to dilemmas or hard cases, in part because utilitarianism and deontologism focused on the question, 'What would be obligatory/permitted/forbidden to do, in situation X?' Issues of character were seen as trite, and of little practical avail in the dilemma cases.

More generally throughout the culture, words such as 'virtue', 'prudence', 'chastity', 'humility' acquired negative connotations, associated with the allegedly uptight, life-denying and hypocritical Victorian world. Virtue still has an 'image' problem.

The reasons for VE's revival are many. First, the dilemmas couldn't be convincingly resolved. Second, ethicists began to realise that even if they could be resolved in some cases, no general conclusions could be derived therefrom. Third, most ethical dilemmas discussed by philosophers were irrelevant to the ordinary person, since he or she probably would never encounter them. Fourth, the effectiveness of Rawls' attack on utilitarianism led to a search for an alternative approach, and while he influenced many young American philosophers in the direction of Kant, not all took that road. In any case, deontologism, while better at the level of norms (the Right) than ulitarianism, was far less clear about value (the Good). The apparent antinomy in Kantian deontologism between moral uprightness (the Right) and happiness (the Good) led a number of philosophers to look elsewhere. Fifth, the slow, reluctant but inexorable realisation by the logical positivists (or of those of them who lived long enough) that metaphysics is ineliminable led to renewed interest in Aristotle's metaphysics and in turn in his ethics. Sixth, the decline of religion's influence in shaping character and personal ideals, and the rise of interest in such VE-related issues as personal growth and professional excellence, indicated growing awareness of an important niche needing to be filled.

FLAWS OF UTILITARIANISM/CONSEQUENTIALISM

The other main ethical systems are utilitarianism and deontologism. Utilitarianism's central claim is that those actions are morally obligatory which lead to good/better consequences, and that what constitutes their goodness is their giving pleasure or being useful. It is thus a combination of consequentialism and hedonism. Hedonism is easily disposed of, but not consequentialism: after all, no serious ethical theory can treat consequences as irrelevant.

The sting in the tail of consequentialism is its view that consequences *alone* determine what one ought or ought not do. It is a seriously flawed system of normative ethics.

The following objections can be advanced.

1. Most consequences are not foreseeable. The more immediate ones are not foreseeable with such clarity that they can be action-guiding to the point of being always over-riding with respect to other considerations.

2. Consequentialism implies that since there is no limit to the consequences of one's act there can be no limit to one's responsibility. That puts excessive moral burden on the agent. Even if there were such a limit, it seems unclear that it could be established on a principled, non-arbitrary basis.

3. Linked to 1 and 2, consequentialism cannot avoid the disturbing phenomenon of moral luck, i.e. that unexpected and unintended consequences also determine the morality of one's action. Amending consequentialism so that expected or reasonably expectable consequences, and not actual consequences, are what count will collapse consequentialism.

4. Utilitarianism's founders (e.g. Bentham) claimed that all consequences (e.g. monetary gain/loss, artistic pleasure, character development) could be reduced to a common measure. Today, the consensus seems to be that this is not possible.

5. If one could calculate all consequences by a common measure, then there would be no room or need for moral deliberation, choice, or decision. There can be no room for deliberation as to whether it is better to earn €10 or €1. Deliberation can take place only when different kinds of considerations enter in, which need to be weighed.

6. Consequentialism can exclude no act-type as immoral. It can offer no list of precepts, of dos and don'ts. One can never say that a certain type of act (e.g. rape, torture, genocide) is inherently wrong. Good enough consequences or a proportionate reason will justify anything.

7. Consequentialism implies that value (the good) resides only in ends or outcome, never in the means or actions directed to them. That is problematic in two ways. First, it assumes that value, well-being, happiness are something passive, never active: fullness of being shrivels to a matter of

Virtue Ethics and Christian Moral Reflection

having nice experiences, much as happens to the computer-controlled humans in the film *The Matrix*. Second, it entails that value keeps receding into the future and is never grasped, since virtually any end is in turn a means to some further end. For instance, one studies in order to pass the exam; but the exam in turn is (merely) a means to getting the qualification, which is in turn just a means to getting a job, which is a means to earning money, which is a means to getting married, which is a means to ... etc. Here we have a kind of moral infinite regress. If none of our acts can ever have value in itself, it is not clear that we can ever grasp or enjoy the good.

8.   Utilitarianism has no concept of the common good, only of the aggregate of individual goods. Yet there are some common goods, indispensable to human well-being (e.g. the rule of law), but not reducible to or explicable in terms of individual desire-satisfaction.

9.   Consequentialism is inhumanly demanding in that it sets no limits to duty. Unlike deontologism, it has one permanently 'on duty'. It has no concept of the permissible or the supererogatory, since one must always be seeking to make the world better, and always to the greatest extent possible. In that framework, one's own projects or life-plans can have no particular importance. In effect, it presents an ideal of being so totally given to universal well-being that one is not entitled to a personal life.[8]

One could argue that utilitarianism/consequentialism's claim to be a moral theory is based on a fundamental mistake regarding what a moral theory is for.[9] While it could be used to assess past actions, it does not seem that it could be action-guiding, for the reasons given in (1)–(6) above.

LIMITS OF DEONTOLOGISM

Deontologism has a more serious claim to be a genuine ethical system, since it is action-guiding. It takes actions (and omissions) as the primary locus of moral value. Motives, psychological intentions and desires acquire their moral character from the type of act to which they tend. Deontologism sees character as determined by action, and virtue as definable in terms of propensity to right action. Act-types are grouped into the prohibited, the mandatory, and the permitted.

In contrast to utilitarianism, deontologism takes some act-types to have a moral character of their own, independently of any further moral character the act-token (i.e. the individual instance of an act) may acquire in a particular context. Rape and lying are inherently immoral act-types. Rights and duties, obligations and entitlements, are among the core-concepts of a deontological ethic.

Kantianism is one of the more famous varieties of deontologism.[10] The ethic of Judaism, Christianity and Islam is wholly or substantially a deontological ethic, presenting a God who is supremely good and whose commands are (in some sense) the foundation of the moral law. A Jew, Christian or Muslim has a moral duty to do justice and avoid injustice because God commands it, regardless of whether or not she has other motives or reasons for doing so.

The drawbacks of deontologism relevant to this paper include:

1. Following the final objection to utilitarianism listed above, deontologism at least allows one to pursue one's own life-projects, since it allows for the zone of the permitted. One can 'have a life'. But deontologism allows it no particular ethical value. Like consequentialism and proportionalism, deontologism is a universalising approach to morality, seeing it as about the duties everybody has, or, in Kant's words, teaching that one should act only on the maxim upon which one can consistently conceive or will that others would act. A person's life-projects and relationships have no ethical significance in themselves. Yet it is one's life-plans, career, relationships and experience-patterns that make up the most interesting and (to oneself) most important elements of one's life.

2. Deontologism, with its focus on acts, classifying them as obligatory, prohibited, or permitted is essentially a law-based view of normative ethics. This is not in itself objectionable. However, on its own, it may generate a legalistic 'How far can I go?' mentality.

3. A law-based ethic must, if it is to be experienced as genuinely normative (i.e. morally compelling), depend on a transcendent Law-giver. Otherwise, it rests on shaky foundations.

4. It is essentially an other-oriented ethic and is unconvincing with respect to how to treat oneself. In the traditional monotheist view, I have duties to God and to my neighbour. If I injure myself, for instance by abuse of drugs, traditional monotheism's comment was that it constituted a kind of disobedience to God, a violation of that body which is a gift from God. That is a reasonably satisfactory answer. But without that religious element, it becomes difficult to see how a deontologist could argue that it is wrong to take drugs or commit suicide, once one can make a half-plausible argument that nobody else is hurt thereby. Saying that one has a duty to oneself not to hurt oneself illustrates deontologism's weakness: talk about duties to oneself is easily deflected by saying that I am surely free to release myself from duties to myself.

Other aspects of deontologism may come in for criticism in my discussion of VE. For the present, those listed above will suffice.

Virtue ethics

Virtue ethics is an ethics of character: 'integrity' or 'excellence' could also serve as synonyms for 'virtue'. It is the approach of Plato, Aristotle, neo-Platonists, Stoics and Epicureans.[11]

Instead of 'What is the most efficient way to reduce harm and maximise well-being?' or 'What norms (duties, rights, etc.) govern my acts?', VE takes the central question to be, 'What kind of person do I want to be? What kind of person would be admirable? What would the good or virtuous person do in this type of situation?'

Consequentialism and deontologism are duty-based ethics, giving priority to the right over the good. In Kant's words: 'The concept of good and evil is not defined prior to the moral law ... rather it must be defined after and by means of the law.'[12] Kant's views go back to Scotus and Ockham, and contrast with those of Aquinas and the ancients who held the good to have priority. Larmore cites Sidgwick:

Sidgwick wanted to describe two very different ways of understanding the nature of ethics. If the notion of right is replaced by that of good at the foundations of ethics, then the moral ideal will no longer be *imperative*, but rather *attractive*. His point was that ethical value may be defined either as what is binding or obligatory upon an agent, whatever may be his wants or desires, or what an agent would in fact want if he were sufficiently informed about what he desires. In the first view, the notion of right is fundamental, in the second the notion of the good. Each view makes use, of course, of the other notion as well, but it explains it in terms of its primary notion. If the right is fundamental, then the good is what an agent does or would want, so long as it conforms to the demands of obligation; it is the object of right desire. If the good is fundamental, then the right is what one ought to do in order to attain what one would indeed want if properly informed.[13]

This indicates something of the shift required in order to think in VE terms: a shift away from thinking in terms of 'What ought one do?' to 'What would be good – for me, first, but not in a selfish sense, so also good for others?'

Ethics then is about the good life, where good is taken in a broad sense, including not merely what we moderns think of as the morally good, but also the rationally good, the aesthetically good, and so forth. The hard work lies in specifying the good, whether by means of an account of intrinsic value (the Platonist option) or by way of an account of human nature and its fulfilment (the Aristotelian option) or some other way. Aristotle and the Stoics largely opt for *eudaimonia* ('an activity of the soul in accordance with virtue' – Aristotle, *Nic. Eth.* 1098b) where happiness is a kind of perfection.

Virtue is the disposition to choose those courses of action which contribute to one's happiness or flourishing. We are rational beings: in other words, our lives go well, according to whether we can exercise our reason successfully. We all have reason to acquire such character-traits as prudence or practical wisdom (*phronesis*), courage, temperance, justice. In acquiring them we acquire emotional dispositions; and from these dispositions spring the motives of our actions.

A virtue has three characteristics:

a. *Dispositional*: it is a state of a person's soul, a way one has made oneself. A virtue is not a feeling (*pathe*) or capacity, since we are not adequately responsible for them. It can be a habit, but this does not necessarily mean it is mindless and devoid of choice, as we tend to assume when we refer to habits today. As Zagzebski notes, natural capacities and skills 'are more closely related to external effectiveness', whereas virtue has an internal element.[14] Virtues, unlike passions, involve choice. We are praised or blamed for them, but not for passions.

b. *Affective*, touching on our feelings, particularly those of pleasure and pain. Developing a virtue involves habituating our feelings in certain ways. One has acquired a particular virtue only when it feels good to act in that way.

c. *Intellectual*, in that it involves the ability to discern the right thing to do, i.e. virtue requires practical intelligence. Virtuous action may come naturally and spontaneously but never automatically or unthinkingly.

Aristotle's *Nicomachean Ethics* discusses cognitive and moral virtues. It deals with courage; temperance; virtues concerned with money, with honour, with anger; the virtues of social intercourse; justice as fairness; continence; and friendship. Christian accounts of the virtues are rather different, as are those proposed by Nietzsche and Hume.

The foregoing is only an elementary sketch of VE. Full book-length analyses of recent vintage include Slote 1992, Annas 1993, Zagzebski 1996, Statman 1997, Hursthouse 1999, and Swanton 2003. In what follows I concentrate on the interesting contributions VE can make.

The attractions of virtue ethics

1. VE offers new ways of looking at ethical issues. The challenge can easily be underestimated, since we moderns instinctively associate notions of duty, obligation and rights with ethics. VE is capable of acknowledging them as part of the ethically relevant context without accepting that they identify what it is in the agent that qualifies her as moral or virtuous. Instead of those concepts, VE takes excellence, admirability, practical reasonableness as the touchstones for moral discernment.

2. Modern VE cannot simply be a return to classical ethics. The Christian view of virtue involved considerable adaptation of Aristotelian ethics, with a different list of virtues. The virtues that today's Christian community might prize could in turn represent an advance on, say, Aquinas's picture of the virtues. In any case, developing a modern VE could be an interestingly creative exercise.

3. VE is *pluralist*. While virtues like justice or honesty are universal, some will be more important to particular people. Some virtues are occupation-specific: soldiers, CEOs and therapists need somewhat different virtues. Furthermore, this pluralism does not lead to moral relativism.[15]

By contrast, deontologism and consequentialism are obliged to find universalizable principles, on the assumption that their universalizability is what confers objectivity or authority on them, and that without it moral relativism looms.

4. VE challenges the notion that the ethical life is inherently burdensome, a dreary fixation on duty. Consequentialism turns every aspect of one's life into a matter of duty, viz. that of maximising universal well-being. It requires that one treat oneself as of no more importance than anybody else, so that one has no moral right to allow special consideration to one's own plans or projects. One's relations, children, and friends can have no larger moral significance to oneself than strangers have. Deontologism is more moderate in its demands, so that there is an extensive zone of moral freedom for one's own projects and friends. But they have no ethical significance, since deontologism is essentially other-directed. By contrast, VE takes it that it is precisely one's projects and relationships that are central for ethical development. The virtuous life is one in which these are experienced as pleasurable and fulfilling. Unlike the other systems, duty is only a part of what the good life requires.

5. VE places *one's own character* at the centre of ethical reflection. Other ethical systems speak more of responsibility, whether for doing one's duty or for trying to make the world a better place. Responsibility is a deontological concept. However, one could adapt it, once one distinguishes between 'responsibility to' and 'responsibility for'. The first suggests the idea of being answerable to, or accountable to, somebody or some group. The second could be taken as a VE notion, where it was understood not as a matter of being accountable but of the prudent, practical person recognising that actions have consequences and that what she does shapes her character, and that person wanting to act reasonably and effectively to promote the good: the good of her own character primarily, that of others along with it.

    With respect to certain action-tokens or action-instances, whether compulsive (the alcoholic having another drink, the addict having another fix) or uncontrolled, or 'incontinent' as discussed in Aristotle, we moderns allow much for diminished responsibility. Deontologism's focus on the particular act in such cases mirrors the proceedings of the law: we can be tried for criminal actions, but not for criminal motives, and there is no legal concept of criminal character. VE by contrast is more concerned with the latter: with the contemporary 'Where is this coming out of?' concern. VE's contribution here is its focus on responsibility for one's character.[16] Deontologism, concerned with the immoral act, sees reduced responsibility as exonerating or mitigating, and so is less able to deal with the character issue.

    VE is not concerned so much with whether one is free with respect to a particular action-token (and so free at that moment), as with how one has made oneself over time. It is reported that President Abraham Lincoln decided against appointing a certain individual to his cabinet because, he said, 'I don't like his face'. When his advisers protested that a man couldn't be to blame for his face, Lincoln replied: 'After 40, he is.' VE makes it possible to see the ethical significance of how one changes.

I take it as established that some alcoholics manage to get sober and that some addicts manage to get off the drug or compulsive habit. So it seems mistaken to hold that, because the addict felt impelled to act out in a given instance, he or she is not responsible, not merely for the particular lapse, but in any way whatever. In the case of drugs, the addict's knowing that they are addictive must imply some measure of responsibility. Even where the addict could not know in advance that he or she would turn into an alcoholic, the period of time, prior to the alcoholic recognising that he has the disease, is usually marked by drunkenness, quarrelling, breakdown of relationships, etc. Failure to deal with these can indicate a head-in-the-sand mentality. It is irresponsible to pay no attention to one's behaviour or to be unreflective about one's character.

Thus, VE is good for ethical analysis with respect to addiction, obsessive or compulsive (e.g. paedophile behaviour) and self-destructive behaviour (e.g. suicide, smoking). Talk about sex addiction or paedophilia as 'incurable' may arise from our being aware of agent's diminished responsibility in the particular instance. Non-VE normative theories focus our attention on the individual act, so awareness of diminished ability to refrain from so acting can push us in the direction of effectively absolving the agent of responsibility and transferring the issue to a non-moral (e.g. medical) realm. This is unsatisfactory, since we also feel that the addict has some moral responsibility for his behaviour. VE directs us to consider character: to consider responsibility, not just with respect to the individual act, but to his or her being that way, i.e. to the character trait. Ethical assessment of character does not lose its point because of obsession.

As mentioned earlier, deontologism has difficulty with self-destructive behaviour, seeing suicide, alcoholism or smoking as immoral, wrong or vicious *only* insofar as it hurts others. There is no obvious answer to the claim that I am free to absolve myself of responsibility to myself in the relevant regard. VE has less difficulty on this point, since self-destructive behaviour is generally not admirable, often a self-indulgent or cowardly refusal to face the challenges of life.

6. VE can deal with the category of the *offensive* or the distasteful. Since the epistemic touchstone of virtue is that it is admirable, that which, while not involving injury or harm, is offensive or in bad taste is by definition not admirable. It captures the intuition that it is bad to be a certain way even though one may not thereby be harming anybody else. Discussion of

responsibility is sometimes hindered by a crude deontological legalism: thus, for instance, few see drunkenness as wrong or ethically objectionable, if it isn't hurting anybody else. Again, it takes VE to articulate the ethical significance indicated by what we feel and think when we witness drunkenness. It is that he or she is disgusting, pathetic, boring, irritating and repulsive.[17]

7. *Business ethics* is an area in which VE has much to offer, as a number of writers have noted. Duty-based ethics tends, when applied to the everyday world of business and finance, to get reduced to observing the law. It is not uncommon for business undergraduates to think that morality is irrelevant to business, except insofar as moral norms are enshrined in law with sanctions to back them up. This reflects a lower level of moral development on the Kohlberg scale, but nevertheless it illustrates an important point: in this, as in other walks of life, a universalised duty-based morality will not get far without the force of the law behind it. Beyond that, an attractive morality is needed, one adapted to the role. So, the starting-point will have to be something like: what does the admirable/good stockbroker, investor, manager, etc. look like?

8. Currently, interest in personal *growth* and *spirituality* is strong in the western world. Bookshops have large sections on self-improvement and myriad ways to achieve excellence in different areas of life, whether managing, meditating, or making love. This is precisely the territory of VE, since a virtue (*arête*) is an excellence. There is a substantial risk that talk of personal growth, divorced from moral or ethical notions, will be soft, self-indulgent and self-deluding. Accordingly, it needs an ethical component and some theoretically rigorous notion of human flourishing or well-being, which is what VE offers (for instance, in Aristotle's *Ethics*). In any event, VE is the kind of ethical system most appropriate to accompany spiritual development.[18]

9. Linked to (5) and (8) is the clarity VE can bring to the confused notion of selflessness found in deontologism and commonsense morality, both of which think of morality as about how one treats others.[19] As the rejection of a focus on one's own interests to the exclusion of others, selflessness is acceptable. But what is sometimes lauded as selflessness is the outright neglect of one's own interests for the sake of others, as a general practice and not just in exceptional circumstances.[20] This is problematic. It turns up in the common idea that an action benefiting others is less morally laudable, even indicative of character flaw, if it also benefits the agent. This applies more emphatically if the agent's motivation for acting was even in part to benefit herself.

But this makes nonsense of the virtue of prudence. Similarly, it makes the modern concern with personal growth morally dubious if not deplorable; and that excludes a significant modern development from ethical reflection and guidance. That would be regrettable, for much of what is today called 'growth' is soft, verging on self-indulgence, and needs the affirmation, as well as the intellectual and moral toughening, that ethical reflection on character-traits can bring.

It also excludes much of everyday life from ethical reflection. Much of our time we are concerned with ourselves: with attending to one's teeth or eyes, with one's projects and relationships, with one's tendency to get impatient, with one's need for a pension. It is unreasonable to hold a moral theory that at best excludes these concerns from ethical consideration and at worst sees them as morally questionable because they involve self-concern. VE can overcome that problem.

10. VE often gives us a better *standpoint* from which to address such general questions as 'Is X-type of behaviour bad/wrong?' Addressing that question, we typically think deontologically: we wonder if it would be wrong for the average (adult) person, unconnected to us, to act thus. If the behaviour hurts or endangers others, the answer is clear. But if not, then, while we do not find it admirable, we are often reluctant to say it is wrong, because either (a) we do not wish to interfere in the lives of others or (b) we do not wish to be 'judgemental'.

However, if instead of thinking of some other adult, we think of some child, our moral intuitions may change. This is even more the case if the child in question is my own, when I consider how I would feel if my child acted thus or whether I would want my child to know that I behave thus. Deontologism, more oriented to universal law, may lead us to say: 'I don't personally like behaviour X, but I don't think we can say that in principle it is morally wrong.' More oriented to character formation, VE would say that the fact that I would strongly object to my child doing it, and that I would be careful not to let my child know I do it or have done it, tells us what my real moral views are. VE places the weight on modelling the admirable person, and takes oneself and those closest to us as providing the epistemic touchstone for our judgements.

Such modelling is primarily oriented to children, of course. But a little reflection shows that one cannot get away with putting on a show of virtue for the children: imposture will be detected, sooner or later. One must believe it, and one can't do that unless one is also consciously practising it. If one has acquired the virtue, then a little more reflection may lead one to see that the modelling is not just for the benefit of children.

If ethical living is *modelling*, there will be little need to articulate 'judgemental' comments. What one's behaviour models will say it all.

11. Duty-based ethical systems lead to focus on *dilemma* cases. In the last few decades, philosophy teachers have concentrated on these, leading to students

thinking that ethics has only to do with problem cases or grey areas. Dilemma cases (or casuistry as it is usually termed in moral theology) are useful when students have strong moral convictions. Today, students imbibe cultural and moral relativism from a relatively early age, or at any rate feel under significant pressure from it, well before they go to study philosophy or ethics at a third-level institute. Heavy focus on dilemma ethics then may deliver the *coup de grace* to any notion that there are some moral truths.[21]

For the same reason, teaching ethical systems in a neutral way is not pedagogically sound. In a pluralist or relativist culture, professors who, like Plato's sophists, either cannot or will not take ethical stands disedify their students.

12. An attractive feature of VE is that it is easily linked to and supported by the great *literature* of the world.[22] Jane Austen's novels, for instance, are studies in character and its importance. In general, novels focus on the development and illumination of character, but rarely to deal with rights and duties or moral dilemmas.

13. VE also makes it easier to be a moral realist at the *metaethical* level. The issue is whether there are any moral facts; if not, there can be no moral knowledge. It is arguable that the abstractness of facts, lacking the 'concreteness' of substances or properties, can make moral realism difficult for some students. However, VE, focused as it is on character-traits, need not commit one to being realist about anything other than the moral properties of persons.[23]

CATHOLIC MORAL THEORY: THE POST-VATICAN II CONTEXT

Prior to Vatican II (1962–65), Catholic moral theology praised the virtues while generally understanding them within a deontological, duty-oriented framework.[24] As was frequently noted, the Christian moral life was often understood legalistically as a matter of obeying the law of God.

In line with Vatican II, moral theologians enthusiastically turned to the task of basing moral theology more centrally on Scripture. They focused particularly on the following of Christ, in an invitation and response dialectic, deploying notions such as conversion, call and response, grace and active charity.

One such notion was that of the fundamental option: the idea that the overall thrust of a person's life reflected his basic choice for or against God and the good. While interesting, it is of use only in the retroactive overall assessment of a person's life. It can play no role with respect to ethical decision-making, since it is uninformative and not oriented to deliberation. While it clearly represented a desire to get away from narrow focus on dilemma cases and the minutiae of casuistry, it nevertheless is too general to be action-guiding, and properly belongs to second-order reflection. It would have been better to aim at particular character-traits that may be developed in action and assessed.

An Irish Reader in Moral Theology

The following of Christ, too, while important as a guiding theme, needed supplementing when it came to moral cases. In the late 1960s, there developed the view that the content of Christian ethics was no different from that of non-religious secular reasoning at its best, a view that represented a kind of 'autonomous ethic' instead of the 'faith ethic' of the immediate post-Vatican II period.[25] That debate has smouldered on since then. By the time that the difficulties were being felt, talk of the virtues had been abandoned.

VE's Advantages

1. VE provides a better framework for *understanding NT moral teaching*. When New Testament authors speak of morality, they cite lists of virtues, common to both Greek and Jewish literature. These lists specify the characteristics of what it is to belong to Christ or to the world, what it is to be 'of the flesh' or 'of the Spirit'. Such texts as Galatians 5:19-24, Philippians 4:8-9, and Colossians 3:5, 8-10, 12-15 emphasise virtue.[26] In the synoptic gospels, Jesus is presented as taking the (deontological) commands of the Decalogue for granted, occasionally refining or adapting them. For the rest, much of his ethical teaching seems best interpreted along VE lines. At times, the VE perspective is explicit, as in, for example: 'What comes out of the mouth proceeds from the heart, and this defiles a man. For out of the heart come evil thoughts, murder, adultery, fornication, theft, false witness, slander' (Mt 15:18-19). For unpacking the beatitudes listed in the Sermon on the Mount, VE is more serviceable than either of the other ethical systems.

2. VE also provides a good angle into the *distinctive content* of Christian ethics, in its focus on such virtues as forgiveness, chastity and humility, and such theological virtues as faith, hope and charity. As noted earlier, VE is also interesting because modern VE cannot be a mere revival of Aristotelian or even classical VE. It could be argued that there are certain modern Christian virtues that Christians of earlier centuries did not advert to or appreciate. VE allows for 'development in morality' precisely because it is not confined to universalizable moral norms.

    Jesus is a teacher of a way of life, in certain respects like the Platonist, Aristotelian, Stoic and Epicurean schools (as early Christian apologists recognised). Beatitude or happiness is presented (e.g. in Sermon on Mount) as the goal and purpose of human life, and ethically central, just as VE makes happiness or flourishing ethically central. It is interesting (and even disconcerting to modern secularist sensibilities) to find that certain types of classical pagan VE identify happiness with becoming like God.[27]

    Even if one were to go along with the 'autonomous' ethic thesis, holding that Christian revelation adds no new content to the general moral norms

Virtue Ethics and Christian Moral Reflection   309 that unaided human reason would arrive at, it would not follow that what would make the Christian admirable would be no different to what would make the secular humanist admirable. In any case, it seems wildly counter-intuitive to hold that Christian virtue is no different from ordinary human virtue: that the character of the admirable Christian is indistinguishable from that of the Buddhist or humanist.

A shift at the level of normative ethics towards VE makes the 'autonomous' ethic position untenable, since it would be impossible to seal off the content of universal moral norms (or our judgement of their content) from the ethical input derived from living a virtuous Christian life. Furthermore, the 'autonomous' ethic was based upon the modern era's excessive focus on the Right (norms for action). Greater attention paid to the Good is unlikely to find that the ethical intuitions of the Christian and the decent humanist are identical.[28] However, both points raise issues that must be dealt with elsewhere.

The 'autonomous' ethic thesis also makes it impossible to see how faith, hope and charity could count as virtues. Faith, hope and charity are gifts of grace, but they are also virtues: they are character traits that are to be sought and practised, that are observable, evident, and (to 'spiritual people') admirable, and for these reasons must have ethical content.

3. It is primarily through the language of the virtues, both natural and theological, that the notion of following, imitating and becoming conformed to Christ can be best articulated. VE's guide to virtue is the admirable person, so the Christian message of imitating Christ can be well accommodated by VE. Paying attention to the virtues within the context of VE shows the importance of developing the appropriate intellectual and emotional dispositions needed to become virtuous as Christ was.[29] At the same time, the fact that treatment of the virtues need not be as rigidly universalizable across the board as deontological norms means that the image of Christ may be found in many ways: 'Christ plays in ten thousand places', in Gerard Manley Hopkins' words.

4. Because virtue is admirable and attractive, VE offers the possibility of linking goodness to beauty, the transcendental that (as Hans Urs von Balthasar argued) has been neglected in recent centuries. With respect to the goals and needs of Christian ethics, that is an important gain.

5. As was discussed earlier, it is widely thought that ethics is inherently other-regarding so that actions benefiting oneself or promoting one's own interests are morally suspect. One of the factors underpinning this distorted notion of moral action may be an exaggerated idea of the meaning of the Christian notion of self-denial.

In an older ascesis, that notion was nuanced by the idea that one had to grow in holiness, so it was accepted that there were certain types of action from which one could knowingly derive benefit, and it would be praiseworthy, not problematic, to do so, viz. actions that reinforced the virtues, natural or theological.

However, with the loss of that ascesis and its valuing of virtue, the problem re-emerged. I remember a Jesuit who remarked in the late 1960s: 'At a certain stage I gave up trying to be holy and started trying to help others.' What he meant was clear: he was giving up an exclusively inward-oriented spirituality, closed to the needs of the wider world. But the phrase was open to misinterpretation, and the move away from talk of the virtues, as well as various other cultural factors, gave rise to a general impression that being concerned about personal holiness (or about 'growth') was a waste of time, and possibly morally questionable.

This was strongest among those religious who were active in social justice, despite the fact that they valued deeply such personal traits as social concern and selflessness in social commitment – which are virtues. Accompanying their focus on making the world a better place is the assumption that concern about character and virtue must be inward-oriented, self-centred, even narcissistic.

But such lack of psychological realism couldn't work. Little wonder that by the late 1970s, religious orders were producing psychologists, counsellors and therapists, because the need for personal growth, holiness, and coping with one's inner demons cannot be brushed aside by saying one ought to be selfless.

VE offers the possibility of an account of personal flourishing that includes social concern as well as acceptance of one's need to become a better person. Aristotle's *Ethics* is a preamble to the *Politics*: before we can identify the kind of society we should want, we had better have the right kind of persons or the appropriately trained characters to develop and maintain it. The Aristotelian virtues are not narcissistic by any means; and while the virtues are good in themselves and benefit their possessors, Aristotle also sees their purpose in the creation of a just society.

6. In the Christian churches, treatment of sexual morality has been almost entirely in the terms of duty-based ethics. It could be enriched by applying the insights of VE.[30] With respect to a wide range of sexual behaviour (including contracepting), there is much to be gained by considering the matter, not so much with regard to whether particular acts are wrong, but with respect to what kind of character traits we would find admirable. Certain kinds of acts might not seem wrong from a deontological viewpoint, yet not seem admirable either and hence not virtuous. A mentality that holds defensively 'I am not harming anybody' may be unable to see that the ethical life is about much more than avoidance of wrong-doing. It is here that VE's strengths lie.

Virtue Ethics and Christian Moral Reflection

VE's attention to character-formation also seems relevant to dealing with sexual abuse of minors. There has been a shift in the direction of seeing the behaviour in question as recurrent and hence (at least in some cases) addictive. In consequence, it has been 'medicalised', i.e. viewed as a medical rather than a moral problem. The loss of the virtue perspective (viz. that of viewing behaviour along the lines of habits being formed over time) has led to an over-emphasis on freedom of the will at any given moment as the crucial, if not the sole, determining moral factor. If the person is seen as 'addicted' (and these days that is not often distinguished from being habituated), then moral responsibility or blame is seen as not assignable, since the person, being addicted or habituated, is not free and so not morally responsible.

Yet we feel morally outraged at sexual assault on minors. When this moral feeling is combined with the belief that the offender being 'addicted' is incapable of stopping himself, it leads to demonization of the offender, presenting him as a mad, uncontrollable monster. This is repellent, as well as ill-founded. Part of the response needed is a view of human behaviour which takes a long-range developmental view of the person, and sees the moral freedom of self-control as something to be incrementally achieved.

It is also interesting to note the kind of 'therapy' frequently provided for sexual abusers. It involves precisely what was once called 'training in virtue': the individual gets support and monitoring in refraining from sexual self-indulgence in the form of masturbation and sexual fantasy, where children are the imagined objects. This highlights the importance of the virtue of chastity or sexual integrity, which is much more than a purely instrumental sexual self-control.

7. Proportionalism is probably the dominant form of normative ethics among Catholic moral theologians today. It relies heavily on analysis, not just of consequences, but of the totality of factors in the context.[31] But 'context' and 'totality' are not the names of solutions: they are the names of problems. Talk of context is like writing an I.O.U.: one still has to pay up – to specify what in the context explains or justifies. Proportionalism's need here could be helped by having a theory of character which was well-developed as regards individual and specific virtues. For instance, with respect to the question of whether it is morally acceptable for a man who is HIV-positive to have intercourse with his wife who is not HIV-positive, it could be approached by asking what virtuous husbands would do or what kind of behaviour we would admire.

Conclusion

There are other factors illustrative of the positive contribution VE could make to Christian moral reflection. Perhaps the most important point to close on is this: living the Christian life is not essentially about moral dilemmas. While they do occur, they are rare. Casuistry is an important part of the Christian moral tradition, but it is only part. The larger part is working at the task of becoming a certain type of person, like Christ.

One can't be prepared for each morally challenging predicament one will encounter in life. Nor can all the dilemmas be resolved in advance in some utilitarian calculus or prescribed for in a deontological rule-book. One can however try to grow as a good person, where goodness is specified in cognitive, moral and other admirable character traits.

This is a way of thinking that will not come back to us easily. When we think of being moral, we think of making the right choices in both easy and difficult circumstances, and we tend to excuse the person who is not able to do so in difficult circumstances. VE suggests that this view is inadequate and flawed, and that the person not able to be responsible may be more to blame, owing to failure to grow during his lifetime. To use a rough metaphor: we need to see that if it is good to be able to save someone from drowning since one can swim, then it is good to be able to swim. It is good to be temperate, it is good to be chaste, it is good to be courageous – even if one never had occasion to use the skills or test the strengths involved. The virtues have value in themselves, and not just as means to other goods.[32]

Notes

1   See Riordan, 2002, p. 12.
2   For the former, see Annas, 1993, and Hursthouse, 1999; for the latter see Swanton, 2003. For a general overview, see Statma, 1997, particularly the introduction.
3   See Baron et al, 1997, where the three ethical systerms are discussed; also Bond, 1996, and Murphy, 1994, pp. 19–26.
4   See Sidgwick, 1907, Book III, Chapter 11, and Book IV, Chapter 3.
5   See Villey, 1975, pp. 182, 213, 385; Wolter, 1990, pp. 17–19, 150–152, 188–198; Pinckaers, 1995.
6   Sidgwick, 1907, is an illuminating example in this regard.
7   It was unfortunate that, at the time when many of today's Catholic moral theologians were looking beyond scholastic Aristotelian-Thomist ethics, secular philosophical ethics was in poor shape and had little to offer.
8   Dickens satirises this type of person in Mrs Jellyby in *Bleak House*. In *Doctor Zhivago*, the revolutionary Strelnikov, dismissing Yuri's poetry as bourgeois and self-centred, says: 'The personal life is dead', representing Pasternak's comment on the Marxist idea that in modern times the political must subsume the political.
9   Bond, 1996, pp. 146, 215–218, argues that it is fundamentally mistaken to imagine that utilitarianism could be a genuine ethical system, as distinct from offering a means of ethical reasoning about public policy issues.
10   The perception of Kant's approach as antithetical to VE may arise from excessive focus on his Groundwork to the exclusion of the later Metaphysic of Morals.

11   See Annas, 1993, Hadot, 1995. It has even been claimed that the ancients did not have morality in our sense, e.g. Browne, 1990: 'moral demands are essentially other-regarding; moral considerations are intrinsically opposed to considerations of self-interest; moral demands are universal and impartial; moral considerations are logically distinct from other kind of practical consideration; moral demands are of over-riding, categorical importance. It is a striking fact that, with the exception of the last, none of these features may properly be attributed to ancient ethics.' (398)

12   Kant, 1788, Ak. 62–63,

13   Larmore, 1996, p. 20; Sidgwick, 1907, p. 105.

14   See Zagzebski, 1996, p. 126; also Slote, pp. 1997, 176–8, 183–8.

15   See Slote, 1997, p. 201.

16   See Audi, 1997, pp. 159–66 for interesting discussion on responsibility and character.

17   See Larmore, 1996, pp. 19–23.

18   See Porter, 1997, and Murphy, 2003, pp. 149–52.

19   See Slote, 1997, p. 194; also Slote, 1992.

20   It is aptly captured by Sydney Carton's thoughts as he waits to be guillotined at the end of Dickens' *A Tale of Two Cities*: 'It is a far better thing I do than anything I have ever done ...'

21   See Sommers, 1993.

22   See Sommers and Sommers, 1989, for numerous examples.

23   Sommers, 1993, reports that Aristotles's ethics seemed to cure moral relativism.

24   See Pinckaers [1985], 1995, for elaboration.

25   See McNamara, 1985, for a good account of the issues between the Glaubensethik and the autonomous ethic.

26   See also Rom 1:29-30, 14:14; 1 Cor 6:9-10; 2 Cor 12:20; Eph 4:32-32, 5:3-5; 1 Tim 1:9-10; 2 Tim 3:2-5; Titus 3:3; 1 Pet 4:3; Apoc 21:8, 22:15.

27   Plato, Theaetetus, 176, see Ammas. 1999, chapter III; also Plotinus, The Enneads, Book 1.

28   See Adams, 1999, for a thought-provoking account of the good.

29   See Newman, 1871, 'Sermon X: Faith and Reason, contrasted as habits of mind'; also Adams, 1995.

30   See Scruton, 1986, chapters 8 and 11; also Murphy, 2002.

31   See Gula, 1989, pp. 272–9, especially 277. However, I confess to finding the doctrine itself vague and unclear.

32   My thanks to Pat Riordan and Joe Lacey for perceptive and helpful comments on an earlier draft of this text.

References

Adams, R.M., 'Moral faith', *Journal of Philosophy*, 92 (1995), pp. 75–95.
     Finite and Infinite Goods: a Framework for Ethics, Oxford UP, 1999.

Annas, J., *The Morality of Happiness*, Oxford UP, 1993.
     Platonic Ethics, Old and New, Cornell UP, 1999.

Anscombe, G.E.M., 'Modern moral philosophy', *Philosophy*, 1958 (reprinted Anscombe 1981).
     Collected Papers, Vol. 3: Ethics, Religion and Politics, Minneapolis: University of Minnesota Press, 1981.

Aristotle, *Nicomachean Ethics*.

Audi, R., *Moral Knowledge and Ethical Character*, Oxford UP, 1997.

Baron, M. et al, *Three Methods of Ethics*, Oxford: Blackwell, 1997.

Bond, E.J., *Ethics and Human Well-being*, Oxford: Blackwell, 1996.

Browne, D., 'Ethics without morality', *Australasian Journal of Philosophy*, 68 (1990), pp. 395–412.

Campbell, K., 'Self-mastery and Stoic ethics', *Philosophy*, 60 (1985), pp. 327–40.

Foot, P., *Virtues and Vices*, Berkeley: University of California Press, 1978.

Geach, P., *The Virtues*, Cambridge UP, 1977.

Gula, R., *Reason Informed by Faith*, New York: Paulist Press, 1989.

Hadot, P., *Philosophy as a Way of Life: Spiritual Exercises from Socrates to Foucault*, Oxford: Blackwell, 1995.

Hursthourse, R., *On Virtue Ethics*, Oxford UP, 1999.

Kant, I. 1788 *Kritik der praktischen Vernunft*, 1788, translated by L.W. Beck, London: Macmillan, 1956.

Larmore, C., *The Morals of Modernity*, Cambridge UP, 1996.

MacIntyre, A., *After Virtue*, University of Notre Dame Press, 1981.

McNamara, V., *Faith and Ethics*, Dublin: Gill and Macmillan, 1985.

Murphy, S., 'The many ways of justice', *Studies in the Spirituality of Jesuits*, 26/2, 1994.

Review of Catholic Ethicists on HIV/AIDS, eds. Keenan and Fuller, *Milltown Studies*, 50 (2002), pp. 160–9.

'Two challenges for social spirituality' in Jesuit Centre for Faith and Justice, *Windows on Social Spirituality*, Dublin: Columba, 2003.

Newman, J.H., *Fifteen Sermons preached before the University of Oxford 1826–43*, London: Longmans, 1898.

Pinckaers, S., *Les sources de la morale chrétienne*, University Press Fribourg, 1985. *The Sources of Christian Ethics*, Edinburgh, T. and T. Clark, 1995 (translation of Pinckaers, 1985).

Plato, *Theaetetus*.

Plotinus, *The Enneads*.

Porter, J., 'Virtue ethics and its significance for spirituality', *The Way*, 88 (1997).

Riordan, P., 'Ethics making sense', *Studies* (2002), 361, pp. 7–14.

Scruton, R., *Sexual Desire*, London: Weidenfeld and Nicolson, 1986.

Sidgwick, H., *The Methods of Ethics*, Indianapolis: Hackett, 1981 [1907].

Slote, M., *From Morality to Virtue*, Oxford UP, 1992.

Slote, M., 'Virtue ethics' in Baron et. al., 1997.

Sommers, C. and Sommers, F., (eds), *Vice and Virtue in Everyday Life*, New York: Harcourt Brace Jovanovich, 1989.

Sommers, C., 'Teaching the virtues', *The Public Interest*, 111 (1993).

Statman, D. (ed.), *Virtue Ethic*, Edinburgh UP, 1997.

Swanton, C., *Virtue Ethics: A Pluralistic View*, Oxford UP, 2003.

Villey, M., *La formation de la pensée juridique moderne*, Paris: Montchrestien, 1975.

Wolter, A., *The Philosophical Theology of Duns Scotus*, Ithaca, NY: Cornell UP, 1990.

Zagzebski, L., *Virtues of the Mind*, Cambridge UP, 1996.

20 Naming Morality

Kieran Cronin

(*The Furrow*, March 2006, pp. 142–50.)

Behind our ethical debates about moral issues – justice and peace, caring for creation, bioethics, to name a few – are complex theoretical issues about whether or not morality is objective, relative or subjective. Our understanding of these concepts will, however, greatly influence our practical decision-making. Sadly, we frequently find these words being used in vague, loose ways when engaging in moral discussions. Worse still, there is a tendency to throw these words around as terms of abuse, as when the Pope spoke recently of the 'Dictatorship of Relativism'. Objective views of morality are, in turn, labelled as 'fundamentalist'. This article tries to clear up some confusions about the use of these basic terms. And it argues that an objective morality must include relative and subjective elements.

Those who take morality seriously tend to claim that the moral life is an objective matter: however, if asked what exactly is meant by 'objective morality', they may have great difficulty in explaining their position. Often an attempt at clarifying the term 'objective' will involve some appeal to opposing terms, 'relative' and 'subjective'. But this terminology, in turn, is far from clear. It's tempting to regard the terms 'relative' and 'subjective' as sharing the same meaning, but I would argue that they actually point to different realities. If asked what our attitude is on hearing these words, I imagine that most people would react positively towards the notion of the objective and negatively in response to the notions of the relative/subjective. After all, talk of objectivity has a reassuring ring to it. The objective is the real, the concrete, the factual. But the language of relativism and subjectivism is suspect; it points to the less real or the unreal. For relativists, it would seem, anything goes – one opinion is as good as the other, it all depends on one's perspective. Likewise, subjective experience centres on the feelings, emotions and perceptions of individuals and these are notoriously unreliable. The subjective sphere is the sphere of the personal, but often understood pejoratively in relation to idiosyncratic tastes. No wonder, then, that we should want to steer clear of any association of morality with these dangerous notions.

In what follows I want to explore and clarify the meanings of these controversial terms and concepts. There is a vagueness and ambiguity about their use that needs to be addressed if ethical discussion is to be carried out coherently and consistently. In particular, I would like to argue against the commonly held impression that, if morality is objective, then it must be totally opposed to the relative and subjective aspects of our daily lives. A comprehensive theory of morality must include relative and subjective elements, and these elements are far from the sworn enemies of the objective as portrayed by some superficial approaches to ethics.

MORAL RELATIVISM[1]

One way to notice the main difference between an objective and a relative view of morality might be to contrast the titles of two books by contemporary moral philosophers. In 1976, the Oxford philosopher, John Mackie, published his work entitled *Ethics: Inventing Right and Wrong*. More recently, in 1990, Louis Pojman of the University of Mississippi entitled his introductory textbook, *Ethics: Discovering Right and Wrong*. The only difference between the titles – one word – is instructive. On one hand, Mackie adopts the more relativistic approach, claiming that morality is a human *invention*. On the other hand we find Pojman arguing for a more objective position; he claims that moral values and norms are 'out there' to be *discovered*. Now, if moral relativism holds that morality is a human invention, the question then follows, 'Who invents moral value?' And the answer to this question leads us to consider two types of relativism, an individual and a group type.

SITUATION ETHICS

There are two main versions of moral relativism in contemporary ethics. One version stresses the great variety of situations or circumstances in human experience. A handy label for this view is 'Situation Ethics'.[2] This form of relativism is sceptical about the value of general moral rules, especially absolute rules that forbid exceptions. It regards the traditional objective view of rules as rigid and inflexible, failing to recognise the uniqueness of each individual life. The other version is less individualistic insofar as it emphasises shared forms of life adopted by cultural groups, especially ethnic and/or religious groups. This way of thinking is sometimes labelled 'cultural relativism', and causes many headaches for the legislators of western-style liberal democracies, given the growing phenomenon of minority cultures in so many European countries.

Of these two versions of relativism, the individual type is the less attractive. First, a moral theory that exaggerates the uniqueness of each individual's experience is likely to undermine what is surely a key function of any moral system – the harmonization of interest and care for others. Second, Situation Ethics tends to play down the value of the cumulative wisdom of generations of moral agents summarised and expressed in basic moral rules. If we exaggerate the uniqueness of each person's circumstances, then moral decision-making will also become quite burdensome, as each decision involves a person starting the process of moral reflection practically from scratch. Furthermore, there is a tendency in Situation Ethics to highlight moral quandaries, often of an extreme kind – the wife/mother who must decide whether to break her marriage vows in order to escape from the prison camp and return home to her family – thus ignoring the realm of ordinary moral obligations which are not so controversial.[3] It's easy to see how an individualistic form of relativism could be used to justify many dubious moral decisions.

Having criticised Situation Ethics, it is still open to a traditional approach to morality with an objective emphasis to allow for exceptions to rules in order to cater for the great variety of moral experience. The tradition of casuistry in Catholic moral theology, especially since the Council of Trent, is arguably an attempt to temper the rigid application of moral rules and may be seen as a form of moderate relativism built into an objective system. Indeed, at times, the practice of casuistry can shade into a situation ethics approach, whereby the casuist can appear to be looking for loopholes in the law to make life easier for someone facing a painful moral crisis. In these cases Church authorities may step in and remind us of the teaching on 'intrinsically evil' acts. Strict moralists often accuse the casuists of favouring a lax moral code.

In addition to this example of casuistry the tradition of moral theology in the Catholic Church has developed a 'three source' theory of morality as an essential guide to decision-making. When making up our minds to act we need to take into account the end in view (what we intend to bring about), then the act which brings about this end (the means), and the circumstances surrounding the proposed act. A positive judgement regarding all of these conditions is required if one is to act well from a moral point of view.[4] It is clear from this teaching that any moral judgement must be grounded in part on an examination of the situation or circumstances before coming to a practical conclusion.

In sexual ethics, for instance, careful examination of the circumstances will influence how we evaluate a particular sexual act between two people. Are they married or single? The answer to this question helps us to differentiate between 'adultery' and 'fornication'. Was the act consensual or forced? The answer here enables us to distinguish between rape and what may be permissible. There is simply no way of coming to a correct moral evaluation of human conduct without taking into account the circumstances of the people involved.

CULTURAL RELATIVISM

Cultural Relativism is more attractive than Situation Ethics largely because it avoids the self-serving and anarchic tendencies of the individualistic approach.[5] This version of moral relativism takes seriously the social and community dimension of the moral life. But there are still major difficulties with this approach mainly due to the great variety of groups and their diverse moral codes. However, it is not clear that this version of relativism is the implacable enemy of ethical objectivity.

I believe an argument can be made for a type of objectivity in morality which distinguishes between universal principles or rules and their relative application in different places and times. At the level of moral principle there is much agreement across different cultures. Practically every social group, in order to survive and to flourish, needs rules promoting safety against aggression and theft, maintaining trust by keeping promises and contracts, encouraging truthfulness, controlling intimate relationships (including sexuality), protecting privacy, respecting the dead, responding to gifts, and so on. But the application of these norms will of course vary given the different circumstances in which people find themselves. If you live in the Himalayas, where there is little earth, the idea of leaving your deceased relatives on the mountain for the animals to consume ('sky-burial') is quite acceptable as a way of respecting the dead. It is not an option to bury people under six feet of clay. Surely we would not wish to condemn such a culture for not respecting their dead? The point here is that objective factors, in this case the absence of soil, influences the cultural/moral norms about showing respect for those who die.

Frequently, those who criticise cultural relativism fail to notice that, underlying the diverse practices of different groups, there is an agreed moral value. A moderate form of relativism could accept that respect for the dead is a universal, even objective, value, while permitting a variety of forms of expression. A similar argument could be made in the case of two cultures each of which respects the institution of marriage, but which advocate different methods of choosing a partner – individual choice based on romantic feelings or arranged marriages guided by family interests. Who is to say for sure which of these ways of organising marriage is best from the objective point of view?

One can easily exaggerate the degree of moral diversity in our contemporary world and put the blame for this on moral relativism. But where are these awful people who think that it is just a matter of personal or group opinion whether it is right or wrong to kill innocent people, to engage in ethnic cleansing, mug old ladies for their pension cheques, betray one's friends, torture people at random, abuse children, burn down homes, rape people, drive while drunk, and so on? A fair amount of agreement in morality today is to be found, and not just at the level of general principles but even at the level of particular applications.

MORALITY AND THE SUBJECTIVE

When contrasting the objective and relative points of view what we should have in mind, I suggest, is the role of circumstances or situations in moral thinking. But when we contrast the objective and the subjective there is a different emphasis and the matter becomes more complex. Here we encounter a number of dichotomies:

reason/emotion, physical/mental, external/internal, impersonal/personal, impartial/biased, acts/agents, and the list could go on. From the objective perspective the first part of each of these dichotomies is privileged while the second part is treated with suspicion. But why this should be so is quite puzzling.

Take the reason/emotion dichotomy which has its classical formulation in the eighteenth century dispute between the followers of the philosophers Kant and Hume. On the Kantian side, morality is based on reason, and emotions or inclinations are marginalised. On the Humean side, morality is based on feeling, and reason is said to be the 'slave of passions'. But this is surely a false dichotomy. A moral agent who acted from reason alone and ignored his or her emotional responses to life's problems would be more like a robot or computer than a human being. A person of good character should be angry at injustice as well as responding reasonably to it. Emotions are not irrational; they have clear objects and a range of appropriate and inappropriate responses. If I am hanging on for dear life on the edge of a cliff, my fear is quite reasonable. If someone steps on my toes by accident, annoyance is a fitting response, not a fury which moves me to torture the perpetrator.

We are used to thinking of reason as the privileged aspect of human life, with part of its role the correction of the emotions, putting them in their proper place. That is still a valid position. However, the role of correction also works in the opposite direction – emotion may correct the reason, since reason as a faculty can be used well or badly. In his essay, *The Conscience of Huckleberry Finn*,[6] the philosopher Jonathan Bennett uses Mark Twain's character to show how the boy's emotional response to his friend Jim, a black slave whom he helps to escape, corrects the corrupt morality Huck has imbibed from his culture. The point is that many reasonable people, like Huck, considered slavery as acceptable. (Specifically, Huck felt guilty at what he saw as stealing from a neighbour, Miss Watson, who had never done anything to harm him!) Bennett claims that Huck was right to listen to his feelings and not to the corrupt use of reason.

Another dichotomy associated with the objective-subjective contrast concerns the distinction between the external aspect of our experience and the internal aspect. There is a danger that those holding the so-called objective point of view about morality place too much stress on external actions and their consequences. But this is disastrous. Again, I must insist that the internal aspect of human life, what goes on in our minds and hearts, is not less real than the actions we perform and the consequences that result. Just because the external realm of acts/consequences is easier to study than the motives, reasons and intentions of moral agents doesn't make these 'subjective' factors redundant.

In fact, arguably, it is the intentions we enact and the reasons which justify our actions that lie at the heart of the moral life. The external actions we perform cannot be understood fully without reference to what is going on internally in the heart and mind. Is this act of killing a type of self-defence or a type of revenge? Is this act of saving a drowning person an act of compassion or an act that is geared to seeking the admiration of one's girlfriend? Is the practice of dieting the same as the practice of fasting? Looking at the external act alone will not get us far in assessing the moral value of what is carried out.

Finally, the whole question of evaluating a person's moral responsibility for acting or not acting demands a careful attention to subjective factors relating to the degree of knowledge and freedom the person possesses. Morality has to do with evaluating acts and evaluating persons. And often the action a person performs is, from the point of view of a comprehensive moral theory, the tip of the iceberg. What lies beneath the surface is most significant.

THE OBLIGATORY AND THE PERMISSIBLE

My final point concerns the way in which an objective view of the moral life is often associated with a legal model of morality. This model emphasises the role of rules and obligations which allow for little or no leeway when it comes to decision-making and acting. There is little room in such systems for relative and subjective factors.

However, the realm of obligation is still only a part of morality, even though it is extremely important. There is also the realm of the permissible, which characteristically involves different degrees of personal discretion. Many important moral decisions are not hedged in by exact rules. In terms of duties to ourselves, for instance, some of these allow for little or no discretion, e.g. to refrain from committing suicide; whereas others, such as the duty to develop our talents, must depend to some extent on our personal judgement, including our desires. In terms of duties to others, the duty of charity is more discretionary than the duty to refrain from killing people. The Catholic Church forbids the use of contraception, but it does not lay down exactly how many children each married couple should have, even though this decision is definitely a moral one.

The permissible dimension of morality has often in the past been dismissed as morally insignificant, precisely because it did not fit the legal model of rules and obligations.[7] If something is important, it must be obligatory, according to the objective view. But the decisions we make to marry or remain single, to have children, to work in this job or that, to live here or there, to make friends, to choose one's hobbies and recreations, to act in heroic and saintly ways, are all moral issues, yet they do not fit into a strictly objective view of the moral life. A moral theory based on strict obligation may well emphasise the impersonal, impartial and disinterested aspects of the moral life, but this is not the whole story. There must be room in a moral theory for the personal dimension; in fact, what is left of true morality when it is divorced from the personal?

CONCLUSION

I have tried to show that relativism and subjectivism involve different approaches to the moral life.[8] It is understandable why people might oppose the notion of the objective to *extreme* forms of relativism and subjectivism, but these positions are pretty untenable when we look at them critically. However, this leaves us with more *moderate* forms of relativism and subjectivism, which I believe do fit into a common sense picture of morality. Any attempt at making sensible moral judgements requires attention to circumstances and situations, while rejecting the silly idea that every circumstance is morally unique. (Usually it makes no moral difference whether you murder a person on Monday or Tuesday, or whether the person you steal from is wearing a spotted tie at the time! Such circumstances are simply not morally relevant.) Likewise, no moral system can afford to ignore the subjective sphere of emotion, intention and motive, while justifiably rejecting the extreme claim that morality is just about one's feelings.

Ironically, the concepts relative/subjective may be clearer than the concept of objectivity in morals. In fact, it is quite hard to picture exactly what this notion means. I think that the answer to this question will depend on how we define morality as a whole. If our view of morality is that it consists of a series of moral quandaries waiting to be solved by arriving at the one right answer in each case, then our view of objectivity will be conditioned by this picture. Abortion, divorce, going to war, capital punishment, artificial reproduction, etc. are either right or wrong. It is just a matter of discovering the moral facts and bringing our minds into line with this truth.

But this view of morality is not the only possible one; indeed, it would seem to be a very limiting one. Another view, related to what is called *virtue ethics*, would emphasise the development of a person's moral character over a lifetime. But this would be judged not simply in terms of how he or she handled controversial ethical issues, but by taking into account thousands of everyday decisions, from the relatively insignificant, to the obligatory and hopefully including actions beyond the call of duty, practices associated with moral sainthood. This picture of morality makes it difficult to see how the lives of millions of people can be evaluated objectively. Just how much goodness must John Smith achieve over a lifetime in comparison with Mary Murphy? How do we combine (quantify) the virtue involved in performing strict obligations with the virtue involved in performing the permissible, but not obligatory?

Much of our public moral debate is depressing because the parties involved soon end up calling their opponents insulting names. Adding the letters 'ism' to the position held by your opponent is a typical strategy. Titles such as Secularism, Creationism, Fundamentalism, Communism and, of course, Relativism and Subjectivism, are nearly always used in a critical way. They may even become terms of abuse. Those who hold an objective/traditional view of morality are called Fundamentalists, while those holding liberal tendencies are labelled Relativists.

But, by criticising extreme forms of relativism and subjectivism, and allowing for the possible value of more moderate forms of these positions, we may be able to construct and bridge between traditional morality and contemporary liberalism. In any case, what is needed is dialogue between these groups, not name-calling!

NOTES

1   A useful introduction to this topic is D. Wong, 'Relativism', in *A Companion to Ethics*, ed. P. Singer, Oxford: Blackwell, 1994, pp. 442–50.

2   See Joseph Fletcher, *Situation Ethics: The New Morality*, Philadelphia: The Westminster Press, 1966.

3   Ibid. Note the case of Mrs Bergmeier's 'Sacrificial Adultery', p. 164.

4   For a clear discussion of this theory see Richard M. Gula, *Reason Informed by Faith: Foundations of Catholic Morality*, New York: Paulist Press, 1989, pp. 265–7.

5   For an excellent critique of Cultural Relativism see Mary Midgley, 'Trying Out One's New Sword', in her *Heart and Mind: The Varieties of Moral Experience*, London: Methuen, 1981, pp. 69–75.

6   J. Bennett, 'The Conscience of Huckleberry Finn', *Philosophy*, 49 (1974), pp. 124–34.

7   See J.O. Urmson, 'Saints and Heroes', in *Moral Concepts*, ed. Joel Feinberg, London: Oxford University Press, 1969.

8   A relativist could be totally opposed to subjectivism, denying that morality is based on feeling, while insisting that local circumstances oblige absolutely only at the local level. 'When in Rome ...' A subjectivist could reject relativism, holding that all humans ought to feel the same about war or abortion or injustice.

21 Morality and Transcendence

Patrick Masterson

(Patrick Masterson, *The Sense of Creation*, Surrey: Ashgate, 2008, pp. 77–84 [extract].)

ETHICS AND RELIGION

For Levinas, an authentic affirmation of God must respect both the separateness and autonomy of the human subject on the one hand, and the irreducible transcendence of God on the other. Consequently the affirmation is not to be achieved through some mystical technique of ecstatic participation whereby the separated knowing self is annihilated or transported outside himself and absorbed into a numinous divine being.[1] Such an approach would treat man as a mere circuit of rupture and reunification within the totality of divine life. It would not respect the truth that precisely as a created existence he is separate from God – enjoys an *esse proprium*, a genuine autonomy.[2] But neither can God, the utterly transcendent, be directly comprehended or thematised as an object of human cognition. God, as he is in himself, infinitely transcends our cognitional resources. As Descartes appreciated, he overflows absolutely any idea we may have of him.

Levinas maintains that in metaphysics, or ethics (he uses the terms interchangeably), man enters a relationship with God, the relation of a separated being with what he cannot in the etymological sense of the word comprehend.[3] This relationship with God, inaccessible to either mystical participation or theoretical cogitation, is accomplished through the ethical relationships with other people such as are portrayed by him in *Totality and Infinity*.

He speaks of the dimension of the divine being manifest in the human face of the Stranger, the widow, and the orphan who solicit us in their destitution. God is supremely present as the ultimate significance of the justice which we render to other persons. Our relationship with him respects his directly inaccessible transcendence and is more effectively disclosed in our ethical welcome of the Other than by any attempt to comprehend him theoretically. Thus he remarks:

> Ethics is the spiritual optics ... Hence metaphysics is enacted where the social relation is enacted – in our relations with men. There can be no 'knowledge' of God separated from the relationship with men. The Other is the very locus of metaphysical truth, and is indispensable for my relation with God.[4]

He sees the ethical relationship between men as the primary irreducible structure upon which all metaphysics rests and as conferring upon theological concepts the only significance they have. This ethical relationship in which a separated self acknowledges concretely the irreducible moral claims of the Other is in its deepest significance the relationship between a person and the utterly transcendent God, and as thus envisaged is what we call religion. Religion is the bond between the same and the Other which is not a function of a totality and does not crystallise into a system.[5]

This claim that a religious relationship with God is achieved through ethical relationships with other people is an appealing but not immediately evident thesis. It strikes a responsive chord in anyone already committed to the Judeo-Christian teaching that access to God cannot be disassociated from the loving welcome of the neighbour. But how might somebody, who is not explicitly a theist or even who is explicitly an atheist, but accepting Levinas's account of ethics, be persuaded that it implies the religious significance which he ascribes to it?

Levinas's text is not entirely helpful on this delicate point. He is generally dismissive of theoretical arguments for the existence of God and tends to assert the relationship between ethics and religion in rather striking terms rather than argue it systematically. His reticence about arguing this religious claim stems from his mistrust of traditional ontology and his conviction that the relationship at issue is unamenable to the totalising movement of thought. 'The relationship between separated beings does not totalise them; it is a "Relation without relation" which no one can encompass or thematize.'[6] He simply asserts that 'the Other, in his signification prior to my initiative resembles God'.[7] Again, speaking of 'the curvature of inter-subjective space' which expresses metaphorically the relationship in which the other person is placed 'higher' than me – in the sense that my ethical responsibility for him is more than I can require of him for myself – he says 'this "curvature of space" is, perhaps, the very presence of God'.[8] Nevertheless, some rational justification of this theistic interpretation is called for if it is not to appear arbitrary or even superfluous. The ethical relation must be shown to imply the alleged theistic interpretation as its ultimate rationale. Although he does not elucidate how this might be shown he does make some perceptive observations which open up an interesting line of reflection.

ETHICS AND METAPHYSICAL ARGUMENT

According to Levinas, the idea of creation from nothing provides the best expression of his idea of the ethical relationship in which the transcendence of the other person is affirmed as irreducible to any kind of totality.[9]

Following up this idea (and recalling the kind of argument advanced by Kant which we indicated above) one might argue that the ethical relationship as envisaged by Levinas requires as its theoretical or metaphysical truth condition the theistic claim that the persons involved in the relationship are created beings. If this were shown to be the case one would have achieved at once a moral and a causal argument for the existence of God as the transcendent creator of moral beings. The argument would be an *a posteriori* and indirect one. It would argue that the concretely experienced ethical relationship turns out upon reflection to be unintelligible and even contradictory unless the terms of the relationship are acknowledged to be created beings.

Such an argument might begin with a consideration of the irreducible significance ascribed to the other person as an absolute and self-possesses source of moral obligation. Each other person appears even, and indeed principally, in their destitution and vulnerability as a being of surpassing worth to whom I find myself obligated.[10] He or she so appears that the only appropriate response in their regard is goodness – even to the point of very great sacrifice, which I cannot on that account reciprocally require of them. (Think of Kant's example of the honest man who is prepared to endure death rather than conspire in the execution of an innocent powerless person.)[11] The other person appears as expressing an absolute moral claim upon my conduct which may not be subordinated to my pursuit of personal happiness or to any global utilitarian ideal.

This ethical relationship, if taken as veridical and not illusory, has metaphysical implications. The order of things must be ultimately such that the other person can validly exercise the irreducible ethical claim upon me which I acknowledge her to do – particularly since what might otherwise appear a better outcome from an impersonal viewpoint is subordinated to this claim. If how things are is not ultimately consonant with, and possibly even wholly inadequate and recalcitrant to, the exigencies of morality, then the ethical life, at least as described by Levinas, is rendered rationally suspect. The absolute claims of the other person and the often very demanding constraints imposed thereby on my action could not be rationally defended – particularly when they appear to impede an objective maximisation of good or minimisation of evil. If absolutist cheques cannot be cashed out metaphysically in ontological currency, i.e. in a compatible and dependable account of reality, then the ultimate subordination of utilitarian considerations to absolutist constraints is, as Nagel contends, rationally indefensible.

How then ultimately must reality be understood to be if the experienced ethical relationship, as described by Levinas, is to be metaphysically confirmed? The most significant features of this relationship are its asymmetrical character and the irreducibility of its terms to any encompassing totality. As Levinas puts it: 'Multiplicity in being, which refuses totalization but takes form as fraternity and discourse, is situated in a "space" essentially asymmetrical.'[12] In the ethical relationship the other is placed higher than me. I respond freely to him as a transcendent and absolute source of obligation exercising a unique, ineluctable, and non-mutual claim upon my service.[13]

Here we come up against what Nagel refers to elsewhere as the sense of incredulity that one should be somebody in particular whose direct inter-personal relationships with other unique individuals constitute the irreducible bedrock of morality.[14] Especially paradoxical is the self-possessed superior ethical status ascribed in the relationship to the other person. This exalted transcendence, irreducible to any totality, orientates our thinking about the structure of reality. It indicates that we should envisage beings as standing in a relationship precisely as separate and independent, as both axiologically and ontologically diverse.

For Levinas beings are characterised by a radical heterogeneity which is resistant to any attempt to totalise them as equivalent instances of the same kind. This radical independence and non-homogeneity of beings (in more traditional idiom the analogical character of finite beings) surpasses comprehension in terms of a naturally dispersed and variously configured break-up of a primordial common stuff. Hence he remarks: 'This impossibility of conciliation among beings, this radical heterogeneity, in fact indicates a mode of being produced and an ontology that is not equivalent to panoramic existence and its disclosure. ... The exteriority of being does not, in fact, mean that multiplicity is without relation. However, the relation that binds this multiplicity does not fill the abyss of separation; it confirms it.'[15]

In effect the ethical acknowledgement of the other person as asymmetrically transcendent impels us to ask how it can be that he thus exists? This exalted transcendence, this curvature of inter-subjective space, is unintelligible in terms of our ordinary scientific understanding of our shared human nature to which utilitarian considerations are so well adapted. It does not make sense considered from below, as it were, in terms of our common appearance as comparable members of the same biological species. We are speaking here more of an innovative emergence of ethically related unique individual subjects than a resultant appearance of objectively equivalent instances of a common physico-chemical structure. As Levinas puts it: 'That the Other is placed higher than me would be a pure and simple error if the welcome I make him consisted in "perceiving" a nature. Sociology, psychology, physiology are thus deaf to exteriority. Man as Other comes to us from the outside, a separated – or holy – face. His exteriority, that is, his appeal to me, is his truth.'[16]

An account is called for of how this remarkable state of affairs can obtain – this coming to be of ethically related individuals possessing conscious moral capabilities irreducible to and underivable from their physico-chemical micro-parts or any connecting or compounding of these micro-parts. As in the case of theoretical knowledge, any attempt to provide a complete account of this interpersonal ethical relationship in cultural, psychological, evolutionary or biological terms is self-defeating. It fails precisely to encompass the radical emergence of the interpersonal dimension of transcendence which characterises the relationship. This dimension of transcendence, expressed in relationships of ethical obligation vis-à-vis the Other, is of a formality disparate from and exceeding the various scientifically comprehensible totalities in which the individuals involved are enmeshed.

How then can the other person, notwithstanding all his manifest limitations and dependencies, present himself to me, a particular non-interchangable someone, as a unique and innovative being, an absolute upsurge of self-possessed value – coming as it were at once from nowhere and from above in relation to where I stand vis-à-vis him? This paradoxical condition of a contingent existent, transcending scientific comprehension in terms of the network of totalities in which he is implicated, suggests that it might be better considered in a different, more metaphysical way, perhaps in terms of the classical account of creation. Let us consider what this suggestion involves.

According to the account of creation, which we have indicated in Chapter 2, finite human beings are not mere emanations of a divine substance. Although wholly dependent they exist and act as distinct substances in their own right. Their self-possessed being, and their activity and achievements as natural causes, depend upon the sustaining power of God's decision to originate them absolutely into communication with his transcendent infinite perfection and goodness. They and their sustaining context are originated, not as the dispersion or transformation of some primordial uncreated stuff, but wholly from nothing – in other words, not from or out of anything. As thus originated to exist and act in their own right each finite human being possesses an ontological exteriority and distinction not only vis-à-vis God but also vis-à-vis other human beings. As created individual beings they stand related to each other not only as similar but also, across the chasm of their respective origin from nothing, as radically separate and diverse.

This exteriority or transcendence which characterises human beings follows from their condition of each having come to be, as the particular incarnate ethical subject she is, through creation from nothing and maintained in her being, action, and interaction by this same act of creation. They relate to each other as personal beings and to the transcendent God across the void of non-being, as it were, of their absolute origin *ex nihilo*. As Levinas puts it:

> To affirm origin from nothing by creation is to contest the prior community of all things within eternity, from which philosophical thought, guided by ontology, makes things arise as from a common matrix. The absolute gap of separation which transcendence implies could not be better expressed than by the term creation, in which the kinship of beings among themselves is affirmed, but at the same time their radical heterogeneity also, their reciprocal exteriority coming from nothingness. One may speak of creation to characterise entities situated in a transcendence that does not close over into a totality.[17]

Now this idea of creation, although it itself raises several deep issues, does make sense of the otherwise unintelligible ethical acknowledgement of the asymmetrical transcendence of the other person, which was the point of departure of our reflections. Ethics, as we have said, achieves a conscious relationship with the other person precisely as other and higher than me in the sense of requiring of me more than I can on that account require of him for myself. Though it commences from my separated self-possessed subjectivity it challenges the tendency to seek the foundation of this self within itself envisaged as *pour-soi* or absolute freedom. Beyond the plane of natural need and arbitrary self-assertion it invests my freedom as desire for the good of the Other.[18] It locates my centre of gravity outside myself at the service of the obligating encounter of the Other.[19]

The Other thus envisaged is separate, unique, transcendent – an absolute upsurge of meaning and value. Although manifestly implicated in all the causality and vicissitudes of a spatio-temporal nature he is welcomed as one whose existence surpasses comprehension in these terms. Thus Levinas remarks: 'The Other remains infinitely transcendent, infinitely foreign; his face in which his epiphany is produced and appeals to me breaks with the world that can be common to us, whose virtualities are inscribed in our *nature* and developed by our existence.'[20] He is welcomed ethically by me as a separate self-referring existence arising from nothing in the world yet ineluctably summoning me to goodness in his regard. He is welcomed as a being who comes to be as existing in his own right, as dependent yet autonomous, as vulnerable to murder yet an expression of authoritative transcendent ethical significance. This ethical acknowledgement of the other person as asymmetrically transcendent, as being from nowhere and above – which is quite unintelligible in terms of any totality or natural process – exemplifies in a concrete way what is reflectively characterised by the abstract notion of a created being.

Thus the concrete ethical experience of the transcendence of the other person constitutes a privileged practical foundation for a metaphysical account of creation. Moreover, this experience appears to require such an account as its ultimate truth condition. It generates a line of metaphysical reflection which contests the totalising tendency of much traditional philosophy and proposes a very different account – a basically religious account of the fundamental structure of being.

In other words, the asymmetrical transcendence of the ethically envisaged other person adduces, as its implicit ontological correlative or ultimate rationale, the theistic account of creation which envisages all finite beings as asymmetrically related to each other and to the transcendent God. Endorsing this contention Levinas writes:

> The dimension of the divine opens forth from the human face. ... God rises to his supreme and ultimate presence as correlative to the justice rendered unto men ... The Other is not the incarnation of God, but

precisely by his face, in which he is disincarnate, is the very manifestation of the height in which God is revealed. ... Totality and the embrace of being, or ontology, do not contain the final secret of being. Religion, where relationships subsist between the same and the other despite the impossibility of the Whole – the idea of Infinity – is the ultimate structure.[21]

Incidentally, for Levinas, the ethical relation which acknowledges the asymmetrical transcendence of the other person not only provides the unique access to a true metaphysical conception of reality. It also provides an elucidation of his original contention that 'The moral consciousness can sustain the mocking gaze of the political man only if the certitude of peace dominates the evidence of war'.[22]

The assurance of peace rests, not on an uncertain victorious outcome to war, but upon a prior, pre-political, ethical relationship whereby I subordinate my egoism to benevolent desire for the well-being of the other person:

Peace therefore cannot be identified with the end of combats that cease for want of combatants, by the defeat of some and the victory of the others, that is, with cemeteries or future universal empires. Peace must be my peace, in a relation that starts from an I and goes to the other, in desire and goodness, where the I both maintains itself and exists without egoism. It is conceived starting from an I assured of the convergence of morality and reality ...[23]

Implicit in this is a repudiation of utilitarian considerations sometimes invoked to justify atrocities.

NOTES

1   Cf. E. Levinas, *Totality and Infinity*, p. 77.
2   Cf. ibid., pp. 104–5.
3   Cf. ibid., p. 80.
4   Ibid., p. 78.
5   Cf. ibid., pp. 79–80.
6   Ibid., p. 295.
7   Ibid., p. 293.
8   Ibid., p. 291.
9   Cf. ibid., p. 293.
10   Cf. ibid., p. 75 and p. 291.
11   Cf. Kant, *Critique of Practical Reason*, par. 305.
12   E. Levinas, *Totality and Infinity*, p. 216, cf. also pp. 35–6 and pp. 290–2.
13   Cf. ibid., pp. 86–7.
14   Cf. T. Nagel, *Mortal Questions*, p. 206, also E. Levinas, *Totality and Infinity*, pp. 304–6.
15   E. Levinas, ibid., pp. 294–5.
16   Ibid., p. 291.
17   Ibid., p. 293.
18   Cf. ibid., pp. 83–90.

19   Cf. ibid., p. 183.
20   Ibid., p. 194.
21   Ibid., pp. 78–80.
22   Ibid., p. 22.
23   Ibid., p. 306.

Part Four
Conscience

22 Toward a Personalist Theology of Conscience

Linda Hogan

(Linda Hogan, *Confronting the Truth: Conscience in the Catholic Tradition*, New York: Paulist Press, 2000, pp. 127–65 [extract].)

I have argued for a personalist model of ethics. This model operates on the basis that ethical values derive their authority, not from some static and abstract notion of human nature but from their promotion of the good of the person 'integrally and adequately considered'. This is the ethical model proposed in both *Gaudium et spes* and in *Dignitatis humanae*. We have already identified some of the implications of moving to this personalist model. These include (1) a greater recognition of the role of history and change in ethics; (2) a focus on the moral significance of intentions and circumstances in addition to the act itself; (3) a greater degree of sophistication in categorising the different kinds of moral norms and the kinds of claims they make; and (4) a rethinking of the relationship between the individual and magisterium on the basis of the relocation of moral authority. Each of the changes mentioned above will inevitably have an impact on the way in which the nature and role of conscience is understood. Some of these changes have already been alluded to. However, a coherent account of conscience against the backdrop of this personalist theology still needs to be developed. The purpose of this chapter is to begin that process.

In the first section we will focus on the renewed relationship between the person and her/his actions. This, above all else, is the most significant change in terms of understanding the role of conscience. In the second section we will develop a holistic account of the operations of conscience, which involves the interplay of reason, intuition, emotion and imagination. And in the final section we will explore the limits of human weakness and sinfulness as manifest in the failures of conscience.

RECONCEIVING THE RELATIONSHIP BETWEEN PERSONS AND ACTS

The traditional understanding of conscience made use of the terms *habitual* and *actual* conscience. The term habitual referred to the innate sense of good and evil that all human beings are believed to possess. The term *actual* focused on the judgements of conscience in which such an orientation must be manifested. The habitual conscience corresponded to the term *synderesis* while the actual conscience corresponded to *conscientia*. It is clear from the deployment of such terminology that the traditional account of conscience, as it developed from the theology of St Paul, had a dual orientation. It involved a focus on the fundamental orientation to the good, which *synderesis* encapsulated, and on the concrete decisions of conscience, which was the work of *conscientia*. However, as the discipline evolved, especially in the centuries when casuistry dominated, attention was ever more focused on the moral act. As a result the Thomistic integration of the habitual and actual dimensions of conscience gave way to a theology preoccupied with the morality of discrete, compartmentalised decisions. So, for example, theologians discussed the morality of contraception, of in vitro fertilization and of warfare, rather than focus on the character and values of the person who chose to use contraception or in vitro fertilization or who engaged in warfare. However, a personalist theology requires that attention be given, not only to actions, not only to the workings of the actual conscience, but also to the character of the person and to her/his orientation vis-à-vis good and evil. In traditional terms the spotlight is once again put on the workings of the habitual conscience. The crucial difference that personalism makes, therefore, is that it places the individual at the centre of moral inquiry and understanding. In terms of a theology of conscience, then, the personalist model involves a radical change of emphasis and a reordering of the significance attached to acts and character.

In this new theological framework conscience denotes both the fundamental orientation of the person to seek and do the good, and the actualisation of this desire in decisions of conscience. Conscience is thus understood to be more than the sum of particular decisions, although each choice is important. Conscience also refers to the integrated and consistent thrust of the person toward goodness. It is the dimension of one's character that determines the direction of one's moral life, one's self-conscious option for good. This kind of language can give a false impression of our reality as persons. It can suggest that the person is constituted by one singular and unitary narrative. In fact we are not at all like this. We do not possess an innate or essential freedom, as though freedom exists in some abstract or unambiguous way. Nor are our commitments necessarily always harmonious. In reality persons are constituted in a complex unity of fragmentary and varying narratives, commitments and values that change over time and that may pull us in different directions.

These issues of personal identity and subjectivity have been the subject of extensive investigations in recent decades. Feminist and postmodern theorists in particular have problematised the traditional liberal assumptions about personhood. Rosi Braidotti talks about persons as nomadic subjects, ever changing.[2] Judith Butler is reluctant to accept any unifying sense of personal identity at all, save as a performative strategy.[3] Others like Seyla Benhabib recognise that the self is in part socially constituted, fragmented and ultimately always in process. Yet Benhabib also insists that one can talk about a self and about personal identity, albeit in a provisional and partial manner.[4] The essentials of

An Irish Reader in Moral Theology

Benhabib's proposal underlie this discussion about conscience. When I speak about the nature of the person or about personal identity it is with a recognition that we are always persons in process and that our identities are multilayered, multiple, ambiguous and necessarily shaped by factors which are beyond either our consciousness or our control. The remit of conscience is thus expanded, to include both the (always incomplete) integrated moral character of the person, and the actions that flow from this and which embody her/his attraction to moral goodness.

This dual emphasis on the direction of the person's life and on the actions that she/he performs has become a cornerstone of the personalist model. The distinction was developed initially in order to rethink the theology of sin, which we will discuss in a later section of this chapter. The central claim is that a theology of sin should focus primarily on the basic direction of a person's life, on his or her fundamental option, rather than on individual acts of failure.[5] This theology of fundamental option, as it has come to be known, is also crucial for rethinking the nature of conscience. The fundamental option is the term given to the basic orientation of a person's life, either toward or against God. At the person's core she/he either responds to the loving invitation of God, or she/he refuses it. A life lived in the context of a 'yes' response is a life oriented toward seeking goodness. A fundamental option that says no to such an invitation is directed away from this search. The theory of fundamental option then highlights that persons can be oriented toward good or evil, that they shape their characters in one direction or the other. Each person's fundamental option is actualised in the particular decisions that she/he makes and the virtues or vices that are cultivated. So, in relation to the conscience, it is not that every single decision is decisive, but rather that daily choices and ways of being, repeated over a lifetime, develop a pattern that reveal the person's fundamental option for good or for evil. In effect the theory of fundamental option ascribes significance primarily to the moral character of the person and directs our attention to the general sensitivity and maturity of conscience. The decisions and judgements of the actual conscience are thus regarded as a reflection of the person's fundamental option and are of significance primarily in this regard.

Many moral theologians have adopted and developed the theory of fundamental option. Bernard Häring, Josef Fuchs and Karl Rahner each have based their theological reflections on the idea that human beings, at their core, opt either for a life lived in the direction of goodness or of evil.[6] Although they each have used different reasoning and terminology to analyse the fundamental option, the central tenets of each explanation are the same. We will use Rahner's analysis to discuss workings of the fundamental option in relation to conscience, but we could as easily use that of either Fuchs or Häring. Rahner suggested that one could think of human freedom as having two distinct dimensions. He distinguished between what he called the transcendental level of freedom and the categorical level.[7] According to Rahner human beings possess a basic freedom, a fundamental and deep-rooted freedom, which enables us to determine ourselves as persons. At this level freedom is not about deciding between particular acts or objects; it is concerned with one's entire orientation and direction in life. This is the person's transcendental freedom. In Rahner's theology the choice at this level is either the acceptance of a loving relationship with God or a refusal of it. Fuchs terms this the person's basic freedom. It is on the basis of this transcendental freedom that the person decides her/his fundamental option and determines whether it is for good or bad.

The choice made at the transcendental level shapes completely the moral character of the person and becomes the basis on which the person exercises choice and makes decisions. Rahner calls the daily exercise of choice categorical freedom, in which the person makes decisions on the basis of the options that are before her/him. The free decisions of conscience exercised in everyday situations are vital, because it is in and through each of these distinct choices that the person concretises her/his fundamental option. Through these free choices, at the categorical level, the person realises and implements the fundamental option for good or evil. Thus, there is a dialectic in operation here. The person's fundamental option is actualised and reinforced by what Iris Murdoch called the ongoing 'acts of attention'[8] to the good. These small, often insignificant acts in which we exercise our freedom are the primary way in which we demonstrate the orientation of our moral lives. They become the incarnation of our fundamental option.

But the choices and decisions a person makes in everyday life not only express the fundamental option, they also reinforce it. This is a point that many proponents of the fundamental option did not emphasise sufficiently. In my view it is unhelpful to conceptualise the fundamental option as radically distinct from and prior to the discrete moments of choosing. Instead, one should think of the person's fundamental option as always in process, as never fully determined once and for all. Rather, it is created in repeated moments of choosing the good over a lifetime. Decisions of conscience, then, are not merely reflections of the person's fundamental option. It is in and through the choices made, both at significant moments in one's life and in the daily routine of minor 'acts of attention', that the person determines her/his basic orientation. It is also in the ways we relate to others and our way of being in the world that our fundamental option is cultivated. Earlier theories of fundamental option did not give due attention to the role that categorical freedom plays in constructing the fundamental option. One always got the impression that the person's basic direction or fundamental option was decided at some abstract level, at some time before the person had to make concrete ethical decisions. However, such a view is completely at odds with the experience of the moral life. People do not choose to be oriented to the good in theory at some transcendental level and then go on to make decisions on the basis of that fundamental option. Nor does this happen in a way that disregards the complex psychological makeup of human beings. Rather, imperceptibly over time, in and through the choices they make and the kinds of dispositions and virtues they nurture, people form their moral characters and thereby determine the orientation of their fundamental option. Thus, the person's fundamental option is created in making choices and cultivating virtues and is reaffirmed through the repetition of such behaviour.

The precise details of the various theories of fundamental option need not detain us here. The primary purpose in discussing it is to suggest a framework in which to think about the relationship between the character of the person and the choices she/he makes. What is suggested by this is an understanding of conscience as the person's orientation to and desire for goodness. However, this orientation toward goodness can only be actualised in the constant and continuous cultivation of a virtuous character. Of course, given the fragile and ambiguous nature of our search for moral goodness,[9] this orientation should not be conceptualised as a single and simple trajectory. In her excellent study *The Fragility of Goodness*[10] Martha Nussbaum reminds us of our limitations as we seek to articulate and live by that which we believe to be good. Our orientation toward 'the good' is more appropriately imaged as a stream making its circuitous and uncertain way toward its as yet unknown destination, rather than as an arrow in flight. It needs to take account of the fact that people change and that what seemed to be a good choice in the past may not seem to be so now. Yet, given these limitations, this is an understanding of conscience that sees an intimate connection between the kind of person one is and the actions one performs. It recognises that the formation of conscience takes place, not by some superficial adherence to rules and laws but rather in working toward goodness rather than evil or indifference in every context, no matter how trivial. It is the way in which these discrete moments of choosing are patterned together that determines the strength and the maturity of conscience. It is through the person's conscience, therefore, that one can see the unity and coherence of the moral character.

We form our consciences over time. We affirm our fundamental convictions through the decisions we have made in the past and the virtues we embody in the present. The mature conscience develops in the attempt to be virtuous and make decisions that further reinforce and continue that pattern. The good conscience, then, is not merely the sum total of good choices made over time. Rather, it is the disposition or orientation to desire good and is the culmination of a life lived consistently in the pursuit of virtue. The focus on the fundamental option enables one to think of conscience as a continuous process, as an orientation embodied in different contexts and related, not only to past and present, but also to the person's future. This conceptualisation of conscience gives most attention to the way in which moments of choosing and ways of relating are patterned into a unity that is the moral self. It allows one to expand discussions of conscience to include considerations of how the emotions, intuitions and imagination of the person shape the moral character. It also focuses attention on the role that the wider community (both secular and religious) has in forming the orientation of the conscience. In short it requires us to abandon the reductionism, characteristic of an earlier theology, which was concerned primarily with acts and with specific, unconnected decisions of conscience.

The role of moral communities will be considered at length in chapter 6. However, it is necessary to mention their significance in the formation of conscience at this stage. It is obvious that individuals attempt to orient themselves toward good and form their moral characters within the context of a community or communities. The social context within which a person operates inevitably has a major influence on the conscience. Leonardo Boff, in his book *Liberating Grace*,[11] developed a convincing argument for the strong interrelation between the individual's fundamental project and the society to which she/he belongs. It is not that we are completely socially determined. Of course people can and do resist the expectations and norms of behaviour that a society may impose on them. However, the values and virtues that a society embodies do play an important role in the formation of conscience. This is true of the limitations and moral blindness of communities and will be important in our discussion of moral failure. But it is also true of the cultivation of positive dispositions.

The values and virtues that shape a person's conscience arise from beliefs about how the good is constituted and how it can be sought. These convictions – such as, it is good to honour the promises one makes or to deal with people honestly – are present in the society's moral code and are conveyed to the individual in a variety of ways. In the same way as a child learns to belong to a linguistic community, so, too, it learns about moral conduct. This moral development takes place at both the formal and informal levels. Parental guidance, school instruction and moral education in religious communities are very important factors in the formation of conscience. But the stories, narratives and traditions of a community are also vital vehicles of moral codes. These operate at a more informal level but are no less significant for that. Stories of moral exemplars, accounts of moral heroism, articulations of a community's moral vision – each play a part in the development of the individual's conscience. The conscience is formed in community. The individual does not construct her/his basic orientation from a tabula rasa. Rather, the person's conscience is shaped within a received tradition, which conveys its sense of moral goodness in a variety of ways. But no matter how regulatory the community or society may be, the responsibility for educating and nurturing the conscience rests ultimately with the individual.

THE INWARD DYNAMICS OF CONSCIENCE

The formation of conscience involves many aspects of the person. It cannot be reduced to tutoring reason and developing intellectual sophistication. Although reason does indeed have a vital role to play in the activity of conscience, so too have intuition, emotion and imagination. Conscience needs an interplay of each of these elements to operate sensitively and successfully. We make choices by attending to and evaluating our responses at a variety of different levels. Good, integrated and fully personal decisions engage the individual at the intellectual, intuitive, emotional and imaginative levels. Good choices reflect a coherence of these important aspects of the personality so that no one level is ignored or silenced. So, far from being objective, dispassionate judgements of reason, decisions of conscience are embodied and emotional, engaging the whole person and not just the intellect.

A personalist model of conscience should highlight the multidimensional aspects of its decision making. When the focus is directed away from the morality of isolated acts and toward the person who performs these acts, then the person's motivations, dispositions, feelings and intuitions gain tremendous significance. Individuals do not engage in decisions of 'pure reason'. However, much of western philosophy and theology operated with the view that 'the subject is rational and objective only to the extent that it is disengaged from natural and social worlds and *even* from its own body which then can be seen as an object of study and a source of deception'. This clearly is an untenable view of the person. Charles Taylor in his *Sources of the Self*[13] has mapped both the emergence and demise of this punctual self, that is, the self who is 'rational, free, but language less, cultureless, history-less ...'[14] In contrast the person at the centre of this theology of conscience is not an abstract mind, but a person who is located in culture and history, one who is relational, embodied and ultimately in progress. Of course this self can and must engage in rational inquiry; however, it is a contextual rationality. Indeed, philosophy since Nietzsche has recognised that the idea of pure reason is a myth. Reason is one aspect of our personhood and as such reflects the particularities and limitations of our contexts. In this discussion of the role of reason in the moral life of the person, rationality is understood as embodied and contextual, shaped by the conventions of culture, by religious sensibilities, by desires both conscious and unconscious, by imaginings and fears. Although it is usually difficult to disentangle the complexities of the inward workings of conscience, it is important to discuss, however briefly, the contribution of these elements.

Reason

This is the element in the activity of conscience that has traditionally been given most attention. Indeed, it does play a central role in identifying the nature of problems of conscience and in evaluating possible solutions. I certainly do not want to underestimate the role of reason in decision making, but I do want to emphasise that reason is always contextual. It reflects the presuppositions, values and limitations of our culture, time and place. It is inevitably shaped and tutored by the person's intuitions and emotions. Reason's contribution to the activity of conscience cannot be limited to one particular phase. From the time the person becomes aware of the existence of some kind of dilemma until its resolution, reason may have a contribution to make. Its ultimate role is to help us find a solution internally coherent and consistent with 'the bigger picture', notwithstanding the fact that our understanding is always limited and our knowledge always incomplete. The task of providing resolutions both internally coherent and consistent with our general framework of understanding is not an easy one.

One of the most important roles that reason has in moral decision making relates to defining the problem or the issue at stake. This is absolutely crucial since many ethical disagreements arise because people differ about the nature of a problem or indeed whether a particular issue has any ethical significance at all. Take, for example, two businesspeople involved in a company takeover, which results in the loss of two hundred jobs in one small town. One businessman may believe himself to have some responsibility for the employees of the company and may be in a dilemma as to what should be done for them. Should they set up a fund to help the former employees retrain for other jobs? Should they try to enhance the local economy in other ways? Should they compensate the workers beyond the minimal redundancy payments to which they are legally entitled? The other businesswoman may believe that they have no additional responsibilities to the work force over and above those required by law. She may be sorry that economic realities mean that they cannot have as large a work force as the former employers. She may regret that the region is so dependent on that particular company. She may feel genuinely sorry for the people who have lost their jobs. However, all this notwithstanding, she may believe that there is no ethical dilemma to be resolved.

These two businesspeople disagree about whether they have some duty to the former work force and the community affected by their takeover. One does not believe that they have a moral problem; the other does. Identifying and defining the problem is thus the first (often contentious) stage in decision making. Reason has an important role in this process since it accumulates all the evidence, identifies which factors are relevant and scrutinises the logic of the arguments. This may result in one person changing his mind about the nature of the problem or may lead to the problem being redefined altogether. Of course at various stages the precise nature and scope of the moral problem may again need to be reconceived. We may discover dimensions of the problem that we never envisaged initially. This constant revision of the nature of the problem is itself an integral part of its resolution.

An in-depth discussion of the nature of rationality and its role in the moral life is neither possible nor appropriate at this stage. Suffice it to say that it has been the object of much inquiry through the centuries. Alisdair MacIntyre is one of the many philosophers and theologians concerned with the changing concepts of rationality in ethics.[15] As with the changing understanding of the self, the consensus among many ethicians is that rationality is always historical and contextual. What appears as rational to us is bound in a significant way to our personal histories, community narratives and symbol systems. Terence McCaughey in his groundbreaking *Memory and Redemption* illustrates this point excellently in the context of the Northern Irish conflict.[16] In this work he discusses the profound impact that a community's traditions and symbols can have in shaping what is perceived to be rational. The rational does not exist apart from these contingencies of place, history and culture, but within them. Furthermore, this does not represent the failure of reason, but rather is part of its nature.

For our purposes, however, it is important to note that reason demands that we concern ourselves with issues of 'consistency, logic, rules of evidence, appropriateness, coherence, clarity, completeness and congruence with received reality and meaning'.[17] Consistency requires that we try to maintain the same standards throughout the whole process of making the decision. Logic points to the need for our thinking to follow a clear and sequential form of argumentation. It helps us to guard against drawing conclusions that are insupportable on the basis of the preceding evidence. The 'rules of evidence' remind us to test all our conclusions so that we take care not to include factors that cannot be justified. Reason also necessitates that we search for and include all relevant evidence and that we give to each element the appropriate weight and importance. It also requires that we conduct our arguments with clarity and an internal coherence. We should attempt to ensure that our resolution should not contain any major contradictions. Furthermore, the way in which a particular problem is solved should not contradict what we know to be generally true of our experience of the world and our relationships. For example, if I resolve a problem in a way that leads me to assume that every single person that I have come in contact with over my lifetime has been lying to me, then I need to reexamine my own thinking, since such a conclusion is at odds with what I have experienced heretofore. The solution to my moral problem ought not to be wildly incongruous with the rest of reality.

The significant role that reason performs is evident right through the whole decision-making process. In addition to defining and redefining the nature of the problem, reason plays its part in gathering and evaluating relevant information, judging whether some factors are irrelevant, proposing solutions, assessing their worth in the situation at hand and in relation to the larger context. The work of reason, therefore, involves the person in a constant appraisal of every aspect of the problem and not just a once-for-all judgement. Although such rational decisions are ultimately personal, they must be made with reference to the wider community. When faced with a moral problem we should also investigate how other rational and informed individuals have resolved similar difficulties. We must test the adequacy of our own reasoning and argumentation in the wider domain. It is not sufficient that we are satisfied with the logic and coherence of our analysis.

We must be prepared to scrutinise it in public, to seek the advice of friends and to evaluate our own reasoning in the light of the values of moral and religious communities. In short, reason itself requires that we test the adequacy of our rationality by comparing it with that of other thoughtful individuals and communities and by assessing it honestly.

Of course there can be difficulties. Incomplete or inaccurate information can make the reasoning process problematic and can result in unsustainable judgements. We may have assumed that certain individuals will act in a particular way and then find out that they do the opposite. We may depend on particular results that don't materialise or we may ignore the fact that much of the relevant data is missing. But in addition to difficulties that arise in relation to the information needed to make decisions, our rational capacity may also be impaired. Various forms of mental illness, including psychosis and delusions of many sorts, make the kind of thoughtful analysis essential to decision making well nigh impossible. The effects of such limitations can be seen in the many instances of moral failure and self-deception that we encounter daily. These will be discussed in more detail later in the chapter. For the moment, however, it is important to note the central role that reason plays in decisions of conscience and the difficulties that arise from its failures.

Intuition

Making decisions of conscience involves evaluating information of various kinds and not just that which we have acquired through the process of reason. Much of the knowledge we have comes to us from sources that are not strictly intellectual. We tend to class knowledge of this sort as intuitive. By describing something as intuitive we generally mean that we cannot test it by purely intellectual means. It is knowledge that we have instinctively. It is not consciously acquired, but is nonetheless known to us in some indefinable way. I can have an intuition not to trust an individual whom I have recently met. I may not be able to articulate why I am hesitant to trust that person. Yet, I may know instinctively that something is amiss. The essence of an intuition is that it comes to us from a nonconscious place. It is not part of our explicit awareness. We make judgements and decisions on the basis of such tacit knowledge all the time. Our instincts – about the reliability of people, about the eventual outcome of events outside our control, about the way relationships are likely to develop and about many other things – are important sources of information in our moral lives. But although intuitive knowledge by its very nature is unconscious, it is amenable to analysis and evaluation.

The person often experiences intuitions as surprising, as being outside conscious awareness. Yet, even though this may be true superficially, if one investigates it carefully one can usually account for an intuition. Let us take the intuition not to trust a particular person one has recently met. If we scrutinise all our encounters with that individual, we are likely to come up with an explanation for our intuition. It may be that she has been indiscreet about someone she knows or that she has made fun of another person's scruples or that she seems cavalier about people's feelings. Although our encounter with the person may have been perfectly pleasant, one may have picked up something almost imperceptible about the person's behaviour that results in the intuition not to trust her. Intuitions usually do have some basis in actual experience. They are rarely completely arbitrary and random. They usually result from being sensitive to the behaviour of another person, or from conclusions drawn from actions in another context.

Women are generally said to be more intuitive than men. Their intuition is frequently referred to as a sixth sense. If women are more intuitive, it is not because of some biologically rooted, gender-specific faculty. Rather, it may come, as most intuitive insight does, from more careful attention to gestures, reactions, unspoken assumptions and valuations. People reveal a great deal about themselves and their priorities without ever intending to. Intuition is usually based on knowledge and insights gained through sensitivity to all that is implicit and nonconscious in other people's behaviour. It may well be that women tend to be more attentive to such things. However, although intuition may be nonconscious knowledge, it cannot remain unexamined. It is never enough simply to act on intuition without evaluating it in the light of our experiences. Intuition can be a very valuable resource for decisions of conscience. It can encourage us to take an unpopular stand on some issue, or it can make one wary of potential but unseen treachery. In short it can operate both as a source of creative insight or as an early-warning signal. However, in order that it does not function simply to reinforce one's prejudices and blind spots, its adequacy must be evaluated.

Our intuition can be affected by a number of complex processes. Memories, dreams, emotions, suppressed experiences and anxieties all contribute to this unconscious knowledge. Sometimes their involvement means that intuition may be mistaken or unreliable. At other times they help explain why someone has come to have such a perception. It is precisely because intuitions are so intimately related to other similarly unreflective elements in the personality that they need to be assessed in many ways, including by the rational, conscious processes of the mind. I may not be able to articulate why I am uneasy in the presence of a particular person or with a course of action, but I can devise ways to identify whether such intuitions are warranted or not. Many of the criteria that have already been mentioned in relation to the operations of reason may also come into play when evaluating the reliability of intuitions. One has to determine if the intuition is well founded, if the conclusions drawn from it are warranted, if this intuition is consistent with the rest of one's beliefs and values, if the normal requirements of evidence are fulfilled. When we are convinced that our intuitions have a reliable basis, then they are a most valuable source of moral knowledge. Intuitive responses to moral dilemmas can cause one to attend to often forgotten or ignored values and can highlight neglected dimensions of the moral life. Many innovative and life-changing insights have occurred because of individuals acting on their intuitive sense of goodness and justice. The key to their reliability, however, rests on the ability of the person to articulate the reasons why such intuitive knowledge ought to be trusted. This clearly points to the integrated activity of conscience.

EMOTION

Contemporary psychological theory and practice indicates that the nature of a person's emotional life is highly complex. Psychologists disagree with one another on almost every aspect of this affective dimension of human experience. There are debates about when a person's emotional responses are learned, whether they can be said to be fixed and constant or whether they are subject to continual revision. There are also debates about whether they can be controlled and whether one can ignore or suppress emotions without some serious psychological consequences. Freudians, for example, identify early infant experience and development as the crucial and often definitive stage in forming and tutoring an individual's emotional life. Others disagree with the weight given to this early infant stage and endorse a more progressive and developmental model of the emotions. Important though they are, these debates cannot be the focus of our attention.

If one were to engage in a comprehensive analysis of the nature and role of emotions in the moral life, then one would need to discuss and come to some conclusions on these and related questions. This is certainly work that needs to be done and would greatly enhance our understanding of the detailed workings of conscience. However, our purpose here is to insist that the emotions do have an essential role in the activity of conscience and to suggest that our understanding of conscience will be seriously flawed if their contribution (both positive and negative) is not appreciated.

There is common misconception that emotion hampers rather than facilitates ethical discernment. Such a misconception is based on thinking of the emotions as essentially irrational and involuntary, that is, outside the person's control. However, such a view seriously misunderstands the nature of the emotions and of reason and misconceives the relationship between the two. The multifaceted activity of conscience has often been incorrectly perceived as primarily or even exclusively an intellectual endeavour. However, the emotions too play a very prominent role in the work of conscience. In the same way as intuition is not an activity of reason but still must be evaluated, so too with the emotions. They may often be involuntary. I may feel envious at the success of a colleague even though I consciously wish him well. I may have a great desire to be liked and accepted by a particular person although I am not comfortable with his values. But although emotional responses may be generated from a place outside the governance of the intellect, this does not mean that emotions are beyond our voluntary recognition and control. Emotions can be evaluated and accepted in much the same way as intuition is.

We can examine our emotional responses and discover whether particular reactions and feelings should be acted upon or whether they should be rejected as unwarranted or inappropriate. I do not want to suggest that the emotional life ought to be determined by rational concerns. Such an approach would be a denial of the vital role that the emotions play in the apprehension of right and wrong. But neither do I want to suggest a model of the ethical life that views the operations of reason and the emotions as completely separate from or even in opposition to each other. Instead, one should think of the emotions as providing important information and insight for moral deliberation, information that cannot be accessed without reflecting on our emotions. However, the key factor here is that we must reflect on these emotions, we must engage critically with them so that we can be confident that the information they provide is reliable.

One can see how true this is by thinking about all that is involved in making a difficult ethical decision. Important decisions of conscience are usually accompanied by a high degree of emotional intensity. If a young unmarried woman finds herself with an unplanned pregnancy, she has to very quickly decide how she is going to deal with it. The decision she will have to make will have to be contemplated amid a range of unexpected, random and often confused emotions. All sorts of problems will confound and pressurise her. Possibilities will arise in a partial and rather confused manner. She will probably be on an emotional roller coaster, with her feelings changing from one day to the next. She will initially have to choose whether to continue with the pregnancy or not. If she decides to have an abortion, many of her subsequent choices will depend on whether abortion is legally available to her and if so, under which conditions. Will she flout the law and look for a so-called back-street abortionist? Will she go to another jurisdiction? Will she invent some psychological trauma in order to convince doctors to allow an abortion on mental grounds? How will she cope with the aftermath? Will she tell her family? Will she tell the father of the child? In any case is it morally acceptable to be thinking in this way? Is she destroying an innocent life? If she has an abortion, is she murdering a child? On the other hand, if she decides to go ahead with the pregnancy what is in store for her? Should she have the child adopted? If she decides on adoption, what kind of life will her child have? Will the child be raised in an institution? Will he be raised by unsuitable parents? Will he be happy and properly cared for? How will he feel about being adopted? How will he regard his birth mother? Will he come looking for her sometime in the future? Again, should she tell the father that his child will be adopted? What if he objects? But if she decides to raise the child herself, how will she manage? Will she be giving her child the best possible context in which to flourish? Will she be able to support him financially? How will her family react?

Will she be putting her job in jeopardy? Will this mean she will be giving up any hope of a future relationship and family? Will her child be discriminated against or ridiculed? Should she involve the baby's father in the child-rearing process, even if she regards him as an inappropriate parent?

Although it is not at all clear what a good resolution of the problem might be for her, it is very obvious that the woman's emotional reactions will play a major part in the process. Emotions – which range from occasional excitement and anticipation, to distress, anger, anxiety about the future, shame and guilt – each has an effect on the decision-making process. In some respects a particular emotion may hamper the resolution of a moral problem. For example, a woman may be so ashamed about being pregnant and unmarried that she may not even consider having the baby, even though deep down that is what she wants to do. She may decide to have an abortion because she could not cope with the shame that she would bring upon herself and her family. On the other hand one's emotional responses may help clarify one's priorities and values. She might decide to acknowledge her mild excitement at the prospect of being a mother and go ahead with the pregnancy, even though conditions are not ideal.

Emotions are spontaneous. We cannot decide how we feel. But we can decide whether and how we are going to act on these emotions. What is most evident, however, is that our emotional reactions are part and parcel of our moral deliberation. The dilemma of what I am to do if I face an unplanned pregnancy has to be confronted in the midst of strong, often conflicting, emotions. The questions I ask myself, the options I am willing to consider and the decision I ultimately come to – all of these are mediated through the filter of my emotions. The fact that I might not consider adoption may be motivated primarily by the fear that someday I may come face-to-face with my child and explain why I gave him away.

But of course one's ethical decisions cannot be completely determined by emotional responses. Part of the process of making a decision of conscience (especially one that is emotionally charged) involves reflecting on such responses. In order for my emotions to be integrated into the decision-making process, I must recognise and acknowledge them. I must try not to deceive myself about the reason for dismissing the option of adoption. I must ask myself if fear of confronting one's child at some time in the future is a good enough reason for dismissing this course of action. In short, I must evaluate my emotional reactions and consider how much importance I should attach to them when making my decision. Evaluation is of a similar kind to that associated with intuition. Are my emotions coherent, proportionate to the situation and consistent with other aspects of my life? Are they reasonable and supportable, or are they illogical and exaggerated?

There is evidence to suggest that, just as a person's rational and intellectual capacities can be impaired, so too one's emotional life can be limited in significant ways. Such kinds of dysfunction are often responsible for serious moral failure.

Inappropriate or disproportionate emotions, lack of control of one's emotions or sometimes the absence of any emotion can lead to unethical behaviour. This and other aspects of moral failure will be considered later in the chapter. Clearly, we cannot decide in advance how we are going to feel about a particular event. Indeed, we may be surprised by our feelings, or by their force. But this does not mean that we should slavishly follow our feelings or that we are prisoners to our emotional reactions. The process of making holistic and integrated decisions of conscience involves an interplay of reason and emotion. Reason shapes and evaluates the emotions; emotion contextualises and gives dynamism to reason. Neither ought to be abandoned, nor should one be considered marginal or peripheral.

IMAGINATION

In some respects this is the most difficult aspect of the integrated activity of conscience to discuss. The operations of the imagination are nebulous and its influence is hard to quantify. We engage our imaginations when we try to come to a decision about what to do in a particular situation. We can imagine different scenarios that would result from various options. We can wonder what a person we admire would do in the same circumstances. We can think about how we will regard the decision in the future. Will we be proud of it, or will we wish we had taken an alternative course of action? Employing one's imagination in this fashion means looking at one's own activity and choices as an outsider would and appraising them on the basis of the decisions made. This involves gaining some critical distance from the problem to be solved. This is often difficult, especially if it is a problem involving great emotional investment. Nonetheless, the imaginative, abstract stage can be very important in allowing one to see possibilities that are not immediately obvious. One's imagination also enables one to view the problem from the perspective of others who may be somehow involved. It helps one to think about how others may be affected, how they might feel, what they might fear or why they might be behaving in a particular manner. By entering their world and experiencing their concerns vicariously we can have a more complete understanding of what may be involved. This is particularly true if a moral problem results in the breakdown of communication between the parties involved. Often, one may not come to appreciate the other person's perspective. Imagination here takes the place of listening.

It can also be vital in situations where one is making a decision that will have far-reaching consequences for people one has never met. Again, engaging imaginatively with their world and their concerns can allow one to empathise with them and to take their interests seriously.

The person's creativity and imagination play a significant role in the moral realm, not only in relation to decisions of conscience made in the present, but also in forming the person's moral character. Here the imagination can cultivate different values, can encourage a person to be more courageous in the pursuit of her/his moral vision and can allow one to confront and then go beyond the boundaries of one's moral heritage. This kind of change and development is vital if any moral tradition or community is to flourish. The process of reevaluating one's commitments and redescribing one's reality is part of the process of being human. As we gain more understanding of ourselves and our world and as we learn from our own and others' moral failures, we need to confront the partiality of our own perspective. Imaginative engagement with other cultures, religious traditions and moral communities can help us to identify the blind spots in our own. So too can creative encounters with literature, drama and art inspire us to imagine different possibilities for ourselves and our moral communities. Far from being redundant in the moral field, one's imagination helps to articulate one's sense of virtue and enables one to engage in the vital task of constantly renewing one's moral vision.

CONSCIENCE AND SPIRITUAL DISCERNMENT

As is evident from our discussion of the inward dynamics of conscience, the process of decision making is not an exclusively rational one. In addition to reason the person's emotions, intuitions and imagination are involved. So also for Christians is the capacity for spiritual discernment, which has a crucial role to play in the moral life. Christians believe that within the conscience each person has an inner source of moral evaluation. However, it is not entirely reliant on the individual's personal resources. It is also an inner source informed by faith and shaped under the guidance of the spirit.

In *The Making of Moral Theology*, John Mahoney reminds his readers that the importance of spiritual discernment was part of the traditional Christian understanding of conscience from the earliest centuries. He characterises it in terms of a Johannine tendency to emphasise 'the role of the spirit as internal teacher of all the faithful (and, indeed of all men)'.[18] Over the centuries for various reasons, the role of the spirit became associated mainly with the passive reception of magisterial teaching[19] and has only recently been reemphasised, primarily in the texts of Vatican II.

However, again as Mahoney argues,[20] it was highly significant in Aquinas's discussions of the role of conscience. Aquinas operated with a theological framework that emphasised the unity of the moral and spiritual realms. He did not regard reason and spiritual discernment to be separate; rather, he thought of them as reflecting aspects of the integrated unity of the person. As a result the rationalism that characterised the later Thomistic tradition is absent in the theology of Aquinas.

As a process of spiritual discernment, the evaluations of conscience involve an element of prayerful reflection and stillness. These are important ways by which the person comes to a deep-seated awareness of the virtues one seeks to cultivate

An Irish Reader in Moral Theology

and to embody in one's life. And although there is 'a personal uniqueness and a human solitariness about the exercise of conscience',[21] there is also a sense that this human endeavour is all the while worked at 'in the shadow of the spirit'. Or, as Mahoney suggests, the conscience is important in discovering where the spirit is leading individuals in response to the call of God in the context of an overall vocation.[22]

Of course we need to engage in a reflective process to help us authenticate the insights arising from this process of discernment, this interior resource, which in the Christian tradition is often spoken of metaphorically as the voice of God. This suggests that the moral insight that comes from genuine and prayerful spiritual reflection forms a significant part of the Christian understanding of conscience. Mahoney describes this interior moral discernment in terms of a taste or a feel for that which is good in a particular context. It is difficult to describe and still more difficult to have confidence in. Indeed, Mahoney recognises the ambiguities inherent in this process of discernment when he acknowledges that 'the moral "feel" for a situation which Christians are believed to possess by reason of their personal adhesion of faith may be unashamedly of the character of insight in search of arguments or, in terms more generally applicable to theology as a whole, of Christian experience seeking understanding'.[23]

NOTES

1   This phrase is characteristic of personalist theologies and is used by both Louis Janssens and Kevin Kelly.

2   Rosi Braidotti, *Nomadic Subjects*, New York: Columbia University Press, 1994).

3   Judith Butler, *Gender Trouble*, New York: Routledge, 1991, and, particularly, *Bodies That Matter: On the Discursive Limits of Sex*, London: Routledge, 1993.

4   Seyla Benhabib, *Situating the Self: Gender, Community and Postmodernism in Contemporary Ethics*, Cambridge, England: Polity Press, 1992.

5   This is developed by Häring in many texts including *The Law of Christ*, Vol. 1, Cork: Mercier Press, 1960.

6   See, for example, Bernard Häring, *Free and Faithful in Christ*, Vol. 1, New York: Seabury, 1978, pp. 164ff; Josef Fuchs, *Human Values and Christian Morality*, Dublin: Gill and Macmillan, 1970, pp. 92ff and Karl Rahner, *Theological Investigations*, Vol. 6, New York: Crossroad, 1982.

7   Rahner, op. cit.

8   Iris Murdoch, op. cit., p. 37.

9   The issue of how we understand the nature of moral goodness is much debated. As is evident throughout this text, I am operating with a view that regards moral goodness not as an abstract ideal or form, but rather something contextual and embodied, something ultimately uncertain and provisional, something our understanding and apprehension can change.

10   Martha Nussbaum, *The Fragility of Goodness*, Oxford: Oxford University Press, 1986.

11   Leonardo Boff, *Liberating Grace*, Maryknoll, NY: Orbis, 1979.

12   Janet Martin Soskice, 'The God of Hope' in *Doctrine and Life*, 44 (April 1994), p. 203.

13   Charles Taylor, *Sources of the Self: The Making of Modern Identity*, New York: Cambridge University Press, 1989.

14   Soskice, op. cit., p. 204.

15   See Alasdair MacIntyre, *Whose Justice: Which Rationality?*, Notre Dame: University of Notre Dame, 1988, for a comprehensive discussion of this point.

16   Terence McCaughey, *Memory and Redemption, Church, Politics and Prophetic Theology in Ireland,* Dublin: Gill and Macmillan, 1993.

17   Callahan, op. cit., p. 126.

18   Mahoney, *The Making of Moral Theology,* p. 222.

19   Ibid.

20   Ibid., p. 207.

21   John Mahoney, 'Conscience, Discernment and Prophecy in Moral Decision Making', in William O'Brien (ed.), *Riding Time Like a River: The Catholic Moral Tradition Since Vatican II,* Washington, DC: Georgetown University Press, 1993, pp. 81–97.

22   Ibid.

23   Mahoney, *The Making of Moral Theology,* p. 209.

23   Conscience Today

Seán Fagan

(Seán Fagan, *Does Morality Change?*, Dublin: Columba Press, 2003, pp. 89–111 [extract].)

WHAT IS CONSCIENCE?

Since the world-wide debate provoked by *Humanae vitae*, more people nowadays feel free to follow their conscience even when their decisions are at variance with what the Church expects. They may be encouraged by the above examples from Church history about torture, slavery, conscientious objectors and lack of respect for individual conscience, which show that Church pronouncements were not always in line with the gospel. But because of this crisis of authority and obedience people can too easily claim to follow conscience when in fact they do not have a mature understanding of what conscience really is and may end up just doing what they please. To say this is not to join the ranks of those unhelpful Church leaders who say, 'Yes, one must follow conscience, but it must be an informed conscience', with the implication that Church teaching will provide the information. Intelligent laity are angered by such statements, and say that in practice this amounts to 'We know best, do what you are told'. They wonder why conscience should be mentioned at all if it is simply a matter of obedience. When large numbers did not accept the encyclical's ban on artificial contraception because they were not convinced by its arguments, authority reacted with the primitive response of most authorities under attack, namely by insistence on obedience, in some cases backed up with sanctions. The mystique of obedience set in motion in the Church during the sixteenth century still colours official thinking in today's Church, and it is often presented as the core of morality. On the other hand, confessors who were confused by the debate and insecure when they found their personal common sense out of step with official teaching, simply told penitents to follow their conscience. This well-meant advice led to confusion among laity insofar as many people had seldom been told this before, and few had ever heard a comprehensive, adult explanation of what conscience really is and how it functions.

The present official teaching of the Church is quite clear in the documents of the Second Vatican Council. The first chapter of *The Church in the Modern World* gives a beautiful description of humanity created in the image of God, and speaks of the essential unity of human nature, of the dignity of human intellect, of truth and of wisdom, of the sanctity of conscience.

Deep within their consciences men and women discover a law which they have not laid upon themselves and which they must obey. Its voice, ever calling them to do what is good and avoid evil, tells them inwardly at the right moment: do this, shun that. For they have in their hearts a law inscribed by God. Their dignity rests in observing this law, and by it they will be judged. Conscience is the most secret core and sanctuary of the human person. There people are alone with God, whose voice echoes in their depths. By conscience that law is made known which is fulfilled in the love of God and of one's neighbour. Through loyalty to conscience, Christians are joined to others in the search for truth and for the right solution to so many moral problems which arise both in the life of individuals and from social relationships. Hence, the more a correct conscience prevails, the more do persons and groups turn aside from blind choice and endeavour to conform to the objective standards of moral conduct. (n.16)

The document goes on to emphasise the importance of freedom for a true exercise of conscience.

It is only in freedom that people can turn themselves towards what is good. People today prize freedom very highly and strive eagerly for it. In this they are right. Yet they often cherish it improperly as if it gave them leave to do anything they like, even when it is evil. But genuine freedom is an exceptional sign of the image of God in people. For God willed that men and women should be left free to make their own decisions, so that they might of their own accord seek their creator and freely attain their full and blessed perfection by cleaving to God. Their dignity, therefore, requires them to act out of conscious and free choice, as moved and drawn in a personal way from within, and not by their own blind impulses or by external constraint. (n.17)

These words confirm the assertion of the first chapter above, that we are most like God in our freedom.

What conscience is not

First of all, conscience is not a special faculty or power distinct from ordinary reason. A conscience decision is made by the same human reason that we use to decide which model of car to buy or where to go for a holiday. Likewise, although some decisions of conscience can involve quite deep feelings, like agonising guilt when we deliberately act against them, conscience is not to be identified with mere feeling or emotion. Furthermore, it is not to be confused with the Freudian notion of 'super-ego'. Freud noticed that his mentally disturbed patients often had the delusion of being watched, even when they were alone. They believed that people were waiting for them to do something forbidden, for which they could then be punished. From this he formed the idea of a self above the normal self, a super-self or super-ego judging the self as an object. In early life this super-ego is formed by internalising the attitudes and rules of parents, and as time goes on the young person accepts these personally, together with the conventions of society, and gradually the super-ego takes on all the functions of early authority figures: observing, accusing, punishing or rewarding. The mature conscience outgrows this, but the childish, immature conscience of some people has many of the characteristics of Freud's super-ego. True conscience is quite different.

It is often said that conscience is the voice of God, but this is only a half-truth. When a Christian has to make a difficult decision in a complex moral situation, it is natural to ask God for help, and the discernment process can be helped by reflection on the truths of revelation, by grace and by one's personal life of prayer. There is no question of private revelation providing easy answers, but there is a strong presumption that one who is habitually in tune with God through fidelity to the gospel will have a special sensitivity towards Christian values and a healthy awareness of personal weakness, blindness and sin. This can be a real help in responsible discernment. On this level it can be said that conscience is the voice of God. Even in difficult, unclear and messy situations, when one is genuinely seeking to do God's will, there is an experience in which morality and mysticism meet. But it is not true that the final decision is literally God's will. It is traditional Catholic teaching that we can be sure of God's will only in general. When it comes to specifics there is no absolute certainty. Those who claimed that Franz Jägerstätter was not justified in his conscientious objection to the Nazi war were just as convinced that their assessment of the situation was God's will as he was of the opposite. In short, it is not quite true that the voice of conscience is the actual voice of God, but it is absolutely true that God's will is that we follow our conscience, always and ever. We may never hand it over to another.

CONSCIENCE NEEDS TO BE FORMED

The Church's current teaching on the dignity and sanctity of conscience and on the need to be free in order to act from personal conviction is a significant change from a long history dominated by the attitude expressed by Pope Leo X in 1520 when he spoke of obedience as the strength of the Church's discipline and the source and origin of all virtues. This tradition left little room for personal responsibility and creativity in moral decision-making. The weakness of this attitude was castigated by the French novelist Georges Bernanos when he said that the sabotage of that sublime faculty of the soul known as judgement can only lead to catastrophes, that people trained to blind obedience are those who are also prone to sudden blind disobedience. If rules are not internalised and personally appropriated, they lead either to passive and external conformity, or to revolt and anarchy. The mystique of obedience that was such a strong feature of Church teaching in the past has now given way to a more balanced approach. When people looked to the Church for guidance, the response was to provide answers to moral questions and lay down rules for moral conduct. There is still a place for this pastoral concern to instruct the faithful, and it is right to insist that only an instructed, well-formed conscience is a sure guide to be followed. But more is required for the formation of conscience than giving information and rules.

FROM INFANT TO ADULT

Since conscience is an exercise of reason, there can be no question of conscience in children who have not come to the use of reason. The human infant is born with the potential or capacity to reason, but the child cannot use it until it begins to use the word 'because' in a significant way, namely when it is capable of giving reasons for its actions. And yet long before reason becomes active on this level, parents begin to train their children in patterns of right living. Initially the young child is totally self-centred, a little bundle of instinctive needs, the most basic of which is the need to be loved, to be accepted, to be approved. The darker side of this is the fear of rejection by the parents, even if objectively this is no more than a frown on the parents' face. The child quickly learns which behaviour brings approval, acceptance and love, and which actions earn disapproval and cause feelings of rejection. This learning extends all the way from toilet training to table manners and the right and wrong way to relate to brothers, sisters and others. Parents lay down the rules on what is right and wrong, and children obey them simply in order to retain the approval and love of the parents. When the child disobeys, it experiences guilt feelings, not because of any appreciation of the wrongness of the actions, but simply because of the fear of rejection.

This kind of conditioning is perfectly normal and healthy; it is all the child can understand in its early years. The child learns that 'good' behaviour brings approval and love, 'bad' behaviour brings feelings of badness, guilt, rejection. Children conform on the basis of reward and punishment, pleasure and fear. This is a pre-moral level of behaviour. But gradually, as the child begins to reason, it discovers that life is more pleasant when it is organised, so it pays to obey the rules laid down by authority. Although reward and punishment may still influence decisions, morality gradually becomes equated with *obedience to social and religious authorities*. Some psychologists claim that the majority of people remain at this level of conscience, which explains their preoccupation with law and obedience. But a higher level is reached by those who accept and obey laws, but are more concerned with the values which the law seeks to protect and promote. People on this level act on the basis of *personally accepted moral principles*. This is the level of mature conscience.

These stages are a logical development of conscience, but they are not watertight compartments with a sharp transition from one to the next. In fact the earlier ones are integrated into the later ones and provide the underpinning for the more developed stage. The felt emotional states inculcated in childhood and early adolescence are quite healthy in themselves and prevent us from doing many anti-social acts. This kind of psychological conditioning frees us from various irrational impulses. Because we are conditioned to reject these impulses spontaneously, we do not have to do battle with them each time they arise, and so we can give more attention to serious matters. Likewise, since we have been conditioned to obey the law without too much questioning, we do not have to puzzle everything out for ourselves, but we trust the authority of others. However, the morally mature person does not accept this conditioning uncritically. Conscience grows towards maturity by internalising and making its own certain *values* and *principles*, and it is these which determine how moral decisions are made. The mature conscience recognises that conditioning which limits us in some areas of freedom is accepted for the sake of the greater freedom it provides in the more important matters of life. This basic conditioning frees us from irrational impulses, endless discussion and unnecessary worry, and so frees us *for* the ordinary business of living, and for the serious moral decisions that require more concentrated discernment.

LEVELS OF CONSCIENCE

Today's world provides us with an enormous range of options. Never before in human history have people had such a variety of choices available to them in so many areas of life. The problem is to know how to choose wisely. Morality is about choice. People become aware of conscience when they have to choose between different courses of action and the question arises: what is the morally right thing to do? Conscience is concerned with the concrete decision about what is to be done here and now.

But conscience is more than just decision. The word is also used to describe the background from which the decision is made, namely the deeper level of consciousness which is a person's general knowledge of moral principles about right and wrong, good and bad. Depending on the individual, it can be more or less extensive. It includes the basic principles: do good rather than evil, treat others as you would wish to be treated yourself, and it can extend to the ten commandments and specific developments of them. This is more than neutral, abstract knowledge. It calls to something deep within our nature, and leaves us with the conviction that we must obey it if we are to be true to ourselves. In this sense, conscience is more than just intellect and will, knowledge and consent. On this deepest of all levels, conscience is the core of our being as free persons. Here it can be said that 'conscience is the whole person'.

In moral terms, an individual is a certain kind of person and has a special pattern of life because of acceptance of, and fidelity to, a set of values like respect for persons, truth, sincerity, integrity, justice, love of God. In this sense, conscience is a special kind of self-awareness. It is a consciousness, not only of what we are doing, but of what we are and of what we are becoming. It tells us the kind of person we are, but at the same time it also tells us the kind of person we ought to be. It is not only a mirror or indicator, but also an invitation and a summons, commanding us to become and to be what we are meant to be, to continually grow into our better selves. In Christian terms it can be said that God, the author of our human nature, calls us through the basic thrust of that nature, towards self-transcendence, through the irrepressible appetites of mind, heart and body, a call which we recognise in the experience of conscience.

It is to this conscience that the words of the prophet Jeremiah apply, when he spoke in God's name: 'I will put my law within them, and write it on their hearts' (31:33). Ezekiel spoke of the transformation of conscience with the words 'I will give them a new heart and a new mind'. St Paul makes it clear that God's call is not restricted to a particular religion, but applies to all human beings when he said of the gentiles that 'what the law commands is written in their hearts'. He is referring to the experience of conscience. This insight of Paul is echoed by the Second Vatican Council, speaking of the salvation of non-Christians: 'Those who, through no fault of their own, do not know the gospel of Christ or his Church, but who nevertheless seek God with a sincere heart, and, moved by grace, try in their actions to do his will as they know it through the dictates of their conscience – they too may achieve eternal salvation' *(Constitution on the Church,* n.16).

Conscience is knowledge of a special kind, namely the awareness of being obliged by a law not of our own making, yet not imposed from without. It is an experience of mind and heart, the innate thrust of our human nature to love the good and avoid evil. This directive of our nature is permanent and ongoing, but not specified in detail as to what precisely is good or evil. Conscience still has the task of discernment, or deciding day by day what is right or wrong.

LEVELS OF CONSCIOUSNESS

The levels of conscience just mentioned are:
1.   decision (this I must do), flowing from
2.   judgement (this is the right thing to do in this situation), which is made after
3.   assessment of the facts of the situation and an habitual knowledge of moral principles and laws, which come from
4.   one's education and experience and ultimately from the core of one's personal being, the kind of person one is morally.

But these levels of conscience are part of a wider context of human consciousness. The most immediate and basic level is *empirical* consciousness, which is that of the five senses (sight, hearing, touch, taste and smell), and of memory, imagination

An Irish Reader in Moral Theology

and perceiving. *Intelligent* consciousness involves the use of intelligence, in inquiry, insight, understanding, formulating ideas or concepts. A third level is that of *rational* consciousness, involving reflection, reasoning and the making of judgements about reality. The fourth and highest level is that of *responsible* consciousness, involving deliberation, decision and action. This is the level of *moral* consciousness or conscience. This fourth level is distinct from the other levels taken by themselves, but is never separated from them. The lower levels are integrated into the higher, so that the human person is all at once empirically, intelligently, rationally and morally conscious, as a whole. Conscience is the highest level of human consciousness. It is the awareness of our personality as a whole and especially of our freedom and responsibility.

These levels of consciousness link up with what was said of the precepts of natural law in the previous chapter: be attentive, be intelligent, be rational, be responsible. These are the basic moral imperatives, essential for all moral decisions and actions. To ignore them is to be irresponsible, and therefore immoral. To be fully faithful to them one needs to recognise and beware of the darker side of our human nature: the risk of ignorance, bias, inauthenticity and sin. To struggle against these requires continual conversion on the intellectual, moral and religious levels. This means that formation of conscience is an ongoing challenge all through life.

Mature conscience is the ideal, but the term is misleading if used in an absolute sense. We can speak of physical, psychological, moral and religious maturity as distinct dimensions of human personality, but they need to be in harmony. One could be psychologically mature and morally immature, or morally mature and religiously immature. A more realistic term would be 'maturity at age'. A person of twenty who is mature for twenty would be immature at forty if no moral growth occurs in the intervening twenty years. There is always room for further growth. It is a lifelong process. There can never be a complete set of ready-made answers, nor can one fall back on slot-machine morality. Moreover, development of conscience is more than just increasing one's knowledge. A crucial element is *fidelity to conscience* and *continual openness* to future development. Conscience can be flawed through habitual neglect, but it may also cease to grow, through routine drifting, through uncritical acceptance of outdated theology, of solutions from the past that no longer respond to new situations. It is the role of prophets, through their words and actions, to shake us out of our complacency and to alert us to new calls on conscience. Human rights activists and liberation theology are in this prophetic tradition.

Both in the formation of conscience and in the use of conscience, it is important to stress that more than mere knowledge is involved. Intelligence and reason are needed to make moral decisions, but feeling and imagination are also important. Pragmatic decisions can be quite cold-blooded and calculating, but moral decisions involve *evaluative knowledge*, since they are a *response to values*. This means that the heart as well as the head is involved. For moral conviction, appeal must be made not only to the intellect, but to the imagination and affectivity. Hence the importance of heroes and saints to fire the imagination and stir the heart. It is important to develop the affective memory in childhood, when, already before it reaches the use of reason, the child is formed in basic trust. It learns to trust its parents and others, to discover that the world is basically good, that it need not fear or be ashamed. Training in morality requires a delicate balance of affection, discipline and explanation. The affective dimension develops through relationships, and the young person eventually becomes what its relationships enable it to be. Feeling and imagination come into play when it is necessary to put oneself in the shoes, if not the skin, of others in deciding what is the moral response to them in different situations.

Peace or guilt

When faced with a moral decision, conscience presents us with the call to do the right thing, and our better self is attracted in that direction, so that part of our being is ahead of the rest. This is a healthy tension, the experience of being stretched towards the good. When we finally do what conscience commands, the rest of us catches up with the better self, the tension is relieved and we experience peace and wholeness, a sense of at-one-ness with ourselves. This is the peace of a 'good conscience'. When we ignore or refuse to do what we know we should, the tension remains, so we lose our basic oneness, we are torn within ourselves, separated from our better self, and we experience alienation and guilt. When there is inconsistency between our knowing and doing we become divided within ourselves. We may make excuses and rationalise our failure, but the very attempt to give 'reasons' for something which is really against reason only aggravates the tension, and we feel guilty. Guilt is the experience of a 'bad conscience'. This lack of inner peace can spill over into our relationships, and we become alienated from our fellow human beings and even from our material environment.

Guilt is the awareness of having acted against conscience. The inconsistency between knowing and doing causes a break in inner harmony, and since conscience is the very core of the whole person there are repercussions in mind, will, body and emotions. Guilt brings feelings of shame, and remorse. This is perfectly normal and healthy body-language reacting to something that is not right. The remedy is to admit, accept and adjust, by acknowledging the wrongdoing, asking forgiveness and repairing the damage. Inner peace can be restored. But guilt is morbid, neurotic, irrational and unhealthy when the feeling is out of all proportion to the wrong done, or is unrelated to any real wrongdoing.

Mature conscience

Elements of unhealthy guilt can be felt at times by mature people, but they are not upset by it. They have a balanced outlook on life. They can respect law and authority, but their lives are governed more by freely chosen values. Theirs is a morality of responsibility rather than of permissions. They see God as a loving creator, Father and Mother interested in their growth and happiness rather than a taskmaster measuring guilt. They are more concerned about their basic attitudes and the overall pattern of their lives than about isolated bits of behaviour, although they are not careless about individual actions. They can accept responsibility for failures and sins, but they do not torment themselves about them. They can forgive themselves and feel loved and worthwhile. They believe God loves them in spite of sin, loves them for their own sake and not simply because they have earned his love by their good behaviour. In repentance and trust, they can leave the past to God, live fully in the present and look confidently to the future. Morally mature people know their own limitations and weakness, but they are constantly open to new information, new insights, new values, and they want to grow in sensitivity and willingness to do good. Their life is not tied to a rigid set of laws, but they are flexible, aware that growth is a slow process, that things take time. Though conscious of the danger of mediocrity and complacency, they do not get into a panic over the occasional lapse as long as they are doing their best. They know that God listens to sentences rather than to isolated syllables.

Mature people know that conscience is their secret core, the very centre of their personality, their sanctuary, a sacred place where others can enter only by invitation. God alone has access to this sanctuary and it is here that they find their deepest peace. Because of their experience of this sacred space within themselves, they try to respect the same mystery in others. They can appreciate the feeling of Moses at the burning bush, when he took off his sandals because he was on holy ground. Conscience, even in the least of our brothers and sisters, is indeed holy ground, truly a sanctuary, a sacred place that must never be violated in any circumstances or under any pretext.

Mature people believe, with Vatican II, that when they come face to face with God on their own personal last day, they will not be judged according to rules learned by heart, or according to the views of their parents, or Church documents, or laws from the Bible, but according to their own personal conscience, not according to whether they did the right thing, but basically according to whether they did what they saw and understood as the right thing. They are bound to follow the guidance of conscience, even if they later discover that it was mistaken, that they acted in ignorance, but in good faith.

The mature conscience can understand St Augustine's words: 'Love God and do what you will.' Theologian Bernard Lonergan was echoing this thought when he said that the continual formation of conscience is as simple and as complex as falling in love. If you really love somebody, you do not have to be constantly referring to laws and rules written somewhere outside of you to guide you in your behaviour towards your beloved. Of course we can be, and often need to be, helped by the experience of the wider community of family, friends and Church, in order to discover what counts as truly loving behaviour, especially in serious and complex matters. Conscience is always personal, but it cannot be isolated from community.

24   Conscience and Decision-Making

Amelia Fleming

(Angela Hanley and David Smith (eds), *Quench Not the Spirit*, MSC, Dublin, Columba Press, 2005, pp. 150–63 [extract].)

SANCTITY OF CONSCIENCE

The Second Vatican Council had attested to the inviolability of conscience in *Dignitatis Humanae* (n.3 and n.14), declaring that one should not be forced to act in a manner contrary to his conscience. Nor, on the other hand, is one to be restrained from acting in accordance with conscience. But, when informing one's conscience, the Christian ought carefully to attend to the sacred and certain doctrine of the Church.

The conflict between conscience and authority erupted in ecclesial circles with the promulgation of Pope Paul VI's encyclical *Humanae vitae* in 1968, and continues to bubble beneath the surface with concerns regarding Pope John Paul II's 1994 Apostolic Letter *Ordinatio Sacerdotalis* and his 1998 motu proprio *Ad Tuendam Fidem*. In recent years, this apostolic letter has pushed the issue of the types of obedience owed to the teachings of the magisterium to the fore in theological debate. The binding force of *Ordinatio Sacerdotalis* seems unclear. It declares that the Church has no authority to ordain women to the priesthood. This letter seems to be a response by the Roman Church to circumstances playing out within the Anglican Church. The Anglican Bishop of Bristol had ordained thirty-two women on March 23, two months prior to the promulgation of *Ordinatio Sacerdotalis*, and pressure was growing within the Roman Catholic Church itself to allow the ordination of women.

Throughout *Ordinatio Sacerdotalis*, traditional Church teaching is cited and repeated, as this traditional teaching is one of the basic reasons behind the declared inability of the Church to ordain women. This teaching on the non-ordination of women is 'definitively to be held' by the faithful, based on sacred scripture as proof of God's plan for his Church, and the 'constant tradition' by the Church. 'Constant tradition' means those teachings that have been believed everywhere, always, and by everyone. Problems have arisen with regard to the assent due to this teaching. Once again, Newman's voice echoes into our own time. He too is critical of this principle quoted from St Vincent of Lerins, rightly pointing out that it is not of mathematical or demonstrative character, but moral, and requires practical judgement and good sense to apply it. For instance, he wonders what is meant by 'taught *always*'? Does it mean in every century, or every year, or every month? Does 'everywhere' mean in every country, or in every diocese? Are we required to produce the direct testimony of every bishop? How many bishops, how many places, how many instances constitute a fulfilment of the test proposed? 'It is, then, from the nature of the case, a condition which can never be satisfied as fully as it might have been. It admits of various and unequal application in various instances.'[1]

If the doctrine is 'definitively to be held', infallibility is implied, yet canon law states that unless a doctrine is *clearly* established as having been infallibly defined, it is not to be understood as infallible. Many theologians believe that the infallibility of the teaching contained in *Ordinatio Sacerdotalis* is not clearly established, as it was not explicitly stated *ex cathedra* by John Paul II. In the official clarification, *Responsio ad Dubium*, issued 18 November 1995 by the Congregation for the Doctrine of the Faith, responding to the doubts expressed as to the doctrinal weight of *Ordinatio Sacerdotalis*, the Congregation declared it to be the intention of the Pontiff to speak infallibly on this matter. It was declared that this doctrine had already been infallibly taught by the ordinary and universal magisterium, *ubique, semper, et ab omnibus* (everywhere, always and by everyone). As this document was papally approved for publication, it would seem that this was indeed the case. In fact, however, this clarification did not retrospectively confer this infallibility unto the apostolic letter, as the pope cannot communicate his infallibility through a curial congregation.

AD TUENDAM FIDEM

The *Responsio* of the Congregation did little to assuage the concerns expressed in theological circles regarding the assent due to this canonically uncertain infallibility. The additions and modifications made in Pope John Paul II's 1998 *Ad Tuendam Fidem* (to protect the faith) were made in order to underline and give canonical status to the type of assent required when dealing with definitive, but non-infallible, Church teachings such as that contained in *Ordinatio Sacerdotalis*. In *Ad Tuendam Fidem*, Pope John Paul II amended the Code of Canon Law. The first change deals with Canon 750, which concerns doctrines which are irreformable and which require the assent of theological faith by all members of the faithful. The proposition of an irreformable doctrine can never be rejected as wrong, although the statement or wording may be expressed differently for a new historical context. These are doctrines divinely revealed, such as the articles of the Creed, the Christological and the Marian dogmas. He also added a new text concerned with truths 'definitively to be held' concerning faith and morals which are necessarily connected with revelation because of a historical relationship or logical connection. Cardinal Ratzinger emphasises in the *Explanatory Note* which accompanied *Ad Tuendam Fidem* (though not specifically linked to it) that there is no difference between the nature of the assent required by truths divinely

An Irish Reader in Moral Theology

revealed and those 'definitively to be held'. Examples given by Cardinal Ratzinger in §11 of the commentary include the Church's teaching on euthanasia, and the ruling out of any possibility of ordaining women to the priesthood. The latter example could hardly have been omitted as it had been proclaimed by the Pope as requiring 'definitive' assent in *Ordinatio Sacerdotalis* (n.4).

There is now confusion about the distinction between infallible and non-infallible teachings by the use of the adjective 'definitive'. Many theologians believe that the Holy Spirit works through every member of the faithful; therefore, in assisting the magisterium in its reformable teachings preserving the Church from defect, the Spirit may also be working through dialogue and dissent to correct a teaching that remains reformable. Some theologians are of the opinion that it is impossible for the Holy Spirit to allow the Church to give erroneous moral guidance, but even a casual reading of ecclesiastical history shows that the Church has been wrong in the past, and there is no *a priori* reason to say it could not be wrong again in some of its current teaching. It is, therefore, highly regrettable that all discussion on the possible ordination of women has been banned. It is only through debate and discussion that the truth can be reached, 'for the human mind has a natural thirst for truth and will only rest when convinced by truth. A teacher may help in the search, but no good teacher would command that seekers stop thinking and searching'.[2] The rights of Catholics to discuss religious matters are included in *Gaudium et spes* (n.62), and in the 1983 code of Canon Law (212.3) and yet often theologians and others are forbidden to write or dialogue on such a question which the Vatican believes settled. Papal authority and power is now used to block theological debate on women's ordination. Trying to inform and educate the conscience of the people of God without open, public and in-house discussion makes it difficult to reach the truth.

A NEW QUESTIONING

It is perhaps the contemporary emancipated female Catholic who, having moved away from her traditional role of mainly wife and mother, questions the authoritative role of the Church and the role of the individual conscience the loudest and longest. Women now not only shape their own home lives, but also wider society through their active involvement in the workplace. In the past three or four decades, they have been consciously transformed by returning female emigrants, media, and an increasing control of their fertility. Several facts reveal this new independent Irish Roman Catholic woman – the widespread use of artificial contraceptives, the increase of births outside marriage, and the increase in legal separations and divorces initiated by the female spouse. This evidences the deepening gulf between women's consciences, their actions and the Church's moral teachings. For many reflective, practicing female Roman Catholics, current Church teaching on marital sexuality in particular causes pain and alienation. Because Irish women were traditionally more religious than the Irish male, society at large feels the repercussions of this conscientious estrangement. Many women are no longer instrumental in the handing on of an unconvincing faith in the home, and are practising their own faith less within the formal Church environment. Education in the faith for the young Catholic is now relegated to the Catholic school and to a lesser degree, the parish. If the majority of Roman Catholics now depend upon their judgement of conscience for moral action, and not the teaching of the Church, and perhaps choose contrary to what is taught, it is imperative that they fully form and inform their conscience to the best of their ability. It is the duty of the whole Christian community to educate our younger members, be it through an established Catholic education system, parish, or by our own behaviour.

THE FORMING OF CONSCIENCE

The Catholic educator has an important responsibility towards the formation and education of the young conscience, especially in a secular society where there is apathy towards religious and ethical formation. Education of the human person who is on a life-long process of creative learning and growing in Christ, is initiated by the lived morality of parents and others, and continued formally in the classroom. It is important, therefore, that we teach young adults to correctly and confidently use their Christian conscience in moral decision making. The Catholic educator is not only the religious educator, but is also the teacher of those other humanities subjects such as English, philosophy, history, media and biology. These areas also raise questions about the human condition and the reality of life, including moral issues which call for a judgement of conscience on the part of the student now or in later life. The Catholic educator is also predominantly a lay Catholic because religious are no longer present in many schools. This should not mean an end to the education of the young in the Catholic ethos. The contemporary religious education teacher has also trained in a different atmosphere than in previous decades. Increasingly, theological studies are offered in secular providers of third level education, and not only in the traditional ecclesiastical institutions. Lecture halls are filling with lay, predominantly female, theology students, being taught by lay theology lecturers. Theology itself is becoming secular. No longer is it dominated by ecclesiastics doing a doctrinal theology from within the Church. Instead, theology has begun to converse with other branches of knowledge, and looks at issues from outside the Church, seeing faith resources in secular culture. Our religious lives have moved from a separate section of our lives, that special world of the divine, to join with our everyday historical world. God and the Church should be a part of this everyday, ordinary world. Our Christian beliefs should permeate our fundamental disposition towards others. It is important to allow valid cultural influences to encourage a practical theology which will enable our teachers to present a convincing and motivating faith context for the education, training, practice and experience of conscientious

An Irish Reader in Moral Theology

moral decision making. The true conscience is enabled and matured by informing and educating it, for we are not born with a conscience, but with a capacity for conscience. We inform our primitive conscience through reason and experience, those human sources of knowledge and also through the divine sources of knowledge: holy scripture and tradition. It is also important to be attentive and respectful to the authentic teaching authority of the Church, and not regard it as merely one opinion among others, for the Church declares natural moral principles determined by God, understood in the light of faith.

In order to make a sincere and correct conscientious decision, we must be convinced that our conscience has all the available information. If we are in doubt in any way as to what our conscience is commanding or forbidding us to do, we must not act according to it. A wilfully erroneous conscience is objectively wrong and culpable. This type of conscience makes an error in judgement through lack of effort or will to overcome any naiveté or ignorance. We must endeavour to overcome any ignorance we may have by being aware that we are limited by our human finitude and sinfulness. Though our reason and past experience may inform our conscience about a given situation, we may not have all the facts, nor fully grasp all the implications of an action. We may also be under the overt or covert influence of personal or social sin. We must be open to any guidance available to us, be it through prayerful dialogue with God, Church teaching or other branches of knowledge. Similarly, there should be recognition that there may be limits to the use of the Bible or Christian tradition due to cultural conditioning or historical context. Scripture has incorporated many cultural meanings over time – and even some that are erroneous. We could use the historical example of women's inferior position in the Christian Church and society to illustrate. Christian feminists often highlight how the Bible incorporates the social and familial patriarchy of the times in which its books were written. For example, the household codes found in the New Testament record contemporary cultural attitudes towards women. These codes, found primarily in Colossians 3:18-4:1 and Ephesians 5:22-6:9, document the inferiority and subordination of women to men. Man is, they claim, the head of the household, and a woman is to obey her husband. For centuries, these teachings perpetuated women's subservience in the Christian Church. However, due to a deepening understanding of sexual equality and knowledge of the importance of the female experience, we now recognise that such teaching is wrong and must be corrected. Moreover, scripture does not deal with the many new issues that we are now facing in different historical and cultural circumstances throughout the world. It does not, for example, address issues of nuclear power, reproductive technologies or genetic engineering. As Christians, we must inform and educate our consciences to the best of our ability in order to live a morally upright lives modelled on Christ.

We must be careful not to over-emphasise any one or more of our sources of knowledge to the detriment of the others. All must act as controls. It is important to recognise that a true and informed mature conscience may sometimes find itself in disagreement with an official Church or secular principle of general application. These conflicts should be regarded as an important source of moral insight into the new dilemmas which give rise to such conflicts. The Church must acknowledge the responsible and faithful attitudes taken by those who engage in these conscientious moral decisions which result in dissent from official teaching. There must be a reaffirmation of the inviolability of the individual true conscience and its importance in the ongoing search for truth.

Notes

1   John Henry Newman, *An Essay on the Development of Christian Doctrine*, 1845 edition, Middlesex, 1974, p. 76.
2   Seán Fagan, *Does Morality Change?*, Dublin: Columba Press, 2003, p. 192.

25 Thomas More's Great Matter: Conscience

D. Vincent Twomey

(Amelia Fleming (ed.), *Contemporary Irish Moral Discourse,* Dublin: Columba Press, 2007, pp. 156–80 [extract].)

Abstract: Poised at the end of the medieval period and the beginning of the modern era, More's understanding of conscience, it is suggested in this essay, belongs to the former theological tradition which the secularised modern era has almost eradicated from our consciousness. This causes some considerable difficulty for us moderns when we attempt to uncover what conscience actually meant for the Lord Chancellor, or indeed when we try to understand the history of this extraordinary man and interpret his writings. This essay is an attempt to explore such methodological difficulties involved in interpreting More and his writings today, before proposing a more comprehensive (ontological) understanding of conscience in order to better understand More himself, in particular his death. To test the validity of this interpretation, the paper applies this fuller notion of conscience to the Utopia, with special reference to the passage on moral philosophy, which, it has been remarked, 'is in fact the cornerstone of the Utopian edifice' (Logan and Adams). Not least because of Patrick Hannon's unique background in English literature and legal studies, this essay on Sir Thomas More, man of letters and lawyer supreme, is offered as a tribute to my colleague in honour of his 65th birthday.[*]

More's first formal biographer described his hero as 'our noble new Socrates'. The parallel is obvious, Chambers adds,[1] noting that Cardinal Pole had first drawn the parallel three years after More's death. Today we call them men of conscience, though Socrates would have asked, what do you mean by that term? And Thomas More would have been not a little amused at our attempt, or rather attempts, for there are many, to say what conscience is. It is doubtful if any of our answers would have made much sense to him, as indeed they don't seem to make too much sense to us. That is precisely our quandary today. What conscience is, is not so obvious any more.

A useful, though inadequate, definition of conscience is given in Lacoste's *Dictionnaire critique de théologie,* namely, the interior guide that approves or disapproves one's actions. Though implicit in the ancient tragedians and adumbrated in Aristotle's *phronesis,* the notion of conscience was first faintly articulated only by the Stoics.[2] The nearest equivalent in the Old Testament is the notion of the 'heart', a fairly vague notion, also found in the New Testament.

Though not a central concept in his writings, St Paul uses the term occasionally. What the New Testament provided, however, was an entirely new context symbolised by personal faith, and martyrdom, as summed up in the words of St Peter (Acts 5:29): 'We must obey God rather than men.' And so, beginning with Origen in the East and Augustine in the West, the Stoic notion was transformed into the uniquely Christian concept it became in the High Scholastic period. One of the most potent influences on that development was the daily examination of conscience. It was central to monastic life, and indeed was not absent from Christian piety in general, forming, as it still does, an essential component of the practice of auricular confession, what one author calls 'the ultimate court of conscience'.[3] By the time we get to the sixteenth century, conscience seems to be on everyone's lips. Beginning with King Henry's scruple about the validity of his marriage, most of the protagonists in More's story at one stage or another appeal to their conscience, including Luther, with whom a new understanding began to emerge, one which has had ramifications down to our own day.

Thomas More stood at the watershed that separates the medieval from the modern period. His understanding of conscience was that of the former. We are, in a sense, products of the latter. And part of our difficulty in trying to understand Thomas More is due to our own notion of, or rather, in the plural, our notions of what constitutes conscience. One could express the difference, rather crudely, by saying that for More conscience was the desire and capacity to know what is, the truth of things and their demands on us, both practical and speculative; on the other hand, for many contemporaries conscience is my own personal conviction, opinion or even my deepest feeling. More sought objective truth. We respect subjective opinions.

Anthony Kenny in his extended essay on More has an instructive discussion of More's understanding of conscience. Central to that discussion is the scholastic theory of an erroneous conscience, namely that one had to act on one's conscience even though it may be in error, provided that one had made sufficient effort to 'inform' one's conscience. Kenny notes that this is the basis of More's defence: he told Cranmer that it was against his conscience to swear the oath since he had informed his conscience. 'But,' Kenny adds, 'for the More in Bolt's play what matters is not whether the Pope's supremacy is true, but the fact that More has committed his inmost self to it.' As he says to Norfolk, 'What matters to me is not whether it's true or not, but that I believe it to be true, or rather not that I believe it but that *I* believe it'.[4] Now, of course, that is precisely what More would never have said, not only because it has distinct echoes of Luther's *Hier stehe ich, ich kann nicht anders*, but because it is a thoroughly modern concept of conscience, alien, I vouch to claim, to all that More stood, and fell, for.

But the problem of interpreting Thomas More is even more complex. All the terms he uses in his moral philosophy or theology are indeed still in use, but they no longer have the meaning or resonance they would have had for More or those

An Irish Reader in Moral Theology

who inspired him, in particular Thomas Aquinas. To take one term: the central concept of 'virtue'. Already in the late seventeenth century the broader term 'moral' is used in its most restricted sense of all, that which has to do primarily with sexual behaviour.[5] By the nineteenth century, colloquial speech had confined the term 'virtue' exclusively to the sexual sphere. One could say that the phrase 'a woman of low virtue' marks its nadir! Despite a recovery of the classical notion of virtue in recent decades, a renowned, contemporary, moral theologian could write (very persuasively) about compassion as 'the virtue of our age'.[6] Such a loose usage of the term would have puzzled any scholastic, since compassion is not a virtue, but an emotion, at best one of those passions, which need to be moulded into the virtues of fortitude and temperance, sometimes by resisting them at their most intense pitch.

In *After Virtue*, Alasdair MacIntyre, as is well known, noted that contemporary public debate is characterised primarily by interminable disputes. This he maintains is due to the lack of an agreed moral language. 'The most striking feature of contemporary moral utterance is that so much of it is used to express disagreements; and the most striking feature of debates in which these disagreements are expressed is their interminable character.'[7] His study of the history of ethics led him to the insight that he describes in terms of a grim parable, which Sachs summarises as follows:

Imagine, he says, that at some time in the future there is a widespread revolution against science. There is a series of ecological disasters. Science and technology are blamed. There is a public panic. Riots break out. Laboratories are burned down. A new political party comes to power on a wave of anti-scientific activity. A century later, the mood subsides. People begin to try to reconstruct what was destroyed. But all they have are fragments of what was once a coherent scientific culture: odd pages from all books, scientific instruments whose use has been forgotten, bits and pieces of information about theories and experiments without the background of knowledge of their context. These pieces are reassembled into a discipline called science. Its terminology and some of its practices resemble science But the systematic corpus of beliefs which once underlay them has gone. There would be no unitary conception of what science was about, what its practices were for, or what its key terms signified. The illusion would persist that science had been recovered. But it would have been lost, and there would be no way of discovering that it had been lost.[8]

The philosophical endeavour of the Enlightenment, which he calls the secularisation of Protestantism, was the beginning of various efforts to reconstruct a moral system made up of the fragments of an earlier revolt against the classical system of medieval Europe. The main object was to find a moral justification for values needed to preserve a minimum of order in society. Each effort to find a philosophical justification for morality failed – as it was bound to fail – until eventually emotivism prevailed, as it does to a large extent today in our western culture. This is, put simply, the denial that in the sphere of morality is there any such thing, strictly speaking, as objectivity. Morality is essentially irrational feeling, personal preference.

MacIntyre does not simply describe the moral debris, or its origins. He tries to recover the original, classical science of morality based on the Greek notion of *aret*, usually inadequately rendered as virtue. It is a term that defies translation, as Professor Thomas Canon Finan has pointed out. The closest English equivalent might be 'human excellence and goodness'. We will return to it.

This has implications for interpreting Thomas More, in particular since he seems to have been one of the first victims of that revolution which eventually swept away the moral language in which he understood his own life and philosophy, and which would have allowed us to understand him. It follows that conscience, whatever it is, cannot be understood in isolation; it is part of a system of thought and life, personal and communal, central to which is virtue as the context of all moral discourse

WITNESS TO CONSCIENCE

This raises the interesting question as to whether or not we moderns can ever really grasp what More understood as conscience.[9] One might argue that sufficient common ground still exits for most people of upright lives to recognise and respond to Thomas More's unique character and integrity (both products of virtue), in particular his readiness to sacrifice everything for what he in conscience held to be, not simply his *opinion* (Plato's *doxa*), but truths of universal validity (*the?ria*). But that answer is not entirely convincing. The real reason why it is possible to recover 'More's conscience', as it were, will I hope become clear in an attempt to do precisely that. Let us begin by glancing at his life and one of his writings.

As one author has demonstrated, More's life and writings give us a unique insight into the way he came to those momentous decisions that marked his life and changed history.[10] He battled for four years with the question of his vocation, monastic life or marriage, before opting for the latter. His crisis of conscience when invited to enter the Royal service is documented dramatically in that wonderful dialogue between Raphael Hytholdaeus and More in Book I of Utopia.[11] His attitude to the Papal Supremacy was the product of some ten days vigorous research as a result of a question posed by Antonio Bonvisi. His decision not to sign the Oath of Supremacy and to remain silent on the King's Great Matter caused him many sleepless nights, as he pondered the consequences for his wife, asleep at his side, and his beloved family all around him, before he could say to a bewildered Roper, immediately after leaving Cheslea for the last time: 'Son Roper, I thank our Lord, the field is won.'[12] He had made his conscientious decision, having counted the cost. In each of these momentous decisions More demonstrated what Aquinas meant when he said that in conscience is our participation in the providence of God, when each of us becomes a lawmaker for ourselves.[13]

It is noteworthy that all his major personal decisions were marked by self-renunciation. At the request of his father, he gave up Oxford and letters for New Inn and law. In deference to the grief he might cause the elder sister of the Colt family, he chose Jane as his first wife rather than the younger sister he really fancied. Just as he was coming into his own as a star among the European humanists, he sacrificed a brilliant literary future, fame, and whatever academic freedom he might have enjoyed, in order to enter into the service of the King. Having no thirst for polemics, he entered the theological fray when requested by the English bishops. Eventually he sacrificed his property, his wife, family, friends and even life for the *unum necessarium* and thought all else as nought. His decisions of conscience were modelled on the *kenosis*, the self-emptying of Christ, as taught in his favourite devotional writings, *The Imitation of Christ*. The hair-shirt was his daily reminder of submission to the will of the Father. In all this More was acutely aware that he was being sustained by that ineffable thing we call grace, that mysterious presence of the love of God poured into our hearts that draws us to union with him. To understand More's conscience, one has to keep both these things in mind: Christ as More's exemplar and Christ as the source of living according to that exemplar. In the Tower, he returns over and over again to the Passion and composes his treatise on the Sufferings of Christ. In a word, his decisions of conscience were his attempt to know and do not his own will but the will of God. His life of prayer and union with God are also the source of the care-free joy and liberating wit that marked his every word and deed, right up to the moment of his execution. He summed up his whole life in his final words: 'I am the King's good servant, [but] God's first.'

As a lawyer, particularly later as a judge and Lord Chancellor,[14] More's fairness and justice would seem to have been based on his attempt to know the truth of each case before him and to see beyond the letter of postive law to the spirit, the origin of the notion of equity, central to medieval English jurisprudence.[15] The ancients called this acquired disposition the virtue of prudence, the highest in rank of, and the precondition for, all the other virtues. If the object of law is justice, then the precondition for justice is to know not simply the legal complexities of a case and the details of the relevant laws, written and unwritten, but the truth about the particular situation involved in each case, before a just judgement could be made. And indeed what modern theologians often refer to as conscience – the ability to judge what one ought to do in a particular situation after one has 'informed' one's conscience – would have been seen by the ancients as an aspect of prudence, *phronesis*.[16] One of the characteristics of prudence is the acquired disposition to get to the heart of the matter swiftly and with a sure touch. The technical terms for this is *sollertia*, which is a '"perfected ability" by virtue of which man, when confronted with a sudden event, ... can swiftly, but with open eyes and clear vision, decide for the good, avoiding the pitfalls of injustice, cowardice, and intemperance'.[17] More's life not only exemplified this *sollertia*. His ability to clear the backlog of cases he inherited from Wolsey and see the day when there were no more cases awaiting judgement is proof that he possessed the virtue of prudence in an eminent degree.[18] After examining the evidence, one author described him as 'a hard-working administrator, a peacemaker more concerned to get at the sources of violence in the country-side than to inflict harsh penalties, a protector of the weak against the strong, and as astute lawyer who could cut through a mass of detail to the heart of the matter at hand.'[19]

Another aspect of conscience is courage, or to be more accurate the virtue of fortitude. It is closely related to the social or communal dimension of conscience and has enormous implications for politics. When the Romans coined the term 'virtue', perhaps it was this aspect in particular which they had in mind. We see it in the way More managed to secure liberty of expression for parliament when appointed Lord Chancellor, the origin of parliamentary privilege.[20] Democracy is based on free speech, which is the prerequisite for a genuine debate leading to a truly prudential decision by the ruler, that dictate of practical reason which is law. But few are ever willing to exercise free speech due to fear of intimidation and reprisals. More, it would seem, did so, but only when prudence dictated. More specifically, the virtue of fortitude is manifested in endurance in the face of unavoidable injustice. Martyrdom is the ultimate expression of fortitude as endurance. It is important to recall that More rejected the popular false heroism of the late medieval lives of martyrs, and, following the words of Christ, insisted that given the opportunity one should flee persecution. Martyrdom is not to be sought out, but, when all else fails, it must be accepted as God's will. Theory became practice in his public silence with regard to the King's Great Matter. His writings in the Tower indicate the source of that fortitude: the theological virtue of hope: that one day we will all be merry in heaven. It becomes almost an antiphon in his final days.

Is there any more to be said? Indeed we have not really touched the core of the mystery of conscience. Here I wish to draw on a recent essay on conscience by Joseph Cardinal Ratzinger, conscience being one of the themes that occurs repeatedly in his writings.[21]

THE NATURE OF CONSCIENCE

It is an essay with the revealing subtitle: 'Conscience and Truth.'[22] What Ratzinger achieves in this essay, it seems to me, is the recovery of what might be described as the ontological level of conscience. In the Middle Ages it was known as *synteresis* or *synderesis*, a term taken from Stoicism, as distinct from *conscientia*, the level of judgement, i.e. conscience in the narrow sense of the term as up to now in discussing More's life. Ratzinger prefers the more Platonic term *anamnesis* to the

Stoic term. It is a term, moreover, that is close to biblical thought, such as St Paul describes in Rom 2:14f: the law that is written into our hearts.[23] This ontological level of conscience was first discovered by Socrates, whom Ratzinger regards almost as a prophet of Jesus Christ, was central to tradition from St Basil the Great and St Augustine to the medieval mystics and the high scholastics, including St Thomas Aquinas.[24] According to Ratzinger it is also central to the thought of the two great Englishmen, Thomas More and Cardinal Newman. But in modern post-scholastic theology it was effectively forgotten,[25] with the consequent shrivelling of conscience to the second level, that of practical judgement. This led in our time to two apparently contradictory but in fact closely related perversions of the notion of conscience, that of the erroneous conscience[26] and that of the infallible conscience. The former has come to mean in effect that it does not matter what one does, provided one is sincerely convinced that it is right, while the latter affirms that conscience cannot err, that what you think is right is in fact right. Conscience is reduced to an 'excuse mechanism',[27] and so neither Hitler nor Stalin can be condemned. Both notions receive their persuasiveness, if not their inspiration, from the prevailing relativism of modernity,[28] the end product of the Enlightenment project built on the autonomy of the subject and the absolute claims of reason. It is now floundering in uncritical conformity to convention and the reduction of reason to empirical or quantitative rationality.[29]

Both notions, in a word, reflect that all-pervasive subjectivity which reduces morality to personal preference, something ultimately irrational. 'In such a "relativistic" context,' Ratzinger mentions in an aside, 'teleological or consequentialist ethics [now also the predominant school of thought in moral theology] becomes in the final analysis nihilistic. And when, in such a world view, one mentions "conscience" the description for it is – more profoundly considered – that there is no such thing as conscience as such, namely co-knowing with truth. Each one determines his own criteria, and in the general relativity no can be of assistance to the other, much less make regulations for him ...'[30]

What then is the ontological level of conscience? It is '... the window, that opens up to man the view of the common truth that establishes and sustains us all and so makes community of decision and responsibility possible due to the common ground of perception'.[31] Pure subjectivity on the other hand disposes of the obligation to search for the truth and removes any doubt about generally accepted attitudes. It suffices to be convinced about one's own views and adjust to the views of others: the more superficial one's views the better. But a firmly subjective conviction untouched by guilt is in fact a symptom of a sickness of the soul.[32] The inability to experience guilt is the sin of the Pharisees.

Interpreting Rom 2:1-16, where Paul undermines the theory of salvation through lack of knowledge of the truth (in other words, due to an erroneous conscience), Ratzinger says:

There is in man the presence of truth which cannot be disallowed – that truth of the Creator which in salvific-historical revelation has also become written down. Man can see the truth of God as a result of being created. Not to see it is guilt. It is not seen, if and because it is not willed. This 'no' of the will which prevents knowledge is guilt. Then the fact that the signal-lamp does not light up is a consequence of an intentional looking away from that which we do not want to see.[33]

According to Newman, who rejected the liberal notion of the subject as a self-sufficient criterion over against the demands of authority in a world devoid of truth, conscience means: '... the audible and imperious presence of the voice of truth in the subject himself; conscience is the cancellation of pure subjectivity in the contact made between the interiority of man and the truth that comes from God.'[34]

The first, as it were, ontological level of conscience, then, consists in the fact 'that something like *a primal memory (eine Urerinneung) of the good* and *of the true* (both are identical) is implanted in us; that there is an inner tendency of being in man made in the likeness of God towards that which is in conformity with God ... This *anamnesis* of the origin, which results from that constitution of our being which is in conformity with God, is not a conceptual, articulated knowledge, a treasury of recallable contents. It is, as it were, an interior sense, a capacity of re-cognition, so that the person who is thereby addressed, and is not opaque within, recognises the echo of it in himself.'[35] St Augustine formulated it more simply as the sense for the good that is imprinted in us.[36] However this sense needs, as it were, help from without in order to become itself; what is external to it performs a maieutic function, to bring its own openness for truth to fulfilment. What is outside is the authority of the Church[37] – but also presumably includes any genuine moral authority.

With regard to the Christian there is yet another dimension to be mentioned that goes beyond the radius of creation: the anamnesis of the new 'we' which has been granted to us through our incorporation into Christ. St John appeals to this Christian memory, that is always learning but which, on the basis of its own sacramental identity, can distinguish between what is the unfolding of memory and what is its falsification (cf. 1 Jn 2:20).[38]

The second level of conscience comes into play in the act of judgement in a particular situation which is always unique. As I have already mentioned above, conscience here would seem to be closely related to the virtue of prudence.[39] Both levels are distinct but interrelated. One must act according to one's judgement or conviction, even if it is objectively wrong – but one may be guilty for coming to the wrong decision. The guilt lies somewhere else, not for judging something right that is in fact objectively wrong, but deeper, ' ... in the desolation of my being that makes me insensible for the voice of truth and its appeal to my inner self'.[40] For this reason criminals like Hitler and Stalin are guilty.

There is a final dimension that Ratzinger mentions in an epilogue, that of grace: the forgiveness of God once we recognise our guilt. It is the divine power of expiation, which, as the Greeks already recognised, would be needed to wash away our guilt. Without attention to this, the real core of the Christian message, truth can become a yoke on our shoulders too heavy for us to bear.

The recovery of the ontological level of conscience throws new light on what is meant by that objective morality which, before the modern period, was universally recognised by the wisdom of humanity. That is 'the conviction that man's being contains an imperative, the conviction that he does not himself *invent* morality on the basis of expediency, but rather *finds* it already present in things'.[41] This conviction is common to all the great religious and wisdom traditions of humanity, which flow like tributaries into the great Christian vision of reality. 'The ethical vision of the Christian faith is not in fact something specific to Christianity but is the synthesis of the great ethical intuitions of mankind from a new centre that holds them together.'[42]

This understanding of the underlying, ontological basis of conscience, it seems to me, is at the core of More's *Utopia*.

THE *UTOPIA* OF THOMAS MORE

Hythlodaeus concludes his discourse in Book I with a comment on the eagerness of the Utopians to learn what they can from anyone coming from another culture or civilization: 'This readiness to learn is, I think, the really important reason for their being better governed and living more happily that we do,' Hythlodaeus says, 'though we are not inferior to them in brains or resources',[43] a jab at European arrogance. Europe was losing the capacity – the humility – needed to learn from others.

Similarly in Book II, Hythlodaeus concludes his account of Utopia and its commonwealth with a description of the content of the Utopians' common worship: they acknowledge God as the creator and ruler of the universe, author of all that is good. They thank him for his benefits, in particular the way of life in the commonwealth and their religious ideas 'which they hope are the truest'. Then Hythlodaeus adds: 'If they are wrong in this, and if there is some sort of society or religion more acceptable to God than the present one, they pray that he will, in his goodness, reveal it to them, for they are ready to follow wherever he leads ...'[44] More here may well be reminding his readers, as some commentators claim, that the supposedly ideal commonwealth is but the product of reason unaided by revelation, which would explain why some of the customs of the Utopians are contrary to Christian practice. But I think that More is drawing his readers' attention to something more serious than the questionable practices of, say, female priests, divorce or euthanasia: namely the closing of the European soul in contrast with the humility and openness of the Utopians. That closure resulted from a new relationship of man to reality as expressed in the way Pico della Mirandola presents God as speaking to the first man:

> No domicile, no form, no special task have I given you, O Adam, so that you may choose domicile, form and task for your self and what you choose should be yours according to your mind. All other creatures have I conceived with a particular nature and thus enclosed them within definite boundaries. You are restricted by no narrow limits. According to your will, in whose hand I have given you, you determine [fix] that nature.[45]

No wonder Rome quaked. This divinisation of natural man is the source of all human hubris: unlimited free choice.

The readiness of the Utopians to learn and their openness to correction about their way of life and their religious ideas are but two sides of the one coin, and that coin is conscience, not the second level, prudence, but the first, ontological level.[46] As far as I can ascertain, the term 'conscience' though used by some translators is not found in the text itself.

Book II is an account of life in Utopia. It begins with a description of the external territory and ends with a discourse on the internal territory of the heart: virtue and religion. Like Plato and Aristotle who provided the main inspiration for Utopia, it would seem that the real discovery the fictional traveller made was not an ideal commonwealth but the perennial truths that order in society is dependent on order in the soul (virtue), that virtue is related to transcendence, and that man is the measure of society because God is the measure of his soul (conscience). As in the Greek experience, this discovery of what one author calls the anthropological principle governing society was made against a background of the dominant cosmological principle.[47] According to the latter, society, in particular its representative, the prince, or, more precisely, the emperor, was in turn the ultimate representative of eternal order so that his word was law and there was no appeal to a higher instance. The Greeks emerged out of this concept of order in society to discover the unmeasured measure of all law (Solon), the unwritten law that measured the licitness of all human laws (Sophocles), the primacy of transcendent truth that could not be exhausted in any human law or teaching but could be glimpsed with no small effort by the just man, whose justice is the fruit of his search for the truth and whose destiny would be that of Socrates.[48] Thomas More witnessed in his day the re-emergence of the cosmological principle that placed the prince above morality[49] and so gave him unlimited power, and god-like status: the so-called divine right of kings. That emergence was cloaked in the garb of expediency and thus, for the sake of the presumed greater good, the individual could, and would, be sacrificed. What could not be tolerated is the man who would give God the primacy over the state,[50] as Thomas More summed up his whole life in his parting words before his

An Irish Reader in Moral Theology

execution. 'God first' pithily captures More's fidelity to his conscience: 'the voice of God within', to quote the Second Vatican Council, following Newman.

It has been pointed out[51] that 'the question of the moral and the expedient interested More deeply, as it did other humanists'. And that indeed the account of Utopia is an attempt, among other things, to answer the question: 'Is it possible, even theoretically, for a commonwealth to be both moral and expedient?'[52] This may indeed be true, but it strikes me as somewhat scholastic, using the term in the somewhat pejorative sense that More used it. Is it possible that what preoccupied More was the more radical question: would morality survive the triumph of the expediency he could observe near and far, where increasingly men were using human laws to set aside the law of God[53] just as preachers adjusted the teaching of Christ to suit the wishes of men?[54] Morality itself was being redefined as utility and so its true nature had to be underlined, namely virtue, understood in the original Greek sense as 'excellence' (aret).

'The passage on moral philosophy,' it has been remarked, 'is in fact the cornerstone of the Utopian edifice.'[55] Indeed, the rest of the account of the ideal commonwealth would seem to be primarily concerned with ideal conditions necessary for virtue to flourish: even one of the two games played by the Utopians was a battle of vices against the virtues.[56] Let us pay a little attention to the passage entitled 'Ethica' by the glossator.

To understand nature of happiness – which as St Thomas Aquinas, following a tradition going back to Aristotle, affirms is the end of all virtue[57] – is almost impossible, the Utopians insist, without reference to two basic tenets of natural religion: the immortality of the soul and reward for virtue, punishment for vice in the hereafter.[58] Without a hereafter, there is no sense in enduring the hardship (aspera) that virtue necessarily involves. Behind this passage is one of the fundamental assumptions of medieval Catholic thought which seems to pervade every aspect of More's life and writings, namely the inter-relatedness of faith and reason: 'Reason is the servant of faith and not enemy.'[59] Under the influence of Nominalism, the Reformation was about to sunder one from the other radically – with enormous consequences, inter alia, for moral philosophy.[60]

The starting point is pleasure.[61] 'Now, indeed, [the Utopians] hold happiness rests not in every pleasure, but only in that which is good and upright. To such, as to the supreme good, our nature is drawn by virtue itself. The opposite school claims that virtue is itself happiness.'[62] The dispute between the Epicureans and Stoics behind these two views may be left aside, since More would seem to have transcended them by interpreting the Stoic concept of the *sumum bonum*, in the light of Augustine's insight that we are made for God and are restless until we rest in him, and so recovering the original Aristotelian concept.[63] What More says is that in us there is an attraction to the ultimate Good, to the extent that we have achieved human excellence (virtue). This attraction is our capacity for happiness. As we will see, this attraction would seem to be the source of conscience.

'The Utopians define virtue as living according to nature since to this end we were created by God.'[64] This is a definition of the Stoics, as the gloss observes, albeit transformed by Christian theology. We moderns have great difficulty understanding this statement, due to the prevailing false, moralistic view of virtue, as mentioned already. The Thomistic description, according to Josef Pieper, is 'the optimum that a human being can be', human flourishing at its best, as God intended we should flourish. The text continues:

> That individual, they say, is following the guidance of nature who, in desiring one thing and avoiding another, obeys the dictates of reason. Now reason first of all inflames [mortals] to a love and veneration of the divine majesty, to whom we owe both our existence and our capacity for happiness. Secondly, it admonishes and urges us to lead a life as free from care and as full of joy as possible, and because of our natural fellowship, to help all other men too, to attain that end.[65]

This is a most significant passage. It opens with the Thomistic concept of conscience: namely that right reason which, according to a recent commentary, 'enables men to distinguish right from wrong with instinctive clarity, that is to apprehend the natural law'.[66] I think that a further clarification is needed: More would have understood the term 'reason' not in the abstract, rationalist sense familiar to us but in the classical sense of *logos*, reason perfected in the cognition of truth,[67] speculative and practical – in other words, wisdom – or the mind of the wise person which has come to recognise the intelligible order of being. The order of human existence is the law. And that law, as More goes on to clarify in the next passage, is the dual commandment to love God and one's neighbour, since, as More comments: '[Concern for, and action on behalf of, others] is the virtue most peculiar to man.'[68] His formulation of the natural law is, however, uniquely his own. First of all, reason (perfected in truth) inflames all mortals to a love and veneration of the divine majesty. More is not talking about a Deistic God infinitely distant from us but the transcendent God who is closer to each one than we are to ourselves. His use of the term 'inflames' is to be noted. Reason, secondly, warns us to live a joy-filled life free of care – this, it seems to me, is but another description of virtue – and to lead others to share that joy, namely love of God and a life free of all care and need, both material and spiritual. More underlines this with a lovely touch of irony ridiculing the long-faced proponents of virtue (the moral zealots of his day, and our day as well): if even they could understand that concern for the poverty and sorry plight of others is humane and so to be fostered, then surely nature, presumed to be good, could be expected to urge everyone to do the same. The Catholic assumption that nature, though flawed, was basically good, was soon to be vehemently denied. The chill announcing the arrival of the storm brewing in Lower Saxony was already in the air. Is this the reason that More makes the epicurean starting point his own in the discourse on moral philosophy we have just glanced at?

Behind this, the central text of *Utopia* is what Ratzinger calls the ontological level of conscience, our capacity to know the truth both at the speculative and at the practical level. It is at this level, it seems to me, that we discover what moved More so profoundly, what moulded his life and death: the truth. Truth is ultimately incomprehensible but capable of some limited though real comprehension, which is often discovered in the process of trying to communicate it to others, as both poet and prophet testify. The truth, though always personal, is not subjective. It is communal and so universal. As Brodsky once said, reason is essentially social. Aristotle, I think, would have agreed, since he used two definitions of man, which, I suggest, are interchangeable: a rational animal and a political animal. More died a witness to the truth (the definition of a martyr), and not simply for his personal subjective conviction. Truth is not individualistic. Though intensely personal and particular in its recognition and expression, truth is by nature universal and communal. It is for this reason that God instituted an ultimate, universal authority – the conscience of a particular person, the successor of St Peter – to be the guarantor of his revealed truth intended for the salvation of all mankind. In More's own words, after he had studied the question of papal supremacy, '... it holdeth up all'.[69] There is, therefore, an intrinsic, and not just an accidental, relationship between More's conscience and the papal supremacy, as he himself seems to have indicated when, after his judgement, it was 'prudent' for him to break his silence.[70]

Individuals may deny the truth, and indeed they may sincerely hold the opposite, in which case (erroneous conscience) they are to be respected. According to the *Utopia*, they should be tolerated, encouraged to debate the issue with the experts behind closed doors – and otherwise left to themselves in the hope that one day they will see the truth and repent, as was the case with Pico della Mirandola, the subject of More's first publication. What they cannot do, according to the *Utopia*, is speak publicly about it, which would amount to imposing their views on society and thus causing social unrest.[71] With regard to those who do wrong, who act unjustly, like the judges who condemned More – God alone knoweth how, as he says – the only thing one can do is pray that one day they too will, thanks to God's grace and mercy, acknowledge their wrongdoing and repent. Because More's own great matter was Truth, or rather conscience understood as the primordial sensorium of truth, he could not only forgive his enemies but sincerely pray that those who condemned him would one day repent – and that they would finally recognise the truth so that they would all be merry together in heaven.[72] His merriment, I suggest, was likewise due to his passion for the truth, not his own convictions. He was literally 'care-free'. The Truth had made him free.

* I wish to acknowledge my gratitude to Ms Clare Murphy, *Moreanum*, Angers, for her most useful suggestions literature re. St Thomas More, and also to my colleague, Thomas Canon Finan for his own suggestions re. relevant material, for his careful reading of the manuscript, and for his encouragement.

NOTES

1   R.W. Chambers, *Thomas More*, London 1935 (1948 reprint), p. 16.

2   Cf. article on 'Conscience' by John Webster, in *Dictionnaire critique de théologie*, under the general editorship of Jean-Yves Lacoste, Paris: Presse Universitaires de France, 1998, p. 256; the earliest reference to the Greek term *syneidesis* is found in Democritus (460–c.357 BC)

3   John A. Guy, 'Law, Equity, and Conscience in Henrician Juristic Thought' in Gordon, J. Schochet (ed.), *Reformation, Humanism, and 'Revolution'*, Vol. 1, Washington: The Folger Institute for the History of British Political Thought, Proceedings, 1990, p. 1.

4   Anthony Kenny, *Thomas More* (Past Masters Series), Oxford, 1983, p. 95. This would seem to be the way some contemporary moral theologians also interpret conscience and even appeal to Bolt's play in support (cf. Richard M. Gula SS, *Reason Informed by Faith: Foundations of Catholic Morality*, New York, 1989, pp. 133–5).

5   Alasdair MacIntyre, *After Virtue, A Study in Moral Theory*, London, 1981, p. 37.

6   Oliver O'Donovan, *Begotten or Made?*, Oxford, 1984, p. 11. I should add that, apart from the possibly ironic use of the term 'virtue' in this context, I am otherwise fully in agreement with his main thesis, which is that emotion, not reason seems to determine moral action in the typically modern world.

7   Ibid., p. 6.

8   Jonathan Sacks, *The Politics of Hope*, London, 1997, p. 32.

9   One of the most impressive accounts of More's understanding of conscience is that penned by the great More scholar, André Prévost, 'Conscience and the Ultimate Court of Appeal' in R.S. Sylvester and G.P. Marc'hadour (eds), *Essential Articles for the study of Thomas More*, Hamden, Conn., 1977, pp. 563–8. See also the account by Brian Byron in his *Loyalty in the Spirituality of St Thomas More*, Nieukoop, 1972, pp. 38–42. Modern readers will find it difficult to assimilate these accounts, not because of any inability on the part of the authors – on the contrary – but rather because of the assumptions we moderns bring to our reading of it; see, for example the quotation below in footnote 13.

10   See Chamber, op. cit., passim. For a succinct and more complete account of the following, see Rudolf B. Gottfried's article, 'A Conscience Undeflowered' in Sylvester and Marc'hadour, *Essential Articles*, op. cit., pp. 520–38.

11   See Gottfried, op. cit., pp. 525–6.

12   Chambers, op. cit., p. 301. Prévost comments: 'Although conscience represents an outstanding value which cannot be "made captive", it is nonetheless dependent upon *objective reality*. Therefore such conscience is not the fixed idea of an obstinate man who will not listen to reason. Before coming to a conclusion which imposed itself to his conscience, More submitted himself to a tremendous amount of homework. And even after forming his conscience, he still acknowledge two authorities that could prevail against his own conclusions: the decrees of a General Council or the unequivocal expression of the 'common faith' of the universal Church, which, in his opinion, have received from God the power of expressing revealed truth' (Prévost, op. cit., p. 567).

13   'Conscience for [More] is an absolute, his own and no one else's concern; no man has a right to exert any pressure whatsoever on it; so highly does he value it that he will offer his life in order to remain true to it. Individual conscience stands above all opinions. It knows no other rule than itself, God and God's will: 'But as concerning mine own self, for thy comfort shall I say, daughter, to thee, that mine own conscience in this matter (I damn none other man's) is such as may well stand with mine own salvation; therefore am I, Meg, as sure as that God is in heaven" (Prévost, op. cit., p. 566; quotation from Rogers, op. cit., p. 528). The extraordinary dialogue between More and Margaret in the Tower as reported by his daughter

in her 1534 Letter to Lady Alice Allington – Chambers compares the letter to Plato's *Crito* – the term 'conscience', according to G. Marc'hadour, occurs at least forty-four times (text in *The Correspondence of Sir Thomas More*, edited by Elizabeth Frances Rogers [Princetown, 1947] letter 206, pp. 514–32). It is well summarised by Prévost (see above, especially footnote 12).

14   'The Chancery was the great secretarial bureau: a Home Office, a Foreign Office, a Ministry of Justice. It was the centre of the English legal system and the political centre of the Constitution. The Lord Chancellor was the highest rank of the King's servants, "the King's natural Prime Minister". He acted as Secretary of State for all departments, and was Keeper of the Great Seal which was, in Matthew Paris' phrase, the key to the kingdom.' (Richard O'Sullivan, QC, *The Inheritance of the Common Law*, The Hamlyn Lectures, Second Series, [London, 1950], p. 110).

15   See the article by Richard O'Sullivan quoted in the previous footnote.

16   Nicholas Madden OCD suggested translating *phronesis* as 'imperative discernment', which is most apt.

17   Josef Pieper, *Prudence*, London, 1957, p. 28.

18   See the chapter entitled 'Law and Conscience' in Richard O'Sullivan, op. cit., pp. 93–118, which maps the development of equity in English law in the course of which the practice of earlier Common Law was perfected by the Chancellor's Court's wide use of its discretionary powers. In exercising such powers, judges (following the principle first enunciated by St Thomas Aquinas) were obliged in conscience to judge purely on the objective facts of the case. There O'Sullivan quotes his son-in-law, Roper, who recalled Thomas's response to judges who objected to the injunctions he granted. After inviting them to his home, he explained after dinner to them how he came to his decisions. They admitted that they too 'could haue done no other wise themselves'. He added, in Roper's words: 'that if the Iustices of euery courte (unto whom the reformacion of the rigour of the lawe, by reason of their office, most especially appertained) wold, upon reasonable consideration, by their owne discretions (as they were, as he thought, in conciens bound) mitigate and reforme the rigour of the lawe themselves, there should from thenceforth by him no more Iniunctions be granted' (O'Sullivan, op. cit., p. 109). But More knew that most judges did not want to take that moral responsibly on themselves, though they were in conscience bound to do so. Conscience, taking the particular circumstances into consideration should modify the law. This primacy of conscience, here understood as *objective* morality, would be challenged by More's contemporary, and religious opponent, Christopher St German, who, in *Doctor and Student* affirmed: 'Forasmuch as it behoveth thee to be occupied in such thins as pertain to the law, it is necessary that thou ever hold a pure and clear conscience: and I counsel thee that thou love that is good, and fly that is evil; that thou do nothing against truth: and that thou do justice to every man as much as in thee is; and also that in every general rule of the law thou do observe and keep equity. And if thou do thus, I trust the light of thy lantern, that is, thy conscience shall never be extinct' (as quoted in Lewis Watts SJ, 'Conscience in Court' in Richard O'Sullivan, QC, *The King's Good Servant: Papers read to The Thomas More Society of London*, [Oxford, 1948], p. 112; see also below, footnote 46, where St German keeps closer to the traditional concept). For a succinct discussion of the Thomistic understanding of relationship between law and conscience, which More shared, see Hilary J. Carpenter OP, 'Law and Conscience' in Richard O'Sullivan, QC, *The King's Good Servant*, op. cit., pp. 49–59.

19   Margaret Hastings, 'Sir Thomas More: Maker of English Law?' in Sylvester and Marc'hadour, *Essential Articles*, op. cit., p. 118.

20   It is captured most forcibly in what may well be the legend of how Thomas More, the young burgess, challenged King Henry VII and forced him to yield to the parliament's just demands. Legends convey their own truths, which tend to be deeper than empirical truths.

21   Cf. Vincent Twomey, 'La coscienze e l'uomo' in *Alla scuola della Verità*, Milan: Cinesello, Balsamo, 1997, pp. 111–45, the following section on the nature of conscience is a slightly revised version of pp. 138–43.

22   Most recently reprinted in English translation in *Benedict XVI and Cardinal Newman*, edited by Peter Jennings, Oxford: Family Publications, 2005, pp. 41–52. Quotations from the text

given here are my own translation of the German original as printed in Joseph Cardinal Ratzinger, *Wahrheit, Werte, Macht: Prüfsteine der pluralistischen Gesellschaft*, Freiburg, 1993.

23 The term also has liturgical, sacramental associations

24 The Thomistic understanding is well articulated by Alasdair MacIntyre as 'that fundamental, initial grasp of the primary precepts of the natural law, to which cultural degeneration can partially or temporarily blind us but which can never be obliterated' (*Three Rival Versions of Moral Enquiry: Encyclopedia, Genealogy, and Tradition being the Gifford Lectures delivered in the University of Edinburgh in 1988*, London, 1990, p. 194).

25 The great exception here, as usual, was Josef Pieper: cf. his *Traktat über die Klugheit* (Munich 1949), pp. 23–36 (in the 6th printing in 1960); see also his book, *Die Wirklichkeit und das Gute* (Munich, 1949). Pieper too speaks about the presence of an *Ur-Gewissen*, which might be translated as 'primal conscience'.

26 Here Ratzinger draws attention to the research of J.G. Belmans, 'La paradoxie de la conscience erronée d'Abélard à Karl Rahner', in *Revue Thomiste*, 9 (1990) pp. 570–86, which demonstrates that, with the appearance in 1942 of Sertillanges book on Thomas, a falsification of Aquinas's teaching on conscience began which has been widely influential.

27 *Wahrheit, Werte, Macht*, p. 39.

28 See Peter Fonk, 'Die Kunst des Steuermanns. Aristotles Beitrag zu einer theologischen Lehre vom Gewissen' in K. Arntz; P. Schallenberg (eds), *Ethik zwischen Anspruch und Zuspruch*, Freiburg, 1996, pp. 267–95 for some useful information about the historical origins of the two notions.

29 Cf. Joseph Ratzinger, *Church, Ecumenism, Politics New Essays in Ecclesiology*, translated by Robert Nowell, Slough, 1988, pp. 153–4; 231–2; ibid. *Turning Point for Europe?*, San Francisco, 1994, pp. 31–5; *Wahrheit, Werte, Macht*, pp. 65–73.

30 Ibid., p. 46.

31 Ibid., p. 32; see also Joseph Cardinal Ratzinger, '*Principles of Catholic Theology*, San Francisco, 1987, pp. 55–7.

32 Ratzinger (*Wahrheit, Werte, Macht*, pp. 34–5) refers to the psychologist A. Görres, 'Schuld und Schuldgefühl' in *Internationale katholische Zeitschrift Communio*, 13 (1984), p. 434.

33 *Wahrheit, Werte, Macht*, p. 37.

34 Ibid., p. 43.

35 Ibid., pp. 51–2.

36 Cf. ibid., pp. 51–3.

37 Cf. ibid., pp. 53–4.

38 Ibid., pp. 54–5.

39 See Josef Pieper, *Traktat über die Klugheit*, op. cit., especially pp. 23–44.

40 Ibid., p. 58.

41 *Turning Point for Europe?* pp. 28–9; there Ratzinger takes up and develops the insights of C.S. Lewis, *The Abolition of Man*, Oxford, 1943.

42 *Turning Point for Europe?*, p. 37; see also his contribution to Heinz Schürmann, Joseph Cardinal Ratzinger, Hans Urs von Balthasar, *Principles of Christian Morality*, translated by Graham Harriso, San Francisco, 1986, pp. 43–66.

43 Thomas More, *Utopia*, edited by George M. Logan and Robert M. Adams, Cambridge: Cambridge Texts in the History of Political Thought, 1989, p. 41.

44 Ibid., p. 106.

45 *De hominis dignitate* Ioannis Pici Mirandulae, *Opera quae extant omnia*, Basel, 1601, p. 208. I am grateful to Ms Penny Woods for locating this book for me in the Russell Library, Maynooth. Isaiah Berlin comments that, like Machiavelli, who 'stressed will, boldness, address, at the expense of rules laid down by calm *ragione*', 'so, too, in his own fashion did Pico della Mirandola in his apostrophe to the powers of man, who unlike the angels, can transform himself into any shape – the ardent image which lies at the heart of European humanism in the north as well as in the Mediterranean' (Isaiah Berlin, *Against the Current: Essays in the History of Ideas*, edited by Henry Hardy with an introduction by Roger Hausheer [London, 1979], p. 74).

46 It is interesting to note that the distinction between the two levels seems to have been

commonplace at this period, if we look at the definition of conscience found in *Dialogue of Doctor and Student* by Christopher St German. He defined it 'as the driving force within the human soul that inclines man to pursue good and eschew evil and which is capable of distinguishing the two at a practical level. Both motive and cognitive in this abstract sense, conscience was an objectivised gauge of ethical evaluation, and it was this gauge that was applied as a theoretical yardstick against the defendant's real-life morality in a particular case in Chancery in order to arrive at a corrective sentence (or decree) should any prove necessary' (Schochet, op. cit., p. 2). However, St German, it seems, modified the earlier understanding of equity quite significantly: for him, 'Equity was not an absolute, but was to be relative to the common erudition of lawyers. It was therefore human and fallible. In particular, it was vulnerable to the political atmosphere of the Inns of Court at a given historical moment' (ibid., p. 11).

47   Cf. Eric Voegelin, *The New Science of Politics: An Introduction*, Chicago and London, 1952, reprint 1983, pp. 52–9.

48   Cf. ibid., pp. 59–75. Voegelin describes this as the anthropological principle, the discovery of the soul as the sensorium of transcendence and with it the recognition 'that a polis is man written large', to use Plato's often-quoted phrase. 'A political society in existence will have to be an ordered cosmion, but not at the price of man; it should be not only a microcosmos but also a macroanthropos' (ibid., p. 61).

49   '*Utopia* is in part, a protest against the New Statesmanship: against the new idea of the autocratic prince to whom everything is allowed' (Chambers, op. cit., p. 131). Two years before the publication of *Utopia* in 1506, Machiavelli had finished writing his treatise on the New Statesmanship, *The Prince* (cf. George Bull in his introduction to his translation in the Penguin Books, 1961, p. 19), which Thomas Cromwell once offered to lend to Cardinal Pole and which evidently suited Cromwell's disposition. 'Parts of *Utopia*,' Chambers notes, 'read like a commentary on parts of *The Prince*' (ibid., p. 132).

50   'More's trial turned on the Erastian question of state dominion or jurisdiction over the Church and his conscience. More died, not so much for any one historic pope – friend of Erasmus and of so many diplomats with Roman experience that he was, he could have had no illusions about Julius or Leo, or Clement VII, their dilatory successor, who helped the Reformation to come to a boil in England through his calculated strategy of doing nothing over Henry's divorce proceedings – or even for the general notion of the papacy. More's death resulted directly from his belief that no lay ruler could have jurisdiction over the Church of Christ, and his concept of the Church was more compatible with a post-Vatican II concept than with a Tridentine one' (R.J. Schoeck, 'Common Law and Canon Law' in Sylvester and Marc'hadour, *Essential Articles*, op. cit., p. 48).Though Schoeck fails to recognise that it is precisely the papacy that guarantees the independence of the local Church in opposition to the Erastian tendencies of the state, his main point is valid.

51   By George M. Logan and Robert M. Adams in their introduction to *Utopia*, op. cit., p. xxiii.

52   Ibid., p. xxiv.

53   Cf. *Utopia*, Book I, ibid., p. 20.

54   Cf. ibid., p. 37.

55   Logan and Adams, op. cit., p. xxv.

56   Cf. ibid., p. 53.

57   Evidently the more severe, not to say pessimistic, extreme Augustinian tradition was gaining, or rather had already gained, the upper hand at the time. It is of interest to note, in an aside, that it was Aquinas who placed the treatise on the Beatitudes at the very start of his discussion of virtue. There is no discussion of morality without first determining our final end, eternal happiness, union with God, eternal beatitudes. The new Catechism of the Catholic Church has restored it to that position after centuries of displacement that seems to have begun in the sixteenth century. More evidently saw the significance of such shifts in perspective.

58   Cf. ibid., p. 68ff. The translation by G.C. Richards as revised by Surtz and Hexter (Yale edition) reads as follows: 'In that part of philosophy which deals with morals, they carry on the same debates as we do. They inquire into the good: of the soul and of the body and of the external gifts ... They discuss virtue and pleasure, but their principal and chief debate is

in what thing or things, one or more, they are to hold that happiness consists. In this matter they seem to lean more than they should to the school that espouses pleasure as the object by which to define either the whole or the chief part of human happiness.

'What is more astonishing is that they seek a defence for this soft doctrine from their religion, which is serious and strict, almost solemn and hard. They never have a discussion of philosophy without uniting certain principles taken from religion as well as from philosophy, which uses rational arguments. Without these principles they think reason insufficient and weak by itself for the investigation of true happiness. The following are examples of these principles. The soul is immortal and by the goodness of God born for happiness. After this life rewards are appointed for our virtue and good deeds, punishment for our crimes. Though these principles belong to religion, yet they hold that reason leads men to believe and admit them.' (pp. 161, 17–163, 5).

59   *Works*, 1557, p. 152, as quoted in R.W. Chambers, op. cit., p. 253.

60   See Servais Pinckaers, *The Sources of Christian Ethics*, translated from the third editon by Sr Mary Thomas Nogle OP, Edinburgh, 1995, pp. 327–53; idem., *Morality: The Catholic View*, with a preface by Alasdair MacIntryre, Indiana: South Bend, 2001, pp. 65–81.

61   We would do well to remember what Aristotle wrote: 'It is not possible to perform virtuous actions without pain or pleasure. The middle-state does not exist.' (No source given, quote found in *The Irish Catholic*.)

62   'Nunc vero non in omni voluptate felicitatem sed in bona, atque honesta sitam putant. ad eam enim uelut ad summum bonum, naturam nostram ab ipsa pertrahi, cui sola aduersa factio felicitatem tribuit.' (Yale ed., 162,15-18.) The translation is my own version of the Yale edition.

63   'The good is that to which all things aim' (Aristotle, *Nichomachean Ethics*. Bk I, Ch. 1, 104a 3, as given in *Fagothy's Right & Reason: Ethics in Theory and Practice*, edited by Milton A. Gonsalves, Ninth Edition, Columbus, Toronto, London, Melbourne, 1986, p. 67).

64   'Nempe uirtutem definiunt, secundum naturam uiuere ad id siquidem a deo institutos esse nos' (Yale edition, pp. 162, 18–21), trans. by Surtz and Hexler.

65   'Eum uero naturae ductum sequi quisquis in appetendis fugiendisque rebus obtemperat rationi. Rationem porro, mortales primum omnium in amorem, ac uenerationem diuinae maiestatis incendere, cui debemus, & quod sumus, & quod compotes esse felicitatis possumus, secundum id commonet, atque excitat nos ut uitam quamlicet minime anxiam, ac maxime laetam ducamus ipsi, caeterisque omnibus ad idem obtinendum adiutores nos pro naturae societate praebeamus.' (Yale edition, 162, pp. 21–28), trans. by Surtz and Hexler.

66   Logan and Adams, op. cit., p. 69.

67   Note, however, Josef Pieper's warning: 'We incline all too quickly to misunderstand Thomas Aquinas's words about "reason perfected in the cognition of truth". "Reason" meant to him nothing other than "regard for and openness to reality" and "acceptance of reality." And "truth" is to him nothing other than the unveiling and revelation of reality, of both natural and supernatural reality.' *The Four Cardinal Virtues*, Notre Dame, 1966, p. 9.

68   Surtz and Hexler use the term 'humanity' for what I have placed in brackets; so do Logan and Adams.

69   Ibid., p. 196.

70   Cf. R.W. Chambers, op. cit., p. 340.

71   The threat to public order posed by heretical movements was fully recognised by medieval society and was the justification for harsh measures against heretics by those who represented the state, such as Thomas More as Lord Chancellor and so responsible for the common good of the State.

72   'Pray for me,' More wrote to his daughter, Margaret, in his last letter from the Tower, 'and I shall for you and all your friends, that we may merrily meet in heaven.' St Thomas More, *Selected letters*, ed. by E.F Rogers, New Haven, 1961, p. 258.

26   The Act of Two Effects

W.J. Conway

(*Irish Theological Quarterly*, Vol. 18, 1951, pp. 125–37.)

To many students of theology there is something vaguely dissatisfying about the teaching of moralists on the 'act of two effects'. For one thing, a principle embodying four separate conditions – each of which must be fulfilled if the act is to be lawful – seems somewhat elaborate and 'unnatural'. One expects the principles of right reason to be more simple. Then it may be felt that there is a certain vagueness about what is often described as the primary condition – that the act must not produce the evil effect *directly*. When does an act produce an effect directly? It cannot be said that the answers given by theologians to this question are always enlightening. Then too there is the question of intention, which at times seems to bedevil the whole problem. Is the intention of the agent a relevant consideration at all? It is often assumed that it is not. Yet in many practical cases common sense seems to indicate that intention is the determining factor. Thus, to modify somewhat a classic *casus* of the older theologians, if a woman jumps from a high window, not *ad salvandam virginitatem*, but with the intention of killing herself, her act is manifestly an act of suicide even though at the time she may be pursued by an *invasor pudicitiae*. Yet it is hard to see what, apart from intention, differentiates this act from that of the woman who jumps in order to avoid rape, an act which theologians regard as lawful.

The present article aims at going over this familiar ground and attempting to show that the teaching of moral theologians on the essential problem of the act of two effects is simply a precise application of the principle that the end does not justify the means. Certain other considerations which are usually added for the sake of completeness follow from equally simple and obvious moral principles. The difficulties experienced in applying this teaching to concrete cases do not derive from any vagueness or over complexity in principle. They are due rather to complexity in the physical structure of the acts in question; they are difficulties of fact rather than of law.

I

We must begin our consideration of this problem by clearing the ground – by excluding various categories of cases where no moral problem arises, either in principle or in the application of principle.

In the first place, no problem of lawfulness or unlawfulness arises when the act is already unlawful in itself quite apart from the evil effect which it produces. Thus we are not concerned with cases like that of the man who causes scandal – and at the same time relieves his own mental depression – by getting drunk. His act may have the two effects of scandal and the relief of depression, but there is no problem as to its lawfulness or unlawfulness since it is already evil in itself quite apart from these two effects. Moral theologians usually state as their first condition that the act of two effects must be either good or at least indifferent in itself. In doing so they are simply stating the obvious fact that if the act is evil in itself, antecedently to the consideration of its effects, no good effect can render it lawful. For our present purposes we may exclude such simple cases from the discussion altogether.

Second, we are not concerned with cases where an effect that is normally evil ceases to be so in the concrete circumstances of a particular case. Thus the effect of grave damage to another's property, which is normally evil, ceases to be so if in a concrete case it is the only means of saving a human life, for example if I must break a stained-glass window in order to rescue a man from a burning church. The damage to the window, which in other circumstances would have been a morally evil effect, ceases to be so in these particular circumstances. Similarly the amputation of a human limb may sometimes be inordinate and therefore 'evil' – but clearly this does not apply to a poisoned limb which is threatening the well-being of the whole body. In other words, these effects are only *conditionally* forbidden by the moral law. In circumstances where the condition is not verified the effect ceases to be evil.[1] In the present article we are concerned only with acts which are unconditionally forbidden, i.e. which may never be willed and which, therefore, are evil in all circumstances.

Such, for example, is the killing of an innocent person. Is it ever lawful to perform an act which will have an effect of this kind? – that is the precise question at issue.[2]

Lastly, no moral problem arises when the evil effect, no matter how it is caused, is intended. If a woman jumps from a window with the intention of committing suicide, then her act is evil even though she may happen at the time to be pursued by an assailant on her virtue. If another woman performs exactly the same act with the sole intention of escaping from the assailant her act is lawful.

This is a point of great importance. It must not be thought that intention is not a relevant consideration in determining the material morality of a human act – that it is something which pertains exclusively to formal morality. That view would be contrary both to right reason and to the consistent teaching of Catholic theology.

Suppose a doctor administers to a woman suffering from dangerously high fever a drug which will have the two-fold effect of lowering her temperature and producing an abortion. If it is a case where the doctor merely intends to save the woman's life by lowering her temperature the act is lawful. But suppose that in an identically similar case the doctor wishes the child to die, and administers the same drug in exactly the same way but this time with the intention of producing an abortion. In this case the act is manifestly evil; the doctor deliberately wills to produce an abortion and he places an act to achieve that end. The fact that his act has also the good effect of lowering the woman's temperature will not make it a good act. Here then we have the self-same act performed twice in identical circumstances; in one case it is a lawful act, in the other case it is evil. Yet the only difference between the two acts lies in the different intentions with which they were performed. The evil intention in the second case makes the act evil.

Moreover in discussing these two cases it is with their material, or objective, morality that we have been concerned; from the facts given we know nothing of their formal morality; that depends entirely on the state of each doctor's conscience at the time he acted. It is not impossible that the conscience of the doctor who intended the abortion was convinced, *bona fide*, that the act was morally justified; if so, there was no formal sin. The point is that, whatever his own conscience may have told him about the morality of his act, objectively it was an evil act, an act of abortion, and that because the abortion was the end he intended to achieve.[3]

This is the consistent teaching, as we have said, of Catholic theologians. Without exception they all teach that an act of two effects, which would otherwise be lawful, is unlawful if the evil effect is intended.[4] And it is easy to see why this is so. The end, or *finis*, of a human act is an essential determinant of material morality, the other two determinants being the 'object' and the 'circumstances'. If the end willed is evil then the act is evil without further ado. We may not do good to achieve evil. Now the end willed is specified, or identified, by the intention; the intention in fact is simply a movement of the will towards the end – and is so defined by St Thomas: *intentio est actus voluntatis respectu finis.*[5] If in placing an act of two effects I intend the evil effect then that effect is the proximate end at which the act is aimed and since it is an evil end the act which aims at it is evil. *Morales actus,* says St Thomas, speaking precisely of an act of two effects, *recipiunt speciem secundum id quod intenditur.*[6]

Etienne Gilson thus sums up scholastic tradition on this point:

> Since the intention of the end is the root, the source, and, to put all in one word, the cause of the choice of means, it is clear that the moral qualification of the intention will affect, and in large measure determine, that of the whole act. If our 'eye' is evil, as the Scripture puts it, that is, if our intention is bad, then the whole series of voluntary choices which determine the means to be adopted to accomplish it will itself be bad: nothing that we can do is good if we do it for the sake of something evil.[7]

The Act of Two Effects

The confusion which is sometimes experienced on this point is due to confounding the material morality of the human act with the 'morality' of the *external act*. The external act, as here understood, is only part of the human act, its outer shell as it were; it denotes the mere physical event, the concrete act performed, prescinding entirely from all internal elements of intellect and will. It is only in a very special sense that one can predicate morality at all of the external act, understood in this sense.[8] But one may ask the question whether a particular external act is in conformity with due order or not. Some external acts are 'evil' in this sense, such as the act of lying; others are 'good', such as the act of almsgiving. Many external acts are indifferent, and it is only when they are informed by an act of the will that we can speak of them as being good or evil.

Now in discussing the question of the morality of the external act, considered exclusively in itself, the question of intention obviously does not arise; *ex hypothesi* all internal elements such as intention are excluded. This was a point stressed a great deal by the late Dr McDonald; and it is perfectly true, as he pointed out, that it is at this level of the external act, *praecesive sumpti,* that the *essential problem* of the act of two effects arises.[9] But it is one thing to say that in considering the mere external act the question of intention does not arise; it is another thing to say that the intention does not enter into the material morality of the *total human act*. The external act, considered in itself is not a human act; the human act is the external act informed by the act of the will.[10] It is defined as *actus qui procedit a voluntate cum praevia cognitione intellectus.*[11] And it is of this total human act that both material and formal morality are predicated. The human act is materially good if it is in conformity with the moral law; it is formally good if it is in conformity with the dictates of conscience.[12] And in determining whether it is materially good or not, the question of intention is of vital importance.[13] If I perform an external act, which is *per se* lawful, as a means to an evil effect, then my total human act is objectively evil –whether my conscience is aware of that fact or not. When we stress therefore, following Dr McDonald, that the essential problem of the act of two effects arises at the level of the external act, and not at the level of intention, we must not be taken as implying that intention does not effect material morality. If the agent intends the evil effect he is guilty of at least material sin. The problem arises only when the act is unimpeachable from the point of view of intention.

Is it ever lawful to perform an act which will have, in addition to a good effect, an evil effect which remains evil in the concrete circumstances of the case, but which is not intended? Therein lies the essential problem which we must now approach.

II

If we analyse the physical structure of external acts of two effects we shall see that they fell into three broad categories.

An Irish Reader in Moral Theology

a.   In certain cases the act first produces the evil effect and then this evil effect in turn produces the good effect. In other words it is *through* the evil effect that the act produces the good effect – as when I give drink to a man and thereby render him intoxicated with the result that he does not commit a robbery he would otherwise have committed.

b.   In other cases the physical structure of the act is the exact reverse of that just considered. The act first produces the good effect and this in turn gives rise to the evil effect – as when a doctor saves the life of a dictator who is persecuting religion, with the result that the persecution is continued.

c.   Finally the act may produce the two effects independently, neither coming through the other – as when the commander of a sunken submarine seals off part of the ship, with the result that some of the members of the crew are drowned while others are saved.

Now the teaching of moralists on the essential problem of the act of two effects is that for the act to be lawful the structure of the external act must not be of the first type described above; that is, *the evil effect must not be the means through which the good effect is achieved*. If the structure or the external act is of the second or third types described above then this act is *per se* lawful, and the human act of performing such an external act will itself be lawful if certain other conditions are fulfilled.

It may be useful at this stage to give a number of quotations from moral theologians to show that this is largely agreed teaching.[14] Most of them state this primary condition in traditional terminology but, as will be seen, they illustrate what they mean by these terms by stating that the condition signifies that the evil effect must not be the means through which the good effect is achieved.

CARRIERE: Licitum esse ponere actum in se indifferentem, ex quo sequuntur duo effectus, unus bonus et alter malus, *dummodo bonus non sequatur ex malo*, saltem compenset malum, et honestus sit finis agentis.

LEHMKUHL: Licet ponere actionem, ex qua duplex effectus oritur, bonus alter, alter malus, modo … 3. effectus bonus saltem aeque immediate atque effectus malus, *i.e. non mediante effectu malo*, sequatur, 4. adsit causa relative gravis …

MERKELBACH: Licitum est ponere causam quae producit simul effectum bonum et malum, si effectus bonus saltem aeque immediate ex causa sequatur ac malus *seu non mediante malo* …

GENICOT: Licet, cum fine honesto, bonam aut indifferentem causam ponere, cuius duplex sit effectus, alter bonus, alter veto malus, dummodo bonus sequatur *non mediante malo* et adsit ratio proportionate gravis.

TANQUEREY: [Requiritur] 2° Ut bonus effectus non producatur *mediante effectu malo*;

DAVIS: It is permissible to set a cause in motion, in spite of its foreseen evil effect, provided … secondly that a good effect also issue from the act, at least as immediately and directly as the evil effect, *that is to say, provided that the evil effect does not first arise and from it the good effect*;

HURTH: Principia de 'voluntario in causea' locum non habent, nisi effectus bonus et malus aeque immediate fluunt ex actions posita. *Ergo non valent, si effectus bonus tandem mediante effectu malo, sive mediate sive immediate, obtinetur.*

AERTNYS-DAMEN: Hinc recte dicunt effectum malum non imputari, si … (c) bonus effectus saltem aeque immediate sequatur ac malus; *si enim effectus bonus sequitur mediante effectu malo,* hic necessario directe et in se intenditur;

VERMEERSCH: Ut indirectus sit abortus, non sufficit ut mors innocentis non quaeratur 'propter se', sed oportet praeterea ut non quaeretur 'in se,' *tamquam medium boni effectus.*

SLATER: It is lawful to perform an action which produces two effects, one good, the other bad, provided that … (3) the good effect is produced as immediately as – *that is, not by means of* – the bad.

NOLDIN: Licet ponere actionem, ex qua sequitur bonus et malus effectus, si quatuor condiciones simul verificantur: Scil … b. Si effectus bonus non sequitur *per effectum malum*, sed aut aeque immediate aut saltem effectus malus per effectum bonum. *Secus malus effectus intenderetur tamquam medium ad effectum bonum.*[15]

This, then, is the essential principle with regard to the physical, or external, act and it is both clear and simple: the good effect must not be achieved through, that is by means of, the evil effect. It is, in fact, merely an application of the more general principle that the end does not justify the means. If my object is to achieve the good effect and if this good effect is achieved through the evil effect, then it is obvious that I will the evil effect at least as a means. I will it, not for its own sake, but in order that through it I may achieve the good effect. And, of course, one may never will evil, even as a means. *Voluntas volendo malum fit mala.*

An Irish Reader in Moral Theology

The condition thus links up with the fundamental principle that morality inheres essentially in the will and that moral evil consists in the willing of evil.[16] I may will evil in two ways, either *propter se,* that is for its own sake, or *in se sed non propter se*, that is, as a means. If the structure of the act is such that it achieves the good effect through the evil effect, then in willing the good effect I will the evil effect, *in se* though not *propter se.*[17] If the doctor saves the mother by killing the child, he really wills to kill the child though he may regret that he has to take this particular means to do so.

This fundamental basis of the principle on the external act has been well analysed in a short passage in Cajetan's commentary on the *Summa Theologiae*, 2-2, 64, 7. St Thomas had said, perhaps over-concisely,[18] that an act of two effects may be lawful if one does not intend the evil effect. Cajetan comments:

> Intellige bene distinctionem litterae ... *Nam finis et medium cadunt sub intentione*, ut patet in medico qui intendit sanitatem per potionem et diaetam. Id autem quod consequitur ex necessitate finis non cadit sub intentione, sed praeter intentionem exsistens emergit; ut patet de debilitatione aegroti quae sequitur ex medicines sanante.

St Thomas's principle, at first sight somewhat startling, is thus seen to contain, in germ, the essential condition. The act is unlawful if one intends the evil effect either for its own sake or as a means, and one necessarily intends it as a means if it is through it that the act produces the good effect.

III

The central principle in regard to the external act, therefore, is not difficult to grasp. To apply that principle in concrete cases is another matter. Where the causal structure of the act is in clear outline there is no difficulty; if the doctor saves the mother's life by producing an abortion, or by amputating the head of the unborn child, the act is clearly unlawful; if he saves a dictator's life by administering penicillin his act does not become unlawful because it has the further effect of continuing the persecution of religion – he does not save the man's life by means of the persecution. But in a minority of cases the issue is not so clear; the two effects may be so closely intertwined with the act and with each other that it may be very difficult to see which, if any, comes through the other.

To facilitate an examination of the causal structure of such complex acts – to help us to study them under the microscope, as it were – theologians suggest certain useful tests, or 'rules of thumb'. Each of these tests is, as we shall see, simply a particular way of applying the principle that the good effect must not come through the evil effect. It is important to bear in mind, therefore, that they are applications of the principle, not substitutes for it.

The Act of Two Effects

The first of these tests could be stated as follows. 'Is it possible to imagine a physically possible situation, however improbable, in which the evil effect would be prevented, but in which nevertheless the act would produce the good effect?' If it is, then the external act is *per se* lawful.

As an illustration of the use of this test we take the case of the Arctic explorer who leaves a companion in the tent and walks out into morally certain death, in the snow, because he knows there is not sufficient food in the tent to keep both of them alive until a rescue party reaches them. The good effect is the saving of his companion's life; the evil effect is his own death. Now it is possible to imagine a situation – not very likely perhaps, but still physically possible – in which the evil effect would be prevented, say if the explorer, after walking for several hours were to come across an abandoned tent with an adequate supply of food and equipment, and in which he too was subsequently picked up by the rescue party. In such a case the evil effect would not take place but the good effect would not thereby be prevented; the favourable position of the companion left in the first tent would not be lessened in any way by the discovery of the second tent. The test thus helps to throw into bolder relief that the evil effect in this case is not a means through which the good effect is achieved. The same test can be applied with advantage to most of the well-known popular moral cases, like that of the sailor who swims away from a lifeboat in mid-Atlantic because it was clear that, while he was in it, the boat was over-crowded and slowly sinking; or the case of the soldier who raises himself into a prominent position in order to draw the fire of the enemy, while his companions make a dash across an exposed piece of ground.

With regard to this first test, however, two points are worth noting. The first is that in imagining the situation in which the evil effect is prevented we must always keep within the bounds of *physical possibility*. Walsh, in writing of this test, speaks of imagining a situation in which the evil effect is prevented 'by a miracle'.[19] The expression can be justified only if by a miracle one understands a miracle in the moral order – i.e. something which, though so unlikely as to be deemed morally impossible, nevertheless does not involve any suspension of the physical laws of matter. It is preferable, we believe, to speak of a situation which, 'however unlikely, is still physically possible'. If we suppose the evil effect to be prevented by a physical miracle then many absurd conclusions would follow; abortion induced in order to terminate a difficult pregnancy, for example, would always be lawful, since it would always be possible that, as a result of a physical miracle, a three-month-old foetus might live and develop into a normal child after the abortion. The object of the test is to throw into bold relief the physical causal structure of the act, and it obviously will not do this if one supposes the laws of physical causality to be suspended or modified.

The second point to be noted is that the test is positive and not negative in its application. In other words, if the act passes the test it may be inferred that the external act is *per se* lawful; it does not at all follow that if the act fails to pass the test the external act is unlawful. Thus, as we shall see, it may be lawful for a surgeon to remove a cancerous womb containing a live non-viable foetus although it is physically impossible to remove the diseased organ without the death of the foetus necessarily resulting.[20] The fact is that both effects of an act of two effects may be physically inseparable *from the act* and yet, they may issue from it independently, neither coming through the other. In the traditional terminology of the theologians, the two effects may issue from the act *aeque immediate in ordine causalitatis.*

The second test is one proposed by Vermeersch for surgical operations or other medical treatment in which the evil effect is the death of the unborn child. 'Could the same act achieve the same good effect, if the woman were not pregnant?' If so then the evil effect is obviously not a means towards the good effect.[21]

Once again it is clear that the test is simply a way of applying the fundamental principle. If the same act achieves the same good effect when there is no foetus in the womb, then manifestly the death of the foetus is not the means through which the good effect is achieved. Thus in the case of the cancerous pregnant uterus it is clear that even if the woman were not pregnant the removal of the diseased womb would have the same therapeutic effect as before. The same holds good for the case of the woman suffering from high fever; even were she not pregnant the drug would be administered to lower her temperature and would do so; it is not the abortion which lowers the temperature, the abortion is rather a concomitant and essentially independent effect of the act.

Not all practical cases are amenable to the application of these tests and in the last resort we must always fall back on the fundamental issue – does the good effect come through the evil effect? In many cases it is not easy to see whether it does or not but, as we hope to have now made clear, the difficulties are of fact rather than of principle.

IV

To complete this summary one further point must be considered. Even when the evil effect is not a means to the good effect, right reason will still demand that the act be not placed without sufficient reason. It would clearly be contrary to right reason to hold, for example, that one may place an act which will cause an abortion merely in order to save the mother from the inconvenience of a few weeks' illness – or that a soldier may expose himself to morally certain death merely to save his companions the discomfort of waiting in hiding until nightfall. Right reason, in other words, demands that in *all* cases in which an act causes an evil effect there must be a proportionate cause for placing the act; the good effect must outweigh the evil. Moral theologians discuss at length the factors which reason will take into consideration in forming this judgement: the gravity of the evil effect, its proximity to the act, whether it is certain or not to follow, and so on. The principle itself, that there must be a due proportion between good and evil, is clear and inescapable.

To sum up: the principle with regard to the *external act* is that the evil effect must not be the means through which the good effect is achieved and the good effect in turn must outweigh the evil. But if we wish to frame a principle which will cover all cases of *human acts* that have two effects, including those categories which we excluded from the main scope of this article, we shall find ourselves with the list of four conditions traditional in Catholic theology on this issue. It is lawful to perform an act which has two effects, one good and the other bad, provided:

a.   that the act is not unlawful in itself, antecedently to the two effects;
b.   that the evil effect is not intended;
c.   that the good effect does not come through the evil effect;
d.   that there is a proportionate cause for permitting the evil effect.

NOTES

1   If it be asked how one is to determine whether a particular effect is conditionally or absolutely forbidden, one must reply, with McDonald (*The Principles of Moral Science*, Dublin, 1903, p. 163), that there is 'no general rule that may be applied'. It is simply a question of right reason forming a judgement in regard to each particular type of effect. In point of fact those prohibitions of the moral law which are conditional have long been recognised as such and are stated by moralists in reasonably precise terms: one may not damage another's property, *domino rationabiliter invito*; one may not amputate a limb, *nisi necessaria sit ad salvandam sanitatem totius corporis*, etc. it is not in regard to the application of these conditional prohibitions that the well-known difficulties of the 'act of two effects' arise.

2   Walsh (*De Actibus Humanis*, 2nd ed., Dublin, 1891, p. 58ff) departed somewhat from traditional terminology in putting the foregoing point. He would regard both the damage to the window and the loss of the poisoned limb as being evil effects even in the circumstances described, but would say that we may will these evil effects as means towards a higher end such as the saving of a human life. In this he is followed by McDonald.

This terminology has not found general acceptance among moral theologians. To say that in certain circumstances one may positively will evil would require far-reaching qualifications in most of the accepted statements of the first principles of morality: such as that the end does not justify the means, *voluntas volendo malum fit mala* etc. Moreover it is difficult to see how an effect which right reason allows me to will positively, even as a means, can be said to be evil in any real sense. The first principle of morality is: *malum est vitandum,* and if right reason also says of a particular effect: *hic effectus in his circumstantiis non est vitandus* it follows that *hic effectus in his circumstantiis non est malus.* Cf. criticism of Walsh's terminology in Tanquerey, *Theologia Nirakusm* ed, 10, Paris, 127, II, p. 152, note 3.

3   The terms 'material' and 'formal' morality are here used in their ordinary accepted sense i.e. formal morality is the morality of the act as determined by the agent's conscience at the moment of acting. Cf. Vermeersch, *Theologia Moralis*, Rome, 1922, I. n.109: *Moralitas obiectiva seu materialis ea est quae obiectum lato sensu sumptum* (i.e. *complectens finem, obiectum stricte sumptum, et circumstantias; ibid., n.113) afficit in se, non considerata persuasione agentis; subiectiva vero ea est quae ex persuasione agentis oritur. Sic abortus voluntarius est moralitatis obiectivae malae, subiectivae tamen bonae in pluribus qui bona fide illum ut honestum vel adeo*

praeceptum in certis adiunctis aestimabunt. Cf. also Hurth, *De Principiis, De Virtutibus, et Praeceptis*, Rome, 1948, n.426, and Coventry, *Morals and Independence*, London, 1949; 'We … distinguish the subjectively good action (done according to what the agent thinks is right) from the objectively good action (which is in fact right).'

4   *nam actio in se honesta fit mala, si agens in ea perficienda pravum finem intendat*: Noldin-Schmitt, *Summa Theologiae Moralis*, ed. 27, Innsbruck, 1940, n.83. Similarily, Gury, Hurth, Lanza, Genicot, Vermeersch, Aertnys-Damen, Davis, Tanquerey, Carriere, Prümmer, etc. etc.

5   *S. Theol.*, 2–2, 12, I, *ad* 4.

6   *S. Theol.*, 1–2 64, 7.

7   Etienne Gilson, *The Spirit of Medieval Philosophy*, ed. 2, London, 1950, p. 348.

8   Billuart, *Cursus Theologiae*, Tome I, *De Actibus Humanis*, 10, 8, *ad* 5; De Lege, 2, 3, *ad* 3.

9   'We want to test whether a certain external action, regarded in itself, is morally good or bad.' (Italics ours.) *The Principles of Moral Science*, Dublin, 1903, p. 149.

10   *Actus internus et externus unum numero actum moraliter bonum vel malum in sua specie completum et consummatum constituunt*: Noldin-Schmitt, op. cit., no.78, *Summa Theologiae Moralis*, ed. 27, Innsbruck, 1940, n. 78.

11   Cf. St Thomas, *S. Theol.* 1–2, 1, 1.

12   Lottin, *Principes de Morale*, Louvain, 1947, '*La conscience, norme de moral – ite formelle*', p. 147ff; Merkelbach, *Summa Theologiae Moralis*, ed. 3, Paris, 1938, I, n. 117; Prümmer, *Manuale Theologiae Moralis*, ed. 7, Fribourg, 1931, I, no. 108; Vermeersch, *Theologia Moralis*, Rome, 1922, I, no. 109. Walsh, *De Actibus Humanis*, ed. 2, Dublin, 1891, n.390.

13   St Thomas, *S. Theol.*, 1–2, 18, 4.

14   Kiselteins' view (*Ephem. Theol. Lovanienses*, III, 1926, pp. 493ff), which appears to take as the essential test the certainty or otherwise with which the evil effect will follow, is rightly criticised by Vermeersch (*Periodica*, VI, 1932, 107ff), and is not found in the classic authors. Lottin, *Principes de Morale*, Louvain, 1947, II, successfully analyses the distinction between a *causa per se* and a *causa per accidens*, with which Kiseltein had been largely concerned, so as to equate it with the almost universally accepted notions of direct and indirect causality.

15   Carriere, *De Iustitia et Iure*, Paris, 1839, p. 243; Lehmkuhl, *Theologia Moralis*, ed. 8, Fribourg, 1896, I, p. 20; Merkelbach, *Summa Theologiae Moralis*, ed. 3, Paris, 1938, I, p. 165; Genicot-Salsmans, *Institutiones Theologiae Moralis*, ed. 18, Brussels, 1946, I, p. 17; Tanquerey, *Synopsis Theologiae Moralis*, ed. 10, Paris, 1936, II, 152; Davis, *Moral and Pastoral Theology*, ed. 5, London, 1946, I, 14; Hurth, *Notae ad praelectiones Theologiae Moralis*, Rome, 1949, I, p. 171; Aertnys-Damen, *Theologia Moralis*, ed. 15, Turin, 1947, I, p. 64; Vermeersch, *Periodica*, VO (1932), p. 115; Slater, *Manual of Moral Theology*, ed. 6, London, 1928, p. 7; Noldin-Schmitt, op. cit., 1940, I, p. 90.

16   *Ex hoc actus moralis dicitur, quia voluntarius est*: St Thomas, *Summa Contra Gentiles*, 3, 10, 4.

17   Cf. Vermeersch, '*De causalitate per se et per accidens, seu directa et indirecta*', in *Periodica*, VI (1932), p. 116.

18   *Il n'en reste pas moins vrai que le texte du saint Docteur prete e équivoque et demande quelques précisions*, Lottin, *Principes de Morale*, Louvain, 1947, p. 157.

19   Walsh, *De Actibus Humanis*, 2nd edition, Dublin, 1891, n.173.

20   The lawfulness of this operation, which is generally accepted (cf. Prümmer, *Manuale Theologiae Moralis*, 7th ed., Fribourg, 1931, II, n.140; Genicot, *Institiones Theologiae Moralis*, 18th ed., Brussels, 1946, I, n.377), has been challenged by Gemelli, but on the grounds that as a matter of medical fact, in order to remove the womb one must first cut veins and arteries and thereby kill the foetus. The death of the foetus would thus not be the result of the removal of the womb but rather a necessary means to make this removal possible. 'Before removing the uterus the surgeon must first ligature the veins and arteries which link it with the internal maternal organism; once this is done the foetus is already killed because its only lifeline has been severed; the removal of the foetus therefore chronologically follows the death of the foetus' (*Nouvelle Revue Theologique*, IX, 1933, 523). Vermeersch replies, rightly, that this argumentation confuses the order of time with the order of causality. It is true that usually, though not always, the foetus will be dead before the uterus has been removed but it does

not follow that the one effect has been the means *through* which the other was achieved; the same sealing of veins and arteries would be necessary even if there were no foetus. This particular discussion, of course, is concerned with fact rather than with principle.

21   *Periodica*, VI (1932), p. 116.

Part Five
Sin

27 What Happened to Sin?

Seán Fagan

(Seán Fagan, *Has Sin Changed?*, Dublin: Gill & Macmillan, 1978, pp. 1–12.)*

Sin is not a fashionable word nor a popular subject in today's world. For non-religious people it is simply irrelevant, a carry-over from a bygone age, now devoid of meaning. Even in religious circles it has not the common currency it once had. Among Christians its meaning has become confused to such an extent that preachers and teachers tend to soft-pedal it. In the flood of religious writing that followed the Second Vatican Council, it received only minor attention. Just a few years ago, its near-disappearance provoked Dr Karl Menninger to write a book with a question for its title: *Whatever Became of Sin?* As one of the most eminent psychoanalysts of our time, he acknowledged the wide variety of factors that can lessen human freedom, and in describing the mess that people make of their lives and the evil they can cause the world, he made full allowance for the influence of heredity, environment, instinctual drives and subconscious motivation. But he insisted that there is still such a thing as moral responsibility. To emphasise this conviction he pleaded for a revival of the word 'sin' and suggested that the world would be a healthier place if we showed more concern for repentance and conversion. As a psychiatrist he explained that it does little good to repent a symptom, but it may do great harm not to repent a sin. He called on clergymen to exercise their spiritual leadership, to preach, to prophesy, to cry out. How? Preach! Tell it like it is! Say it from the pulpit, cry it from the housetops! Sin! Sin! In calling for a revival of the moribund word 'sin', Menninger asked the clergy to reassert their oral leadership, to study sin, identify it, define it, warn people about it, and promote measures to combat and rectify it.

This is indeed the mission of priest, prophet and spiritual leader. There are plenty of biblical precedents for it. The Old Testament prophets continually denounced the misdeeds of the Jewish people as sins. John the Baptist urged his hearers to be converted from their sins. Jesus himself preached repentance, conversion, and told his followers that his body would be broken and his blood poured out for the forgiveness of sins. Sin is a fundamental concept in Christian faith. In fact, we cannot really be Christians unless we are conscious of our sinfulness and recognise our need of Jesus Christ.

Is sin changing?

But sin has had a bad press in recent times. It is no exaggeration to say that there has been a wide-spread loss of the sense of sin, not only in the world at large, but even within the Christian churches. A variety of reasons can be suggested for this. Among church-going people, it may be a reaction against overemphasis on sin in the past, both in its hell-fire punishment aspect and in the detailed labelling that attached a degree of sinfulness to even the simplest of human activities. Benjamin Rush, the first American psychiatrist, dashed off an open letter to clergymen of all faiths on the subject of American morality in 1788, in which he condemned as sins 'smoking, drinking, the popular election of judges, the country fair (a temptation to extravagance, gaming, drunkenness and uncleanness), horse racing, cock fighting, dining at men's clubs, and enjoying oneself on the Sabbath by swimming, sliding, and skating'. It is easy to smile at such a list and murmur condescendingly about the Puritan ethic. But Catholics have no grounds for complacency. Until a short time ago it was considered a venial sin for a priest to celebrate Mass without a biretta; it could be mortal if it were done out of contempt. Many people still think that to miss one Sunday Mass deliberately without sufficient reason means hell for all eternity. Though their number is diminishing, there are still people who feel that they need confession before communion if they have a fleeting sexual thought during a television programme. Today's common sense rejects such attitudes, but the rejection is often accompanied by an impatience with any talk of sin, and so the real meaning of sin is weakened or lost.

The worldwide decline in respect for authority is another factor. Sin has traditionally been preached as disobedience to God's law as expressed in the Bible, Church teaching and the commands of lawful authorities. But people are nowadays more alert to the abuses and exaggerations of authority, and find it difficult to see any convincing link between obedience to rules and fidelity to God. This too may be a healthy enough reaction, rejecting the notion of God as primarily legislator and taskmaster, but it can blunt our sensitivity to God's call and blind us to the possibility of sinful refusals.

A new, but not always correct, understanding of conscience may also lessen the sense of sin. Reacting against the blind obedience sometimes preached in the past, many people now confuse personal conscience with doing as they please, without any reference to guidance from authority. 'What is right' very easily becomes 'what I like', and since there is no strong urge in human nature to do what one dislikes, the lines between right and wrong become blurred, moral conflict disappears, and with it the whole notion of sin.

A more general reason for the weakening of the notion of sin is the lessening of the sense of God in today's world. Western society is becoming more and more secularised, with little direct reference to God, so the faults of men are seldom understood as religious realities, as sins. Affluence is a factor here, insofar as riches often bring a sense of independence and self-sufficiency, with little room for God. Jesus himself warned us about this: 'How hard it will be for rich people to enter the kingdom of heaven' (Mt 10:23).

FREEDOM AND RESPONSIBILITY

In the area of freedom and responsibility, the discoveries of psychology about subconscious motivation and the influence of heredity and environment tend to lessen people's sense of guilt and consequently their admission of sin. It is frequently believed that because a motive for an action can be identified, that the action was not fully free, and so the evils in the world can be attributed to outside forces and circumstances beyond our control. It is too easily forgotten that no human action can be without a motive, that our motives are freely chosen, notwithstanding outside influences, and they are often sinfully selfish without regard for our true good or for the needs of others.

Paradoxically, a somewhat similar form of escapism may be our greater sensitivity nowadays to collective responsibility for sinful situations and structures, for social evils like discrimination, racism, economic exploitation on national and international levels. We can become so righteously indignant about these social injustices not of our making that we forget the personal sins in our own lives. The enormity of some of these unjust structures and our helplessness in the face of them make our personal misdeeds seem trivial by comparison.

Psychologists have discovered a great deal in recent decades about neurotic guilt and the influence of what Freud called the 'super ego'. The general acceptance of these findings by the public at large has tended to weaken the sense of sin, since sin is usually associated with guilt. But writers of popular psychology often fail to distinguish between the irrational guilt feelings produced by infantile conscience and the real guilt acknowledged by a morally mature person who has acted against his conscience. Psychiatrists and counsellors sometimes undermine a person's morale and sense of personhood by telling him that he was not responsible for his actions, instead of helping him to accept his responsibility and real moral guilt. There is a sure-fire remedy for the pain of real guilt: acknowledgment, repentance, atonement. To treat it as neurotic in those cases in which it is clearly not such, is to ask for trouble. A rehabilitation of the word 'sin' and a greater understanding of how to cope with it through repentance and forgiveness would be more helpful to many people than the guesswork and groping of some psychiatrists.

An over-optimistic view of evolution and human progress can also blunt the concept of sin. It is possible to contrast today's moral sensitivity to human fights with the barbarism and cruelty of former times, but it would be a mistake to conclude that mankind is therefore less sinful. Our greater awareness of certain moral values and our deeper insight into the dignity of man do not mean that we are morally better than our grandparents. The developments of technology that

What Happened to Sin?

have made life more comfortable and offer us possibilities for a new humanism have also opened new roads to unprecedented forms of inhumanity. The old are often lonelier today than in most times in the past, people are less capable of coping with the problem of death in today's society, and the living conditions in modern cities have not produced greater friendliness or neighbourliness. We can feel self-righteous in condemning apartheid abroad, but what happens to our convictions when we are in a position to do something about racial discrimination in our own neighbourhood or in our business? The torture and oppression practiced by so many governments throughout the world should be a warning against a too easy optimism. Sin is still a reality in our world, and the world might be a healthier place if it were more sincerely and realistically admitted.

The 'sin-grid'

Catholics have been affected by many of these factors, but there were elements in our own religious tradition to weaken or distort the notion of sin. Our experience of the sacrament of penance was not always helpful, and it left many with a very inadequate notion of sin. They were frequently provided with what has been called the 'sin-grid', a precise set of categories of sin for use in the examination of conscience in preparation for confession. Anything which did not easily fit into this grid might be considered wrong, but was not always seen as sinful. Sins were clearly divided into original and actual, mortal and venial, formal and material. Actual sin was any thought, word, or deed contrary to the law of God. It was serious when the matter was grave and the sin was committed with full knowledge and full consent. If the matter was not grave in itself, or if the sinner was ignorant of its gravity, or did not fully consent to it, the sin was less serious, i.e. venial. Serious sin was mortal, involving the loss of sanctifying grace, which is the divine life in the soul. A sinner dying in this state would go to hell for all eternity. The infinite punishment for a finite act was thought necessary since an offence is measured by the dignity of the person offended. Since God is infinite, the offence was infinite, and so the punishment would be infinite or eternal. This picture was clear and simple; all one needed to know was what constituted grave matter (hence the sin-grid), and the main burden of conscience was to decide on the degree of knowledge, or consent.

Large numbers of Catholics lived happy and holy lives with this simple understanding, and there may be some for whom it is still meaningful, or at least not too harmful. But growing numbers are dissatisfied with such an over-simplified picture. It does not speak to their condition, and it raises too many questions for which they have not been given convincing answers. There is a reaction against a legalistic, formalistic, juridic notion of sin as a thing, a breaking of an external law, a disruption of order and stability. There is a greater awareness of man's personal responsibility, a realisation that the established order itself, whether in Church or state, may be an obstacle to full human development, and so not in accordance with God's will. The dissatisfaction with the older presentation is not always clearly defined or understood, but there is real need for a new understanding of sin. Such a new understanding has indeed developed over the past few years. There is no question of a 'new theology' to do away with sin or encourage the so-called 'permissiveness' of modern society. There is continuity between the old and the new, though a considerable shift of emphasis has taken place, and in many ways the whole question is seen in a new light. Sin is as much a reality as ever, and is taken quite seriously by the new theology. In a sense, the new understanding makes far more demands than the old.

It could be objected that what is needed for the renewal of the Church is a positive theology of love rather than a negative theology of sin. This is certainly true, but there is room for a book which will meet people where they are, which will take what understanding they already have, and help them to see where it needs to be corrected and developed. A book on sin need not be a negative treatment. The good news of the gospel is that God loves us with an everlasting love, and that this love became incarnate in Jesus through whom we have the forgiveness of sins. We cannot repent and be converted unless we take sin seriously. But a defective notion of sin can produce distorted ideas of God, the Church, conscience, law, sacraments (particularly penance), and Christian morality itself. It may be helpful, therefore, to take a critical look at those aspects of the common understanding of sin which need correcting and development. A new presentation will not be helpful to people who are still under the influence of inadequate notions from the past. To identify and admit that influence can in itself be a liberating experience.

PROBLEMS FROM THE PAST

The old 'sin-grid' focused attention on measurement, both of the matter of the sin and of the degree of responsibility and guilt. This needs re-examination today. Are the old categories sufficient? They emphasised law, which was always clearly defined, and therefore easily measured. But with the multiplication of Church laws, people felt that where there was no clearcut law, there was no moral obligation. Besides, many came to believe that things were wrong because they were forbidden instead of seeing that they were forbidden because they were wrong. This is hardly moral maturity. Among the commandments, the two relating to sex were singled out for such disproportionately special treatment that many people today automatically think of sex when the word 'sin' is mentioned. If sin is feared, it is often because of the punishment attached to it, but the traditional notions of purgatory and hell are unconvincing to many modern Catholics, so their sense of sin is affected. Not only can parents no longer instil the fear of God into their children by invoking the threat of hell-fire, but they are at a loss when it comes to explaining and handing on the moral principles they themselves were brought up on. They feel particularly helpless in trying to form the consciences of their children, because they themselves were seldom encouraged to explore the full meaning of conscience or to use it in a really personal way. The teaching Church, as a loving mother concerned for the safety of her children, at times developed an overprotective attitude amounting to a nervous distrust of the presence of the Holy Spirit in the faithful. A narrow view of the 'teaching Church' restricted it to the government in the Church, and it was forgotten that the whole Church is both a teaching Church and a learning Church. Because of an individualistic notion of sin, the sacrament of penance became, for many people, a private guilt-shedding process with little reference to the Church itself as a community of reconciliation. Preoccupation with law and measurement, coupled with this individualistic notion of sin, left Catholics less conscious of collective responsibility and the general sinfulness of the community itself. Likewise, individual sinful actions were often assessed in isolation from the overall pattern of life. Bits of behaviour were often given moral labels in terms of their physical component, without reference to the full human meaning of the action.

CHANGE IN THE CHURCH

While these various factors have left many Catholics with an inadequate or even distorted notion of sin, it is also true that the confusion they experience is part of the general upheaval in the Church since the Second Vatican Council. Changes were not limited to dogmatic theology, liturgy or ecclesiastical organisation, but affected some of the basic principles of Christian morality. The interpretation of the Bible, the extent of the Church's teaching authority, and modern insights about the nature of man, all gave rise to new questions in the area of morals. The old black and white answers were no longer convincing, the lines became blurred, and soon people were confused as to what could be labelled sin, or indeed what sin really meant.

Since a defective notion of sin can result in distortions in so many other areas of Christian belief, the following chapters will treat of sin in relation to law, measurement, sex, guilt, punishment, conscience, forgiveness, teaching and preaching, and conclude with a summary of what Christian morality is all about. It could be objected that this is an inversion of the logical procedure, that one should begin with the positive call of God, the fullness of Christian life, and see sin as failure and refusal. It is true that it is more attractive, consoling and challenging to be presented with the ideal before discussing the failure. But it can also be helpful to begin where people are, and many people already have a notion of sin which can be an obstacle to their understanding of the ideal. For example, to judge by the almost neurotic repetition of sins from their past life confessed in their weekly or monthly confession, one wonders if some people really believe in God's forgiveness. Even at the risk of seeming to paint a caricature, it may be a service to such people to bring out into the open and face explicitly whatever it is that distorts their notion of sin. It is not a question of the private aberrations of a few immature or neurotic people. All the factors in question are elements in the experience of the Church itself down through the centuries. In describing and analysing them, there is no intention to criticise simply for the sake of criticism or to make fun of previous generations of Christians. It must be recognised that any new understanding of the Christian message must grow out of, and be in continuity with, the past. But it is a false loyalty to the Church to pretend that it was always perfect, that it could never be short-sighted or one-sided in its understanding and practice. There is no need for us to disown our past; without it we cannot fully understand the present. However, there is no question of merely highlighting the negative elements. We need to rediscover the valid insights from the Church's long experience and develop them in the light of today's needs.

REHABILITATE SIN

What is needed is a rehabilitation of the word 'sin', not for its own sake, but in a way that will re-focus and revitalise our understanding of Christian morality, help us to accept responsibility for our wrongdoing, and enable us to appreciate the incredible, liberating and re-creating gift we have been given in God's forgiveness. To speak of sin and to reflect on our own sinfulness is not necessarily an exercise in introversion, a pessimistic navel-gazing. On the contrary, it can be a very healthy and profoundly Christian experience. We cannot be Christian unless we feel a real need for Christ, and it is our sinfulness that brings this home to us. The English mystic, Julian of Norwich, was not ashamed to write: 'We need to fall, and we need to realise this. If we never fell, we should never know how weak and wretched we are in ourselves; nor should we ever appreciate the astonishing love of our Maker ... We sin grievously, yet despite all this it makes no difference at all to his love, and we are no less precious in his sight. By the simple fact that we fall, we shall gain a deep knowledge of what God's love means ... It is a good thing to know this.' Indeed, it is a very good thing. It makes all the difference between simply knowing about God and actually knowing God. St Paul assures us that 'all things work towards good for those who love God'. Commenting on this, St Augustine added: 'Yes even sin', and he knew what he was talking about.

* This book has been completely rewritten as *What Happened to Sin?*, published by Columba Press in 2008.

28   Sin

Hugh Connolly

(John Bowden (ed.), *Christianity: The Complete Guide,* London: Continuum, 2005, pp. 1114–20.)

While the word sin may seem very familiar to us in the twenty-first century, over the years its meaning and ethical content have become somewhat elastic. Sin is synonymous with life's little luxuries: gourmet food, designer clothes, refined perfumes, deluxe automobiles and so on. Of course, the older religious meaning endures, but often this becomes a caricature in the popular mind in the form of the 'sins of the flesh' and such like. So if we want a more focused account of what sin means today, like a restorer we must peel away the layers of varnish and overlay that distort the original picture. This task has been greatly aided by the enormous flowering in biblical scholarship and enquiry over the last century.

THE BIBLICAL BACKGROUND

If we turn to the Bible and look at it in its own terms, the picture that emerges is an integral one, giving a multi-dimensional picture of humankind. Right from the opening pages of the book of Genesis, the story of human weakness begins to unfold. Chapter 3 tells the story of a man and a woman, Adam and Eve, who are the original sinners, but if we read on we soon find a couple, a family, a dynasty, a city, an entire nation, indeed all of humanity described as in some sense sinful.

The effect is to chart the irreversible domino effect of sin after the first act of disobedience and transgression. As Genesis sees it, that initial rebellion brings a disorder into the relationship between God and creation because creatures try to become like their creator. The nub of the issue is that human beings reject the truth about themselves, they overstep their status as creatures and sin puts a separation between them and God. The ultimate effect of sin is alienation and isolation.

Yet in the earliest scriptural accounts it is not just the relationship with God that has been disordered; life itself takes on a very different complexion. Chaos enters the web of human relationships and even the relationship with the natural world is upset. Sin no longer simply concerns the lives of the first parents (Adam and Eve); it begins to cast its shadow over the entire human race and all creation. The emphasis here is on the universal; the consequences of sin have rebounded not just on Israel and the Hebrews but on all of humankind. All humanity is represented in the symbolic name 'Adam'. Recrimination and rationalisations abound, but despite the best efforts, the consequences of sin cannot be undone (Gen 3:14-24). Adam is henceforth to be a tiller of the soil; he and his descendants will have to engage in a silent combat between man and soil in order to win their livelihood. Eve, in turn, is destined to suffer in giving birth and the story of Cain and of the subsequent generations down to the tower of Babel in the chapters of Genesis that follow is a litany of jealousy and envy, giving rise on occasion to violence, bloodlust and even death.

These mythical narratives attempt to account for the replication and reproduction of sins from one generation to the next. The estrangement of Adam and Eve is mirrored in Genesis 4 in the life story of Cain, who becomes the archetypal fugitive. Here, in this narrative of origins, we can already discern some key elements of the underlying understanding of sin. A first element is the damage which sin does to the relationship between God and God's people, a relationship that set Israel apart from the other nations. Here, human pride and rebelliousness are not simply the hubris of Greek tragedy, which brings about the downfall of the flawed hero through the blind forces of fate. They are an expression of rebellion against God: the Lord who has loved his creatures into being. Sin is a wilful breaking off of the loving dialogue through which God converses with God's creation and calls it to fullness of life. This dialogue will later take the form of a covenant – the pledge of intimate love, which God calls upon God's people to reciprocate.

For the Hebrew prophets in turn, the essence of sin is the deliberate rupture of personal relations between humankind and God. God 'knows' God's people with an irrevocable love (Amos 3:2; Hos 13:5); Israel must therefore 'know' God (Hos 13:4). The expression 'to know' here has a profound conjugal sense of mutual gift and intimacy. Sin is the rejection of this intimacy with God, the refusal of the dialogue, the rebuff of the call. It is the injury done to the heart of God and a damaging of the conjugal bond. This understanding of sin is also the backdrop to the prophets' frequent use of the figurative vocabulary of adultery and prostitution (Hos 3; Jer 3:1-5, 19-25 and 4:1-4 as well as Ez 3). Sin therefore brings about a rupture and a separation between creature and creator (Isa 59:2). But God never leaves the sinner without hope. Consciousness of sin is the first step to conversion. To the Hebrew mind, this awareness can only be born out of a sincere acknowledgement of the truth, a frank confession of one's recognition of the unlovely spectre of sin before the blinding holiness of God. In the words of the psalmist, 'My sin is always before me' (Ps 31:5).

So in the Old Testament we find a searingly realistic view of humankind and of its fallibility. We find here a truthful anthropology, a view of human beings that is credible. There is no pretence that human beings are anything other than creatures prone to all the foibles and frailties of the human condition. Nevertheless, they are loved by a God who will never abandon them, no matter how great their sins may be. New Testament thought and its understanding of sin is also dominated by the horizon of covenant. This covenant continues to be understood in terms of God's loving intimacy, but now it finds its most vivid expression in the gift of God's only-begotten Son.

As depicted in the gospels, the earthly ministry of Jesus too is consistent with the Father's loving care. The gospels are replete with examples of his tenderness and compassion towards all who encounter him, especially those who are publicly identified as sinners. On numerous occasions this attitude is a source of scandal to the civic and religious leaders of the day, notably many scribes and Pharisees, who (not unreasonably perhaps) considered it entirely inappropriate that a rabbi should have such familiarity with tax-collectors, women and foreigners without first insisting that they repent. Nevertheless, the world in which Jesus lived tended to make a marked separation between respectability and sinfulness, so that some states of life were seen as sinful in themselves. It is this judgemental, human tendency, which is of course by no means limited to first-century Palestine, which Jesus seeks to challenge and to change.

Thus Jesus is pictured as having overstepped the rigid conventions of his society and disregarded many of the traditional taboos. In so doing he also demonstrated his wish to move beyond the prevailing cultic notion of sin. External impurities that could be washed clean, omissions in the ritual prayers and sacrifices, eating proscribed foods, all of these understandings of sin, though having a valid cultic basis, were not in themselves capable of encapsulating the moral meaning of sin. Even though the prophets had already struggled against deficient conceptions of sin, Jewish morality at the time of Jesus (in common perhaps with much of human morality before and since) still tended to measure guilt by the external material act rather than the internal disposition towards good or evil. By contrast, Jesus taught that sin, like goodness, is a quality of the inner self, for it is from within the human heart that all good and evil thoughts and deeds come (Lk 6:45; Mk 7:2lf). Jesus therefore demands interior disposition as the decisive factor in moral action. And so, for example, by way of a lustful look at another, the sinner is deemed to have already committed adultery 'in the heart' (Mt 5:27). In this way Jesus radically redefines sin, not by evoking what went before but by drawing out the full implications of a morality centred on the 'heart'.

Since sin is a failure in a relationship of love, it necessarily involves the 'heart'. For Jesus, as for the prophets before him, the response to God is rooted in the heart and to sin is really to 'harden one's heart' to God's love. This is a metaphorical vocabulary that emphasises the inward thrust of the New Testament message. For Jesus, this table fellowship with sinners is central to ministry. 'I came not to call the righteous but sinners' (Mk 2:17). The righteous here are those who, like the elder son in the parable of 'the prodigal son' (Lk 15:11-32), are too concerned with their own status and standing to appreciate their sinfulness and need of salvation. Self-absorption and excessive self-preoccupation are the sinful pitfalls for the 'righteous'. These are diametrically opposed to the call to discipleship, which is a call to love one's neighbour and to take up the cause of the 'poor, the widow and the orphan'.

Jesus' parable of the Pharisee and the tax collector (Lk 18:9-14) demonstrates the point lucidly. A Pharisee enumerates all the religious actions he has performed; the tax collector can only beat his breast and ask for mercy. The proud and self-satisfied 'holy man' is so infatuated with his own exemplary but purely external generosity that he loses the measure of true justice. The humble tax collector by contrast knows his sins and in that acutely painful self-knowledge is profoundly aware of his need.

God is therefore like the loving and compassionate father who seeks an errant child, the good shepherd who searches for a lost sheep and the woman who combs the house for a lost coin. There are to be no limits to love.

For the authors of the first three gospels, all human failure and personal sin are to be seen in the light of the Great Commandment, to love God with all one's strength and to love one's neighbour as oneself. Sin can therefore be understood as a betrayal or neglect of love. For the evangelists, this manifests itself in negative stances and attitudes towards others and is seen especially in the insensitivity, selfishness, vengefulness and coldness of the Pharisees.

Here, though, we must be on our guard. When the evangelists paint their negative picture of the Pharisees, they are influenced by the rift between the Jews and the followers of Jesus that was taking place in their time. Modern New Testament scholarship has taught us to distinguish between the reality of the Pharisees in Jesus' day, who often represented the best in contemporary Jewish religious practice and ethical seriousness, and the presentation of the Pharisees in the New Testament, where they unfairly come to represent an approach to religious practice that can be found in almost any religion.

Given that all sin is an offence against God's love and providence, which seeks humanity's own good, refusal to acknowledge the power of God working in Christ is seen as the unpardonable sin. This is the sin against the Holy Spirit, because it is a closing of oneself to the very source of love and of life (Mt 12:30-2). It is also a refusal to grow, to interact, to live in communion and to give of oneself. It is undeniably a refusal of God, but also a refusal of the truth about oneself. As such it is the most radical form of revolt open to humankind. It represents the deliberate abandonment of good and the choice of evil under the influence of what Matthew and Paul were to call *anomia*, that iniquity which can make its way into the heart and gnaw away there like a disease.

Viewed thus, sin eventually cuts the individual off from God as a branch is cut from the vine. The sinner's heart is hardened so that he or she refuses to be receptive to God's love. Sin becomes a refusal of the Father's love, a refusal rooted in the free, self-determining choice of the sinner. In the end the starkness of this choice is as striking as the difference between light and darkness, and this imagery is taken up by the gospel of John to describe sin's mysterious and pervasive presence in the world.

ORIGINAL SIN

If Adam and Eve were not historical figures, clearly original sin cannot simply be about eating a piece of fruit offered by a serpent. Nevertheless, Christian tradition has always insisted that the sinful inheritance of Eden affects the very being of men and women and is not just symbolic in a narrow way. It is through the new Adam, Christ, that the human heart is re-orientated towards the infinite love of God.

Augustine, despite his certainty about the power of baptism, recognised the reality of sinful inclinations. Baptism in a sense was a down payment on a new life which would be experienced fully only in the hereafter. Many centuries later Martin Luther was to pick up on this point. Unlike Augustine, he came to identify concupiscence and original sin as one and the same thing. For him, original sin was no longer simply a question of a sinful disposition but of a 'profound and total upset in the human economy, whereby ... man is constituted in a permanent state of sin'. The Council of Trent disagreed. It was not simply a question of original sin not being imputed; rather, in baptism the sinner was buried with Christ, and so the 'old man' was thrown off and the 'new man' emerged. The merits and demerits of the respective position of Luther and Trent were to be the subject of much lengthy and detailed historical analysis. That episode in the gradually unfolding theology of sin is richly expressive of a conundrum that is at the very heart of the human condition. Human beings are at once free and yet somehow slaves to themselves. They are convinced of a call to the greatness of God and to partnership with God, yet everywhere they are confronted by the signs of their own fragility and finitude. The nature of original sin therefore resonates with the fundamental realisation that as well as individual transgressions and acts of rebelliousness, sins also have a kind of transpersonal and even cosmic dimension. As well as being evidenced in categorical acts, sin at another level also represents the very ground from which these acts spring.

CONTEMPORARY ACCOUNTS OF SIN

What is our understanding of sin today? Gradually, a more biblically based account of sin has begun to replace the legalistic and narrow understandings of sin that dominated much of western Christian thought for the better part of four centuries. Chief among these was an unhealthy preoccupation with sin and an excessive casuistry aimed at avoiding punishment. Sin had come to be seen as infringement of the law. Further, there was often confusion between positive (man-made) law and moral law, as well as a tendency to neglect the Bible and to emphasise individual rectitude over social awareness.

Some of the reasons for this are obvious. From the time the Church began to regularise the formation of clergy and train them for the confessional, it had become imperative that pastors should also be equipped to deal with the practicalities of sin as manifest in the concrete lives of penitents. This probably tilted the balance, especially in the Roman Catholic tradition, away from a dynamic approach and towards the more static understanding of sin expressed in the manuals of moral theology as failure before the law.

With the development of psychology and the human sciences in the twentieth century, the need was increasingly felt for a theology of sin which could combine the dynamic account by the Church fathers with precise applied pastoral, ethical and human wisdom. The stage was set for a thoroughgoing renewal of the theology and language of sin. Gradually, the Great Commandment with its inescapable link between love of God and love of neighbour became central to moral theology. Rediscovery of Jesus' interpretation of neighbourly love in an absolute and universal sense brought with it inevitable criticism of a theology of sin which was legalistic and minimalist. Renewal of moral theology in favour of a positive accentuation of discipleship and the imitation of Christ also re-awakened interest in the virtues, vices and 'tendencies of the heart' which underpin human action. Understanding the roots of sinful behaviour was now more important than precise enumeration of misdeeds. This approach also re-focused scrutiny on sins of omission as well as commission. Sin was no longer merely the contravention of law and the transgression of boundaries. The sins of not doing enough, of not caring enough, of not serving enough and ultimately of not loving enough re-emerged.

Influenced by a strong renewal of interest in personal relations, contemporary theologians have described how the call to life and the call to love are fundamentally a call to relationship with God and with one's fellow human beings. The meaning, substance and consummation of life are summed up in love of God and love of neighbour, and the entire force of the Great Commandment insists that these two loves may not be separated. It therefore follows that the path towards discovering that meaning, substance and consummation is to be found in human relationships and the virtues such as justice, tolerance, fraternity, respect and forgiveness which sustain them. For Paul, Christ showed true love, self-denial and self-emptying. For humankind he therefore becomes the new creation, the personification and incarnation of the call to love. In future all human actions are to find a reference in Christ; every moral failure is to be viewed in the light of this new ethical criterion: the call to love as Christ loved. Consequently, Christian morality is more intensely personal, for it takes place within the framework of relationship with Christ.

The struggle against sin here loses some of the negative character that served to fossilise its true meaning. It is no longer simply a question of fleeing from a taboo or 'avoiding occasions of sin' as if treading through a minefield. Instead, sin is now conceived as all that keeps the individual (or community) from making real that 'newness of life' (Rom 6:4) which is their fundamental calling. In other words, it is a failure to do the good that one could do in order to develop one's own insight, sensitivity, freedom and creativity. Sin is a refusal to grow, a refusal of responsibility and co-responsibility.

Sin thus understood presupposes a certain freedom and ethical awareness. It takes for granted an adequate internalisation of moral principles and beliefs. Without such internalisation, the capacity to act morally is significantly impaired. As a result, a basic understanding of the process of human growth towards psychological maturity is central to the new vision. The internalisation of moral responsibility also presupposes the capacity conscientiously to weigh moral values and to embrace them by personal choice. If, as psychologists have suggested, in the early years human conduct is regulated from outside by means of taboos and promises of reward or punishment, it then becomes paramount for the individual will to attain a sufficient level of personal maturity to achieve moral autonomy. Where such autonomy has not been achieved, the capacity to sin will also be significantly reduced.

There is always, of course, the danger of regression towards a Pharisaic concept of sin. As in the attitude of the prodigal son's mistaken elder brother in Jesus' famous parable, the emphasis can too easily be placed on obeying orders and observing law to the detriment of deepening the relationship with the Father.

The renewal of biblical scholarship, spearheaded by the Reformation tradition, has also led to an increased emphasis today on the corporate or collective dimension of sin. Some of the great prophetic texts in scripture such as Isaiah 1–5, Deuteronomy 4–7 and Matthew 23–7 are clearly about the totality of humanity in both its personal and social dimensions. Careful emphasis is laid here on the responsibilities held by people in different roles and functions: heads of families, civic leaders, parents and religious leaders. Similarly, the misdeeds and uncharitable dispositions of all manner of groups and assemblies are denounced. Gently, the people of God are led to assume, distinguish and articulate the responsibilities that belong both to individuals and to groups and indeed to the multiple collective expressions of humankind: families, tribes, tongue, peoples and nations. Amid this great diversity of historical and social forms the preaching of the law of the covenant is designed to engender both individual responsibility and community solidarity.

The gospels make clear the close parallel between 'hardness of heart' and the 'perversity of the world'. This double symbolism lies at the heart of their concept of sin, sometimes referred to as 'the sin of the world'. The animated debates about the sabbath, what is clean and unclean, the precepts of the law and table fellowship with sinners, are all directed against a collective hardness of heart. It is sin born in the human heart, born in the hearts of the learned, those who 'know' much but 'understand' little. It takes expression in the life of the group.

Although the refusal to open one's eyes and one's heart to Jesus' saving message is individual, the structures, the social ties and pressures are such that this refusal appears to be the embodiment of a single attitude. Sin is therefore more than the accumulation of individual acts of sinfulness; it is, as Paul writes, a power that seeks dominion over our lives. 'Sin abounded ... sin has reigned' (Rom 5:20-1). The inward disruption of the sinner is mirrored in the dismemberment of society. For Paul, sin has a very real corporate dimension. Because through baptism the individual is admitted to the community, the *koinonia* of the body of Christ, thenceforward he or she cannot be considered a mere individual nor can their acts, attitudes and dispositions be solely private. 'None of us lives to himself and none of us dies to himself' (Romans 14:7). All are members of the body of Christ.

This does not mean that traditional distinctions such as capital, mortal and venial sin are dispensed with. The notion of capital sin has been with us since the time of the Church fathers. The spiritual writer, Evagrius Ponticus (346–79) drew up a list of eight generic malevolent thoughts that he maintained were at the root of every sin. This list became a classic text of Eastern Christianity. It explains that 'there are eight generic thoughts: gluttony, fornication, avarice, sadness, anger, sloth, vainglory and pride'.

One can see a similarity here with the western idea of the seven vices. In fact these were a version of Evagrius' list taken up later by Gregory the Great. The order was inverted to take account of the prophet's view that 'pride is the beginning of all sin' (Sir 10:13). He also reduced the number of vices by combining vainglory and pride and replacing sadness with envy, i.e. destructive and selfish sorrow. Evagrius' list may have been inspired by the three temptations of Jesus, to which the others were added. Noting that Jesus responded to each of the devil's temptations with admonitions from holy scripture, Evagrius later set out to provide a compendium of scriptural passages which would equip the follower of Christ to combat every temptation. This text, too, was divided up into eight parts according to the eight generic vices, and this scheme has become a regular feature of subsequent classifications of sin.

Augustine is largely credited with the introduction of the mortal sin/venial sin vocabulary. He sought to make a distinction between sins *ad mortem* (mortal sins) that broke the bond of communion, and more easily pardoned sins (*veniabiliora*). This division laid the foundation for the classic distinction between mortal and venial sin that has largely remained, although it was later taken up and developed into a coherent system by the scholastics. With the gradual sophistication of theological enquiry, the subjective condition of the sinner was open to ever-greater scrutiny. In time venial sin came to be seen as a transgression of God's law without 'complete commitment to the evil end' in comparatively unimportant matters or in important matters that were carried out with imperfect knowledge or imperfect consent. By contrast, mortal sin was viewed as a decision in radical contradiction to God's will which always presupposed full knowledge and full consent of the will.

Doctrine traditionally argued, therefore, that three conditions had to be verified for mortal sin: grave matter, full knowledge and full consent.

In more recent times the shift to a personalist focus has led to a re-evaluation of this traditional doctrine. In particular, the previous emphasis on 'the gravity of the matter' was called into question. Was there not a danger that the manualist method had to some extent 'materilised sin', thus glossing over the personal component and interior disposition? Moreover, were not categorical acts expressive of interior attitudes which ultimately determine whether or not sin is present? The theologian, Karl Rahner, among others had argued that actions spring from different levels of our being. Not everything we do emerges from or is expressive of our deepest core. The human decision-making process is constructed in layers starting at that core and becoming more and more external. Thus it is possible to do one and the same thing and have several motives and intentions for it, contradictory in themselves. The difficulty for Rahner and others was the traditional insistence on identifying mortal sin with one specific act. Was it possible for one specific decision or deed at the outer level completely to alter the moral orientation of one's existence?

And so the theory of the fundamental option was advanced, as giving a more credible anthropological basis to this aspect of the moral life. Mortal and venial sin are held to be expressive of the basic disposition of the sinner. They cannot simply be considered in themselves, because choices and deeds alone are ambiguous. Mortal sin is to be understood as any action or series of actions or attitudes that change, or are equivalent to changing, one's fundamental option towards God. Venial sin, on the other hand, does not concern one's fundamental option at all. It is a step off the right path, but still generally headed towards God.

There is a danger that in attempting to correct an overly materialist conception of sin one can unwittingly encourage the opposite fallacy, namely an excessively spiritualised notion. Certainly, the fundamental option defines a person's moral disposition. But it can be completely changed by particular acts especially when, as often happens, these have been prepared for by previous more superficial acts. Thus it would be wrong to say that particular acts are not enough to constitute mortal sin. The usefulness of the fundamental option theory is therefore counter-balanced today by an insistence on the importance of evaluating sins according to their gravity and of not underestimating the consequences of losing sight of the sinful character of particular acts.

MODERN CORRECTIVES TO THE THEOLOGY OF SIN

The contribution of political, ecological, liberationist and feminist writers has been central to recent efforts to move away from mono-dimensional accounts of enquiry towards a more representative, synthetic and holistic approach development.

While feminists have tended to concentrate less on the theme of sin and more on the patriarchal identification of women with sin, their work has on occasions lucidly demonstrated how prone our religious imagery and theological paradigms are to distortion and bias. Such bias may also express itself in ethical theory and in the basic understanding of the moral life. Spiritual and moral machismo may be found in inordinate preoccupation with victory over individual sins to the neglect of responsibility for nourishing and nurturing relationships. Some critiques go further and argue that there is a tendency with traditional conceptions of morality to legitimate so-called 'feminine virtues', thereby perpetuating injustice and oppression. Whatever the validity of these claims, there is no doubt that feminist thinkers have done a service in highlighting the 'sin' of sexism. The blatant dishonesty at the root of a belief that gender is the primary determinant of human characteristics, abilities and talents and that sexual differences produce an inherent superiority of one sex has been clearly exposed.

This critique also raises questions about the accuracy of hubris as a type for universal sin, as this very concept mirrors chiefly the experience of men who aspire to positions of power and influence. It argues that patriarchal structures and sexist attitudes are still a reality in society generally and in Christian churches and communities more particularly. Like liberation theologians, feminists have drawn inspiration from the prophetic tradition of Jewish and Christian ethics, which emphasised God's defence of the oppressed as well as the need to criticise oppressive power structures and to recognise ideological elements in religious belief. They have also criticised an overly spiritualised account of original sin. In doing so they are broadly at one with theologians who argue that sin is essentially about refusing the invitation to play our part in the human family's journey towards becoming more fully human. The fact that Christian theology and in particular its reflection on sin and evil has until recently been constructed predominantly by men, to the near exclusion of the experience of women, means that there is corrective work to be done.

A new awareness of the fragility and delicate ecological balance of the environment has led to increased reflection on the duty of stewardship for all creation and what this means in terms of concrete individual and collective moral responsibility. Here there are ready parallels with the classical Christian view of justice as right relationships. Ecological sin is a refusal or neglect to share these resources with those who are most in need of them. It is also a failure to recognise the inherent goodness of the natural world. That goodness is a deeply rooted scriptural conviction. After each of God's acts of creation, 'God found it very good'. Similarly, the Psalms proclaim that the 'earth is the Lord's and all that is in it' (Ps 24:1-2).

There is a pervasive recognition here that the world is not ours and that human beings are a part of the created world. Made in the image and likeness of God, human beings are to reflect God and to look after and care for the world and its resources. There is the implication here of a care-taking role, a duty of stewardship, which is part of a respect for the integrity of all creation. Such an attitude is directly opposed to the purely utilitarian stance, which considers natural resources to be expendable and disposable commodities. It is also a relational attitude, an attitude that calls for a rediscovery of our dependence on the earth. This sense of justice towards all creation had once found expression in the ancient Jewish tradition of the sabbath law and the jubilee year. There was a sense of allowing the earth to replenish its resources and restore its energies during a fallow period. One can speak, meaningfully, therefore of ecological sin and of the need to encourage awareness of sustainability.

Reverence for the earth is an ethical and religious imperative that touches our self-understanding in a profound way and asks searching moral question of our individual and collective lifestyles. In so far as we refuse to recognise these questions or reject their import or fail to answer them, we also disregard the perennial summons to 'act justly, love tenderly and walk humbly with our God'. This rejection is what we have learned to call sin.

The fields of political theology and liberation theology are the context of some other recent attempts to contextualise the concept of sin. In large measure the preoccupations of these theologies are those connected with 'social sin'. 'Political' theologies have sought to develop theological reflection on sin and guilt in the context of contemporary social relationships in the modern world. Their approach sets out specifically to challenge and criticise the individual bias, which is part of modern western culture. Some of this theology has been influenced by the traumatic experiences of the Second World War. These raise the question of the suffering of innocent victims and of the large groups of people who are denied the opportunity of becoming 'subjects' due to political and social repression. People need to liberate themselves from the structures that impede their integral growth and development. A collective conversion, an 'anthropological revolution', is required whereby people emancipate themselves from the influences of 'privatism' and from the sinful tendencies of consumption and domination. This can only be achieved by a collective abandonment of the competitiveness and egotism of the 'success ethic' and a realisation of the full implications of the status of men and women as social beings who accept responsibility for the human family, the world and themselves.

BIBLIOGRAPHY

Coll, R.E., *Christianity and Feminism in Conversation*, Mystic, CT: Twenty-third Publications, 1994.

Connolly, H., *Sin*, London and New York: Continuum, 2002.

Fagan, S., *Has Sin Changed?*, Dublin: Gill & Macmillan, 1978.

Gula, R., *To Walk Together Again*, New York and Mahwah, NJ: Paulist Press, 1984.

Kierans, P., *Sinful Social Structures*, New York and Mahwah, NJ: Paulist Press, 1974.

McCormick, P., *Sin as Addiction*, New York and Mahwah, NJ: Paulist Press, 1989.

Müller-Fahrenholz, G., *The Art of Forgiveness*, Geneva: WCC Publications, 1996.

Theissen, J.P., *Community and Disunity: Symbols of Grace and Sin*, Collegeville, MN: St John's University Press, 1985.

Schoonrnberg, P., *Man and Sin*, London: Sheed & Ward, 1965.

29   Understanding Sin Today

William Cosgrave

(William Cosgrave, *Christian Living Today: Essays in Moral and Pastoral Theology*, Dublin: Columba Press, 2001, pp. 61–89 [extract].)

THE RELATIONAL MODEL OF SIN

The relational model of sin is one element in the relational model of the Christian moral life generally – a model that is dominant in Catholic moral theology today.[1]

In this section we will outline the basic elements of this relational model of sin, beginning with a brief description of sin itself and moving on to discuss the main presuppositions and implications of that starting point as they emerge in this understanding.

WHAT IS SIN?

As the name indicates, the relational model of sin sees the moral life of the Christian, and hence also sin, as being concerned with and taking place in relationships between people. Christian morality is a relational reality and so too is sin. The Christian community and its members are called to live their lives in these relationships with other people and in community and to do this in a loving manner. This they do by relating responsibly and appropriately to the individuals, groups and communities they come into relationship with. In this context sin is understood as any selfish attitude, disposition, tendency, habit or activity that damages or destroys a relationship a person or persons has/have with another person, group or community. It is unloving activity; it is a failure or refusal to love another or others. It involves saying no to a person(s) in a relationship. In a word, sin is selfishness in relationship. This means that to commit sin is to be irresponsible in our relationships, to fail to respond positively and appropriately to others, to fail to love.

For the Christian this failure or selfishness in human relationships involves failure and selfishness in our relationship with God, since to fail to love other human persons is to fail to love God. It follows that sin is, at one and the same time, both a refusal to love another human person or persons and a refusal to love God. Refusing to love others is refusing to love God. To offend against another human person or persons is to offend against God. It may be mentioned here that it is also possible to sin against oneself in one's relationship with oneself, i.e.

to fail to love oneself appropriately, e.g. by damaging one's health through over-work, by substance abuse, by over- or under-nourishing oneself physically, by isolating oneself excessively from relationships.

PERSONAL AND SOCIAL DIMENSIONS OF SIN

In Catholic theological thinking on the moral life today, there is a noticeable shift from talk about human nature to talk about the human person. Thus Christian morality is seen today as, above all, personal, involving persons in relationship and in community. In this context there is a concern to take account of the fact that human activity must be judged morally by reference to the human person integrally and adequately considered. This means that the human person adequately considered is the criterion by which we discover whether an act is morally right or wrong. Hence, we need a good Christian anthropology, or understanding of the human person, if we are to think fruitfully about morality and live well as moral beings.

In this context, it will be clear that sin, like morality generally, concerns persons or groups of persons, not in isolation but in relationship with other individuals and in community. It is persons who sin, whether individually or in groups, but it is also persons who are affected by sin and who suffer damage in one way or another. Sin hurts people in their persons and in their relationships. It also hurts or damages the sinner, because it makes him/her more selfish and less loving and so less human.

Special attention needs to be given to the communal or group dimension of sin, since this has been neglected in the past and even today is poorly understood and inadequately presented in Catholic moral theology. We have done, and still do, most of our thinking and theologising about morality and about sin in terms of individual persons. While this is basic, it is not by itself adequate. Some improvements has taken place in this matter in recent times and we find, in consequence, valuable reflections on immorality and sin from the group, communal, social, national, international, structural, institutional and systemic points of view. We are still, however, far from having an adequate theology of social immorality and social sin. In particular we need a fuller account of the group as moral agent and as sinful, and of structures, institutions and systems in their relation to causal and even moral responsibility.

SINFULNESS AND SINS

Our focus on persons in all their dimensions enables us to look for and find sin in areas other than specific actions or individual concrete deeds. As a result there is in the relational model a tendency to speak of sinfulness as well as sins, or of sin as distinct from, though not opposed to, sins. This arises from the fact that sin is more than a specific act done at a particular time and place. We can be sinful in

Understanding Sin Today   421 our attitudes, tendencies, dispositions, habits, intentions, values, goals and priorities, and this sinfulness can and will express itself in concrete choices and actions. Here we find the sources or roots of our individual acts of sin and these sources or roots are in important ways more significant than the fruit they bear. In other words, the sinfulness in a person or within a group is the primary reality; the sins that flow from that sinfulness are, of course, important but they are not the source or root of the evil. In this context it makes sense to speak of sin as a condition or state of the person or group or even of a whole community, nation, institution or system. Some, like St Paul, consider sin as a power within us pushing us to commit particular sinful acts. So sin is primarily in the heart of the sinner or deep within the group or community. This is sin at its deepest and most significant and it is in relation to this sinfulness within that conversion and reconciliation are most needed but usually most difficult.

One can easily understand that sinfulness in the sense intended here, as well as the individual sinful acts that flow from it, may well have very serious consequences for and effects on one's relationships or those in a group or community. Such sinfulness or selfishness will weaken and perhaps destroy some of our relationships, since the person or group concerned is selfish in some real degree and so is less capable of loving others and of responding to them positively and appropriately. There are, of course, degrees or levels of sinfulness and they vary from person to person and from group/community to group/community as well as from time to time. These degrees or levels can range from minor to basic or profound. Experience would seem to indicate that every person and group/community has some degree of sinfulness and commits some sins.

SIN AS PRIMARILY A CHOICE FOR EVIL

One of the criticisms of the legal model of sin is that it gives too much importance to the matter, the external deed, and underplays the significance of the other factors in the choice to commit a sin. The relational model seeks to redress this distortion and so changes the emphasis in relation to the factors that are central in the commission of sin. This results in sin being described as primarily a free choice for evil, where the main element of the sin is the commitment of the sinner to the evil on which he/she has set his/her heart. Care is taken to avoid identifying the sin with the external deed and, in consequence, sin is seen as being, first of all, in the choice the agent makes of some particular evil or immoral reality. What really makes an action sinful (as distinct from just being immoral) is the degree to which the sinner puts his/her heart into it and makes the evil in it his/her own. Hence, sin is seen as being, firstly, in the heart, in one's commitment to evil and this expresses itself in and through one's choice of a particular immoral deed or evil.

This does not mean that the external deed, the matter of the sin, is unimportant. It is very important, because one's choice expresses itself in the

An Irish Reader in Moral Theology

doing of that external deed. When one chooses morally, one has to choose something. One's choice has to have an object, a reality one decides to commit oneself to in some real degree, in this case, some evil. We can say in fact that the object of one's choice evokes that choice and in a sense determines it. So, the matter is a pointer to the sin and to the degree of sinfulness in the choice. But it is no more than that, since in some cases one can make a deep choice about a small thing or a superficial choice in relation to a major evil. So then, the sin remains primarily in the choice as expressed in what one does. Hence, the object chosen, the external deed, is in itself correctly spoken of as immoral rather than sinful. One can, then, observe or see the immoral deed, the external act, but the sin considered as one's choice of evil is rooted deep in the sinner's heart.

We cannot, therefore, know with certainty if another has committed a sin, and even less can we know the degree to which he/she has committed him/herself to the evil involved in the choice made. Only the sinner can know that, and even he/she cannot always be certain. Clearly, then, we should refrain from saying such things as: Michael has committed a serious sin; Joan has fallen into mortal sin. We should, rather, confine ourselves to saying something like: Michael has done something immoral; Joan's action is gravely wrong. Leave the judgement about sinfulness to the person him/herself, to the confessor and to God.

In the light of this line of thought, it seems clear that it will often be far from easy to distinguish between serious (or mortal) and non-serious sin, certainly in regard to other people and even in one's own case. This is true but it is not of primary importance, since the main thing is to repent of one's sin and not agonise over which category of sin it is to be put in.

SIN AS A PROCESS

It would seem to emerge fairly clearly from what has been said above that sinfulness or sin, as distinct from specific sin-acts, is not usually something that happens in an instant or on the spot, as it were. There is fairly obviously an element of process about our becoming sinful persons or groups. It takes time and effort; it is something that happens gradually and usually imperceptibly. It seems true also that some of our individual sinful actions do not take place in an instant but involve a process that can go on over quite some time. We may consider these points briefly here.

In relation to the person (or group) becoming sinful, it seems clear that one does not normally become a sinful person in one fell swoop, in an instant. Generally, one grows into sinfulness over a period of months and even years, until finally one is in fact a sinful person in some degree. (The same sort of process takes place, it would seem, in relation to becoming a virtuous or holy person.) Such growth is a process and it would seem to consist of many individual choices for evil, serious and not so serious. One's sinfulness, like one's virtue, builds up gradually and usually seems to occur without any very noteworthy, much less spectacular, actions on the surface of one's life. Many people don't even notice this development in sinfulness or vice in themselves. It seems to creep up on them without them being explicitly aware of it. And yet one must be aware of it at some level, since it involves one's free commitment of oneself to evil. It will be obvious from experience also that one's sinfulness or sin can vary in depth and strength, and can become stronger or weaker, depending on the moral choices the person (or group) makes from time to time.

In regard to individual sinful actions, not all of them seem to take place in an instant or solely at the time and place when the external deed is done. Some do, especially the smaller or more superficial ones, e.g. a minor theft, a small lie. But it can and does happen that a particular sin or moral choice for evil may take quite some time to get under way and come to completion. Since a human action is not to be identified with a particular visible object or thing done, we must reckon with the fact that a person (or group) may make a choice for evil that takes time to work itself out in external behaviour. In other words, an individual sinful action may involve a process, spread over a notable interval, that is made up of many lesser choices for evil (venial sins), as the major or deeper choice unfolds. We have only to think of a vocation to the priesthood or to marriage and all that is required for and involved in such a profound choice to see this. This would seem to be true also, at least sometimes, in relation to significant choices for evil like adultery, murder, serious theft. Such immoral and sinful actions are not to be identified with the external event of physical sex or physical killing or actually putting the money in one's pocket. It will likely be the case here that these sins will have begun long before the external deeds or physical acts themselves actually occur. Such sins will probably include selfish desires and attitudes, deteriorating relationships and perhaps increasing conflict, with much thinking and planning beforehand, etc. Doing the external deed would, then, be the culmination of a long and profound internal process, the visible expression of a single but complex human choice for evil, a major sin. In a word, these sins involve a process and take time and effort to bring to completion.

AWARENESS AND CONDITIONING IN RELATION TO SIN

The above discussion of the person as sinful and of individual sinful actions brings with it, in contemporary moral theology, an important reflection on the levels of awareness that we have in our human choices, whether for good or for evil. Today two such levels are usually distinguished. In our specific choices for evil, i.e. our acts of sin that fall into a particular category like lying or theft, we are explicitly aware of what we are choosing and doing. This is referred to as explicit or reflexive awareness or consciousness and means that we are thinking about our choice and have concepts about it in our head, e.g. when one decides to steal a sum of money and does so. Implicit or non-reflexive awareness, on the other hand, is the awareness or consciousness which we have of ourselves as subjects, as we make a basic choice for evil (i.e. commit a mortal sin) or for good. This awareness is obscure and elusive, since the choice is too personal to be viewed as one views an object or even a specific deed one does. Hence, it is difficult to be sure one has committed a mortal sin or is in the state of mortal sinfulness (or of grace). This fact would seem to be borne out in our experience.

In the relational model of sin, it is also presupposed that freedom and knowledge in the sinner are always conditioned, situated, limited and frequently imperfect. This is simply how the human condition is. Part of this conditioning and limiting is due to social influences and attitudes and part of it comes from psychological and emotional factors within the agent(s). It will clearly be very important to take account of this in assessing the sinfulness of oneself or one's action in any particular case. In short, we must reckon with the fact that responsibility for sin is real but seldom total.

DISTINGUISHING KINDS OF SIN

In this relational model of sin one soon comes to realise that it may be rather difficult to make a clear distinction, in practice at least, between the different kinds of sin and in particular between mortal and venial sin. In many cases there seems to be no very obvious dividing line between them, as we will attempt to do shortly. When we emphasise that sin is primarily in the subject, in the sinner and in his/her choice for and commitment to evil and selfishness, and only in the second place in the matter or external deed, then it becomes clear that we cannot always in practice distinguish mortal and venial sin as neatly as in the legal model of sin. The boundary line between the human free choices involved in serious and minor sin can be somewhat blurred and far from always clearly discernible in our daily experience. This seems to be how things are in reality and we must live with this relative lack of clarity. It may be said to be compensated for by the greater sense of realism that attends this relational understanding as compared to that in the legal model. This understanding rings truer to our experience, it seems to many, and that points to its basic correctness.

It will be important to add here that in the majority of cases there is no pressing need for a person or group to spend a lot of time trying to decide if a particular sin is mortal or venial; much less should they worry about it. The reason for this is that, when a person or group has sinned, the primary thing is to repent of and be converted from that sin. It is less important and very often not really a priority to be able to label one's sin as mortal or venial. One will normally have a general impression about its seriousness or lack of it and that usually suffices.

MORTAL SIN

In the relational model of sin, our understanding of mortal sin runs along the following lines. Avoiding identifying the sin with the external deed, as tended to happen in practice at least in the legal model, and remembering that what really makes an action sinful, as distinct from simply immoral, is the degree to which the sinner puts his/her heart into it and make the evil his/her own, we may describe mortal sin as follows. Mortal sin is one's deep personal commitment to evil, a profound choice of selfishness. To make such a commitment or choice one has to have a real appreciation of the values and evils involved in one's choice; one has to gather one's resources as a person, as it were, and then one has to commit oneself to evil in a big way, in and with one's heart or deepest self. Mortal sin in this sense is referred to today by theologians as a fundamental option for evil, a basic choice not to love, to be selfish. Such a deeply personal choice is difficult to make; it cannot happen by accident or on the spur of the moment. It will usually take time and involve a process that includes lesser or more superficial choices (venial or minor sins), until finally one completes or finalises one's basic choice and commits mortal sin. Thus one comes to be in the state of mortal sinfulness, which means that one is now a basically selfish, unloving person who has broken his/her relationship with God and his/her relationships with other people and so has lost the state of grace. Mortal sin thus understood is, of course, a specific human action but, since it is a choice made deep within the agent, even the person who does it will find it hard to identify it as a mortal sin. We may add that such a mortal sin will shape the person who does it profoundly. By it he/she takes up a particular stance or direction morally or as a person; one is now directed towards evil and selfishness and away from other people and from God. And this stance or direction is fundamental, as the choice for evil was. In short, the fundamental option for evil that is mortal sin gives rise to a fundamental stance or direction in the agent that is also set on evil or selfishness.

Viewed in this manner, it would seem correct to say that mortal sin can come about in two ways. One may commit a mortal sin as one makes a wholehearted choice of a specific gravely evil object or matter, e.g. murder, adultery, major theft. Such a choice, because it is so basic and profoundly personal, will very likely have an element of process in it; it will take time and develop gradually within the agent as he/she moves towards completing his/her commitment to the major evil involved. On the other hand, there is the possibility, as experience would seem to indicate, that one can make a fundamental option or basic choice for evil in a more hidden, subtle manner and without necessarily doing any specific external deed that is spectacularly evil. Such a basic choice will also come to completion gradually as one moves deeper and deeper into selfishness over quite a long time. The end result in both these cases is that one loses the state of grace and enters the state of mortal sinfulness.[2]

In this conception it will be true to say that mortal sin will be a rare thing in the life of a Christian, especially if one is trying to live a good life. It will be rare, because it involves a profound and difficult choice and we do not make many such choices. In addition, it will be a choice that only one with significant moral maturity can make. Only those with such a level of moral maturity will have the personal capacity to make a deep personal commitment such as is required for mortal sin. In other words, mortal sin is an adult reality; it is not something of which children are capable. So only those who are adults in the moral sense can commit mortal sin. Furthermore, it is important to say that, though it is hard to be sure one is in mortal sin oneself and virtually impossible to know if others are, this is not a matter for worry. It is generally not of prime importance to have certainty about this. Since conversion or repentance is the main thing, one should focus on that and do all possible to achieve it.

We have said above that it is hard to commit a mortal sin and get into the state of mortal sinfulness. This is a reassuring and comforting point, particularly since the legal model of sin gave the impression that it was rather easy to fall into mortal sin. We may add in this context, then, that it is highly unlikely that a person who has lived a good life for decades will fall into mortal sin at the last minute and so be lost for all eternity. On the other hand, it has to be said that a sudden death-bed conversion after a seriously sinful life is equally unlikely.

NOTES

1   For a brief account of the relational model of the Christian moral life in general, see chapter 1 [in original], pp. 16–22; also Cosgrave, 'Models of the Christian Moral Life', op. cit., pp. 564–7; Richard M. Gula, *Reason Informed by Faith: Foundations of Catholic Morality*, New York: Paulist Press, 1989, pp. 63–4; Harrington, pp. 16–17.

2   See Harrington, p. 71; Kevin T. Kelly, *New Directions in Moral Theology: The Challenge of being Human*, London: Geoffrey Chapman, 1992, p. 133; Richard M. Gula, op. cit., p. 111.

FURTHER READING

Cosgrave, William, 'Understanding Sin Today', *The Furrow*, October 1999, pp. 538–47. This article is a summary of the present chapter.

Gaffney, James, *Sin Reconsidered*, New York: Paulist Press, 1983, especially chapters 1, 8 & 10.

Gula, Richard M., *Reason Informed by Faith: Foundations of Catholic Morality*, New York: Paulist Press, 1984, chapters 7 & 8.

Gula, Richard M., *To Walk Together Again: The Sacrament of Reconciliation*, New York: Paulist Press, 1984, chapter 4.

John Paul II, Apostolic Exhortation, *Reconciliation and Penance* (1984), nn.13–18.

May, William E., 'Sin' in *The New Dictionary of Theology*, ed. by J. Komonchak, M. Collins & D. Lane, Dublin: Gill & Macmillan, 1987, pp. 954–67.

O'Connell, Timothy E., *Principles for a Catholic Morality*, revised edition, San Francisco: Harper & Row, 1990, chapters 7 & 8.

O'Keefe, Mark, OSB, *What are they Saying about Social Sin?*, New York: Paulist Press, 1990.

30   What is Mortal Sin?

Denis O'Callaghan

(*The Furrow*, Vol. 25, No. 2 (February/May 1974), pp. 71–87.)

It's a mortal sin to get drunk, to indulge in unlawful sexual pleasure, to steal a substantial amount of property, to miss Mass on Sunday. Presupposing certain general qualifications in the matter of advertence and voluntariety, that list would pass as a popular itemisation of mortal sin. As against this ready reckoning there is the feeling that the whole idea of mortal sin and of the hell which attends it contradicts what is known of God, the Father of love, as revealed in Christ. Does not the idea suggest at worst a deity who scrupulously balances the debit/credit account and punishes with implacable decisiveness, at best a Lord who at a certain moment sets mercy aside and lets justice take its toll?

When one thinks of the infinite love and goodness of God and of his power to change the most hardened heart, and of the inherent weakness and blindness of man, one may feel that mortal sin and an eternal penalty just do not make sense. But, then, one recalls Christ's parables of the Net of Good and Bad Fish, of Dives and Lazarus, of the Sheep and the Goats; one remembers his warning to fear God who can destroy both body and soul in hell, his direction to cut off hand or pluck out eye rather than end up with all one's faculties in a hell 'where the worm does not die nor the fire go out', his remark that the road to perdition is a broad well-beaten track while the road to life is narrow and little travelled. Granted that Christ, prophet that he was, was concerned not with statistics but with the urgency and need of repentance, one must at least read in his words the *possibility* of final impenitence for everyman. This is essentially what Christians have always accepted. Generations of preachers have stretched imagination to the utmost in describing the horrors which would make hell an ultimate deterrent. In his *Portrait of the Artist as a Young Man,* James Joyce presents an unforgettable account of the retreat sermon on hell which he had heard as a boy. But, perhaps, the fiery torments of which the good Father Arnall spoke would be a welcome distraction from the cold despair and self-recrimination which hell must be!

In any terms the concept of mortal sin is a problem, but we may well have compounded it by approaching it from the wrong side, that familiar to us in confessional practice. We have ended up in identifying the theological concept of mortal sin with the more disciplinary concept of grave sin. Mortal sin should be understood primarily in terms of the God-man relationship described in scripture. Here one must bring together the concepts of the infinite love of God and the real possibility of man's final impenitence. Grave sin should be understood primarily in terms of the Church's discipline of penance within which it has developed. This discipline requires that sins of particular gravity be submitted to the priest acting in the name of the community so that the 'excommunicated' sinner may be reconciled in Christ's name with the Church and through Christ and the Church come to die to sin and live for God. The aim of the process is, first, the achievement of a genuine and effective *metanoia* in which God 'forgives' sin, that is, transforms the heart of the sinner, and, second, the protection of the community from the rot of sin.

MORTAL SIN

Mortal sin or, better, mortal sinfulness, should be seen as a state, a situation in which the sinner has come to reject God and make something other than God the end and purpose of his life. If a sinner has committed himself to this way of life, and dies in it, then Christian tradition holds that he is irretrievably bound to its consequences. Hell, 'life' without God, is not imposed on him as punishment. It is the logical continuation, the final phase of the choice which he has made. God takes man and man's decision seriously. Admittedly, this must require in the individual a degree of freedom and self-determination which no one except God could estimate. Circumstances of personality and situation, moral obtuseness and the various mechanisms of rationalisation and exculpation, all kinds of unconscious influences will affect the degree of guilt. The Parable of the Talents shows that the effort to compare oneself with others is quite arbitrary. 'When a man has had a great deal given him, a great deal will be demanded of him' (Lk 12:48).

Scripture refers constantly to the fundamental choice which is placed before man. It is a choice of life, of doing God's will, or a choice of death, of attaching oneself to one's own will and of manufacturing false gods. 'I set before you life or death, blessing or curse' (Deut 30:19). 'When God in the beginning created man, he made him subject to his own free choice. If you choose you can keep the commandments, to behave faithfully is in your power. He has set fire and water before you; put out your hand to whichever you prefer. Man has life and death before him; whichever a man likes better will be given him' (Eccl 15:14-18). Ezechiel 18 provides a flesh and blood description of this choice when he explains how each man is responsible for his own life and how the just or the unjust man may change his way of life for bad or for good in quite dramatic fashion.

Christ expressed the choice simply: 'You cannot serve God and Mammon' (Mt 6:24). Man's inmost and predominant life direction is either the service of God in terms of the double precept of love, or, in the Qumrâm phrase, the setting up of 'idols of the heart' through various forms of self-indulgence, such as

What is Mortal Sin?   429 ambition, pleasure, wealth, power. This inmost direction which gives unity to life is referred to by contemporary theology as 'basic orientation', 'core decision', 'fundamental option'. Christ used the words heart and eye, 'From the heart comes evil intentions: murder, adultery, fornication, theft, perjury, slander' (Mt 15:19); 'Where your treasure is there will your heart be also' (Mt 6:18); 'The lamp of the body is the eye. It follows that if your eye is sound, your whole body will be filled with light. But if y our eye is diseased, your whole body will be all darkness. If, then, the light inside you is darkness, what darkness that will be (Mt 6:22-23).

Those descriptions certainly set out the principle, but they do not resolve the ambiguity of the human experience. In effect one's life-policy will be far from black and white and unvarying. Freedom and self-determination do not inhabit some citadel apart from one's chemistry and psychological make-up, apart from the pressures and influences of life. All these enter into and condition one's most personal and fundamentall decisions. The terms responsibility and imputability which we use so readily in the abstract raise difficult questions when it comes to assessing an individual case. Here the intelligent person – not just the charitable one! – will simply have to say: 'God alone knows.' He will agree with Jeremias. 'The heart is more devious than any other thing, perverse too; who can pierce its sercrets? I, Yahweh, search to the heart, I probe the loins, to give each man what his conduct and his actions deserve'(17:9-10).

There is no inconsistency in assuming the existence of a predominant life-direction in the normal individual while admitting that it may be beyond one's capacity to identify this with any certainty in the particular case. The hypocrite may even be fooling himself! Acts of apparently calculated malice may spring from causes other than malice. In our own human experience we know of the perverseness which injures and apologises at the same time, which persists in inflicting pain on the person whom one has never ceased to love. In his *Procès à Jésus* Diego Fabbri has Simon Peter say: 'Despise me if you will! But what you cannot understand, what I shall never make you understand perhaps, is that a man can at one and the same time believe and betray, love and deny. Yes, I tell you, that is possible. And even as I stood in Annas' courtyard saying: "I do not know him! I have never seen him!" at that very moment I loved him.'

We have referred to mortal sin as a state. It is described by St James as the end result of a process of hardening the heart: 'Everyone who is tempted is attracted and seduced by his own wrong desire. Then the desire conceives and gives birth to sin, and when sin is fully grown it too has a child and the child is death' (1:14-15). This idea of 'sin unto death', from which we derive our term *mortal*, recalls St John's warning about the sin which *is* death, the sin which has closed the sinner's heart to grace (1 Jn 5:16-17). There is even no point in praying for one so disposed! John here refers to a particular sin, the sin of those who have deliberately refused to accept Christ, the sin which, in the words of the Synoptics, is unforgivable and eternal (cf. Mt 12:31-32; Mk 3:28-30). James describes sin unto death in a wider context and his language is less radical and less heated. He is stressing the end result of an unrepented sinful life rather than the unforgivable quality of a particular kind of sin.

Rejection of God, or rather introducing something else in place of God, need not be seen as a sudden decision; it will more likely be the result of a process of moral and spiritual decline; it will have a history and time dimension. How does one relate the development of this sin-attitude, the state of being closed in on self away from God, to particular sin-actions? Obviously, the guilt of a particular sin-action depends on the state of mind, the *mens rea*, the conscience which lies behind it. It is not so much that one did something as that one was capable of doing it!

On the whole, behaviour must be accepted as a fair index of nature. Moral is as moral does. One's overall life direction and attitude will objectify and ratify itself in appropriate action; action will consolidate and confirm a life direction. But if it is difficult to judge a whole life pattern, it is also difficult to judge the moral significance of a particular action.

It is possible that a single episode may mark a turning point, a radical change in one's moral life as relationship with God. The identity or gravity of the external act need not be the key factor. The importance of the act will lie in its sign-value as moral gesture of rejection or change of heart. In a relationship it is the malice which lies behind the more or less casual remark that counts. The biblical description of the sin of Adam and Eve comes to mind as a classic case. In the Paradise story the eating of the fruit is portrayed as an act of rebellion, all the more coldly deliberate in that the first pair are presented as free from the moral weakness and concupiscence which could otherwise be invoked as extenuating circumstance. This is why St Thomas maintained that the sin of the First Parents could not be but mortal.

One wonders whether a cold-blooded gesture of rebellious self-will, involving a cataclysmic disruption of the God-man relationship, is psychologically possible for a human creature, since it demands a degree of malice which can only be described as diabolical. If this explicit outright rejection of God with its extreme degree of spiritual malice were required, mortal sin would be a matter of academic interest. In practice, the anti-God decision must be seen as something much more human. It will be a constructive rejection, a choice of Mammon rather than a rejection of God, a *conversio ad creaturam* which incorporates an *aversio a Deo*. Some other value offers and is accepted in place of God. The actual account in Genesis suggests this kind of psychological pattern even for the first sin: 'The woman saw that the tree was good to eat and pleasing to the eye, and that it was desirable for the knowledge that it could give' (3:6). This human character is even more evident in the case of David's sin with Bethsabee (2 Sam 11). Here lust induces the king to have the loyal Uriah done to death so that he can have his way with Bethsabee.

One may admit that a particular episode or episodes may mark a turning point in an individual's moral life, but most probably these episodes will be the culmination of a process rather than isolated occurrences. Such episodes could be described as mortal sin, provided one applies this term not just to the action but to the mentality, the *mens rea*, which carries through the actions. The type of episode which implies such spiritual drama must be of its nature unusual in the experience of the ordinary person. No one – unless he is some kind of moral hysteric! – makes a practice of swinging from one pole of the moral compass to the other. At any rate, if such an episode happens out of character, the sinner's heart will still be 'in the right place' and his predominant life policy will reassert itself in terms of repentance.

Apart from these crucial and decisive moments, most of life's actions are joined by a thread of unity in that they conform to type. They reflect and confirm a policy or moral life. One can read the kind a man is from the kind of actions he does – admittedly with reservations unless one claims to be God! The familiar text in Galatians 5 where Paul contrasts the works of the flesh and the works of the spirit is relevant here: 'When self-indulgence is at work the results are obvious: fornication, gross indecency and sexual irresponsibility; idolatry and sorcery; feuds and wrangling, jealousy, bad temper and quarrels; disagreements, factions, envy. I warn you, as I warned you before: those who behave like this will not inherit the kingdom of God.'

Moralists have too often invoked this type of sin catalogue as if Paul had claimed that each of these items excluded from the kingdom was a 'mortal sin' in its own right. The items are in fact a random selection varying in gravity. What Paul does say is that the general lifestyle represented by this kind of behaviour betrays the unredeemed man who serves the flesh, who is in the way of death. These are the symptoms which enable one to diagnose the nature of his moral life.

The psychology of sin in St Paul finds a possible parallel in Ezechiel 18. The language and general approach in this passage of Ezechiel must have influenced the Christian understanding of repentance/impenitence, reward/punishment, and the whole concept of mortal sin: 'The soul that sins shall die.' The prophet explains how the wrongheadedness of the wicked shows itself in a life of sin; he itemises the typical crimes which this attitude produces; like St Paul he is concerned to bring out the general attitude which finds expression in wrong actions rather than to analyse these various actions in themselves; he repeatedly mentions life and death as the respective destinies of the man confirmed in justice and hardened in sin – even though at this date these terms must indicate long happy life and premature death; he teaches his audience that if they wish to live they must make themselves 'a new heart and a new spirit'.

The biblical phrase 'hard-heartedness' pretty well describes what we mean by the state of mortal sinfulness. It is the way of life of one who rejects the claims or the reign of God. What is at stake is the quality of one's attachment to a wrong way of life rather than a computation of the gravity of particular actions taken in isolation. In effect, each act should be rated in terms of a general life policy or programme. In view of the irreparable nature of final impenitence one must presuppose a high level of culpability in this hardening of the heart. There are problems here no matter how one approaches the question. If it is difficult to see how in a single episode a person will radically change his life direction, to invoke a gradual process of decline seems to lessen the cold-blooded quality required in so momentous a decision!

Even St Thomas failed to answer all the questions and produce a satisfactory synthesis of mortal sin, but without doubt his approach is the correct one. In his theology of the Christian life he distinguishes the virtue of charity as *virtue of the goal*, from the moral virtues as *virtues as the means*. Mortal sin is *contra caritatem*. It destroys charity, the virtue which attaches man to God as to his last end. Venial sin is *praeter caritatem*. It deflects charity and lessens its power to make love of God and love of one's fellow man operative in one's life. The failures which this tendency to weakness occasions are casual occurrences; they are inconsistent and illogical in terms of one's overall life policy. Man being man, they are par for the course; they are understandable and pardonable – hence the name venial.

> When the soul is so disordered by sin that it turns away from its ultimate goal, God, to whom it is united by charity, then we speak of mortal sin. When the disorder stops short of turning away from God, then the sin is venial. As in the body the disorder of death which results from the destruction of the vital principle cannot be repaired, whereas sickness can be overcome because the vital principle is intact, so too is it in matters concerning the soul.
>
> The man who sins by abandoning the ultimate goal fails irreparably, as far as the nature of sin is concerned and is said to sin mortally and deserve eternal punishment. However, the man who sins without turning away from God fails in a way which can be repaired because the source of order has not been destroyed.[1]

The reader will hardly quarrel with this statement of the fundamentals, but he will be curious to discover how St Thomas brings it down to lived experience, how he identifies mortal sin in the concrete. It seems that St Thomas was as unhappy here as any contemporary theologian, but he does get the emphasis and starting point right: in judging malice one begins with the internal state of mind rather than with the external action. In the matter of gluttony 'a turning away from God as last end occurs when a person attaches himself to the pleasure of eating as the purpose of his life and because of this he holds God in contempt and is prepared to transgress his laws so that he may indulge his pleasure'.[2] To the objection that it is illogical to suppose an infinite difference in the scale of punishment between mortal and venial sin since they are both human actions he replies: 'Although there is an infinite distance between venial and mortal sin as regards turning away from God, this does not hold as regards turning to the object which identifies the sin. Accordingly, a given species of sin can be either mortal or venial, e.g. the preliminaries to an act of adultery might be venial, and a casual remark which is usually venial might be mortal.'[3]

The text just cited is significant in that it pinpoints the limitations of a distinction which became the stock in trade of the moral manual, the distinction between wrong actions which are of their nature matter for mortal sin (*ex genere suo mortalia*) and those which are of their nature matter for venial sin (*ex genere suo venialia*).[4] It is clear from St Thomas that this is an extrinsic criterion and nothing more than a general indication of the kind of sin which these matters involve. Perhaps if he spoke today's language he would say that some actions should be regarded as sufficiently significant or sufficiently serious in human experience to qualify as real moments of decision, as moments when one might expect the normal person to come face to face with the fundamental moral question: Where do I go from here? Do I serve God or Mammon? It follows, then, that *a priori* judgements about the psychological significance of various kinds of actions and as to whether or not they should serve as matter for a mortal sin decision are fairly arbitrary and are useful only when one admits the limitations of a rough and ready assessment.

In formulating his concept of mortal malice St Thomas encountered the perennial difficulty of drawing together the two points of reference – the anti-God decision and the concrete immoral act. At least his starting point was correct when he stressed the heart and mind of the sinner and left the guilt of the individual action in that ambiguity which is part and parcel of the human condition. One may say that he read the external act for its sign value, for its capacity to indicate the wrongheartedness of the sinner, and keeping to our metaphor of language, the onus of proof was on the one who asserted that the action was not a statement of the intent.

GRAVE SIN

Whereas mortal sin centres on sin as state or situation of the sinner, grave sin centres on sin as event or episode in his moral experience. But, even in this latter case of sin-action, sin always denotes individual guilt or culpability, and therefore assessment of its intrinsic meaning or malice must necessarily end in a question mark. There is a great difference between saying that an action is wrong (i.e. objectively immoral) and saying that it is sinful (i.e. subjectively immoral). Naturally, then, there is a temptation to short-circuit the imponderable of individual culpability and to make the verdict more manageable by seeing sin primarily as wrongdoing and applying more external criteria to it. Scripture has a very important lesson to teach us here.

The nature and source of culpability in the individual sin-action is a very complex chapter in the theology of the Old Testament. From every early period the concept of personal guilt was obscured by an idea of corporate responsibility in which the sinful action was attributed to a whole community (2 Sam 12:10, 21:1, 24:13-17), and even more by the notion of material transgression or chance occurrence as morally imputable, as implying sanction and requiring expiation (1 Chron 13:9; Num 3:4). Numbers 15 and Leviticus 4–5 deal specifically with these 'sins' of ignorance or of inadvertence (shegagôth) and they establish the complex ritual by which these unintentional transgressions of the law should be expiated. Numbers contrasts this sin of ignorance with deliberate sin, 'sin with a high hand', and rules: 'The man who sins deliberately, whether native or stranger, must be outlawed from his people; he has despised the word of Yahwah and broken his command. This man must be entirely outlawed since his sin is inseparable from him' (15:30-31). One is readily tempted to read our terms grave and light sin into this distinction of sin with a high hand and sin of ignorance, particularly in view of the severity of the punishment imposed for the former. While it is possible that this text had some influence on the Christian discipline of excommunication, it would be anachronistic to read it otherwise than as drawing a distinction between purely material infringement of the law and deliberate or intentional transgression. The former we would simply not regard as sin, nor would we admit that moral guilt is incurred in the sense that 'a man realising it later becomes answerable for it' (Lev 5:3).

Against this background the Prophets did set out to teach the concept of individual responsibility and of genuine moral guilt. Ezechiel cites the proverb: 'The fathers have eaten sour grapes and the children's teeth are on edge', and counters it with the pronouncement: 'The son shall not suffer for the iniquity of the father, nor the father suffer for the iniquity of the son. The righteousness of the righteous shall be upon himself, and the wickedness of the wicked shall be upon himself' (18:2-20). Jeremiah in his turn teaches that the malice of the particular sin-action springs from the heart. In effect, the sin-action is sin because of the evil mind which inspires it. 'Can an Ethiopian change his skin or a panther his fur? And can you work the right you who are hardened in wrong?' (13:23). His linking of the terms *awon* (wickedness) and *hattat* (faults) suggests that the guilt of the sin-action springs from man's inherent wickedness. 'Because of your great iniquity your faults have multiplied' (30:15); 'I will purify them from their iniquity with which they have sinned' (33:8).

The efforts of the prophets against formalism with its emphasis on external transgression must be set against certain opposing influences in post-exilic Judaism.[5] During the century-and-a-half of the Babylonian exile, in the absence of Temple and homeland, the law became the point of reference for Jewish religion and piety. The emphasis on observing the law led to a situation in which obedience became the sole virtue or, as one commentator has said, a cannibal virtue. The rabbinic schools came to interpret the law in ever more detail and 'to build a hedge around the law', ending up with as many as 640 precepts. All this led to an externalisation of sin in terms of the illegal act, a matter of calibrating particular trespasses rather than of recognising the basic corruption of the will which gave to sin its deep-lying unity and coherence. This atomistic view of sin was set off by a similarly atomistic view of merit. Guilt and merit balanced out. Good works done within the law would weigh down the scales on the side of reward. The boasting Psalms, which extol the singer's impeccable observance of the law and his certainty of reward, betray this weakening of the sense of sin and could and did lead to a closing of the heart to genuine conversion and to the call of God. The gospel account of Christ's preaching shows that this self-righteousness made many of his audience impervious to his message and occasioned his strictures on the mentality of the Scribes and Pharisees (cf. Mt 23). Is there irony in his remark, 'I am not come to call the *just* but *sinners* to repentance' (Mt 9:9-13)? Is it suggested that these latter, the non-practising Jews, the 'people of the land' in the contemptuous phrase of the Pharisees, have avoided a false righteousness and so are more ready to lend an ear and heart to Christ's message? Is this interpretation borne out by those parables in which Christ contrasts Pharisee and Publican or two sons, the elder portraying the loyal Jew and the younger the 'sinner' (e.g. Mt 21:28-32; Lk 15:11-32)?

This background is of more than academic interest for the Christian experience. The manner in which the Church's penitential discipline has developed over the centuries bears within it the hazard of formalism. There is always some degree of risk that it may lose sight of the wood for the trees, the sinner for the sins. It should not surprise us that one strand in the tradition came to see the confessional as a slot-machine which dispensed pardon on the insertion of the proper token.[6] This was a hardening of the arteries rather than a genuine development of the theology of sacrament.

That this risk of formalism is endemic in our penitential discipline calls attention to the fact that this discipline in its essence and from the very beginning concentrated on sin-action. This was a practical way of identifying the sinner in the context of the community and of determining who should submit himself to the penitential process. The concern was not simply the community interest of law and order and the need to have objective criteria to identify the sinner; it was also, and primarily, a concern for the genuine personal reconciliation of the sinner – *salus animarum suprema lex*. Behaviour is rightly regarded as the best index of character. By your fruits you shall know them; *actio sequitur esse*. 'To consider that action is secondary and that only the intimate being of a person is of value, is one of the worst errors. Man is incarnate spirit and the act is the truth of the intention. But it is also true that the intention creates the truth of the act, for without the intention the act would be no more than a physical fact. Intention and act are two aspects of the one inseparable reality, and it is a mistake to favour one at the expense of the other.'[7] To pass up behaviour in favour of more psychological

An Irish Reader in Moral Theology

and ambiguous tests would lay the way open for hypocrisy and self-deception. If the self-knowledge which comes from the acknowledgement of oneself as sinner is essential for repentance then it is difficult to imagine how one could gain this in any manner other than in passing one's life in review and singling out particular areas of failure. It may also happen that some of these failures have caused injury to others, injury which must be put right if repentance is to mean anything.

From the very beginning of the Church's discipline of penance certain sins were judged grave by the community and for these the guilty person was in effect excommunicated and had to undergo canonical penance before readmission was granted. We can see the beginnings of the process of excommunication/reconciliation in 1 Cor 5:3-5 and 2 Cor 2:5-11. As the discipline came to be systematised it was decreed that the sinner could avail of the process only once in his lifetime, but then comparatively few sins attracted the sanction of canonical penance. These were described as *crimina, peccata gravia, peccata capitalia*. The three chief ones were idolatry, homicide and adultery, but there were others. This suggests a parallel with our institution of reserved sins. In time, the sinner was allowed access to penance after relapse and, as readmission became more widely accepted, particularly under the influence of the Celtic missionaries, the classification of 'grave sin' became more extensive. These missionaries drew up *Penitentials* which allocated tariff penances for the various sins on a sliding scale. These *Penitentials* and the *summae Confessariorum* of later years served to specify grave sin in the concrete. The Council of Trent canonised the position in decreeing that by divine law penitents were obliged to confess all mortal sins according to number and species.[8] It was natural that the moral manuals after Trent in their explicit aim of instructing confessors should have given a great deal of attention to setting out the species and the gravity of the various sins.

Given the actual position which Church law possessed in the matter of determining moral obligation, it does not surprise one to discover that infringements of Church law were most readily specified in terms of gravity. This was rarely done in the actual statement of the law, and so the moralist was expected to answer the concrete question: 'What is grave matter in the laws of fast and abstinence, of Sunday Mass, of the Breviary obligation?' St Alphonsus did protest at the importunity of those who plied him with such questions as 'How many grams constitute a grave infringement of the fasting law?', but, unfortunately, he still supplied the required answers. After all, I suppose, his questioners would have said, this is what moralists are for! It would not have been too confusing if he, and they, had understood by 'grave matter' matter which should be submitted in confession and therefore matter the specification of which fell within the competence of the community.

The medieval discussion as to whether sexual pleasure admitted of parvity of matter provides us with a classical example of the manner in which a consensus emerges as to what is or is not grave mater. In this case it was not the conviction of the serious intrinsic evil of each and every jot of unlawful sexual pleasure that won the case as much as the prudential factor that any weakening of the sanction in so parlous an area (*res lubica*) would open the door to lust.[9] This places in relief the predominant pastoral concern which coloured the concept of grave sin.

CONCLUSION

In the above pages it is accepted that if one is to answer the question: what is mortal sin? one must sort out the confusion between the concepts of mortal sin and grave sin. This involves a measure of linguistic analysis starting from the data of scripture and the history of Church penance. In reference to a particular individual the descriptions mortal sin and grave sin may both be valid ways of assessing his moral guilt, but one must remember that these descriptions operate from quite different viewpoints and, since we are dealing with distinct concepts, the verdicts may or may not converge in the particular case; in fact, it is more likely that they will not converge. If one neglects to recognise this one ends up in theological chaos where the sanctions of hell-fire and Church penitential discipline are employed indiscriminately and where the nature of the Christian God becomes incomprehensible. Some theologians propose a way out by demanding a very high level of evaluative knowledge and freedom of consent for grave sin/mortal sin. This would in effect transform 'grave sin' into 'mortal sin' and justify the sanction of eternal separation from God. One agrees with their conviction that it is the quality of decision rather than the quantity of matter which is the determining factor in mortal sin, but an escalation of culpability to the extent of identifying grave sin with mortal sin does not do justice to the Church's discipline of penance at any stage of its history. Certainly in the discipline with which we are familiar grave sin is a sin committed in a human way, indeed a sin of weakness which does not presuppose any extraordinary clarity of knowledge or any outstanding malice. It is the kind of sin which is usually committed more regretfully than maliciously. Without any doubt, then, it is more consistent and more in keeping with the evidence to treat the two kinds of sin as distinct concepts.

A pastoral theology which is concerned with deterring people from sin may feel it useful to trade on the confusion of grave sin and mortal sin. Even the theology of sin of a St Augustine is marred by this confusion. In particular, it often leads him to interpret the sin-language of St Paul in a manner which does less than justice to the latter's emphasis or pattern of thought. But when he takes up the question on a wider theological front he puts everything in better perspective. We may instance his very apt use of the metaphor of Christ, the foundation stone, as set out in 1 Cor 3:10-13.

> Let no one charged with the criminal acts which exclude from the kingdom of God delude himself and say: Because I have received the sign of Christ and the sacraments of Christ, I shall not be lost for eternity; and, if I do pass

438 An Irish Reader in Moral Theology

through purgatory, the fire will save me ... If on the foundation which is Christ man has built up sins, that is, if his edifice is of wood, of hay, or of straw, he will be saved but only as through fire, in view of the foundation on which he has built. As for those others (i.e. whose foundation is not Christ) their lot will be an eternity (of fire).[10]

When he comes to speak explicitly of individual grave sins (*crimina*), he short-circuits this analysis of the foundation or life-direction and connects the sin-action directly with final impenitence and with the sanction of hell:

I have said that we cannot be altogether without sin here on earth, but it does not follow that we should commit murder, adulteries or other mortal sins which kill at a single blow (*coetera mortifera peccata quae uno ictu perimunt*). A Christian inspired with a sincere faith and a firm hope will not be guilty of such sins. He will only commit those sins which daily prayer (i.e. the Our Father) serves to cancel.[11]

This tendency to attach the term mortal to the individual sin-action judged grave or serious by the Church leads him to interpret the sin list in Gal 5 in an uncritical manner as so many mortal sins:

The word of God teaches us precisely, openly and clearly that those who lead a bad life will have no part in the kingdom of heaven ... St Paul does not say that those who have all these vices together will not possess the kingdom of heaven ... As regards exclusion from the kingdom of God the least of these vices produces the very same effect as all of them together or as the greatest of them all.[12]

After this, one does not wonder that St Augustine takes the various sin-lists in Paul (Gal 5, 1 Cor 6, Rom 13, 1 Tim 1) as so many explicit inspired enumerations of mortal sins and states in support that it is God and not man who decides the gravity of the various sins. Indeed, he says, were it not for the explicit words of scripture certain sins would be judged by us much more lightly than they are in reality. For instance, are we not astonished to discover that the penalty of hell-fire is imposed on one who calls his brother a fool![13] He admits that it is difficult to explain why certain sins cut one off from heaven and merit hell. He himself failed to come to any understanding of this question in spite of repeated efforts. He ends up by suggesting that God keeps us in the dark about it in case we should relax our vigilance or cut our cloth too fine.[14] These views of Augustine were invoked in the middle ages by the Nominalists to justify their contention that certain sins were mortal simply because God willed then to be so. Search for further reason was presumptuous. In fairness to St Augustine, one feels that he

What is Mortal Sin?   439

might have avoided or solved the confusion between mortal sin and grave sin if the express question had been put to him from the viewpoint of the Church's discipline of penance. Here he employs the term crime for grave sin. Every crime is a sin, but every sin is not a crime. Crimes are those which require submission to Church penance and therefore when one sees a Christian in the queue of penitents one knows that he is guilty of a crime. The Church judges both the seriousness of the sin which qualifies as crime and the duration of penance:

> When a crime is committed which is of such a nature as to merit separation from the body of Christ one should really take account more of the sincerity of sorrow than of the duration of penance. But since ordinarily no one except ourselves can recognise the sincerity of our repentance, and since we can prove it neither by words nor by signs, it is for those who govern the churches to decide the duration of penance so that satisfaction may also be made to the Church within which the sinner receives the remission of his sins and outside of which our sins cannot be remitted.[15]

In this text St Augustine takes for granted that within the Church's discipline of penance the gravity of sin and the duration of penance are established by criteria established within the community. It is obvious that he would have rejected any suggestion that these criteria were arbitrary or extrinsic. Their purpose was not just to safeguard moral law and order in the external forum but to bring those who had sinned in serious degree to acknowledge their sin and to undertake a salutary process of repentance. Naturally in preaching penance St Augustine constantly invoked the sanction of final impenitence which hung like the sword of Damocles over those who led an immoral life. It was not in his interest as pastor to draw too clear lines of demarcation between the two types of sin which we have termed mortal sin and grave sin. However, there is a time for distinctions, and the questions asked by the Christians of today do make such distinctions necessary. They in no way lessen the fact or the extent of man's capacity for evil nor do they exercise the threat of final impenitence in all its scriptural reality. They simply clarify the logic of all this.

NOTES

1   1a 2ae, q.72, art. 5.
2   2a 2ae, q.148, art. 2.
3   1a 2ae, q.72, art. 6.
4   The distinction is set out in 1a 2ae, q.88, art. 2, but as explained there it leaves many questions unanswered.
5   On these see Walther Eichradt, *Theology of the Old Testament II*, London: SCM, 1967, pp. 419–23.
6   Martin Luther presented in his *De Captivitate Babylonica* a caricature, too close for comfort,

of a popular view of the mechanics of sacrament.

7   Jean Lacroix, *The Meaning of Modern Atheism*, Dublin: Gill, 1965, p. 87.

8   The phrase 'divine law' as used by Trent has been exhaustively analysed in recent years. It does not in itself refer to law promulgated by God or by Christ. It refers rather to the Church's interpretation of the mission given her by Christ, as is clear from the manner in which some of the sacraments were instituted. The Fathers of Trent knew enough history to appreciate that the catalogue of grave sins or, as it called them, mortal sins, had been specified by consensus in the community down the centuries.

9   See Anton Meir, *Das peccatum mortale ex toto genere suo*, Regensburg: Pustet 1966, pp. 359–61, on the well-known 1612 decree of Claudius Aquaviva, the Jesuit Superior-General, and posthumous retraction by Sanchez (+1610) of the view published in his *De sancto matrimonii sacramento* (1602).

10   *In Ps.*, 80, 20, PL 37,1044. In similar vein many of the Fathers, including St Augustine, described man in a state of sin which separates him from God as being in a strange land 'a land of unlikeness'. This very rich phrase (*locus dissimilitudinis,* topos tes anomoiotetes) originated with Plato and Plotinus, who referred it to the soul's sojourn on earth, an alien land of shadow existence. In the sin-language of Christian authors it refers to the thorough-going *conversio ad creaturam* which constitutes an *aversio a Deo* or, in other words, the state of mortal sin. Here the term incorporates the concept of sin as distorting that likeness or image of God which gives the human soul its true value (cf. Gen 1:26) and as removing man to a strange land far away from his true country as in the case of the Prodigal Son (cf. Lk 15:13). For a particularly powerful medieval use of the metaphor, see Amedee Hallier, *The Monastic Theology of Aelred of Rievaulx*, Shannon: Irish University Press, 1969, pp. 10–18.

11   *Sermo* 181, 6, 8, PL 38, 983.

12   *De Bapt contra Don.*, 4, 18-19, PL 43, 170–171. Augustine does justice to the Pauline teaching here if he has expressly used *vitium* rather than *peccatum* to indicate 'commitment to a vicious way of life rather than commission of a single sin'. I have not succeeded in discovering a text where he has consciously clarified this ambiguity. Indeed was it ever in his interest to clarify it?

13   *Enchiridion*, 88–89, PL 40, 269–270.

14   *De Civitate Dei*, 21, 27, PL 41, 750.

15   *Enchiridion*, 64–65, PL 40, 262.

31   Overcoming Sin:
Conversion and Reconciliation

Hugh Connolly

(Hugh Connolly, *Sin*, New Century Theology Series, London: Continuum, 2002, pp. 125–145.)

Contemporary psychology has identified four essential moments in the process of conversion. There are:
1.   Disorientation.
2.   A sense of gathering up the fragments.
3.   An experience of mercy and the forgiveness of failures.
4.   A sense of the Other, of being as it were 'grasped by God'.[1]

These elements form a classic pattern which charts the 'reversal of sin into forgiveness, of suffering and pain into generous love, of death into life' and which is reflective of 'the law of the cross'. This is what Rahner calls: 'a resolute radical and radically conscious, personal and in each instance unique adoption of Christian life.'[2]

The idea of conversion also gives rise to a further series of questions. Does the term describe a sudden event or a gradual process? It is a once-only experience or may it be repeated? Is this an entirely personal experience of the heart or is there a necessary social dimension? Contemporary theology tries to answer these questions by distinguishing between three types of conversion. In particular it points to the separate meanings of intellectual, religious and moral conversion. This is not the occasion perhaps to rework a question which has been explored at great length and with great technical expertise in the writings of Lonergan, Rahner, Tillich, Erikson and Kohlberg – to name but a few. One can nevertheless affirm that their work in exploring the multidimensional and multi-layered nature of conversion allows for a much more nuanced understanding of the idea today. At one level it can be considered a definitive moment which reshapes and refocuses the entire life of the individual, while at another level it is a process which continues to actualise itself in and through daily life and the normal web of human relationships Conversion is at once a deeply personal need as well as a moral imperative for communities, people and even nations. It can be described in terms of an event, while at the same time being recognised as an attitude that pervades the moral life.

As well as charting the stages and kinds of conversion, one can also meaningfully speak of conditions of conversion. Perhaps it is this facet of conversion which most clearly illustrates the struggle against sin. The first such condition is simply awareness and admission of sin and guilt.[3] Honesty, truth and a willingness to acknowledge the reality of one's weakness are prerequisites on the path to *metanoia*. 'God be merciful to me a sinner' is the prayer of the publican (Lk 19:9-4) who seeks Christ's forgiveness. It also mirrors the first step of contemporary recovery programmes. The moment of truth is where the addict admits that they are powerless on their own to effect real change and that their lives have become unmanageable. It is a decisive time of acceptance of reality and of the need for assistance from without. The parallel has been adverted to by several theologians who see strong similarities between addiction as a pathological relationship with a substance or process and the idolatry of sin. Both in a real way are constructed on what we have called a false anthropology – a refusal to accept one's own limitations, imperfections and creatureliness.[4] Both involve a 'progressive enslavement' and a vicious circle effect. The experience of being attracted to an elusive and illusory freedom, devastating personal disintegration and isolation, and the self-destroying spiral of deterioration and despair are themes which are common to both the pathology of sin and that of addiction. Recovery likewise in both scenarios entails a commitment to the truth and to an attitude of honestly and is born in that moment of that candid and humble acknowledgement which in clinical terms might be called an admission of powerlessness. In more religious terms one might simply speak of humility before God.

Honesty and candour are the starting points for the individual's process of turning away from sin and returning to the loving presence of God. In analogous ways communities, societies and cultures need to make a decisive break with the sinful past in order to recover collectively from the poisonous effects of sin. In mid-1990s South Africa, for instance, the collapse of apartheid left behind a legacy of distrust and hurt. By way of a remedy the old National Party favoured a Reconciliation Commission, whereas the African National Congress (ANC) sought nothing less than a painstaking investigation of the truth. The resultant compromise, the Truth and Reconciliation Commission, provided a much-needed cathartic process and its very name gave expression to a basic prerequisite for the healing of collective hurt. Similarly, the Church of France, in acknowledging its share of responsibility for wrongs perpetrated during the Nazi occupation, especially those against Jewish fellow citisens, recalled the words of the novelist François Mauriac: 'A crime of this magnitude falls in a not insignificant way on all who were there, on those who didn't cry out and who kept silent for whatever reason.'[5] In like manner, international enquiries into old wounds in Northern Ireland and the Balkans have been important steps along the laborious path to peace in both regions.

By way of support for this approach, Müller-Fahrenholz suggests that there is much more wisdom in the Jewish proverb 'Forgotten prolongs captivity. Remembering is the secret of redemption' than in the popular adage 'Forgive and forget'. He speaks of the 're-membering' in the original sense of bringing together the members and pieces of something that was once complete – a restoration of what has been lost and a joining together of what has been broken. Remembering is therefore a process which calls to mind the deepest convictions and possibilities of people, encourages them to heal forms of dis-memberment and to work toward a better, more integrated society.[6] Confession, admission and acknowledgements of responsibility and ultimately of sin are necessary purgative, purifying and ultimately healing acts.

A second condition is some kind of interior readiness for moral renewal. In an older theological language this would have been described as a 'firm purpose of amendment'. What was meant here was a realisation that conversion entailed personal and, on occasions, collective effort to overcome the effects of evil, whether from within or from without. This disposition is encapsulated in the first plea of the Lord's Prayer: 'Thy kingdom come'. It is a plea which first and foremost demands a real personal commitment and engagement. Two things are immediately apparent here. First, on a theological level the wholly gratuitous nature of God's pardon is unquestioned. The Christian understanding of grace has always been thus. The Reformed tradition in particular has insisted that grace comes 'unprevented': it is definitely 'prevenient grace'. The initiative in the reconciliation between God and humanity lies with God alone. The same revelation which gives us an insight into the religious meaning of evil and thus a fuller grasp of the reality of sin also gives us the proclamation of God's commitment to forgiveness and to his faithful and all-enduring love for his people. The sinner nevertheless does not experience himself or herself solely at a spiritual level, for human beings are embodied. The New Testament witnesses to the episode where a paralytic's friends were asked by Jesus 'which is easier to do – to say to this man "your sins are forgiven" or to say "get up, take up your bed and go home"?' would have had no difficulty in identifying the first statement as the easier, for forgiveness is not so readily susceptible of external verification. The episode ends, however, with the paralysed man's mobility being restored. Morally he had already been healed by the divine word of forgiveness; humanly it became much easier to realise this when it found a resonance in his physical cure.

The great tradition of asceticism rests, in large measure, on the same insight. Grace can never be purchased, forgiveness cannot be earned, but neither can one ignore the serious duty of reparation, the need to reconstruct one's own life and the obligation to undo sinful effects in the lives of others. Human beings give expression to the reshaping of their lives in reparative and ascetic acts. There is an inescapable logic in that sin and those effects of sin that are primarily physical in expression should be countered in a physical and tangible way. For en-fleshed human beings it makes sure that the entire human person – body, mind and spirit – should be somehow engaged in the process of conversion. Seen in this way, asceticism is not at all about self-hatred, still less is it about personal feats of endurance or showing 'what one can do for God'. Spiritual 'machismo' can have no genuine point of contact with a gospel of humility and truth. But asceticism does have a very real role in recalling salvation history, and in particular Christ's sacrifice in shouldering the cross so as to defeat sin and complete the will of the Father.

So the practice of penance is ultimately about identification with the cross, even though it may also have a very real human role to play in personal reintegration and in reparation for wrong which has been done. The example of Zaccheus is notable here: 'Behold Lord the half of my goods I give to the poor; and if I have defrauded anyone of anything, I restore it fourfold' (Lk 19:8). What is more, the traditional forms of penance, namely prayer, fasting and almsgiving, show us that the ancient ecclesial wisdom was keen to give penance an orientation toward outreach, concern and support for others.

This idea of making satisfaction or restoration is paralleled again to a certain extent in the process of recovery from addiction. The 'steps programmes' lead recovering addicts to an awareness of the people who have been harmed as the result of their addiction, to a resolution that direct amends will be made whenever possible. They also insist on the recognition that no recovery will be possible until their lives have been 'surrendered to a higher power'. Here the importance of restitution is not simply that it does justice to those who were initially wronged, but that it also marks a further step in the process of personal acknowledgement and acceptance of responsibility for one's life. The comparison between recovery from addiction and the conversion from sin can also yield two further insights. The first is that both processes involve the entire human person. Like the pathology of sin, the pathology of addiction permeates the whole of human experience and so recovery needs to be holistic and integrative. A resonance may be observed here with those who argue, convincingly for the most part, that the true theological meaning of concupiscence is moral disintegration and fragmentation of human existence caused by sin. Conversion from sin and toward moral coherence and consistency implies by definition an integrative and all-embracing advance. It implies a new focus and cultivation of inner attitudes as well as of patterns of behaviour that bring about changes, which truly heal and make whole again.

A second observation is simply that conversion, if it is to be taken seriously, has to be considered a lifelong task. It needs to be understood as a process and not simply an experience. The recovering addict is under no illusion that recovery is anything other than a lifetime commitment. He or she must commit to an 'honesty programme'. Similarly conversion implies a pilgrim's process of progressive liberation from sin through a gradual increase in sincerity, integrity and candour. Although the experience of and engagement with repentance and reconciliation may be seen as identification with the cross of Christ, it is equally the case that for most people the *via crucis* is not condensed into the space of a few days but is woven instead into a life journey. Recovery from sin and reorientation toward the gospel is therefore for them an integral, organic and permanent task. It is 'the process by which we untie the multiple knots and webs of our cross-addictive sins and progressively integrate ourselves into a new reality'.[7]

Neither is the process capable of being undertaken alone. Recovery requires the simple honesty of confrontation. In the Christian tradition this has long been acknowledged through the confession of sins to a third party where confession is made to one who is entrusted with the ministry of reconciliation and forgiveness. It is also recognised in the centrality of the word of God. It is not one's own fears, guilt or shame (all of which are subject to fluctuation, fixation and indeed manipulation) which in the final analysis provoke contrition and repentance, but confrontation with the message and mission of Jesus Christ. Recovery manifests itself also in progressive reconciliation with other people. Analogously it is to be seen in the efforts made by communities of faith to initiate the process of repentance within themselves. It is borne out also in their efforts to foster the central values of unity, solidarity and respect for creation. Communities of faith, churches and even nations and blocks of nations have therefore a responsibility for integral human development and must also be prepared to open themselves to the same dynamic of repentance, reform and reconciliation. The succinctly expressed aspiration *ecclesia semper reformanda* is a time-honoured acknowledgement that as well as being an individual imperative, conversion is also a shared duty and responsibility.

In their final document at the end of the second Pan-European Assembly held in Graz, Austria in 1997, the Christian churches of Europe clearly recognised this collective and corporate dimension to reconciliation:

> Although we bear the bruises of our lack of reconciliation, we believe that this reconciling power is still at work today among us. It can already be seen in our longing for reconciliation (cf. Rom 8:26f.) and makes us prepared to let our thoughts and behaviour be transformed.[8]

There is here an ecclesiology of the *ecclesia peregrinans*, a faith community which takes as its model the *koinonia* of the early Church, and which sees itself not simply in terms of an institution but as a true *communio* exhibiting genuine regard for all who live in it.

The same document is also at pains to point out that the search for corporate and collective repentance and reconciliation is not about glossing over the very religious, cultural, ethnic and ethical differences which are a fact of life in a multicultural world. Still less is it about whitewashing over the deep differences between the guilty and their victims. Reconciliation is never a substitute for justice and truth. If separated from these it merely contributes further to sinful divisions and discrimination in the world. True community, true belonging and true solidarity are not qualities that can somehow be bestowed or superimposed in an artificial way. They only come about when people have the space to discover the basic truth of inter-connectedness. The encyclical *Redemptoris Missio* once memorably noted that for genuine dialogue to take place three conditions must be respected:

1. It must be genuinely mutual.
2. There must be no false 'irenicism'.
3. No party must try to impose its view on the other.

The horizontal thrust of reconciliation depends on this kind of candour and honesty and on a recognition of 'the fact of human inter-dependence on a global scale. A realisation of the fact that one's own life and the lives of countless others, whom one may never come to know personally are intertwined for good or for ill'.[9]

A third and final condition of conversion might be described as openness to the gift of grace. Christian tradition insists that every step to conversion is taken in the light of divine grace. Jesus reassures his followers: 'Ask and it will be given to you: seek and you will find, knock and the door will be opened to you' (Mt 7:7-8). The invitation that is placed before us is ultimately a call to life: 'I have come that you may have life and have it to the full.' It is an invitation to consciously choose to live and to 'seize the day', to grasp the *kairos* moment. It is also a decision that requires courage. Saying yes to the *Sequela Christi* is in some respects like saying yes to the unknown. It is a journey in faith, hope and love, but it is also a journey where the itinerary is not predetermined or mutually agreed.

The element of risk is quintessential to discipleship whereas avoidance of risk smacks of the sinful. In the parable the steward who buried his talent in the ground was described as wicked by his employer because he had closed off all new possibilities including the in-breaking grace of God. Thévenot describes this essential aspect of the process of conversion as the journey from 'idol' to 'icon'. The sinful attitude is idolatrous because it is fashioning of oneself and one's life in the light of and at the whim of one's own needs and desires. It is a narcissistic strategy, which halts the journey and arrests progression toward true freedom by offering an alternative, but ultimately static, goal. Iconic attachment, on the other hand, renders us open to the mystery, to the adventure of discovering God, to the other and ultimately to oneself. It fosters a readiness to be drawn even deeper into the mystery of the One who is the icon of the invisible God, the God whose name is 'love'.[10] This kind of dramatic reorientating and transformation of horizons is very evident in celebrated conversion stories such as those of Mary of Magdala, Paul, Augustine, Francis of Assisi, Blaise Pascal, Paul Claudel and many others.

Overcoming Sin: Conversion and Reconciliation 447

Within each individual conversion a new and loving God discloses the world of generosity from which everything originates. Suddenly even what was evil in the past is seen as having led toward a God who forgives. Betrayals are disclosed as wounded trusts; modest faith in the other is refined into a greater freedom to embrace God and neighbour. All of this comes about through the transforming power of conversion.[11]

Psychologists suggest that the situation is akin to falling in love. Suddenly the world takes on a whole new prospect – what once appeared dull and uninteresting is now charged with interest and with meaning. It is as if one has suddenly found the means to access a whole new universe that was previously unavailable. Where the experience is one of recovery from addiction the contrast may be even more vividly experienced. Deeply ingrained patterns of thought and behaviour, which had kept the addict on a treadmill of self-preoccupation and self-loathing, are gradually replaced with the discipline of honesty and transparency that allow the charting of a new course. Senses that had been inured and deadened are reattained, as the individual emerges from the tunnel of despair into the light of new hope. The power of divine grace erupts in the human heart, the shackles of enslavement are broken, and the journey, which had been abandoned, is once again resumed.

It is recorded that when the creators of the first twelve steps programmes adopted the neutral, perhaps somewhat insipid language of 'Higher Power' they did so not out of an aversion to Christianity nor even primarily in consideration of those from other cultures and traditions who undertook the programme. Instead, their choice of terminology was above all a recognition that many who suffered from addiction had also suffered alienation and disaffection from God and faith. Yet withal, the thrust of such programmes remains God-oriented, it continues to be a complete surrender of life to the all-powerful, all-loving Other. The baggage of sin, decay and self-inflicted suffering is left behind and the world becomes a place in which God dwells and reaches out in compassion to all creation.

Consumerism, colonialism, militarism, sexism, racism, sectarianism and terrorism are just some of the collective sinful addictions which have manifested themselves, and indeed continue to manifest themselves, often dramatically, in the world today. For this reason there is a renewed urgency in re-discovering the collective dimension of prophecy. Challenging popular conceptions of pluralism and tolerance and their claim to be moral absolutes will also be an import task if societies and communities are to be persuaded to collectively open themselves to the prompting of Divine Grace. But such profound change is not just wishful thinking, and the dream of solidarity is not utopian. The power of grace is truly transformative, and just as the twentieth century is strewn with examples of man's inhumanity to man, so too are there striking examples of that *metanoia*, that change of heart, which brings about new life and new hope.

Another little detail from the recent ecumenical journey of the European churches, in particular a contrast between the circumstances of the two Pan-European Ecumenical assemblies, graphically illustrates this point. As part of the first such assembly held in Basle, Switzerland in 1989, and by way of a symbolic gesture to show the human spirit's capacity to transcend all man-made barriers, all the participants were invited one morning to go on a short walk in the outskirts of Basle. Since Switzerland, France and Germany meet at the city of Basle, the walk took them through three national frontiers. Some of the delegates from Eastern Europe found that simple exercise so overwhelming that many of them ended the walk in tears. The idea that one could simply stroll through a frontier with a wave of the passport without having to queue endlessly for a visa was incredible to them. That one didn't have to trot back and forward between one government department and another, perhaps having to bribe some officials as might have been the case in their own countries, was too much to take in. This free, almost blasé, crossing of frontiers was, for some, like an impossible dream. Yet in a few short months, as we now know, that impossible dream was to become a reality for almost all the peoples of Eastern Europe. The Iron Curtain was torn open; the Berlin Wall was demolished brick by brick and peoples of Eastern Europe moved freely across frontiers. The two lungs of Europe, East and West, breathed freely again for the first time in half a century.

The gospel insists that dreams can become reality. Sometimes symbolic gestures and celebrations are necessary in order to peel away the mask of sin, to reignite our hopes and to nourish and sustain our visions and dreams.

NOTES

1   S. Happel and J. Walter, *Conversion and Discipleship*, Philadelphia: Fortress, 1986, p. 9.
2   K. Balmer, 'Conversion', in *Sacramentum Mundi*, London: Burns and Oates, 1968, pp. 291–2.
3   This is an adaptation of a schema to be found in K. Peschke, *Christian Ethics: Moral Theology in the Light of Vatican II*, Alcester: Goodliffe Neale, 1993; New York: Seabury, 1975, Vol. 1, 332ff.
4   For a fine analysis of these parallels see McCormick, Patrick, *Sin as Addiction*, New York: Paulist Press, 1989, esp. pp. 146–77.
5   Eglise de France, *Le Repentir*, Paris: Desclée de Brouwer, 1997, p. 28.
6   G. Muller-Fahrenholz, op. cit., 36–7 and 59.
7   McCormick, op. cit., p. 186.
8   CEC/CCEE, Final Document EEA2, Christian Commitment to Reconciliation, 1997, p. 3.
9   Irish Bishops, *Work is the Key*, Dublin: Veritas, 1993, p. 3.
10   X. Thévènot, *Compter Sur Dieu*, Paris: Éditions du Cerf, 1993, 297ff.
11   Happel and Walter, op. cit., p. 16.

Overcoming Sin: Conversion and Reconciliation

Acknowledgements

When we first came to compile the articles and essays for this book, we quickly realised that this was a far bigger undertaking than we had originally believed, and so began to look for advice and, above all, practical research and organising assistance. Through the good offices of Margaret Tyrrell of the Faculty of Theology in Maynooth we met, interviewed and integrated into the team two outstanding doctoral students, Aoife McGrath and Siobhán Mooney. Their interest, intelligence and industry combined with brief judicious notes on the material researched made this work feasible for two ageing theologians. Without their assistance it is doubtful if this Reader would have appeared in our lifetimes. Their research work, combined with the very effective secretarial work of Mary O'Malley and the splendid editorial work particularly of Caitríona Clarke at Veritas, finally enabled us to fulfil our ambitions. Our sincere thanks naturally to all our contributors and to the many colleagues and friends whose advice we sought and sometimes followed.

Index – Contributing Authors